**Archbishop
Oscar
Romero:**

# A
# Shepherd's
# Diary

**ARCHBISHOP OSCAR ROMERO:**

# A
# Shepherd's
# Diary

Translated by
Irene B. Hodgson

Foreword by
Thomas E. Quigley

Introduction by
James R. Brockman, S.J.

First published 1993

Catholic Fund for Overseas Development (CAFOD)
2 Romero Close, Stockwell Road
London SW9 9TY, UK

Catholic Institute for International Relations (CIIR)
Unit 3 Canonbury Yard, 190a New North Road
London N1 7BJ, UK

British Library Cataloguing-in-
Publication Data.
A catalogue record for this book
is available from the British Library.

ISBN 1 85287 109 1

Cover and book design by Julie Lonneman

Translated from the Spanish by Irene B. Hodgson

Published by St. Anthony Messenger Press, Cincinnati, Ohio, U.S.A.

Printed in the U.S.A.

# Contents

# Foreword

Archbishop Romero began this diary on March 31, 1978, when he had headed the see of San Salvador for just over a year. He made his last entry four days before he was murdered on March 24, 1980. For two of his three years as archbishop, then, this volume provides a unique look into the life and thought of one of the outstanding public figures of contemporary Latin America and one of the Church's best known and most revered priests.

## The Social and Political Context

The year following Romero's 1977 installation as archbishop was one of the most turbulent in the country's history. The installation itself had been a hurried and low-keyed affair just two days after the February 20 elections, in which the government candidate for president, Carlos Humberto Romero, was declared winner despite evidence of massive fraud. Protests followed, then more repression: the massacre of demonstrators in the Plaza Libertad on February 28.

It was also a time of repression directed against the Church. Several priests had recently been detained, threatened or expelled. Two U.S. priests had been unceremoniously shoved across the border just before Romero's installation. Several other priests (including Ignacio Ellacuría, S.J.) had been denied reentry into the country that very day. And before Romero was archbishop for a month, his deeply-admired friend, the Jesuit Rutilio Grande, was killed.

A year later, in 1978, the situation was, if anything, worse. The role of the Church and the voice of its archbishop were clearly central to the drama that was being played out daily in El Salvador. It was then that Romero determined to provide an additional record of his and his staff's activities in the fast-moving events of the time—additional, because for all the detail found in this diary, his recorded talks and homilies comprise one of the most dramatic and detailed collections anywhere.

Romero was a well-known preacher long before he came to San Salvador; he often spoke on the radio. On becoming archbishop, however, he added to his distinctive homiletic style a new feature—indeed, a news feature. Because the national media rarely reported and often distorted the news concerning the popular organizations or the Church and almost never presented the truth concerning the lengthening litany of human rights violations in the country, the archbishop took upon himself the task of informing a public eager to know what was happening.

His Sunday homilies were broadcast nationally by the Church's station YSAX, the *Voz Panamericana*, except when it was bombed off the air. My own first meeting with the archbishop in June 1977 coincided with one of these times. I was able to convey a check from the U.S. bishops' conference to help rebuild the station, which had recently been damaged by a bomb. My last meeting with him was on March 23, 1980, the day YSAX returned to the air after a bomb had destroyed it five weeks earlier. It was the last time YSAX would carry Romero's voice.

According to listener surveys at the time, seventy-three percent of the rural population and forty-seven percent of the urban regularly tuned in to the Mass from the cathedral to hear the homily, which rarely lasted less than an hour and a half. Romero's recounting of the *hechos de la semana*, "the events of the week," was a recital of both good and bad news, of both *anuncio* and *denuncia*—proclaiming the Good News of the liberating gospel and, with the prophets of old, denouncing the evils of the day.

## The Diary

According to James Brockman, S.J., whose *Romero: A Life* is the indispensable and so far definitive biography of the archbishop, Romero's awareness of the historic importance of what was happening in the Church of San Salvador impelled him to maintain this other and more personal record of his pastoral activities. For two years he kept notes on each day's meetings, visitors and conversations and then, daily when possible, used a portable tape recorder to preserve a summary narrative of the events and his own thoughts.

This is where the diary is of signal importance. It is not a "diary of the soul," not a private record of his spiritual life and personal reflections. But it does for the first time reveal aspects of Romero's personality and convey his most deeply felt views on a range of topics in ways that his public utterances never could. One cannot know the essential Romero without being familiar with his diary.

It is, of course, also a private document in the sense that some of the problems and persons that filled his days (and thus this record) were themselves of a sensitive and confidential nature. It would not have been appropriate to make public some of the archbishop's comments and observations at the time they were recorded, and even today there will be some who cannot be pleased with the publication of the diary. But it is the essential Romero, and it provides an unparalleled opening into a drama that has captured the interest of much of the world beyond tiny El Salvador.

It was apparently Romero's intention that more than his own personal activities be preserved. In his entry for December 11, 1979, he describes a meeting with his key administrative staff in order to straighten out the matter of the taped diary. He complains that he had hoped it would be an account of the life of the archdiocese, recording the activities of the whole pastoral team, but it was so far "only the views and activities of the bishop himself." He observes with typical modesty (but mistakenly, one must say in hindsight) that it is this fuller history, encompassing the life of the whole archdiocese, that would be of greatest interest to others in the future. As it happened, the decision reached at that meeting—that information from each of the archdiocesan offices should be pulled together so as to complement the archbishop's own record—apparently came to naught.

It's worth observing as a kind of literary footnote that the priest who agreed to pull together the data from the other offices, Father Rafael Urrutia, figures in a special way at the beginning and the end of this diary. The Sunday before Romero began the taping (Easter 1978), he had conferred the ministry of acolyte on a young seminarian, Rafael Edgardo Urrutia Herrera; he ordained him to the priesthood the following November 4. The diary's final entry, March 20, 1980, mentions Father Urrutia, who was then chancellor of the archdiocese and part of the core team.

It may not have been possible, given the speed with which events were unfolding in the first months of 1980, for Father Urrutia to do much about the diary project, but it has now fallen to him once again to gather all the information he can about Oscar Arnulfo Romero. Urrutia is the postulator of Romero's cause: that is, the one charged with pursuing the case for the canonization of the man already acclaimed by many as St. Romero of the Americas. And it is Urrutia, chancellor once again, who has authenticated that the published diary is the faithful transcription of the thirty original cassettes Romero used.

Another key aide of Romero's whose name bookends the diary,

appearing in the very first entry and in the last (and often in between), is Roberto Cuéllar, the young lawyer who directed the archdiocesan human rights office. The diary's first entry deals with the human rights issue and the requests that come to the Church to investigate and denounce the numerous violations of that era. "We have a small office for human rights," Romero tells a group of lawyers and law students on that March 31, "but it is powerless to deal with the huge number of cases that come in."

It's appropriate for the diary to begin on the human rights theme, for it was this issue and the Church's response that first drew world attention to El Salvador. The same praise and the same criticism were to mark the years following Romero's death, when his successor and Cuéllar's, Arturo Rivera Damas and María Julía Hernández, continued the same gospel commitment to defending the rights and dignity of human beings.

## The Publication of the Diary

As the war escalated in the months following the assassination and the offices of the archdiocese were themselves targets of attack, copies were made of the original master tapes of the diary as well as those of the archbishop's broadcast homilies and brought for safekeeping to the U.S. Catholic Conference (USCC) in Washington.

In 1982 John McAward, then of the Unitarian Universalist Service Committee, brought up to the USCC 153 tapes of the recorded homilies from May 12, 1977, to March 23, 1980. A little over a year later, Father James Brockman, who had been working in the San Salvador archdiocesan offices with the diary and other archival material in preparation for his life of the archbishop, brought up the thirty diary tapes. Both sets have been kept in the climate-controlled archives of the USCC. While they no longer represent insurance against the potential destruction of the master tapes in El Salvador, they are still a prized resource of the Conference and a symbol of the close relationship between the two Churches.

To commemorate the tenth anniversary of the assassination in 1990, the archdiocese of San Salvador published *Monseñor Oscar Arnulfo Romero: Su Diario*. At the commemoration that March 24, Archbishop Rivera Damas raised the matter of an English-language edition of the diary with both Cardinal Roger Mahony, representative of the USCC, and Julian Filochowski, director of the British Catholic Fund for Overseas Development (CAFOD), who had been instrumental in getting the Spanish edition published.

The USCC undertook the translation and publication and chose St.

Anthony Messenger Press to be the U.S. publisher. Because the diary is long and unavoidably repetitive in places, some readers recommended editing the text to a more manageable size. But Archbishop Rivera urged (and both the USCC and the publisher fully agreed) that the text should be published whole lest distortions, however unintentional, result from trimming.

This insistence on fidelity to the original has guided Dr. Irene B. Hodgson's fine translation throughout. It is intentionally a highly literal rendering, departing from the original chiefly in providing the correct spelling for a number of foreign names and in breaking into smaller units some of Archbishop Romero's often lengthy and elliptical sentences. The text may not always flow in either language; presumably the archbishop might have done some further editing himself had he lived. But the translation here does convey the sound and texture of the spoken tapes. It is the authentic voice of Oscar Arnulfo Romero.

Thomas E. Quigley
Latin American Affairs
U.S. Catholic Conference

# Introduction

Born in an isolated mountain village in eastern El Salvador in 1917, Oscar Romero left home at thirteen to study for the priesthood. At the age of twenty, he was sent to Rome for his theology studies and was ordained a priest there in 1942. Returning to El Salvador in 1943, he worked energetically as pastor of the cathedral parish in the San Miguel diocese until 1967, gaining great renown among the people as a preacher, newspaper writer and organizer of diverse activities in the diocese. But he at the same time irritated some of the clergy and other persons with his demanding and, at times, harsh personality.

## The Church and the Council

Deeply devoted to the Church and the papacy from his youth, Romero watched with interest as the Second Vatican Council, called by Pope John XXIII, worked from 1962 to 1965 to update the Catholic Church. The Council prepared a set of documents to be applied to the Church's life, and it left an exciting atmosphere of change and development in the Church. Going back to the Church's roots, the Council recalled that the Church is basically God's people in spite of the institutional form it has acquired over the ages. The Council reminded the clergy and hierarchy that they must be servants of the people, not a privileged class. The Church itself was to be the servant of the world, as God's instrument of salvation.

Among the developments that came directly from Vatican II was the formation of bishops' conferences in each country (although a few countries had already formed conferences well before the Council). The conferences have enabled bishops to formulate a unified course of action in matters of interdiocesan significance and to speak with a single voice on national questions. Each bishop, however, remains the supreme Church authority in his diocese. In 1967, at the age of 50,

Romero was named secretary of the bishops' conference of El Salvador and he moved to San Salvador, the capital city.

In 1970 Romero himself was ordained a bishop, as an auxiliary bishop of the San Salvador archdiocese. (An auxiliary bishop is an assistant to the bishop who heads a diocese or archdiocese.) As auxiliary bishop, Romero served at times as rector of the seminary and as editor of the Catholic weekly newspaper, besides giving sermons and talks and performing liturgical functions.

After the close of Vatican II, the bishops of Latin America had called a meeting of their own to implement its reforms in their area. Bishops from all the national hierarchies of Latin America met at Medellín, Colombia, in 1968. Adopting Vatican II's basic ideas that the Church must be the servant of society and that it must try to understand the world in order to serve it and proclaim the gospel of Jesus to it, the Medellín conference recognized that massive and oppressive poverty was Latin America's basic reality. They called upon the Church to work for the people's liberation from that injustice as part of the work of human salvation. Within a short time, theologians were writing on the same theme, and thus was born what came to be called liberation theology. Liberation theologians have continued to develop in various ways the theme that salvation involves liberation from present evils as well as from final damnation.

The Archdiocese of San Salvador eagerly followed the direction of Vatican II and Medellín, but Romero as auxiliary bishop clearly disagreed with much that was done in the archdiocese. He avoided the meetings of the Priests' Senate and the monthly meetings of the clergy for discussing and implementing pastoral policies. He accepted the pronouncements of Vatican II as he understood them but was unwilling to accept many things that others were saying or doing in the aftermath of Vatican II and Medellín.

In October 1974 Bishop Romero was appointed to head the small diocese of Santiago de María. It was a largely rural diocese in the eastern mountains and included his own hometown. Once again he plunged into the busy pastoral work that had marked his years as a priest in San Miguel, including visits to parts of his diocese accessible only by horse or mule. His visits made him more aware of the hardship and injustice of the Salvadoran peasant's life. In 1975 the government's rural police massacred five peasants in his diocese, and Romero visited the bereaved families, celebrated the funeral Mass and protested vigorously in a letter to the president of the republic. His public comments, however, were more restrained.

In 1976 a timid land-reform law initiated the barest beginning of a transformation of the country's unequal distribution of farmland, which for generations had kept the peasants in bondage to a few wealthy owners of huge holdings. The landowners immediately got the congress to repeal the law. Peasants began to organize to protect their rights and agitate for reform, even though Salvadoran law denied their organizations legal recognition. The landowners grew alarmed.

A few rural pastors were showing sympathy for the peasants' organizing and were preaching about the Church's social teaching. At the same time, the archdiocese was encouraging the formation of small Christian communities among the peasants as a means of furthering the people's Christian life. The communities helped make the Church present in areas that parish priests could barely reach. (In a rural country where most peasants lived in hamlets of a few families and farmed the surrounding land, priests often had thousands of parishioners and dozens or hundreds of hamlets to tend.) But the landowners viewed the communities as undercover organizing that threatened their control. By the end of 1976, tensions were high, and the media were attacking the archdiocese and its priests, especially some who were working in peasant parishes. Several foreign priests were expelled from the country in early 1977.

## The New Archbishop

The aged archbishop, Luis Chávez, was about to retire and a new archbishop was to be named. There were at the time only five dioceses in El Salvador, including the one archdiocese; thus, the archbishop was automatically the preeminent Church figure in the nation.[1] Most of the archdiocesan clergy wanted the new archbishop to be Bishop Arturo Rivera Damas, an auxiliary of the archdiocese since 1960. In opposition, El Salvador's oligarchy of wealthy landowners and business people wanted an archbishop who would change Archbishop

---

[1]Dioceses are grouped into ecclesiastical provinces. One of the dioceses is called the metropolitan see or archdiocese, and its bishop is called the metropolitan or archbishop. Although he has no authority within the other dioceses in ordinary governance, he has the responsibility to report abuses occurring in them to Rome. The other dioceses are called suffragan sees and their bishops are called suffragan bishops.

In El Salvador there is only one ecclesiastical province, but it is not the same thing as the national bishops' conference. Its members are the individual dioceses, whereas the members of the bishops' conference are the individual bishops, including auxiliary bishops. Readers of Romero's diary may find it helpful to bear in mind that as archbishop he held a special place in the country's ecclesiastical life and structure, but he held no special place in the bishops' conference.

Chávez' policies and stop the preaching about social justice and the rights of the poor. Their preference was Bishop Romero. From his record and his conservative character they judged that he would meet their desires. They rejoiced when the Vatican chose Romero.

Less than three weeks after Romero's installation as archbishop, gunmen murdered a rural pastor, Father Rutilio Grande, along with a boy and an old man riding with him in his jeep. Having worked in the seminary for many years, Grande was well known and highly respected. Romero regarded him as a friend; it was Grande who had planned and coordinated the ceremony of Romero's ordination as a bishop in 1970.

The murder shocked the country. For generations the government, the armed forces and the police had served the interests of El Salvador's wealthy landowners, who could virtually order the police to eliminate troublemakers. Grande had publicly denounced the expulsion of one priest from the country, and his parish was active in promoting small Christian communities. Past history gave everyone good reason to think that the landowners and the government were responsible for the killing. Now the clergy and people of the archdiocese wanted a strong reaction from the archdiocese and its new archbishop.

After careful consideration, Romero adopted measures requested during a day-long clergy meeting. He closed all Catholic schools for three days of mourning and of reflection on the nation's situation. He ordered only one public Mass celebrated in the archdiocese on the Sunday following Grande's funeral in the central square before the cathedral. It turned out to be the largest religious demonstration in the nation's history and for many a profound religious experience. But it also led to a serious clash with the Vatican's ambassador, the papal nuncio, who had pressured Romero not to hold the single Mass lest the government think it provocative. It was the beginning of an enduring lack of understanding and support on the part of the nuncio.

For the next three years, Romero was a center of conflict. Disappointed in his performance, the government and the oligarchy maintained their fierce opposition to him. He in turn held to the course he had begun, finding that he had the people with him and sure that he was following his duty as revealed in the gospel and in the teaching of the Church. Five more priests were murdered after Rutilio Grande during those three years; Romero himself would be the sixth. Countless members of the small Christian communities were killed by military or security forces.

The media attacked Romero relentlessly, calling him a

communist, a subversive and a madman. He was saddened by the opposition, the "hardness of heart," as he said, of so many members of the upper classes, some of whom had been his friends. But the people responded to him with their love and support, and he was not disheartened.

The hardest trial Romero endured was the opposition of his fellow bishops. Except for Bishop Rivera, the others contested what he was doing. In some of the meetings of the Salvadoran bishops' conference the other four bishops—including even his own auxiliary—fought him and accused him of causing most of the country's problems. At least once he was moved to tears as he talked about the bishops' opposition.

## A Man of Prayer

In one of his letters to Rome, Romero wrote that he had always tried to do whatever God asked of him, and so he felt he had to act as he did in the circumstances he found in the archdiocese, especially because of the persecution of the Church's priests and small communities. A few such remarks in his letters, in his sermons and in this diary, plus the notes from his retreats that have survived and the memories of those who knew him, give us clues to his inner life, the source of his strength. Staff members would sometimes see him leave important meetings where they were discussing what action to take in a crisis, so that he could go to the chapel to pray. After a while, they would tell him to go and pray when they could not agree on what advice to give him, judging that he would make the best decision that way.

In his last weeks he saw that the growing violence and division would likely lead to his own death. In his last spiritual retreat he wrote:

> ...I express my consecration to the heart of Jesus, who was ever a source of inspiration and joy in my life.... I place under his loving providence all my life, and I accept with faith in him my death, however hard it be.... For me to be happy and confident, it is sufficient to know with assurance that in him is my life and my death, that in spite of my sins I have placed my trust in him and shall not be disappointed, and others will carry on with greater wisdom and holiness the works of the Church and the nation.

Three weeks later an assassin's bullet struck him as he preached at Mass. While he was only one of thousands of martyrs in El Salvador in recent years, his life was unique. He has often and rightly been called the voice of the voiceless, one which made known the sufferings and hopes of his people. He nourished that hope in them during his life and he continues to do so now.

James R. Brockman, S.J.
Author of *Romero: A Life* (Orbis Books);
editor-translator of Romero's *The Violence of Love* (Harper)

# A Note From the Translator

The three sources with which I worked on this translation are the tapes in Romero's own voice, the typed transcription prepared by the archdiocese and the version published in Spanish.

Before I began, I read as much as I could about El Salvador and about Romero himself, especially *Romero: A Life*, by James R. Brockman, S.J. (Orbis, 1990). I traveled to El Salvador in August 1990; I visited Romero's little house at the cancer hospital and the chapel where he was shot, as well as the archdiocesan offices.

Most of the difficulties in translation arise from the spoken nature of the work. Sometimes he spun out extremely long sentences; other times he left thoughts and clauses hanging as he changed direction in mid-sentence. Sometimes he recorded the accounts of two or three days at once (probably aided by a list of his appointments) with inconsistent verb tenses. Speaking for an audience who already knew what he was talking about, he also referred to more details in other documents in "the files"—the archdiocesan files.

When I met with Jon Sobrino, S.J.,[1] to ask some questions about an article of his I was translating, I told him that I was going to translate this diary. His response was that I could make all the errors I wanted translating *his* articles, but that I'd better "get Romero right." I hope I haven't let Sobrino down.

I offer thanks to the many people who helped in this project:

> to St. Anthony Messenger Press managing editor Lisa
> Biedenbach and editor Carol Luebering for their support
> and patience;

---

[1]Sobrino teaches philosophy at the Universidad Centroamericana José Simeón Cañas in San Salvador. He worked closely with Archbishop Romero and is the author of *Archbishop Romero: Memories and Reflections* (Orbis Books, 1990).

to Susan Harper, Margaret Warminski and especially Carol for their improvements to the manuscript;

to my friend Bruce Pulliam for his encouragement and the many hours he spent typing the translated text and keying corrections into the computer;

to Gail Nurre and Monica Rivera of Xavier University for their typing efforts;

to Thomas E. Quigley, Latin American Affairs adviser in the United States Catholic Conference's Office of International Justice and Peace, for his review of the manuscript;

to Father James R. Brockman, S.J., Father Jon Sobrino, S.J., and others with special knowledge of the Church, the history of El Salvador and the Spanish used there;

to Monsignor Ricardo Urioste and María Julia Hernández of the Archdiocesan Human Rights Office and to Conny de Huezo, Monsignor Urioste's secretary, for their kindness and help during my visits to the archdiocesan offices in August 1990;

to my family and friends and colleagues, who have put up with me during these long months.

Irene B. Hodgson

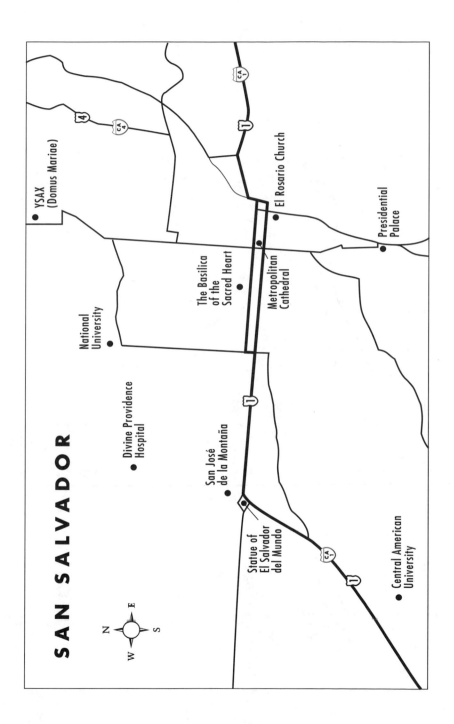

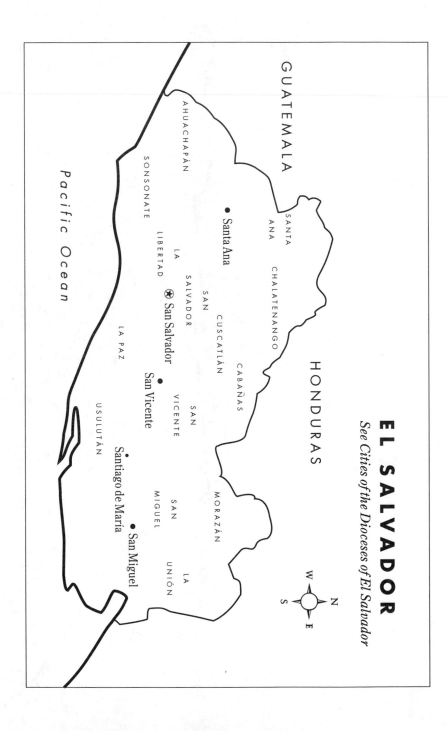

# EL SALVADOR

*See Cities of the Dioceses of El Salvador*

GUATEMALA

HONDURAS

*Pacific Ocean*

AHUACHAPÁN

SONSONATE

SANTA ANA

CHALATENANGO

LIBERTAD

LA SALVADOR

SAN SALVADOR

CUSCATLÁN

CABAÑAS

LA PAZ

USULUTÁN

SAN VICENTE

SAN MIGUEL

MORAZÁN

LA UNIÓN

• Santa Ana

✪ San Salvador

• San Vicente

• Santiago de María

• San Miguel

W N E S

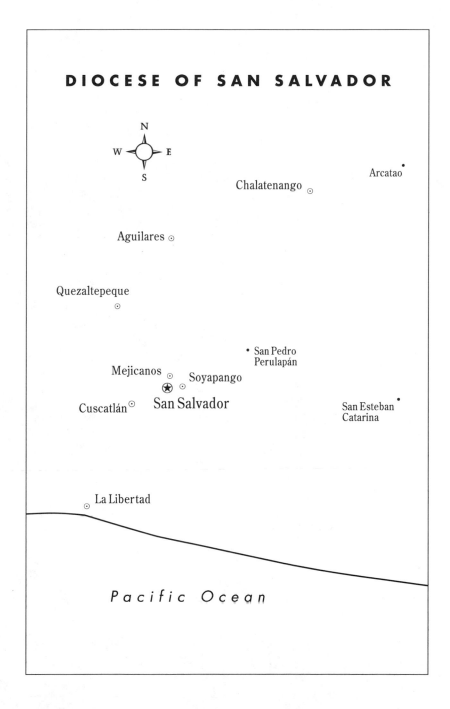

# DIOCESE OF SAN SALVADOR

Arcatao

Chalatenango ⊙

Aguilares ⊙

Quezaltepeque
⊙

• San Pedro
Perulapán

Mejicanos ⊙  Soyapango
⊛ ⊙
Cuscatlán⊙  San Salvador

San Esteban
Catarina

⊙ La Libertad

*Pacific Ocean*

# March 1978

 **Friday, March 31**

The most important meeting today was one we had with lawyers and law students we had brought together to explain to them the difficulties the Church encounters and to ask them for legal help with so many cases of abuses of human rights.

We have a small Legal Aid Office housed in the Externado San José[1] that is called Socorro Jurídico, but it is powerless in the face of so many different kinds of cases. And so we suggested to them that they organize a permanent team of distinguished lawyers and law students the Church could call on for advice of a legal nature.

Our invitation had been enthusiastically received because almost twenty people—both lawyers and law students—came. For the specific names, ask Bachiller[2] Roberto Cuéllar, of the Legal Aid Office; he has the list of those who were invited and those who attended. Among the concrete ideas that were enthusiastically proposed was that of seeking amnesty for those who have been detained because of the events at San Pedro Perulapán.[3] Next week a petition to this effect will be presented to the Assembly,[4] asking for amnesty for them. The idea of helping the Legal Aid Office was well received. The Office was asked to pull together cases needing help and to send them to the lawyers present, who offered to provide help in their own offices as long as it involved routine matters, and to work together in a collaborative effort when necessary.

Also suggested was the idea of organizing a lawyers' association that could be joined by others who had not been invited to the meeting or were

---

[1] The Jesuit elementary and secondary school.

[2] An honorary title for someone who holds a *bachillerato* (a bachelor's degree or, more often, a pre-university diploma).

[3] A town 12 miles east of San Salvador where two weeks of violence during Holy Week and Easter Week of 1978 left at least six dead, 68 missing, 14 wounded and many peasants' homes destroyed.

[4] The legislative body of El Salvador.

from other areas in order to create a consulting body as the Church had requested for its difficulties of a legal nature. It was also suggested meeting periodically to discuss these matters.

I thanked them, and told them how satisfied I was with their response to my appeal and the goodwill they had shown as lawyers with Christian conscience.

# April 1978

 **Saturday, April 1**

As I always do on the first of the month, I preached the Holy Hour and celebrated Mass in the Divine Providence Hospital.[5] After Mass there was an audience that had been requested by the Confederation of Catholic Schools of the Archdiocese, the Director of the Colegio[6] de la Asunción, Sister Inés, and of the Colegio Sagrado Corazón, Mother Nelly Rodríguez.

They informed me that they had met yesterday as well as today to consider the possibility of demonstrating solidarity with the peasants of San Pedro Perulapán and also their solidarity with the appeals made by the archdiocese for accurate information and other matters on behalf of the peasants of that place.

I explained to them my concerns about the idea, especially that this demonstration of Christian, evangelical solidarity might be confused with the strike being called for the same time by the ANDES[7] teachers' organization and that I didn't want the Catholic schools to be manipulated by ANDES. They told me that they had considered this risk and that there

---

[5] Hospital de la Divina Providencia, a hospital for indigent cancer patients where Romero lived, first in a room off the chapel and later in a little house built for him on the grounds.

[6] Elementary or high school.

[7] ANDES 21 *de junio,* National Association of Salvadoran Education, a major teachers' union.

were also difficulties within the confederation itself because they were not all in agreement. I told them that I would leave it to their judgment and would appreciate if they would not bring my name into their discussions.

Afterward they were going to meet again, later in the evening, and I did not learn that day what the results of their deliberations were.

## Sunday, April 2

At eight o'clock, as usual, I celebrated Mass in the cathedral, always filled to overflowing with the faithful, who extended all the way to the park in front. I read, with a few comments, the statement from the archdiocese about the events at San Pedro Perulapán, which can be found in its entirety in the archdiocesan files.

The main theme of my comments was related to the biblical readings on the theme: "The risen Christ lives and he lives in his community of Christians on this earth."

I first explained the characteristics of the risen Christ according to St. Thomas: Lord and God, messenger and instrument of the redemption of humankind. His greeting of peace is the synthesis of the gift that the Father sent us in Christ; that is, salvation. I presented the Risen One also as the object of our hope as the Church makes its pilgrimage through life, always desiring the encounter with that Christ who is to return.

My second point was to explain the characteristics of the Christian community that carries the spirit of Christ in the world. The Gospel tells us how the resurrected Christ sent the Church in the same way that the Father had sent him, and that by breathing on the new Church, like God in paradise breathing on Adam's clay, he inspired in it the new life that the Church has to bring to the world: "Receive the holy Spirit" [John 20:22]. The characteristics of that community are in the first reading from the Acts of the Apostles, which says that the multitude all lived together and shared with each other; that it was a community where prayer abounded, where the members came together in the breaking of bread and lived in great hope.

I explained that these were indications of what the Church should be like, the community that follows Christ and is the presence of Christ in this world, the saving mission of Christ. A community of life that grows and a community where life finds salvation. The Book of Acts says it this way: "...[E]very day the Lord added to their number those who were being saved" [Acts 2:47]. A community of life that showed its communion by mutually sharing together the goods of the Lord; even the goods of the earth were put at the service of all. A community of life for its increasing repute under the authority of the apostles.

But, secondly, it was principally a faith community, and this is what distinguishes the Church from any other social group or human organization. I emphasized this because the Church should not be confused with other organisms and be falsely accused, as it is now when it is accused of being responsible for violence. I told them that this community of faith and of the Spirit had to be a community in conformity with the teachings of the apostles, a community of prayer and a community nourished with the sacraments and, finally, an eschatological community that lives, then, the hope of something beyond.

At three in the afternoon I had been invited by the Salesian Sisters to the Colegio María Auxiliadora, where they were having an oratorio for the girls. They had prepared a group of young people for Confirmation and the Mass was very beautiful. The music vibrated with a unique enthusiasm. When the time came for the Gospel, I explained to them that the breath of Jesus was on the community: It was the Spirit of God given to those who would believe in Jesus Christ. I explained Confirmation to them—the rite and its meaning. And I administered to them this sacrament of the Holy Spirit. There were about forty young women who had been prepared to receive the Sacrament of Confirmation this afternoon.

In the evening, at six-thirty, in Colonia[8] Miramonte, in the parish Church of the Resurrection—they are celebrating the patronal feast of this parish named for the Resurrection of the Lord—the parish community came in great numbers, filling the church. The Augustinian Fathers and other priests of the vicariate of this part of the city concelebrated Mass with me.

I preached on the Gospel and made reference to the empty tomb of the risen Jesus and to the sealed tomb of Father Alfonso Navarro,[9] who just last year, in this very celebration, had showed such a pastor's enthusiasm in a parish that bears witness to the resurrection of Christ. His tomb was sealed after he was murdered, one of two priests shot dead this last year. His sealed tomb could be perceived as a failure of the redemption and resurrection of Christ and yet it is a sign of hope. Our dead will be raised and the tombs of our dead that today are sealed by the triumph of death will one day also be like that of Christ—empty tombs. Christ's empty tomb is a sign of the final victory, of redemption realized. Until then, we must struggle, we must work so that the message of that

---

[8] A word used to describe different neighborhoods or parts of a city.

[9] Shot in his rectory, along with a 14-year-old boy, on May 11, 1977.

empty tomb of Christ may enlighten all our work on earth with hope until the fulfillment of the Lord's redemption.

After Mass the community of the parish of Miramonte had prepared a light meal for all of those at Mass—a wonderful experience of the family feeling of the parish. The Augustinian Fathers who run this parish are to be commended because they have worked with enthusiasm and continue to work toward a model parish community.

 **Monday, April 3**

The Bishops' Conference of El Salvador called an urgent meeting. My first impulse was not to go, since the invitation arrived only on Monday morning. I was advised to go, however, and I did because it had to do with the matter of the letter from the priests to the nuncio,[10] and I could, therefore, by going give an opinion in defense of the priests.

As I expected, when I arrived at the meeting, I found that everything had already been decided prior to the meeting. Bishop Rivera's telegram saying that he could not come because of a meeting in Guatemala and asking them to wait since the topic required a meeting at which all the bishops would be present was not heeded, even though I seconded Bishop [Arturo] Rivera's request. With the vote, naturally, four bishops against my one vote, the meeting was held. I also protested that the document to be discussed had been prepared in advance. They told me that there was always a draft document presented, but I could see that it was not just a draft, since it was not discussed. Rather they began right away to sign it in spite of my giving my reasons against it.

My reasons were these: The priests have written a letter to the nuncio, so what should happen now is that the nuncio should invite the priests to talk with him. Another reason is that the document of the bishops against the priests accuses them of offending the Holy See. I made a distinction between the Holy See—mainly the person of the pope with whom these priests feel themselves united in the faith—and the person of the nuncio who represents the pope but does not always do so effectively. In order to show this, I pointed out some things that have

---

[10] A letter to the papal representative, Emanuele Gerada, signed by 200 or so priests and religious, criticizing the nuncio for disagreeing with Romero's policies and openly supporting "a repressive and unjust government."

made the nuncio an unpopular figure both here and in Guatemala.[11] Another reason is that the document written by the priests should itself be analyzed, not just to criticize the composition or the inadequacy of expression, but rather to see concretely what the nuncio has done to cause them to say that his witness is less than Christian. The priests should not be accused without a hearing, and it seems to me that publishing this document will only foment division among the bishops, since I would not agree to sign it.

In spite of all of these reasons, the document was already being passed around so that the four bishops could sign it: Bishop Aparicio, president of the Conference; Bishop Barrera, bishop of Santa Ana; Bishop Alvarez, bishop of San Miguel; and Bishop Revelo, auxiliary bishop of San Salvador.

The document was approved, and I was subjected to many false accusations by the other bishops. I was told that my preaching is subversive, violent; that my priests provoke a climate of violence among the peasants; and that we should not complain about the abuses that the authorities are committing. The archdiocese was accused of interfering in the other dioceses, causing division among the priests and pastoral unrest in other dioceses. The archdiocese was accused of sowing confusion in the seminary, and they said that it was urgent that the archdiocesan offices leave the building of the San José de la Montaña Seminary.[12] And other caluminous and false accusations to which I preferred not to respond.

It has been a bitter day because of this event and I lament that the division among the bishops will be worsened by this step, which seems to me not to be very wise.

---

[11] At that time Archbishop Emanuele Gerada was nuncio for both countries.

[12] The archdiocesan offices occupied space in the building which housed the major seminary serving all the dioceses of El Salvador.

**Tuesday, April 4**

I give personal thanks to God because today is the thirty-sixth anniversary of my ordination as a priest in Rome.

The meeting of the clergy was held. The topic for study was base communities.[13] It was presented by Father Jesús Delgado, structuring it as a consultation for the Latin American Bishops' Conference to be held in Puebla next October.

The second part was an explanation of and information about what happened Holy Week and Easter in San Pedro Perulapán and in parts of the archdiocese, where the repressive governmental forces have done many things to destroy the tranquility of the villages and the dignity of human rights.

On our side, we have published a statement commenting on this situation and expressing our solidarity with the people who are suffering.

Some parish priests brought catechists, peasants who have lived through these tragic hours of a terribly bloody and repressive Holy Week.

It was agreed to send to Rome on behalf of all the clergy and women religious present there a vote of solidarity with the archbishop to counteract the document of the bishops who, at their meeting, insulted the Archbishop of San Salvador and have attacked him in their statement, which is to be published.

In the afternoon an interview with a Swedish journalist and a conversation with Father Jesús Delgado on many topics relating to the Bishops' Conference and the archdiocese.

 **Wednesday, April 5**

As we do every Wednesday, we had a study breakfast with representatives of the Priests' Senate[14] and members of the Justice and Peace Commission. Today's consultation centered around the document published by the bishops in support of the nuncio, Archbishop Gerada, because of a letter addressed to him by some priests and nuns calling his attention to what they see as an anti-Christian witness in his actions. The bishops, in their document, express their solidarity with the nuncio and, to some extent, insult the priests a little. I explained in the

---

[13] Small groups who meet regularly, usually under lay leadership, to explore Scripture and its relationship to their lives.

[14] An advisory body representing the priests of the archdiocese.

meeting what I had said about this to the bishops and why I did not sign this declaration.

My reasons were these: In the first place, because the meeting of Monday, April 3, called urgently by the conference, did not seem right to me. Bishop Rivera of Santiago de María was not present and, in spite of the fact that in his telegram he asked them to wait for him, they would not accede to his request and voted against it. As for me, I agreed with Bishop Rivera's request and voted for it. But since the other four wanted to hold the meeting, my vote seemed very small compared to those four: Bishops Aparicio, Barrera, Alvarez and Revelo.

In the second place, I asked that we discuss the appropriateness of publishing, at a time so given to division, a statement that would cause an even greater division of opinion in our Church and that would make the bishops look bad, given the present atmosphere. Bishop Revelo answered that he did not care about the atmosphere, but only about carrying out his duty.

Another of my reasons was that, before making a statement against the priests, it seemed to me only fair to hear and talk with them and, if it were possible, to have the nuncio present so that things could be cleared up first there and that then perhaps it would not be necessary to do anything further.

Another of my reasons was that a dispassionate analysis of the letter from the priests and religious to the nuncio perhaps would not find it merited this condemnation, for it would require analyzing the facts referred to in the letter—facts that seem to indicate rather that the nuncio should think about how to provide a more Christian witness. And I referred specifically to those facts, principally to his having supported Father [Rogelio] Esquivel,[15] knowing that he was going against the opinion and pastoral line of his bishop.

Bishop Aparicio took advantage of this occasion to say that what I defended in the priests against the nuncio was the same thing I was doing with the dioceses of El Salvador; that my preaching was violent, subversive; that it was dividing the clergy and the dioceses; that the priests now looked more to the archdiocese than to their own bishops.

I do not remember how many more accusations he made that were also supported by my brothers: Bishop Barrera, who also called my preaching violent; Bishop Alvarez, who took the opportunity to voice his disagreement with me; and the strangest part was that Bishop Revelo, recently named my auxiliary bishop, also took the opportunity to say he disagreed with my approach. He said I was not infallible when I explained

---

[15] A priest Romero had removed from pastoral office.

that my orientation was precisely that outlined by the documents of the Council [Vatican II], the recent encyclicals of the popes and Medellín.[16] According to Bishop Revelo, I could be wrong in the application of those documents and that, therefore, he was not obliged to agree with this approach.

I preferred to remain silent for the rest of the meeting since the document that was published was only read one time and there was no opportunity for clarification. Rather, it was signed in this rather tense atmosphere, which only confirmed for me what I said at the beginning: "This has all been arranged in advance."

Then the advisors at breakfast this morning gave me their opinions. They thought it better for me not to issue any clarification, that the absence of my signature from the signatures of the other bishops was testimony enough and that everyone thought that the letter published by the bishops in support of the nuncio would rather arouse curiosity about the letter, which many have not seen and would therefore require them to see what the clergy thinks of the nuncio. And, also that the letter itself is badly written—it even refers to personal accusations against the priests that have nothing to do with the matter—and that the letter itself will be more likely to defame the nuncio and the hierarchy itself. "It is a shame," they said, "for this action even further to divide Catholics who were already divided." And that if I wanted to issue a clarification, it would be better to write to the bishops' conference and send a copy to the nuncio and to the Holy See explaining my reasons for not signing and describing in it how the process took place. The same thing could be asked of Bishop Rivera, to write a separate letter expressing his unhappiness with the meeting in which it was agreed to write this letter of support to the nuncio.

After the meeting, this morning at nine o'clock I was in the Externado San José in the Legal Aid Office, where there were several lawyers and law students gathered to sign the petition for amnesty that they later took to the legislative assembly on behalf of the men and women arrested because of the events in San Pedro Perulapán.

I was very glad that the lawyers and law students took this occasion to strengthen even more their desire to stay united, to meet frequently, to study legal problems together and support the needs of our people, especially those of the poor. Specifically, they promised to study and analyze the Law for the Defense of Public Order[17] and prove that it is

---

[16] The Second General Conference of Latin American Bishops, held in Medellín, Colombia, in 1968.

[17] Enacted in November 1977 and immediately criticized because of the restrictions it placed on political activity and because it gave wide powers to the security forces to detain suspects. It was finally repealed in 1979.

unconstitutional. They will meet next Monday at seven o'clock in the evening in the same place to decide on the frequency of their meetings from then on and the way in which they will proceed.

Afterward in the chancery[18] there was a series of very interesting meetings, such as that of the Ricaldone missionary group, which includes several students from that Salesian school and women students from the Colegio de la Asunción.

Mother Lidia Valle also came, who is currently assistant mother superior of the Congregation of the Oblate Sisters of Divine Love, and she explained to me several problems that congregation has.

Another interview was with Ingeniero[19] Galván, who contributes in an exemplary fashion to the organization of the diocesan curia.[20] He told me about some different situations related to the Caritas[21] Commission, which do not sound very good and which we will have to look at more closely, as well as some projects on the social communication of the archdiocese. It seems that our programming on YSAX[22] is widely received but is not enough to neutralize the growing feeling against the Church. According to him, we must try for shorter programs, broadcast often during the day so that they reach into those spheres where the longer programs are not listened to and which have wrong ideas about the Church.

Today the letter from the bishops (Aparicio, Barrera, Alvarez and Revelo) to the nuncio, denouncing the priests who wrote demanding that he take a more evangelical position, appeared in the newspapers. The publication of this letter has caused a very negative reaction against the bishops, as it is considered an imprudent demonstration of the lack of unity, since the letter was not signed by Bishop Rivera, who was not at the meeting, or by me, since I did not agree with its publication.

As usual on Wednesdays, I was interviewed today on the radio. This time it centered around the events in San Pedro Perulapán and some questions posed by YSAX listeners.

---

[18] The archdiocesan offices.

[19] A title used for one who holds a degree in engineering.

[20] Administrative offices.

[21] The main social assistance group of the Church in most Latin American countries.

[22] The archdiocesan radio station.

## Thursday, April 6

After breakfast, I left with Father Leopoldo Deras for San Juan Opico, where I turned over the parish to Father Jorge Salinas, who had been in Tacachico. He will now have to administer the parishes of both Opico and Tacachico. After the inauguration Mass we had an interesting meeting with the catechists, celebrants of the word and others who cooperate in the parish life in that fervent parish of San Juan Opico. On a personal level, I was especially moved to find myself in the birthplace of my bishop, Bishop Juan Antonio Dueñas y Argumedo, and of my brother in the priesthood, good friend and companion, Bishop Rafael Valladares, who was auxiliary bishop of San Salvador when he died.

Afterward we went to San Rafael Cedros, where Father Deras had a great number of people gathered all the way from the entrance of the town to the church. In church, I officiated at the Confirmation of some forty children, a ceremony held during Mass, at which all of us present renewed our Confirmation vows.

I also talked with groups from ecclesial base communities and with the sewing academy that is producing much fruit there in San Rafael Cedros.

In the afternoon, after San Rafael Cedros, we went to Santiago de María, where I talked with Bishop Rivera, particularly about the disagreeable incident of the publication of the letter from the bishops to the nuncio. This and other subjects that concern us a great deal as pastors in this divided atmosphere of the bishops' conference filled nearly an hour of conversation. Afterward he invited us to stay for dinner, and I left very late. To top it off, we had a flat tire on the road and did not arrive at my residence until about eleven o'clock.

 ## Friday, April 7

Among the many visitors who arrived at the archdiocese, I want to single out the Vincentian Fathers, gathered here from all their Central American houses, who came to express to me their solidarity and offer me their prayers in the difficult service of the archdiocese.

Also, a group of women students, with a professor, who brought tape recorders to interview me on various matters relating to the situation of the Church in this country and its mission among us. The young women showed great interest in questions that worry many Salvadorans today. With God's grace, I believe that I was able to answer and to let these young people see the message of the Church.

Lunch was at Don Pepe Simán's[23], where there was also an Englishman, Mr. Julian [Filochowski], who brought a letter and a special greeting from the Cardinal of England [Basil Hume], which showed a very pastoral, very affectionate solidarity. His words are a message of great encouragement for me. I asked him to take back to the Cardinal of England my fraternal embrace, my appreciation and a promise to write him very soon.

The opportunity has been offered me, possibly in June, to speak in England and to travel to other countries of Europe to explain the situation of our Church. The conversation with this Catholic gentleman who has traveled through many countries of Latin America and who knows all of our problems was very encouraging to me and provided me with some guidance. He told me that, just as my situation is very difficult in El Salvador, so there are bishops in other Latin American countries in very similar situations: Many times neither their brother fellow bishops nor the people around them understand them and the commitment which the gospel and the present teaching of the Church ask of pastors. I hope, then, to be faithful to this teaching, and I pray for all my brother bishops faced with similar difficulties.

From four p.m. until about six-thirty or seven, I was with the major seminarians[24] of the archdiocese discussing different topics, and we ended with a celebration of the Holy Eucharist in which we meditated in the light of God's word.

In the evening, finally, I went to the Colegio de la Asunción, where women religious from Guatemala, Nicaragua and El Salvador have been meeting this week to review their work and the spirit of their congregation in their communities. After Mass, which was celebrated with great devotion, we had dinner together and shared our thoughts on the situation of our three neighboring countries: Guatemala, Nicaragua and El Salvador.

---

[23] José "Pepe" Simán, prominent businessman and president of the archdiocesan Justice and Peace Commission.

[24] Students in advanced training for the priesthoood.

**Saturday, April 8**

A visit to the town of Dulce Nombre de María in the department[25] of Chalatenango, arranged with the Oblate Sisters of the Sacred Heart, who work in that city and have some problems locally. Nevertheless, my arrival there and my visit were very moving experiences for me: the meeting in the town, the celebration of Mass, the meeting we had later with the celebrants of the word, catechists and other groups active in the Church. It is a community that gives real hope, a community that is alive. The Carmelite Missionary Sisters and members of the neighboring community of La Laguna, also in the department of Chalatenango, were present as well. These communities also participated in the meeting we had at the end of my visit, a little before lunch.

It seemed to me that the problem the sisters had with some people in the town was automatically solved, given the enthusiasm of all the other Catholics of the town and of the little villages who showed their support for the sisters who had called them together.

A disagreeable detail when I entered the town was the aggressive posture of a member of the National Guard, who only got out of the middle of the street when the crowd that accompanied me at that time was very near. I noticed how surprised people, especially the children, were by this gesture, and I could easily see that they are planting seeds in Dulce Nombre de María of what they call "a psychological war." I saw this in the people who arrived from the small villages—a kind of fear, worse because they had circulated a rumor that I was going to come with some guerillas and they tried to dissuade the people from going to participate in the ceremony and the meetings that we had planned.

 **Sunday, April 9**

Mass, as always, at eight o'clock in the cathedral, with a homily on the theme of the feast of the Paschal Mystery. I discussed the Jewish origin of the Paschal feast and how Christ, at Passover time, achieved the redemption and so the mystery of the death, resurrection and ascension of Christ was called the Paschal Mystery and, later, the Christian Pasch or Easter. The readings of the day give these characteristics of the Paschal Mystery: It is a mystery of liberation. Christ

---

[25]*Departamento*, a territorial division equivalent to a province or a state.

through his Paschal Mystery redeems us from sin, from death, from hell and from every kind of slavery. I pointed out that Christian liberation is more complete and deeper than any other liberation that is merely political, social or economic.

The second thing I pointed out was the sacramental nature, the sacrament, of the Church of Christ, and thus a hidden presence of the Lord, but a true presence with all of its grace and its redeeming power in the Church. The passage about the disciples at Emmaus points out this hidden nature of Christ and how he is present on humankind's pilgrimage.

The third characteristic of our Paschal Mystery is its communitarian and ecclesial aspect. It is a mystery that creates a Church that is communion. And finally, its eschatological nature. In this Sunday's readings this eschatological aspect is evident when Christ reproaches the disciples at Emmaus, who were sad because they expected a very temporal liberation, and he teaches them through the prophets that it was necessary to suffer and enter through that suffering into the glory that is the ultimate goal of Christian liberation.

The cathedral seemed fuller today than on previous Sundays.

In the afternoon, invited by the Parish of the Divine Providence in the Colonia Atlacatl, I went to celebrate Mass and to share in the celebration of the anniversary of the Legion of Mary in that parish, where the Redemptorist Fathers are in charge.

 **Monday, April 10**

As I do every Monday, I have given precedence to meetings with priests. I talked with Father [Rafael] Palacios, who informed me about his work in the ecclesial base communities and his work of motivating group pastoral work in the city of Santa Tecla. His news is very comforting, and I hope that this difficult task will progress if, trusting in the Lord, we work to unite the diverse sectors of that parish or of those parishes that are already well supplied with priests, women religious, Catholic schools and laypeople who are already well prepared.

With Father Rafael Moreno [S.J.] we also talked about problems having to do with the social communication of the archdiocese. Father Abdón Arce, from the Diocese of Santiago de María, paid me a visit to invite me to the fortieth anniversary of his ordination as a priest.

At night, an interesting talk with Father [Juan] Hernández Pico [S.J.], with whom we are preparing a pastoral letter on faith and politics, on which all of the advisory committee with which we meet on a weekly basis are working. Besides the work on the pastoral letter, we spoke of some very important topics relating to the pastoral work in our archdiocese and in Latin America in general, especially about its perspective on the Third Latin America Bishops' Conference in Puebla.[26]

 **Tuesday, April 11**

I celebrated Mass in the morning in the Colegio de la Asunción with the students studying for their *bachillerato*. I took the opportunity to introduce myself and tell them that I was glad to meet them personally this way since they had heard, undoubtedly, about the two different images of the archbishop that are presented in San Salvador. For some, he is the cause of all evil, a monster of evil; for others, thank God—for the simple people, especially—I am the pastor. "And how I wish you had been witnesseses to the reception they give my word and my presence, especially in the very small towns!"

I introduced myself, then, as pastor and gave them the message I give everywhere, applied, naturally, to the particular situation of the Colegio de la Asunción. And I spoke to them in this way, developing these three concepts: the young woman, the woman, the Christian woman, using each of these categories to ask them to be the true hope of the Church, of their family, of their country. According to what the director of the school, Mother Inés, told me later, the comments were very favorable and a good impression was left at the school.

Later I went by Mr. [Adolfo] Rey Prendes's house, where some members of the Christian Democratic Party had invited me to have breakfast and talk with me about their political perspective and about our Church. It was a very enriching dialogue, in which I had the opportunity to clarify once again the mission of the Church, which must not be confused in any way with a political party—even though they sometimes try to achieve similar objectives like social justice, political participation of all citizens, etc. They also made some very insightful comments to me

---

[26] Originally scheduled for October 1978, the conference was postponed because of the deaths of Pope Paul VI and Pope John Paul I. It convened in Puebla, Mexico, in January 1979.

about how a Church can be truly autonomous, independent of all political hue.

In the archdiocese I found the priests and laity of the Vicariate[27] of Cuscatlán and of the Commission of Laity meeting in order to discuss how better, as Church, to serve this sector of the department of Cuscatlán, which is being so tormented by military operatives, by ORDEN[28] and by other political elements that try to repress any demonstration against the regime in power.

It was agreed to develop as a mission of the Church a campaign to calm people down and also to help in an impartial way with all the needs of that sector of the archdiocese. We can take the opportunity to organize the aid commissions in all the parishes and towns and small villages. That can be a beginning for the parish committees of Caritas.

In the afternoon representatives of the board of the Confederation of Catholic Schools visited me to inform me about the meeting they had this last Saturday, called by the bishop who is president of the Education Commission, Bishop Aparicio. According to them, Bishop Aparicio intended to remove the current board and to single them out because of the letter that the board of the Federation had sent to the nuncio—along similar lines as the letter from the priests asking the nuncio to have a more evangelical attitude. It seems the session was very stormy, and there were very serious complaints against Bishop Aparicio and his less-than-pastoral attitudes. One of these is his suspension of ten priests for signing the letter against the nuncio, a suspension that has caused a good deal of disturbance in the whole country, principally in the Diocese of San Vicente.

In between, there were different visits of a personal nature that kept me busy all day.

---

[27] A sub-unit of a diocese.

[28] Democratic Nationalist Organization, the government's antisubversive paramilitary organization, composed mostly of peasants.

**Wednesday, April 12**

Besides the private audiences, it has been a very transcendent day. The breakfast meeting with the Justice and Peace Commission and with representatives of the Priests' Senate turned out to be very interesting; its theme was the confusion that could arise between the Church and the BPR, the Popular Revolutionary Bloc, because many people from the Bloc have taken refuge in the seminary in these times of persecution, principally in the department of Cuscatlán. The criticism has been made that many from the Bloc have taken advantage of this situation to make the seminary a kind of general headquarters for their activities. They said that when there was a large group gathered in the seminary, those of the Bloc had planned the occupation of the cathedral and the embassies that has filled today's news. We discussed at length the need to clarify the position of the Church, for it is always obligated to give aid to those who are persecuted and to be the voice of the voiceless, but we must clearly separate the mission that is purely of the Church from any partisan aspect, especially if it has a revolutionary nature.

We discussed also the rumors we hear about a committee that will go to Rome planning to give a negative report about the archbishop with the intention of having him removed. I was advised that it would be useful to go to Rome to report personally, making use of intermediaries who know that atmosphere well (and specific mention was made of the Curia of the Society of Jesus), and to be sure also that other religious and laypeople will give testimony favorable to the pastoral work of the archdiocese in order to neutralize the official reports of the nunciature and the powerful information from the government and the capital.

I spent the greater part of the afternoon at the minor seminary.[29] We had agreed to have a meeting and it turned out to be very interesting, since the young men who are studying for the bachillerato love their vocation a great deal and are closely linked as well to the concerns of the people and of our Church. In responding to their questions and in my summary, in the meeting as well as in the Mass we had at the end, I spoke to them about the beauty of a vocation lived thus in obedience to God's call, and, because of that, the efforts to become holy and live united with God. And, on the other hand, from God, from that contemplation of God, to manage to reflect God's thought toward so complicated and difficult a people as the one that they will have to guide spiritually when they are priests—or even if they do not become priests, as laypeople who had the chance to form themselves, even if only for a few years, in the seminary.

---

[29] A preparatory school for aspirants to the priesthood.

At night we had a report from the committees that have been working to provide information and aid to the victims of the situations in Perulapán and in the department of Cuscatlán. It also turned out to be a very animated meeting in which there was honest recognition of errors, but also one in which a program of assistance and justice for the archdiocese was planned for even when this emergency is over. There was talk already about formally creating a Vicariate of Solidarity,[30] but for now, it is only a solidarity committee.

Today we also had a meeting with the leaders of the Popular Revolutionary Bloc. To represent the Church, the Vicar General[31] went with me, the priest in charge of social communication and some laypeople, specifically, from the emergency or solidarity committee that works in the area where problems have occurred. It was about the occupation of the cathedral and the embassies, what their goals are and how they will respect the role of the Church and not confuse the two, although the Church is providing help. It is not aiding the Popular Revolutionary Bloc as such, but because from a Christian perspective, the Church, like a Good Samaritan, has tried to help everyone in need, of whatever stripe. In this sense, we begged them to continue, and have their followers continue, to respect the autonomy of the Church and not to use it in any way to advance their own ends.

For its side the Church promised to continue aiding them and all who need help because their human rights are abused. Specifically, they asked to use the premises of the archdiocese for a meeting with the ambassadors of the occupied embassies; they were advised to try for a diplomatic location, where the diplomats could feel more at ease. If they could not get one, they could, as a service offered impartially by the Church, use the premises of the diocesan curia for such a dialogue.

---

[30] Modeled after the human rights agency of this name in the Archdiocese of Santiago, Chile, created in 1976.

[31] Monsignor Ricardo Urioste.

**Thursday, April 13**

This morning the leaders of the Popular Revolutionary Bloc are waiting at the chancery for the response of the ambassadors of the embassies occupied by the Bloc, so as to explain to them their situation and what they want. It mainly has to do with getting the ambassadors to influence the government to withdraw its military forces from their villages so that they can return to their homes and get on with cultivating their lands. They need to do that now, for winter is already approaching. They also have occupied the cathedral with this same goal: to call the attention of the people of the city of San Salvador to that situation. They will also ask that the ambassadors make known to their governments and, through their governments around the world, the Salvadoran situation.

Since they have asked for mediation, the archdiocese has committed the auxiliary bishop, Bishop Revelo, to represent the Church. According to conversations by telephone, Bishop Revelo would be present at one in the afternoon, the time at which the ambassadors were going to meet with the representatives of the Bloc at the chancery.

The situation of those who occupy the cathedral is rather difficult since the National Police have surrounded the cathedral and are blocking all access. And in the cathedral there are many people, among them women and children, who will suffer greatly if they do not get food. On its part, the archdiocese has issued a bulletin to express its position on the situation—a situation of anguish, to which the archdiocese has responded in a spirit of genuinely impartial charity. It has said that the situation in the cathedral is serious and it asks, above all, that the presence of women and children be taken into consideration. This bulletin has also denied the rumor being circulated that there will be a Mass today at five o'clock in the cathedral. The archbishop has not been told about this, nor has he called or authorized any Mass. It does call on the authorities and those in charge to normalize the situation without violence.

This morning I also had a meeting with the team preparing the pastoral letter that I want to have ready for Pentecost, which will be titled: "Faith, the Church and Political Commitment," since it urges needed clarification of our situation, which is so politically sensitive and where there is so much danger of confusing true faith with political action. The need, then, of clarifying these points has made it essential for me to prepare, with a team that is intelligent, united and enthusiastic, some norms that will serve as guidelines for our people.

In the evening we prepared a recording with the seminarians that will be broadcast tomorrow on the *Young People's Program,* which will be especially directed to next Sunday's theme, which is World Day of Prayer for Vocations. Very sensibly, the team responsible for this program has gotten the views of two seminarians about their priestly vocation, of a woman religious about her vocation and of a married man to point out also to the young people that marriage is a Christian vocation. The recording ends with choral recitation of the prayer that the pope composed and has published at the end of his message for the Day for Vocations next Sunday.

 **Friday, April 14**

In the morning, a great deal of activity with the Committee for Information and Aid that has been organized around the situation of San Pedro Perulapán and of the department of Cuscatlán. There are problems with the group that is occupying the seminary, or rather, the parish house of San José de la Montaña, since they do not want to accept the authority of the Aid Committee. It seems that, controlled by the Popular Revolutionary Bloc, they are trying to turn this occupation into a center of operations for their political activities.

We pointed this out to them, since the Church does not want to be identified with any activity of a purely partisan nature, but rather serve those who need it with the Church's own charity, which is that of the gospel. We have managed, on the other hand, to convince the faithful to keep a distance from whatever political side or group or organization in order to be able, as the institutional Church, to serve all who need its message and its salvation. This has served to purify our service with a true sense of Church.

I had meetings with several priests, since they are arriving from all over the country for the meeting called by the priests' cooperative[32] that was to be held in the parish of San José de la Montaña, but that, out of prudence (given the police vigilance there), it was agreed it would be better to move it to the parish of Cristo Redentor, at the end of Escalón Street. At noon, worried about the Christians occupying the cathedral and especially about the parish priest of the cathedral, Monsignor Modesto López, we debated about what could be done, since they are surrounded by the police and they are not letting anyone in, not even to take them food.

---

[32] A buyers' co-op which purchased in bulk for the parish.

A committee of teachers from ANDES asked for the Church's help, since they have food for these people but cannot figure out how to get it to them. It seemed to me to be prudent to go first to speak with Monsignor López. I was accompanied by the auxiliary bishop, Bishop Revelo, but at the corner of the cathedral facing the National Palace we ran into a lieutenant, the one who commands the operation that has the cathedral surrounded, and he told us that he was very sorry but that we could not go in without his first communicating with the ministry or with his commanders. He had me wait in the sun almost—over half an hour. When I saw that it was taking so long, I told him that I was very sorry but that I was leaving and that it would better if I came back in the afternoon.

The same thing happened when we went to the door of the cathedral rectory. I wanted a policeman who guarded that entrance to let me go in, but that was not possible either. Because of this, I was only able to talk with Monsignor López on the telephone and assure myself that everything was all right with him and also that nothing new had happened to those who had taken refuge in the cathedral, or rather, those who had occupied the cathedral.

Bishop Revelo went this afternoon to meet with the president of the republic [General Carlos Humberto Romero] after having talked with me, to explain to him that the concrete request being made of him was to guarantee to the peasants who are occupying the cathedral or who are fleeing from their villages that they can go back, that they will find a peaceful atmosphere and be able to begin to work after being obliged to flee. The president agreed and said that, if they left the cathedral in small groups and let him know when they would leave, he would immediately withdraw the army or the police. He also said that he would guarantee to these people a peaceful return to the villages they are from.

At the same time, in the afternoon, the ambassadors of the embassies occupied by the Popular Revolutionary Bloc—that is, the embassies of Panamá, Venezuela, Costa Rica and Switzerland—talked with the negotiating team from the Bloc. The Bloc presented the objectives that had led them to these occupations. In the first place, they want a peaceful return to their villages and therefore the withdrawal of all military forces and an end to all activity causing violence in their lives in the villages. Second, they asked that the prisoners taken as a result of these military operations in those villages be released. They also asked the ambassadors to pressure the president to agree to their requests and to ask their respective governments to make the situation of the country known.

After a long dialogue between the ambassadors and the Bloc they arrived at an agreement, but those representing the Bloc said that they still had to consult with their leaders about this latest agreement and would have to leave a definite resolution for the next day. If it had not been for this condition, the ambassadors themselves would have gone that very same afternoon to talk to the president.

I insisted that they should move with all speed, because it meant another night that the people involved in the occupations would be obliged to sleep poorly when such lack of comfort could be avoided. Also, the next day was Saturday, and it would be more difficult to get meetings and have access to offices.

Nevertheless, it was left until tomorrow (Saturday). The ambassadors will be notified by the representatives of the Bloc when they are ready to reach a definite agreement, and the four ambassadors will be able to join in the petition that the diplomatic corps will make to the president.

In the evening I went to the cathedral with Bishop Revelo to visit Monsignor Modesto López and those occupying the cathedral since, in the audience Bishop Revelo had with the president, the president told him that we could go to the cathedral whenever we wanted to and that he would notify the police, who were still guarding it.

As always, the commanders of the forces that stand guard were on the corner closest to the National Palace. They made us leave the car there, so we went on foot, accompanied by the colonel, to the rectory of the cathedral. We talked with Monsignor Modesto López, who is calm, normal, and later we went to talk with those who are occupying the cathedral. Their spirit is good; no one is seriously ill; they have food that Caritas has provided for them.

I took advantage of the opportunity to give them a little Christian guidance, calling them to the true liberation which is that from sin and to a love of Jesus Christ free of all resentment, all hatred, whatever is out of harmony with their faith. And then we talked with the leaders (some five young men), with whom we shared the news we had brought, of both the meeting with the ambassadors and the interview with the president. They are waiting for orders from their leaders to end the occupation of the cathedral, which will not happen until they have some assurance of achieving their objectives. For this reason, although they are hopeful that everything can be resolved tomorrow (Saturday), nevertheless, they think that this occupation of the cathedral could be prolonged.

It is obvious that they do not have a negative attitude toward the Church, but it is also clear that they are not very interested in the concerns that the Church has in regard to the celebration of the Sunday Masses and that they give precedence to the group interests of the organization to which they belong. They asked me to say Mass for them, and I promised to do so.

When we left, after a long time, the colonel who had escorted us was still there along with other policemen, and he commented that we had been in there for a long time. To which we responded: "It is not strange at all, since we were in our own house," and also that there was also a great deal of talking to be done to promote a situation that would avoid violence—that our visit had been, then, of benefit to the rector of the cathedral and to the group that is occupying it.

The colonel told us that he had accompanied us from our car to the door of the rectory when we arrived because he had heard that they were going to throw a bomb at me—that, for that reason, he had protected me. Of course, I realized that it was one of those exaggerations that they often use to justify their military actions. He offered also to send an escort with me so that nothing would happen to me on the way home. I thanked him, but I told him that it was not necessary.

I headed to the Externado San José where, convened by the Legal Aid Office, there was a group of some fifteen lawyers and law students, more or less, who had been called together by a letter that I signed, in order to continue this hopeful effort of law professionals who want to work together in a more noble way in what is a noble profession. I was very glad that at ten o'clock at night, when I arrived, they were still working with great enthusiasm.

They had already heard as a group those in charge of the Aid Committee who had come to ask them to help resolve the occupations and for other legal aid that they could provide in that situation. I noticed their great sense of the law and their real sorrow at the extent of the violation of the law in our country. They want to make the rule of law respected and, specifically, they spoke about the petition of amnesty for the political prisoners who had been taken in this military operation in the department of Cuscatlán, as well as of studying the Law for the Defense of Public Order, which is the cause of so much uneasiness, so many attacks on our peasants and in our cities as well. In short, an organization of jurists that, God willing, will create a great hope for our people.

**Saturday, April 15**

I had invited the new auxiliary bishop, Bishop Revelo; the vicar general, Monsignor Urioste; the chancellor, Father Brito; and the diocesan treasurer, Father Barrera, to have breakfast together in the dining room of the Divine Providence Hospital. After commenting on the status of our activities with regard to the problem of the cathedral and other related matters, I told them that the purpose of having breakfast together "as a family" was to share and discuss our ideas about the functioning of our diocesan administration, since we are the ones principally responsible for that.

Father Brito, whom I asked to present the situation as he saw it, knew how to handle the meeting with a very human-oriented dynamic, having us look first at the material aspects of the curia—the situation of the offices, the concrete work, the personnel aspects—and we made some very satisfactory decisions. It was already the time at which the ambassadors were expected, and Bishop Revelo preferred that we continue at another time. And so we have agreed that every Saturday we will have breakfast together to evaluate the week at the curia and plan for the next week.

I was very happy when I left because it is a hope and a joy to see that Bishop Revelo is trying to incorporate himself into our work team and see the true situation of our archdiocese and also to see the collaborators so content, so that we are able to have a very friendly union through which we try to serve this local Church that the Lord has entrusted to us in the best way we can.

From eight o'clock until one, there was a meeting of men and women religious in the Colegio de la Asunción. They had invited me, but I could not get there until noon, when they were almost through with their meeting. But I was able to express to the group present my joy, my satisfaction in being able to count on this religious force in the archdiocese, to encourage them to always be true to the Church, of which the reading for that day from the Acts of the Apostles said: "[The church] was being built up and walked in the fear of the Lord, and with the consolation of the holy Spirit grew in numbers" [Acts 9:31].

We also talked some about the current situation, chiefly about those who have occupied the cathedral and of the places that have been destroyed by the recent repression. I asked all of them to pray a great deal and, from our calling in the Church, to have a great sense of solidarity with our suffering people.

Bishop Revelo was waiting all day long to mediate in the dialogue between the diplomats and the Popular Revolutionary Bloc, but it does not seem that the peasants intend to resolve the problem of the occupations, but rather to continue holding the cathedral and the embassies in order to exert more pressure toward obtaining their objectives.

 **Sunday, April 16**

Because the cathedral was occupied by the Popular Revolutionary Bloc, I celebrated the traditional eight o'clock Mass that is carried on the radio in El Rosario Church. The crowd was enormous and although the Mass could not be broadcast live, the technicians from YSAX were good enough to tape it and broadcast it from the station an hour later.

 **Monday, April 17**

The bishops met today to continue studying the preparatory document for the Third General Conference of the Latin American Bishops. Bishop Rivera reported on the Central American regional meetings that he had attended. Also, Monsignor Revelo reported on the meeting held in Bogotá by those in charge of ecumenism and the problem of nonbelievers, whose deliberations were also directed toward the meeting at Puebla.

I have the impression that in this meeting of bishops as well there were some machinations beforehand, since in the voting for the delegate there seemed to be total agreement among Bishops Aparicio, Barrera and Alvarez, who voted for Bishop Revelo—who, naturally, won against the votes of Bishops Rivera, Revelo and me. The result was that Bishop Revelo got three votes, Bishop Rivera two (possibly Bishop Revelo's and mine) and I received one vote— undoubtedly Bishop Rivera's.[33] The same thing happened in the election of a priest from the diocesan clergy: The same bloc elected Monsignor Fredy Delgado. I have faith that the inspiration of the Holy Spirit will prevail over all human intrigues and that the meeting in Puebla will be truly like that of Medellín, a Pentecost for our America, in spite of all the fears and intrigues of human beings.

---

[33] The bishops were not permitted to vote for themselves.

In the afternoon, representatives of German television interviewed me and did some filming to be shown in that country. The main topic of the interview was the persecution of the Church in El Salvador, also how I see the Puebla meeting and the accusation of socialism made against our Church. I think I expressed my thoughts with total frankness and sincerity, and effectively defended the Church's position.

That night there was a new and terrifying fire. It left in ashes a commercial zone of San Salvador located between Rubén Darío and 11th Avenues.

 ### Tuesday, April 18

I went to the mission meeting that takes place in the Institute of the Somascan Sisters. The new president of the commission, Bishop Barrera, and the new national director of Missionary Works, Father Enrique Gloden (also from the Santa Ana diocese), conducted the meeting. As former national director, I turned over the accounts to the new national director and participated in the discussions about how to encourage the missionary spirit in our country.

In the chancery this morning, the dialogue continued among diplomats of the embassies occupied by the Popular Revolutionary Bloc and the representatives of the Bloc; Bishop Revelo acted as mediator for the Church. They arrived at a final agreement and, at noon, those occupying the embassies and the cathedral will end the occupation. The Red Cross will also mediate to enhance the safety of the evacuation.

In the afternoon, this operation was carried out, but it seems to have been rather disorganized. There was not sufficient transportation to take those who had been occupying the different places back to their villages. I am afraid for them, of the reprisals that could take place on the road or when they arrive back at their villages. God grant that will not happen!

But a new occupation began at eight in the morning. FAPU,[34] which is another popular organization, occupied El Calvario Church. I have talked with the representatives of this organization in order to find out what their goals are and their reasons for being in a Catholic church. They have said that they want to talk with the archdiocese to ask for its cooperation with their objectives; they want to show their protest of the attacks on the peasants, principally those in the zone of Suchitoto, that

---

[34] United Popular Action Front, a coalition of popular organizations.

have followed those of Perulapán. They want to send a letter to the Holy Father to ask him to condemn the government of El Salvador because of its abuses of human rights. I told them that the best way to reach the pope is through the nunciature and that they could ask the parish priest of El Calvario to be an intermediary and talk to the nuncio.

In the evening, I went to visit Monsignor Modesto López, rector of the cathedral, to thank him, congratulate him and encourage him, since he has been present during the entire time of the occupation of the cathedral, contributing through his presence the order that, thank God, was maintained during the days of the occupation. Monsignor Modesto indicated to me that, as far as the police that guarded the cathedral, they had in general been very considerate of him, although he regrets an incident that occurred when a policeman (perhaps not knowing who he was) stopped him and forced him to go back into his rectory when he wanted to go outside, as he was accustomed to doing. Monsignor López has given spiritual aid to the occupants of the cathedral; he has celebrated Mass for them and has also offered them the use of the rectory facilities.

After going to the cathedral, I went to visit the priests at El Calvario and I also spoke with the leader of the occupation, repeating to him what I had said to the commission that came to the archdiocese. He told me that possibly they would leave El Calvario Church tomorrow. We hope that this new situation does not become more complicated.

 **Wednesday, April 19**

As I do every Wednesday, I had breakfast and a meeting with the Justice and Peace Commission and representatives of the Senate. The principal purpose was to look over the outline and ideas for the pastoral letter that will be called "Christian Faith, Church and Political Commitment" with the objective of clarifying the great confusion that exists today about the popular organizations and the commitment of the Christians who belong to those groups or the uneasy consciences of other Christians who feel they have an obligation to organize themselves politically. The discussion of the ideas that are being prepared is very rich and I hope that it will be a highly useful pastoral.

In the meeting, we also studied other events of current interest, principally relating to the occupation of the cathedral, El Calvario Church and the embassies.

Among the morning's audiences, one which seemed to me to be very important was a visit from some teachers from the National University and the José Simeón Cañas University.[35] They are in solidarity with the ideas of the archdiocese, and their organization as a solidarity committee composed of university instructors responds to the need to defend themselves, since there are so many abuses also in the field of university teaching. I thanked them for their visit; I encouraged them to continue to cultivate the sense of solidarity and I took the opportunity to communicate to them the thoughts of the Council regarding the culture and the legitimate autonomy of temporal values. I also asked them to collaborate in the area of university pastoral work, which I am so concerned about since I have no priest dedicated to this pastoral work.

 **Thursday, April 20**

I had invited some members of the Christian Democratic Party to have breakfast with me, since they had invited me last week. Only two came, but we had a very enlightening conversation, both for the Church in its evangelizing mission and for the party in its specific political mission. We are agreed that the two missions must not be confused, but that they can work together to help the people break out of this spiral of violence in which we find ourselves.

Among the morning visits, that of Dr. Salcedo also stands out. He had just written some articles against me, placed as paid advertisements,[36] and it seems he was on a sounding-out mission on behalf of the government or some of the economically powerful. I tried to clarify for him that it is the Church's mission to point out where the root of so much evil is, and that it is not the Church that is the guilty party.

Also Don Pepe Simán brought me some very interesting news from the United States about the concern they have there to help us in the defense of human rights. Possibly there will be a visit there by a group of Salvadorans to give them a more complete idea of the Church, also to bring more complete information, so they can inform the North American politicians who can influence the Secretary of State, the House and the Senate.

---

[35] The Central American University (UCA), also referred to as the Catholic or the Jesuit university.

[36] Articles or letters, called *campos pagados,* are placed as paid advertisements in many Latin American newspapers.

In the afternoon I went to participate in the meeting being held in Apulo by the women religious working in the different towns and parishes of the archdiocese. Monsignor Urioste was presiding and they were sharing their experiences and trying to get more guidance. I was very glad to be able to share, in an atmosphere that was truly one of Church, of evangelical concern, my thoughts on the current situation which the archdiocese is experiencing. The meeting ended with a Mass in which I expressed to them my feelings of hope and optimism that must be inspired by the risen Lord that we have to preach to our communities. The Prayer of the Faithful was a true expression of the concerns that all the sisters in these communities share.

 **Friday, April 21**

Among this morning's visits, I received a brother of the Marist congregation, their provincial, Brother José, with whom I share a longtime friendship. The principal subject we discussed was the situation of the Marist schools, especially the Liceo Salvadoreño, in the context of the entire Federation of Catholic Schools.

Very frankly, I remarked to him on the negative attitude of one of the Marists who comes to the meetings and seems not to trust in the coordination of the pastoral work with the archdiocese. I expressed regrets about some of the attitudes of the Marist school, which seems to collaborate very little in the pastoral goals of our archdiocese. The meeting ended on a positive note, after we had told each other many things very clearly.

He also protested against the somewhat aggressive and marginalizing attitude of other schools against the Marist school. We ended saying it would be good to promote a meeting of a spiritual nature, so that we could achieve agreement on criteria for the pastoral work. He reiterated to me the solidarity of the Marists with the hierarchy and with me personally, since we have very solid bonds of friendship with the Marist congregation.

Also, another important visit was a delegation of teachers from the ANDES 21 *de junio* group who came to also express their solidarity with the pastoral work of the archdiocese and to seek my help in asking that a professor in Argentina be released, as with other professors who have disappeared here in El Salvador.

Another very important group who came for an audience is CUTS,[37] a workers' organization. They came to talk to me about their plans for May Day[38] as well as to express their solidarity with the Church. I took the opportunity as I thanked them to invite them to continue this kind of dialogue in which they can learn about the social doctrine of the Church. We agreed on another visit for next month, and I hope that the workers will pay attention to some of it, although at times it seems like they have a different ideology.

I spent the afternoon with the seminarians of the major seminary of the archdiocese—a group which inspires a great deal of hope. The dialogue is very frank. Today's theme was "why other dioceses do not approve of the approach of the archdiocese." They had heard seminarians from other dioceses and communities express very frankly the good they see in the archdiocese, as well as certain shortcomings, but because of their solidarity with their own bishops, they are unable to follow any more closely the pastoral line of the archdiocese. We celebrated Mass, by way of conclusion, in which I noted an authentic youthful and manly fervor.

 **Saturday, April 22**

This morning in the Guadalupe Hall of the San José de la Montaña Seminary, I attended the meeting of Catholic secondary and elementary schools. It's the first time they've met at the diocesan level, since the federation has operated on a national level up to now, but at the last national meeting it was agreed that each diocese would coordinate its own schools through a diocesan federation.

It gave me the opportunity to remind them of the document on Catholic education that encourages them to follow on the same pastoral line as the diocese, and says that the school must be a pastoral instrument in the coordinated pastoral work of the diocese. And I called on them to overcome differences and divisions and to be all in agreement in such a difficult time when the Church cannot be seen as disunited or divided. They were agreed in planning a daylong meeting to reflect on this aspect of unity. Afterward, there were studies of the ideology of the current

---

[37] *Central Unitaria de Trabajadores Salvadoreños*, Central Union of Salvadoran Workers.

[38] May 1 is International Workers' Day, as well as the Feast of St. Joseph the Worker.

seminar on educational reform and other matters that are very important in the life of our schools.

At the time of morning Mass and in the evening dinner hour, I had the opportunity to talk with Father Hernández Pico and Dr. Eddie Stein, with whom we are preparing a pastoral letter on "Christian Faith, the Church and Political Commitment"—a subject that becomes more important every day to clear up the confusion that reigns, even in priests and very Christian laypeople.

 **Sunday, April 23**

Mass of the Fifth Sunday of Easter at the cathedral, well attended as usual. In the homily I presented the idea of the resurrected Christ who returns to his Church in the Holy Spirit. And this Church is presented using the three images presented in today's readings: the house of God, of which Christ is the cornerstone and the foundation for everyone who builds in a Christian manner and becomes a stumbling block for those who do not structure their lives in a Christian way. The second image is the people of God, with the beautiful qualifiers that St. Peter uses in his first letter, "a chosen race, a royal priesthood, a holy nation, a people of his own" [1 Peter 2:9]. And the third idea and comparison is the Church as communion, a community, that has its crisis of disunity like that between Greeks and Hebrews that is recounted in the Book of Acts, but which is overcome through the sense of service, of *diakonia*, the first seven deacons and a service of love, prayer and faith, the Church community.

 **Monday, April 24**

As I do every Monday, I have spent my time receiving the priests who always come and I am happy to talk to them very openly.

In the evening, by prior arrangement, we dined at the Hospital of Divine Providence with those who are in charge of the training at the seminary: Father Gregorio Rosa, rector, and Father Abel Morán, prefect of studies. We talked at length about problems of the seminary, especially those which have been created by Bishop Aparicio's biased communications with the nunciature and the Sacred Congregation for Catholic Education. The fathers complain that he has never asked them for input on these problems and that he has bypassed those in charge of training and given information that does not reflect the reality of the situation.

That is exactly the same problem I deplore and I have received a letter from the Sacred Congregation reproaching me about this, based on the accusations of Bishop Aparicio. We are going to study how to answer both letters, the one from Bishop Aparicio, accusing me of being responsible for a lack of discipline in the seminary and even of sowing leftist ideas among the students, and the one from the Sacred Congregation, using the data I already have. And together with the priests at the seminary, we will deal with these false accusations.

 **Tuesday, April 25**

Feast of St. Mark, evangelist. Invited by Father Zanconato, parish priest at San Marcos, I went to celebrate the patronal Holy Mass in that parish. The little church was full of the faithful, who generously applauded me when I arrived. In the homily, I thanked them for this warm reception and tried to explain to them the thought, the message of the Gospel of St. Mark, concentrating principally on three ideas that are the foundation of St. Mark's theology.

First, in his Gospel, St. Mark says that the hour of the salvation of the world coincides with the kerygma, that is, with the proclamation of the message of the Kingdom, a message of conversion: "Repent, for the kingdom of heaven is at hand" [Mark 1:15]. The second theological theme in St. Mark is that this Kingdom of God is a mystery that Christ carries in his own personality. And more than his doctrine and his miracles, St. Mark focuses on Christ's personality itself, revealing his person, discovering him as Messiah and as Son of God, as the Kingdom of God. And the third thought is that not everyone understands this mystery and Christ tried to make it accessible through parables and other comparisons, and that it only became clear and evident when he announced his passion. This is to show that the mystery of Christ as Messiah, as the Son of God, as the Kingdom of God, cannot be understood if we do not enter with Christ in the mystery of his passion, of his cross, of his humiliation.

Afterward, I talked with some of the communities or congregations of the parish and I congratulated the priest for his work in the parish. Through him, I greeted all the Franciscan Fathers of the Province of Venice, who have St. Mark as their patron saint, so that St. Mark may protect the apostolic labor that the Italian Franciscan priests have developed in our archdiocese.

Also, the sisters who work in parish communities organized a trip to the villages of San Pedro Perulapán and they informed me that afternoon of the desolation, the anguish, the affliction and the fear that have remained as a consequence of the abuses of human dignity that have been perpetrated there by elements of the army and ORDEN, who repress any attempt those poor peasants make to organize.

 **Wednesday, April 26**

A study breakfast in the seminary with the Justice and Peace Commission and representatives of the Priests' Senate. Until ten-thirty a.m. we studied the next pastoral letter, which will be about Christian faith and political commitment. It is a well-done study, but very long, and we agreed to summarize it and organize it in a more practical and pastoral form. And this very afternoon we will meet with the principals responsible for its writing.

With a worker and a seminarian, we prepared the interview that is broadcast on the radio every Wednesday at one p.m. The worker, naturally, talked about the approaching May Day; the seminarian read to me some questions from letters sent in by radio listeners.

At noon, I gave the secretaries of the curia a lunch prepared in the Colegio of the Somascan sisters, since today is Secretaries' Day. It was a cordial gathering. I think it was encouraging for these humble and self-sacrificing women employees.

In the afternoon, a visit from the Mother General of the Maryknoll Sisters, who expressed her admiration for the pastoral work of our diocese and her congratulations for the defense of human rights that we are carrying out. I took the opportunity to thank her for the services of her Maryknoll congregation in our diocese, and she promised me to do everything possible to send more personnel and to start more communities.

Afterward, I met with Monsignor Urioste and Fathers Jerez[39] and Jon Sobrino to study a new way to present the pastoral letter. It was a very

---

[39] César Jerez, S.J., then Jesuit provincial.

constructive, very profound dialogue, and I think that we have found the pastoral outlines for this document, which is intended to be, above all, an exposition of Christian principles—to guide, especially, the peasants faced with the appeals of the popular organizations and the danger of government repression and of using the Church not for religious ends, but rather for other ends of those same groups. I think we will come out with a document in which, I pray to God, it will be very clear that the dignity of the Church and the clarity of the doctrine for those for whom it is intended will shine forth for the glory of our Lord.

In the evening, at night, a visit from Nelly Rodríguez, a Sister of the Sacred Heart, who told me of the problems at the seminary with educational reform and how the Catholic schools will be involved to prevent the Ministry of Education from trying to manipulate this instrument of culture of our people—that is, education, school, the *colegio*. There are some real experts among the Jesuits in the Central American University who can direct this presence of the Church through the directors and the professors of our Catholic high schools and parochial schools.

 **Thursday, April 27**

In the morning there was a meeting of the Priests' Senate in which we discussed matters suggested by the correspondence I read to them, principally an anonymous letter from a priest—not because it was anonymous, but rather because of the ideas in it, which call for reflection on our part. It gave us the idea to have a meeting of the Senate with the idea of an open dialogue, in preparation for a plenary meeting of the clergy in which we would try to bring out all the resentments, reticences and everything else that impedes a more honest unity among the clergy. The minutes of the Senate this morning have many important details.

In the evening I celebrated the patronal Mass of the Virgin of Monserrat in the colonia of the same name, together with the parish priest, Father Amado Molina, and the vicar[40] of that sector, the priest of the parish of El Calvario. Afterward, I visited Father Eleodoro Orellana in the Colonia Guadalupe of Soyapango. He has been very ill; his health seems to have deteriorated a great deal. I left him some money to help pay his medical costs.

---

[40] An administrative assistant empowered to act for a bishop in certain matters.

**Friday, April 28**

In the afternoon, an interview with workers of CUTS (which is a federation of unions), whom I had invited together with other priests who are suited to do pastoral work with the workers, with the object being a discussion to learn more about the workers' organizations and to better offer them the Christian guidance of the Church. In spite of being very informal, the dialogue was very enriching and created interest on the part of the workers, who will continue to talk with the priests.

In the evening, a visit of Licenciado[41] Atilio Viéytez, who worked very closely with the previous president of the republic, Colonel Molina.[42] He is a very enlightened man, very Christian. He offered me his opinions on the situation of the Church. He is supportive of the present Church and offers his unconditional support of this Church.

# May 1978

 **Sunday, May 21 (continued)**[43]

In the afternoon I visited Ciudad Arce, where I had been invited for a First Communion, but there was a misunderstanding with the parish priest, who had held the First Communion in the morning. At any rate, what I was most interested in was bringing a message of unity to the entire Christian community, since there have arisen difficulties there between the parish priest and the sister who promotes base communities. And for that reason, after the Mass we had a meeting in the parochial school, which was attended by the priest, Father Brizuela, the sister and all of the most direct participants in the pastoral work, which turned out to be very constructive.

The message of the day about the Holy Trinity and the explanation of the specific circumstances of that place gave a marvelous opportunity to

---

[41] A title given to one who holds an advanced or professional degree.

[42] Colonel Arturo Armando Molina, president of El Salvador from 1972 to 1977.

[43] The gap in the tapes here is unexplained.

talk in an indirect way about the topic that worried me and I think it was resolved through a sincere desire always to work together in a unified fashion.

 ## Monday, May 22

I had lunch in the Jesuit community at the Church of Carmen in Santa Tecla. It is a community in which the majority of the Jesuits are rather elderly and have a great deal of experience. And I was very pleased to hear that they all agree with the pastoral work and preaching that I am trying to do. They encouraged me greatly, and the support that I felt from them is worth a good deal to me, since it comes from a group of people who are very sensible, prudent, and who have a great deal of experience.

 ## Tuesday, May 23

I called together the council of the seminary this morning and also all the diocesan priests who work in the Vicariate of La Asunción, Flor Blanca (that is, the parishes in the Miramonte zone: San Benito, La Ceiba, etc.) to talk about the problems with the training at the seminary as it concerns the pastoral aspect, since these diocesan priests of this vicariate have been called to constitute a kind of pastoral reflection. We agreed that the seminarians have to be trained so that they will be the servants of the people, under the inspiration of the Church in whatever situation they may have to work. For this reason, these parish priests will be incorporated a little more into the life of the seminary and will have the seminarians work with them in this region that is so difficult for pastoral work. This is because it is the region where the most powerful members of our society live but, at the same time, there are marginalized and rural zones in the area.

We also talked about a substitute for Father Segura in the rectorate of the minor seminary, and we agreed to ask the Jesuits for a substitute, preferably a Mexican priest who has already worked in the seminary and who continues to have great affection for this work: Father Himes. And only as a last resort would we choose a diocesan priest, which would be the best solution if there were sufficient clergy. But for now, we need the help of the Jesuits.

In the afternoon I went to bless the facade and towers of the church of Carmen in the department of Cuscatlán, where Father Miguelito Rodríguez, although he is rather elderly, has managed with a parish team to renovate that picturesque church. I enjoyed myself very much because of the warm reception of that community. I urged them to always be in harmony with their parish priest and their bishop; that is, always "to be of one mind and heart with the Church."[44]

 **Wednesday, May 24**

The feast day of María Auxiliadora.[45] I celebrated Mass for the students of the Salesian schools in the morning and, in the afternoon, the parish Mass after the procession. Both events were very solemn and give the immense consolation of a people who are very devoted to the Holy Virgin. I congratulated and thanked the Salesian Fathers for cultivating these Marian feelings among our people.

The Wednesday radio program, the usual interview, was with Licenciado Magaña, who is the person in charge of the Centro Familiar, a center which is doing great good in family pastoral work.

I also received today a letter from the Sacred Congregation for Bishops in which they invite me to come to Rome[46] to dialogue about the situation of our archdiocese. Afterward, I visited my spiritual director, Father [Segundo] Ascue [S.J.] and the psychologist Dr. [Rodolfo] Semsch,[47] and they agree that it is a magnificent opportunity offered me by the Holy See to clarify, with the sincerity and good will with which I am doing it, the pastoral work of this archdiocese.

---

[44] Romero's episcopal motto, *Sentir con la Iglesia.*

[45] Patron of the Salesians of Don Bosco.

[46] Every bishop is obliged to journey to Rome (an *ad limina* visit) to report on the status of his diocese at five-year intervals. Romero had not been in office for five years at this time, but other Salvadoran bishops were making the journey this year. Romero's purpose in going was to defend his policies against their accusations.

[47] Romero's relationship to Dr. Semsch was that of a close personal friend, not a patient. Romero consulted him for a psychologist's viewpoint on his life, according to James R. Brockman's *Romero: A Life.*

**Thursday, May 25**

I had lunch with the priests of the Oratory of St. Philip Neri: Fathers Brito, Fernando Abad, Manuel Reyes and Abrego. Theirs is a community in which I felt a very priestly and friendly atmosphere. We reminisced about Father Juanito García Artola, with whom I had a very deep priestly friendship and who was the founder of the Oratory of St. Philip Neri in the Colonia San Benito in San Salvador.

In the afternoon, an audience with the Escuela Rural Mixta of the village of Cojutepeque. They had come to ask me to let them use my name for their school and, if I accepted, that I please give them my curriculum vitae. I explained to them my concerns about the idea and the objections that the government could make. They insisted, however, and I very gratefully accepted their petition, saying that I expected them to let me know when they hear what the Ministry of Education decides.

Another important audience this afternoon was one with the Union of the Electrical Industry, who came to ask me for moral support for their complaints about their pension fund. I promised them the help of our Legal Aid Office and everything I could do to help them, insofar as their claims are just.

In the evening, the meeting of the Commission of Laity, which has become a reflection group on the lay pastoral work. The group has goodwill and I believe, being able to reflect with them about such a crucial section of the Church, the laity, I will be enriched by their judgments.

I could not go, as I had been invited to, to the seminary, which celebrated the festival of Corpus Christi in a very original and solemn way. I dined with its leaders, however, and with the auxiliary bishop, who had presided over the ceremony.

 **Friday, May 26**

The plenary session of the Bishops' Conference was held to look at the results of the study for the Puebla meeting. The work of the dioceses has been collected. We are still lacking that of San Miguel. The most complete and deepest study is that of the archdiocese. After reading them, we will prepare a summary which will include all of the contributions from the laity, the religious and the priests. And, in the name of all the people of God, the Bishops' Conference will send it, so that

CELAM,[48] the Latin American Bishops' Council, will be able to develop the document that will be used as a foundation for the meeting in October in Puebla.

In the afternoon I presided at the funeral of Francisco Martínez Saprissa. In the homily, I eulogized his sense of generosity and his spirit of poverty, reminding people that "poor" does not refer only to those who have nothing but also to those who are good stewards of what they have, according to the will of God and love of neighbor, among whom I included the dead man; and also because he was one of those of whom Christ said: "And blessed is the one who takes no offense at me" [Matthew 11:6 and Luke 7:23]. I said that today many Christians are scandalized by the gospel in all of its demands and would like preaching that would be more in accordance with their likes, and that Paco Martínez Saprissa had understood the demands of the true gospel. As a participant in the Cursillo de Cristiandad,[49] he had preached the social, temporal implications of the Kingdom of God. Without a doubt, he had a prophetic vision of what was needed in preaching, of the evangelization of our time.

In the evening, the Secretariat of the Cursillo de Cristiandad gave a dinner for me at the home of Doña Julita de Núñez's house, where we discussed some very interesting matters having to do with the lay apostolate and especially about the Cursillo de Cristiandad movement.

 **Saturday, May 27**

Breakfast with those who work in the curia: Father Brito, Father Barrera, Monsignor Urioste. Bishop Revelo was not there. We talked about some rather important matters, especially among the clergy. We studied the article by Father Juan León Montoya, in which he criticizes the archbishop. We agreed that we should not worry about it, but lamented that he is siding with the government.

---

[48] The administrative body of the Latin American episcopates.
[49] A three-day program of spiritual renewal.

**Sunday, May 28**

The Acies[50] of the Legion of Mary was held in the Sacred Heart Basilica. It was very well attended because the legionnaires came mostly from the capital but also from other parishes of the diocese. I commented on the pastoral value of devotion to the Virgin as it is presented by the pope [Paul VI] in his exhortation *Marianus Cultus*.

In the afternoon, the celebration of Corpus Christi in the cathedral. It was very beautiful. There were representatives of different communities who made the procession around the park a very eucharistic Church spectacle.

 **Monday, May 29**

Among the visits I received, the one from Don Lencho Llach, ambassador to the Holy See, stands out because he insisted on the necessity of dialogue with the government. I expressed to him the goodwill on my side, but said that we were waiting for a response to our letter, which had been sent before Holy Week, as he himself could verify.

The throat specialist, Dr. Silva, has ordered me not to speak for two days, and because of that I have canceled all my appointments for Tuesday and Wednesday.

---

[50] A unit of the Legion, from the Latin word for a line of soldiers drawn up for battle.

# June 1978

 **Thursday, June 1**

I preached again after two days of resting my throat, and I am pleased to have dedicated the service of my voice to the Eucharistic Holy Hour in the chapel of the Divine Providence Hospital. Many people attended.

 **Friday, June 2**

A welcome visit from Bishop Pablo Vega[51] from Nicaragua and Bishop Rivera, with whom I conversed. And we concluded that it would be a good idea to have a meeting of the Central American bishops that would be along the lines of the new documents of the Church to share our concerns, particularly about the next meeting at Puebla. They put me in charge of issuing the invitations and we agreed that on the Feast of the Savior of the World,[52] if possible, they would come to concelebrate and then to spend the day reflecting on the indicated topics.

In the afternoon, since today is the Feast of the Sacred Heart of Jesus, I presided over the celebration at the basilica, which is dedicated to the Sacred Heart. The immense church provided a beautiful spectacle, since it was completely filled with the faithful and all of them in an attitude of prayer.

---

[51] Prelate of Juigalpa in Nicaragua; his brother, Father Juan Ramón Vega, worked at the time in San Salvador.

[52] The patronal feast of El Salvador ("the Savior") and San Salvador is called the Feast of the Divine Savior of the World and is celebrated on August 6, the Feast of the Transfiguration.

## Saturday, June 3

From eight in the morning until one in the afternoon we talked with the directors of Catholic colegios and representatives of the parochial schools. We discussed the exhortation on Catholic schools which came from the Sacred Congregation for Catholic Education. It touched on a sensitive point with the Catholic colegios, who felt challenged by the question: Do we really evangelize? The concern was strong enough that we will have another meeting about this.

In the evening, with Father Gregorio Rosa, rector of the seminary, we studied how to answer the letter from Bishop Aparicio and the Sacred Congregation for Catholic Education in order to answer the serious accusations that, originating in reports from Bishop Aparicio, have produced a lack of confidence in the archdiocese and in the team responsible for formation at the seminary. Father Gregorio was able to come up with very insightful, energetic and scientific responses to these very superficial accusations inspired by Bishop Aparicio's lack of goodwill.

## Sunday, June 4

After the Mass at the cathedral, accompanied by Mr. Salvador Barraza, I went to Guatemala to meet with Father Juan Deplanck, who has come from Belgium and with whom I spent long hours conferring in the afternoon. He shows great interest in and has great joy about the position of the Church in El Salvador. He assured me that many people in Europe who had lost faith in the Church are recovering it, thanks to the evangelical attitudes they see in the Churches of Latin America. And he asked me always to maintain this credibility that, thank God, the Church in El Salvador is awakening.

Today the meeting of the Scouts of Central America was also beginning in Guatemala but, unfortunately, I had to return today because I have many commitments at the chancery. But I delegated the auxiliary bishop to participate in the meeting of the Scouts in Guatemala. Unfortunately, he did not go either and did not send a message, so that we had no Salvadoran representation.

**Wednesday, June 7**

As usual, we had breakfast together and we reflected in an attempt to assess the situation of the Church and the country.

 **Thursday, June 8**

I had the pleasure of meeting again with Dr. Dárdano, a psychologist, with whom I discussed in great depth the pastoral attitude that I have tried to convey and about which I have to report to the Holy See. Dr. Dárdano's advice has been, as it usually is, very encouraging for me and very orienting. I have also talked about this with Dr. Rodolfo Semsch, who agrees completely with the pastoral attitude of the archdiocese.

This afternoon, in Zacamil with Father Rogelio[53] and his lay collaborators, we had a very nice pastoral reflection in which we discussed current points, especially the relationship of the Church to the popular organizations.

In the evening, I participated in the Holy Hour of the Cursillo de Cristiandad, since a group of ladies are in Planes de Renderos beginning their Cursillo de Cristiandad, which will end this next Sunday.

 **Friday, June 9**

Father Gonzalo López has returned and he has been assigned to the parish of Comasagua and has accepted with very good will. Next Thursday will be the formal installation, to be presided over by the auxiliary bishop, Bishop Revelo.

---

[53] Father Rogelio Poncelle, a Belgian priest.

**Saturday, June 10**

We met with the representatives of the administration of the archdiocese, including Bishop Revelo, and we mainly discussed how the archdiocese will be governed during my fifteen-day absence while I go to Rome to render an account of our situation to the Holy See.

In the evening, a meeting with the major seminarians, with whom we discussed a dynamic for integration and collaboration that resulted in a great deal of practical information.

 **Sunday, June 11**

After Mass at the cathedral, I presided at the consecration of the lovely church dedicated to St. Anthony in Planes de Renderos which is directed by some Italian Franciscans. It was a ceremony deep in its catechetical and liturgical aspects. It is a great satisfaction for a pastor to share such a beautiful morning with such good people.

Also there was great pastoral satisfaction in the closing night of the Cursillo. The ladies who had heard my homily from the cathedral in the morning on the radio expressed great solidarity and encouraged me greatly to continue the work of the archdiocese along a pastoral line in conformity with the modern thinking of the Church.

 **Monday, June 12**

Very early in the morning, because of an invitation issued yesterday, the young Franciscans studying philosophy came to meet with me. There were some very interesting questions. I learned later that they had left with a very good impression and had all felt that the interview was a veritable class on modern pastoral work. I'm so glad!

In the evening, representatives of FAPU, a popular organization, came to tell me of their desire to help the Church, but I warned them strongly that it must be without any danger of manipulating it. They agreed and will only, they said, lend their aid, their help and their support to the Church because, while they respect its autonomy, its independence of any political group, they believe the Church guides and stimulates the people's struggle for freedom. I insisted strongly in this autonomy of the Church, and also that the Church, from its evangelical perspective, is in agreement with and supports all initiatives that have as their object justice, well-being and the peace of all humankind.

 **Tuesday, June 13**

Today, St. Anthony's feast day, I was unable to attend the patronal feast in Soyapango, but I asked the auxiliary bishop to go since I had to preside at the Senate meeting at the Somascan sisters' house—a meeting that turned out to be very useful and very full. At the Somascan sisters' house, I also received the visit of the Italian ambassador.

 **Tuesday, June 13 (continued)**

While the Senate meeting was going on, the Italian ambassador came for an appointment and I met with him, and he expressed his desire to collaborate with the Church, since he is a professed Catholic. He is a member of the Christian Democratic Party of Italy, about which he spoke at great length, comparing it to the party of the same name here in El Salvador and suggesting that a well-organized Christian democracy would be of great help in achieving the political and social ideas of Church doctrine.

**Wednesday, June 14**

The first visit this morning was from the president of the Legislative Assembly, who is a professed Catholic and offers the Church his help unconditionally. He wants to serve his country well in this important post. I conversed with him, expressed the position of the Church simply and frankly, and its desires and fears relative to the government. He expressed his desire to serve as intermediary, if the Church should want to make use of him, of services that he offers unconditionally as a Catholic.

In the afternoon, I was grateful for the time spent at the seminary of the Somascans, near La Ceiba. I celebrated Mass with the priests who are the directors. And afterward, at dinner, we shared concerns, for I invited them to dialogue and they expressed some very interesting questions. I noted a youthful concern to be up-to-date on the pastoral work of the Church. With such an agreeable group and very deep reflections, the time passed by quickly.

In the Divine Providence Hospital, several priests from the diocese of San Vicente were waiting for me. They have been suspended by their bishop[54] and wanted to take the opportunity of my visit to Rome to ask for my support on their behalf. Naturally, I offered in fraternal charity to do all that I can in this sad situation. Bishop Aparicio has been in Rome since Friday.

I forgot to mention that last Friday I made a courtesy visit to the nuncio, who was very attentive and cordial.

 **Thursday, June 15**

In the curia, various priests and women religious came to express their best wishes for my trip to Rome. There were some very nice gestures from lay communities and even from some communities which are not in the diocese, by way of greetings to the Holy Father. The community of La Palma, where they have organized craft workshops called La Semilla de Dios, "God's seed," send some of their typical handicrafts to the Holy Father. Also there are letters from some of the seminarians of the major seminary of the archdiocese and from some of the laypeople. It is very moving how our people love the Holy Father.

---

[54] For signing the letter to the nuncio.

In my private time, I have been organizing the things that I have to take and arranging my trip. Tomorrow, Friday, I have to be in the airport at eight o'clock to catch an Iberia flight to Spain and Rome. I can count on many prayers. It makes me feel very secure to have priests, men and women religious and the faithful so united spiritually with me, and I hope that this opportunity to commune with the Holy Father will be of great benefit for our Church.

 ## Saturday, June 17

At eight o'clock in the morning, some priests and several other friends came to see us off. I am traveling with Bishop Rivera and Monsignor Urioste. The trip has been very enjoyable, an hour's flight to San José, Costa Rica and, afterward, four hours to San Juan, Puerto Rico, and from there seven hours to Madrid. After a three-hour layover in Madrid, in three hours we were in Rome.

The Oblate Sisters of Divine Love were waiting for us because Mother Scarglietti had notified them from San Salvador that we were coming, a kindness that was much appreciated. We stayed at the Pensionato Romano and, after resting for a while—this was already Saturday noon—in the afternoon we went to visit the Basilica of St. Peter. At the tomb of the first pope, I prayed intensely for the unity of the Church, for the pope, for the bishops and for the whole universal Church, especially for our archdiocese, commending to St. Peter the interests of our Church and the success of this dialogue with the Holy See.

Afterward, we visited the curia of the Jesuits, where we were able to greet the superior general, Father Pedro Arrupe, who was very nice and very generously offered us all the services of the Society of Jesus. He gave us the names of some priests we could talk to who could give us all the help we might need.

We returned to the Pensionato, where a good night of deep sleep has helped us to adjust to the change in time that certainly shakes up our poor human bodies.

**Sunday, June 18**

We celebrated Holy Mass in the Pensionato together with a priest from India, and after breakfast we went to arrange some details of the interviews in Rome with the Procurator of the Jesuits. A very interesting conversation, going deeply into points of theology, of pastoral work, of diplomacy, of relations between the Holy See and individual Churches. It was a true master class of pastoral practice that was very interesting to us and oriented us a great deal to begin the official *ad limina* visit and especially about the specific report of our diocese before the Holy See and its accustomed manner of proceeding.

We left at the time at which the immense crowd gathers in St. Peter's Square every Sunday at noon to wait for the pope [Pope Paul VI] to come out on his balcony, to pray the Angelus with him. The Holy Father addresses them first with a few words that today were about the Christian meaning of life: that in the midst of all of the present trials, the Christian must have great faith, great strength, great optimism, trusting fully in God to protect people's lives and oversee the march of history.

We also saw the pope last night on television in a magnificent concert given for him in the Hall of Audiences, where there were many cardinals, bishops, priests, religious and laity. The pope seems to be very lucid in his thought and is also agile enough in the physical realm, in spite of his being eighty-one years of age. It gives us great confidence to find in Rome a pastor of the Church with so much experience, so much wisdom and, above all, with so much love for God and humankind.

In the afternoon, a visit to St. Paul's tomb, in his church Extra Muros [St. Paul-Outside-the-Walls]. It was the hour for vespers, and the basilica was fully illuminated. We heard the organ filling the air and the choir of monks singing in Gregorian chant. Kneeling by the tomb of the Apostle to the Gentiles, the great St. Paul, in that atmosphere of prayer that was almost heavenly, I felt stirring in my memory, in my heart, in my love, all those emotions from my days as a student and, once I became a priest, my visits to Rome, my prayers beside these tombs of the apostles have always meant inspiration and strength. Above all, this afternoon in which I feel that my visit is not a simple visit of private piety, rather in carrying out the official *ad limina* visit, I bring with me all the interests, concerns, problems, hopes, projects, anguish of all of my priests, religious communities, parishes, base communities—that is, of a whole archdiocese that comes with me to prostrate itself, yesterday in front of St. Peter's tomb, today in front of St. Paul's tomb.

**Monday, June 19**

The principal work today has been making arrangements for interviews or audiences with the Sacred Congregation of Bishops that was granted us for tomorrow, Tuesday, in the morning; with the Secretariat of State, where we left documents and they said they would let us know when we would be received; with the Office of Audiences, to see if it would be possible to have a private audience, but the preparations for the celebration in honor of the Holy Father and also his health problems have reduced a great deal his private audiences, although there was some hope of a very special audience after the general audience next Wednesday.

In the Sacred Congregation for Bishops we were told to converse with Monsignor Michele Buro, with whom we conversed for a long time, but we noted a series of concepts and prejudices in his mind-set that leave us little hope that he will understand the pastoral work our archdiocese is carrying out. Nevertheless, the talk was very useful, for it allowed us to express—in the brief moments he let us speak, since he talked most of the time—our points of view.

In the afternoon and evening, with no commitments or official duties, we enjoyed the beautiful atmosphere of Rome that in June is already beginning to get rather warm. The climate is rather similar to that of El Salvador. Also, in the evening, Father Juan Bosco Estrada, a Mexican Jesuit, visited us and invited us to take a walk after dinner through St. Peter's Square, from which we contemplated the famous window where the Holy Father studies and where he prays for all of humankind.

 **Tuesday, June 20**

Our most important interview has been with Cardinal Sebastian Baggio, Prefect of the Sacred Congregation for Bishops. I have written an account of this interview, which was very important for me, according to what I am able to remember, to leave a written record of my response to the observations the cardinal made about my pastoral work. I think I have managed to correct a great deal of information that was not accurate and that, rather, came from interests opposed to those I try to defend in the line of the pastoral work and preaching of the archdiocese. I recommend reading the confidential account of this interview with the cardinal.

In the afternoon, we received the news that the Holy Father will receive Bishop Rivera and me in a special audience after the general audience. In the evening, we were invited to dinner by the Oblate Sisters of Divine Love. The atmosphere was very cordial and we shared good memories of the work of this congregation in San Salvador in the Colegio de la Sagrada Familia, and in the archdiocese in the direct pastoral work in the village of Citalá, Chalatenango.

Also today I had the opportunity to greet personally a great friend of the Sacred Congregation for Catholic Education, Monsignor De Nicoló, who is in charge of the seminaries in Latin America. I gave him the correspondence which includes my response to the false information the Congregation has received about the relationship of the archdiocese with the interdiocesan seminary, San José de la Montaña. Monsignor De Nicoló demonstrated a very priestly and intimate friendship to me, giving me some confidential warnings, and he advised me to be very frank in the dialogue with the cardinal that we would have the next day.

 **Wednesday, June 21**

The general audience and the special audience with the Holy Father has filled this unforgettable morning. It is June 21 and the main thing I remember about the general audience is that today it has been fifteen years since the June 21 when Cardinal Giovanni Batista Montini was elected to succeed St. Peter with the name of Paul VI. This circumstance caused great joy in the immense audience of all languages, who through their interpreters showed their affection, their prayers, their loyalty to the successor of St. Peter.

The pope, responding to this explosion of love, said that the election being commemorated meant for him an absolute giving of himself to the People of God. And in the name of this giving, his message was inspired in a task that has belonged to the pontiffs throughout history: that of making the beauty of the Church seen in spite of the human characteristics and personal deficiencies of the pontiffs. He referred especially to that great mission of the Church: to sow unity, peace, joy in Christ in the midst of humanity. He urged his listeners to be Christians who are very faithful to the Church and to live with all faithfulness the teachings of the Second Vatican Council, which are a true gift of the Holy Spirit for our time.

At the end of the audience the Holy Father called on the bishops present—there were eight of us—to give the benediction to the crowd

with him. Afterward, he led us to a private chamber where we awaited for
the exciting moment we would speak more intimately with His Holiness
Paul VI.

When our turn came, we entered the chamber where the pope was,
and we greeted him with the emotion such moments produce. The pope
made us sit one on each side of him and addressing himself to me in
particular, he took my right hand and kept it between his two hands for a
long time. I also took the pope's hands in my two hands. I would have liked
to have had a photograph of that moment, which expressed such intimate
communion between a bishop and the center of Catholic unity. And holding
my hands that way, he talked to me for a long time.

It would be difficult for me to repeat his long message exactly because,
besides being more detailed than I expected, and rather cordial, ample,
generous—because of the emotion of the moment—I cannot remember it
word for word. But the principal ideas of his words were these: "I
understand your difficult work. It is a work that can be misunderstood; it
requires a great deal of patience and a great deal of strength. I already know
that not everyone thinks like you do, that it is difficult in the circumstances
of your country to have this unanimity of thinking. Nevertheless, proceed
with courage, with patience, with strength, with hope." He promised me
that he would pray a great deal for me and for my diocese, and said that I
should make all possible effort for unity. And that if in anything he could
personally be of help, that he would do it with pleasure.

He spoke later of the people. He said that he had known them since he
had worked in the Secretariat of State some fifty years before and that they
are a generous, hard-working people and that today they suffer a great deal
and demand their rights. He told me that I had to help them, work on their
behalf, but never with hatred, fomenting violence, rather basing my action
on great love. He spoke about making them aware of the value of their
suffering, about preaching peace, about letting the people know how much
the pope loves them and how he prays and works on their behalf. He also
spoke about difficulties that can only be overcome through love: difficulties
with the dominant powers, difficulties with some who work with us,
because not all of them understand the effort that must be made.

I told him that this was exactly the way in which I tried to preach,
announcing love, calling for conversion. I told him that many times we had
repeated his message of the Day of Peace: "No to violence, yes to peace."
I expressed to him my unshakable allegiance to the magisterium[55] of the
Church. And that when I denounced the violent situation of the country, I
always called for conversion and showed my compassion for those

---

[55]Teaching authority.

suffering, for the families of the victims. And, at the same time I denounced sin, I called for the conversion of the sinners.

The pope repeated that he would pray for us a great deal, and that we should tell him what he could do to help us. Then he addressed himself to Bishop Rivera, words of encouragement for him as well. And finally he said to us: "Let's have our picture taken." And the photographer came in to give us the pleasure at the wish of the Holy Father. That was our great desire, to have the witness in images of that unforgettable moment.

I am sorry I cannot remember his words better. But, in essence, they were as I have said. It gave me the satisfaction of a confirmation of my faith, of my service, of my joy in working and suffering with Christ, for the Church and for our people. I think that this moment by itself would be worth all our effort in coming to Rome: receiving comfort from our communion with the pope, being illuminated by his guidance. Naturally, the pope himself indicated, we will have to deal with the Sacred Congregation. In particular, he mentioned the Secretary of State, Archbishop Casaroli, who will be the one to talk with me whenever the Secretariat of State grants me an audience.

Because the pope in his brief message was, I thought, very well-informed about the situation, and wanted us to explore the concrete problems more deeply with his different secretariats. But his word is the important one in this sharing—a word of hope, of encouragement which, as I have said, served to reinforce in me my will to serve our people in love through the Church of Jesus Christ.

During this audience, I gave the Holy Father the portrait of Father Navarro that his brother Napoleón had sent him, also the objects from the workshops of La Semilla de Dios in La Palma, in Chalatenango, and letters from some communities, also a gift that Francisco González sent him from San Miguel. I left him a memorandum in an envelope marked "private."

I left the Holy Father a memorandum, in the form of a brief letter to express to him that we were already visiting His Holiness' different dicasteries[56] and I explain to him how difficult it is to carry out the archbishop's ministry in the situation of my country, trying to be faithful to the present magisterium of the Church. I also tell him that the information I bring to Rome is supported by documents and publications that reflect that situation and, at the same time, either defame the Church or express solidarity with the archbishop—testimonies that come from all over and, above all, from the people it is my job to guide. And all of this encourages me to continue my pastoral work the way I do it.

---

[56] Or deaneries; the main offices of the Vatican.

I also tell him that I am sorry that, based on comments that some secretariats have made on my pastoral behavior, it seems that a negative judgment prevails that coincides exactly with that of the most powerful forces that there, in my archdiocese, try to stop and discredit my apostolic effort. But I end saying that "you can be sure, Holy Father, of my faithfulness to you as the Successor of Peter and of my unconditional allegiance to your magisterium, since in this faithfulness and allegiance I have always found the secret and the certainty of walking with my flock in accordance with the Spirit of the Lord."

I saw this letter later among the papers that Archbishop Casaroli brought with him to talk to me in the dialogue or audience at the Secretariat of State. And I could see that at the end of my letter there was some writing that doubtless was that of the Holy Father making some comments for Archbishop Casaroli to keep in mind when he talked with me.

That same afternoon of June 21, as I had arranged with Father Pedraz, we talked on the telephone so I could tell him about my impressions and my activities in Rome on tape, a recording that I am sure was broadcast on YSAX that Wednesday, June 21.

 **Thursday, June 22**

This morning we had an audience with the Sacred Congregation for Catholic Education. Cardinal Garrone himself, the secretary, Archbishop Antonio Javierre, and another bishop were present. They explained to us the origins of the two letters about the problem of the archdiocese and the seminary that arrived through the nunciature. There is a summary of this audience that was prepared by Monsignor Urioste, who was present, as was Bishop Rivera y Damas. The conversation was based around the letter of response I wrote to the Sacred Congregation on June 5 that I delivered personally. My letter of June 5 in reply to Cardinal Garrone and the brief document written by Monsignor Urioste about this audience can be found in the files.

I should say that our clarification was very useful because the truth about the relationships between the archdiocese, the curia and the operation of the San José de la Montaña Seminary had been very twisted. We realized that some very disagreeable things had been reported behind our backs. And they had even asked for an apostolic visitation[57] to the

---

[57] A preliminary investigation carried out by a Vatican-appointed "visitator."

seminary and the archdiocese—something that even the Sacred Congregation thought would be inopportune, thank God!

We hope that after these clarifications there will be more respect for the life of the archdiocesan curia in San Salvador and the property it has in its present location in the San José de la Montaña Seminary, that, as has been proved, belongs—physically, as a building—to the Archdiocese of San Salvador. This does not change our intention to build archdiocesan offices independent of the seminary when necessary.

We were able to leave the Sacred Congregation for Catholic Education well-informed as to our goodwill and of the difficulties and sometimes emergencies that occur in the life of the diocese and that, of course, affect the seminary that is included in the life of the archdiocese.

Afterward we visited Archbishop Maximino Romero, Secretary of the Sacred Congregation for Clergy. It was a very wide-ranging, very extensive conversation and provided great guidance for relations with our priests. I also talked to him about the problem of Quezaltepeque and he promised to issue a declaration about the situation with the usurper, Father Quinteros.[58] We also talked about the problem of the ten suspended priests,[59] speaking on their behalf, and he said that instructions to resolve the situation had already been given to the bishop of San Vicente.[60]

At twelve o'clock we went to the Pontifical Justice and Peace Commission in the San Calixto Palace in Trastevere. We conversed extensively with the secretary, a French monsignor, who was very knowledgeable about the social situation and also about the situation of injustice and abuses in our country. And he provided valuable guidance in the conversation and showed himself to be very interested in the situation of our country.

---

[58] On November 20, 1977, a dissident priest, Father Pedro Antonio Pineda Quinteros, forcibly took over the church and parish house in Quezaltepeque, ejecting the lawfully appointed pastor, who continued to serve the parish in the school chapel.

[59] Priests suspended by Bishop Aparicio of San Vicente for signing the letter criticizing the nuncio.

[60] Aparicio.

**Friday, June 23**

The day was left almost entirely for personal concerns because, besides the problems we brought as a group, each of us also brought his own specific problems and so we left the whole day Friday for that.

 **Saturday, June 24**

The Oblate Sisters of Divine Love, who have been very attentive during our stay in Rome, provided us with a lovely excursion to Tivoli that lasted the whole day. Those picturesque fountains, the natural surroundings, the reminder of so much history provided a real rest for the spirit in the midst of the problems that create turmoil in our pastoral work. On our return, we went to Piazza Navona, one of the most typical in Rome, to have a capuccino, as coffee with cream is called in Rome, there.

In passing, on the way to Tivoli, we stopped to visit the St. John Lateran Basilica; it was his [John the Baptist's] feast day, June 24. The solemn Second Pontifical Mass of Perozzi was being sung. That chorus and that organ and that lighting that made the mosaics of the old basilica shine brought me so many memories. And the crowd present, that mass of humanity that throughout the centuries is always present and vital in the Church. A moment to reflect and be encouraged and be a humble, faithful servant of the Church. St. John Lateran is the pope's cathedral and is the mother church of all the churches.

 **Sunday, June 25**

We went to St. Peter's Square at twelve noon to pray the Angelus with the pope. Before beginning the prayer to the Virgin, the pope told the moving story of an Italian boy named Mauro (I do not remember his last name), eleven years old, who, when his fifteen-year-old brother was kidnapped, offered himself to the kidnappers in place of his brother because he was ill. And from April until now nothing has been heard because the ransom demanded is very large and the family cannot get that much. His mother has also offered herself. And the pope protested this ingratitude at the same time that he offered his solidarity to the family and addressed words of encouragement and admiration to young Mauro, whom the pope called a "little lamb of goodness" in contrast to the evil of the kidnappers. This declaration of the pope filled me with satisfaction because this gesture of understanding of human suffering coincides with my way of preaching. I thank God that I have found here a new inspiration to go on with my pastoral work.

At midday, the ambassador from El Salvador to the Holy See, Don Prudencio Llach, invited us to lunch at the Grand Hotel, where he is staying.

In the afternoon, we had a very extensive audience with the Father General (the superior of the Jesuits), Father Pedro Arrupe, with whom we analyzed the steps we are taking in Rome and our situation in El Salvador. He understands well that there are some very different currents in the Church and that we must consciously follow where our consciences lead us and try to keep the pope well-informed of our actions and of our intentions. He has a great deal of experience with the misinterpretations that often occur of the work of the Jesuits, an experience that has helped us as well to be serene in moments of misunderstanding and difficulty. He is a very holy man and it is obvious that the Spirit of God has enlightened him for him to have a spirit that is so open and understands the present moment so well. He again offered us the complete collaboration of the Jesuits—which, in fact, we already receive.

 **Monday, June 26**

At the invitation of Monsignor Michele Buro of the Sacred Congregation for Bishops, I went to talk with him as the Secretary of the Congregation. I gave him my letter accepting the invitation to be a special guest at Puebla. I also took him the account I prepared for Cardinal Baggio about the meeting we had last week. Monsignor Buro insisted on his well-known ideas about prudence and of "purely evangelical" preaching.

At eleven o'clock in the morning we had an appointment with Cardinal Pironio. It was a pleasure to find this great friend of the Latin American bishops had been promoted to the position of Cardinal Prefect of the Congregation for Religious and that he still always manifests that same spirit of simplicity and humility, that friendly reception, with which he was able to make wise comments about different matters we consulted him on about religious life, about women religious in parochial work. He was referring to this when he told us that women religious are fully developing their vocation as long as they meet three conditions: love of Jesus Christ, fidelity to their charisms[61] and a service useful to the local Church where they work.

I also asked him about the different currents in the Church and about the meeting of bishops to be held in Puebla. He responded to everything in the open way in which he has always given his words of guidance. When we were saying good-bye, when I told him that I was accused of being an instrument of communism in Latin America, Cardinal Pironio told me: "It does not surprise me, since they have even published a book with the title of *Pironio, Pyromaniac*." So this is the legacy of everyone who tries to preach social justice and promote our Latin America.

Bishop Rivera and Monsignor Urioste also visited the Sacred Congregation for the Sacraments to consult them about some things, especially about Confirmation, about which Monsignor Urioste wrote a brief memorandum.

In the evening, at six-thirty, at the Secretariat of State we were received by Archbishop Casaroli. Monsignor Urioste also wrote up a short document about this conversation, which was very interesting. I refer you to that so that I may keep these notes brief. At this meeting Bishop Rivera, Monsignor Urioste, the ambassador to the Holy See and I were present.

 **Tuesday, June 27**

Today, only a private visit to Monsignor de Nicoló who, as I said before, is a good friend, and with whom this time we talked very privately and confidentially about different things, which was very useful for me.

---

[61] Particular gifts. In a religious order, the gifts and vision imparted by the founder.

## Wednesday, June 28

Since today is a day without any particular commitments, I took the morning to go again to the general audience of the Holy Father, mixed in with the crowd. It gave me great pleasure to feel myself just another one of the Christians who come from different parts of the world and wait with such longing to see the pope. As it is the eve of St. Peter's feast day, it was a very meaningful, very joyous audience. Before the arrival of the pope, there were some songs in all the different languages and, when the pope arrived, the sound of the applause was enormous. The pope spoke of St. Peter, of his tomb, of his basilica and of how all of us Christians there are very close to the rock that is the foundation of the Church. He invited us to be faithful to that Church.

I took with me the things I had bought to take home as souvenirs with the blessing of the pope.

In the afternoon, a visit from Mother María Castro Llerena, who assured me that my petition to start a branch of her order in El Salvador was progressing and that, possibly, after the founding of the one in Panamá that was already taking place, it would be El Salvador's turn next.

After the visit of Mother Llerena and the Mother General of the Oblates, I went to St. Peter's when they were singing the vespers of the patron saints, Sts. Peter and Paul. Both of them are patron saints of Rome. I also heard here the solemn vesper song in a festive atmosphere, with people from all over the world filling the choir area of the basilica, which brought me many memories. And there, near St. Peter's tomb, I recited the Apostles' Creed, asking the Lord for the faithfulness and clarity to believe and preach the same faith as the apostle St. Peter.

In the evening, on our nightly walk that we take with Father Juan Bosco Estrada, we again went around St. Peter's Square, remembering there so many historical things that are evoked by the names of Peter and Paul in Rome.

## Thursday, June 29

Preparations for the return trip. Visit to St. Peter's. The solemn Mass in the morning is impressive. Many people come and go, filling the square and the adjacent streets—a true patronal feast, but with a universal implication. In the same way that in our towns the patronal feast days bring in all the people from all the neighboring villages and towns,

St. Peter's feast is ecumenical. Instead of villages and towns, we see here people from all nations of the world. But the spirit is the same: a popular celebration, a joyous occasion inspired by Christian faith and hope. Some selling, some buying, people coming and going, joy: This is the result of being in contact with those heroes who have conquered and reign in eternity, while we are pilgrims in this life trying to follow their examples.

In the evening, departure for the airport and return to my country. In spite of the fact that I am going home, back to my country, I am sad to leave Rome. Rome is the home of everyone who has faith and a true sense of Church. Rome is the homeland for all Christians. The pope is there, who is the father of us all. I have felt him so close. I leave very grateful to him because my heart, faith and spirit continue to be nourished by this rock where the unity of the Church is felt so palpably.

Tomorrow, June 30, the fifteenth anniversary of the pope's coronation, we will be busy with our trip, in getting home, unpacking, etc. Rome will always be mother, teacher, homeland in our hearts.

 **Friday, June 30**

This day began for me in the Madrid airport. Last night, from eight to eleven p.m., the flight from Rome to Madrid. At two a.m. departure for San Juan, Puerto Rico, San José, Costa Rica and El Salvador. The infinitely long night over the ocean. An uneventful trip. Many thoughts fill my mind, many intentions my heart. We are coming back after having been in such intimate communication with the pope and the Holy See, to our see that Divine Providence has given us. We have collected impressions, conversations, recommendations—everything good that the pope and Rome can offer to a bishop who wants to remain faithful to the unity of the universal Church.

The long night of traveling dawns on Latin American shores and, around nine a.m., we arrive at Ilopango Airport, where a crowd of good people receives me with applause, with words of welcome. An interview with the press to explain to them that my visit to Rome has been very satisfactory, to send my greetings to everyone reached by such methods of social communication, among which there is a radio station in Guatemala.

Bishop Revelo, the auxiliary bishop, is among the friends who have come to welcome me, and he tells me that there is a Mass organized at the cathedral to welcome me and so that I can greet the people. I head to the cathedral, celebrate the Mass and, at the time for the Gospel, Bishop

Revelo welcomes me very formally and I reply by giving my impressions of Rome, issuing a call to work, to continue building this Church, thanking the pope for his words of encouragement, feeling myself confirmed in my work, in my hope, in my ideals, inviting everyone to celebrate together this Mass to begin a new stage in our pastoral work.

My preaching was broadcast on the radio. This homily was repeated on several different programs today and the next day.

# July 1978

 **Saturday, July 1**

I am trying to adjust to the change in time that upsets sleep and work patterns to such a great extent. In the morning, I went to deliver letters I had brought for religious from other religious, for communities in the archdiocese. Among the communities I went to are Bethany in Santa Tecla, the Oblates of Divine Love, the Colegio La Sagrada Familia, the parish of Centro América, the Josephite Fathers, the Jesuit Fathers. I have had the pleasure of taking to them personally greetings from their own religious who live in Rome.

In the afternoon, I preached the Holy Hour that is said the first of every month in the Chapel of Expiation at Divine Providence Hospital.

 **Sunday, July 2**

The Mass at the cathedral was offered in honor of the pope and of all the communities of the archdiocese. Also some priests, religious and especially laity filled the cathedral completely. It was even necessary to use the choir area. It was a marvelous response to the call to celebrate the pope's day. I recounted my impressions of my trip to Rome.

I gave witness to the confirmation of the path that we are following in the archdiocese. I have tried to leave the impression of robust faith, hope and love, of faithfulness to the pope. The people applauded the homily, and there was also some very affectionate applause as I entered and left the cathedral. God be praised for the love that our people feel for their pastors!

 **Monday, July 3**

I think the most memorable of today's visits has been that of Mrs. Matsumoto, wife of the Japanese gentleman who was kidnapped in the month of May and about whom there has been no news. With the manager of the textile factory INSINCA as interpreter, she expressed her desire for me to help her find her husband, that I might mention him in one of my homilies. I offered, if she wanted me to, to write an article to be put in the newspaper, and she thought it was a good idea that I should write it and that she would pay the cost of the ad in the newspapers.

Mrs. Matsumoto said that even though she was not a Christian she would like to pray with me for her husband. I introduced her to Mother Luz, who gave her some words of comfort, and together we went to pray before the Blessed Sacrament in the chapel of the hospital. I asked with great confidence in the Lord that he bring Mrs. Matsumoto's anguish to an end.

# October 1978

 **Sunday, October 1**

The previous cassette was recorded only on one side and covers the period from June 21 to July 4. This diary was interrupted there by circumstances, perhaps my fault. I hope that this gap between July 4 and today when we begin again, October 1, 1978, can be filled in.

Today, October 1, is Sunday. I celebrated Mass in the cathedral. In the homily I told of my week's activities, especially about visiting different communities and telling about the fervent religious life of our diocese and other ecclesial activities—among them, the round table organized by the Catholic university to discuss my third pastoral letter,[62] which is also Bishop Rivera's first.

Also, I denounced the outrage perpetrated in the National University, and especially the disappearance of an employee of ANDA who lived near the university and was taken by guards of the university itself. He was beaten and is considered disappeared.[63] I also denounced the continued repressions, especially in the peasant sectors of San Pedro Perulapán and Cinquera, and the disappearance of a young woman who was shot in Colonia Nicaragua and taken to the hospital, where she was under police guard who later took her out of the hospital to some unknown destination.

After the Mass at the cathedral, I went to a celebration in El Plan del Pino, part of the parish of San Sebastián de Ciudad Delgado. The Carmelite Spanish missionary sisters work in the community El Plan del Pino, the same ones who are in charge of the Salvadoran Policlinic and also work in La Laguna in the department of Chalatenango. It was a very rich, fervent experience. A group of young people had been prepared to receive Confirmation and, naturally, the main part of the liturgy was addressed to them.

But I also met several different groups there, organized by the sisters, that are promoting a truly admirable pastoral work: a group of young people, a group of the Family of God, a group of catechists, a group of ladies of the Guardia del Santísimo.[64] This is a beautiful combination of piety and action. I congratulated the sisters and their collaborators in a nice meeting that took place after the Mass. The crowd that came out to meet me and that attended the Holy Mass was very large, and I noted their great cordiality and warm reception for the sisters and for the bishop.

In the afternoon in the chancery, we talked with Father Moreno, with Bachiller Cuéllar, to question one of those who had disappeared who has escaped from jail. And he has told us about horrible things that happen in the mysterious realm of the jails of the security forces where, I am sure, are several people we mourn as disappeared. It is a very sensitive secret; some really dreadful revelations!

---

[62] "The Church and Popular Political Organizations," on their relationship and on violence.

[63] Known to have been taken away by security forces but whereabouts and fate unknown. Often used as a noun.

[64] A pious group with devotion to the Eucharist.

At night, I celebrated the Holy Hour in Divine Providence Hospital. And afterward I went out again to celebrate the tenth anniversary in the priesthood of Father Samuel Orellana of the parish of Ayutuxtepeque. It was also a very nice event in a community that feels great affection and appreciation for their parish priest.

 ### Monday, October 2

The morning was dedicated to sharing with the group of priests of different dioceses who meet monthly in the minor seminary of San José de la Montaña. They had asked me to explain to them the origins and theological foundations of the third pastoral letter. I noted a great deal of interest on the part of these dear priests because after my presentation, which I tried to make brief, a discussion began in which most of them participated. And if it did not go on longer, it was because it had gotten to be nearly noon. But they promised me that they would meet in groups to reflect on everything we had discussed and that, in the next meeting, they would give me their opinions and tell me the results of their group discussions.

I also invited them, in response to a question they asked me, to use one of their sessions (at which I would like to be present) to talk about the problem of the seminary and of the priests who do not make a serious effort to follow the pastoral line of the archdiocese seriously.

I had lunch with Father Luis Armijo, whom I had seen yesterday. He was the director of the Crusade of Family Prayer when it developed here in El Salvador, and continues to have great affection for us. He has collected recommendations from different Latin American bishops in order to try to get a subsidy from Adveniat[65] and thus encourage this prayer crusade in the different Latin American countries.

By telephone from Guatemala, the secretary of the nunciature consulted me about the commemoration of the funeral of the Holy Father.[66] I told them that, as far as the archdiocese was concerned, it would be held next Tuesday (that is, tomorrow) with the participation of all the clergy, and I invited him. He accepted the invitation to come. And as to what he consulted me about, I told him that we could follow the nuncio's custom of holding it in the nunciature, but that I would recommend avoiding so much

---

[65] The German bishops' agency to assist the Church in Latin America.

[66] Pope John Paul I, who died after just a month in office. Pope Paul VI had died August 6.

publicity. For it seems like the government is more interested in publicity which makes the newspapers than in prayer and paying homage to the Holy Father. The secretary thanked me and he said that he would take my observations into account.

 **Tuesday, October 3**

Today, as on all first Tuesdays, was the meeting of the clergy, which was attended also by numerous women religious who work directly in the pastoral work. The topic to be studied was the third pastoral letter. A very original and interesting note was that the exposition of the first part was presented by two women religious. The doctrinal part and the conclusions were presented by Father Fabián [Amaya]. The discussion was very interesting, many ideas were clarified and amplified as well. The meeting ended at 11:30 in order to attend the Mass at 12:15 in the cathedral, offered in suffrage for the eternal rest of His Holiness, John Paul I. The cathedral was completely filled with women religious and laypeople.

In the homily I emphasized three concepts in honor of the Holy Father. How during his brief pontificate, he was a luminous response from God, showing forth these three concepts of the Church: its hierarchical nature (God has called us intensely to reflect on the papacy with the death of two popes and two elections), but the hierarchical nature is subordinated to service to the Church, in the same way that the Church is subordinated to service to the Kingdom of God and to the world as a whole.

And because of this (the second concept), that hierarchy and the Church must be, above all, Christian. And this is the great lesson left us by Pope John Paul, because his humility, his poverty, his disregard for the vanities of life, the sureness of his teaching, a discipline not based on legalism but on conviction and on love, are all expressions of a pope at the apex of the hierarchy in the service of the Church, but, above all, of a Christian who, like Paul, can say: "Be imitators of me as I am of Christ" [1 Corinthians 11:1].

And therefore the third concept: devotion to Mary. I pointed out the affection that the pope showed for the Virgin and I ended reading the brief message that the pope addressed to the Third Marian Congress in Ecuador, his only radio message addressed to Latin America.

At night, I participated in the Mass of the Franciscan Fathers in the Concepción parish, which was already celebrating the feast of Saint Francis of Assisi. In my sermon I presented St. Francis as a Catholic man and I explained the structure of the Church with its human deficiencies in the hierarchical aspect. And, therefore, St. Francis as a Christian. This is the hierarchical Church at the service of Christianity. And for this reason it must express holiness and an evangelical sense in all of its structures. And Francis is an example for us of a truly Christian Catholic and, therefore my third thought, the perfect man. Francis, because he was an authentic Christian, is also the fully developed man: joyful, ample, etc.

 **Wednesday, October 4**

St. Francis' feast day. I went to celebrate it with the people of San Francisco Morazán in the department of Chalatenango, who had invited me several times. The reception from the people was enthusiastic. They led me to the temple, where we celebrated Mass in a church that was completely full. Sister Imelda, an Oblate Sister of Divine Love, works there although she lives in Citalá. But through an agreement with the episcopal vicar of Chalatenango, Father Fabián, she is doing good work in that town, which has not had a priest for some time.

I preached the same idea again from yesterday's homily in honor of St. Francis, naturally making applications to the difficult situation of those towns of Chalatenango: accused, watched, terrified. And I invited them to live authentic and brave Catholicism and Christianity in spite of all the difficulties. After the Mass we held a meeting with the pastoral agents. And with joy I realized that there are very good pastoral cores in some villages. Father Fabián planned with them and with Mother Imelda the work that is to be done, always building the same line of the pastoral work.

Upon returning to San Salvador, I learned the news that they had finally found the body of Mr. Fujío Matsumoto, with whose wife and daughter I have talked several times to console them, to guide them. And they were waiting for me this afternoon to bring me the news. And through their tears, they indicated they also felt satisfaction at being able to take his ashes back to Japan.

Also, people were waiting for me at the archdiocesan offices to discuss the case of our refugee. A woman lawyer participated in the meeting and things seem to be very interesting at the same time that they are very secret.

**Thursday, October 5**

The first visitor was a member of FAPU, an organization that is interested in having news about and communicating with the probable refugee supposed to be at the archdiocese. I tried to be evasive to keep the secret, which will be revealed later. The Christian Democratic Party has taken responsibility for this refugee and has secured him asylum in the Venezuelan embassy, where he was taken by members of that party. Before that they heard his very interesting testimony about the tragic situation of the people who have disappeared but who are in the jails, still alive.

Today I also received a report that, in the early morning, Father David Rodríguez was taken along with Piquín, an announcer—or rather, singer— on YSAX, on the program that is broadcast at five p.m. They were taken to the police and also Father Trinidad Nieto was taken, near Apopa. He was also taken to the National Guard. There was word in the afternoon that Father Nieto had been freed, but the others were still prisoners, still at the police station.

 **Friday, October 6**

This morning they freed Father David Rodríguez and Piquín and they came to the archdiocese to report on the treatment they had received from the National Police. The priest was treated with great respect in an attempt to give the impression that they have not maltreated priests, that there is no persecution of the Church. Bishop Aparicio was present at the police station, and they wanted him to see the respect they had for priests and that what they were after was Marxist infiltration. Unfortunately, Bishop Aparicio, instead of defending the cause of the Church, agreed with the motives the police gave—which could be dangerous for the archdiocese, because their purpose is to give the impression that the archdiocese exaggerates, that there really is communist infiltration and that we are not being fair when we denounce so much abuse of the people and the Church.

This morning we have resumed our working breakfasts. We study the reality of the country at this moment and the role of the Church. I expressed my admiration for the loyalty of these priests and laity who provide such valuable service to the archbishop. We ended with the decision that we will have a morning of reflection to study the working document for the Third

Conference in Puebla in order to help me prepare some specific points that it would be good for the Latin American bishops to hear.

This afternoon we celebrated the Mass for Mr. Fujío Matsumoto, who had been held by kidnappers since May and whose body was found on the Cerro San Jacinto in a plastic bag, not yet decomposed, so that they were able to identify him. According to the Japanese ritual, he was cremated and his ashes in a small urn are what were present at the Mass. The family, that is, his wife and daughter, will take these ashes back to their country.

 **Saturday, October 7**

On the personal side, I have spent time in reflection and I have not done any work in the office. The only thing I did was to ask Father Pedraz to get the copy of the Puebla document for the study we referred to yesterday.

 **Sunday, October 8**

At the eight o'clock Mass at the cathedral we had Dutch television filming the Mass with the homily and all the events of this Mass that, thanks be to God, is becoming an ecclesial event. I saw in the crowd the ambassador from Ecuador and the cultural attaché of the United States Embassy. The people who came from Holland to film for television told me that they thought it had been magnificent. They were very impressed by the crowd and by their attentiveness. The Dutch crew promised they would also go to the Mass that would be celebrated that evening in El Calvario in Santa Tecla.

In the afternoon I attended a meeting of base communities that took place in the parochial convent of Soyapango. It was very interesting, especially the participation of the young people who, in discussion with me, were searching for answers to many interesting questions. The lack of relationship between the parish priest and the communities was explained. And I encouraged them to look for a solution that would make this parish a true Christian community, of which the parish priest must be the head. And there must be very open discussion with him in order to present the Christian witness of a community that truly follows Jesus Christ. We celebrated the Eucharist in honor of the Virgin of the Rosary, whose feast day was being celebrated there.

And in the evening, as was already mentioned, I celebrated Mass in El Calvario in Santa Tecla to present solemnly the new parish priest, Father Francisco Xavier Aguilar, a Jesuit. The vicar, Father Benito Tovar, assisted, as well as other priests and representatives of the religious communities of Santa Tecla, and a crowd of the faithful filled the church. The parish priest was very pleasantly surprised by the reception offered to him. After Mass, we talked cordially with some of the parishioners.

And in my room in the Divine Providence Hospital, the Dutch television people interviewed me about the situation of the Church and the country. We finished rather late but with the satisfaction of having completed one more day of work toward spreading the Kingdom of God on earth.

 **Monday, October 9**

In the afternoon I went to celebrate Mass in the village of La Loma in the territory of San Pedro Perulapán, a Mass offered for two murdered peasants who were found near the Apulo Highway. I was surprised by the size of the crowd waiting for me. I addressed words of comfort to them. The mother, wives, children and other family members and friends of those murdered were present there.

All of them reflected the fear being sowed in these sectors of our dear people—fear that is justified by the repression and abuse of authority by the security forces and, especially, by the armed peasant groups like the organization ORDEN. In fact, while we celebrated Mass, they appeared with their curved knives, some of them unsheathed, and they stood where they could watch the crowd. They wrote down the license number of the van in which we had come with the sisters. And there was an aggressive attitude, or, at least, a mistrustful wariness.

And I understood the peasants' fears, why many men sleep somewhere other than at their homes for fear of being taken by surprise at night. It is a shame that the authorities support an organization that is against their brother peasants. This is what I analyze in my third pastoral letter. I was pleased by the comfort that we were able to offer to the suffering families and the encouragement and spirit that we tried to inject into the Christian community also.

In the archdiocesan offices, a visit from two university representatives of AGEUS[67] in order to ask for the support of the archbishop in their demands at the university, which is controlled by armed men that have destroyed their confidence in that atmosphere of culture. With pleasure, I offered to help them to the extent that I am able. And, in order for me to be able to do that, they agreed to invite certain other people to the archdiocese on the following day.

 **Tuesday, October 10**

Among the visits I had one from some poor workers or peasants from La Unión in the diocese of San Miguel. One of them had marks of the torture to which he had been subjected unexpectedly in a meeting of Christians when a National Guardsman, who arrived by surprise, hit him on the back of the neck and then kicked him in the stomach. And the man thinks that these blows have affected his health. He even thinks he has symptoms that may mean he is losing his eyesight and wanted to tell us about it so that a complaint could be filed and we could see what else could be done for them.

Also the visit of Dr. Hugo López from the Cursillo de Cristiandad, who since Saturday has not known the whereabouts of his two daughters, university students, who were taken prisoner by agents of the National Police. And they are not acknowledged to be in any center of the security forces. We have also taken notes so that we can denounce the situation on our radio program.

This Tuesday we also began again the practice of having breakfasts at which we evaluate and plan the responsibilities of the curia. The group which met at the Divine Providence Hospital included Father Brito, Monsignor Urioste and Father Chus Delgado.[68] And we discussed matters related to the Pastoral Commission, which needs to be reorganized. And for that reason, we agreed to have another meeting with other specialists in pastoral work.

In the afternoon, the meeting suggested by the students of AGEUS took place. A representative of the parents' organization, a representative of the Human Rights Commission and Father Brito, representing the archdiocese, were present. Yet another meeting was called for tomorrow.

---

[67] A student organization.
[68] Father Jesús Delgado.

In the evening, dinner in the house of the architect Romeo Jovel with members of the Secretariat of the Cursillo de Cristiandad. There was a very interesting conversation about how Christianity should be lived in our time. It was very encouraging to me to see how well they understand these new commitments that the Church, without betraying its ancient traditions, has to accept to understand the present moment and what the world expects from it as service on the part of Jesus Christ.

 **Wednesday, October 11**

Two principal activities at the curia today. At noon the meeting of the economic administration with the priests' cooperative in which they studied the advantage of transferring the money from the curia to the account of the priests' cooperative, which gives interest and offers special attention to our curia. We agreed and asked for the greatest cooperation possible to respond to the economic needs of our archdiocese. I have realized that the situation is precarious and that it is necessary to study ways to provide more economic security for our activities.

In the evening the meeting of Caritas—the archdiocesan meeting that I called so that they could advise me about what the statutes say about whether or not it is the archbishop who is to select the national board and the president. Bishop Aparicio, once he was named by the Bishops' Conference, had to be approved by Archbishop Chávez.[69] And, according to the statutes, the term is only for a year. I feel responsible for naming an efficient board that will direct this institution that has so much responsibility honestly and with a sense of Church. A committee composed of the Ingeniero Galván and one of the ladies from the archdiocesan board was named to talk with Bishop Aparicio and express our point of view to him: that is, that the archbishop should name the national board of Caritas.

---

[69] Luis Chávez y González, Romero's predecessor, was archbishop from 1938 to 1976.

**Thursday, October 12**

Today I was visited by the British ambassador, who seemed very interested in learning about the situation of the Church and of El Salvador in general, and especially about the relationship between the Church and the government.

At noon, I celebrated Mass at the María Eugenia House, which belongs to the Sisters of the Assumption. All of the communities that work in El Salvador were assembled, reviewing their own charisms in order to put them at the service of the people. Since it was the feast day of the Virgin of Pilar, I talked to them about confidence in the Virgin and about how providential their presence was for our continent.

 **Friday, October 13**

I celebrated Mass at the Colegio Santa Teresa of the Carmelite Sisters of Saint Teresa. They wanted with this activity to anticipate the celebration of their patron, St. Teresa of Jesus.

Afterward I accompanied Father Cristóbal Cortés in the Sacred Heart Basilica in the awards program, or rather, the graduation from the bachillerato of their first bachilleres from the Colegio San Antonio in Soyapango. I encouraged the young people to achieve the two syntheses they should in a Catholic school: the synthesis between culture and faith and the synthesis between faith and life.

Afterward I went, along with the Carmelite Sisters from the hospital, to rest for a while at the house of the Oblate Sisters of Divine Love in Planes de Renderos.

 **Saturday, October 14**

I participated in the meeting of laity held at the convent at Soyapango. This is a national meeting, held every month, of laity who work with priests.

I have asked the diocese to intensify its prayers, since today in Rome the cardinals will begin the election of a successor to John Paul I.

## Sunday, October 15

At the Mass at the cathedral at eight a.m., I gave the homily as usual, denouncing especially the case of a person disappeared since December 1977 who escaped from the Treasury Police jail September 29 and who presently has asylum in the Venezuelan Embassy. It is certainly proof that many of the disappeared are prisoners of the security forces.

The theme of my homily, the three Gospel readings, was called: "God's feast with humankind"—how God prepares a feast, invites all humankind, but not all of them are worthy of this invitation; how the Church is the messenger bringing this invitation of God to the feast.

At eleven o'clock, I celebrated Mass at the Colonia Roma, where the Carmelite fathers are honoring their patron saint, St. Teresa.

And in the evening I was in Colonia Atlacatl in Divine Providence Parish, where the Redemptorist Fathers are doing very good work. After Mass, we had a meeting to organize the board of directors of the parish Caritas Committee.

## Monday, October 16

Today we received the welcome news of the election of the new pope, Cardinal Carol Wojtila, who has taken the name John Paul II. On the Vatican radio we received his first blessing and heard his first words. We felt the joy of the Church and asked God for his blessings for the tremendous responsibilities John Paul II faces.

## Tuesday, October 17

A very busy morning of visits. In the afternoon, an interesting meeting on the problem of the pastoral work of the archdiocese, in which we decided to study the reality of the pastoral situation we have in order later to study the organization, so that our pastoral work may be more productive.

With Father Enrique Gloden, national director of the Pontifical Mission Works, we prepared the tape as we do every Wednesday for broadcast on YSAX, the Pan American Voice.

I had a pleasant visit from a group of young people from one of the sections of the Miramonte Parish, who have been preparing for First Communions and Confirmations and came to invite me. And we discussed their pastoral work at great length.

In the evening, a dinner in Santa Tecla that the community he organized has planned to celebrate his birthday.

 ## Wednesday, October 18

In the evening, a meeting with pastoral workers in Soyapango. We discussed very frankly the lack of communication that exists with the parish priest. But the discussion was very positive and I was left with great hope for mutual collaboration.

 ## Thursday, October 19

I celebrated Mass in the Colegio de la Divina Providencia in the elementary school. Today is the feast day of the founder of the Passionist Sisters, St. Paul of the Cross. And I talked to them about their charism, encouraging them to submit to the will of God as the best cross one can bear.

In the afternoon, an interesting visit arranged by Father Walter Guerra with someone who knows a great deal about the secret depths of the political situation of the country. We agreed to talk again.

Afterward, a visit from representatives of peasants' organizations to explain to me the situation of the workers on the coffee, cotton and sugarcane plantations and the improvements in conditions they seek from the Labor Ministry in order to ask for my support for their just demands. I made them see also that, to be just, it was necessary to take into account the needs of the owners, and they agreed. And I consider many of the peasants' demands to be just ones—another reason to continue this effort to support our dear people.

**Friday, October 20**

An interesting visit from Mr. Eugenio Araujo, who wanted Monsignor Urioste to be present, to explain his plans for expenditures in the cultivation of sugarcane and how what the peasants demand is impossible, given the situation of the cane owners. I had the impression that he had already made his decision and that discussion was of little use. As I told him, I understood the needs of the cane owners, but that it was also necessary to understand the pressing needs of the peasants who work with them and that it was necessary to look for intelligent solutions.

Another visit this morning, a very important one, was that of the president of CEBEMO.[70] CEBEMO is a Dutch aid organization that has shown a great interest in learning about the situation of the country and of the Church. We talked at great length and he offered his full collaboration in support of our pastoral line. I thanked him for the marvelous contribution they have made to the improvement of our diocesan press. And when he asked what was the next program we needed help with, I talked to him about improvements needed to coordinate the services of the communications office and the Legal Aid Office. He liked our proposal a great deal and promised to help us be able to have a more formal kind of Vicariate of Solidarity.

At lunchtime, a meeting with representatives of the archdiocese and the Christian Democratic Party to discuss the situation of the country and search, each one in his own area of expertise, for a way to resolve the situation. There was much talk of democratization, meaning allowing more participation of the Salvadoran people in public action—something that the political parties will have to work on—and also meaning normalizing the situation of the country so there is legality, so there is more respect for democratic institutions. We accept the pastoral responsibility and from our evangelical perspective will work for an improvement in the country. Privately one of them, Licenciado [Alberto] Arene, made some very perceptive observations about the role being played by my preaching, which I appreciated, because it seemed to me very constructive criticism.

In the evening the problem with my stomach got worse and I called Dr. Saca, who ordered me to go to the hospital. And I have been in the Emergency and Diagnostic Hospital since that night.

---

[70] Mr. Thom Kierstiëns.

**Sunday, October 22**

Saturday, October 21, and Sunday, October 22, I have been in the hospital, where I have been very well attended by Dr. Saca and the director of the hospital, Dr. Badía, a good Catholic with whom I have talked about the social situation. He is a doctor who is very sensitive to social problems and who believes that a profession is not only for oneself but rather must be seen as a service to the people. He gave me a copy of a book he has written and some journals of which he is editor in which he maintains this principle of health for the people.

The Sunday Mass was celebrated by Father Jesús Delgado, who gave a very brave homily, denouncing the anomalies at the university and other unjust situations in the country.

 **Monday, October 23**

I returned to my residence after being well taken care of in the Emergency and Diagnostic Center. I prepared a brief message for the day I was in the hospital, to be broadcast on the radio. And according to the doctor's instructions, I will not be able to carry out my commitments this week. I regret this, but it is God's will, as shown by my health which I have not recovered completely.

 **Tuesday, October 24**

St. Raphael's feast day, patron of hospitals. I was unable to go to San Rafael, Chalatenango, where I had agreed to celebrate this patronal feast, nor to Paraíso, where there was to be a meeting of catechists, but I was able to celebrate Mass at the Diagnostic Hospital and thereby could express my gratitude for the attention I received very generously at no charge from Dr. Saca and the doctors who work there and were there at that time, as well as the nurses and employees. They indicated their appreciation of this unexpected Mass at their hospital.

### Wednesday, October 25

Because of my health I also had to cancel the commitment I had to Father Sergio Moreno, parish priest of San José Guayabal, to celebrate with him his twenty-fifth anniversary as a priest. But I have joined him spiritually in his expression of thanks.

### Thursday, October 26

Today at noon, in the cathedral with the priests and faithful, we celebrated Mass for the new pope, John Paul II. As usual, it was very fervent and I was able to demonstrate to the faithful and to the archdiocese my unshakable adherence to Peter's successor.

### Friday, October 27

Today the meeting in Puebla would have been ending, the meeting that was supposed to have begun on October 12, which, due to the deaths of Popes Paul VI and John Paul I, the new pope, John Paul II, has postponed to a later date that has not been announced yet.

### Saturday, October 28

Because I was still weak, I had to cancel the visit I was so looking forward to making to San Antonio los Ranchos, which today celebrates its festival of the corn. It is a typical festival in which they use all the products of corn. And I was only able to send them a written message, praising this tradition and showing them how the Church supports any initiative of the people and how we wished that this product of our earth—corn, the grain of which is the base of our nutrition—could be on every table when, many times, even this is absent.

There was also going to be a meeting in San Antonio Abad that day, but I asked Monsignor Urioste to preside at it since it had to do with somewhat complicated difficulties in the pastoral work of different groups.

**Tuesday, October 31**

A meeting with the major seminary and with parish priests who have seminarians and with the seminary team and with the Pastoral Commission. It took place at the house of the Passionist Sisters on the road to Planes de Renderos, and it was a very honest session in which we discussed the problem of the seminary on a very deep level, analyzing the year which is coming to an end and finding many deficiencies, but being encouraged to overcome them through a very sincere desire to have an authentic pastoral work in our archdiocese.

# November 1978

**Friday, November 3**

I celebrated the festival of St. Martín with the parish of Quezaltepeque. There were Confirmations of young people who had been very well prepared by Father Roberto and those who work with him. The parish church and El Calvario and the convent are still occupied by Father Quinteros, who is truly a usurper but receives support from political forces which are against the Church. I encouraged those present (and they were many) to remain firm in their union with the true Church and reminded them that the temple of God is not a physical Church but is rather each one of us and that all of us as a community form the living temple that is built to the glory of God.

**Saturday, November 4**

This day of St. Charles Borromeo I had the satisfaction of ordaining Rafael Urrutia,[71] who has finished his studies of theology in the seminary in Guatemala. He is a young man of great promise. And especially, he shows great solidarity with the hierarchy of his archdiocese. He will form part of the pastoral team of Chalatenango.

 **Sunday, November 5**

At noon, I participated in the celebration that the parish of Santo Tomás has organized to commemorate the twenty-five years Father Teodoro Alvarenga has been in parish work. I praised his work. I pointed out how a good priest is truly a blessing of God and encouraged the community to continue in its solidarity with its parish priest.

 **Monday, November 6**

We had a meeting with Ingeniero Galván, Dr. Fuentes and other advisers to discuss the change in the national board and presidency of Caritas that we have been trying to achieve, so that the statutes that make the archbishop responsible for national Caritas be discussed in a fair way and Caritas recover its true mission in this country. Everyone is inclined to support the position of the archbishop in promoting a new national board, of which some of those present would be members.

Also, today marks fifty years that Father Platero has been part of the Jesuit Community of Carmen in Santa Tecla. Although his pastoral work is in the parish of Guadalupe in the department of San Vicente, I sent him congratulations from the archdiocese.

---

[71] Later chancellor of the archdiocese. A chancellor is responsible for transacting the business of a diocese.

## Tuesday, November 7

At midday, in the Divine Providence Hospital, I celebrated with the priests who at that time were celebrating their twenty-fifth anniversary as priests: Fathers Sergio Moreno, Cristóbal Cortés, Roberto Torruella, Pablo Castillo and Carlos Ayala of the diocese of San Miguel and others. It was very nice that three others who had been ordained on the same day but no longer are part of the priestly ministry and who, having received dispensation, have married came as well. They were Luis Alonso Machado, Maeda and Matías Romero. Not only the priests but also the other three who have returned to lay status demonstrated very priestly emotions.

Father Garrido was present also. With him they reminisced about the days in which these priests were seminarians and he was a professor at the seminary. Also present was Father Platero, with whom they also shared pleasant memories, and they celebrated his fifty years as a religious. Afterward, we lunched together in the dining room of the Carmelite sisters of the hospital where the cordial sharing continued.

In the Vicariate of Mejicanos, together with Monsignor Urioste, we discussed with the parish priests of that vicariate the situation of the parish of Mejicanos, for Father Barrera is leaving, and how the vicariate, all together, will decide the question of a substitute.

## Sunday, November 12

In the afternoon, I went to officiate at Mass and Confirmation of some young people in the village of El Carmen of the Cristo Redentor Parish, under the direction of Father Angulo. A group of catechists directed by a seminarian had prepared this group very well. And they had invited other communities that came and gave witness of their Christian experience at the end of the Mass.

**Monday, November 13**

At the house of the Passionist Sisters on the road to Planes de Renderos, we spent the day with a group of priests and laity so that they could advise me in my study of the document that will serve as a basis for the Puebla meeting. I have listened to many people's experiences and acquired a great deal of knowledge to use in Puebla to support my actions as pastor.

 **Tuesday, November 14**

There was a meeting of the Pastoral Board. In it we were trying to list, in the form of an inventory, all the tasks, organizations, etc., of our pastoral work, in order to achieve better coordination. In the vicariate at Mejicanos there was also another meeting for further discussion on the replacement of the priest of the parish of Mejicanos.

In the afternoon a meeting with the archdiocesan board of Caritas for an update on the situation of the change of statutes about the national board and national Caritas—a change of statutes brought about through the initiative of the current president (Bishop Aparicio) with the support of the Vicar General (Bishop Revelo) who, subverting the authority of the archbishop, have gotten the Minister of the Interior to change the statutes.[72] Because of this, there has been an exchange of letters between the archbishop and the government protesting this abuse, and, at the same time, demanding the rights of the archbishop, without whose authorization such changes cannot be made. But the archdiocesan board, which is totally in agreement with the position of the archbishop, is willing to work for a Caritas in the archdiocese that is moved by the spirit of an institution that truly would demonstrate the charity of the Church.

---

[72] On November 23, 1978, Romero removed Bishop Revelo as auxiliary bishop because of insubordination.

**Wednesday, November 15**

A very interesting meeting with the episcopal vicar of Chalatenango, with Father Hector Figueroa, also from Chalatenango, who is in charge of the minor seminary, and with the Pastoral Commission of the archdiocese, with Father Cortina[73] acting as consultant on the repair of the house. He also promised to draw up the plans for a new minor seminary that, with God's help, we will build in Chalatenango, because this presence in the village will be very beneficial for the vocations of the young men who study for their bachillerato and go on from there to the major seminary of the archdiocese.

In the evening, the graduation of the Catarina di Maggio School, which was dedicated to the archbishop. I thanked them and I expressed my appreciation also for the solidarity they have always demonstrated with the pastoral cause of the archbishop. The director of this school is an Oblate Sister of Divine Love originally from Nicaragua, Sister Socorro, who has always shown herself to be very enthusiastic and supportive of everything connected with the present direction of the archdiocese of San Salvador.

 **Thursday, November 16**

Ilopango is celebrating the patronal feast of St. Christopher. And for this occasion the parish priest, Father Fabián Amaya, and the catechists had prepared a very good group of young people for Confirmation. After Mass, there was a very interesting discussion with these young people.

In the evening, a meeting with the laity advisory committee in order to plan a meeting of ecclesial base communities and lay movements that will take place on December 17, the Sunday before Christmas, as an opportunity for the Christians of the archdiocese to share in a celebration of Christmas in a Christian spirit.

---

[73] Jon Cortina, S.J., a Jesuit with degrees in engineering.

**Saturday, November 18**

In Chalatenango with the entire pastoral team of the vicariate— that is, the Episcopal Vicar, Father Fabián Amaya, some of the parish priests (because some were absent), the religious communities and some laypeople—we evaluated the work of the vicariate. I found interesting the sincerity with which they discussed their own defects, but also the great hopes that are being created by the pastoral work directed by Father Amaya.

In the evening I attended the graduation ceremonies of the academy of the parish of La Luz, where Father Brito gave out diplomas as seamstresses to the young women who were just finishing their course of studies at the academy. The Catarina Di Maggio School attended, and I greeted them very affectionately, for it is a school that is very devoted to the archbishop.

I was unable to go in the evening, for lack of time and because of poor health, to the academy of the Emmanuel Baptist Church where they were also having their graduation at the close of the school year, to which I had been cordially invited by the pastor and other members of that church.

 **Sunday, November 19**

After Mass in the cathedral, I went for a while to the meeting of laypeople from different vicariates who were meeting in the parish hall of San José de la Montaña. It is very exciting to see how the lay presence is growing in our archdiocese. It seemed to me that the meeting was not well enough coordinated and could have produced some sense of frustration in some who, perhaps, expected more. On my part, I tried to inspire them with my talk: What is the laity? What does the Church expect? What do we hope to accomplish through these meetings of laypeople from different vicariates? An organization that will make the strength of the laity felt and be sure it fulfills its responsibilities.

In the afternoon, I was in Chiltiupán, a picturesque town on the coast of La Libertad where the pastoral work is directed by the Sisters of the Rosary of Fátima. We had many children to confirm, but all of them old enough to understand. I saw how the sisters are working. Although there are deficiencies, it is easy to see the presence of someone who is encouraging the pastoral work in that picturesque region.

## Monday, November 20

I went to San Miguel to honor the patron, Our Lady of Peace. The bishop of Santiago de María, Bishop Rivera, wanted to go with me on my trip. And together we celebrated Mass at eleven in the morning in the cathedral of San Miguel because on the feast day itself, tomorrow, we would not have the chance to honor her in a more intimate way as we would like because of the presence of the highest civilian authorities and because these authorities tend to use the situation because of the publicity involved and are not as interested in the religious tribute involved. The Mass was private but, in spite of everything, there were several friends from San Miguel who accompanied us and, on leaving, lamented that they had not known in time to have organized a more solemn Mass.

## Tuesday, November 21

Festival of Our Lady of Peace. The other bishops, the president and his wife, and other officials were present in the cathedral of San Miguel. The nuncio presided at the Mass.

I said Mass in the Divine Providence Colegio, attended by the Superior General of the Passionist Sisters and also the Passionist Fathers who work in Jiquilisco, in the diocese of Santiago de María, and all the women religious, since they are celebrating the hundredth jubilee of their congregation. In my homily, I reminded them that it was a day to honor the Virgin of Peace, an opportunity I welcomed—also to be able to celebrate it in such an ecclesial atmosphere, since the congregation had a close relationship with this feast of the twenty-first of November.

In the afternoon we had an interesting pastoral meeting, talking about the realities and the current pastoral work to see how we could work together to organize a better pastoral effort.

### Wednesday, November 22

The group of priests of the archdiocese who meet with other priests from other dioceses wanted to meet specifically with me, and we held the meeting at the Lourdes farm of the Passionist Sisters. We discussed very interesting, very priestly topics like the seminary and other aspects of the administration of the diocese—very constructive criticism and sincere desires to work together to have better organization of our archdiocesan service.

### Thursday, November 23

On the same farm belonging to the sisters at Lourdes, I had a meeting to consult with some priests and laypeople, to study together the working document that will be used at Puebla. The suggestions, especially those about the realities of our country and our archdiocese, were very good for me to hear and will be helpful for my participation in Puebla.

### Friday, November 24

I had a meeting with the parents at the Vicariate of Soyapango in the convent of the church of Soyapango. It is clear that there is a great deal to do. There is no cohesiveness. They do not have a unified program, but I could see there were efforts being made to work more effectively as a team. They complain about the parish of Ilopango, since Father Fabián is the episcopal vicar of Chalatenango, and think that it would be better to have a priest assigned to Ilopango. The same complaint is made about the sisters that work in Apulo and do not attend the meetings of the vicariate. I noted this and asked them to help me visit them and to work as well for greater enthusiasm in the pastoral work of the vicariate.

**Saturday, November 25**

I visited the village of María Auxiliadora de Tenancingo in the department of Cuscatlán, which was celebrating its patronal feast. I felt a very deep satisfaction as a pastor, since the people were very fervent and receptive. After Mass, they took us to a house where they gave us dinner and offered us a small literary and comic program.

 **Sunday, November 26**

Today Father Fabián Amaya, in my name, turned over the parish of Dulce Nombre de María with its affiliated town of San Francisco Morazán to the Maryknoll Fathers. I am pleased to count on the cooperation of these priests, who are very dynamic and self-sacrificing. Also, it is a very difficult region but, with God's help and the goodwill of these Maryknoll priests, I hope that much will be accomplished in the department of Chalatenango.

The festival of St. Joseph that was to be celebrated today in San José Villanueva was canceled because a few days before two sacred vessels were stolen and it had been announced that, if they did not turn up, there would be no solemn celebration but rather some act of atonement.

In the afternoon, I went to San Marcos to administer Confirmation to a fine group of young people who had been prepared by the community.

 **Tuesday, November 28**

A meeting of the Senate was held in the Divine Providence Hospital and, in the afternoon, a pastoral meeting at the archdiocese. But today was disturbed in a dramatic and tragic manner by the violent death of Father Rafael Ernesto Barrera, who was killed in a feigned attack by the security forces on a house in the Colonia Divina Providencia, where Father Neto was found shot to death. But there are theories that he was already dead when he was taken there. The different bulletins put out by the investigatory commission which contradict different aspects of the official version can be consulted on this.

In the evening, there was a vigil held with the body of Father Neto in the church at Mejicanos, where his brother Manuel Barrera is parish priest.

 **Wednesday, November 29**

The principal event today was the funeral of Father Neto Barrera in the church at Mejicanos. His grave was dug right there, since it was feared that a procession to the cemetery could be used as an opportunity by clandestine groups and create more havoc. The Mass was impressive, perhaps more than sixty priests, with the church and nearby fields completely filled—a Mass that showed the affection many people felt for Father Neto, principally the workers he had worked with in a special way. There continue to be rumors that Father Neto belonged to the FPL, the Popular Liberation Forces, which are considered to be the violent forces of the Popular Revolutionary Bloc. We still cannot with certainty either confirm or deny this idea, which worries the Church a great deal.

# December 1978

 **Saturday, December 2**

I was invited to a sewing academy that was founded in Mercedes Umaña in the diocese of Santiago de María while I was there, and I went to join Bishop Rivera and take part in this very simple and beautiful celebration—but, above all, to share it with the bishop of Santiago de María. There is a great deal of affection in that town, principally at the home of Miguelito and his wife, where we had lunch.

In the evening, we held a solemn act of atonement in the parish of San Martín, where the Blessed Sacrament had been stolen. From the moment

I entered the town, the people gave me a very warm reception and the Mass was very impressive.

## Sunday, December 3

Today I had been invited by Father Ernesto Barrera—may he rest in peace!—to a meeting of workers in Ayagualo. It was not held since he is dead now, but we prayed for him with his friends, for his eternal rest.

This afternoon I met with three British legislators who had come to learn about the situation of the country and to communicate to me personally that the English Parliament had nominated me for the Nobel Peace Prize. This news, which was circulated here some days ago, has been received in very different ways: For my friends, naturally, it has caused joy and many congratulations, but on the official side and in the media, there has been a very significant silence. Nevertheless, the Britons talked extensively with me this Sunday, also with several of my advisers, who informed them about the political, social and economic situation of the country, and they seemed very interested in learning about this reality. At the end, one of them told me that they were three of the one hundred eighteen legislators who had proposed my name for the Nobel Peace Prize and that, now that they had seen the reality, they would ask doubly for this prize for me.

I took advantage of the opportunity to express my gratitude for this gesture on the part of the English Parliament, which is of great support for me, as is such an important visit from these three British legislators. Later they visited jails, peasant areas, farms and, in essence, take back very valuable information and a very deep conviction of the violation here of human rights. Naturally, the governmental or governing sectors in our country have not been pleased by this either.

## Monday, December 4

Today several priests of the archdiocese began their spiritual retreat in the novice house of the Somascan Fathers.

## Tuesday, December 5

Meeting of the clergy in the San José de la Montaña Seminary. The priests on spiritual retreat also attended.

In the evening, a meeting of the archdiocesan board of Caritas. I informed them of the state of affairs in respect to the change in statutes made without the consent of the archbishop as required by the statutes, and the legal means they have taken through the Ministry of the Interior. The spirit of the archdiocesan board about this situation is admirable: neither vengeance nor anger, rather a desire to work intensely for an authentic Caritas in the archdiocese.

## Wednesday, December 6

Today is the celebration of the patronal feast of Tonacatepeque, in honor of St. Nicolás, bishop, and there I had the joy of presiding over a very solemn Mass and then of talking with several priests of the Vicariate of Cuscatlán who had come to this celebration.

In the afternoon, an interesting meeting promoted by the Christian Democratic Party with representatives of ANEP,[74] that is, of the private sector. We had a dialogue among three sectors, the Christian Democratic Party, the business leaders and the Church. Monsignor Urioste, Father Jesús Delgado and I represented the Church. They showed a willingness to dialogue, but they also are still clinging to their own advantages. Nevertheless, the afternoon was very productive. There was a great deal of interchange of ideas and these dialogues will continue. We ask God that this may result in something positive for the good and peace of the country.

In the evening I presided at the Eucharist in Plan del Pino, to pray for the eternal rest of one of the workers who died with Father Neto Barrera,

---

[74] *Asociación Nacional de la Empresa Privada* (National Private Enterprise Association).

since this worker was from there and worked in that pastoral effort. The Spanish Carmelite Sisters who direct that community testify to the affection that the village had for Father Barrera. And they themselves recognize that he was a very helpful priest, very dedicated to pastoral service.

## Thursday, December 7

On the farm of the Passionist Sisters at Planes de Renderos, another meeting with my advisers to study the working document for Puebla. This consultation is progressing and has been very fertile for my participation in the Puebla meeting.

In the evening, a visit from a group of young people from San Antonio Abad, who explained their political and pastoral concerns, and I had the opportunity to clarify several situations, given their way of thinking.

## Friday, December 8

Feast of the Immaculate Conception. Many parishes and religious institutions are celebrating it. I cannot go to all of them, in spite of my goodwill and also the wishes of the different communities. I went to the parish of La Libertad, which has her as a patron and where the participation in the Eucharist indicated a community that is very alive.

And after the Mass we met to talk with the pastoral workers. The parish pastoral council for La Libertad was established. The pastoral work there is directed by some North American priests from the Cleveland diocese and some women religious, also North Americans, who really dedicate themselves to our people through their work.

In the afternoon, an ecumenical encounter with brothers from the Emmanuel Baptist Church and also with Mr. Asper[75] present, a representative of the World Council of Churches and also of Human Rights. He brought greetings for our archdiocesan Church from the World Council

---

[75] Dr. Charles Harper, Director of the World Council of Churches human rights office in Geneva.

of Churches and also the Seminar or Symposium on Human Rights[76] held in Santiago, Chile. He expressed his admiration and affection for our pastoral labor and we had some very interesting dialogues in which both the Catholics and Protestants participated.

We also talked with our separated brothers about how to celebrate Unity Week next year. The idea that predominated was that of a more intimate work of conversion rather than public manifestations that cause problems, given the political sensitivity of the atmosphere and given, also, that many Protestants are following a line that is sympathetic to the government and the status quo of the republic.

 **Saturday, December 9**

Visit from a journalist. In the afternoon, First Communion in the Divine Providence Hospital for a little girl who had been very well prepared.

 **Sunday, December 10**

In the afternoon, Mass in Potrero Grande, a village in the parish of Aguilares, where they were already celebrating, early, the feast of Our Lady of Guadalupe. The parish priest of Aguilares and the Oblate Sisters of the Sacred Heart who contribute to the pastoral work of that parish were there. It is obvious that Father Grande[77] and his pastoral work in this sector of the archdiocese are remembered.

---

[76] Sponsored by the Santiago archdiocesan Vicariate of Solidarity.

[77] Father Rutilio Grande, S.J., pastor at Aguilares, was machine-gunned to death March 12, 1977.

**Monday, December 11**

Meeting of the Senate at the Divine Providence Hospital. In the evening, also at the hospital, a meeting with a group of friends that Father Neto Barrera advised. The object was to hear testimonies of the attitudes and actions of Father Neto. And all of them have a great feeling of gratitude, a deep sadness at his death and all of them praise Father Neto's Christian work. None of them spoke of violent attitudes or ideas in this priest whom they have tried to vilify in the official reports.

 **Tuesday, December 12**

The Day of Our Lady of Guadalupe. In the Church of Guadalupe in La Ceiba there was a large gathering of the faithful. The parish priest, Cataldo Papagno, told me that some sixty thousand persons came to visit the Virgin during this festival. I went to celebrate it in Dulce Nombre de María. I had the opportunity to greet the Maryknoll Fathers and to share some time with that community, which seems to be very alive.

In the evening I celebrated the Virgin of Guadalupe in Colonia Las Delicias in Santa Tecla, where Father Francisco Xavier, a Jesuit, is working with great enthusiasm. I was introduced by him to a group of young people who told me many of their problems and with whom I also spoke rather frankly.

 **Wednesday, December 13**

I went to celebrate the feast of St. Lucy, patron of Suchitoto, in that parish temple, which was completely filled by the faithful. After Mass, we had a very animated meeting with all the priests of the Vicariate of Cuscatlán except for Father Sergio Moreno, who is ill with throat problems. I had the impression, being with the priests, that their confidence and unity has increased; they themselves said that.

In the afternoon, a meeting of the pastoral workers to continue collecting, like an inventory, the realities and activities that have occurred in our archdiocese. We discussed different aspects of our pastoral work in order to coordinate it better.

## Thursday, December 14

Today, the town of Tacachico celebrated its traditional patronal feast in honor of the Immaculate Conception and the apostle St. Paul—two devotions that I used, in presiding at the Eucharist, to focus St. Paul's doctrine on redemption and on the privileged redemption of the Immaculate Conception. It is a very nice community, very alive, and I felt very great satisfaction there. It was a shame that I was not able to stay after Mass, since I had an appointment in the apostolic nunciature at eleven with the commission that has been created to mediate in the kidnapping of the two Englishmen captured by FARN, Armed Forces of the National Resistance.

In this meeting, we were informed that the president had not granted the audience that had been requested, since he denies the existence of the political prisoners that the members of FARN are demanding in exchange for the freedom of the two Englishmen. We prepared a document in which we made clear our intention of interceding with the president of the republic and our failure.

In the afternoon, at the Divine Providence Hospital, I received a commission from the parish of Santa Lucía, in Colonia Santa Lucia, who came to greet me with their parish priest, Father Astor Ruiz, and to give me a pretty notebook where they had recorded their conclusions after meditating on my pastoral letter. I thanked them and saw that they had really worked hard. And I felt that the pastoral letter had helped to illuminate their minds about the popular political organizations and their relations with the Church's pastoral work.

## Friday, December 15

A meeting with representatives of the national clergy. In the afternoon, I also met with a group of priests and seminarians to talk about the matter of the seminary, to learn about the reports to the extent that they can be divulged in public, since each one of the individual reports would be given to each one of the seminarians. But, in general, we talked about many difficulties with respect to the present situation of the seminary having to do with this group from the archdiocese, and we created a committee to study this matter on a continuing basis.

## Saturday, December 16

In the morning, I celebrated Mass and gave First Communion and Confirmation to a group of youngsters in the Calvario church presided over by the Somascan Fathers.

At twelve-thirty, a Christmas gathering with the archdiocesan board of Caritas in a private home, where we were well treated.

At five in the afternoon, in Colonia Santa Lucia, the patronal feast, where First Communion was given and Confirmation was administered to a good group of young people and children.

And even later in the evening, at nine o'clock, the wedding of a niece in La Ceiba in Guadalupe.

 ## Sunday, December 17

The outstanding event today was the meeting of ecclesial base communities and lay movements from the different vicariates of the Archdiocese of San Salvador. In the meeting hall of the Colegio Guadalupano, principally, some eight hundred persons talked about their pastoral work and the life of the communities of the archdiocese. The Eucharist that I went to preside over at noon seemed to me to be extremely impressive because of the participation and the active consciousness with which these people came to the Eucharist, the fruit of their reflections and of their lives, which are committed to the Church.

At four in the afternoon I was in Rosario de Mora, where the Oblate Sisters of Divine Love do their pastoral work. They had prepared a group of children for First Communion and Confirmation. A very picturesque outing, some very lively children, a very affectionate community.

At eight o'clock in the evening we were in the parish San Sebastián de Ciudad Delgado to turn this parish over to its new parish priest, Father Juan Antonio Gutiérrez, the replacement for Father Neto Barrera, deceased. The enthusiasm was really impressive. The Mass could not be held in the church so we had it in the patio. After my homily, Father Guty[78] spoke, committing himself to the work. And after Mass several laypeople took the microphone. There was a joyful atmosphere, a reception indicating goodwill and willingness to work with the new parish priest.

---

[78] Father Gutiérrez.

**Monday, December 18**

Today in the archdiocese we celebrated the feast of Nuestra Señora de los Remedios, who is honored in the church or chapel of la Vega, where Father Raúl Alberto Flores serves, and I celebrated Mass there. And this same festival is also celebrated in the village of San Laureano de Ciudad Delgado, where I also celebrated Mass this afternoon.

 **Tuesday, December 19**

Today the parishes of Quezaltepeque and San José Guayabal are celebrating St. Joseph's Day. I could not, of course, go to both places, but I went to San José Guayabal where the parish priest, Father [Sergio] Moreno, is somewhat ill and where this festival of their holy patriarch was celebrated with great piety. My visit to Father Moreno was, I think, very constructive.

In the afternoon, another meeting about the problem of the seminary. In the evening, I was invited to dinner at the home of Licenciado Viéytez, where the Jesuit Father Paco Estrada[79] and the rector of the UCA, Román Mayorga, and his wife were also present. A very interesting conversation about the problems of the country and the university and on the situation of our archdiocese.

We also spoke confidentially about the apostolic visitation that is taking place this week in our archdiocese. Bishop [Antonio] Quarracino[80] has come. He is from the diocese of Avellaneda in Argentina, commissioned by the Holy See on behalf of the Sacred Congregation for Bishops, to make an apostolic visitation to assess the pastoral work of our archdiocese. Relations with the auxiliary bishop are of particular interest. I know that many people have come to report to him on the pastoral work of our archdiocese and the result of the visit seems to me to have been, up to now, very positive.

---

[79] Father Francisco Estrada, S.J., later rector of the UCA.
[80] Later president of CELAM.

## Wednesday, December 20

In Potonico we celebrated a Mass of atonement for the sacrilegious robbery of the consecrated hosts from that church. From the moment I arrived in the village, the reception was very enthusiastic. But before most of the crowd arrived, a group of children approached me with signs in their hands and with a letter in which they told me (also in a little speech that one of them gave) of their solidarity with the many orphaned children, victims of this situation of abuses of human rights, and that they were asking me to support their cause. They asked me for an audience on December 26, which I granted them with great pleasure.

Accompanied by the people, I headed to the church. There were some very meaningful signs in the streets. I particularly liked the one that said "our pastor and friend." I celebrated the Mass with Father Fabián Amaya, with Father Efraín, parish priest of Chalatenango, and with Father Luis Recinos, the new parish priest—temporarily at least—of the parish of San Antonio los Ranchos and Potonico, and Father Rafael Urrutia, who is working in Chalatenango and will be in charge of the seminary and of the Secretariat of the Vicariate.

After Mass, we met with the pastoral workers, and it turned out to be a very animated discussion.

## Thursday, December 21

A very interesting meeting on matters of economic administration, listening to the auditor and Ingeniero Galván and Monsignor Urioste about very practical matters of subsidies and ways to administer our assets.

In the afternoon, also, a meeting on our pastoral work which we spent developing the list of pastoral activities of the archdiocese.

### Friday, December 22

I celebrated Mass at the Asilo Sara at noon. It is an old people's home in Colonia Costa Rica that looks rather run-down. It is clear they are not receiving spiritual care and we must do something to help the many old and sick people in that place.

### Saturday, December 23

This afternoon I celebrated the Holy Mass in Fátima Church in Planes de Renderos. The church was completely full of Franciscan sisters led by the superior general of the congregation and four provincials. Today marked the end of the jubilee year that they have been celebrating to give thanks to God for the fifty years they have been in this country. It is a congregation that has houses in Zacatacoluca, in Cojutepeque, in Usulután, in Berlín and, in San Salvador, the Colegio del Espíritu Santo and the novice house in Planes de Renderos. God has blessed them with many vocations and I urged them to carry on a profoundly ecclesial work.

In the evening, a farewell for the superior general of the congregation of the Passionist Sisters, who has been with us for several days. She leaves with a very good impression of the work her sisters are doing in this country.

### Sunday, December 24

I celebrated the Christmas Vigil in the morning, after the Mass in the cathedral, in Colonia Amatepec, where they greeted me with affection, carrying palms that made me think of Palm Sunday. We blessed the new hermitage. Father José Luis Bourguet, in charge of the pastoral work in this colonia, has managed to win the affection and esteem of all of these people, who work with him very enthusiastically.

This afternoon in Colonia Bernal. It is a part of the parish of Miralvalle that is under the Augustinian Fathers. I think that this Colonia Bernal, with the enthusiasm of its youth, is called to be the yeast of the new parish. We met there with a group of young people prepared by Father Plácido for

Confirmation and a Eucharist with great participation. After Mass, there were tamales and coffee and bread for the children who had had their First Communion and for the guests.

In the evening, I celebrated the seven o'clock Christmas Eve Mass in the cathedral and at ten o'clock in the chapel of the Divine Providence Hospital.

 **Monday, December 25**

In the morning, wedding masses and First Communions in Soyapango parish. In the afternoon, as well, many weddings. There were forty couples, and a small group of children celebrating their First Communion. The two communities gave me great comfort this Christmas because of the preparation with which they were ready to receive the sacraments, especially Matrimony.

 **Tuesday, December 26**

In the morning, a group of children from San Antonio los Ranchos who had organized themselves into a solidarity committee for orphaned children came to see me. They had requested an audience with me and they spoke to me of their ideals, of wanting to empathize with these children, who are their friends, who have become orphans because their parents have been killed or disappeared or are in prison.

On this Christmas, they feel the sadness of so many children without parents and they want to do something. I congratulated them and offered them all the support I can give for their projects.

I had lunch in the Opus Dei[81] house. They are recently installed in a new house, since they are leaving the Doble Vía.

I was visited by a representative of the International Red Cross principally to discuss the matter of the kidnapping of two men from England, one from Japan and another from Holland. And he will intercede

---

[81] Founded as a secular institute in 1928, now an international prelature of both priests and laypersons.

with the authorities of the country and asked for my help, and I offered it, within the limits of my abilities and what I can do.

In the afternoon, a meeting of the pastoral team to continue listing information, activities and what could be better organized.

 **Wednesday, December 27**

Patronal feast of San Juan Opico. We were able to concelebrate with Father José María Dueñas, who was ordained in this very church fifty years ago by his uncle, the bishop of San Miguel, Bishop Juan Antonio Dueñas. I preached and shared very pleasant memories of Bishop Dueñas and Bishop [Rafael] Valladares. And I cordially congratulated the guest of honor. After Mass, we met with catechists from this parish community and from Tacachico. The problem of a priest for Tacachico was discussed again and I left them charged with helping me to think of a solution.

In San Juan Opico, we discussed the problem of a priest for Tacachico. I asked the catechists and priests for their help in resolving, through consensus, such an urgent problem.

In the afternoon, I ordained deacon the young man Jaime Paredes, for he has almost finished his studies of theology in the seminary in Guadalajara, Mexico. He will go back to finish his studies and then come to be a deacon for a time and then he will be ordained a priest. In the basilica, there were many distinguished people, some from Opus Dei, and I tried to greet all of them.

In the evening, I was interviewed by a North American journalist at the Divine Providence Hospital.

**Thursday, December 28**

In Old Cuscatlán we celebrated the traditional Feast of the Innocents. The message I brought was one of respect for life, the sense of solidarity and how Christ is the source of all of our merits. I talked with Father Hector Figueroa, who will leave the diocese to enter a religious community and go into mission work according to the call he feels in his vocation. I respect his vocation, his wishes, and I told him the diocese will be open to him if he should wish to return.

In the afternoon we marked the thirty-day anniversary of the death of Father Neto Barrera in Domus Mariae with a group of workers who used to meet with him, and they shared with me their impressions of him. I really feel that Father Neto did not always convey a purely priestly message but rather acquiesced greatly with the political and revolutionary ideals of these groups. Nevertheless, they tell me, they thought he always tried to guide them as a priest. We still do not know what the deepest beliefs of this priest were.

This same day there was a gathering of priests at the seminary. The priests' cooperative was celebrating its Christmas party—very lively and well attended.

 **Friday, December 29**

In the evening, a nice time shared with some young people at the pastoral house of San Antonio Abad—some sixty young people giving their opinions, reporting on their pastoral activities and asking anxiously about their problems, which are typical of the times.

 **Saturday, December 30**

In the Colegio Belén in Santa Tecla, the Carmelite Sisters of St. Joseph were celebrating the fiftieth anniversary of the death of their founder, Mother Clarita Quiroz. I officiated, talking to them in the homily about their charism, of the need to be faithful to it and to adapt it to the present situation and to that of the local Church.

I participated for a while in the meeting of the Vicariate of the Department of La Libertad, which was meeting in the convent of Concepción Church. Almost all the priests, religious communities and laypeople who work in the pastoral work were present.

This afternoon, I learned that FARN, which has the four men who were kidnapped, had accepted the mediation of the Human Rights Commission, but they wanted me to become part of the Commission. When I was notified of this by the Human Rights Commission, I told them that I would accept with pleasure and that I was at their service to help to save these lives and also the lives of the prisoners that these forces are asking the government to free.

## Sunday, December 31

We have come to the end of the year. The Mass in the cathedral was well attended, as was the Mass at seven in the evening, at which we already were celebrating the Mass for January 1.

At noon I had lunch with the seminarians that work in the cathedral at the Colegio Sagrado Corazón. Lunch was provided for us there.

In the evening at ten o'clock we had a meditation before the Blessed Sacrament and I celebrated Mass in the chapel of the Divine Providence Hospital. And in the sisters' dining room together with other special visitors, in the midst of the explosions of fireworks, we witnessed the passage from an old year to a new one. And we predicted happiness for the new year. Happy New Year!

# January 1979

## Monday, January 1

Not much activity during the day, since almost everything took place during the night. I was able to rest a little at the farm belonging to the Oblate Sisters of Divine Love.

This evening I celebrated the usual Holy Hour in the chapel of the Divine Providence Hospital. The attendance was unusually large. I talked to them about the meaning of time in the biblical sense: the experience of God visiting human beings and the human obligation to respond to time as a visit from God.

## Tuesday, January 2

When the workers return to their tasks, the chancery resumes its normal routine. I took care of several private audiences. In the afternoon, the taping of the interview program I have every Wednesday.

## Wednesday, January 3

A great deal of activity in the archdiocese. Among the most important visits was that of Miss Doris Osegueda, who has taken charge of the communications office. An interview with Ingeniero Galván to talk about concentrating all our efforts so that this year we will improve the organization of our diocesan curia.

An edition of one of my homilies is being prepared in the secretariat, the one from the first Sunday of Advent. We hope to continue issuing the rest of the homilies in booklets, but I wanted to do this first one as a token of appreciation for all of those who have been so kind as to remember me with greetings at Christmas and New Year's and to congratulate me on my nomination for the Nobel Peace Prize.

I also received a visit from the International Red Cross delegation to talk about the kidnappings of the two men from England and the one from Japan, Mr. Suzuki. The Red Cross cannot act as intermediary if there is already another intermediary and, in this case, the Commission on Human Rights has been mediating. At the request of the kidnappers, I have been made part of the Commission.

In the evening, during dinner, I had an interesting conversation with the rector of the seminary, Father Gregorio Rosa, who informed me about the activities of the other bishops with regard to the seminary, which they want to educate only the seminarians from the suffragan dioceses, thus eliminating the group from the archdiocese which, according to the other bishops, is the one that is causing problems.

Naturally, the seminary team reacted in a very ecclesial way, saying that they are at the service of the Church as regards the formation of priests and that the Holy See had issued a directive that it wanted an interdiocesan seminary. I was pleased by this ecclesial reaction from the team, as well as by the reports given to the apostolic visitor, who was here investigating the archbishop's actions and the pastoral work of the archdiocese.

Finally, very late in the evening, a visit from Dr. Roberto Lara Velado[82] and Dr. Napoleón González, members of the commission that is acting as intermediary to try to resolve the kidnapping of the two Englishmen and the Japanese gentleman. They told me that today a formal petition, signed by many of our people, was presented to the Legislative Assembly. It asks the government for a general amnesty for political prisoners and abolishment of the Law for the Defense of Public Order. They talked with the president of the Assembly, who indicated his desire to help with the petition, but made them understand that, because of his political position, he cannot do anything more. We discussed how to support this petition since the extremist groups engage in violence, which could weaken the requested petition for amnesty.

In the chancery there was a meeting of parish priests and of the seminary commission. It was very interesting to see the concern of all the priests that the seminarians from our archdiocese be understood, be supported in their concerns and be formed in the way they should be as priests, in the way that the pastoral work of our archdiocese needs them to be. Father Sigfredo, rector of the minor seminary, was put in charge of continuing to coordinate reflection on this problem. All the priests present will have to take part in this reflection, as well as those who want to continue collaborating in this great concern, which is the principal one of our diocese—the formation of a clergy which is at the proper level and ready to respond to the needs of the present time.

 **Thursday, January 4**

I went to the village of La Junta, in the parish of Concepción in Quezaltepeque, where Father Eduardo Alas[83] is doing very efficient pastoral work. In the village of La Junta, there had been a sacrilegious robbery of the Blessed Sacrament, and we went to celebrate an act of atonement. It turned out to be very impressive. Beginning at the entrance to the town, a group of children with little flags, the colors of the Church, announced the joy and warm reception that the bishop and the parish priest inspire there. Also the collaborating catechists, women religious— the Spanish Carmelite Missionary Sisters work there with Father Alas with

---

[82] An important figure in the Christian Democratic Party, president of the Commission to Investigate Political Assassinations and Disappearances.

[83] Later the first bishop of Chalatenango.

great intensity—and a large number of the faithful were waiting for me at the edge of the village to take me to the shrine. Because it is not large enough, we had to celebrate the Eucharist on the porch of the rectory, above the plaza, shaded by some picturesque almond trees.

In the eucharistic message, I spoke to them about the presence of Christ in our midst, which he has revealed in diverse forms: in the Church community, in its ministers, in the proclamation of his word, and, especially, in the Eucharist; about how many times the Lord's loving presence is answered by indifference, persecution and slander; and how, therefore, atonement is necessary.

After Mass, we held a eucharistic procession. After I gave the benediction, I invited them to join in a moment of fellowship—that is, for the different communities which had brought beautiful signs to come to the microphone and read their signs or express their feelings in ecclesial communion. And it was very impressive to hear their different voices: men, women, adults, young people expressing their feeling of profound solidarity with the Church and its pastor. As Father Alas told me, "Through these gatherings, one grows in faith."

I returned home, having truly grown, feeling confirmed in my desire to serve this noble people of God that the Lord has entrusted to me.

When I got back I found some important messages about matters of the life of the archdiocese waiting for me, and also a confidential message transmitted to me directly by someone who has received information about threats against me. With the help of God, I hope to overcome this and continue loyally to serve the gospel and our people.

 **Friday, January 5**

In the morning, we had a meeting of the archdiocesan communications office. The new executive secretary is Miss Doris Osegueda, who worked with me a long time ago in San Miguel. Today, skilled in her chosen profession and with a degree in journalism, she has left her job at the university and will add her services to this important office, which we tried to restructure in this morning's meeting. Along with the Secretariat there will be an advisory group which will give advice on the direction to take and will also serve to advise the hierarchy itself. Under the Secretariat, there is the radio, publishing house and all other information services. They also will try to increase the circulation of the newspaper *Orientación*,[84] and especially to interpret in the newspaper as well as on the radio the ideological direction defined by the archbishop. It was a very constructive meeting and comforting as regards the possibilities for diffusion of the Church's message.

I also had a brief interview with a North American journalist who showed great admiration for what he has seen in our archdiocese. He thinks that this direction of the Church is the one that can attract people, since a spiritualized emphasis—disembodied, unconcerned with the realities of the earth—would no longer be very credible in the present situation. I thanked him for his words of encouragement. And to his questions about the religiosity and the problems of the country, I tried to respond with the loyalty with which I have always tried to do so.

Also another interview with a woman religious from Ciudad Barrios, who told me about the conflict that has arisen at Don Carlos Boillat's farm. It is a conflict on a coffee plantation where the owner, someone very well respected, many times does not realize what his underlings—the administrators and foremen—are up to. Conflict occurred and resulted in the death of one person in that city.

In the afternoon, I visited the community of San José Villanueva, where the Passionist sisters work. We had a very interesting dialogue with them, and with the catechists of the parish of Huizúcar, of the communities of Huizúcar, from Nuevo Cuscatlán and San José Villanueva and from several other villages, about their pastoral activities and about the difficulties and, at the same time, the hopes, and the projects the parish priest, Father Benito Tovar, directs there. The meeting ended with some delicious pupusas[85] and hot chocolate served to all those attending.

In the evening, in the Divine Providence Hospital, a visit from the representatives of the Commission on Human Rights to talk about the matter of the kidnappings, which still doesn't show any signs of being resolved.

---

[84] The archdiocesan weekly newspaper.
[85] A typical Salvadoran pastry usually filled with pork, cheese or beans.

### Saturday, January 6

Today, after a long time, we had an advisory breakfast. I was still asking for advice about my appearance at Puebla. They gave me a great deal of information and made many suggestions. We are hopeful because several bishops and experts who agree completely with the pastoral direction of our archdiocese will attend. We also tried to analyze the current situation of the country, the results of the apostolic visitation the archdiocese had recently, the problem of the seminary and other topics. Consultation on these topics with these priests and laypeople greatly enriches my pastoral criteria.

At noon, a meeting with Father [Rafael] Moreno and Beto Cuéllar to put together the information on the week's events and comments for tomorrow's Sunday homily.

In the afternoon, a visit to the parish of Apopa, where Father Oscar Martell had prepared the Confirmation of some young people and a dialogue with the pastoral agents.

 ### Sunday, January 7

We celebrated the Mass for Epiphany in the cathedral. I took the title for my homily from the Bible readings—"Christ: Epiphany of the Saving Love of God." I presented it in three parts: first, how the Epiphany shows us a transcendental salvation (I spoke of the need for any movement of revindication to make itself part of the salvation that God can provide and that Christ alone came to carry out). The second thought was that the Epiphany offers us a universal salvation: No one is excluded, for there are no distinctions in the saving love of God. And the third thought, the necessity of faith (of which the three wise men are an example) in order for us to make the salvation revealed and offered in the Epiphany our own. The cathedral was full of people—as usual, thank God!

In the afternoon, I attended the installation of Father Samuel Orellana as the new parish priest of Mejicanos, and of Father Octavio Ortiz as vicar of the area, replacing Father Manuel Barrera, who has asked for a temporary leave of absence.

This was also a beautiful ecclesial event. The church was completely full; a great deal of affection was shown to the priests, a great solidarity with the pastoral direction of the archdiocese. The three priests spoke and all of the priests of the vicariate attended.

## Monday, January 8

This morning a week of study of our priestly identity began at the seminary, San José de la Montaña. More than seventy priests were there, but there were some unexplained absences and those priests will be asked to come. The participants have been asked to stay for the entire week and to be punctual, since the topic is a problem that concerns our priestly ministry so profoundly in order to be able to fulfill it as God wants us to—and the Church needs us to—at this time.

The survey made about the pastoral direction of the archdiocese and the actions of the archbishop is being used as a base. The survey was my suggestion and was carried out by the Priests' Senate. In this encounter of priests, it will be studied from sociological, theological and pastoral points of view, leading us to a priestly identity that will truly reflect the thought of the Church in our archdiocese.

The participation, the group reflections, the plenary sessions have already been very promising from the first day. The problem has been examined very deeply. Father Carlos Mejía, priest of the parish of La Asunción Flor Blanca, reported on the survey. Fathers Octavio Cruz and Walter Guerra, both specialists in sociology and members of the diocesan clergy, presented the survey from a sociological perspective. Father Astor Ruiz, representing the Pastoral Commission, is in charge of the week.

In the evening, Mass in the church at Colonia Miramonte, with the participation of all of the parish priests of the Vicariate of Mejicanos and Zacamil. Memorial Mass for the mother of Father Rogelio, priest of the parish of Zacamil, attended by....[86]

## Monday, January 8, continued

After returning from the church in Colonia Miramonte at nine o'clock at night, a press conference with a Mexican journalist, another from Costa Rica and another young woman who was also Mexican. Our conversation about the situation of the Church in our country was very interesting.

---

[86] Tape ends here.

### Tuesday, January 9

The week on priestly identity continues at the seminary, San José de la Montaña. In the morning the plenary continued, drawing conclusions and discussing very interesting topics of our pastoral work—about the relations between the bishops and the priests and many concrete aspects of our pastoral work. Immediately afterwards, Father Jesús Delgado gave a theological interpretation of the survey that we are studying. Seen from a theological perspective, the survey seems rich in details about our pastoral work.

At noon, we had a meeting on the seminary. Present were the commission on the seminary, parish priests who have seminarians from their parishes and the seminary formation team. Discussion was primarily about the six students from the archdiocese whom the team is trying to remove from the seminary and whom the parish priests and communities are defending because they consider them to be hopeful signs for the Church through their pastoral work in the towns and small villages. The formation team promised to study the problem of these six seminarians again. Father Sigfredo will be in charge of calling a new meeting to reveal the results.

### Wednesday, January 10

Today was the third day of the week on priestly identity. Father Torruella was responsible for presenting the central theme, a pastoral interpretation of the survey. The pastoral aspects were very interesting and they praised the concern on all sides to find the true position of the Church, and to be in solidarity with the direction that historically was begun during the time of Archbishop Luis Chávez y González and has been continued by the present archbishop. The discussion in the plenary session was also very interesting, the theme of the search for the true concept of poverty prevailing. I said that I thought that it was all a matter of conversion, that the poor person is one who has been converted to God and puts all his faith in him, and that the rich person is one who has not been converted to God and puts his confidence in idols: money, power, material things. And that all of our work should be directed toward truly converting ourselves and all people to this authentic meaning of poverty. For Christ said that the secret is this: You cannot serve two masters, God and mammon.

In the evening, I went to a dinner given by the sisters of the Colegio de la Asunción. Their community has been increased by the sisters who have come from Santa Ana and from Guatemala to take part in an educational program.

 **Thursday, January 11**

This day in the week on pastoral identity was spent on a synthesis. The groups worked according to the different vicariates, reviewing all the rich material of the previous three days to arrive at a synthesis to present to the plenary session. The result was a rich abundance of ideas. There were suggestions about the nature of the pastoral work that can enable us to live our priesthood in its true identity of service to our people.

I took advantage of the meetings in smaller groups to take care of different appointments. The most important audience was one at noon with the ambassador from Venezuela. We spent a long time remembering my former Venezuelan companions in Rome with whom I got along better perhaps than with any other group. The ambassador also showed great interest in learning about the situation of our country and of our Church.

In the evening, I went to bless the home of Dr. Guerra, a professional and very good friend, who was celebrating his fourteenth wedding anniversary and, at the same time, his wife's birthday.

 **Friday, January 12**

We have come to the end of the reflection on our priestly identity. The plenary session from yesterday continued for a long time yet this morning. Afterwards I gave my presentation, which I used to thank, congratulate and encourage my dear brother priests. And I took as the subject of my reflection the different chapters indicated by the *Decree on the Pastoral Office of Bishops*,[87] telling the priests how happy I was to find such wonderful parallels between the points that we have brought up in our

---

[87] From the Second Vatican Council.

reflection this week and the indications that, under the different aspects of the episcopal ministry, the Church gives the bishops.

I presented, as the decree does, a perspective on the Church on which our identity as priests is to be modeled. Then, the offices of teacher of the faith that we, together with the priests, have to live, always being careful that our preaching and our doctrine be the true doctrine of Christ. As minister of the liturgy, together with the priests, we must sanctify. All our liturgy must be appropriate and must respect the hierarchical understanding. Therefore we must obey the norms that make our worship, the administration of our sacraments, the celebration of our Mass a true act of rational obedience to the discipline of the Church, searching always for the greatest good and edification of the people. I also spoke here of the rich popular religiousness among us, of our personal devotion, of being sure that we also know how to profit from the sacraments in our individual lives.

The bishop as center and minister of the hierarchical society that is the Church, together with the priests, have to care for all the people of God and be united among ourselves: Here I tried to emphasize the multiple reflections that had been made about the relationship between the bishop and the diocesan clergy, as well as between the religious clergy and the life of the diocese. We must work to bring the women religious, the laity and everyone who is part of the people of God closer and closer in the unity that Christ wants.

Then the decree presents the bishop as president of the community of love and charity and speaks to us of promoting the sense of Christian love and also of social justice. I emphasized how in our time we cannot overlook this aspect of educating our people: promoting awareness and a critical sense among our people that can lead to the more just society God wants.

And finally, about the organisms of the curia, the vicariates, the parishes. The priests have a principal role in these realities and I asked them for all the cordiality of their service to the people—and to our Lord, of course.

We ended at noon around the altar of the parish church of San José de la Montaña. And this Mass, concelebrated by all the priests, was quite impressive. At the end of the Mass, in a ceremony truly reflecting the mission of our priests to their parishes, the ministerial licenses were awarded after we had renewed our ordination vows. We had lunch together and there was a true sense of sacramental brotherhood that seemed to have increased as a result of this successful week of reflection and spirituality.

After lunch, the vicars stayed to have a preliminary meeting to organize the Pastoral Council of the archdiocese, which has been one of the most profitable initiatives to come out of this week on the priestly identity. The women religious who work in the pastoral life will also be represented, as well as the laity. Father Astor Ruiz was named executive secretary. He will be in charge of this commission or council of the archdiocesan pastoral work which is so necessary to coordinate all the pastoral richness and activities in the archdiocese.

A journalist from Norway interviewed me for an article in his newspaper and for the radio of his country, asking about different matters of the life of our Church and about its relationship with the people and with the government.

In the evening we celebrated the Mass for Peace in the cathedral. Bishop Arturo Rivera Damas, Bishop of Santiago de María, was there because he is also president of the National Commission on Justice and Peace. This commission had organized this evening, which turned out splendidly, with Mass concelebrated by several priests and a talk by Bishop Rivera that received much applause, especially at the end when, in conclusion, he repeated the desires expressed in the pastoral letter that he and I have published about the popular political organizations and their relationship to the Church. His conclusions referred to support for the petitions that are being made at present for amnesty for political prisoners, for free entry into the country for those in exile, for abrogating the Law for the Defense of Public Order and also for the freedom of those kidnapped. The cathedral was filled and, when we were leaving, we spent some very cordial moments with the people, who have a great deal of confidence in our Church.

 **Saturday, January 13**

There was a gathering of catechumens in the Franciscan church in Planes de Renderos. I was not able to go. I have spent my time in reflection and personal tasks since I had no time during the week.

At noon, I had lunch with Father Moreno and Bachiller Roberto Cuéllar to prepare the report that we give every Sunday in the homily.

**Sunday, January 14**

Mass at the cathedral was well attended and there were representatives of the foreign press. After the Mass I was interviewed by some of these journalists. Then I left for San Antonio Abad, where I celebrated the Mass as part of the novena[88] that the community is holding in preparation for its patronal feast. I talked to them about an effort to achieve unity and to overcome any difficulties like those which, unfortunately, they have suffered previously.

In the afternoon, without having made plans to do so, I decided to visit the Santo Cristo of Esquipulas[89] in the parish of San Bartolomé Perulapía. I surprised Father Luis Montesinos, who was very flattered by my visit and introduced me at the microphones at the romería.[90] I had to say a few words, and I spoke of the popular religion and of profiting from these popular centers and devotions to grow in our faith.

In the evening, I visited another sanctuary of our diocese in honor of the Christ of Esquipulas. It was in the parish of Colón, where Father Nicolás Menjívar had invited me to celebrate a Mass for youth in honor of the Holy Christ. After the Mass, during which I directed my message to the large group that filled the church to visit the Holy Christ, we shared an enjoyable time with the pastoral agents.

 **Monday, January 15**

Monday the fifteenth, Feast of the Lord of Esquipulas, the parish of Aguilares celebrated the crucified Savior under the title "Lord of Mercies" as its patronal feast. Invited by Father Octavio Cruz and the Sisters of the Sacred Heart, I presided over the Eucharist attended by nearly all the priests of the vicariate and many other people, since they have great devotion there to the Black Christ. I took the opportunity to explain a passage from the Epistle to the Hebrews that speaks to us of the sacrifice of Christ and of his entry as redeemer and savior of humanity into the perfect sanctuary, heaven.

---

[88] Nine days of prayer.

[89] A popular shrine and pilgrimage site in Guatemala containing the statue of the "Black Christ" of Esquipulas. Here Romero refers to other statues of the Santo Cristo de Esquipulas.

[90] Pilgrimage.

Among those attending were many people who belong to popular political organizations. I tried to orient them so that the strength for justice of their organizations does not deviate from a Christian sense, but may rather be included in the profound and universal redemption of Jesus Christ—that is, that it begin in liberation from sin.

### Thursday, January 18

I had a breakfast meeting for consultation with my usual advisers in which we focused, at my request, on an outline for my participation in the Bishops' Conference in Puebla. Also we talked some about the reality of the situation of the country. These meetings are very useful. I have been neglecting them a little but, on returning from Puebla, I will have these meetings on a more regular basis.

The ecumenical week has begun. It is principally the Baptists and the Catholics who, with great enthusiasm, have organized a week of prayer for Christian unity. Tonight was the opening ceremony in the First Baptist Church. I was asked to participate in the welcome—to greet those attending, who were very numerous. A Baptist minister gave the principal address about how the Holy Spirit is a unifying force and how we have great confidence in him and ask for his enlightenment and his strength for the objectives of the ecumenical movement.

### Friday, January 19

In the afternoon, we had an interesting meeting on the problem of the seminary, where six young men have been singled out by the formation team. According to the team, they should not return to the seminary, but parish priests and base communities who know the work of these young men oppose this judgment and have asked us to intercede so that these vocations are not lost. The discussion was very interesting and we are inclined to continue to support the vocation of these seminarians unless we receive evidence to the contrary.

## Saturday, January 20

A very tragic day. It dawned with the news that there had been a military operation in El Despertar in the parish of San Antonio Abad. It was at a house frequently used for retreats designed to deepen the participants' Christian faith. Father Octavio Ortiz, along with Sister Chepita, as they call the Belgian sister who works there, was leading a program of introduction to the Christian life for some forty young men. But at dawn today, the National Guard with a riot squad set off a bomb to break down the door and then entered violently with armored cars and shooting. Father Octavio, when he realized what was happening, got up just to meet his death, as did four other young men. The rest of the group, including two women religious, were taken to the headquarters of the National Guard.

We did not learn about the murders of Father Octavio and the other four young men until the afternoon, when their bodies already had been taken to the morgue at the cemetery. Father Octavio's face was very disfigured; it looked like it had been run over and flattened by something very heavy. He was taken to La Auxiliadora funeral home along with three of the others (one of the bodies had already been claimed by relatives, but these three had not yet been identified by their families). We had them taken to the funeral home to be prepared and then to the cathedral for the viewing of the bodies. There they would be identified by their families, who then would take charge of them.

In the evening, this tragic funereal cortege was taken to the cathedral. A great many people were there; the cathedral was almost full. There were many prayers for the slain and gospel messages preached to the crowd. I got there at about eleven p.m. The crowd greeted me with applause. I led an intercessory prayer for Father Octavio and the others and also explained to the crowd how we would proceed the next day. I invited all of them to come to the eight a.m. Mass at the cathedral. All the priests will be there, having suspended their normal Sunday schedules to concelebrate this Mass for their brother priest.

**Sunday, January 21**

The Mass concelebrated at the cathedral was beautiful and filled the whole morning. There were more than a hundred priests around the casket of their dead brother, Father Octavio. The other three caskets were there too, those of the young men that the Church had arranged to bring there from the cemetery morgue.

We could not celebrate the Mass inside the cathedral, so we set it up in the street and the park. At the time for the Mass to start, it was very moving to see such a concentration of people, especially because of the pious way in which the crowd participated in the prayers for the dead. A representative of the bishop of Cleveland was at my side, and there were other priests from the United States. In my homily, I analyzed the crime perpetrated against Father Octavio and the four who had been sacrificed with him. I called for a rational response rather than resorting to violence and force. I protested this attack on the dignity of our Church. I reminded my listeners of the sentence of excommunication destined for those who planned, as well as those who carried out, this crime against a priest. Among the crowd, there were people from all the parishes of the archdiocese and also representatives of many communities from other dioceses.

Father Octavio's casket and those of the other young men were moved back into the cathedral after the Mass so that they could continue to be viewed by the faithful, who expressed their affection through prayer and reflection as they filed past the caskets.

The community of San Francisco, in Mejicanos, asked permission to bury Father Octavio's body in their church. And after talking over the situation, figuring out how to avoid anything that could provoke a violent situation, we decided that they should move the body secretly. His body belongs to them, since it was there that he was ordained and it was there that he worked during his five-year ministry. I was the one who ordained Father Octavio on March 3, 1974, representing Bishop Luis Chávez y González.

By afternoon, Father Octavio's body had been moved to his parish of San Francisco in Mejicanos, and I went there to preside over the concelebration. There were forty priests and the crowd was huge. The street in front of the church was not big enough to hold the numerous crowd that had come from all over. Because of this, the celebration was held out of doors and, after Mass, the visitation of the faithful to Father Octavio continued with lines that stretched all the way to the furthest stop of the Mejicanos bus line—a truly wonderful demonstration of solidarity, suffering and love, of surrender to the cause of Jesus Christ. The crowd expressed great affection to the priests and to their bishop, greeting him with applause, kissing his hands, etc. I left there filled with a spirit of satisfaction, thinking how well people respond to those who know how to love them! Father Octavio's body remained on view until the line of people, which was still very long then, had all entered.

 ## Monday, January 22

At 8:20 p.m. I left for Mexico on a Pan American flight to attend the Puebla meeting. When we stopped in Guatemala City, we greeted the priests who met us there and were interviewed briefly by a journalist who was particularly interested in the declarations just made in Mexico by the president of the republic,[91] who said that the Church is not persecuted in El Salvador. He also wanted details of the attack on the youth retreat center where Father Octavio was tragically killed.

In the Mexico City airport, too, when they realized that the archbishop of San Salvador was arriving, there was a press conference with Mexican journalists, television crews and representatives of the press who also were interested in the situation of the Church in El Salvador and its relationship to the government. In this interview, we clarified certain inaccuracies in the declarations made by the president in Mexico. One of the journalists told me in confidence that the visit of [Salvadoran] President Romero and, above all, his departure for El Salvador had been very cold—"icy," the journalist said.

We were warmly received by the Carmelite sisters of St. Theresa, who had been notified of my arrival time by the sisters of that congregation at the Divine Providence Hospital in San Salvador. They came to meet us at the airport and took us to their novitiate in Colonia Santa María de la Rivera. I was accompanied by Fathers Jesús Delgado and Astor Ruiz; Father Rafael Moreno had also come with me, but he went to stay with his Jesuit brothers. We have been in constant communication because he is in charge of reporting to the public information secretariat of the Archdiocese of San Salvador on the Puebla meeting and all the events of this trip.

After resting for a little while in the sisters' house, I went with my two priest companions to the Basilica of Our Lady of Guadalupe, making our first offering on this trip to her. It was six in the evening and a group of pilgrims was to arrive from the market. I asked the chaplain of the basilica

---

[91] Carlos Humberto Romero.

to let my two companions and me concelebrate. He was very nice and let us participate in the celebration that had been prepared to welcome the pilgrims.

At night, we talked with Father Moreno, who came to where I was staying to tell me about the relationships he was establishing with bishops and other priests. I also received a telephone call from the bishop of Cuernavaca [Mexico], Don Sergio Méndez Arceo, who told me that there was going to be a meeting of magazine editors, that he was going and that we could talk there. I told him that I would be very happy to go, because I wanted to talk with him also. He was to confirm this early the next day.

On television at ten o'clock that night, I saw part of my interview at the airport. I also learned that Cardinal Pironio[92] had arrived and been interviewed. Also Father Moreno told me that the bishops from Chile would arrive tonight as well as other bishops. He will keep me informed.

 **Tuesday, January 23**

After a night of rest and peace, thank God, I celebrated Mass in the small sanctuary of the novices, where we also shared some reflections on the word of God, meditating on its implications for this moment that is so important for Latin America. And I asked them to be a living force in their prayers, so that the Puebla meeting and the visit by the pope to our continent would mean a true Pentecost for our peoples, who have such hope in the Church.

I greeted the Dominican provincial, accompanied by Father José Luis, who is staying with them and has come to help me with reports for our communications office so that our people will receive the true account of the pope's visit and especially of the Puebla meeting. We went with them to get their press credentials; these were being given out at an office that has been set up to help the archdiocese and CELAM communicate with the media.

At eleven-thirty a.m., I went to meet Bishop Méndez Arceo, who had asked me to meet him at that time in the house where the magazine directors were meeting. Unfortunately, he wasn't there, but shortly before I had to leave, I was able to talk with him briefly. It was obvious that he was glad to see me and that we support each other in our position as pastors of a Church that wants to be faithful to a gospel at the service of the poor. He

---

[92] Argentine archbishop and prefect of the Vatican Congregation for Religious.

told me some of his adventures as a pastor, of his meeting with Pope John Paul II and of his joy at being able in this way to serve the people of God.

In the evening, I was invited to the motherhouse of the Carmelite Sisters for dinner. After dinner, we saw on television some scenes of the preparations for the pope's arrival.

Also in the evening, I was visited by two journalists with whom I talked in greater depth about my ideals of service to the Church and the problems that this creates.

 ## Wednesday, January 24

I went to see Mexico City Cathedral and the immense plaza of the Zócalo where the Holy Father will meet with the peoples of Latin America. They were preparing the cathedral with stands of seats in the choir section and in the main part of the church for the crowd that will attend the Mass celebrated there by the pope. While we were there, we heard the song of a choir that was rehearsing—a wonderful choir accompanied by an orchestra and the organ.

In the evening, a press conference. Alan Riding[93] had invited a group of journalists—actually, correspondents from press agencies. We were not expecting so many people, but I was glad to see before me some fifty journalists with their television cameras, photographers and, especially, with a series of very interesting questions. They seemed to have a special sympathy for the Church. There was respect and also sincerity in the questions asked.

I began by thanking them for this opportunity to project my voice on behalf of the voiceless and to make the thought of the Church known through the diffusion of its messages, a Church that wants to be true to the gospel. I described briefly the economic, social and political situation of my country and how, in such a difficult atmosphere, the Church tries to carry out a prophetic mission that will awaken the conscience of the Salvadorans so that they will react not merely as a mass, but rather as true sons and daughters of God, formed into communities ruled by true love. This is why the Church denounces everything which destroys individual dignity and especially whatever limits our ability to build a country which has love, justice and peace as its foundation.

---

[93] Latin American correspondent for *The New York Times*.

After the press conference, I had the satisfaction of hearing some very positive comments: how many of them didn't know anything about the reality of El Salvador before and how, thanks to this interview, they had learned what the Church is able to do in that difficult situation.

In the evening, we again went to have dinner with the superiors of the Carmelite congregation. There we also saw on television the final hours that the pope spent in Rome before his trip. The television encouraged everyone to continue watching since, at one a.m. Mexican time, they would be transmitting the pope's departure for America live. He will be flying directly to Santo Domingo.

 **Thursday, January 25**

In the brief homily of the Mass I celebrated in the Carmelite novice house, I reminded them of the events taking placing in these days: the pope's visit to America, the bishops' meeting in Puebla (beginning that very day) and the eight-day period of prayers for Christian unity that concludes today—the feast of Saint Paul's conversion—with special prayers which, in San Salvador, will be held in the cathedral. We prayed strongly for these intentions and I asked them to pray especially for the Puebla meeting.

Today is the day scheduled for us to assemble in Puebla. A Carmelite sister very kindly drove us from Mexico City to Puebla. We arrived at noon, at lunchtime, at the home of a very warm Salvadoran, Arquitecto[94] Gonzalo Yáñez, who, along with with his wife, María Teresa, and his daughter, offered us a very cordial welcome and fed us a delicious meal.

Afterward, close to five p.m., they took me to the Palafoxian seminary, headquarters of the Third General Conference of the Latin American Bishops. I registered; they gave me the materials to study and put me in room 325. Many cardinals, archbishops, *periti,*[95] priests and laity, as well as deacons and women religious, had already arrived. It will be a good representation of our Church to deliberate on evangelization in America both now and in the future. When I had finished registering, I went with Father Jesús and Father Moreno to see the downtown area, which is very nice. We visited the cathedral and then we had a cup of coffee in the plaza.

---

[94] A title used for one who holds a degree in architecture.

[95] Advisers to particular bishops.

When we got back to the seminary, I saw several bishops I knew: Cardinal [Raúl] Primatesta [of Córdoba, Argentina], who went to school with me; the chancellor of the diocese of Puebla, Father Miguel Navotrato, who embraced me effusively; the bishop of León, [Nicaragua] Bishop [Manuel] Salazar; the archbishop of Panamá, Archbishop [Marcos] McGrath; some bishops from Chile and several other bishops who I felt showed sympathy for me and my archdiocese. There are still many other bishops to make contact with, but tonight at dinner I was able to continue to greet casually others to whom I have not yet been introduced.

## Friday, January 26

This morning we celebrated our first Mass. The place we will use for the plenary sessions will also serve as the chapel; it is a large room parallel to the dining room of the Palafoxian seminary in Puebla. The whole day was spent in registration, preparation, getting acquainted with the building and, naturally, making contact with different participants. In the Saint Joseph Hospital of the Josephite sisters, there is a Maryknoll priest from the United States who used to be in Opico. He greeted me very affectionately and I promised him I would go see a companion of his who was ill and in the hospital. Unfortunately, the time and my lack of familiarity with the city prevented me from going to visit him.

Father Jesús Delgado, who was traveling with me to act as secretary, as well as Father Moreno, as adviser for information and communication with the press, are staying in the home of Arquitecto Gonzalo Yáñez, where his wife, María Teresa, has treated them very well, giving them a place to stay and taking care of them.

## Saturday, January 27

The high point was the pilgrimage that we made by bus from Puebla to the Basilica of Guadalupe in Mexico City to concelebrate with the Holy Father. Our arrival at the basilica after a reflective journey, saying the rosary and singing to the Virgin, was quite complicated. We had great difficulty getting down the wide Avenue of Guadalupe because it was filled with people who were waiting for the Holy

Father to pass by. The people greeted us very affectionately, for they recognized our buses as those of the bishops who were meeting in Puebla.

The crowd was even greater in the plaza and it was very difficult to get through. All the bishops even had to climb over a railing in order to get into the old basilica, where we were to vest for the concelebration. This unexpected development delayed us and when we got to the old basilica the Holy Father was already in front of it because he was also going to vest there. He was carried on top of a specially prepared open van decorated in red. His white figure stood out, affectionately greeting the crowd, who never tired of applauding him.

From the old basilica, the procession of priests and bishops seemed unending in the midst of the crowd, which by then had been better organized so that the concelebrants could get through to the new basilica. With the applause and the singing, emotion was increasing as the procession went by, culminating with the Holy Father in his pontifical vestments. In the basilica, a very impressive choir welcomed the episcopal procession when the Holy Father entered. Those in the procession were seated in the seats or presidential chairs behind the altar and also filled the pews, since just the bishops of CELAM and those from Mexico and other places who had come to this solemn opening ceremony of the bishops' meeting filled a good part of the section of the basilica intended for the people. The Holy Father gave a homily in honor of the Virgin and emphasized the solemnity of the inauguration of the meeting at Puebla. His homily is contained in a special volume published by CELAM that includes all of the speeches made by the pope on his trip to Latin America.

On the way back to Puebla, on the bus I was on, the different bishops and priests from various countries talked about the devotion to the Virgin that is typical of our countries. I was very glad to be able to give testimony in honor of Our Lady of Peace.[96]

When I got back to Puebla, I went out again in the evening to take tickets to Fathers Moreno and Chus Delgado and the family they are staying with so that they can attend the pope's Mass at the seminary in Puebla. I realized that many people from nearby towns have come to wait for the Holy Father to arrive. They are sleeping on the sidewalks while other Catholics who have come from farther away or who are a little better off have parked their cars in places near the seminary where His Holiness is going to celebrate Mass.

---

[96] The title under which Mary is venerated in El Salvador.

## Sunday, January 28

The whole morning was filled with expectation of the pope's arrival at the seminary in Puebla, where bishops, priests and participants in the meeting were ready for his arrival. Prior to that, we had had Morning Prayer and a concelebrated Eucharist, since the pope will celebrate the Mass in the seminary alone. The large sports field of the seminary was completely full. According to the calculations of the experts, there were around a hundred fifty thousand people.

From Puebla, and from neighboring areas, many Catholics have come with a natural eagerness to see the pope. Many who could not come here were able to see him and greet him along the highway from Mexico City to Puebla, which had been reserved exclusively for the travel of the pope and his retinue. The pope traveled in the open van so that he could greet all the people who had gathered along the highway. Naturally, the crowd was even greater in the towns and amazingly so at the entrance to the town of Puebla and along the whole route through the city to the seminary.

In the cathedral we were anxiously awaiting him; the lights had been turned on. But the pope arrived an hour late and was very sorry not to be able to satisfy everyone, since it is like him to try to understand and comply with all the wishes of the people. An hour later than expected, that is, at one p.m., the Holy Father arrived at the seminary and, after putting on his pontifical garb, he came out to a great acclamation from the bishops, who filled the hallway running from the platform prepared for the celebration, and from the people, who were on the other side, facing the altar. The applause, the enthusiasm typical of the city of Puebla, were so overwhelming that it brought tears to the eyes. The pope, very moved, greeted the people and began the Mass. The archbishop of Puebla, Archbishop [Rosendo] Huesca, welcomed him and the pope began the eucharistic sacrifice.

In the homily, the pope discussed the theme of the family from a very interesting social focus. When it came time for the Presentation of the Gifts, it was very moving to see representatives of the indigenous peoples and their native customs bringing him the products, flowers and fruit that are typical of these fertile lands. The pope seemed very moved when he received them and presented these offerings to the Lord in the symbols of the bread and the wine. It was a shame that they had not planned for a practical way to distribute Communion and that, therefore, only a group of seminarians was able to receive Communion from the hands of the Holy Father.

In the dining room of the seminary, we had the honor of having lunch with the Holy Father. He seemed very tired from the trip from Mexico City to Puebla and from the celebration, and soon retired to the room that had been prepared for him so that he could rest for a while. At four or five p.m., in the hall used for the plenary sessions, we had the honor of listening to the pope's message to the bishops gathered at the Third Conference. It was the principal address given by the pope during his trip to America, for that was the specific reason for his trip; he had been specially invited to give it. The pope's address is also in the collection of the speeches he made in Latin America. The speech provided direction for the work of the Puebla meeting.

Afterward, the pope took leave of the bishops and returned to Mexico City quietly. Archbishop [Girolamo] Prigione, the apostolic delegate, who previously had been nuncio in El Salvador, was traveling with the pope, and I had the pleasure of greeting him. Archbishop Héctor Santos, president of the bishops' conference of Honduras and archbishop of Tegucigalpa, presided at the Vespers service. The way we are to proceed in our work had been announced previously, but it was now announced that the entire next day would be used to learn about the system of....[97]

 **Monday, January 29**

In Puebla, at the Third Conference of the Latin American bishops. At eight a.m. we celebrated Lauds[98] and the Eucharist and afterwards we began our work in the first plenary session. Cardinal Aloisio Lorscheider, president of CELAM, along with Cardinal [Sebastiano] Baggio and the archbishop of Mexico, Archbishop [Ernesto] Corripio, were the copresidents. Cardinal Lorscheider made a presentation of the goals and of the working document. The general secretary, Bishop Alfonso López Trujillo, discussed how the working document was prepared: consultation with all the bishops' conferences, the reference material, the working text, the meetings, etc. In this way, then, we have come to this moment in which the assembled bishops will evaluate their pastoral work through discussion of the theme: evangelization in Latin America now and in the future.

The associate secretary, Father Héctor Urrea, read from the list of the participants in the Third General Conference of Latin American Bishops. Presiding: Cardinal Baggio, Cardinal Lorscheider, the archbishop of Mexico, the general secretary; as vice-presidents, Cardinal [Juan]

---

[97] Tape ends here.
[98] Morning Prayer.

Landázuri of Lima and Bishop Luis Manresa of Quetzaltenango [Guatemala].

The presidents of the different departments of CELAM were: Archbishop Luciano Cabral Duarte, archbishop of Aracajú, Brazil, and president of the Department of Social Action of CELAM; Bishop Francisco de Borja Valenzuela of [Valparaíso] Chile, president of the Bishops' Conference and of the Department of Catechetics; Bishop Darío Castrillón of [Pereira] Colombia, of the Department of Social Communications; Archbishop Carlos Quintero Arce of [Hermosillo] Mexico, president of the Education Department; Bishop Antonio Quarracino of [Avellaneda] Argentina, president of the Department of Laity; Bishop Romeu Alberti from Brazil, president of the Department of Liturgy; Bishop Roger Aubry from Bolivia, president of the Department of Missions; Bishop José Gottardi of [Montevideo] Uruguay, president of the Department of Men and Women Religious; and Bishop Román Arrieta Villalobos from Costa Rica, president of the Department of Vocations and Ministries.

In addition to the departments, CELAM also has sections and those in charge are: Archbishop Samuel Carter from the Antilles, in charge of the Section on Ecumenism; Bishop Ovidio Pérez Morales from Venezuela, in charge of the Section on Nonbelievers; and Bishop Willem Ellis from the Dutch Antilles, in charge of the Section on Youth. Also, the financial committee, under the presidency of Cardinal Luis Aponte Martínez from Puerto Rico. These, then, are the nineteen cardinals and bishops who are presiding over this meeting, or are presidents or heads of the different divisions of CELAM.

Participants from number twenty to 187 include the bishops who are presidents of episcopal conferences or who were elected by their conferences to represent the different countries of Latin America; some of them were named directly by the Holy Father. The list continues from 188 to 211, including priests who are also representing their countries or who were named directly by the Holy Father. Then there are four permanent deacons and the list continues from numbers 216 to 235 with religious representing different regions or named by the Holy See. From number 236 to number 266 a list of laymen and -women, also representing the different regions or approved by the Holy See. Numbers 267 to 271 are religious from CLAR, the Latin American Confederation of Religious.

Afterward come the invited guests beginning with number 272: first those who are part of the Commission for Latin America; then other dignitaries from the Holy See or superiors general named as papal representatives by the Holy See; representatives of the episcopal conferences of the United States and Canada, from Europe, Africa and Madagascar, and Asia; representatives of national episcopal organizations that provide aid to the Churches of Latin America, up through number 329. And there are the observers who are non-Catholic Christians, whose status is only that of observers, from the Orthodox Church, the Anglican Church, the Lutheran Church, the Methodist Church and also Judaism. That makes five observers. And finally, certain experts nominated by the episcopal conferences, and thus we arrive at the number 350, which is the total number of participants.

If anyone wants to know their names, where they are from or other data in greater detail, they will find all of this in the records of the meeting that are preserved in the files of our archdiocese.

When Cardinal Lorscheider presented the working document to us, he also gave us a summary that will help in the work that we are being asked to do. It is a large sheet of paper that we have informally begun to call the "bed sheet"; it lists different themes and aspects of the working document arranged by main ideas, by topics, so that some provisional alphabetically grouped committees can try to deal with the working document and see if they agree with the topics proposed or if they want to omit some or suggest others, with the idea of beginning to establish the topics around which the final committees will be organized.

My group, naturally, is composed of those whose last names begin with R: among them, Archbishop Maximino Romero de Lema, secretary of the Congregation for the Clergy; Cardinal [Agnelo] Rossi, prefect of the Congregation for the Evangelization of Peoples; Archbishop Ladislao Rubín, secretary-general of the Bishops' Synod; Bishop Andrés Rubio, a bishop from South America [bishop of Mercedes in Uruguay] whom I met at some previous meeting.

A committee called the Interface Committee will collect the fruits of today's work in order to organize the definitive outline for the document we will write later, working in committees organized according to the number of main ideas and themes that come out of today's work.

Bishop Francisco de Borja Valenzuela, president of the episcopal conference of Chile, presided over the Vespers service.

 **Tuesday, January 30**

At the Puebla meeting. The whole day was spent on the hierarchical ministry, as yesterday was spent on the unity of the Church. Cardinal Agnelo Rossi, prefect of the Congregation for the Evangelization of Peoples, presided over the celebration of Lauds and the

Eucharist. The reciting of the psalms and the celebration of the Eucharist were very fervent, even sublime, with the participation of the seminary choir and a choir of women religious. It turned out really to be a celebration that filled the spirit and made the presence of God felt in this meeting. In his homily, Cardinal Rossi talked about the hierarchical ministry and also directed it toward the missionary task of the Church.

In the plenary session the way in which we will work was explained. Two well-known experts will be in charge of it, the Jesuit priest Manuel Vela from Colombia and Father José Marins from Brazil. They are going to organize the committees to study the topics outlined in yesterday's work. The participants can choose which committee they want to be on based on the topic which most interests them. But in case it is necessary to make any changes because of numbers, we were each given two other slips of paper on which to indicate, in case we could not have our first choice of a committee, our second and third choices.

In the afternoon, with the committees organized according to the preferences each of us had expressed, they announced where we would meet and which topics we would work on. So we began the work of writing the final document, which will go through four lengthy revisions. For now, we are to look for the different aspects of the topic that need to be covered, taking into account the working document and the suggestions or proposals that might come up in the committee. In this work, which will produce an outline for each topic, we spent the entire afternoon. It ended with the Vespers[99] service conducted by Bishop Román Arrieta from Costa Rica, who also spoke to us about ministry, giving special emphasis to the work of encouraging vocations.

 **Wednesday, January 31**

Today was spent talking about the religious life. Because of this, the Eucharist was presided over by Cardinal Eduardo Pironio, prefect of the Sacred Congregation for Religious and Secular Institutes, who previously was secretary-general and then president of CELAM, a prelate who is very highly regarded in the Puebla meeting. His homily, with his characteristic fervor, urged a great spirituality of the Mystical Body of Christ, in which he singled out the religious life for its way of following the Lord.

---

[99] Evening Prayer.

The work of the study committees will last all day and will produce a preliminary draft (called that because it is not exactly a draft, but rather an outline that will have to be developed into a draft). This work will be turned over by the different coordinators to the Interface Committee, which will make its comments and return it to the committees for a second draft.

There are twenty-one committees working on this first draft and they include the following themes: first, the pastoral vision of reality; the second committee, Christ as the center of history; third, the Church; fourth, the dignity of human beings; fifth, evangelization as a universal destiny and the criteria for it; sixth, the one I am working on, is evangelization and human promotion.

I want to mention that on this sixth committee, I have had the pleasure of finding among the seventeen bishops and priests that make it up Archbishop Helder Cámara [of Olinda and Recife, Brazil] and my good friends Gerardo Flores from [Vera Paz] Guatemala; Domingo Roa Perez [Archbishop of Maracaibo, Venezuela]; Constantino Maradei from [Barcelona] Venezuela and Manuel Talamás of [Ciudad Juárez] Mexico. The topic of our committee is very important for, as part of it, we will study liberation theology.

The seventh topic is evangelization, culture and popular religion; the eighth topic is evangelization, ideology and politics; the ninth, the family; the tenth, Christian base communities, the parish, the local Church and communion with the universal Church; the eleventh committee will study the hierarchical ministry; the twelfth, the religious life; the thirteenth, the laity; the fourteenth, vocations; the fifteenth, prayer, the sacraments, liturgy, popular piety; the sixteenth, catechesis, witness, education, media; the seventeenth, dialogue for communion and participation; the eighteenth, the preferential option for the poor; the nineteenth, young people; the twentieth, action for the foundations of a pluralistic society. And the twenty-first committee, which is the last one, is studying the topic of action in relation to national and international reality.

All the participants in the Puebla meeting are divided up into these twenty-one committees, studying through this division of labor, as can be seen, the different topics that all together will make up the definitive document.

The evening Vespers was presided over by Bishop Claude Angénor, Bishop of [Les Cayes] Haiti, a black bishop. Since it was the day devoted to men and women religious, he talked about the Mystical Body and the different charisms in that Body.

# February 1979

 ### Thursday, February 1

Today has been spent on the topic of the laity and lay ministries. Morning Prayer and the Eucharist were presided over by Cardinal Juan Landázuri, president of the Episcopal Conference of Perú. There were many representatives of the laity from Puebla in the chapel, and Cardinal Landázuri talked in his homily about the great possibilities for the Church among the laity of Latin America. We continued to work in the groups or committees organized yesterday, studying the document passed out to the twenty-one committees that correspond to the topics projected for that document.

In the afternoon we had free time and could spend time on personal things. I went to find the priests who are staying with Arquitecto Yáñez and it was a restful afternoon. I also went to the cathedral where I was surprised to meet Father [Juan] Ramón Vega,[100] who told me that he wants to go work in Nicaragua again, in the diocese of León. The bishop of León, Bishop Salazar, who is at the conference, has suffered problems with his diabetes and has been hospitalized. It seems to have gotten worse and there is even danger that they may have to amputate his foot.

 ### Friday, February 2

Today is called the Day of Reconciliation and Peace. It is the day on which we celebrate the feast of the Virgin of Candelaria,[101] as is the custom in our countries. A procession with candles

---

[100] A Nicaraguan priest who headed the Salvadoran Interdiocesan Social Secretariat and the Justice and Peace Commission.

[101] The Feast of the Presentation of the Lord, called in English Candlemas Day because candles are blessed on this day.

went from the front of the seminary to the chapel, and Cardinal Avelar Brandão Vilela, who is president of the General Council of the Commission on Latin America, presided over the Eucharist. It was a very intense day of work. The different committees progressed in their drafts. They will present tomorrow, without fail, the second draft.

 **Saturday, February 3**

Today is the day devoted to the family. It was impressive to see so many families in the chapel: husbands and wives who came with their children to pray for the bishops and to hear a message from the Latin American bishops and to pray for all the families of the continent. Cardinal Luis Aponte Martínez from Puerto Rico presided over the Eucharist and spoke very beautifully about the mission of the family and the Church's hope in it for the evangelization of the continent.

Today we have written intensely and will present the second draft, which is already finished, tonight. Vespers was celebrated this evening by Bishop Angélico Melotto from [Sololá] Guatemala.

I forgot to say that every day this week I have had appointments with journalists who wanted to ask me questions about the situation of the Church and of El Salvador. Some of them have been broadcast on television on Channel 13, where every night they broadcast the program *Seven Days*; others have been printed in the newspapers—not only in Latin America but also in Europe and the United States. I have felt great satisfaction at being able to bear witness to the life of my Church on a world level.

Unfortunately, today they also published a statement by Bishop Aparicio in which he blames the Jesuits for the violence in El Salvador and accuses them of having come to Puebla to defend the archbishop's position, which, according to his statement, is "indefensible" since (he says) the archbishop in his actions has even personally offended the government—which is false.

The Jesuits, whose superior general, Father [Pedro] Arrupe, is here with us, have expressed their resentment at his making such dangerous statements publicly, especially when there is so much repression in El Salvador and so much prejudice about the work of the Church. Father Arrupe and I talked about this situation. He is going to consult with his Jesuits and they will arrive at some decision—not so much to defend ourselves personally, but rather for the good of the Church and to avoid the danger that this statement could release against the Company of Jesus.

## Sunday, February 4

Today is the day devoted to the ministry of the word. At the Puebla meeting they had the good idea to take the bishops to different parishes of the diocese. It was inspiring to see the vans that came from each parish with groups of parishioners, many of them young people, to accompany the pastors to visit and share the morning, the Eucharist and lunch with the parishes to which each bishop went.

## Monday, February 5

Today was titled the "Day of the Beatitudes." The archbishop of Mexico, Archbishop Ernesto Corripio Ahumada, presided over the Morning Prayer and the Eucharist. Then the task for today was explained to us. It is what they call "interchange," that is, the different committees are going to divide up into delegations to go to other committees, to supplement in this way the documents written last week. We have in our hands a very thick folder with the twenty-one topics that have been written by the twenty-one committees and on which we have to report in the different "interchange" committees.

At noontime, I visited the group of theologians who are working at 14 Washington Street at the call of the bishops, giving us valuable collaboration, advising us on theological matters. The other night I had dinner with them. Archbishop Helder Cámara was also there and other bishops who indicated their appreciation for the self-sacrificing work that these priests and religious are doing.

Also at noon I had a television interview for a program that is famous in Mexico: *24 Hours*. They asked me about the situation in El Salvador and were interested in the process of our meeting in the seminary of Puebla.

Today I spoke by telephone with Monsignor Urioste to ask him about the situation at the archdiocese; I was especially interested in knowing the reaction to the declarations made by Bishop Aparicio. And frankly, it is a shame, because in El Salvador it is being used against the Church and has created a dangerous situation for the Jesuits. But Monsignor told me that tomorrow there will be a meeting of the clergy and the Senate to discuss what measures to take. I gave them my authorization, only asking that they not do anything that would make the present situation worse. He promised me that they will approach the matter very calmly and that they will always act for the good of the diocese and not compromise their bishop. He also informed me about the situation at the seminary. I thank God that the problem of the seminarians who had been removed has been resolved.

 **Tuesday, February 6**

We called today the "Day of the Poor." Cardinal José Clemente Maurer from Bolivia presided over the liturgy in the morning, and there was a large group from the old people's homes, where many poor people are cared for by women religious. The day was spent, in the morning, finishing up with the "interchange" committees, supplementing in this way all the themes of the document. And, in the afternoon, the plenary session began so that everyone could bring in all the documents.

At noon, I had an interesting visit with some journalists and television reporters, mostly European correspondents who are here in Mexico for the program *24 Hours*.

In the afternoon the bishop from Havana, Cuba, Archbishop Francisco Oves Fernández, presided over the liturgy. In the evening entertainment was provided by the people of Puebla, who were very warm.

 **Wednesday, February 7**

Today was a special day because it was devoted to ecumenism. Among those attending the meeting are representatives of other Christian Churches as observers, among them the abbot of Taizé,[102] who has become a good friend of mine. Cardinal Pablo Muñoz Vega, archbishop of Quito, Ecuador, celebrated the morning liturgy. Today has been quite intense. There were plenary sessions in the morning and the afternoon. Many people have taken part because they didn't allow more than three minutes per participant. Many topics were discussed. There were also contributions from the advisers, who are outside the meeting and are giving valuable service.

---

[102] An ecumenical monastic community in eastern France. Its prior and founder is Brother Roger.

In the afternoon, Vespers was an ecumenical celebration in which ministers from other faiths participated dressed in clerical garb, and Archbishop Samuel Carter of the Antilles presided over the Eucharist.

At noon I also was interviewed by journalists and learned that yesterday they had been expecting me in a press conference, which I thought it wiser not to attend because Bishop Aparicio's statements were so recent and I didn't want to be involved in any conflict. So I have postponed it until next Friday. The Central American Provincial of the Jesuits, Father César Jerez, has arrived and we had lunch with him, as well as with our friend Julian Filochowski from England, who has been giving me valuable assistance with the press and with establishing relationships with other bishops. He knows a good number of the South American bishops.

From Father Jerez I learned about the scandal caused by the news of Bishop Aparicio's statement and about the letter that he, as provincial, wrote respectfully protesting and asking him to do something to neutralize the danger of the threat resulting from his declarations. I know that several of the Jesuit bishops have gone to the president of CELAM to ask for an audience with Cardinal Baggio to explain to him this very painful situation; those who have commented to me privately on this situation tell me that it has been the undoing of Bishop Aparicio, for it has created a very bad impression in the atmosphere of the Puebla meeting.

What I have done is to ask the Lord to help us be above these human miseries of the Church and I said that today when I transmitted to YSAX by telephone the dialogue that we have every Wednesday (thank God it has not been interrupted). Father Sigfredo interviewed me by telephone from El Salvador and told me of the interest there was to know what role I was taking in the meeting, what the atmosphere was like—here inside—and what were my reactions to the expulsion of Father Plácido.[103] I tried to give an optimistic and hopeful message in spite of the difficulties. I also dictated by telephone an article for *Orientación* called "From Puebla to My Archdiocese." May God bless this effort to take advantage of the different kinds of media so that the message of the gospel may continue to encourage our dear archdiocesan community.

---

[103] Plácido Erdozaín, a Spanish priest expelled by the Salvadoran government while Romero was at Puebla.

**Thursday, February 8**

Today was designated to honor the Eucharist. Cardinal Raúl Primatesta from Argentina presided over Morning Prayer. The whole morning was spent reading so that we could prepare the new draft of the document. The afternoon was free. In the afternoon, I was interviewed for German television and by the *Times* of London. And I was invited to have lunch with my old schoolmates from Pío Latino[104] by special invitation from the archbishop of Mexico, Archbishop Ernesto Corripio, who also had studied with me, but other circumstances prevented me from having this pleasure.

In the evening we had dinner with several bishops and some of our theological advisers at the house at 14 Washington Street. It was a great comfort for me to be able to tell them about the loneliness that a pastor feels when he tries to be faithful to all the instructions given us by the gospel, Vatican II and Medellín, and how colleagues such as those who have come with me from El Salvador to Puebla think differently.

The response to my testimony was very warm. Father [Luis] Patiño suggested that they write a letter expressing their solidarity with me and with the bishops of Guatemala and Nicaragua who are in similar circumstances.[105] The idea was approved and signatures will be collected from bishops who wish to express their solidarity.

 **Friday, February 9**

The problem with my vision has persisted. I thought it was merely that something got in my eye, but when I saw the oculist, he found a small wound on the retina. He has ordered me to rest my eyes and given me some medicine that will force me to keep my eye closed. I canceled the other appointments that I had with journalists. Thank God, the Josephite sisters who run the San José Hospital have received me warmly and I spent the whole day Friday at the hospital.

At seven p.m. in the evening, however, there was a press conference that had been postponed from Tuesday and, with the approval of the oculist, I went. It turned out to be a real tribute to my archdiocese. I went with

---

[104] *Colegio Pío Latinoamericano*, Roman secretary for Latin America, founded in 1859.

[105] The bishops of Guatemala and Nicaragua were in conflict with the governments of Lucas García and Anastasio Somoza, respectively.

Father Plácido Erdozaín and Father [José Luis] Ortega[106] in testimony to the expulsion of priests from my country. I invited them to share the pastoral experiences of an archdiocese that can give testimony to suffering as well as to the fruitfulness of sacrifice. There were some very interesting questions; the room was completely full. And, at certain moments, there was enthusiastic applause; especially, when I was leaving, there was a chorus of "Nobel, Nobel!" Several of them wished to continue with private interviews. I tried to oblige them and then returned to the hospital, where they gave me the first treatments.

 **Saturday, February 10**

I spent the whole day in the hospital. Resting my eyes and my whole body has been very good for me.

 **Sunday, February 11**

Again today I was not in the meeting at the seminary but rather in the San José Hospital where I shared prayers and the Mass with the community.

 **Monday, February 12**

The doctor gave me the good news that the wound was healing, that I could uncover my eye—continuing, nevertheless, a treatment with colyrium and vitamins. And so at noon I returned to the seminary to rejoin the meeting of the bishops.

The atmosphere was so optimistic about the documents that they had already begun to vote, although there was strong pressure from the conservative bishops. Nevertheless, we have a good committee for writing and interface, and it is holding to the ideals of an evangelization along the

---

[106] A Spanish Jesuit expelled from El Salvador in May 1977.

line of the demands of our people. I have also seen the outline of the message to the Latin American people; the television and the press have asked me for it. I have had the occasion to share moments of great trust with the journalists, very interesting questions. I have become friends with the majority of them. With the theologians I have shared some very useful ideas; those who came from El Salvador were sharing very cordially this evening.

I have begun to pack my suitcase for the return trip.

 **Tuesday, February 13**

We have come to the end of the Third General Conference of the Latin American Bishops. We spent the morning polishing and refining the final text of the document. It is clear, however, that everyone is ready to prepare for their journeys home. Nevertheless, those in charge of the writing are working feverishly so that everything will be finished by this afternoon.

At four p.m. the final plenary session started. The last topics were passed out and, together with the first part, will be put to a final vote after Mass.

We left the plenary already vested for the closing concelebration. Today everyone is wearing a miter that was given to each of the bishops by Mexico. The Mass was celebrated facing the seminary fields, since the public had been invited and were waiting for the arrival of the bishops in great numbers and greeted them enthusiastically. It is estimated that there was a crowd of no less than fifteen thousand people.

The Scripture readings narrated the origins of the apostolic college, whose successors are the bishops surrounding the altar of concelebration. The homily by Cardinal Baggio connected this reality with the prayers and demands of Christ when he chose his first twelve bishops. When it was time for the Offertory, all the documents that were going to be given to the presidents of the national bishops' conferences were presented as fruit of the conference. Each national president received them in the name of the bishops' conference of his country and under the protection of the national devotion to the Virgin. In this way, the giving of the documents was a real litany to the Virgin in Latin America. The people responded to the invocations to the Virgin: "Pray for us!" And the announcer said "Viva!" for each country.

When the Mass ended, the gathering became a celebration. The candles that all the faithful had brought were lighted. The Archbishop of Puebla commented on the event as if it were a celebration of Easter, saying that Christ's candle illuminates the roads of Latin America. Cardinal Baggio also reminded us of how the priests of the Council of Ephesus[107] went with a procession of candles when they proclaimed the divine maternity of Mary. Through this and other comparisons, this celebration of light comes to mean the faith of a people that accompanies and inspires the ministry of the Latin American bishops. Then explosions of fireworks, a rain of lights and great joy—a greeting to each of the bishops, who were lost in the crowd. Finally, we gathered again in the plenary session to take a final vote on the entire text of the Puebla document. The majority of it was approved.

In the dining room there were also farewells, Mexican songs appropriate to the occasion. Many of the participants have already left to have dinner with the families that have adopted them, and then the families will take them to Mexico City or to the airport. The press is anxiously awaiting the text. There weren't enough copies to go around, even for all of the bishops, and they were asked to come back in the morning to pick them up. I was affectionately received at the home of Arquitecto Yáñez with dinner and a long conversation in which we shared many memories of our homeland.

 **Wednesday, February 14**

The return trip to Mexico City was provided by the congregation of the Carmelites of St. Teresa, who sent their new van to pick us up and take us to our lodgings at the congregation's novice house. The superior general invited us to have lunch with her.

We were also invited to a meeting of Christian base communities held at the Marist school, where about one thousand Christians who are living the experience of ecclesial base communities in different parishes in Mexico have gathered together for an in-depth study of the phenomenon in our Church. And they asked me to tell them about the experience of my archdiocese. Along with Fathers Jesús Delgado and Astor Ruiz, I gave testimony of the life and suffering of our archdiocese. Among those attending were Fathers Ortega and Plácido, who have been expelled from El Salvador. They also talked about that reality, which really seemed to

---

[107] A fifth-century council which declared Mary Mother of God.

impress the listeners. They showed me affection and solidarity and I left this fraternal gathering very encouraged. Also, another bishop who had been invited talked about the situation of Chile.

In the evening, we were visited in our lodgings by representatives of the young people expelled from the country, who had taken over the Mexican embassy. Also other countrymen who have suffered the pain of exile in Mexico for a long time. We talked with them a great deal to encourage them in their situation; we see that their spirits are very good and that they are still optimistic. We tried especially to help those who have arrived only recently and are staying in a hotel under the protection of the Mexican government. This is only for a period of forty days, at the end of which they will have to prove to the Mexican government that they have obtained work in the country in order to be able to legalize their situation in Mexico.

 ## Thursday, February 15

Very early in the morning, when I was getting ready to go visit the group of exiled Salvadorans, a large group of them came to tell me that, for my good and their own, perhaps it would not be a good idea for me to go to their hotel. And they thanked me and said they would accept the help which I had offered them and that, instead of my visiting them, they would come visit me later.

Father Vicente Nieto, who had helped us in training Father Elías Morales, paid me a visit. We discussed the result—or rather, the failure—of this effort, since Father Elías currently has left his ministry in Santiago de María diocese. I went with Father Nieto to the Basilica of the Virgin of Guadalupe, where, in no hurry, I spent the rest of the morning in prayer, ending with the celebration of the Mass.

And afterward, a visit to my old friends Tepito, as I call the adopted family of Father Antonio Aguadé, a friend that I remember very dearly. We shared many pleasant memories. They invited me to have lunch and even gave me a place to take a nap. It was raining when I returned. Thank God I found a taxi that took me to the Carmelite Sisters' house, where I was staying.

In the evening, another visit from the exiles. I tried to encourage them with my words and offer them what help I could, given my situation. I will continue to offer help, not from any political ideas, but simply in a spirit of Christian brotherhood and charity.

**Friday, February 16**

I had breakfast at the motherhouse of the Carmelites of St. Teresa, where I also celebrated Mass. I spent the morning packing my suitcase for my return.

The last thing that happened was a program in my honor by the novices, in which they sang several songs and talked about some very interesting ideas. One of the sisters took us to the airport and we began our return trip. There were many other participants from the Puebla meeting at the airport, also waiting for flights to different parts of Latin America and Europe.

Nothing special happened on our Pan American flight to Guatemala City. I was interviewed briefly for Guatemalan television about aspects of the Puebla meeting and about the situation of my country. When I arrived in El Salvador near seven p.m., I was surprised by my reception at the airport. A group of priests—Fathers Cortés, Victor Guevara and Fabián Amaya—were waiting for me at the foot of the steps from the plane, and they had a car ready for me, Father Guevara's car. The director of the airport himself took my passport to take care of all the arrangements for me and offered me the diplomatic lounge. But I saw that many people had come to the airport to wait for me, and so I didn't use the car to leave immediately. Rather I walked out to greet all my friends: nuns, priests and laypeople who greeted me very affectionately.

At that time, they told me that there was a Mass scheduled for seven-thirty p.m. in the cathedral. We invited everyone at the airport to come, and I headed straight to the cathedral. In reality, the cathedral was already full and, when people realized that I had arrived, they began to applaud. And the cries of "Viva!" grew stronger because the crowd also continued to increase. I vested for the Mass. Many priests were waiting for me to come in to begin the entrance procession and the Mass, while more priests and more people continued to arrive.

At the time for the reading of the Gospel, Father Cortés welcomed me warmly in the name of the clergy and the people. He received great applause because he interpreted in a simple but moving way the sentiments of the people who filled the cathedral.

In my homily, I expressed my thanks for the greeting and the welcome, and I talked about the theme of Puebla, making the following three points: First, how I went to Puebla as the representative of a diocese that was praying, and I emphasized this a great deal. As I thanked them for the prayers that I felt so strongly, I asked them to continue praying so that this would be the greatest strength of our diocese: prayer.

The second point was that in Puebla I gave testimony of a diocese that has a pastoral direction which coincides with what we studied at Puebla. I talked about the many examples in the life of the archdiocese that I thought of so often during the Puebla meeting. I thanked the vicar general, the other vicars, the parish priests and the communities for their pastoral work and for the way they continued to have a rich Christian life during my absence. And I told them how happy I was to have been able to tell people in Puebla about the living testimony of my archdiocese.

And the third point that I brought from Puebla to my archdiocese was the experience, richness and friendship of many pastors and dioceses of our continent and worldwide. The people interrupted me with affectionate applause several times.

When the Mass ended, I took leave of the priests, almost all of whom were present, and I went out through the acclamations of the people to greet those outside, for there were people all the way to the street outside the cathedral. It was a very caring moment of greetings, embraces and even kisses from some people, giving me such a welcome that I felt almost that they were my family, and that I was at home where I felt comfortable!

 **Saturday, February 17**

I went to the chancery and there was nothing out of the ordinary there. Work has proceeded normally. There was news of different events which have taken place that I had already heard about in Mexico.

In the afternoon, I prepared the homily for Sunday. In the evening, I had been invited by the sisters of the Assumption, and I went to greet their superior general, who is here with us. And I told her that her congregation is doing great good in the archdiocese. I also felt that I received a very cordial reception here, very much in the spirit of the Church, from these sisters who work in Colegio de la Asunción and in the communities of the marginalized zones and in Chalatenango.

**Sunday, February 18**

For the eight o'clock Mass the cathedral was as it has been on previous Sundays: full of people. I presented, through the Scripture readings, the message of Puebla to the peoples of Latin America. I gave my homily the title: "Christ, the Word That Is Always New in the Church." I developed three points, based on readings from Isaiah, St. Paul to the Corinthians and the Gospel of St. Mark. First, historical reality: that God saves in history and how, through the readings, we see an Israel that leaves behind the history of the Exodus to refer to a moment in the history of Babylon and also how the Gospels show Christ in a specific historical situation, the struggle against the Pharisees. Thus the Church has been living the history of the world since that time up to the Puebla meeting, which is also a historical fact that God wills to use as a salvific moment for the peoples of Latin America.

The second point was a reflection on history, a theology of history. In the readings from Isaiah and the Gospel, I pointed out this meditation on history, how the only thing that matters is building the Kingdom of God, but how many human beings oppose it because of their sin. Here the message of Puebla served me wonderfully to show how historically sin is denounced, and not just in my preaching, but rather how all the bishops denounce the great sin in Latin America, especially the sin of social injustice.

And the third point is that in the reading from St. Paul, his Second Letter to the Corinthians, Christ is the constant *yes* from God and the *amen* from human beings. I tried to give a message of hope, the message the bishops wanted to communicate in the Puebla message, based on faith and hope in Christ, who always makes the salvation of peoples new. I suggested that we should trust in Christ and open our hearts to hope and all offer ourselves, each one in his or her own profession, to work for a more just world but with a great trust placed in Jesus Christ.

In the afternoon, or rather, when the Mass ended, I went to Tamanique, where Mother Juanita had prepared a group of catechists to be ministers of Communion. There were sixteen of them and I took the opportunity to explain the Sacrament of the Eucharist to the people and also the charisms that God gives to the people of God. I called on the families to encourage vocations as priests and nuns and for all the laypeople to look for their own gifts for service to the Church. Afterwards we shared some very happy moments in a truly fraternal spirit of *ágape* love. The communities expressed thoughts, poems and songs, and it was clear there was a spirit of solidarity between the people and their pastor. I felt at home.

When I returned to the Divine Providence Hospital, I received a visit from the superior general of the Belgian nuns, who came with a counselor and two priests. I planned to intercede so that Sister Chepita, who had been captured in El Despertar in San Antonio Abad and then freed in the custody of the nuncio, might stay with us. The vicar general intervened at the right moment with the government, with the ambassador of Belgium, and she was not to be expelled as the government had wanted, but the superior general has decided to take her with her. And although I did everything I could to plead with her to leave Sister Chepita here, the decision has been made and they will leave tomorrow.

In the evening, Sister Chepita came to have dinner and talk about her impressions. I tried to encourage her in such a difficult obedience and also to leave the door open for the hope that she could come back and work with us again.

 ## Monday, February 19

In the chancery I found that everything has gone on as usual. There is a lot of mail to be dealt with and it also needs to be organized so that I can look through it and answer it.

At night, I celebrated Mass in the Ana Guerra de Jesús Center to open a new course for women from the market.

I also went to the ultreya[108] where a group of cursillistas welcomed me warmly and where I explained the opinions that some of the Latin American bishops had expressed about the Cursillos de Cristiandad. Many of them complained that they are too set on their method and are not willing to adjust to the local pastoral situation. And I told them that my perspective was that, although I can say that some have been set on their method and have distanced themselves, I can count on a dedicated group of Christians who have matured and have identified themselves with the pastoral direction of the archdiocese. I congratulated them and encouraged them to continue on this path, which is the true one for the Church.

---

[108] A reunion of cursillistas, people who have made the Cursillo, part of the follow-up program.

**Tuesday, February 20**

In the morning, interviews with priests, with some laypeople and a journalist. In the afternoon I had an especially interesting press conference attended by nearly all the major media. I told them that the principal topic would be to inform them about the Puebla meeting, but many questions came up about the situation of the archdiocese, and especially about its relationship with the government. In my answers I reaffirmed the position of the archdiocese to be ready as the true Church to serve the people in the things that refer to God, and that its relationships with the government, as with any other organization that is part of the world, will always be in function of its mission as Church.

The interview, which turned out to be very cordial and very interesting, will be published in *Orientación* this week.

Later, I met with some people who have suffered in the jails and who, miraculously, were able to escape. They tell of such difficult situations and of the hope they have in the Church when it defends those who are suffering.

At eight p.m., I went to the Church of Carmen, in Colonia Roma, at the invitation of a Marriage Encounter group.[109] I addressed a word of hope to them and told them how the Puebla message considers work with married couples and families a pastoral priority.

 **Wednesday, February 21**

Among this morning's visits was one from the dean and other members of the School of Humanities of the National University to invite me to give a lecture on the Church in Latin America. I suggested to them that instead of a lecture it would be better to have a roundtable, and they liked the idea. And they authorized me to get other participants on that same topic.

In the afternoon, I was visited by the Inter-Church Committee on Human Rights[110] from Canada, who showed great interest in learning about the human rights situation in El Salvador, having already gotten a great deal

---

[109] A movement which organizes weekend meetings designed to improve communication between husband and wife.

[110] ICCHRLA, the Inter-Church Committee for Human Rights in Latin America.

of informative material from the Secretary of Information. I also talked with a Dutch journalist who asked about the same topic.

At night, along with some of the Jesuits, we had dinner at the home of Doña Ana Margot Méndez and talked about very important topics on the life of the Church and about the UCA.

 **Thursday, February 22**

Today the first meeting of the Pastoral Council took place in the parish hall of San José de la Montaña. I really wanted to attend, but something unexpected kept me from going to this meeting that is so vital for the diocese. I asked the vicar general, Monsignor Urioste, and the secretary of the council, Father Astor Ruiz, to take my place and lead this new instrument of archdiocesan pastoral work in a good direction. Unfortunately, many of the lay members who were to represent their different vicariates did not attend and a date was set for a meeting next month.

In the afternoon I went to a spiritual retreat of the seminarians in Apulo. I celebrated the Eucharist in the patio outside the church, where we shared around the altar, in the light of the word of God, our concerns about the pastoral vocation and the seminary. I was very pleased with the confidence and frankness with which the seminarians explained their concerns. These young people provide great hope for our archdiocese.

 **Friday, February 23**

In El Calvario parish in Santa Tecla, a meeting to prepare catechists and also to promote Christianity in the whole Vicariate of La Libertad is ending today. Father Benito Tovar, vicar of this department, along with Father Xavier, the priest of El Calvario parish, concelebrated with me. They have directed the Cursillo, which seems to have been very fruitful, based on the contributions of the participants during the Mass.

Today also Mr. Zeledón from the Toyota agency brought me the new car my current one is to be traded for, since they still estimate it to be worth a lot and because I need a car for my ministry.

**Saturday, February 24**

In Colegio de la Asunción, there was a meeting of CONFRES to talk about the results of the bishops' meeting in Puebla. All of us who attended this general conference—that is, Fathers Jon Sobrino, Jesús Delgado, José Luis Bourguet and the president of CONFRES, Father Francisco Estrada. The attendance was extraordinary. I think that there were more than three hundred people, including men and women religious, and it was clear that there was a positive good spirit to adopt the document and make the conclusions from Puebla real in the pastoral work of our archdiocese.

I was glad to be able to say that Puebla was not a surprise for our archdiocese, for its pastoral directions, thank God, are along the same line as we have been working. And so I encouraged them to continue to be faithful in communion with the archbishop and to the entire pastoral line that we have inherited from Archbishop Chávez. And that, thanks to everyone's effort, it is making our archdiocesan community, our parish communities, our religious communities and Christian base communities flourish. I invited them to feed the diocese with the irreplaceable force of prayer and the testimony of a consecrated life that will be a faithful reflection of the presence of Christ among us.

 **Sunday, February 25**

The Mass in the cathedral is always well attended and very animated with a truly liturgical participation: alive, ecclesial. The answer that Christ gave to the criticism that his disciples did not fast while those of John and the Pharisees did gave me the theme of the homily: "Christ, Bridegroom of the Church." I talked about this newness, joy and enthusiasm, the hope that Christianity gives when there is faith that Christ lives with all his love within our Church.

After the Mass I received many visits from people from the villages, who always are anxious to speak even briefly with their bishop.

I had lunch with the sisters of the Colegio de la Sagrada Familia. In the afternoon, I participated in the celebration of the tenth anniversary of the parish of Zacamil in the Externado San José. Their work with the Christian base communities seems to be very fruitful, since the great crowd that filled first the theater and then the church of the Externado shows that there is a great consciousness of Christian and community life among the members of that parish. The celebration was attended by communities from different parts of the archdiocese.

In the evening I went to the Church of San Jacinto to turn it over to the new parish priest, Father Eduardo López Molina, who is going to substitute for Father Bobadilla, who is moving to Ilobasco. I spoke of the long tradition being established by the work of the Vincentian Fathers in this San Jacinto parish. I thanked them and I encouraged them to continue giving us the rich charisms of Saint Vincent de Paul in this part of the archdiocese.

I greeted the Sisters of Charity with great affection in their old people's home, where they have earned such great merit through the sisters who have given their lives for Christian charity. Also the enthusiasm of the faithful, especially of the children who approach the bishop, shows the care taken with the pastoral work in that area.

## Monday, February 26

This afternoon, I presided over the Mass in memory of Don Abraham Rodríguez, an old friend from San Miguel, father of one of the sisters of the Sacred Heart. We were some fourteen priests who concelebrated, which really demonstrated the sympathy for the family.

In the evening I was visited by a young businessman who had been introduced to me by his mother before. He talked to me about the concern young business leaders like him have to talk with the Church about the very difficult situation of the country. I saw a desire to move closer to the Church that I really liked and, of course, I took advantage of this invitation and agreed to a meeting that will take place this very week.

## Tuesday, February 27

I had breakfast with Monsignor Urioste and Father Brito to talk about the functioning of the curia during my absence. Ingeniero Galván also came to evaluate the progress in the organization at the curia. Father Astor Ruiz was also present to report to us on his work in the pastoral counseling office.

I had lunch with the ladies of the archdiocesan Caritas and their coordinator, Father Tilo Sánchez, and other friends of Mrs. Trigueros in Colonia San Benito, where we shared a very Christian feeling.

In the afternoon, in the María Eugenia house of the Assumptionist Sisters in Planes de Renderos, I participated in Mass, celebrating the twenty-fifth anniversary in the religious life of one of them. I talked to them about the relationships between the hierarchy and the religious. And afterward, we participated in a friendly party with family members. Sisters from all over the country were there. I realized the depth of the affection that they have for their pastor, and I thank them for it.

 **Wednesday, February 28**

It is Ash Wednesday and the principal event, in terms of liturgy, was the beginning of Lent at seven-thirty p.m. in the Corazón de María Church. The vicariate of this residential zone of San Salvador had invited me to celebrate the beginning of Lent with them, and I took advantage of the occasion to invite the whole archdiocese and give a diocesan character to the ceremony. This helped to fill the church completely, and the participation of the people added to the fervor. All the priests of the vicariate concelebrated.

The ceremony of penitential ashes turned out to be very impressive, the people of that neighborhood receiving the testimony of true humility and human equality of the ashes and the sense of penitence along with humble people from the villages. A general absolution with the appropriate cautions and a homily that reminded them of the sense of conversion to which the Church calls us—all this contributed to a fervent Lenten beginning. I hope, with the grace of God, that this will result in great blessings for the entire archdiocese.

# March 1979

 **Thursday, March 1**

In the morning, a great deal of activity and many visits at the chancery. One of the most interesting was that by a group of pastoral workers who prepare people for Baptism who are coming to work with the catechumens[111] that already exist among us.

In the afternoon, celebration of the traditional Holy Hour at the Divine Providence Hospital.

I had dinner with Bishop Rivera, with whom I talked mainly about our life as bishops in El Salvador and about the Puebla meeting. We also talked about the visit to San Miguel that will take place soon, on March 10, when all the bishops will take the Puebla document to Our Lady of Peace. We agreed that we should provide a united front while, at the same time, expressing our disagreement with the anomalies of the Bishops' Conference.

I had a conversation with Dr. Semsch that was very helpful for me psychologically.

At night, a meeting with the young business leader, Mr. Muyshondt, to plan the meeting that will take place tomorrow at his house in Colonia San Benito.

---

[111] Candidates for Baptism.

**Friday, March 2**

Again a morning of great activity at the chancery. Mr. Sigfrido Munés had breakfast with me, and we talked extensively about the situation of our country and about dialogues that might be arranged, that could make the Church a good mediator in such a difficult moment. We agreed to meet again the next day with Monsignor Urioste, Dr. Chávez of the Christian Democratic Party and Mr. Munés.

In the afternoon, the meeting with the business leaders initiated by Mr. Muyshondt had very positive results. Monsignor Urioste, Father Ernesto Abrego, priest of San Benito parish, and I represented the Church. I asked the business leaders to explain everything they have against the Church in order to get out any resentments, anything causing separation from the Church. They were very frank. They gave us the chance to defend the Church's position, and, at the same time, to demonstrate to them that, in areas where we thought that they were right, we were willing to accept that. At the end of the meeting, a very positive atmosphere had been created, and we decided to meet again within two weeks.

In the evening, in the retreat house in El Despertar where Father Octavio and four young men were killed, we celebrated the Eucharist on the fortieth day after the tragic death of our brothers. Many communities came. The size of the group assembled and their participation was very impressive. When it came time for the Offertory they gave a bouquet of red flowers to the mothers of each of the four young men. They also gave one to Father Octavio's father, who was there too, and this was very moving for the people present. In my homily, I also thanked the families for having given us those four brave young men who had been chosen by God to offer the ultimate proof of love.

 **Saturday, March 3**

Breakfast meeting with Monsignor Urioste, Sigfrido Munés and Dr. Chávez. A very interesting conversation on the current situation of the country and on the usefulness of a dialogue that could be of some benefit to our people. I was assured that the moral stature I have achieved would not be at all compromised by looking sincerely for a private dialogue with the government. I said that I think that dialogue among groups in the Church, the business sector and the government seems a necessary preparation for the dialogue we had discussed.

At noon, a visit from a family who told me that their son, who had been captured near the San Carlos barracks and taken to the headquarters of the police or the National Guard, had been cruelly tortured and taken to the hospital. I went to the hospital and saw how serious his condition is. Actually, I think he is dying. I have realized once again how little respect there is for human beings in the present situation of our country! I made notes so that I can denounce what has happened in my homily tomorrow.

I spent the afternoon and evening preparing the homily.

 **Sunday, March 4**

First Sunday in Lent. The subject was Lent, renewal of our covenant with God. After this Sunday's readings, I talked about the history of the covenant. Christ is the key to our covenant, and Baptism makes individual human beings part of that covenant with God. I challenged the people to prepare themselves to be worthy to celebrate Easter, since that is the goal of the celebration of Lent.

When I was finishing the doctrinal part of the homily, the power went out and I had to stop preaching and continue the Mass. After the Mass ended and the benediction was given, I said that those who wished to stay would hear the part in which I give news and denounce cases of injustice. Almost everyone in the cathedral remained in their seats until they had heard every one of the announcements and then went out to greet me in the doorway of the cathedral.

In the afternoon, I went to San Antonio Abad for a meeting with the principal leaders of that community. We studied the situation in depth, discussing with great honesty errors that could lead to great tragedies. We decided that an unwise mixture of politics with pastoral work can cause great evil, and we have agreed that all pastoral workers will keep their pastoral work completely separate from the implications caused by mixing it with political organizations.

In the afternoon my homily was broadcast on the radio. It had been taped and thus could be heard by those who had been there in the morning, when it was interrupted by a power failure.

**Monday, March 5**

From today through Friday, March 9, I went to do the Spiritual Exercises[112] at the María Eugenia house of the Sisters of the Assumption, along with twenty other priests. The exercises were led by Father Fermín Aranguren, a Redemptorist priest, who was helped on two days by Father Fabián Amaya. Both of them gave us guidance which was helpful, opportune, spiritually deep and very timely. The group came together in a marvelous spirit of unity and our reflection was deep. Truly priestly spiritual exercises, of great benefit to our ministry—thanks be to God!

During the period of the Exercises, we all had to leave temporarily to attend the meeting of the clergy Tuesday at Domus Mariae, at which the Puebla document was presented and some practical information was given for the life of the diocese, principally for Lent and Holy Week. That same Tuesday night, I presided at the opening of the course of formation in the faith that, for the second year in a row, has been organized by the Vicariate of La Asunción, Flor Blanca, at the parish house of Corazón de María. This year there will be two courses since the group that took this course the first year (the initiation of a very timely program set up by the priests of this vicariate, who are committed to having a more engaged ministry) will do a second course. At the end of the opening ceremony, the cultural attaché from the U.S. embassy offered his help in making better recordings of the homilies at the cathedral—an offer that I appreciate and that I accepted.

 **Friday, March 9**

In the afternoon, after the Spiritual Exercises, all my time went to helping to look for a solution to the strike at La Constancia and La Tropical,[113] where they have not been able to resolve a labor dispute for several days.

---

[112] A retreat based on the principles of St. Ignatius, founder of the Jesuits.

[113] La Constancia produces and distributes beer and cola drinks; La Tropical, other soft drinks.

**Saturday, March 10**

I was invited by the Bishops' Conference to attend the presentation of the Puebla document to the Virgin of Peace, according to the initiative taken at Puebla of bringing the document to the Patroness of each of the countries of Latin America. They had invited the clergy, the women religious and all of the faithful, and a large number of people were assembled in El Rosario Church. From there we headed to the cathedral to take part in the solemn concelebration. The largest group of priests was from the archdiocese, some eighty of them. The ceremony had been organized according to instructions from the Bishops' Conference. It was obvious to everyone that they had excluded me from participation in the ceremony. The people honored me with unexpected applause when I left, for which I am deeply grateful.

When the entrance procession arrived, Bishop Aparicio explained the occasion for the celebration. Bishop Revelo was in charge of presenting a summary of the document, which he did after the reading of the Gospel. And the nuncio, who presided at the ceremony, said a few words at the end about devotion to the Virgin and evangelization in Latin America.

In El Calvario convent, Monsignor Pablo Castillo and Father Villacorta had prepared, at my request, some refreshments that really turned out to be a lunch for all the priests of the archdiocese.

When I got home, there was a message that I had received several calls about the conflict at La Tropical and La Constancia. Father Rafael Moreno and I have tried to help as much as we could; we spent the entire evening encouraging dialogue between the management and the workers' side. We worked on this until very late at night—Father Moreno until the early hours of the morning. But we only succeeded in one thing: keeping open the possibility of dialogue, to try at least to get representatives from the management and the workers' side together to discuss how talks could take place. This gives us hope, given that the situation is such a difficult one, since the factory where the strikers are has been cordoned off by heavily armed men, and we are worried about the tragic consequences this may have.

### Sunday, March 11

Starting very early in the morning, Father Moreno and I continued our efforts to help. The Human Rights Commission was exerting its influence to try to get some agreement. In my Sunday homily, after the doctrinal discussion of Lent as renewal for the People of God, I spoke about several specific cases among us, but particularly stressed the strike at La Constancia and La Tropical.

Father Moreno stayed to wait for any phone calls, since I had to go to San Pedro Perulapán, which turned out to be impossible anyway because of the traffic problems created by the strike. Therefore, I had to authorize the vicar of the department of Cuscatlán, Father Montesinos, and the priest of the parish of San Pedro Perulapán, Father Solórzano, to administer Confirmation to the young people and children who had been prepared for it.

In the capital, our mediation along with other efforts has managed to reestablish talks, which are being held beginning this afternoon and, I think, all Sunday night.

 ### Monday, March 12

I celebrated Mass in Colegio San Cristóbal, part of a week dedicated to St. Joseph that begins today. It was a beautiful demonstration by the youth. I spoke of St. Joseph as a just man, that is, a man who understood his role in life and tried to put himself in the role God had designed for him in the overall picture of history. And that is the challenge for all young people: to discover what God's project is and what role each one is called to play in that project.

At noontime I went to have lunch with the seminarians at the minor seminary in Chalatenango, where we shared a celebration of the Eucharist and a dialogue that was very useful for their vocation. The Sisters of the Assumption and the Bethlemite Sisters were there, since they work in that department.

In the afternoon, I attended a meeting in San Antonio Abad with the leaders of the communities of the different sectors. We talked extensively, using the word of God to guide us, and I think that there is a new resolve to continue, in spite of the difficult situations that have resulted from the murder of Father Octavio and the events at El Despertar.

In the evening, the talks about the strike at La Constancia and La Tropical continued. I personally took a worker who is part of the negotiating committee to the Red Cross, where the two sides are talking. This young man belongs to the committee, but he didn't feel safe going by himself.

 **Tuesday, March 13**

Today has been a very intense day. In the morning, we continued to hope that management and the workers' side from La Constancia and La Tropical would arrive at an agreement. The negotiations went on all day up until about six p.m.

Meanwhile, at noon, I made the recording for my Wednesday program. And I had been invited to have lunch with a group of ladies at Colonia San Benito, where I had the opportunity to challenge certain ideas. I was pleased to see the spiritual concerns that have been created by the current preaching of the Church. I consider this to be a wonderful opportunity to evangelize a very difficult sector of the diocese. And if we can reach a group of women like those who were at lunch today, through their goodwill, I believe that we can take the word of God into many other homes.

In the afternoon there was a meeting with the workers at the archdiocesan press, who expressed their desire to join together and develop themselves in the Christian faith; at the same time they complained about certain anomalies at the press. Also two young men who had an audience came to discuss concerns about their ideology of violence, which they do not want to give up in spite of the effort I made to explain to them the force of Christian love. They think that only violence can resolve the unjust situations in our country.

At the invitation of the nuncio, I went to the nunciature, where he offered me his help in resolving the strike. I thanked him for his goodwill and told him there was a threat that if, by midnight, the workers had not evacuated La Constancia and La Tropical, they would take military action, which could lead to tragedy. And since the talks were ending, could he ask the president to restrain the security forces from any acts of violence and ask them to exercise a little patience so that the talks might end peacefully?

Tonight I had dinner at the home of Ingeniero Girón and his wife María Elena. There was no special topic, for they had the kindness to create a completely restful atmosphere for me.

But when I got home at eight-thirty p.m., I still had to talk with lay representatives of a vicariate that is really developing Christian base communities. We talked for a long time about this evangelization based on small communities, and I asked them for their collaboration, even to try to win the goodwill and cooperation of the parish priests.

I received word that everything had been resolved in the conflict-filled situation of the La Constancia strike, and I thanked God on the radio—our YSAX and also in an interview with Radio Sonora. On both radio stations, I made my comments thanking both groups for their goodwill, congratulating them on their willingness to talk, and pointing out that, at the same time, it is necessary to work to remove the causes of this crisis, for they could provoke new conflict as long as the root of the problem is not resolved.

 **Wednesday, March 14**

I was notified that the evacuation of the strikers and others who had been with the workers in La Constancia and La Tropical was very slow. For it was only in the early hours of the morning that they arrived at the hall at San José de la Montaña—which is where the workers had asked to go because they had more confidence in the Church. I regret that the priests whose presence had been requested by the workers for their protection were not given sufficient respect by the security forces. They did not let Father Cortés and the assistant parish priest from Calvario, who had gone to carry out this commission, go inside the place or even get off the Red Cross bus or even open the windows to breathe some fresh air. And they had to wait there through the long hours of the night, nearly until morning, until they were finally taken to the hall at San José de la Montaña.

In the afternoon I visited the novitiate of the Oblate Sisters of the Sacred Heart in Colonia Costa Rica and celebrated Mass there.

 **Thursday, March 15**

I had lunch with the parish priests of the capital, with whom I needed to arrange some coordination for the upcoming Holy Week so that we can combine some activities and plan a joint celebration. We agreed, primarily, to celebrate Palm Sunday in the cathedral and El Calvario Church and to give more pastoral attention to the silent procession[114] in Concepción, since it is an immense crowd with no one in control. To do this I will give an address at the beginning and YSAX will continue to encourage other parish priests to schedule other events at the same time, be they other silent processions in other parishes or some other event that will attract people so that the crowd will not be so large and can actually reflect on Holy Week. Also, the Procession of the Entombment[115] will be broadcast on the radio for any parishes who want to take advantage of this radio transmission.

I said that we should give the greatest importance to the Easter Vigil and especially that they should bring communities and young people early because we are going to have it at seven p.m. in the cathedral.

Since I felt a little indisposed today, I canceled a luncheon date with Don Pepe Simán and a planned trip to Monte San Juan to turn the parish over to the new priest, Father Benjamín Rodríguez. These cancellations leave me very unhappy because I want to carry through on my promises, but my health does not always cooperate. This is complicated, perhaps, by some negligence on my part.

At night, however, I had a nice, lively meeting with the young men of the archdiocesan minor seminary that lasted for two hours, in which the young men expressed some very interesting concerns, appropriate both to their age and to their vocation.

 **Friday, March 16**

For the same reason, I canceled the visit I had planned to the town of El Paraíso in Chalatenango, where the Bethlemite Sisters were expecting me with great affection. The people were prepared to express their affection for me, but I was able to let them know in advance that I couldn't go and that the vicar general would go in my place. It was a meeting of pastoral agents from the whole vicariate and I know that it turned out well in spite of my not having been able to go.

In the afternoon, along with the other priests who went with me to Puebla, we reported to the students of the major seminary from the archdiocese on this event. We had an interesting discussion with them.

---

[114] The Holy Thursday procession in silence to the altar of repose with the Blessed Sacrament.

[115] A popular devotion reenacting the burial of Jesus—a procession through the streets.

Later we went to a second meeting with some young business leaders. They expressed their hope in the Church and also their concerns about the difficult moment through which our country is passing.

At night, I visited Colonia Atlacatl, a parish where they are developing a catechumenate group. I talked to them about the need for this kind of biblical program but, how, at the same time, they should try to adapt themselves to the pastoral work of the local Church, to show in this way the authenticity of their Catholic intentions.

 **Saturday, March 17**

In the morning, I was visited by a British television crew. I had a short talk with them on the situation of the country and on our Church, which they filmed for their television.

This morning, Father Jesús Delgado and Father Octavio Cruz and I planned the roundtable that we will have at the National University on the theme: "The Role of the Church in Latin America."

In the afternoon, at Mass at the hospital, I baptized Dr. Semsch's grandson.

 **Sunday, March 18**

This has been a rather intense Sunday. After the usual Mass at the cathedral, which is always encouraging for the pastoral life of the diocese, I went to San José Villanueva where, as preparation for the patronal feast of St. Joseph, I celebrated Mass as part of a nice celebration that had been organized there by the Passionist Sisters, who work in that village along with the parish priest, Father Benito Alfaro.

In mid-afternoon, I went to the community of San José Cortés in Ciudad Delgado, a very large and enthusiastic community. I celebrated Mass there and then talked to the pastoral agents. There are many catechists. This good number creates a great pastoral hope in that sector.

And in the evening I went to the parish San Francisco de Mejicanos to turn the parish over to the new priest, Father Rafael Palacios, who will fill the vacancy left by Father Octavio Ortiz—who, as everyone knows, was murdered at El Despertar in San Antonio Abad.

 **Monday, March 19 – Friday, March 23**

I went to the Dominican Republic because they were holding a seminar on the devotion to the Sacred Heart of Jesus in Santo Domingo. It was held by an international institution that organizes these events in different parts of the world. From El Salvador, Father Santiago Garrido, director of the Apostleship of Prayer, also went. The seminar was very useful for theological, biblical and pastoral knowledge, especially in discussions with the other participants from different countries of Central America and the South American continent.

We studied how to make this devotion attractive to the people of today—this devotion that undoubtedly continues to be important, but that, perhaps because of not having been brought up-to-date sufficiently, is considered by some to be antiquated. Nevertheless, enlightened by our reflections, we understood that it needs to regain the attention that it deserves. For this reason, those of us attending from Central America decided to organize a small committee which, working with the international center, will look for ways to carry out the ideal renewal of the worship of the Sacred Heart in our countries.

I had the honor of being named president of the small Central American group. I accepted with pleasure because it has always been my preferred devotion and because I know that devotion to the Sacred Heart could be very fruitful for the pastoral work of our diocese.

The seminar took place at the Jesuit Loyola House, in a picturesque location near the sea. I also had the opportunity to talk about the situation of our archdiocese, for there was great interest on the part of the participants in the seminar, the religious and some of the media, such as the television for their daily news one day. Father Arango, a Jesuit who has a program on Sundays, dedicated his entire program to a conversation with me.

**Saturday, March 24**

Today with Fathers Moreno, Fabián Amaya, Walter Guerra and Miss Doris Osegueda, we met (as from now on we will every Saturday) to talk about changing the direction of our media office. This meeting, in which we analyzed the different aspects of the week and the impression being created by our radio and *Orientación*, can have some interesting implications for my governance as well.

In the afternoon, in Suchitoto with many priests assisting, we celebrated the priestly ordination of Deacon Ezequiel de Jesús Gámez. The Mass was held outdoors in the atrium of the church; it was very nice and very impressive. Among the communities attending (and they were numerous) the community of Chalatenango stood out, since Father Gámez, in spite of being from Suchitoto, has become part of that community and has made a kind of bond with them to pursue his vocation as a priest.

 **Sunday, March 25**

After Mass in the cathedral, I went to participate in the twenty-fifth anniversary of the minor seminary in Santa Ana, the John XXIII Seminary. I had been invited by Bishop Barrera. The nuncio and many priests from the diocese were also present. The Mass took place at noon. Among the crowd that attended I heard some call out "Monseñor Romero,"[116] which worried me. Because of that, I left as soon as the Mass had ended in order to avoid any problems. Besides, I had other fears to attend to in the capital city, since we were dealing there with some very serious labor problems, which are often brought to the archdiocese for our help. The principal problem is at the Delicia[117] factory. Among the hostages is a man whose mother has died, and they will not let him leave. I interceded on his behalf but, unfortunately, it was impossible to achieve what we wanted.

---

[116] In Spanish, both bishops and monsignors are addressed as "Monseñor." In El Salvador, *Monseñor* used alone usually refers to Romero.

[117] La Delicia produces corn chips and other processed foods.

**Monday, March 26**

At breakfast I met again with the priests with whom we are planning Holy Week. Father Gutiérrez has taken the organization of Holy Week very seriously, and, thank God, proposed some plans. We have the celebration arranged now.

At noon we had lunch with all the chancery personnel, both priests and laity, in order to relate on a more personal level. The conversation that we had before and during lunch was really human and warm, and I was glad to be able to relate on a more human and Christian level in a work that is so important for the entire archdiocese.

In the afternoon, I talked with two representatives of the guerrillas, and I tried to persuade them to the Christian ideal of nonviolence. But these people are firmly convinced that it is not the force of love that will resolve the situation, but rather the force of violence. They do not want to listen to reason, much less hear about Christian love. I realized that there is a very deep gap between the way a whole sector of our society, represented by these people, thinks and the Christian position.

I ask God to light the way for his Church so that it be understood even by those who want the good of the country but use very different means than those Christ taught us.

 **Tuesday, March 27**

Surprisingly, before breakfast, I received a visit from Dr. Nelson Segovia, who has been named judge in charge of the hostages that are being held in the strike at the Delicia factory. He told me about the problem, which is very serious, and I am trying to help him in any way that I can. I also offered him the assistance of Monsignor Urioste, with whom he went to talk afterwards. I talked to him later and I think that things are going in the right direction.

The whole morning was occupied with the meeting of the Priests' Senate at the house of the Somascan Sisters, where we also had lunch. We made an interesting attempt to evaluate the archdiocese. It was so interesting that we discussed doing it periodically—if possible, not just in a morning, but spending sufficient time to go into more depth, to see how the diocese is functioning in order constantly to improve the direction of our pastoral work.

There was some discussion of selecting new senators since, according to the rules, their term is for two years, which is ending now. But we left it to Father José Luis Bourguet to study the rules and we will decide the matter at a future meeting.

The roundtable in the School of Arts and Sciences at the National University was at five p.m. The chosen theme was the role of the Church in Latin America. The participants were Father Jesús Delgado, who gave the theological perspective and explained liberation theology; Father Octavio Cruz from the parish of Aguilares, who holds a degree in social sciences, who presented the social, economic and political context of our country and of Latin America in general. I spoke last, talking more specifically about the role of the Church in Latin America in light of the recent documents from Puebla.

The reception our university gave to these representatives of the Church was very moving. The auditorium of the Law School (the largest auditorium in the university, where the roundtable took place) was not large enough to hold the crowd; it overflowed into the corridors and the terraces around the hall. There was great respect, complete silence during the presentations. And when there was an opportunity to ask questions, the questions also reflected the great interest that the message of the Church has for the university community of professors and young graduates, some of them already professionals.

I expressed my appreciation and offered the Church's cooperation in this effort to promote culture at a national level. The dean of the School of Humanities and the rector of the university invited us afterward to a small reception, where we exchanged impressions on the event—positive, of course, on all parts. The comments that we heard later were also quite positive.

In the evening I went to a dinner with the cursillistas, who often offer me this chance to talk with them in an informal setting.

 ### Wednesday, March 28

Among this morning's audiences, the main one was one with some progressive military men, now retired, with whom I talked extensively. Monsignor Urioste went with me so that there would be a better representation of the Church. They talked a great deal about the history of El Salvador and proposed some solutions to the present situation. Speaking for the Church, we expressed our admiration for their goodwill.

We expressed our appreciation for the insights they gave us through their analysis and we offered to work with them. The Church is always willing to cooperate when we see a true desire on the part of the government to serve the people that the Church is also here to serve.

The meeting turned out to be very interesting, and I think that we all left feeling a little bit more hopeful. We agreed to meet again to talk about this further. They carried a message back to the people they talk to, including the president of the republic, conveying the view of the Church about this situation.

I canceled a private lunch that I was to have with the Redemptorist Fathers and a meeting with the typesetters, also my visit to a catechumenate group at María Auxiliadora. I was sorry because these cancellations, sometimes against my will, make me unhappy, but sometimes my health does not match my goodwill.

 **Thursday, March 29**

This morning, we had a meeting with the Pastoral Council of the archdiocese. It is still very early in the process, but the meeting was very positive. The question that I threw out, purposely before any of the other items on the agenda was whether or not they understood how important this Pastoral Council is, and what suggestions they could offer for making it work in a truly effective fashion. Answering this question took up almost the whole meeting, but a useful result was the decision to create a smaller committee in which there will be only one representative of the priests, another of the women religious and another from the laity to study all of the suggestions that were made in order to figure out how to make this organism, recommended by the Council, which will without a doubt do great good for the pastoral work of the diocese, function more effectively.

In the afternoon, Sister Nelly Rodríguez of the Colegio Sagrado Corazón, along with a group of mothers, visited me to express their concerns about the dangerous currents they see among the young people, their own sons and daughters, especially certain Eastern, Gnostic religions that sometimes are accompanied by other kinds of alienation. We spoke extensively about the young people and suggested some measures that the Catholic schools can take. It was, as one of them said, really a therapy session, because it also touched on some spiritual points that were especially pertinent to them on a personal level.

In the evening, I was invited to a dinner with CONFRES to congratulate Mother Vanegas, who has been elected vice-president of CLAR,[118] and also to express solidarity with the archbishop. I thanked them and expressed my satisfaction with the life of CONFRES, encouraging them to promote even more the spirit of religious life in a manner that supports the direction of the Church.

 ### Friday, March 30

Dr. Roberto Silva came to have breakfast with me. I have always told him that when he has something to say to me that he should do so freely. And what he wanted to do today was to ask me to clarify for the people who listen to me that the left must not be confused with terrorism, accompanying this with any necessary explanations. In his words, "There are many who listen to you, and not just your people, but also those who listen to you and attack you."

He said that this was necessary because the justification that is always given is that of attacking terrorism, of defending against communism. And that it was necessary to point out that there is a great deal of justice on the part of what is called the left. Also, there is also much to condemn in the left when it becomes terrorism and fanatic violence. I amplified the idea, saying that I would also like to distinguish in the right what there is of good from the evil that exists as well. I thanked him for his suggestions and asked him always to come talk with me whenever he had any suggestions.

I went to have lunch with the priests of Opus Dei in their new house. I left them my portrait, inscribed "to the Opus Dei in the archdiocese, with my blessing as pastor and friend."

In the evening, I had another interview with a journalist from Finland who, besides his reports now on El Salvador, said that he was collecting data for a book that he is writing.

---

[118] *Confederación Latinoamericana de Religiosos*, the continent-wide federation of men and women religious.

## Saturday, March 31

We had our second breakfast meeting to reflect on the problem of communicating information. Monsignor Urioste was there, Fathers Rafael Moreno, Fabián Amaya, Walter Guerra and Miss Doris Osegueda. We discussed a letter that has been received. It was signed by several different communities who complain that the commentaries of YSAX and the presentations in *Orientación* do not follow the pastoral direction of the archdiocese, but rather present biased political options, and that they do not cover the Christian base communities. We analyzed it in great depth and decided we would have a meeting with these communities to explain some situations that they are not aware of and also to listen to their ideas.

In the afternoon, I went to San Antonio Abad with the coordinating team of the community. We discussed some aspects of the problematic of this parish where El Despertar is located, which was the site of the murders of Father Octavio and the four young men. We agreed to celebrate a Eucharist on Monday of Holy Week, in the evening, to install Father Rogelio in the house, since he will temporarily take charge of the parish until Father Coto, whom the parish is expecting with great affection, is ordained.

Tonight again a visit from a Finnish journalist, who promised me that, in addition to the information he took down, he would accompany me to Mass at the cathedral tomorrow and to the Salesian oratory, where he will share my experience with the children and their catechists.

# April 1979

 **Sunday, April 1**

The Mass at the cathedral had a special note, encouraging and exemplary: the presence of the community of Somascan Fathers, who wanted to concelebrate with me and, at the same time, bring us their institutions, their seminary and other Somascan works. There were six priests, and I greeted them at the beginning of the Mass, introducing them to the community as a model gesture of communion that should be imitated. At the Gospel one of the priests, before my homily, expressed the intention with which they had come, their charism of founding institutions specifically for orphans and the homeless. And since this line of working with the poor is precisely the true direction of the gospel for the saints of all times, they want it to be their direction, and also be in solidarity with the pastor of the diocese.

After Mass I went to celebrate another Eucharist at the Oratory of the Ricaldone Institute, where they had invited me and where I shared the Salesian joy of those catechists and the children, more than a thousand of whom will benefit in the rural areas. There I administered Confirmation to some young people and explained to them what it meant to be baptized and receive the strengthening of the Holy Spirit, which is what Confirmation is.

In the afternoon we celebrated the Holy Hour, which was well attended and fervent, in the Chapel of the Divine Providence Hospital. I also baptized the firstborn son of Roberto Cuéllar, who aids the work of the archdiocese greatly through his service in the office of the Legal Aid Office.

In the evening we celebrated Mother Juanita's fiftieth anniversary in religious life. She is an Oblate Sister of Divine Love who is very old, and who for many years has worked in the Colegio de la Sagrada Familia. We shared with that community our impressions that they are working in great harmony with the pastoral work of the archdiocese.

## Monday, April 2

I had planned to rest today, but there has been too much to do in the chancery. But through an arrangement with Monsignor Urioste, the vicar general, I will stay away as much as possible from these duties this afternoon and for the next two days.

## Tuesday, April 3

Even though there was a meeting of the clergy today about the spiritual retreat during Lent, Monsignor Urioste was kind enough to take my place and advised me to rest today, which has been good for me.

## Wednesday, April 4

Today marks the thirty-seventh anniversary of my life as a priest. I was ordained during Holy Week in 1942, on Holy Saturday, April 4. When I said Mass at the Hospital, the sisters were aware of this and offered their Communion for me and congratulated me. Complying with my plan to rest for three days, I did not go to the chancery; I only signed some letters that were ready for my signature. I appreciate this cooperation.

## Thursday, April 5

Today was the first meeting of the Executive Committee or Secretariat of the Pastoral Council, which is composed of a representative of the vicariates, Father Carlos Mejía from the vicariate of La Asunción, Flor Blanca; a representative of the women religious, an Oblate sister of the Sacred Heart who works in Aguilares; and a representative of the laity. Also there was a lay representative of the parish of Miramonte. This core group, along with the secretary of the Pastoral Council, will have the responsibility of carrying out all those things that are agreed upon in the

Pastoral Council. They will also take to the Council suggestions, criticisms and other things that need to be studied from a pastoral perspective.

This meeting coincided with an interview that had been requested by the representatives of Marriage Encounter, a movement similar to the Cursillos de Cristiandad and the Christian Family Movement.[119] It was created by a group from the Cursillos de Cristiandad and already has grown a great deal because they already have held many encounter sessions. They explained their problems, especially some in relation to the other family movements, and we listened to them all and suggested some possible solutions, especially offering them all the services of the Secretariat of the Pastoral Council.

In the morning I also received a visit from a journalist from the United States who brought a new package of signatures from France expressing solidarity with our archdiocese. There were other visits on this work-filled morning.

Father Benito Tovar took me to have lunch with the newspaperman Jorge Pinto.[120] We shared our concerns about the present situation with a university professor[121] who was also at lunch.

This afternoon I went to the María Eugenia retreat house to a meeting of Baptist ministers from all over Central America. Some forty ministers wanted to see me and talk with me about Christian problems, evangelical problems, of our Central American region. I responded to them, greeting them and expressing my admiration for their sense of Christian openness, and offering them my friendship and cooperation in ecumenical work. The dialogue that took place was very interesting, for we touched on several topics relating to the realities of Central America and the commitment that Christians who believe in the gospel must make in these situations and realities.

I could not go to the meeting that had been set up with the young businessmen, but Monsignor Urioste and Father Ernesto Abrego went, had dinner with them and talked to them about the situation of the country. It seems that my absence will delay a project that they want to talk about in another meeting with me.

---

[119] A movement whose purpose is to Christianize family life and to create supportive communities.

[120] Editor and owner of the newspaper *El Independiente*. It was a memorial Mass for Pinto's mother Romero was celebrating when he was killed.

[121] Carlos E. Martínez.

**Friday, April 6**

At eight-thirty a.m., in the Colegio de la Sagrada Familia, a spiritual retreat for teachers at different Catholic schools began. With Father Isidro, secretary of CONFRES, we talked about the theme of Holy Week and the present reality of the country. And we encouraged discussion with the teachers, which also was very interesting and showed the interest that these teachers, who collaborate with the Catholic schools, have in the Church and in Jesus Christ.

A British journalist visited me with an interpreter. We conversed about the situation of the two Englishmen who were kidnapped. They indicated their concern and their disagreement with the attitude of the British government, which has not been willing to do anything to free its subjects. We talked extensively about the situation of the country and the Church. His paper is one of the most popular in England and has a circulation of more than a million. For this reason, I was particularly interested in the interview with this newspaper. I renewed the offer of the services that the Church has been giving and will continue to give help on behalf of the kidnapped Englishmen.

I went to have lunch with the Jesuit Fathers at the UCA, and we talked especially about my plan to write a pastoral letter [122] to be released on August 6; I want it to be about the current problems our archdiocese faces, such as the relationship to the government in a police state and, more importantly, to present a Church that wants to be authentic and does not want to ally itself with any political organization. It tries to understand and support them insofar as their cause is just, but without becoming identified with any of them. And I want to ask all Christians to help build, through our Christian base communities, the true Church defined without any ambiguity, clearly the Church Christ wants us to build. The Jesuit Fathers understood my concern, and we talked for a long time about this subject. They will help me write an outline for this pastoral letter that, God willing, will be published next August 6.

In the evening, Dr. González of the Salvadoran Human Rights Commission visited me, and we talked about the very difficult situation that the country is facing, the aid that the Human Rights Commission and the Church are giving and what we can do to attract more energy to the restoration of peace to the country.

---

[122] Romero's fourth pastoral letter, "The Mission of the Church in the Nation's Crisis," published in August 1979.

Immediately afterward, a committee of workers came to inform me that a fight had begun in the ADOC[123] factory, where some one thousand workers who are on strike have shut themselves in. They were being attacked by a military force as we spoke. I tried to communicate with the parish priest of Soyapango, Father Villarán, who went to the factory to find out what was really going on. He told me that it was true that there was a siege in that place and that he had not been able to get any closer because the military has surrounded the factory. I also called Father Moreno in Santa Tecla to tell him to be ready because I would call him if necessary so that he could help to defuse this new situation.

Today I saw the doctor and, thank God, he found me to be in good health.

 **Saturday, April 7**

I had breakfast with the Communications Committee at the house of the Somascan Sisters, and we discussed aspects of the Church-government relationship. There are some new situations that seem to be creating hope in different sectors. We will try to encourage these good intentions, which we hope will produce results. We also discussed the concerns we have about transforming ideologies and political customs with the faith and practice of our religion during Holy Week. A suggestion was made that we should clarify this and ask for greater respect for the religious feelings of the people. Then we studied the summary of the week's events that will be used for tomorrow's homily. And there was not enough time for us to study the policy we should follow in regard to the use the archdiocese makes of the mass media. We will do this in another meeting in another two weeks.

In the morning, I received a visit from the ambassador to the Holy See, Dr. Lencho Llach, who came to say good-bye before he leaves for Rome to participate in the pontifical Holy Week events. I told him that I will also go to Rome for the beatification[124] of Father [Francisco] Coll, founder of the Dominican Sisters of the Annunciation. I asked him to intercede well enough in advance so that I can get a private audience with the Holy Father.

In the afternoon, I visited the village of El Pepeto in the parish of Soyapango where the Sisters of the Colegio de la Sagrada Familia have

---

[123] ADOC is the largest manufacturer and distributor of shoes in Latin America.
[124] The semifinal step in the process of canonization, declaring someone a saint.

organized a nice catechetical program. I shared the joy of the group. I ended up in a little house where they served pupusas and hot chocolate.

It appears that the fight in the ADOC factory has had tragic consequences that I will explain later.

 ## Sunday, April 8

Today is Palm Sunday. We had agreed with the priest of El Calvario parish, Father Francisco Sanggiano, to have the blessing of the palms in front of that church. There was a very impressive crowd of people with palms. After the blessing of the palms, the procession headed toward the cathedral. There the Mass was celebrated in the atrium, since the crowd was so numerous that it would not have fit inside.

I preached a homily presenting Christ as the mediator of the coming new covenant—a covenant whose mediator identified himself with the people so completely that he called himself the Servant of God and faced humiliation in his death. But the new covenant that God makes with humankind makes us participants in the glory that Christ achieved through that humiliation.

Unfortunately, this was the second Sunday in which there was interference with the radio transmission. It is very probable that we are dealing with interference coming from the ANTEL[125] headquarters itself. The intention seems to be to interfere with the transmission of my homilies.

The Salesian seminary had organized the choral part and the Seminary San José de la Montaña the ritual. The ceremony as a whole was splendid. Thanks be to God!

At noontime, I went to a family gathering with my brothers. We had lunch at one of their homes.

In the afternoon, I went to bless the new tower of Concepción Church in Santa Tecla. The parish priest, Father Andrés Alvarenga, the mayor, many guests and other people filled the large atrium of the Santa Tecla church. I spoke, as did some laypeople who addressed the crowd in the name of the parish. I celebrated Mass there and afterward I greeted the people cordially.

Afterward, I went to visit a group holding a retreat for a renewal of the Spirit in the parish school. I encouraged them to "be of one mind and heart

---

[125] *Asociación Nacional de Telecomunicaciones,* National Telecommunications Company.

with the Church" and not to respond only on an emotional level, but rather to go deeper for an authentic renewal in the Spirit. I sensed their feeling of solidarity with the bishop, a determination to be faithful to the Church hierarchy and not to disobey their pastors in anything.

 **Monday, April 9**

My principal concern this morning was to talk with those in charge of the radio and the media in the archdiocese to see what yesterday's interruption of the transmission of the ceremony in the cathedral meant and what can be done about it. Father Pedraz had begun investigating already, and he thinks it is very probably intentional interference with the Catholic radio. I thanked him and asked him to continue to try to clear this up and to do all that he can to normalize the situation.

During the day there was new interference with precisely the radio programs that give opinions critical of the situation of the country. A technical attaché from the United States Embassy, speaking privately with Father Pedraz, told him how disgusted he was that this kind of measure had been taken against our radio. He is a good Catholic and expresses great solidarity with the position of the archdiocese. And he has promised his help.

Today I taped the interview for next Wednesday for the radio program with Ingeniero Oliva.

In the evening, I went to San Antonio Abad because they were celebrating a beautiful Mass in El Despertar to turn the parish over to Father Rogelio, who will live there and take charge of the parish of San Antonio Abad temporarily. It was a communal gathering with a great family spirit.

## Tuesday, April 10

I have ordered that copies be made of the letter that Pope John Paul II wants all the priests to have for Holy Thursday. Since our press has acquired a modern offset system, it is now much easier to make five hundred copies of a letter. It will be given to all the priests of the archdiocese. I also have sent the letter to the other bishops for their priests.

Efforts to ensure good transmissions for Radio YSAX and investigations into the interference have continued today. It has been confirmed that the interference was deliberate, to impede the broadcast particularly of the programs that talk about the situation of the country. Station YSKL, which shares the YSAX channel, declared publicly that it was not their fault, that their principles would never let them commit such an ignoble act. This makes it clear that it was done intentionally and, concretely, the comments on the radio today show that the government is guilty—or is at least an accomplice if it does nothing to stop this interference. In this sense, a polite but firm note has been sent to ANTEL, requesting better service to try to avoid this interference.

At noon, Father Pedraz, a lady from the United States and Dr. Italo Vallecillos from the UCA came to visit me to confirm the information that Father Chencho [José Inocencio] Alas had given me on the telephone about the visit of a senator from the United States who will come on Holy Thursday. We planned what people should be included in this meeting. It will be held on Holy Thursday at the Colegio Belén in Santa Tecla, where they will prepare lunch for us.

In the evening I went to visit Father Crespín, who had been in the hospital, but I didn't find him in his parish of Santiago in Ciudad Delgado. I could only leave a message for him, since he was in one of the villages of his parish in spite of his weak health.

I also visited the other parish in Ciudad Delgado, San Sebastián, where Father Gutiérrez is the priest, but I didn't find him either. The parishioners were arranging a statue of the Nazarene in the traditional Agony in the Garden.

And, finally, I visited the community of La Madona, where the Bethlemite Sisters work, in order to tell them about the trip I will soon make to Costa Rica and to offer my services in case they want to send anything to their provincial, since she lives there.

## Wednesday, April 11

Father Brito and I organized the distribution of the pope's letter to all the priests so that all of them in the archdiocese will receive it by Holy Thursday. I also asked him to help me to get a priest who, in the meeting Thursday with the congressional representative from the United States,[126] will explain the following two points: the influence that the multinational corporations have on the social injustice in our country and the situation of our countrymen who are undocumented aliens in the United States. We want to ask this representative for his cooperation on both problems.

In the communications office we talked extensively about the problem of interference with the radio. In the noon commentary, there was again serious interference that prevented this program from being heard, and also in the one from the communications office on which I do my usual Wednesday interview. But, thanks be to God, it could be heard on the evening broadcast.

In the afternoon, I went to the Colegio of Fátima in Santa Tecla, to visit the congregation of the Dominican Sisters, who are preparing for the beatification of their founder, Father Coll. I will have the honor of attending the ceremony in Rome at the invitation of the congregation. We talked a great deal about the work of this congregation in our country, especially in the Colegio de Fátima and the Colegio de Suchitoto, and the other areas of human promotion here and in the rest of Central America. I praised their willingness to adapt to the wishes of the archdiocese. I got the impression of a congregation that is truly faithful to its charisms and knows how to put them at the service of the local Church.

 ## Maundy Thursday, April 12

I began the Chrism Mass[127] at nine-thirty a.m. in the cathedral. There were a good number of priests present, around sixty of them, which is a very significant number since they are so busy on Holy Thursday. The title of the homily was "The Holy Spirit: Soul of the New Covenant." After Mass, we went down to the crypt with all the priests and

---

126 Then Representative Tom Harkin of Iowa.

127 The Holy Thursday Mass at which the sacramental oils are blessed.

had a small reception there, thus promoting the brotherly feeling of this day in the priests.

In the vicariates, especially in the one in Chalatenango, they had meetings with the priests who could not get to the cathedral, and, in these meetings, they were given recently blessed holy oils.

Eleven-thirty a.m. was the time for the meeting with the congressman from the United States, Mr. Tom Harkin, as well as the others he brought with him and, along with me on our side, the rector of the UCA,[128] Don Pepe Simán, some members of the Commission of Human Rights, Beto Cuéllar from Socorro Jurídico and Miss Doris Osegueda, in charge of social communications. The purpose of the meeting was to inform them about the situation of the Church and the country.

We began by analyzing what he had witnessed himself: the interference with our Catholic radio station and the programs from the archdiocese. Father Ellacuría gave him a summary of the situation of the country, and Beto Cuéllar told him of specific cases of human rights abuse. We had lunch there in the Colegio Belén, and when they left, I had the impression that they were satisfied with the meeting.

The congressman, who is a Catholic, told me that in spite of the enormous distance that separates us, he felt himself to be a member of this diocese. It is Congressman Harkin who has worked to get the support of the Congress of the United States for my nomination for the Nobel Prize. I thanked him for that and also for the interest he has shown during his visit, and we told him that we hoped that this dialogue would create some moral support for our Church.

In the afternoon, this U.S. congressman went to the services at the cathedral, which were very beautiful and fervent, for the cathedral was filled with the faithful. We celebrated the Eucharist and the theme of the sermon was love: the law of the new covenant. I related it to the message of Puebla to the people of Latin America, the call to build a civilization of love.

In the evening a group of seminarians and announcers from the YSAX studios described the silent procession that took place in San Salvador and in several different villages.

---

[128] Román Mayorga.

**Good Friday, April 13**

Thanks be to God, we were able to broadcast the three events scheduled for today: the Way of the Cross, the afternoon liturgy and the Holy Entombment. We had the help of Aníbal Romero and of several seminarians, and I think that it left a good impression of this day that is so significant for the life of our Church. And the radio enables so many more people to hear it.

One disagreeable detail was the presence of the National Guard band in the procession of the Entombment. The most serious part was that some of the members of the *cofradía*[129] of the Entombment were opposed to the broadcast through the loudspeakers along the route of the Holy Burial, preferring the band and thus rejecting the message from the archbishop that was being transmitted by radio to the entire archdiocese. This was noted by the parish priest, Father Sanggiano, to whom I plan to suggest that it would be better for this band not to be present, since it is part of a security force that has offended the Church and all Christian people in many ways. Also, we must look at the faith and solidarity with the archbishop of all of those who belong to groups associated with the parish.

I think that in other parishes as well there have been similar incidents of rebellion against the authority of the Church: processions or events for Holy Week organized without the authorization of the parish priests. Therefore we will evaluate Holy Week with the Pastoral Commission in order to improve the conditions for our celebrations, which should be totally in accordance with the Church.

 **Holy Saturday, April 14**

In the evening we celebrated the solemn Easter Vigil. The people's response was wonderful, and the cathedral could not hold them all. We opened the door to the choir loft; even so, many people were unable to get in. The participation of the young people was very meaningful, also the readings—we did all of them[130]—which were read by

---

[129] A brotherhood devoted to a particular image in a particular parish. In many Central American parishes, they exercise nearly total control over the processions they sponsor, regardless of the Church's wishes.

[130] Nine Scripture readings are offered for the Easter Vigil; the number may be reduced to as few as four.

members of different non-Catholic Christian communities. In this way we made the Liturgy of the Word a truly ecumenical celebration. Their friendly joy was obvious, especially at the end when I greeted people at the door until the rain made it impossible to leave. I went back inside among the people who were still waiting to leave, where I received affectionate greetings and wished everyone a happy Easter.

## Easter Sunday, April 15

The principal event today was the solemn Mass at the cathedral at the usual hour of eight a.m., but with a special ritual and an especially large attendance. The title of the homily was "The Resurrection: Seal and Key of the New Covenant." At the end of Mass, I gave the papal blessing and explained the meaning of indulgence[131] and the essential condition of repentance and faithfulness to our Lord.

## Monday, April 16

My principal worry has been the situation with Radio YSAX, since there has continued to be interference with the messages from the archdiocese. I agreed with Father Pedraz and Monsignor Urioste that they should make an official visit to ANTEL and make them acknowledge their responsibility in this situation. We will also encourage the religious congregations and the laity to insist to the government on the Church's right to freedom of expression, urging them to investigate and put an end to this interference with our radio.

In the afternoon I left for Costa Rica for the SEDAC meeting, the Episcopal Secretariat of Central America and Panamá, where I will be all week. On the airplane I had the company of a Protestant minister who had been visiting me during the morning at the hospital, expressing his solidarity with the direction of our Church and worried also about ecumenism in Latin America because of the new guidelines[132] of CELAM. I told him that the pope himself had pushed ecumenism in his new

---

[131] The remission of temporal punishment for sin after death.

[132] A strong denunciation of fundamentalist sects in the Puebla document overshadows the positive references to ecumenism.

encyclical and that each bishop is responsible for the actions of the Church in his diocese. Because of that, neither CELAM nor any other guidelines opposing or marginalizing ecumenism has any real authority. I think that I gave him enough guidance and encouragement to continue working in the way that the Church desires.

When I arrived in Costa Rica, I found several bishops from different parts of Central America who are friends of mine also arriving. With Bishop Manresa, especially, and Bishop Luna, we stayed at the house of the Bethlemite Sisters. The Carmelite Sisters, who had been notified of my arrival in San José, were also kind enough to come out to the airport.

During dinner at the house of the Bethlemites, I received two telephone calls: one from Father Plácido, who is in San José taking a course on ecclesiology, and the other from Father Higenio, who is in Heredia. They both offered to arrange meetings for me with people who are interested in the situation in El Salvador. I told them that I first wanted to see what the atmosphere was like in the bishops' meeting and see the schedule before I decided on the possibility and wisdom of such meetings. Father Plácido and another colleague, Agustíno, arrived a little later to visit me in person. They took me out for a beautiful evening view of the city of San José.

 **Tuesday, April 17**

At nine a.m., I went to the place where they were holding the SEDAC meeting, the retreat house of the Claretian Fathers. The meeting would not begin until evening, so I took advantage of the free morning and afternoon to visit the Carmelite Sisters in Alajuela. When I returned, I found that many more bishops had arrived, although some were still missing.

At five p.m., the opening Mass was celebrated, presided over by the bishop of Alajuela, Bishop Bolaños, who is also apostolic administrator[133] of San José. He welcomed us and expressed his hopes for this meeting.

After dinner we had our first meeting to develop the agenda and decide on the mechanics of our work. The prevalent idea was to present the ideas of the Puebla document briefly and also other doctrinal points on which there would be presentations. They were to be presented briefly as ideas for further reflection. Then we will divide into groups according to countries in

---

[133] One appointed to administer a see that is temporarily vacant.

order to study the guidelines from Puebla and use them to analyze our own national realities. Then we will reconvene to see what the constants are. Groups then will be organized around the constants that appear in the reports on the different countries. In the plenary sessions after that, we will arrive at some conclusions and talk about the future of our evangelizing work.

### Wednesday, April 18

The Eucharist was presided over by Archbishop Miguel Obando Bravo, archbishop of Managua, in his role as president of SEDAC. In his homily, he offered our work to God, welcomed all the bishops (who numbered around thirty by then) and thanked the bishops of Costa Rica who have welcomed us so warmly and challenged us to do a pastoral work that will be truly useful for our Central American region and Panamá.

The work this morning was rather heavy because we heard the papers that had been prepared and they have been rather boring, although there have been some good perspectives (especially that of Archbishop McGrath [of Panama]) on the Puebla document. We did not finish in the morning and we had to spend part of the afternoon listening to the rest of the six papers that had been prepared. After that, we were organized into committees according to our episcopal conferences to study, in light of the Puebla document, the opportunities and difficulties in our countries for carrying out the ideals proposed at Puebla, such as present and future evangelism.

In one of the plenary sessions, the one at noon, we read the telegram we are going to send to the Holy Father, which I had been in charge of writing, along with Bishop [Miguel Angel] García Aráuz from [Jalapa] Guatemala. We wrote it in the name of all of the bishops of Central America, and it was approved on the first reading.

The work of the bishops' conferences was very interesting. Our group from El Salvador was studying several different aspects presented in the papers. I suggested that we ought to present our ecclesial and national reality very frankly—beginning with the divisions between the bishops and the different problems in our relationship with the government, and with those who have suffered greatly for the Church and other aspects that are matters of dispute among the bishops. The topic was very fruitful. As Archbishop Luis Chávez y González, who was also there with us, said, "The bombing was intense," referring to how they accused me of many things they said, as if I were the one responsible for all the divisions and problems, even of the politicizing of the clergy.

In the evening, I received a visit from two university students who offered to bring me a copy of the report issued by the Human Rights Commission of the OAS,[134] which they have had copied for distribution in Costa Rica. I also was interviewed by Channel Six television and the interview should be shown tonight.

The evening plenary session was for us to report on the meetings of our bishops' conferences, and the six conferences gave reports that were very realistic, brave and frank. From these, at the end, we abstracted the factors that were constant. We came up with twelve very important themes, and tomorrow we will meet in groups to study them in greater depth.

 **Thursday, April 19**

Bishop [Román] Arrieta, bishop of Tilarán and president of the bishops' conference of Costa Rica, presided at the Eucharist. In his homily he spoke to us about episcopal unity, about the sense of service in our ministry and about a fraternal understanding of all of our priests.

After breakfast, I prepared a report that had been requested on the ex-seminarian Mauricio Oliva. Unfortunately, it had to be a negative report.

The plenary session this morning was devoted to an explanation of CELAM and its last meeting held in Los Teques, near Caracas, Venezuela, given by Bishop Arrieta, who is vice president for Central America, and Bishop Manresa, the previous vice president.

The activities continued with more small-group meetings and also plenary sessions. We are outlining a conclusion that will be announced in a press release. It will be very clear in its objectives, according to the guidance we have been receiving from the Puebla document, which will without a doubt be the Magna Carta for our pastoral work for a long time to come.

Today I went to have lunch with a group of ecumenical Christians. They are from different parts of Latin America and do pastoral work, principally with peasants and indigenous peoples. They were very interested in knowing about our experience in El Salvador. Some other Salvadorans also went with me: Father Plácido, Fathers Higenio Alas and

---

[134] Organization of American States.

Miguel Montesino, and two seminarians who are studying in San José [Costa Rica].

(Here there is a problem with the recording and I apologize. Wait and, after a short silence, it will continue with the afternoon's activities.)

The meetings in the afternoon were a plenary session to gather the conclusions from the morning and from each of the bishops' conferences in order to draw conclusions specific to each of our countries, and to formulate suggestions to be given to SEDAC, which will take place during the plenary session tonight. I couldn't participate much in the afternoon meetings because of the visits I received.

The first one was from Colonel [Ernesto] Claramount, who had been a candidate for the UNO[135] party and is now in exile. He expressed to me his optimism and his hope of soon returning to our country to continue to work for its good. I tried to encourage those hopes.

The second visit was in the evening, from some reporters from a university newspaper who wanted to interview me for their paper. We talked about the relationship between the Church and the state and the situation of the Church, particularly in my country. They also asked me about my reaction to having been nominated for the Nobel Prize.

The third visit had to do with this too: It was from a group called the Committee for the Nobel Prize and for human rights in El Salvador. Father Higenio Alas is one of their advisers. Father Plácido was there too, also Dr. Castillo, Licenciado Baires' brother, and other Salvadorans and Costa Ricans. I thanked them for their noble gesture and I accepted it—not for me personally, but as part of the pastoral work I try to direct in the archdiocese, which reflects the concerns of pastors and communities from different parts of the continent.

The last visit, at eight-thirty p.m., was from the Salvadoran consul, Dr. Granillo, whom I have known since my childhood in San Miguel—I was wrong, the last visit was from a group of Christian Democrats in exile, among them Ingeniero Napoleón Duarte and Dr. [José] Antonio Morales Ehrlich,[136] who wanted the latest information about the Church in El Salvador. They also wanted to express to me their wish to help me and serve me and to ask me for my help within the limits of my pastoral responsibilities. We talked extensively and I explained to them what service means to me and my hope in politicians who really love the Church, especially if they are of Christian inspiration.

It was midnight by then, and I had to get up early to go to the seminary, where I had promised to celebrate Mass at six-thirty a.m. Today has been

---

[135] An opposition coalition in the 1977 elections.

[136] Major figures in the Christian Democratic Party.

a day of great satisfaction for me—and of moments of disillusionment too, when I think about the divisions that exist among the Salvadoran bishops.

 **Friday, April 20**

At the invitation of the major seminary, I went to celebrate Mass for them at six-thirty a.m. In the homily, I praised the characteristics of youth and said how God wants to use the youth in a seminary to rejuvenate the priestly vocation so that even we priests who are further along in life may find in the youth of the seminary the image of the resurrection of Christ: always youthful, always joyous, never bored—that is, the life of the Church that we as priests are bound to serve. On this theme, I also used the words of the pope in his letter to priests of praise for the raison d'etre of the celibate: to serve as a testimony of a life different from a worldly life, a witness to the people of God.

Father Montesinos, who had taken me there and concelebrated with me, brought me back, stopping briefly at the retreat house to pick up some papers, since I would not be able to stay for the last part of the bishops' meeting. According to what they told me later, it turned out to be very edifying, and they recognized the importance of continuing to support the organization of the Central American bishops, SEDAC.

The Carmelite Sisters who are in Alajuela were waiting to take me to the airport but, before that, since there was still time enough, we went to see the beautiful beach area Ojos de Agua, near Alajuela.

In the airport, I found I would be traveling with Bishop [Richard] Ham,[137] auxiliary bishop of Guatemala, and Bishop Gerardo Flores from Alta Verapaz, also in Guatemala, which made the trip very enjoyable. We had a very interesting pastoral conversation all the way from San José to San Salvador.

In San Salvador, the Barraza family[138] and my sister were waiting for me and took me to my residence at the Divine Providence Hospital. In fellowship with the community there, which has provided me with lodging with such great affection, I told them my impressions of the meeting, and they also told me the news of the week.

---

[137] An American Maryknoll priest who was then bishop of Huehuetenango, later auxiliary of Guatemala City.

[138] Close personal friends.

And finally, in the evening, we saw some beautiful slides provided by the Dominican Sisters of the Annunciation of the different activities of the order in El Salvador, Guatemala, Costa Rica and Nicaragua. It is very timely since the founder of the order, Father Francisco Coll of Catalonia, will be beatified in Rome on Sunday, April 29, in the first such ceremony to be celebrated by Pope John Paul II. I will have the good fortune to attend, God willing, thanks to the generous invitation from the sisters.

 ### Saturday, April 21

As we do every Saturday, we had our breakfast meeting about communications. We studied some requests from workers' organizations, from peasants, to buy air time on the Catholic radio station. The Human Rights Commission of El Salvador also has asked for some time on our radio. We approved the idea, but we reserve the right to censor anything broadcast. There are special programs planned for May 1 to present the Church doctrine on the worker, on work. We will quote texts (and there are many of them) from Pope John Paul II, speaking principally to workers.

In this meeting I also consulted them about what I should do in Rome on my impending trip and about the audience that, God willing, I will have with the Holy Father.

There have been some very serious revelations of complicity in certain acts of violence and murder—complicity on the part of the government. One case was the attempt to murder Dr. Méndez, one of the members of the Human Rights Commission, who was wounded in the leg by a bullet when they shot at him, trying to kill him. Tomorrow evening, God willing, I will visit this man who, because of his efforts to help, has faced the danger of an attempt to murder him.

We also talked about other projects with the media. At eleven-thirty a.m., I was interviewed by Mr. Lewis Wilton, member of the Associated Press, on whose behalf he interviewed me about the situation of the Church in this country and on some points of doctrine related to our pastoral work.

At the invitation of Father Modesto Villarán, I went to Candelaria in Cuscatlán to celebrate Mass for Father Villarán's mother and father, who are celebrating their fiftieth wedding anniversary. The celebration was made even more interesting when one of Father Villarán's brothers and his wife knelt alongside the parents because they were also celebrating their twenty-fifth wedding anniversary that same day.

## Sunday, April 22

In my homily in the Mass at the cathedral, I announced the program of sermons for the Easter Season.[139] We will be looking at the different gifts of Pentecost, that is, all those treasures of redemption that the biblical readings offer us. This Sunday I talked about the gift of the Holy Spirit, given by Christ on the very day of his Resurrection.[140] Second, the gift of faith, based on the story of Thomas and on the second reading in which John tells us that this is the victory that overcomes the world, our faith. And the third gift, the supernatural love that creates true community.

Unfortunately, today too there was interference with the Catholic radio station that made a good transmission of the homily impossible, but the station found a way to broadcast it after the Mass from the antenna itself.

After that I went to San Pedro Perulapán, where I have been supposed to go on several occasions but been unable to because of unforeseen circumstances. Today I went to help that community renew their Baptism and Confirmation vows. I explained to them the meaning of Easter and of the Christian community that lives because of this mystery.

I was very sorry not to be able to stay to have lunch with the priest, especially since he insisted. But because of some advice I had received, I did not want to go eat in the public restaurant where the lunch had been prepared. I also noted a certain watchfulness in the National Guard barracks that it seemed prudent not to encourage by my continued presence in the village.

In the evening I celebrated Mass in Resurrección parish in Colonia Miramonte, where the Augustinian Fathers, following the tradition of previous parish priests, made it a patronal feast and after the Mass offered a fraternal *agape* feast to the entire community. The theme of the sermon was, "The parish community, with the breath of the risen Christ, continues the mission that Christ gave to the Church": a mission that presupposes the cross and martyrdom, as witnessed by the tomb of Father Navarro, a parish priest murdered in his parish. But the grief is later assimilated and transformed into the victory of the risen Christ, as he transformed his cross and the humiliations he suffered into the glory of his Resurrection.

After Mass, I went with Father Moreno and Mr. Cuéllar to visit Dr. Méndez, who was the victim this week of an attempt on his life. Thank God, the doctor was only wounded in the leg and is recuperating; it is probable

---

[139] The fifty days from Easter Sunday until Pentecost.
[140] See John 20:1-9, the Gospel for Easter Sunday.

that he will be well very soon. I know that this attempt was motivated by actions of the government itself—of which the doctor himself is unaware.

 **Monday, April 23**

A brief conversation with Father Rafael Palacios, parish priest of San Francisco in Mejicanos, and with the Belgian Sister María. We were able to establish that there has been a great deal of political infiltration into the pastoral work of that parish. Father Palacios is willing to work to remove all of this interference so that the parish's work will be truly pastoral.

I went to Chalatenango to converse with the minor seminarians and have lunch with them. We had a very friendly and very interesting dialogue in which, by the end, the Sisters of the Assumption, who have a community in that parish, were also participating.

When I got back, I met with Monsignor Urioste, Father Pedraz, who is in charge of the radio, and Father Moreno from the Secretariat of Social Communications. The main topic we discussed was the interference at YSAX. We agreed that Father Pedraz, as head of the radio, and Monsignor Urioste will go to ANTEL with a letter asking them to find an effective solution to this problem.

Tomorrow, as a follow-up, we will meet to see what is to be done, based on the conversation they have with the president of ANTEL when they visit him tomorrow.

In the evening there was a very interesting meeting in the parish of San Sebastián in Ciudad Delgado. The priest of this parish, Father Juan Antonio Gutiérrez, invited me to meet with those who direct the pastoral effort, but when I got there, I found the Church completely filled with people. The meeting had to be held with all of them!

I asked them to think about what the true mission and shape of the Church should be and then, beginning with that truth, to discuss the divisions that exist in the parish. There were very frank comments from both the more traditional sectors and the elements of renewal, which, under the title "Family of God," do the kind of pastoral work the archdiocese has requested. All of the comments were very useful. Whenever I spoke, I recommended unity, talked about the importance of the work the Church does and especially recommended that they study more and more deeply what the Church is in order to make our pastoral work a more concrete effort to build the true Church of Jesus Christ.

**Tuesday, April 24**

I went to Santa Tecla in the morning to make my confession and to visit Father Isidro, who had had an accident on the way to Santa Ana. Praise God, it was not very serious and he is already on the road to recovery. After stopping briefly at the office of the archdiocese, I went to Domus Mariae to attend the meeting of the priests' cooperative. There was good attendance and the directors of the cooperative reported at great length on how the priests' cooperative, ARS, was flourishing economically.

In the afternoon I prepared with Monsignor Urioste the program that is broadcast on the radio every Wednesday at one p.m. Among the themes we discussed were my trip to Rome and my impressions of the bishops' meeting in Costa Rica. We also talked about the interference with the radio and the conversation that Monsignor Urioste and Father Pedraz, head of the radio, had today with the president of ANTEL.

 **Wednesday, April 25**

We spent the whole morning in a meeting of the Pastoral Council. The ten vicars came and the representatives of the women religious and the laypeople who participate in the pastoral work. This organism is becoming better and better defined, and I have great hope in it for the coordination and encouragement of the pastoral work in the entire diocese.

The sisters at the Colegio de la Sagrada Familia were very kind and provided us with refreshments. Because of that, we were able to continue the meeting until one-thirty p.m.

Monsignor Urioste, vicar general, and Father Pedraz, in his position as head of the radio, met with the Minister of the Interior. The reason for the meeting was the interference with the Catholic radio station. This morning at breakfast I met with Father Pedraz, Father Moreno, Monsignor Urioste and Bachiller Cuéllar to talk about that same matter of the interference, after Father Pedraz and Monsignor Urioste had gone to meet with the president of ANTEL. The president of ANTEL received them very cordially and promised to do everything he could to stop the interference. They also told us about a very interesting conversation in which Monsignor Urioste reminded the minister how popular our radio is and how any attack on our station is a violation of freedom of expression.

## Thursday, April 26

I spent the day preparing for my trip to Rome. I especially wanted to prepare a package of documents and declarations of solidarity with the archdiocese in case I need to talk about that. But mostly I am going there to listen, since we have already provided them with many reports on our situation.

Many people have come to tell me good-bye, showing me great affection. In the afternoon I went to see the major and minor seminarians. After expressing to them my admiration for the vocation that the Lord has given us, I asked them to be faithful and loyal to this vocation that they have received from God. They asked questions, particularly when we talked about our pastoral work involving Holy Week. It is comforting to see how our young men in the seminary, who share the pastoral life of the Christian base communities and identify with them, also bring them the thought of the gospel and of the Church.

I also celebrated the Eucharist with the priests at the seminary and with all the young men in the chapel. In my preaching, I emphasized how youth is a sign of renewal, of concern, of praiseworthy boldness. I challenged them to let all of their youthful energy be guided by criteria that is evangelical and Christian and ecclesial, so that their youth be a continual Easter, a Christ who is resurrected and will never die again!

I stayed up very late packing my suitcase for tomorrow.

## Friday, April 27

After celebrating Mass in the Divine Providence Hospital, I was taken to the airport in a car belonging to the Dominican Sisters of the Annunciation. We took a TACA[141] flight that took me to Guatemala, where the provincial of the congregation that has given me this trip to Rome was waiting for me. We left on an Iberia flight around noon for Spain. We stopped in Managua, then in Santo Domingo, where we had to wait for three hours because there was something wrong with the plane, but it was nothing major. We explored in the large duty-free store in the airport. And we left very late, when it was almost dark, for Spain. Nothing important happened on the flight; we were flying over the ocean all night. They try to keep the passengers occupied with movies and meals. Because of the

---

[141] *Transportes Aereos Centro Americanos,* the national airline of El Salvador.

delay, we did not arrive in Madrid until around noon, after a very short night, since we are flying toward the sun when we fly toward Europe.

We missed our connection....[142]

 **Saturday, April 28**

A night spent flying from the American continent to Europe is a very short night. We arrived in Madrid on what was the morning of April twenty-eighth for us but, because we were delayed so long in Santo Domingo, it was already close to noon on Saturday there. Because we had missed our connecting flight to Rome due to the delay in Santo Domingo, they put us on an Alitalia flight, but they did not put our two suitcases on the flight with us. When we realized this in Rome when we arrived about three p.m., we complained to Alitalia, where they only said that they would pass our complaint on to Madrid.

We were not satisfied merely to wait for the results of a trace so, thinking that our luggage would arrive that same afternoon on a later flight, we waited there until ten p.m., when the last flight came in—still without our luggage. At that point, we confronted the person in charge of Alitalia and asked him to do something more because it was urgent for us to receive our luggage. He promised to send it to our lodgings as soon as it arrived.

Our taxi driver was rather elderly but very nice. He took us to the house that the Dominican Sisters of the Annunciation keep for guests in Monte Mario. We found some Spanish bishops still having dinner, for they had arrived late too, and so we were able to have dinner with them, since we hadn't eaten yet.

Thus ended another day of blessings for me, because being in Rome is always a blessing of the Lord for me.

---

[142] Tape ends here.

**Sunday, April 29**

The dawn in Rome brings back so many memories. The scenery that became familiar to me when I was studying theology here, when I was ordained as a priest and spent my first few months as a priest here, brings a sense of renewal to my spirit. Now, when I have responsibilities that I didn't have then, I feel that being able to be in Rome is a blessing from the Lord that confirms me in my mission, my work that God shares with me by giving me the happiness of being able to help in a modest way in building the Kingdom in this world.

Today was the day Father Francisco Coll, founder of the Dominican Sisters of the Annunciation, was beatified. But only today did I realize that he was not the only one being beatified. There was also Father Laval, a Frenchman who worked spreading the gospel to Negroes freed from slavery. The two figures were both great missionaries, both great evangelists. In his homily the pope pointed out this characteristic that coincides with his great concern for catechesis. He will prepare a document soon on this theme, taken from the 1977 Synod,[143] which was precisely on catechesis.

Since I do not have a change of clothes because my suitcase has still not arrived, one of the other bishops, the bishop from Tarragona [Archbishop José Pont y Gol], lent me a cassock and a cincture that were exactly my size. This was also the Lord's providence, because it enabled me to go with the other bishops to the prominent place reserved for us in the beatification ceremony.

I saw the Holy Father up close; I enjoyed the choir and the participation of the people. There is no doubt that the new liturgy has noticeably changed from the triumphalism of other days, and we now have a true atmosphere for prayer, for reflection.

The pope who, with characteristic simplicity, did not use his pontifical chair but walked along with the concelebrants, is the object of ever-increasing enthusiasm.

At the moment of the beatification, as they always do, before the Bernini columns they uncovered the tapestries of the two being beatified and greeted them with warm applause and the *Te Deum*—or, rather, the "Glory to God in the Highest." The readings came next. The first one was in Spanish in honor of Father Coll; the second in French in honor of the newly-beatified Father Laval and the Gospel was read in Latin.

---

[143] A gathering of representative bishops elected by their national or regional episcopal conferences.

The pope gave a beautiful homily in which he talked about the gifts of the two being beatified and related them to the present-day concern of the Church for true evangelism and catechesis of humankind.

When we came out, it was almost noon. The pope, in spite of how tiring the ceremony was, held an audience for the Dominican Sisters and for all of those who were interested in and had participated in this beatification. And at a little after noon, as is his custom, he went out onto the balcony of his room and from there he talked more about the concept of catechesis and of how the two people beatified are examples of great evangelists. He said that it was a very important day for him because, for the first time as pope, he had performed this ceremony for the Church, giving them two new examples of saintliness, and he hoped that they would be advocates for him in heaven.

The speech was interrupted several times by applause from the square, which was completely full. At the end, he talked about specific events of the week, he wished them happiness and he joined in prayer for many intentions in Rome and throughout the world. He mentioned the conflicts in Uganda and in other parts of the world, asking the people to pray for peace. With this motivation, we prayed the Regina Coeli, which is the noon prayer to the Virgin during the Easter season.[144]

When I returned to the house of the Dominican Sisters, I met several people that I knew among the nuns, bishops and priests that the sisters had invited for a reception and lunch, which was fraternal and animated.

I spent the afternoon resting and in the evening, after dinner, I went out to familiarize myself with how to get to Risorgimento Square, where I will go for my errands in Rome. It is only a short trip from the Number Fifty bus stop at the hospital at the Gemeli University to Risorgimento Square, which is very near the Vatican, where there is another stop. It appears, then, that this bus line will be very useful for me. After walking around Saint Peter's Square, I saw that the window of the pope's room was no longer lighted. It seems that it needs some repairs and that he is staying in another room. I returned with the satisfaction of having spent a very full and happy day in this immortal Rome.

---

[144] Instead of the Angelus.

**Monday, April 30**

The Central American provincial of the Dominican Sisters, Mother Nieves, gave me the good news that Alitalia had informed her that they had finally found the suitcases and that she would go to the airport and get them. I left for the Vatican to get the answer to my request for an audience with the Holy Father.

A torrential rain kept me from walking very fast, and I unexpectedly came upon a shop where they make cassocks and sell all that ecclesiastical paraphernalia. I spent a good part of the morning in this shop, which was really very good because it means there is enough time for them to make me two new cassocks.

I bought a clerical suit and went to the Vatican, where, unfortunately, the prefect of the Pontifical Household was not in. He is the one who will have the answer for me about the audience. They only told me that I should come back tomorrow and inquire again.

This afternoon in a Dominican theater there was a very artistic dramatization of events from the life of the newly beatified Father Francisco Coll. The majority of the scenes were enacted by young people from Barcelona.

And from there we headed to the Dominican Church in Minerva Square, where we concelebrated—some sixty bishops and priests, presided over by the Cardinal of Barcelona. The church was completely full of nuns and pilgrims who had made the pilgrimage, who had come for the beatification of Father Coll. The concelebration was impressive and a new inspiration for the sanctification of the congregation founded by this illustrious Dominican. I myself felt the joy of this life in the Church that constantly sanctifies us.

In the evening, at dinner, they showed us more than a hundred and fifty photographs taken at the beatification ceremony so that we could choose which ones we want to buy. But, as they are extremely expensive— over three dollars each—we had to limit our orders.

# May 1979

 **Tuesday, May 1**

On May 1, International Workers' Day, all commercial activity ceases in Rome but, since the buses don't run either, it is difficult to go anywhere. To be able to do anything today, I had to take expensive taxicabs, but that way I was able to go again to ask at the Pontifical Household about my audience with the pope. But the Prefecture was closed, too. And even though one of the Swiss Guards let me knock on the door, I realized that it was useless to wait.

After that I went to the Jesuit curia, where one of the father general's assistants from South America received me very graciously and told me that the priests from Central America would not be there until evening. And I can hope for a meeting with Father Arrupe as well. Once the assistant knew who I was, he was much more attentive and expressed his thanks for what has been done for the Company of Jesus in our diocese.

Then I went to the motherhouse of the Oblate Sisters of Divine Love. My visit was a pleasant surprise for the mother general, Mother Gloria. I also greeted Mother Valle and all the sisters of the executive council. They invited me to have lunch with them and we shared some very cordial moments. The mother general and Mother Juana, with whom I became friends on my last trip, were kind enough to drive me back to where I am staying at the Dominican Sisters' house in Monte Mario.

I spent the evening at the concelebration, at six p.m. in the beautiful Basilica of Sacra Cuore di Maria. The Claretian Fathers, in sign of their long-standing friendship with the newly beatified Father Coll, had invited the Dominicans. The father general of the Dominicans and the father general of the Claretians assisted the principal celebrant, who was Cardinal Tarancón [Vicente Enrique y Tarancón]. I greeted him and he kindly offered me a place to stay in his house in Madrid when I go there.

The concelebration was really splendid, like the one yesterday, with some sixty bishops, eight priests and the large church completely filled with nuns and pilgrims. The father general of the Claretians preached on the similarities between the two holy men, St. Anthony Mary Claret and Father Francisco Coll.

When I got back to the house, they told me that Father Arrupe was very interested in talking to me and that I should call to set up the visit. I will do that tomorrow, God willing.

 **Wednesday, May 2**

Today I went to the pope's general audience. It took place in St. Peter's Square, since the number of pilgrims was around 130,000 people, among them the large group of Dominican nuns and pilgrims who had come to the beatification of Father Coll as well as the religious and pilgrims who had come for the beatification of Father Laval. There were many other pilgrims, too, and the square was completely filled.

The pope came out through the Portico of the Bells and went around the square in different directions in a jeep, greeting everyone affectionately. The crowd naturally applauded when the pope came near them. When he got out of the jeep and headed toward his chair, he stopped for several more minutes, talking and shaking hands with those who were in his path. Then from his throne he made the Sign of the Cross and began his address after the secretary had pointed out to him which groups spoke Italian.

The theme the pope spoke on was that of the Holy Virgin Mary, since we are beginning the month of the Virgin, which coincides with the Easter Season.

The ideas coming from the mouth and heart of the pope were deep and pleasant. He ended by expressing the nostalgia he felt when he mentioned the patron of his people, Our Lady of Czestachowa.[145] He used to visit her at the beginning of May when the patronal feast is celebrated there. Today it is impossible for him to be there, but he will go in June with all the bishops and other pilgrims who come to meet the pope when he visits his country.

The pope also repeated his greetings and an abbreviated version of his message in French, German, Spanish, Catalán and Portuguese. When he finished his address, he called all the bishops—some forty of them—to his throne and we gave the benediction along with him. After that, seated on his throne, he greeted us one by one. When I took his hand and asked him for a blessing for the Archdiocese of San Salvador, he told me that we should

---

[145] Patroness of Poland.

speak privately—which was, I told him, my greatest wish; I had requested an audience.

I hope that the pope will grant me this private audience. Therefore, I did not give him the papers that I had brought in the form of a memorandum, in case it was not possible to get an audience—various papers which should be included with the report of the apostolic visitator. In the memorandum, I ask the Holy Father for his guidance, after the abundant information I am sure he received from the apostolic visitator. Also I will leave him a copy of the letter I sent in November about the variety of problems that I as archbishop had to inform His Holiness about regarding the situation of the Church and the state in our country.

Immediately after leaving the pope's throne, I talked to Monsignor Martin and Monsignor Monduzzi, who are in charge of arranging his audiences, to ask them more urgently for the audience I have been requesting since before Holy Week. They told me it might be possible, but not before next week. I will insist, because it is my greatest desire and also my greatest need to talk with the pope on this visit to Rome.

In the afternoon I went to the Jesuit curia, where I spoke with Father Juan Bosco [Estrada]. I made the arrangements with him for the Wednesday telephone call that will be transmitted by our station YSAX. I talked with Monsignor Urioste in El Salvador. The conversation referred to the different ways in which I have experienced Rome, and, principally, to the beatification ceremony on Sunday, today's audience and also the praying of the Regina Coeli in St. Peter's Square.

I reported that the pope, during this short period of time that I have been in Rome, has been teaching many points of doctrine. Mainly they have had to do with the Blessed Virgin, with catechesis—the two being beatified were models for this—and with the life of the religious, who are represented in Rome in such great numbers now because of the beatification of two religious. I also referred to how the pope congratulated and thanked all catechists. He recommended to his listeners that they be like the two being honored, whose lives were a living witness: people who really live the Resurrection of Jesus Christ. As the Lord said in last Sunday's Scripture: "He who keeps my commandments knows me."[146]

The Jesuits invited me to have lunch with Father Arrupe tomorrow, also with other Jesuits who are interested in talking with me about the situation of El Salvador and about other situations that would be helpful to me also. I also was invited by the Claretian Fathers to go for dinner tomorrow to Sacra Cuore di Maria. Church with their father general.

---

[146] See 1 John 2:1-5a.

I will do so, thinking with gratitude of the Claretian communities who work in our archdiocese.

 **Thursday, May 3**

The Spanish bishops and priests who had come for the beatification of Father Coll and were staying in the house belonging to the Dominican Sisters have been leaving all day today. I have been left almost alone, but I spent the day trying to resolve certain matters. First of all, I went to the Prefecture of the Papal Residence to try to arrange for my audience with the pope. It will possibly be Wednesday or Thursday of next week, for they explained to me today that there are many bishops on their *ad limina* visits and they will be given preference at this time. I explained that it is urgent for me to see the pope because of the situation of my diocese and because my country is so far away and I want to use the time to talk about some other matters as well. Nevertheless, I must be patient and await my turn.

Later I went to ask for an audience with Cardinal Baggio, Prefect of the Congregation for Bishops, and with Cardinal Pironio, Prefect of the Congregation for Religious—the latter more out of friendship.

I went to have lunch at the Jesuit curia. They did me the honor to put me at the same table with Father Arrupe. I talked to him before lunch about the ecclesial situation of my country. And he also told me about different projects the Company has in Latin America. Father Juan Bosco Estrada, a very good friend at the curia, let me use his room after lunch so I could take a nap. I also talked with several Jesuits who were interested in the situation of my country, which is very important, given the worldwide significance of the work that is done there.

Later, enjoying the spring afternoon, I went to visit the Church of the Twelve Apostles. The tombs of the apostles Sts. Philip and James the Lesser, whose saint's day is celebrated liturgically today, May 3, are located under the main altar.

I forgot to say that in the morning I also visited Saint Peter's Basilica again, and close to the beloved altars dedicated to St. Peter and his recent successors in this century, I asked for great faithfulness to my Christian faith and the courage, should it be necessary, to die as those martyrs died, or to live a consecrated life as those modern successors to Peter did. More than any of the other tombs there, I am impressed by the simplicity of Pope Paul VI's tomb.

Today I visited the Gregorian University. I went in the principal classroom and wandered around those cloisters that remind me of my years as a student in my youth. It brought back so many memories!

Then I went to visit Father López Gall, and I had a very interesting conversation with him in which I learned the opinion of my conduct as archbishop held by different sectors of the Roman Curia. And he told me that the impression is very positive and that I should keep on as I am. He also told me, with friendly simplicity, that some sectors have a negative opinion of Father Jon Sobrino's[147] theological writings.

And finally, I went to have dinner at the curia of the Claretian Fathers. I was seated at the head table with the father general, who leaves tomorrow for Germany to honor his predecessor, who is over eighty years old. I remembered with them my days in the minor seminary and also my first Mass, for I celebrated it here in the chapel next to the Claretian headquarters, Sacra Cuore di Maria Church. And when they asked me to sign their visitors' book, I wrote, "Today I have returned to my origins. Having dinner with you, I have recalled the time I spent in the minor seminary when I studied with the Claretian Fathers. And it was here that I celebrated my first Mass in 1945. I thank you and ask God to bless you."

 **Friday, May 4**

Since I was worrying about the principal reason for my trip to Rome, besides attending the beatification of Father Coll, I went again to the Prefecture of the Papal Residence to try to get them to grant me an audience with the Holy Father. I did not find Monsignor Martin, but I left a better address where they could notify me of the answer and said that I would call him later when he would be in the office.

I am still very concerned about the attitude they show to the pastor of a diocese, considering that I asked for this audience some time ago. They keep delaying the response and I am afraid that they are not going to grant the audience because there are many bishops in *ad limina* visits. And there are also other reasons they could give preference to other requests.

I have put it in God's hands. I told him that I have done everything in my power and that, in spite of everything, I believe in and love the Holy Church and, with his grace, I will always be faithful to the Holy See, to the teaching of the pope; and that I understand the human, limited, defective

---

[147] One of the leading Latin American theologians of liberation.

part of his Holy Church, which is the instrument of the salvation of humankind and which I want to serve without any reservations.

These supernatural and very ecclesial thoughts enriched my visit to Monsignor De Nicoló, an old friend who is at the Congregation for Catholic Education. I conversed with him with great affection and brotherly confidence about my relationship with the other bishops, with the government and with the nuncio. And he knew that—he was sure that— given my temperament and my formation, the negative information that has reached Rome about my conduct as archbishop must be exaggerated.

Immediately afterward, I went to visit the community of the Bethany Sisters. They are four Salvadoran and Guatemalan nuns who run a house for university students at 172 Via Aurelia. They invited me to have lunch there, and the young men, some of whom are already professionals, showed great interest in learning about the situation of my country and set up a meeting for me with other journalists that evening before dinner. I accepted with pleasure, given their sincerity and the Catholic climate that pervades at the publishing house where they work.

From there I went to visit the Passionist Sisters who run the house for the Passionist Fathers, as well as their curia and the retreat house next to the famous Church of St. John and St. Paul, where Saint Paul of the Cross, founder of the Passionist Orders, is buried.

The majority of these sisters—there are ten of them—are Mexican and have been to El Salvador. They were very happy I came to visit them, and they asked me to have lunch with them tomorrow and celebrate the Holy Hour for them. I agreed, given their affection and the prayers they offer to God about the situation of our Salvadoran Church. They kindly drove me to the community of the Bethany Sisters, for it was already time me to be there for dinner and the interview with the press I mentioned earlier.

 ### Saturday, May 5

Today I went to reiterate my request for an audience with the pope. Monsignor Martin went to speak with his colleague and when he came back told me happily: "I have good news for you—you will be received on Monday. Tomorrow, Sunday, in the afternoon, you will receive the notice we always send giving the time of the audience." I thanked him cordially and, naturally, I have thanked God.

Afterward, I went to Minerva Square to look at the sacred art to see if I could find the kind of bishops' staff that I have always wanted. It is similar to the one Paul VI used and that John Paul II still uses. I was able to find an artisan there who will make me one. Mother Gloria promised to find someone who will pay for it, because my spending the money might be interpreted in a negative way. It would then be a gift from the people. It will represent the Holy Christ in the form of a staff.

I went to have lunch with the Passionist Sisters at the Sts. John and Paul convent. And there I rested and celebrated Mass, preaching to them on the theme of vocations and how all of us who have been called by God must collaborate with God in his work and practice the spirit of the Good Shepherd with human beings. The Passionist Sisters took me to my lodging, where I had dinner with the Dominican Sisters and shared their evening recreation.

### Sunday, May 6

After celebrating Mass privately in the Dominican Sisters' chapel, I went to St. Peter's Square to be part of the public that goes on Sunday at noon to pray the Regina Coeli with the pope. Mother Gloria and Sister Juana were waiting for me there, and afterward we went to have lunch at Castel Gandolfo. It was a beautiful excursion, and it was a shame that it was so cloudy and at times was raining. And in the picturesque dining room that looks out on the lake, it was very humid; there was no visibility and I couldn't even see the countryside. But I have been able to see how picturesque is this area where the Holy Father goes to rest on his vacations. It is surrounded by poor areas and, given these surroundings, the immensity of the property of Castel Gandolfo, summer home of the pope, is perhaps too noticeable.

### Monday, May 7

When I got up, I finished preparing the documents that I plan to give the Holy Father when I have my audience with him. There are four reports from foreign delegations who came to El Salvador to study the situation of the country. There are also expressions of solidarity, documents denouncing the situation, also my nomination for the Nobel Prize and other documents from the period after the apostolic visitation from Bishop Quarracino that should be included with the documentation from the visitation. I also included the letter I wrote to him in November because I doubt it ever reached him.

At 12:20 p.m., I was received by the Holy Father in a private audience. He was seated at his desk and he asked me to sit down too. I had taken off my zucchetto and had it in my hand, and he told me I could put it back on. He began to ask me questions about the situation of my country. I respectfully suggested that we follow the memorandum I had written, and he willingly agreed. We began to read and I handed him the appropriate documents. When I took out the folder of reports from the foreign delegations on the situation of the country, he smiled, seeing how thick it was, knowing that there would not be time to look at it. I asked his pardon, explaining that my intention was for him to order that it be studied and summarized for him, but that I wanted him to have an idea of how impartial observers describe the situation of injustice and the attacks that happen in our country. I also gave him a folder with a photograph of Father Octavio [Ortiz], now dead, which included extensive information on his murder.

After I gave him each of the seven folders with a brief explanation of each one, the pope began his comments with the last point on my list. It referred to my wish to learn through this meeting the true ideas of the pope and how to better serve our people. He acknowledged that pastoral work is very difficult in a political climate like the one in which I have to work. He recommended great balance and prudence, especially when denouncing specific situations. He thinks that it is better to stay with principles, because there is a risk of making errors or mistakes with specific accusations.

I clarified for him (and he said that I was right) that there are circumstances—I mentioned, for example, the case of Father Octavio—in which the accusation has to be very specific because the injustice perpetrated, the attack committed, was very specific. He reminded me of his situation in Poland, where he was faced with a government that was not Catholic and where he had to develop the Church in spite of the difficulties. He said the unity of the bishops is very important. Again recalling his time as a pastor in Poland, he said that keeping the bishops unified was the main problem. Again I clarified, telling him that this is also something that I want very much, but that I was aware that unity cannot be pretended. Rather, it must be based on the gospel and on the truth.

He referred to the report on the apostolic visitation of Bishop Quarracino. He had realized that the situation was an extremely delicate one, and he had recommended that to resolve the deficiencies in the pastoral work and the lack of harmony among the bishops, an apostolic administrator *sede plena*[148] be appointed.

At the end of the audience, after he had given me the chance to express my thoughts and had also expressed his opinions, he suggested we be photographed together and gave me some religious articles as gifts. He put the folders aside to continue with the remaining audiences.

And I left, pleased by the meeting, but worried to see how much the negative reports of my pastoral work had influenced him, although deep down I remembered that he had recommended "courage and boldness, but, at the same time, tempered with the necessary prudence and balance." Although I did not feel completely satisfied with the meeting, I think that the audience and our conversation were very useful because he was very frank. I have learned that one cannot expect always to get complete approval and that it is more useful to hear criticism that can be used to improve our work.

After the audience, Father Toral was waiting for me, and he took me to his residence of Josephite priests and brothers in Villa Santa..., and I had lunch there. Mother María Castro Llerena was also there. She had come from the village where she lives, more than an hour away from Rome, to see me. We talked about her cousin, Monsignor Castro Peña, and shared other memories of our dear country (she is also Salvadoran).

In the afternoon, Mother Gloria and Sister Juana took me in their van to see the artisan who is making my staff, and Mother Gloria managed to get a significant reduction in the price and make a change in the design of the work. Then we went to pick up the garments I had ordered at the tailor shop for clergy. Then I went back to have dinner with the Oblate Sisters of Divine Love. Afterward, I returned to the Dominican Sisters' house where I was staying.

 **Tuesday, May 8**

In Rome it seems like time just gets swallowed up. I had planned to do something else before the audience I had today with Cardinal Baggio at eleven in the morning. But I was only able to make a few arrangements with the tailor, who hasn't finished what I ordered yet. And I went to St. Peter's Square to commend myself to the great pontiffs

---

[148] "With the see occupied"; that is, Romero would still be bishop but the administrator would run the diocese.

who are buried in the Vatican crypts and who have given me so much inspiration and guidance in my life, and to hold that moment of introspection before going to talk about very important matters at the Congregation for Bishops, presided over by Cardinal Baggio.

In St. Peter's Square I ran into Monsignor Eduardo Cásuli, who had been secretary at the nunciature, I think when Archbishop [Bruno] Torpigliani was in El Salvador. He was very warm. We shared many memories, and he understands how difficult my situation is. He said that he thinks of me often and prays for me to be a worthy pastor in those circumstances.

My conversation with Cardinal Baggio was very cordial, even though I had expected some severity like the last time, which was last year. He really wanted to meet with me and told me that it would have surprised him if I had come to Rome without coming to see him. I told him that I had been trying to get an audience with him since the first day I got to Rome, but that, because of his commitments, it had not been granted earlier.

He expressed his concerns, especially about the division among the bishops and about the situation of the auxiliary bishop. And he very frankly acknowledged that the auxiliary bishop had made a mistake in signing the permission to change the statutes of Caritas, which should have been signed by the archbishop; and that he, as vicar general, must have agreed with the changes. But if he knew that the archbishop did not agree, he should not have done it. But he also said that I had been very severe in my decision to remove him and that I had left him hanging.

I tried to explain that whole situation, because I also realized that one of the reasons Bishop Revelo had given to justify his action was that Caritas was being politicized and becoming controlled by the guerrillas. Also the excuse that I was ill and in the hospital. I explained to the cardinal that neither the one nor the other was reason enough to justify his action.

There was reference made to the apostolic visitation and to the idea the pope had touched on in our conversation yesterday, that is, to resolve the situation by naming an apostolic administrator *sede plena*. But Cardinal Baggio thought it was not a very practical solution, because he did not see that any one of the present bishops who could be the apostolic administrator could work well with me. And to bring in someone from outside the country also seemed an absurd idea, given the situation of our country. Because of this, it is still being studied. I indicated to him my willingness to do anything I can to resolve the situation.

I referred to the reports I gave the pope, which are impartial, and told him that they express a situation of true persecution of the Church. I specifically mentioned the OAS report and its insistence on telling the government to prevent the systematic persecution of the Catholic Church in its evangelical mission. The cardinal was very cordial when he told me: "We are not dealing with enemies, rather with people working for the same cause and we are, therefore, ninety percent agreed already. And the one hundred percent is based on the truth and on the gospel." I told him that his words gave me great encouragement and that the depression I had been left with after my audience with the Holy Father had here, in my conversation with him, been replaced by a hope that my situation and that of my diocese have solutions if we continue to look for them in goodwill and with love of the Church.

He seemed satisfied. We talked about other things, and the time was up. He gave me two books and expressed to me his willingness to help me in my service to the Church.

I was satisfied when I left there and, upon leaving, it was providential that I ran into Monsignor De Nicoló, a good friend. I told him that I would like to tell him in confidence, so that he could provide me with spiritual guidance, how I had felt, my state of mind, yesterday and today. He provided me with very clear guidance inspired by his great love for the Church. He told me how virtue, especially humility, is in such cases a very good key to unlock a solution. He was sure, he said, that goodwill reigns in the Curia, which has changed greatly, and that he, as one who has experienced it, can tell me that there is a great readiness to help those who serve the Church in different places in any way possible, and that the influence of the present pope has been very beneficial both for the Curia and for the Church as a whole.

He gave me some practical guidance on how to approach the Secretary of State—referring to the previous suggestion, that I regard all of it as a message from God who is looking, even in my situation, for a solution that will benefit the Church. That I be very careful not to react more strongly because, possibly, the Holy Father and Cardinal Baggio could be trying to gauge my reaction when they suggest the idea of an apostolic administrator to me. That if my reaction were negative, then everything might be lost. That I be humble and patient and write to the Secretary of State, giving him my impressions and my suggestion, for example, that some future nuncio who can work well with the archbishop could carry out the difficult role suggested for a possible apostolic administrator.

I think I understood what he was trying to tell me and I will try to do as he suggested with the goodwill toward the Church that, with God's help, I have always tried to keep and develop.

After that I went to the Vatican radio station where I had been invited by Father Suárez, in charge of transmissions for Latin America. He taped an interview with me on the situation of the Church in El Salvador, on my work and on my impressions of my visit to the Holy Father. I summarized our situation and my work, what I intend for it to be. And, most importantly, I said that I was very optimistic after my visit to the Holy Father, because I had realized that he knows how to listen and it is easy to see that he wants to learn about the reality of our Latin American world. Because of this, I think that all of us who have the honor and joy of talking directly to the pope have a great responsibility to inform him—not based on our own perspective, but as much as possible about the true reality of the Church in our countries.

With Father Suárez and the person in charge of programs for Spain, I went to the Jesuit house, where all the writers and workers at the radio live (some thirty people), to have lunch with them and then later to share their conversation after the meal, which is very fraternal. Father Juan Bosco let me use his room, as he did the other day, to take a nap, which was very nice.

Afterward Father Juan Bosco went with me to make the arrangements for my return trip, with stops in Barcelona and Madrid to visit the birthplace of the Dominican congregation that has been so kind as to provide me with this trip to Europe for the beatification of Father Coll.

Afterward, I picked up my clothes at the tailor shop of my friend Mangenelli, who has been very cordial in all of his dealings with me. I also bought some prints of His Holiness John Paul II to put in all the parish houses, but the famous Soprani[149] seemed to be a beehive of shoppers and it was difficult for me to buy anything else. I spent the last part of the day dining with the Oblate Sisters, who offered me transportation both to go to their house and to return to my lodgings with the Dominican Sisters, where tonight I packed my suitcase for my trip tomorrow.

 ### Wednesday, May 9

After thanking the Dominican Sisters, represented by the superior general and the Central American provincial, for their generous gift of this trip to Rome, I congratulated them on the way the ceremonies and celebration for their beatified founder Father Francisco Coll went. I said good-bye to them, since tonight I will begin my return trip, on which I will stop in Barcelona, Madrid and then El Salvador.

Later I went to visit Cardinal Pironio, with whom I had an audience scheduled for eleven-thirty a.m. The traffic around the Vatican was impossible. The general audience attracts crowds of people and vehicles;

---

[149] Luciano Soprani, a very traditional men's clothier in Rome.

large buses of tourists and pilgrims invade all the streets adjacent to St. Peter's Square.

But I arrived only a few minutes late, and I still had to wait a little while for Cardinal Pirinio, who received me in such a fraternal and cordial manner that this one meeting was enough to fill me with consolation and encouragement. I explained to him in confidence my situation in my diocese and with the Holy See.

He opened his heart to me, telling me what he also has to suffer, how deeply he feels about the problems of Latin America and that, even though they will never be completely understood by the highest levels of the Church, nevertheless we must keep working, keep giving them as much information as we can about the truth of our reality. "The worst thing you can do is to become discouraged," he said. "Have courage Romero," he said to me many times.

And when I left after thanking him for other advice, for a long and fraternal conversation, I found that he had left me with greater strength in my heart as a result of my trip to Rome.

When I was on my way back from the Congregation for Religious, of which Cardinal Pironio is prefect, I stopped in St. Peter's Square, where the pope was still giving his messages in different languages and the people received him with fervor and applause. But, on the outskirts where I was, there were many distractions. Young boys and tourists were distracted and weren't listening to the voice of the pastor. This allowed me to see what our listeners are like, but nevertheless we must sow the seed. And the pope is tirelessly doing so and acting as a shepherd who gives the abundant spiritual food of doctrine to the people, and it depends on them whether or not they choose to accept it.

Later I headed to the Jesuit curia, where the good Father Juan Bosco took me to see the garden and later to have lunch, after which he lent me his room for my siesta. Afterward, we concelebrated the Eucharist. Later, he did me the favor of placing a phone call to El Salvador, to Monsignor Urioste, and our conversation was taped to be broadcast on YSAX.

He told me about the difficult situation of violence in the country. The most serious incident has been the confrontation between the Popular Revolutionary Bloc and the security forces near the cathedral. And he told me that in the cathedral of San Salvador they have laid out nine bodies of people killed in this incident and it is believed that there are more dead.

I used this opportunity to send a message of peace and to transmit the message of the pope to them. In my audience with him, he recalled the murder of Aldo Moro[150] a year ago.

---

[150] Former prime minister of Italy, kidnapped and murdered in 1978.

After the telephone conversation with El Salvador and the information Monsignor Urioste gave me and what I communicated to him, especially about my private audience with the Holy Father, relating everything to the tragic situation today in the cathedral of San Salvador, I went to visit St. Peter's Basilica one last time. And near the tomb of St. Pius X, I prayed intensely, thinking about all the intercessions that the tombs of St. Peter and those of the most recent popes mean for me. Later I went to buy some souvenirs at the market near St. Peter's Square where they sell *Osservatore Romano*,[151] and then the Oblate Sisters of Divine Love took me to the airport.

The trip from Rome to Barcelona was very smooth. And in Barcelona, at eleven p.m., Mother Grau and another Dominican sister were waiting for me. They took me by taxi, with a very nice driver, very talkative, through the main streets of Barcelona, especially around the Sagrada Familia Church.[152] After that we went to Vich, where they put me in a little house that the Dominican Sisters have as a guest house for priests. We made plans tomorrow to go to the birthplace of Father Francisco Coll. The town of Vich is very significant for me, since it is where Father Claret was from. His missionaries inspired me in my first years in the seminary.

 **Thursday, May 10**

In Spain it gets light an hour earlier because of the official time difference between Italy and Spain. I felt like it was very early, but it was already eight a.m. I got dressed quickly and went to have breakfast with the sisters of the house that the Dominicans have in Vich. It is a large community, since they run a school, a nursing home for their own sisters and another series of very productive apostolic centers in this city, which is the congregation's birthplace.

After breakfast, I went with Mother Grau and another nun who keeps the archives and a collection of memorabilia of Father Coll to visit this museum. There is a great deal of information about the activities of this religious order all over the world. I have taken notes in order to be able to talk about the vitality of the order as a response to their generous invitation for me to participate in the beatification of their founder.

---

[151] The Vatican newspaper.

[152] Gaudí's famous unfinished church begun in 1882. Construction continues today amidst controversy over design and funding.

Afterward, we went to visit the cathedral of Vich, which has been rebuilt twice, the last time after the Spanish Civil War. It is beautiful and its modernism is a healthy kind; in the crypt one can still see part of the original church. There have been two later ones up to the present. The paintings were done three times, according to what they told me, because the first time they were lost along the way, they were stolen. The second time they were destroyed by the Communists during the civil war. Finally, the artist, who was doing the decoration from Paris on his own, did the design that presently adorns the cathedral so beautifully. The cloister is the original one, Gothic style, and is very interesting.

Afterward, I had the pleasure of visiting the tomb of Father Antonio María Claret, founder of the Claretians. There are many relics and a magnificent church. At the center is his body, wearing a silver mask and bishops' garments. And, most interestingly, they have rebuilt the places that witnessed the birth of this religious institute dedicated to the Immaculate Heart of Mary. A portrait at the back gives his height, one and a half meters;[153] Father Claret was small in stature. It also gives the names of the other founders: names that I learned in my first years in the seminary, since I began my formation for the priesthood with this congregation that later was moved by Monsignor Dueñas to San Miguel. I reminisced about this with the priests there, who thanked me for my visit. I thanked them for their very cordial reception.

After lunch we went to the town where Father Francisco was born [Sallent]. It is about forty kilometers[154] from Vich, a very picturesque journey on a brilliant spring afternoon. The small town, on the side of a mountain, speaks of the origins of that saintly man, whose house has been reclaimed for use by the religious order he founded. They also have a retreat house there with very beautiful and peaceful views, adorned with gardens, where through nature one truly feels himself near our Lord.

I also went to visit the Church where he was baptized and, when I got back, I celebrated Mass with four nuns in the little chapel that contains Father Coll's original house. It was a very intimate Eucharist, remembering the great needs of my country. The sisters and I have prayed strongly that our life in the Church and in the country be resolved in a way that is in accordance with the will of God.

---

[153] Just under five feet.
[154] About twenty-five miles.

**Friday, May 11**

I celebrated Mass at the chapel of the sisters who are elderly and infirm, where I invited them to join together in prayer for the needs of the Church and told them that they are a very great force in the universal Church. We left after breakfast by the highway to Manresa and we passed very near the cave where St. Ignatius did his Spiritual Exercises and wrote his famous book on them.

Then we took a beautiful highway up to the monastery of Monserrat. The Benedictines were preparing to sing the Mass in the abbey. It was in Catalán, but with a piety and a Gregorian rhythm that are truly moving. There were many people. Afterward I said the rosary to the Virgin of Monserrat. And then we went back down to Barcelona.

Mother Grau was very attentive during the trip to Monserrat, to Vich and to the town Father Coll was from. In her generosity, she also took me to the airport, and left me at the so-called "air bridge," a service that has flights between Barcelona and Madrid every hour.

In Madrid, Sister Raymunda was waiting for me. She is from the same congregation and is the sister who was expelled from Guatemala. She was very glad to see me again. She took me to her residence where, with other sisters, they take care of a residence for employees and students. They do great good at this house. I called Father Pedro, of the Passionists, who brought María with him, the writer who writes in *Vida Nueva*[155] and who did a fine article and gave the proceeds to the poor of the archdiocese. I was very pleased to meet her and to talk with Father Pedro Ferradas and share with them many memories and impressions of our life in El Salvador.

We agreed on a press conference in the evening and I left with the sisters, after lunch and a siesta, to visit their retreat house in the beautiful sierra some fifty kilometers[156] outside Madrid. The house is called El Roble and many people go there to spend time in spiritual retreat or in fellowship.

After dinner in Madrid some reporters came, not just to interview me, but also to talk in friendly intimacy about the situation of the Church, their fears for Latin America, their impressions of the pope and a series of concerns. I was very glad that we were able to share our concerns about the problems of Latin America. I told them that they had a great mission from the Church because they are sensitive to our problems. In Europe in general I have noticed a good deal of indifference or lack of knowledge of the problems of our America.

---

[155] A well-known Spanish Catholic weekly.
[156] Thirty-one miles.

I had dinner at ten p.m., Madrid time, and the sisters, Raymunda and another one who drives very well, took me to the airport, where I said good-bye to them, thanking them for all of their kindnesses to me while I was in Europe. I then went to wait for my flight, which will leave at 2:55 a.m. and arrive at eight-thirty a.m. San Salvador time.

 ### Saturday, May 12

When this Saturday, May 12, dawned, we were in Costa Rica after a very long night, eight hours longer than a normal one because of the time change involved in the flight from Europe to America. We passed through San Juan, Puerto Rico, and through San José, Costa Rica, and we arrived in El Salvador right at eight-thirty a.m. There were no problems on the trip. I spent it praying, putting myself in the presence of God, asking him to enlighten me and to help us to resolve the serious situation that I am going to be faced with when I get back to my country.

When we arrived at the airport, there was a torrential rain. We had to descend from the plane with umbrellas. I saw that there were several friends, both priests and laity, waiting for me, and the Dominican Sisters, faithful to the end in their generous gesture of giving me this trip to the beatification of their founder. After greeting everyone at the door of Ilopango Airport, I went in the sisters' car to my residence. Before I left, I also spoke briefly with Monsignor Urioste about the problems, and we agreed to meet that evening with some others who would help to inform me about the situation in the diocese in such a tragic week. They have told me so many violent, tragic things that have happened, but with God's help we will know how to deal with them in the light of the gospel and the Church.

In the airport, there were several reporters taking photographs, but none of them asked me any questions. Some foreign journalists had announced today that they would interview me tomorrow after Mass, which will be at El Rosario since the cathedral is still occupied by the Popular Revolutionary Bloc.

Some reporters arrived unexpectedly, however, and I received them. I told them that I was not yet able to give them any opinions on the latest events because I had just arrived and that tonight we would be meeting to analyze the situation. And, in fact, in the evening I met with Monsignor Urioste, Father Moreno, Father Brito, young Doris Osegueda and Bachiller Cuéllar.

We analyzed many interesting points having to do with the current situation of the country. We decided it would be a good idea to spend a day or even longer reflecting on certain factors that prevent a better understanding of the climate and, in any case, to go deeper in our analysis of the Church and our political and social situation. After this very interesting conversation, we prepared the summary of the week's events that I will use in my homily tomorrow.

Two young people from the Popular Revolutionary Bloc came to ask me to say a Mass at the cathedral in intercession for four more people who had been killed by government forces while they were carrying out activities of the organization. I analyzed this request with the priests who were meeting with me, and I told them it was difficult for me to understand how they think that I could even consider celebrating a Mass at the request of the Bloc, even if it is for the dead, in a cathedral they are occupying, when I cannot celebrate the regular official Mass there at eight a.m. because of the occupation by the Bloc. If I did that, then our Mass would seem to be subordinated to the strategy and ideals of the Bloc. Because of that, I told them that I thought that, as Christians, we ought to celebrate a Mass for these dead, but I proposed that we have it in the basilica. And the parish priest of the basilica, Father Cortés, will be in charge of planning the liturgy. They accepted, and I think that this has resolved one of those unforeseen problems that are difficult to solve because of the possible complications.

 **Sunday, May 13**

Since the cathedral is occupied, this Sunday's Mass was held in El Rosario Church, which was completely full, and there were people outside—caring people, who when they realized that I had arrived, greeted me warmly with applause. I went to vest and then, with the Dominican Fathers and the seminarians, we began the procession toward the altar. The Dominican Sisters of the Annunciation and some students from their schools had a prominent place, since this Mass is in honor of the newly-beatified Father Francisco Coll Gitard, and the Dominican Sisters had been in charge of planning the liturgy for today.

The homily was a report on my trip to Rome at the invitation of and with the sponsorship of the Dominican Sisters, which had as its principal objective my participation in the beatification of Father Coll. I told them about my travels in Spain, and my impressions when I heard there about what was happening in El Salvador. The principal point of doctrine in my homily was the Gospel reading on the vine and the branches,[157] which gave me the theme of "grace as a gift of the Easter Season." I focused this doctrine on the reality that has been lived in El Salvador this week, and especially on the massacre of May 8. Anyone wanting more information on these insights on our national reality in this tragic week can get the homily (transcribed each Sunday) containing the exact words that I spoke on this occasion.

There were many reporters and television crews at the Mass, who were recording many details of our Mass. When the Mass ended, we held a press conference with them in the hall of the parish school of El Rosario. It was quite interesting, since the questions they asked brought up some current problems and were very timely, given the situation of the country and how it relates to what is going on in the rest of the world.

Afterward, I went to have lunch with the Dominican Sisters in the Colegio de Fátima in Santa Tecla. The Dominican priests, the Marists from Santa Tecla and the different groups of Dominican nuns who work in our archdiocese were there.

This was the most important—no, I forgot that in the evening we were invited to the Camino Real Hotel to see a documentary about the happenings at the cathedral that was filmed by a television reporter. Unfortunately, the tape is circulating outside the country now, but tomorrow the reporter who filmed it will himself inform us about arranging a showing of this film for us.

These are the most important things that happened on the first Sunday after my return from Rome.

 **Monday, May 14**

I spent the first morning after my return from Rome working in the chancery, and it was a very full morning. With regard to pastoral work, I met with Father Benito Tovar, vicar of the department of La Libertad. He introduced a young man, Astul Guirola, to me. He has already finished his studies in theology—he is from the diocese of Santa Ana—and he will be ordained and possibly work for a time, if he wishes, as a priest in our archdiocese. I wrote a few lines for him in support of the petition he will make to his bishop, Bishop Barrera, for permission. I also greeted the

---

[157] John 15:1-8.

priests who have come to the chancery and nuns also, with whom, I thank God, we share the same pastoral and ecclesial concerns.

The most important events today had to do with political and diplomatic matters, because I received a visit from the Peruvian ambassador, who brought a request from the Venezuelan ambassador who is a prisoner of the Popular Revolutionary Bloc in his own embassy. He asks the Church to mediate. I told him we were willing but told him that it would be necessary for the request also to come from the Bloc, since mediation supposes a request from both sides. Nevertheless, I promised him that I would study the request and asked him, of course, to convey the comfort of the Church to the Venezuelan ambassador and assure him of our desire to do all that we can to help normalize this situation.

There was also a visit from a special envoy from France trying to resolve the occupation of that embassy, where the ambassador and others are being held hostage. I also promised him all our help and asked him to come to a meeting that the vicar general, Monsignor Urioste, and I were having with those in charge of the communications office, Father Rafael Moreno, Father Pedraz and Father Fabián Amaya and the secretary, Father Brito. With all of them and the French envoy we discussed all the ways in which the Church could act effectively in this situation, which also affects it, since the cathedral is occupied by the same Bloc. And we learned this morning that they have also occupied the churches of Suchitoto and Apopa.

In the afternoon, we heard that they had occupied the church at Aguilares too. We came to the conclusion that what was most urgent was to make contact with the leaders of the Bloc, and the French envoy offered to do this through the people occupying his embassy. Once he had arranged for a meeting place at the National University, he would invite the leaders of the Bloc to a meeting which would also be attended by a delegation from the Church, composed of Father Fabián Amaya and Father Brito and doctoral candidate Roberto Cuéllar from the Legal Aid Office.

In the afternoon these three met with the vicar and the secretary of communications so that they would have specific ideas to take to the meeting but, unfortunately, only they and the representatives of the Bloc showed up. The representatives of the Bloc refused to go in unless the representatives of the embassies that are involved, especially the French envoy who had invited them to the meeting, were present also. Therefore, no progress could be made in spite of all the effort that had been made.

We continue to pray and hope because the situation looks like it might get worse. The Popular Revolutionary Bloc has announced a huge demonstration for tomorrow in memory of those murdered on May 8 by the National Police.

And, finally, I went to have dinner with the Oblate Sisters of Divine Love and to give them letters from their motherhouse and convey the personal greetings of the superior general, who was so kind to me during my stay in Rome.

In the evening there was a detail that provided great comfort. The call I made to nurses on Sunday in my homily to celebrate Eucharist with us in the chapel of the Divine Providence Hospital was received with great enthusiasm and the chapel was filled with nurses. Monsignor José López Sandoval, ecclesiastical adviser to the national nurse movement, concelebrated with me. My message to them invited them to see in each patient the double face of Christ: a suffering face, in pain, dying, and the glorified face that is precisely the result of that passion. He learned obedience through his suffering and, because of that, he became the beginning of, the reason for hope in everyone who believes in him.

When the Mass ended, there were very cordial greetings and also a few words from Father López Sandoval, and a good-bye that made us feel the communion the Church creates in our hearts. Many expressed the wish that we could meet with greater frequency.

 **Tuesday, May 15**

In the morning, with a small group of advisers, I analyzed the current situation and what role the Church could take. We wrote down our conclusions in the form of a statement in which we show how different groups may have some of the responsibility for creating this difficult situation.

In the afternoon, there was a press conference in the library at the archdiocese. Many reporters came, maybe around twenty-five or thirty, including foreign and national journalists and television cameras. They were given our statement, which will be communicated to the public through them.

**Wednesday, May 16**

I had breakfast with Monsignor Urioste and Dr. [Fidel] Chávez,[158] who is the unifying force in the dialogue being held between ANEP, the Christian Democrats and the government, in which the Church has also participated. He informed me about the efforts at agreement during the last few months, which have opened a number of channels of hope for mutual understanding—especially in looking for a solution in which there would be more participation of all of the active sectors of the nation in a search for the common good. I wrote immediately afterwards the article I will send to the press. It refers to my return from Rome and to my hope placed in God in spite of what seem to be insurmountable difficulties. After that, I took a few hours to rest at the farm belonging to the Oblate Sisters of Divine Love.

At four p.m. at the chancery, I had a very interesting conversation with the rector of the University of El Salvador and the rector of the Central American University José Simeón Cañas. They were accompanied by high administrators from both universities. Monsignor Urioste and Father Rafael Moreno were with me.

The initiative for the meeting had come from the rector of the University of El Salvador, and he spoke first. He referred to the statements that the two universities and our archdiocese have made with respect to the state of conflict that exists between the government and the Popular Revolutionary Movement, searching for a way they can work together to resolve that conflict. Both of the rectors said that they had a very positive view of the call made by the archbishop for all of the active forces in the country to do their part, to the extent of their abilities and possibilities, to resolve not only the immediate problem, but also to go deeper and look for a solution to the roots of the problems caused by the social injustice in our country.

The conversation went on until very late in the afternoon, and we agreed to encourage the participation of all the sectors to which the archdiocese has appealed. The universities will work primarily in the professional and cultural sectors of the country. In order to facilitate this, there will be a roundtable that will analyze and discuss the archdiocese's statement and there will be programs to look for solutions to our social, political and economic problems.

During this conversation with the rectors, the superior of the Guadalupana Sisters came to notify the archdiocese that two Mexican sisters who work in Arcatao in the department of Chalatenango, had been

[158] A leading Christian Democrat.

taken away by a red car from Immigration to some unknown place. We have tried to investigate to see what this is all about, and not until very late in the evening was the superior able to communicate with the Ministry of the Interior, who told her that Immigration had received many complaints against the sisters and that they had taken them to the frontier with Guatemala.

The Catholic radio station has reported this news along with the protest from the archdiocese calling this a new form of persecution of the Church and a violation of human rights, because no proof is offered of any crime committed that would cause the sisters to be deported in such an unexpected way. The sisters, not just the Guadalupanas but other congregations as well, are notifying their sisters in Guatemala, so that they will look out for the well-being of these sisters who have arrived in another country in such an unforeseen way.

 **Friday, May 18**

The most significant visit this morning was from Spanish television. They talked with me briefly to find out what is going on and what the position of the Church is with regard to this conflict between the popular organization, the Popular Revolutionary Bloc, and the government.

Also there was a visit from CUTS, an organization of labor unions, to express its solidarity with the call the archdiocese has made for talks. It is willing to organize a forum with a roundtable to analyze the situation. An interesting conversation, especially in the way it shows how advanced and sensible in political and social matters our workers are.

Bishop Rivera also came to see me—a pleasant surprise—and we talked about the secret document of denunciation the other four bishops are preparing. In it, they denounce me to the Holy See in matters of faith, say I am politicized, accuse me of promoting a pastoral work with erroneous theological grounding—a whole series of accusations that completely impugn my ministry as a bishop. In spite of how serious this is, I feel great peace. I acknowledge my deficiencies before God, but I believe that I have worked with goodwill and that I am not guilty of the serious things of which they accuse me. God will have the last word on this. I am at peace and hope to continue to work with the same enthusiasm as always, since I serve the Holy Church in love.

In the afternoon I received a visit from the special envoy from France, who is very discouraged because his efforts to free the embassy from the occupation of the Popular Revolutionary Bloc have not been successful. The Bloc insists on the government freeing or giving information on three of their members who were taken, but the government insists that it does not have them. There is a rumor circulating privately that they are already dead. In my call, I have asked the Bloc to end these occupations, since everyone suspects the worst has already happened to the disappeared and that it is enough to have put pressure on the government. Whatever else it does, the Bloc itself is contributing greatly to an unrest in the country that is out of proportion to their objectives.

I said these same things to the envoy and expressed to him the willingness of the Church to do everything it can, but that the only thing it can do now is to join with him in his feeling of impotence in the face of human willfulness. He told me about the bad conditions in which the hostages in the French embassy are living and how they even have to sleep on the floor. They are keeping all of them in the same room. He has managed to improve their human condition a little, but it continues to be a very serious situation, and the crisis has been going on now for two weeks. The Venezuelan embassy is still occupied too, but the occupation began a week later than that of the French embassy. The cathedral, as I pointed out to the ambassador, was occupied on the same date as the French embassy. The cathedral is being used as a center of operations by the Bloc. This doesn't bother me, but I feel a sense of impotence at not being able to rescue it and use it only for worship, as it is intended.

I met with the seminarians of the archdiocesan major seminary. Father Gregorio Rosa, the rector of the seminary, was also present. It was very cordial and frank. I was able to use the discussion and their questions to express my fears of the Church being politicized and to call on them to work together for the unity of the Church, and to shape themselves through their identity as priests, to which their vocation calls them.

It was a meeting that left me very satisfied on seeing the concerns that the young men have and also, as a pastor, on having the opportunity to guide my priests as I would want to. I continued talking afterward with the rector. I took him to dinner and we walked for a while, during which he also talked with me very cordially and more freely—not just in his position of rector reporting on the seminary but as the good friend he has been for a long time.

In the evening, in the Divine Providence Hospital, I met with Dr. [Roberto] Lara Velado, Dr. González, director of the newspaper *La Crónica*, and a group of university law students to plan a roundtable on human rights that the law students are organizing for May 22 at the

National University. I am supposed to speak on human rights from a moral and a theological perspective.

After making plans for the roundtable, we talked for a long time and talked particularly about a call made by the president of the Republic for a national dialogue to involve different sectors in solutions to the problems of the country. Almost everyone was pessimistic about the credibility of an offer of freedom and democratization from the government. At the same time, however, there were some who thought that we should take what is offered in a positive sense and with our goodwill bring forth among all of the different sectors on a national level (organizations, professionals, etc.), the enlightenment and strength that the country is asking of all of us.

 ### Saturday, May 19

From early morning until about three p.m., I went to visit a small town in Colón parish, a picturesque place on the slope of the volcano of San Salvador, where Father Nicolás, parish priest of Colón, and the Sisters of the Sacred Heart had prepared a group of children and young people to receive Confirmation. When I got there, the atmosphere seemed to be rather cold, and I never managed to reach a warmer level of contact with those people, who seem to be very repressed. It appears that their situation of having to work at a hacienda[159] causes them to depend totally on the administrator. This seems to me to be rather despotic. I recommended to Father Nicolás that he visit these people frequently and encourage them, and to be careful not to be identified with the owners of the hacienda.

I was sad about this when I returned, and also had decided that I would never again agree to participate in a celebration on a hacienda or ranch, and was even more determined not to accept the landowners' generosity to me while they keep the people who work for them in this marginalized state.

At dinner we had a meeting of the information team to prepare the report that I give weekly in the homily. There was some controversy over my commentary on the president's speech, because I have to manage to show the Church's goodwill in spite of our skepticism about some of the promises, which will need to be proved by subsequent events. We cannot simply believe the president's promises, as the people in general do not believe them, when they were made in an atmosphere in which lies,

---

[159] A large estate.

distortion and deception have predominated. I asked for the opinions of everyone at the meeting and, with the help of the Holy Spirit, I will prepare the statement that will be my responsibility to give in the Sunday homily.

Later in the evening, a visit from some journalists, from seven to nine, and at nearly ten p.m., I had an interview for French television, Guatemalan television and a journalist or reporter from a German magazine.

Mother Juanita also came to tell me about an attempt to set fire to the convent at Tamanique. She was not able to give me any details except that gasoline had been poured on the doors and a fire had been started, but, thank God, it was controlled in time.

 **Sunday, May 20**

Since the cathedral was still occupied by the Popular Revolutionary Bloc, I again had to ask for the hospitality of El Rosario Church in order to celebrate my Mass at eight a.m., which, praise God, was very well attended. The singing of the minor seminary from Chalatenango inspired the crowd, who all participated. There was a great deal of participation in the Mass.

The homily was on the theme of how Easter gives us the gift of love, since all the readings tell us about the God who is love and about the new commandment Christ gave, to love one another as he loved us. This leads to a new definition of the Church as an institution designed to construct a community based on love. This is what distinguishes it from any other group and movement of political, social, earthly character. I defined, once again, the autonomous position of the Church, which does not identify itself with any system or movement or political group.

After Mass the journalists and television reporters, who were very busy during the Mass, asked me to meet with the press, and I agreed with pleasure. Among the journalists, I remember a reporter from *Le Monde* in Paris and two Venezuelan television channels. Afterward, I went with my family to Apopa for a few restful hours that were very nice.

In the evening I had dinner with the Oblate Sisters of Divine Love in a very cordial atmosphere. And when I got back to my residence, they told me that the Venezuelan ambassador had managed to escape from the embassy held by the Popular Revolutionary Bloc, and that he has taken refuge in the nunciature. I spoke with the chancellor, Father Brito, and asked him to go in my name to see what the ambassador needs and to let me know if I need to go in person.

**Monday, May 21**

Stopping briefly at the chancery, I met with some priests, nuns and laity and, in particular, with the Caritas group from Aguilares, who were concerned about how to get foodstuffs to distribute in that region since the stores are in the cathedral, which is occupied. My response was that we should wait because it would be risky at this time to try to get anything out of the occupied cathedral.

After this brief stop at the chancery, I went to Chalatenango. I had been invited by the episcopal vicar, Father Fabián Amaya, to meet with the sisters who do pastoral work in that department. The purpose was to express our solidarity with the Guadalupana Sisters, who are suffering the temporary exile of the two sisters in Arcatao who were taken to Guatemala. They should return today or tomorrow and, meanwhile, this meeting was held to evaluate the sisters' work, based on the complicated political reality that we are living in our country.

This afternoon, when the plane arrived from Guatemala, the Guadalupana Sisters were not on it as we had expected. We will wait and see tomorrow.

Tonight Father Gregorio Rosa was with me, and we talked a great deal about the accusations in the document prepared by the other bishops and about the reality of our archdiocese. Father Goyo [Gregorio] thinks it is a moment of truth and that we have to use it as an opportunity to reaffirm the position of the Church and remove all the obstacles that keep us from doing a more authentic pastoral work. There is some truth in their accusations, and it is necessary to correct the mistakes, but there is also a great deal of exaggeration and it is almost calumnious.

We are not going to answer it, except through our actions as we continue the pastoral work of our archdiocese.

 **Tuesday, May 22**

Father Chus Delgado came to have breakfast with me and brought me up to date on the progress of the talks with ANEP, the Christian Democrats and the government. According to Father Chus, it seems that there has been no great progress because there is insincerity and each group is protecting its own interests. At any rate, I told him that I thought that we should continue to be present so as to not give the impression of bad faith on the Church's part.

I did not go to the chancery because I decided to spend the time preparing my presentation to be given at the University this afternoon. At five p.m., there was a roundtable at the National University that I took part in, along with Dr. González, the director of *La Crónica del Pueblo*, a worker and a peasant. We talked about human rights. My part was the theological and moral aspect. The Law School hall was so completely full that even the hallways were filled. My arrival was greeted very warmly. I thank God for the opportunity to take a message in his name to such a crowd.

At the end, an announcement was made to the crowd that, at that very moment, there was a new massacre taking place at the Venezuelan embassy. The hostages—that is, the ambassador and other employees of the embassy—were already out and a demonstration organized by the Bloc was heading there to incorporate those who were still inside.[160] And the security forces opened fire on them. They have announced there are at least six dead and many wounded.

There were several journalists and also television reporters at the roundtable. A Mexican reporter followed me to the Divine Providence Hospital to interview me for the newspaper *Uno más Uno* in Mexico.

The Sisters of the Sacred Heart came to ask what they could do to help after the massacre at the Venezuelan embassy, which is very near the Colegio Sagrado Corazón. We asked the Red Cross for information and offered it our services, but they said at the Red Cross that even they had not been able to get in there because the security forces would not admit them.

They notified me from the Colegio Guadalupano that the two sisters who had been taken to Guatemala have returned. Both of them talked to me on the telephone, very moved and very happy to be back in the country. I promised them I would have lunch with them tomorrow.

 **Wednesday, May 23**

I had breakfast with the usual advisory group of priests and laity. The principal topic was to evaluate the dialogue being held by ANEP and the Christian Democrats, to which the Church had been invited. Lately, a representative of the government has been attending also. The question is whether it is worthwhile to keep going, if there is any benefit to be gained. We decided that it is always useful to participate and

---

[160] They would mix with the crowd and leave safely.

to use any opportunity in which the Church can provide insight and guidance in our situation.

Another topic was the National Forum that has been called for by the president. The general feeling was that we must wait for it to have more credibility so that we do not let ourselves be manipulated by political interests.

And a third point was the relationship between the Church and the Popular Revolutionary Bloc which, in this recent conflict with the government, has shown little consideration for the Church; it has seized churches and made declarations against the archbishop. The thought was that we do not want to break off relations now even though it is a difficult moment in their defense of the people's rights, and that we will have to wait to decide about our relationship with them which has always been that of two autonomous realities: the Church and the Bloc.

Dr. Guillermo Ungo[161] and a member of the Christian Democratic Party came about the National Forum called for by the president. They wanted to talk with the Church to agree together on whether or not to participate in this National Forum. Although I thanked them and expressed our goodwill, I made it clear that we cannot have any kind of a joint position that would make it seem as if the Church were associated with any political party. While I was meeting with them, we got the tragic news of the murder of Dr. Rebollo, Minister of Education. It appears to have been in retaliation for the murder of the fourteen demonstrators killed by the police and the National Guard near the Venezuelan embassy yesterday.

I was interviewed by a Spanish journalist who expressed to me his opinion of and sorrow about the condition of our press. For he was a witness yesterday to what happened near the Venezuelan embassy and had read today the information given the press by the government and business sectors.

I went to have lunch at the Colegio Guadalupano to talk with the two sisters who have returned from Guatemala, where they had been taken by the immigration authorities. Thanks be to God, they have managed to survive this moment of calumny and attack and are willing to go back and work in that remote village in Chalatenango with the same love as before.

In the afternoon with Father Moreno I prepared a statement about the death of the demonstrators and the murder of Dr. Rebollo. I expressed my solidarity with the suffering of all the many families, said I was praying for those killed, and I called on both sides, the government and the Bloc, not to be willful in this conflict. And I called on those who can to intercede so that

---

[161] Vice-presidential candidate with Duarte in 1972, later president of the Democratic Revolutionary Front (FDR).

this is resolved soon, since it is costing so many lives and so much discomfort to our people.

All day long there has been a meeting of ministers at the Presidential Palace because of the seriousness of the situation and also a meeting of the National Assembly, and the result has been a decree of a state of siege [martial law] for thirty days.

Monsignor Urioste and I prepared the dialogue for the radio, and this time we commented on this situation of conflict between the government and the Popular Revolutionary Bloc. We expressed the Church's ideas on this, which I have already explained. We called on both sides to return to a peaceful state soon. I also spoke about the roundtable at the University and the Day of the Seminary and the Confirmations of young people that will take place on Pentecost, June 3. I ended by reading my statement on the tragic events of yesterday and today.

 **Thursday, May 24**

Today passed in an atmosphere of nervousness because of the violent situation in the country, plus now martial law. Nevertheless, we must bury today the bodies of the fourteen riddled with bullets by the police and National Guard at the Venezuelan embassy, as well as the Minister of Education, Dr. Carlos Herrera Rebollo. The funeral at the cathedral was not for all fourteen, since seven of the bodies had been taken by the families.

Seven bodies were on display in the cathedral last night, and this morning they were buried, accompanied by a crowd calculated to be some seven to ten thousand people. The people who had been occupying the cathedral took the opportunity to mix with the crowd and leave too, thus ending the occupation of the cathedral after three weeks. Thanks be to God, there were no unfortunate incidents with all the movement surrounding the burial of yesterday's victims.

Dr. Rebollo's funeral was in the afternoon. His body was laid out in a community center. He was a simple man. He loved the people a great deal and because of that wanted the company of the poor in his last moments.

Today's newspapers carried my call for an effort to end this conflict. I said that this is not a time to try to show who is the strongest, who can win, but rather who is more humane and is willing to yield and forgive so that we do not have to continue to mourn tragedies in different sectors of the country.

I met with four seminarians from the major seminary who took part in the May 1 demonstration. They justify their participation as an act of solidarity with the peasants and workers, the class of humanity to which they themselves belong. Frankly, I do not believe that they have done anything wrong. I only pointed out to them that, given the situation in the country and especially that of the Church, the seminary and the archdiocese, that it would be wise for them always to ask for the advice of someone who can guide them well. I especially asked them always to maintain their communication with their bishop. I tried to understand their concerns and not take away from the nobility of their motives. But I also called on them to be sure to express them in such a way that they will provide an effective witness that serves the just claims of the people. As priests—or as those called to the priesthood—they cannot be involved except in a fully evangelical sense.

Tonight there was new violence. It was in the San José de la Montaña area and the parish priest, Father Víctor Guevara, has been surrounded by a cordon of the police who patrol that area. And also Father Pedraz, the head of the radio, was stopped and they made him get out of his car when he was on his way to the Divine Providence Hospital; he was ordered to go back to his residence. It appears that the reason for all the vigilance in that zone is that there have been attempts by the Bloc to occupy the Mexican embassy, which, along with the Panamanian embassy, was the next occupation planned. But the security forces have prevented it.

At an accounting office near Plaza Libertad, Contador[162] Montoya—I cannot remember his first name—was murdered when he left his office. He is someone who has worked with our cooperatives on the financial records of the construction of the cathedral and in the Interdiocesan Social Secretariat.[163] We do not know who killed him or why he was killed.

On a different note, the feast of María Auxiliadora was celebrated with great fervor today, May 24. The celebration was held primarily at the church which bears her name, directed by the Salesian Fathers, and in the schools and other institutions run by the sons of Don Bosco.[164]

---

[162] Accountant.

[163] An office dealing with social concerns serving all the dioceses directed by Father Juan Ramón Vega.

[164] St. John Bosco, founder of the Salesians.

**Friday, May 25**

The whole morning was spent in a Senate meeting trying to assess the situation of the diocese within the very complicated picture of the country as a whole. We talked about our relationship to organized groups and with the government, especially in an attempt to draw conclusions as to what our priestly and ecclesial attitude should be. We also planned the next meeting of the clergy along the same lines. It will be organized so that, first, there will be a presentation of the events that have so shaken up the country during the month of May; then, the Church's attitude. And then each priest will be asked to express his feelings, his thoughts and his opinions, freely and with total frankness, on the attitude of the priests and of the Church in general. All of this will be looked at in light of the Church documents, and we will end with a summary of practical conclusions that are the product of all the reflection, to be presented by the archbishop. I was very pleased with the sincerity and interest in being sure that we are acting truly as the Church to avoid confusion and ambiguity in a climate as critical as the one in which we are living.

The Senate also reviewed its rules and proposed some amendments that will be taken to the clergy for their opinions. It also heard about a document that Bishop Alvarez read in a meeting of the clergy in his diocese in San Miguel, which denounces the attitude of the archbishop and of the archdiocese. I told them that, as far as I was concerned, we should use this criticism as an opportunity to review our actions sincerely and with humility.

In the afternoon, I received a visit from the rector of the Central American University (José Simeón Cañas), who expressed, with a sincere feeling of love for this country, his worry about the decision that the universities not participate in the forum called for by the president of the republic, since the necessary climate of confidence and credibility does not exist. Because of that, they believe that by attending they would somehow be legitimizing attitudes that have caused so much suffering in the country. And that it would be, in a way, support for these injustices and also the pretense of democratic ideals, but would actually deny the liberty necessary for a true democracy.

I told him that there are absences that are painful but necessary, and that not participating in the forum under the circumstances did not reflect a lack of goodwill on the part of people who sincerely want to work; rather it is a request for an appropriate atmosphere in which to cooperate willingly.

I also received a visit from the Panamanian chargé d'affaires to ask me to intercede with the negotiating committee of the Popular Revolutionary

Bloc and offer, on behalf of his government, asylum to those who have occupied the Venezuelan and French embassies, telling them that arrangements have already been made with the chancery of El Salvador so that they can leave for Panamá. Since the members of the Bloc carrying out the occupations are refusing this offer of asylum, they want me to try to convince them for their own good since, if they do not accept asylum in Panamá, they will be tried for the crimes of occupation and taking of hostages in both the embassies they have occupied. Until very late at night, I have searched for ways to get this letter from the Panamanian embassy to the negotiating committee for the Bloc, but I have been unable to find the necessary contact. And so I will leave it for tomorrow morning, God willing.

 ### Saturday, May 26

In the Somascan Sisters' school I had a meeting with my advisers on communications for them to report to me and help me, with their different perspectives, to prepare the part of my homily in which I give this information. This study that we do every week is very interesting because it gives us the pulse of the reality of the country.

This time we mostly analyzed the continuing violence, which has left many dead and wounded, the occupations of the Venezuelan and French embassies, the declaration of martial law on May 24 and the National Forum that the president of the republic has called for and to which many have responded with skepticism and decided not to participate. As regards the Church, the bishops' conference was invited and has chosen as its representatives Bishop Revelo and Monsignor Fredy Delgado.

I said that I did not oppose such dialogue, but that I would want to see a confidence based on actions showing that the government had decided to respect again the precepts of the constitution that it is violating and that, without that, its desire to have dialogue is not credible. I suggested to the conference that, rather than bishops going, we send others to represent us.

Afterward, I was interviewed by a reporter from the Mexican newspaper *Uno más Uno*, who is frightened by the situation in El Salvador. I also had a meeting with the Guadalupana Sisters, the superior at the school and the two sisters who had been deported to Guatemala and then allowed to return. The minister has said that, in his view, their work is not of a religious nature. The sisters asked for concrete examples and proof and none was offered. Father Fabián Amaya and I listened to what they had to say and we encouraged them to continue with their work, always basing it on truth and the true evangelization, because they are doing a great deal of good in the remote village of Arcatao. But we told them that during the period of martial law they should avoid any action that could provoke an unfortunate reaction on the part of the government.

Father Brito and Bachiller Cuéllar managed to deliver the note from the Panamanian embassy offering asylum to those occupying the Venezuelan and French embassies. They promised, according to what Father Brito told me, to think about the matter.

 ## Sunday, May 27

I thank God that the cathedral has been evacuated and we were able to have our eight a.m. Eucharist there. But, unfortunately, they had not been able to repair radio YSAX yet, and we were unable to broadcast the Mass. The number of questions we have received about it shows that many people listen to it. Today was Ascension Sunday[165] and I preached on transcendence, how our mission and our vocation as a Church and as Christians is always to work in this world but with the intention of transcendence. There were many journalists at the Mass and they also took pictures for television. I did not recognize all of them, but it seemed to me that some were from Europe and Mexico and from other places as well.

The Panamanian chargé asked the Church for its cooperation, since a special delegation has arrived from Panamá, in arranging asylum for those who were occupying the Venezuelan and French embassies. I asked Father Brito to be in charge of this service.

In the evening, an interview with a reporter from the United Press.[166] We talked about the Church and the country.

---

[165] The celebration of Ascension Thursday is moved to the following Sunday in some countries.

[166] The wire service United Press International (UPI).

## Monday, May 28

Today I finished polishing the letter that I will send to Cardinal Baggio with a copy to the [Vatican] Secretary of State about Bishop Quarracino's suggestion that an apostolic administrator *sede plena* be named. I said in the letter that it seems to me that this solution would not only be an ineffective one but also very harmful to the archdiocese, because it would cause a complete break and would give the archdiocesan community a double situation to deal with. The problem is not just to resolve the personal conflicts. The voice of the archbishop, which must speak for all the people of God, would lose much of its effectiveness if an apostolic administrator were to be named. It would be clear that such an action would express a lack of confidence in the bishop. I have suggested, as a solution that would resolve the deeper problems, the naming of some new bishops, with the criteria of Vatican II, in order to inject new pastoral criteria into the Bishops' Conference and thus avoiding a split that should not occur, since it would be in violation of the Council's principles.

I was visited by three representatives of French organizations that work for human rights, who have come with the purpose of investigating the human rights situation in our country.

I had lunch with Fathers Ellacuría and Sobrino to talk with them about my project for a pastoral letter on the situation of the country and the mission of the Church, which I hope to publish by this coming August 6. We will meet again in a week to concretize the outline that we hope to have prepared by then.

I went to the communications office to investigate the situation of the work at the radio, which is still not back on the air. Many people are waiting anxiously for this situation to be resolved. It appears that we lack some part that has to be brought from the United States and they expect will arrive at any moment. But I asked the priest in charge to hurry it up and, if necessary, for someone to go personally to the United States to get the parts.

I also learned that a young man who works at Criterio Press, which produces our weekly paper *Orientación*, had been arrested and tortured and, that when he was being interrogated, they asked him many questions that show the attitude of persecution that the government has toward our communications media.

In the evening I wanted to go to the ultreya of the Cursillos de Cristiandad, but, there was....[167]

---

[167] Tape ends here.

## Tuesday, May 29

At breakfast I had an interesting conversation with Father César Jerez, the Jesuit provincial,[168] who had just returned from a trip to South America. He told me about the interest there in following the pastoral orientation of our archdiocese and how there are echoes of our episcopal teaching. It was very interesting to hear the impressions of a Church and episcopal conference as powerful as that of Brazil; comparatively, we are very small. It is spiritually filling to see the Church decide to identify with the people and to confront—or be forced to confront—governments that do not understand the people. The necessity of choosing, as Puebla advised, the option for the poor is a recognized fact and is gaining ground in a Church that is trying truly to be the Church of Jesus Christ.

The whole morning was dedicated to a meeting of the newly formed Pastoral Council. It was very comforting to recognize and analyze the deficiencies we still have and then, with great enthusiasm, propose ways to make this Council's work a true force for coordinating the pastoral work, for guiding the pastoral work of the entire archdiocese.

During the meeting, I had to leave for a while to attend to a seminarian from Chalatenango and, of particular importance, to an employee of the press who had been tortured and asked some very malicious questions about the archdiocese. And also with Father Martel from Apopa, who gave me a negative report on a young man we have been watching to see if he truly has a vocation. From this conversation, it seems, unfortunately, that we must for now give up hope of his proceeding with his studies at the seminary.

In the afternoon, I was interviewed by a reporter from the United Press and another who writes for several magazines in South America and the United States. All the reporters want to know what the Church thinks and what its relationship to the government is. And I always try to be very clear and very sincere. And I also denounce the manipulation of the press I sometimes see occurring in this atmosphere.

I have continued polishing the letter to the Congregation for Bishops that I will soon send with my response to the proposal that an apostolic administrator *sede plena* be appointed, and about possible ways to resolve our ecclesial conflicts.

---

[168] The head of a religious order in a particular region.

**Wednesday, May 30**

Again it was a very intense day. We awoke to the news of the murder of a business representative with the rank of ambassador of Switzerland in Paseo Escalón in Plaza Alegre. He was attacked as he headed toward the embassy and killed by a burst of machine-gun fire.

The secretary of the nunciature wanted to talk to me. I promised him I would come to the nunciature because it would be calmer there, but I could not get there because that area, near where the murder had taken place, was blocked off by police barricades. The secretary of the nunciature came to the chancery to tell me confidentially that France has asked the Holy See to intervene to resolve the problem of their embassy in El Salvador, occupied by the Popular Revolutionary Bloc. There the ambassador and others who are held hostage are in a precarious state because of the inhuman conditions in which they are being held, and this has been going on for over twenty-five days. He made some suggestions to me. I appreciated his suggestions and will take them and use them, in a pastoral sense, to talk about the crime that has just been committed and other attacks on the liberty and dignity of ambassadors and other citizens of foreign nations.

A delegation of two French lawyers came to the archdiocese, and also Maurice Barth. They came in the name of several different French organizations to show their solidarity with our Church and to collect data on our situation. We talked extensively, and their good understanding of our situation is a source of strength for me. I also expressed my gratitude to them and asked them not to abandon us, but always to give us the same moral support as today.

In the afternoon, a meeting with those in charge of communications and Father Pedraz, head of the radio, to study the situation of our radio station. In regard to the technical aspect, we expect to have the problem that still is keeping it off the air resolved soon. Rather, we were analyzing ideological aspects and decided to form a committee composed of Father Pedraz, Father Fabián Amaya, Miss Doris Osegueda and Fathers José Luis Bourguet and Gregorio Rosa to be responsible for the content of our broadcasts. All of them were present at the meeting.

I also used the opportunity to ask their advice on the statement the nunciature had suggested and that I would like to make it into a pastoral statement. They gave me some ideas, and Father Gregorio will help me to finish drafting the document. Because of this, after dinner he came to the Divine Providence Hospital and we worked there until very late at night. As a result, I had to decline the invitation I had received from the *cursillistas de Cristiandad* to have dinner with them, an event I would also have used to talk about some aspects of the lay pastoral work. But I asked them to pardon me and promised we would get together very soon.

 **Thursday, May 31**

Father Gregorio Rosa and I continued our work as soon as we woke up. After a night's rest our minds were fresher, and we were able to finish it by about ten a.m.

I invited the secretary of the nunciature and the people in charge of the French embassy to see what we had written. The secretary of the nunciature made various comments and made me think that the French would not be very happy with it because it did not give the problem of the French embassy a prominent enough place. I cautioned him that it was a pastoral declaration and could not limit itself to the situation of the French diplomats, but must also refer to the situation of the Swiss ambassador who had been murdered and touch on all the events affecting foreign diplomats and citizens of foreign countries, to which the Church also has a pastoral responsibility.

After some observations made privately with the secretary of the nunciature, the two French envoys arrived and I let them read the draft of my statement. They expressed their complete agreement; they only asked me if I could stress that the ambassador and the others, among them an elderly lady seventy years old, had been held hostage now for more than twenty-eight days in inhuman physical and hygienic conditions.

I made this change gladly and then released the statement publicly, with the rest just as we had written it. I did add one further comment suggested by the secretary of the nunciature about the request by the government to intercede in the situation at the French embassy, but always with absolute respect for the lives of the people involved in this occupation.

The initial reactions to my statement that have begun to circulate this afternoon were very positive.

In the afternoon, I had a welcome change in my pastoral work, for I had accepted Father Cayo Ayala's invitation to celebrate in San José Villanueva, the town he was born in, the sixtieth wedding anniversary of his parents, Don Francisco Ayala and Doña Herminia. It coincided with the end of the month of May, and the May flowers were arriving at that little village church from the different parts of that parish, where the Passionist Sisters work. It made a lovely combination for a pastoral afternoon to talk about the Virgin Mary, about the sanctity of marriage and faithfulness, about the gift of life and the blessing of children—themes appropriate to that simple atmosphere. There were also many schoolchildren, for they had brought the entire school. A talk in simple pastoral language and a parting greeting, when I left shaking hands with everyone, leave in me the peacefulness of being rooted in and loved by a people who know how to return that love.

# June, 1979

 **Friday, June 1**

In the chancery I shared a cup of coffee with Fathers George, Trinidad Nieto and with Modesto Villarán from Soyapango, with whom I talked at greatest length, since he had been attacked in the newspapers yesterday. He was presented as if the people of Soyapango were asking for him to be transferred, saying he was a priest who had offended the people who have the market around the church—all of which is completely false, knowing him and the regard they have for him in the town. I encouraged him to continue his efforts. He is also very enthusiastic, for these lies serve more than anything else to animate the pastors.

I told him how, on my side as well, I had received telephone calls, threatening me with death and a card with the swastika of the UGB, the White Warrior Union,[169] ordering me to change the way I preach, telling me I must condemn communism, that I must praise the members of the security forces who have been killed, etc., and that if I do not do what they say, they will kill me. I understand these to be psychological threats, attempts to silence a voice that in good conscience cannot be silent but must bring light amid so much confusion and so many spurious interests.

At ten o'clock in the morning, we expected a visit from the ambassador of the United States.[170] He came accompanied by the new secretary of the embassy, with the political affairs officer and the representative for

---

[169] *Unión Guerrera Blanca*, a rightist terrorist group.
[170] Frank J. Devine.

international aid for Latin America. He respectfully expressed his admiration for our Church and touched on several topics in which the relationship of the United States embassy to the archdiocese could produce great good for our country.

There was also a delegation of medical students. Two young men who are very dedicated to their profession, very close to graduation, expressed to me their surprise at the amount of power that the medical profession has in the clinics with regard to the origin of life. So many mutilations! So many sterilizations of men and women, carried out with such ease and on such a massive scale! I was particularly moved by the expression of one of these young men when he said to me: "The fruitfulness of our people is being castrated and we must do something."

They suggested holding a roundtable on this topic at the university and that I take part in it. I accepted with pleasure, congratulated them and asked God that they may always have minds as pure as they do now so that they will be doctors who defend life, not destroyers of humankind. We agreed that on June 11, close to Medical Students' Day, we will hold this forum with other representatives of the medical profession and some economists to study this violation of the fundamental right to life.

I also was visited by two workers who came to invite me to come or to send a representative to a meeting on unifying workers' goals that will take place tomorrow. I agreed with pleasure at least to send a representative, since my time is already committed to a meeting with some women religious.

Also there was a visit from a Japanese journalist. I had to use an interpreter as he does not speak Spanish and I do not speak English. This interview also had to do with clarifying the archdiocese's position with regard to the current political situation of the country.

In the afternoon, a telephone interview with a journalist from Colombia about the occupation of the cathedral by members of FAPU, who are holding it again since the day before yesterday but who have promised to leave there tomorrow, that is, Saturday. I talked about this with Father Moreno and with Ingeniero Ricardo Navarro of the Commission on Human Rights in El Salvador, who came to visit me in the name of FAPU in order to explain to me the reason for the occupation: to draw attention in protest against the violent death of one of the women in the group. I took the opportunity to ask him to intercede with FAPU so that they would leave the cathedral free for us by Sunday. He said that there was no bad feeling toward the Church, but rather they were only using this as a way to make themselves heard and they asked me to forgive them.

Since today was the first of the month, we held the celebration of the Holy Hour that, thank God, is regaining its importance, as shown by the number of people attending and even more by the quality of the prayers on behalf of the many needs of the Church and of the country.

My brother Gaspar, who holds an important post in ANTEL, has been unexpectedly demoted. Without a doubt, this is revenge on the government's part because he is a relative of mine. I am sorry that my family is suffering as a result of the prophetic task I must carry out. I have tried to raise his spirits and to tell him that, whatever the situation, we must always keep our hope strong and also be firm in our struggle for justice for our people, although it is difficult for people with little religious and Christian formation to understand the role of the Church in the present day—a very difficult role if one wants to be faithful to the gospel.

 ### Saturday, June 2

At the advisory breakfast on the homily, we spent a long time discussing the topic of faith and politics—the need for a specific pastoral work to cultivate the political concerns of the most active Christians— principles and ideas that cannot be dealt with in a massive pastoral effort. Meanwhile, we must do what we can so that those who have become involved in popular political organizations do not lose the faith that perhaps inspired their political commitment in the first place. For lack of an adequate follow-up by the Church, they could lose that faith and follow the wrong path.

At nine o'clock we had a meeting with the superiors of the women religious to analyze the case of the sisters expelled from Arcatao—an expulsion rectified by the government itself, which has declared that the sisters may return, although they are waiting for the permission of their superior general. The account of one of the sisters was very moving, especially because of her desire to continue her work in that area, to which she feels extremely committed. She believes that her absence will be harmful and will retard the progress that has been made through their reflections. The sisters of the other congregations expressed their solidarity with these exemplary sisters. I urged them to frequent evaluation and reflection of this kind, which allow them to identify more closely with the pastoral work of the archdiocese, which does not try to impose its will but rather to engage in dialogue so that we may walk together in great conviction on the path the Lord wants us to take.

I had lunch with the Oblate Sisters of Divine Love since, sadly, they are saying farewell to their present superior, Mother Carmen María Scaglietti, who has decided to leave the religious life and return to Costa Rica, where she is from. I could see that all the sisters were upset and I tried to encourage them in an ecclesial spirit. And Mother Carmen as well, so that even though she will no longer be a sister, she may still be a faithful servant of the Church.

### Sunday, June 3

Because Radio YSAX is not operating, more people come to the cathedral for the eight o'clock Mass. Also, there was a group of young people and children who were to be confirmed on this Pentecost Day, along with their family members, godparents and communities, which made this a very solemn Mass.

A team from the BBC of London was there to film parts of the liturgy for British radio and television. They filmed throughout the Mass and after it ended, when they asked my ideas about how to find a peaceful solution to the situation in the country and my thoughts regarding violent solutions. My responses were what I have always preached: that the best solution is a return to love and a sincere desire to achieve dialogue; that this requires that a level of trust be first established so that the people can freely express their opinions; and that all groups must be included in any dialogue designed to arrive at a solution. In regard to violence, I explained the principles already written in my pastoral letter.

### Monday, June 4

After Mass, two representatives of FAPU were waiting for me in the Divine Providence Hospital to propose a meeting and ask me to set a date. I told them I would have to consult with some other people first, which I did during the day. I suggested the following Thursday at six o'clock in the evening.

Also, a representative of FENASTRAS[171] came to ask me to celebrate a Mass for the young woman gunned down in La Reubicación, in Chalatenango. She suggested the following Wednesday at noon in the

---

[171] *Federacion Nacional Sindical de Trabajadores Salvadoreños*, National Labor Federation of Salvadoran Workers.

cathedral for the Mass. I told her that I had already been asked to celebrate a Mass for the young woman and that it would be held in the chapel at the Divine Providence Hospital. She was not happy with this because, she said, it needed to be more public in order to denounce the crime that had been committed. I told her that the principal purpose of the Mass was to pray for the person who had died and that the Church had already made very clear statements denouncing what had happened.

In the morning, I attended the meeting of the parish priests of the Vicariate of La Asunción, in Flor Blanca. I explained to them my idea of setting up pastoral work in the metropolitan area and asked for their cooperation, since they are established in the heart of the city, in the most conspicuous part. It was very pleasing to hear a positive response to the idea of a better service in the capital city. I also presented to them the problem of the parish priest of San José de la Montaña, who is planning to leave the country. And I used this occasion to ask the vicariate for a nomination that will give San José the same spirit as the rest of the parishes in the vicariate. They suggested either Father Carlos Mejía, current priest of the parish of la Asunción, or Father Ernesto Abrego, parish priest of San Benito.

An important reason for attending this meeting was to encourage them, because I have had reports that some of them have suffered a certain erosion of spirit. I told them I am pleased with the way they have organized their work and with the sense of teamwork they have brought to all their pastoral labors. I congratulated them on this and encouraged them to press forward.

In the chancery I was visited by Father Jorge Benavides, parish priest of Suchitoto, who told me of some interesting problems relating to political division and about other aspects of that interesting town. Father Cazares from Tonacatepeque and Father Julio Orellana from Cuscatancingo were also present.

In the afternoon I celebrated another Mass in the chapel at the hospital, this one for the soul of Professor P. Ramos, who was killed April 24 after being tortured. His wife, his three children and his mother were there, as were other members of the family and a number of teachers from different schools. The sermon was based on a text from St. Paul: Because of a man death came into the world.[172] I said that our situation as a whole shows the victory of sin, sin that expresses itself most clearly in the death of others, in the killing of others, but that Christ was the beginning of a justice in which we are to base all our just demands without needing to resort to violence and hatred.

---

[172] See Romans 5:12-14.

A journalist from San Juan, Puerto Rico, came to see me. He had some difficulty speaking Spanish, as his language is English. We managed to understand one another and had an interesting discussion about the situation of our country. When he left, he praised me greatly and said that it had been a significant experience for him to speak with me. I thank the Lord for giving me the personal character not to want to indulge my vanity but, rather, to channel it to the Church as best I can.

In the chancery, a great deal of material has been prepared for the clergy meeting that will be held tomorrow, God willing.

 **Tuesday, June 5**

I spent this morning at the monthly meeting of the Priests' Senate. Many priests attended from all the vicariates, and also the women religious who work directly in the archdiocesan pastoral effort in the towns. Father Fabián Amaya chaired the meeting; Fathers Benito Tovar and Trinidad Nieto had planned it. The intent was to analyze the events during the month of May, which were so serious, so bloody, so complicated. After a summary of the events, prepared by the media office and read by Father Nieto, Father Jesús Delgado spoke about *Evangelii Nuntiandi*[173] and about my second pastoral letter, about the principles in which we can find criteria and insight that will help us illuminate and reflect on the reality.

Afterward, this information and insight was amplified by some contributions in the plenary so that, after a break for refreshments, they could divide into groups and then return again to the plenary. There they made some interesting observations and suggestions for a pastoral work that would define us more clearly as a Church and allow us to distinguish easily among the different political tendencies and demands for justice existing in today's climate. Thus identified, we can be what Christ wanted when he put his Church, guided by his word, at the service of the world.

The last presentation was mine. I congratulated them for the richness of the thought they had contributed. And I tried to encourage them to continue in this kind of reflection and to summarize, in the form of a motto, all of this in the words "Clarification, identity of the church, priestly unity—in order to present the ministry of our clergy as the nucleus and the focus for all the activities of the Church—and discernment" (so that the

---

[173] "Evangelization in The Modern World," Apostolic Exhortation of Pope Paul VI, 1975.

Holy Spirit may enable us not to let the Church become confused by other tendencies, to be truly Church and to understand everything and everyone else from our own identity). I felt great cordiality and much enthusiasm at the meeting. I have the impression that our clergy is maturing and is ever more in solidarity with the pastoral ideal of the archdiocese.

 ### Wednesday, June 6

In the morning, a meeting with reporters. A newspaper that is committed to denouncing abuses of and attacks against human rights has been traveling around El Salvador and has collected many facts. It asked for the information the Church has and the criteria it uses, which are well known.

A meeting of the women religious involved in pastoral work was very lively. Father Chus Delgado presented a panoramic view of the real situation of El Salvador. Although it seemed to be somewhat one-sided and politicized, it still gave us a basis for focusing in a pastoral way on the task of building a Church that is authentic, able to dialogue and to save what God has entrusted to us. Almost all of the women religious were present. They were also especially interested in the case of the sisters in Arcatao who had been expelled and then had returned to their work.

In the afternoon, I celebrated Mass for Mercedes Recinos. She was a working woman shot during the current repression because she was a union leader; she was killed in her own house, in La Reubicación, in Chalatenango. In addition to her family, the Mass was attended by many of her fellow workers, by FAPU, a popular political organization that includes several groups of workers. I used my homily to support the justice of their meetings and of their demands as workers, but directing them to a more transcendent cause toward which the departed Mercedes now points us, for dying for a cause on earth has complete meaning only when we have not lost sight of eternity. And I said that a Christian ought to have, in order to become part of the redemption of Christ, all the redemptions those groups work for. Afterward some interpreted this to mean that I was opposed to organizations and that I only wanted "good Christians." I told them, "Now you see how difficult it is to make yourself understood and, therefore, how easy it is for the Church to be criticized unjustly."

In the evening, I met with the ladies who make up the archdiocesan council of Caritas so that they could express freely and frankly any anomalies and shortcomings they see in the office staff and in the advice given by Father Rutilio Sánchez as the representative of the Church. They were very frank. I agreed to meet with the director and with Father Sánchez, along with a representative of the archdiocesan council, in an attempt to guide them and correct any shortcomings so that Caritas may be what it always should be: a school that serves to promote charity and love, not only using the programs already in existence, but also providing an example for the charitable work of the Church.

 **Thursday, June 7**

Again a journalist, this time Jennie Traf, is interested in learning the thoughts of the archbishop directly and in hearing about the pastoral direction of the archdiocese. I also gave direction to a Belgian nun who works in Cojutepeque, who will help me to organize the archdiocesan Pastoral Office and the periodical archives.

With the Vicariate of Aguilares, a meeting of the coordinating team, composed of priests and nuns, to study the case of Ciudad Arce, where Father Joaquín Brizuela and the woman religious represent two opposing pastoral currents. There have already been several attempts to organize them, to coordinate their work, but it appears there is no other solution except to remove them both and replace them with a more united effort. In fact, Mother Josefina came and we spoke to her very frankly. She is willing to leave. Father Martel will be in charge of notifying Father Joaquín and of convincing him of the expediency of changing parishes for the good of the Church, and will give him the opportunity to express his preference in a transfer.

We also studied some other situations in that vicariate, such as the cases of Quetzaltepeque, Guazapa and Opico. I was very glad to see such goodwill for resolving problems in an ecclesial way.

In the afternoon, a group of catechists from the Ricaldone Oratory came for an appointment. Unfortunately, since it had not been confirmed, I was unable to be there. I asked Father Brito to talk about what I had wanted to tell them, that is, to see how the system of Salesian oratories could be extended throughout the archdiocese, but integrated with the concerns of our pastoral work.

From five o'clock in the afternoon on, in the Divine Providence Hospital, a meeting between representatives of FAPU and, representing us along with me, Beto Cuéllar, Father Moreno and Miss Doris Osegueda, to discuss some points of disagreement between the Church and that organization—especially the occupation of churches, the relationship between their group and our Christian base communities, their criticism of the pastoral direction of the Church. The conversation turned out to be very interesting because we were also able to resolve the matter of the Church's concern about certain political movements. For even though the Church is not a specialist in politics, it can attend as an invited guest, always respectful of the autonomy and the responsibility that laypeople and political parties and organizations have in this area. But as Church, it always has something to say in support of a just cause or to denounce an injustice.

 **Friday, June 8**

I had a meeting with the board of directors of the Federation of Catholic Schools in which they informed me of their concern about the selection they are to make of a new board. They have some problems with the representative of the bishops' conference, Bishop Aparicio. I encouraged them to proceed freely and also to include members favorable to the federation chosen from other dioceses, for there are certainly individuals—for example, a Marist brother, Brother Izquierdo, who is in San Miguel, and a sister of La Asunción in Santa Ana—and that they not stop their efforts to move the schools toward a true pastoral labor. I also asked them to concern themselves with getting the parochial schools to take an active part in the federation. There are efforts at conscientization and pastoral work in the federation and it is worthwhile for the Catholic schools to continue working together as a federation.

I had lunch with the Jesuit provincial and three other Jesuits to ask them for their advice in the present situation. They were very explicit and sincere in giving me their opinions and also in developing the next pastoral letter through a survey taken in all the parishes and all the communities, which represents a kind of vote. The opinion of the archdiocese in the national forum turned out to be very one-sided, but the Church feels the obligation to express this opinion as best it can for the public good in the situation of the country. We already have an outline and we are waiting for the responses from the communities so that we can include them in the final version.

This afternoon we evaluated the organizing efforts of the chancery. Father Ibáñez helped us, along with others from the Vivienda Mínima.[174] Although it may be only a small step, they told us they can see progress in the organization of the chancery, through which we are trying to achieve better functioning of the ecclesial institution in our archdiocese. One of the most useful conclusions was that those most directly responsible for the chancery and the diocese will meet on a weekly basis on Tuesdays at eight o'clock in the morning, with a layperson from the housing foundation, who can give us an outsider's view, also attending.

Afterward, with the same collaborators from the foundation and Father Pedraz, the director of the radio, we spoke about the situation of our station and the need to install new equipment, but this would require spending one hundred thousand colones[175] for a new antenna. I asked Ingeniero Galván to send in my name a cable or telex to Misereor,[176] an institution which has already helped us a great deal. We will ask for new help for this installation, since we do not know whether or not we will be able to repair the old equipment, presently out of service for lack of a part we have been unable to get. It is urgent that we have a radio station that expresses the Church's thought.

 ### Saturday, June 9

As we do every Saturday, we had the advisory breakfast to prepare the notes for the homily. And it turned out to be a very interesting meeting because we evaluated the communications office. We criticized the new format of *Orientación*, asking that some overly pious notes be discontinued to leave space for information and criteria more useful in this moment when our newspaper is our only voice, since the radio station is off the air. It was agreed that Miss Doris Osegueda, who directs *Orientación*, will seek advice from some individuals who may be a bit aggressive. Although it may be necessary to restrain them, it is always good also to have people who push in this way.

As usual, I spent the rest of Saturday preparing the homily for Sunday and on other spiritual and personal matters.

---

[174] Also called FUNDASAL, *Fundación Salvadoreña de Desarrollo y Vivienda Mínima*, a foundation for community development and housing.

[175] About $40,000.

[176] International aid agency of the German Catholic Church.

**Sunday, June 10**

Thank God, the Mass at the cathedral is always very well attended, especially now when we do not have the radio station. Many people come to hear what they previously listened to on the radio. It is Trinity Sunday and I presented in the homily the idea of the God of our fathers as he is presented in the Old Testament in the first reading,[177] a God who accompanies his people in history. From there, I related it to our history, applying it specifically to this week, inviting people always to have the faith Israel had in the God who was with them even in the greatest difficulties they faced. The second point was the God of Jesus Christ: the revelation of the Holy Trinity, the love of the Father, a God who became present in the man Jesus, who incarnated God's mercy, love, self-sacrifice for humankind. And, finally, the second reading from St. Paul,[178] which speaks to us of the sending of the Holy Spirit to carry out in humans a process that would unite them with God, making them children of God who have received a Spirit of love—not of fear or of slavery, but of holy freedom and great hope, since we are the heirs of God and coheirs with Christ.

At noon I went to celebrate with the Oblate Sisters of the Sacred Heart the twenty-fifth jubilee of Sister Ana de Jesús Ovín. The Mass was deeply moving; that is to say, everyone participated wholeheartedly. At the time for the homily, some little girls from a community they have in Ciudad Arce also participated. The participation of the honoree, Sister Ana, was also very moving.

The provincial, responding to a call that I made in the homily, said that, with the consent of the superior general, they would offer me their help in spreading the devotion to the Sacred Heart of Jesus, not just in El Salvador but in all of Central America, as I was commissioned to do in the recent seminar on the Sacred Heart devotion held in Santo Domingo, where they made me president of a small committee to spread the devotion in Central America. We agreed that we would meet very soon with the sisters who will commit themselves to this work. I see all this, then, as a gift from the Sacred Heart of Jesus and I hope that, with our humble efforts, his kingdom will grow and be deepened among the Christians of Central America.

In the evening, in the Colonia Atlacatl they were celebrating the festival of the patron of the parish. (It is the parish of the Divine Providence, whose feast is celebrated on Trinity Sunday.) The Redemptorist Fathers, who are in charge of the parish, concelebrated with me. The church was filled to overflowing; affectionate applause greeted me when I arrived. I

---

[177] Deuteronomy 8:2-3, 14-16.
[178] Romans 5:12-14.

preached to them about the meaning of divine providence, which does not exclude intelligent and generous collaboration by human beings, and how the parish, in God's designs, is an instrument that must be used for sanctification, since the purpose of God's providence toward humankind is to make them his sons and daughters, his heirs, to share his life with them—precisely the pastoral work we must do so that all of us may live in the grace of God.

 **Monday, June 11**

I was visited by a group of fourth-year students in the Technological Institute of Usulután, who came to ask me to speak at their graduation and also asked for permission to use my name in the title of the program. I thanked them sincerely and told them I had no objections; that, on the contrary, it was a great honor and satisfaction for me. I only said that the bishop of the diocese, Bishop Rivera, would have to agree to my participation in their graduation ceremony and that they should let me know when it was to be held.

I spent the rest of the day preparing my presentation for the roundtable on the topic of birth control, which was held at the National University this afternoon at five. Those participating in the roundtable were a doctor from the demographic society, an economist and a doctor from social medicine. With me were Father Guillermo Gibbons, a doctor in charge of the St. Luke Center in San Miguel, who explained Natural Family Planning, and also Mrs. Reyes, Licenciada, who is in charge of the Population and Family Center, another archdiocesan initiative to help guide our families.

I explained the doctrine of Paul VI's *Humanae Vitae*, emphasizing human rights, the dignity of man, respect for life—that is, all the positive parts of the encyclical, which seemed to make quite an impression—in order to deduce from there the moral laws that control the sacred act which transmits human life.

After the presentations came some interesting questions from the audience, who showed their concern with the uncontrolled distribution of contraceptives. The medical students courageously challenged the policies of the demographic society and even demanded, in the name of professional ethics and of the freedom and dignity of our people, that they not be so servile to this policy, which does not provide a solution to our problem. I indicated this to them in my presentation when I said that the problem of demographics must be conceived more broadly as part of an integrated social problem, and that merely trying to decrease the birth rate—even worse, encouraging abortions—is merely putting a patch, a sinful one, on a very complicated social problem such as our situation.

 **Tuesday, June 12**

At eight o'clock in the morning we held the first weekly meeting to evaluate the organization of the chancery. We especially talked today about the problem of YSAX, which by now has everyone concerned, and we agreed on certain things to speed up the return to the air of this station so necessary to the whole Church.

At ten o'clock in the morning I participated in a meeting in Santa Tecla to which I had been invited by the board of directors of the Salvadoran Communal Union.[179] It was very interesting to talk with these peasants from different parts of the country about their social concerns. I admire their capacity for autonomy and for respect and the hope they have in the Church. I promised them all my help and encouraged them to continue being faithful to the goals of our Latin American Church and to the preferential option for the poor, thinking primarily of the peasants and their attempts to get their rights.

Some priests also came this morning, since Tuesdays are left open especially for them. At four o'clock in the afternoon, I had a meeting at the archdiocesan major seminary that I was very pleased with because of their concern with the liturgy in the cathedral and because of their efforts to get closer to the minor seminarians, with whom they are organizing a gathering soon, and also because of other aspects that point to a certain level of maturity in these young people who are being prepared to renew the priestly ranks of the diocese.

In the evening, an interesting conversation with Dr. Castro Salazar, who had been taken prisoner and tortured, and who is extremely angry about what can happen in the present climate. He says now, "I had thought that I had hung up my gloves, because I had always been a fighter until I experienced exile; however, I believe that our country requires me to put on my gloves again and I am ready to put myself at your service for whatever little I might be able to do." On my side, I admire him and I thanked him

---

[179] UCS, funded by a U.S. labor organization AIFLD (American Institute for Free Labor Development), sought to represent peasants participating in agrarian reform projects.

because this gesture of solidarity on behalf of the country really provides encouragement for me.

 **Wednesday, June 13**

I celebrated the Mass of St. Anthony in the parish of Soyapango, where he is considered patron. It was very well attended. I concelebrated with the three priests from Soyapango: Father Villarán, the parish priest; Father Pedro Cortéz, associate; and Father Heliodoro Orellana, the chaplain of Colonia Guadalupe of Soyapango.

In the homily I tried to apply the message of St. Anthony to the current situation of Soyapango, inviting them, based on the doctrine taught by St. Anthony (which is the same doctrine as that of the gospel), to communion, to saintliness and to commitment.

After Mass, I attended a gathering with a group of young people from that parish and with great confidence they asked me questions which have been very useful for my own reflections. I encouraged them always to continue to be faithful and to have their own criteria so they will not be easily swayed by what they hear and will rather know how to judge things personally. I promised them that we would spend a whole afternoon, when it fits into their schedule and mine, to study these problems in greater depth, especially those of faith and politics, which seem of particular interest to these young people.

I spent the rest of the day resting at the house of the Oblate Sisters of Divine Love in Planes de Renderos, where I stayed until the evening, when I came back because the sisters of la Asunción had invited me to have dinner with them. There I met Father Fabián, the acting vicar general and Father [Cristóbal] Cortés, with whom I talked about the problems of our clergy and the diocese, especially about the parishes of Chalatenango, San José de la Montaña and about other specific situations.

**Thursday, June 14**

I went to the chancery earlier than usual to see several seminarians who had requested a private meeting with me. I admire the goodwill of these young men and their concerns about how to live in the present moment. It would be easy to confuse this healthy concern with other political or revolutionary concerns and it could be dangerous if they do not receive proper guidance. But, if they are channeled correctly, these are impulses that seem to me to be very healthy for a priest today. For this reason, I have emphasized that in their own sense of identity as men called to the priesthood they are, above all, messengers of the transcendence of God in the midst of a world concerned with the present. But they should know also how to keep their identity with their people.

I also talked with Father Pedraz about the radio and with Arquitecto Morales, who happened to arrive and who suggested some very good ideas on how to get our new transmitter into operation soon.

Some priests also came to the chancery and I talked with them; also some women religious. The meeting with Sister Socorro, Oblate Sister of Divine Love, particularly stands out. She is concerned about the situation of her congregation and rather depressed by the departure of the one formerly called Mother Scaglietti, who has left a big void by leaving her congregation. Also a visit by the provincial of the Franciscan Sisters of the Immaculate Conception, who now work as teachers in the Liceo Salvadoreño but want to do pastoral work more directly involved with the people. I suggested Chalatenango, Amatepec and also, finally, pastoral work with the sick, which is so needed in the capital. Another parish will also need help from women religious soon: that of San Juan Opico and, associated with it, Tacachico.

In the afternoon, I visited the Sara Asylum and celebrated Mass there. Five hundred elderly people and invalids live in this place, where they are not very well taken care of. But, thank God, the Oblate Sisters of the Sacred Heart go there to do a difficult and useful pastoral work. The fruits of this were apparent in this Mass, which was well attended and in which I presented a message of consolation and Christian hope. Among the invalids confined to wheelchairs, I found a catechist from La Reubicación in Chalatenango, who became handicapped precisely because a National Guardsman shot him in the back. I wondered how many more like him there must be, how many handicapped people with families without resources because of this senseless violence we are living in.

I visited the novice house of the Oblate Sisters of the Sacred Heart, where I had dinner and we talked about an apostolate to spread devotion to the Sacred Heart of Jesus, appropriate to our times. They were very enthusiastic, and we will try to organize a small group to think about how we are going to carry out the commission for all of Central America that was given to me in the seminar on the devotion to the Sacred Heart held last May in Santo Domingo in the Dominican Republic.

I went to the Policlinic to visit Father [Abdón] Arce, parish priest of Jucuapa. It appears that his condition, even though the doctor has not said this, is definitely leading to a conclusion that he himself senses. I tried to encourage him and he appears to be in good spirits. He asked me, if this turns out to be his last illness, to do what I can with Bishop Rivera so that he can be buried in his parish church in Jucuapa. I encouraged him not to dwell on such things, but told him that he could count on me completely and that he was entitled to this honor, since he built the church and has been the much-loved parish priest in that area for a long time. I also visited another patient, a teacher, who is recovering from gunshot wounds received in a period when more than nineteen teachers have died.

When I went back to my residence, I found General Medrano waiting for me, and we had an interesting conversation. He is well versed in current politics, a principled man who criticizes the many unwise decisions, the disorder and the errors proliferated by the present government and the armed forces and the representatives of the capital city. We found ourselves in agreement on many things and he promised me his help. I also offered him my cooperation, which is always directed toward the good of the country.

### Friday, June 15

There were numerous visits today, but it seems to me that the most important was with the director and the manager of the archdiocesan Caritas, Father Tilo Sánchez, and Rafael Medrano and, representing the archdiocesan board of Caritas, the treasurer, Mr. Mauricio Merlos, with whom we shared our impressions of how the Caritas office is operating—criticizing some imperfections but, at the same time, acknowledging the many positive things that it is doing throughout the entire archdiocese. Caritas is taking on an original form. It is promoting meetings in all of the parishes and villages it can; organizing the respective committees and promoting charity that truly promotes—is a school for—love in our diocese. I congratulated them, but at the same time, I insisted they make an effort to improve the office, which should be the center for all this work.

I had another very important conversation, this one with the rector of the seminary, Father Gregorio Rosa, with whom I had dinner. Then we went for a ride in the car as far as La Libertad, talking about different things: about the archdiocese as well as about the seminarians, about relations with the other bishops. He seems to me an individual who contributes to the good of the Church and the unity of our hierarchy. I thanked him for all his suggestions; at the same time I explained my thoughts on how he can improve his work as rector, especially as regards the group from the archdiocese and its relationship to the minor seminary.

I received the welcome news that they have found the part to make the radio, which has been off the air for three weeks because of technical difficulties, operable again.

 **Saturday, June 16**

Breakfast with my advisers to prepare the list of this week's events for my homily. It has been an especially bad week as far as abuses of human rights are concerned. Especially notable are the murders of teachers; the total is nineteen at the present time. This is detailed in the international bulletin prepared by the communications office.

After a visit to the eye doctor because of a vision problem, I went to the Policlinic, where Father Abdón Arce, parish priest of Jucuapa, had just died. I expressed my condolences to some parishioners who were there from Jucuapa, as well as to his family, especially his niece Elena. I tried to help them organize the transfer of the body to Jucuapa and its burial in the parish church. I have promised them that I will come tomorrow for a while at least, since I have the Corpus Christi Mass in the afternoon at the same time as the funeral Mass.

When I arrived back at the hospital [Divine Providence], I found a delegation from Catholic Relief Services, who had visited the diocesan Caritas. They wanted to tell me personally of their willingness to help, to express their congratulations for an organization that is breaking traditional patterns to represent a true Caritas in the diocese and to say that they are willing to provide all the help they can for programs that grow out of this new inspiration of Caritas. I felt great satisfaction and thanked them for their valuable cooperation.

In the afternoon, I confirmed some twenty youngsters, boys and girls, who had been prepared by the sisters of la Asunción in one of the most complicated areas, Colonia Morazán. I shared some very happy moments with this community and, when the Mass was over, those who had been confirmed expressed feelings of solidarity and of great pastoral value.

 **Sunday, June 17**

I was listening to YSAX's transmission of the six o'clock Mass at the cathedral, but it was soon cut off again and was therefore unable to transmit the eight o'clock Mass, which was very well attended, also because it was the celebration of Corpus Christi. I presented my theme, framing in the festival of the Body and Blood of the Lord my denouncement of such attacks against human life, whether as a result of the repression, of the terror or of all the sins against new life—abortion, sterilization and all the criminal methods of contraception. On the last point, I spoke about the roundtable at the university and issued a call to the people to avoid such great sin that, without a doubt, has influenced the social unrest of our people.

A journalist from Colombia who represents several different media groups in America congratulated me on my homily and asked me to say a few words for Radio Caracol in Colombia.

After the Mass at the cathedral, I went to Jucuapa, where I had promised to celebrate a Mass at noon for the soul of Father Arce with his body still present. He will be buried tomorrow. I was able to greet many friends and give a Corpus Christi message in the presence of a dead priest—telling them that the priesthood never ends and that its mission, while life's pilgrimage lasts, is through the symbols of the sacraments, but that in eternity it is the liturgy mentioned in the day's reading from the Letter to the Hebrews,[180] where Christ as high priest makes us see and enjoy ultimate good.

When I returned, it was four o'clock in the afternoon, and it was time for the celebration of the Corpus Christi Mass at the cathedral. At the time of the homily, I announced that the radio station was back on the air and that our Mass was being broadcast. The people who filled the cathedral applauded with great joy, since the silence of the radio for technical reasons this week had left people hungry. I took advantage of this first message

---

[180] Hebrews 9:11-15.

heard on the radio to invite those who were listening to join the procession that would leave the cathedral within half an hour to process around the park in honor of the Blessed Sacrament. And the announcement was effective, because many people began to arrive and made the procession a beautiful cortege for Jesus in the Sacrament. After the blessing in the atrium of the cathedral I received many congratulations, which I passed on to the congregation, since we are celebrating together the joy of once again having the radio at the service of our community.

 **Monday, June 18**

The same Colombian journalist I mentioned yesterday interviewed me again. Also an Italian journalist who specializes in Latin American problems wanted to interview me to ask me about the situation and the role of the Church in our country.

There was a meeting of secretaries with Miss Godoy, who specializes in records and with whom we are trying to work out a better-organized filing system in our chancery.

I received great satisfaction from a conversation with Father Rafael [Urrutia], who works as rector of the minor seminary in Chalatenango. I was very moved by his honest expression of his happiness in his first months as a priest. And he said that our community and the role of the archbishop strengthen him; in his exact words, "They confirm me in my faith and in my priesthood." He will have a few days' vacation and then return with new plans within his pastoral vocation. He seems to me to be a fine young man who will bring great honor to our Church.

Also, I found consolation in knowing that this very day the priests of the Vicariate of Flor Blanca in San José de la Montaña are meeting to try to provide more pastoral direction for the life of that parish, which at present has no parish priest. And that the vicariate, as a team and as part of the diocese, intends to follow the lines of our pastoral work.

At the same time, there was a meeting in the seminary of women religious who work in the archdiocesan pastoral ministry to analyze and evaluate the work in each of their pastoral areas. The work of the women religious in the archdiocese is more providential each day.

In the evening I participated in the ultreya of the Cursillos de Cristiandad. I used the opportunity to propose two projects to them and to ask for their help: first, in the planning of an urban pastoral project; and second, in the writing of a pastoral letter.

About the planning, I told them that the metropolitan area of San Salvador requires serious study and that, since their Cursillos de Cristiandad has as one of its goals gaining knowledge of different atmospheres, they can help me direct this planning according to the different atmospheres. With respect to the pastoral letter, I commented that in their own newspaper they had printed the questions I had raised for opinions from the most basic levels. There seems to be much enthusiasm about providing this help as there also is in helping me to plan the pastoral effort. We agreed on another meeting to discuss these proposals in greater depth. But I pointed out, as I told them, that the fruit is ripe and that, thank God, the Cursillo can really be a tool for the pastoral work in the archdiocese.

## Tuesday, June 19

At eight o'clock we had the meeting we had planned to have every Tuesday to assess how the organization of the archdiocese is progressing. We spent this meeting talking specifically about the workings of the radio and the communications office. Arquitecto Morales offered to resolve the problem of where to install our new antenna. We also clarified different aspects of responsibility and areas of expertise in the parts of the communications office. We talked also about changing the format of *Orientación* because of financial considerations, but that was left for consultation with the clergy in their next meeting.

After that, I met with the priests, sisters and lay workers of the Vicariate of Mejicanos. It turned out to be a very interesting meeting. Father Rafael Palacios started it off with a Scripture reading and a reflection, followed by an evaluation of the pastoral work of this vicariate, presented with a true spirit of humility and sincerity. Proceeding in this way, they expressed their difficulties, problems between priests and lay workers, and everything related to functioning better, unifying different aspects of the criteria that should control the pastoral efforts in that area. The meeting was dense with suggestions, discussions, proposed initiatives. It was agreed to continue it next week.

In the afternoon, I had an interesting interview with the provincial of the Marists and some of the directors of their schools in El Salvador. They complained about the distance that exists between their community and the archbishop. I explained clearly my goals, my concerns; they also spoke very frankly about the difficulties which exist. As mediator we had, by common consent, Sister Nelly Rodríguez, who is part of the board of directors of the Federation of Catholic Schools, in order to assess with her the pastoral relationship of the Marist schools in the important area of education, which is seen as a pastoral effort of the archdiocese. It was agreed to strengthen relations and to try together to achieve a pastoral labor truly in harmony with the archdiocese that will be at the service of our people with their special characteristics.

 **Wednesday, June 20**

This morning while I was preparing the tape of the interview to be broadcast on the radio today, I received the tragic news that Father Rafael Palacios was murdered in Santa Tecla at that same time, around nine o'clock in the morning. I ended the tape by referring to this tragic event and I headed to the meeting of the Senate being held at the Somascan Sisters' house to consult with them about what we should do, faced with this new tragic situation. It was urgent that I hear the opinion of the Senate in order to resolve the immediate matters of arrangements for the funeral and the participation of the clergy and the people. And later, a deeper study of the situation reflected in this event.

In regard to the first matter, we agreed that we should pick up Father Rafael's body and, after preparing it, return it to Santa Tecla, where he is well loved, for viewing in El Calvario Church. And to hold a Mass there in the evening. And then the next day, to take the body to the cathedral for rites there and afterward take it to Suchitoto, following the wishes of his family, who is from there. After another Mass in Suchitoto he will be buried in the parish church.

While the Senate continued its discussions, I went to Santa Tecla, where they had already brought Father Rafael's body. I only announced that he would be brought back for viewing in El Calvario Church and that they should issue the invitation for the evening. From there I went to the place where the forensic examination of the body was made. It was riddled with bullet holes; his face had been hit and other parts of his body. The group of Christian base communities in Santa Tecla, who had such great affection for him, was there and they cried inconsolably. I tried to comfort them and then returned to the Senate meeting, which was already over.

In the chancery, however, there were people who wanted to talk about this event, among them his sisters and his brother. With them and with other priests and seminarians, we talked—an enlightening discussion of what Father Rafael had been like from his childhood, how he carried out his vocation as a priest up until the hour of his death. It is a marvelous thing to have a close look at a life about which there have been some doubts and some prejudices. I believe we learned a great deal from this familial reflection that took place in a room in the archdiocesan offices.

In the afternoon, I was interviewed by Brazilian television about the situation of the Church and the country.

Also, I was offered assistance in fixing up the room for religious and secular meetings in the Colegio de la Sagrada Familia, which I greatly appreciate, for it will be done with great love and very competently as well.

In the evening I went to celebrate Mass in Santa Tecla at El Calvario Church, which was completely filled. There were many priests beside Father Palacios's body; no less than twenty-five from all parts of the archdiocese concelebrated with me. We discussed how to celebrate the next day. We agreed that we would assemble in the Sacred Heart Basilica at ten o'clock in the morning, and that we would take the coffin from there to the cathedral and hold funeral rites there.

In my homily I spoke on the idea that Father Palacios had found in Santa Tecla what every faithful priest encounters where he works: great love and great hate. And the proof of the hate was his tragic death, his murder, which also showed how the Church, which has the responsibility of denouncing sin, must be prepared to suffer the consequences of having wounded the monster that is responsible for so much evil in the world—the monster of sin.

 **Thursday, June 21**

The sisters at the hospital have been the first to remember that today is the anniversary of my ordination as bishop. Frankly, it has been nine years since I was anointed to the fullness of the priesthood. Although I was to celebrate the funeral Mass for Father Palacios, the sisters wanted me to celebrate a more private Mass in the hospital chapel to give thanks to God and to reflect on this ninth anniversary. It has seemed to me very significant that I celebrate this anniversary with a priest having been assassinated and in the fullness of solidarity with all the priests of the archdiocese and with many others who have come from other archdioceses, including the bishop of Santiago de María, Bishop Rivera. Because of this, even though I celebrated the private Mass very intimately with the Lord and a small group of sisters and patients representing the people of God, it seemed to me that the funeral of Father Rafael Palacios was another, more grandiose, way of observing this anniversary.

His body was brought from Santa Tecla and all the priests, sisters and many of the faithful were waiting at the Sacred Heart Basilica to accompany it in an impressive silent procession to the cathedral, where we held a Mass that was also quite solemn. I think that no fewer than sixty priests filled the sanctuary and surrounded Father Palacios' coffin.

In my homily I tried to interpret the message of the blood of a murdered priest, which reveals three things to us: first, the mystery of evil, pointing out the unjust situation of sinful structures in our country and the sin of the Church as well, which many times becomes an accomplice by singling out or doubting priests because of their efforts to renovate the pastoral work of the Church. The second point: the mystery of faithfulness—how dying in such a way does not mean a priest was bad, but rather that he was faithful, like Christ to the Father, like the Church to Christ. And third, to provide a message of hope, since this death shows us what should be the dimensions of the Church's work: to form a people made new through love and to open their eyes to the vision of the eternal that death shows so clearly.

Around three o'clock in the afternoon, Father Palacios' body was moved to his adopted town, Suchitoto, where it will be on view. Tomorrow at ten o'clock there will be a funeral Mass and he will be buried in that church. I hope to be able to be there with him.

This afternoon I went to keep a promise to celebrate the patronal festival of San Luis Mariona,[181] a town in the parish of Father Julio Orellana in Cuscatancingo, where there was a reception and a cordial, affectionate celebration. Father Orellana had prepared a group of young men and women to receive the Sacrament of Confirmation. It was a good catechesis; they were well prepared. We celebrated the Mass of the Holy Spirit and I referred to their patron saint, St. Aloysius Gonzaga, as an example of a Christian who knew how to live his Baptism and his Confirmation.

In the evening, I responded to an invitation from Licenciado Atilio Víeytez along with Father [Paco] Estrada and the rector of the Central American University, Ingeniero Román Mayorga. A very interesting conversation about the current political problems of the country and the situation of our Church.

---

[181] St. Aloysius Gonzaga.

9999999999999999999999
9

### Friday, June 22

In the morning, I went to Suchitoto to celebrate the funeral Mass for Father Rafael Palacios. That large church was completely filled with the faithful of Suchitoto and other communities that had come. Many priests, many sisters. In my homily I related the celebration of the Sacred Heart of Jesus to the death of Father Rafael. The priest makes present the mystery of Christ, which is the mystery of love. If Rafael Palacios had to return to his adopted town dead, the Feast of the Sacred Heart of Jesus was a good time for him to be able to say, "Mission accomplished!" Father Rafael Barahona and Father Palacios' brother Carlos also spoke. We carried the coffin around the park in a procession of many people; afterward it was buried in the chapel of the Sacred Heart of Jesus. Amid the Easter hymns, the tears seemed to be illuminated with great Christian hope.

I had lunch with the community of Dominican Sisters, whose school there is operating very well. I congratulated them and encouraged them to continue.

In the afternoon, the Mass of the Sacred Heart of Jesus in the Basilica. It was well attended, even though Father Cortés, parish priest of the Basilica, told me that there had been more people the previous year, possibly due to a torrential rain that fell a little while before the Mass, or because of the fear that, in general, the people feel in the present atmosphere.

When I preached, I tried to explain how the Church was present in the heart of the historical Christ, and how the Sacred Heart of Christ continues to be present in the Church to sanctify it and to put it at the service of the world with the mission he brought from the Father. And, finally, always in the spirit of a parish, we went to have dinner at the home of Dr. Mario Levy Van Severen, who is a member of the parish council.

### Saturday, June 23

As we do every Saturday, we met over breakfast at the house of the Somascan Sisters to review the week and make notes for my homily. I wanted to express a feeling almost of frustration at the coldness with which the tragic death of Father Rafael Palacios has been received. I cited, for example, the basketball game between two Catholic schools played while Father Rafael's body lay in state prior to the funeral

Mass at the cathedral and the lack of sensitivity in the atmosphere. I said that we need to analyze this to see how people were responding to events that should have produced a greater reaction of solidarity in the entire Church.

For this reason and because of some other matters that also show the need for us to reflect more deeply, we agreed to meet next Monday with the people whom we normally consult for advice. And we will spend the entire morning, so that we have enough time and can arrive at some conclusions, since also we have the responsibility, given us in the meeting of the clergy to carry out the initiatives discussed then.

Of course, the bells are being rung every night at eight, but it is lamentable that on the radio it seems as if they referred to the death of Father Palacios on the day of his funeral only as a courtesy and have not followed this up with any other mention of this or with any demand regarding this event.

Also we announced and are continuing to announce that there will be only one Mass in the entire archdiocese a week from Saturday after a novena in memory of Father Rafael.

I went with Father Estrada to visit Dr. Badía, rector of the National University, to try to convince him not to resign, since his presence represents great hope for the university. It appears, however, that he sees great difficulties because of the disorder in groups of university students who seem uncivilized and are seemingly being manipulated to ends that have not been revealed. They are causing great damage to the university, and he, Dr. Badía, thinks that he cannot carry on alone, for many others are also resigning. I continued to try to give him the spirit to carry on and also offered him my moral support.

 ### Sunday, June 24

We celebrated the Mass of St. John the Baptist at the cathedral. As on every Sunday, the attendance provided great pastoral encouragement.

At eleven o'clock in the morning, I celebrated the patronal Mass in Chalatenango in honor of St. John the Baptist. This also provided great spiritual consolation. The minor seminary sang at the Mass. It is celebrating today its second anniversary and is flourishing with the grace of God and under the direction of a very active episcopal vicar and rector, Father Urrutia, who provides great priestly understanding to the young men. After Mass, we shared lunch and a little party with the families in the seminary. The atmosphere was truly Christian, very warm.

In the afternoon, a very interesting conversation with the family who treated Father Rafael Palacios very affectionately during the time he lived in our archdiocese. They revealed to me some important details that clarify some aspects of Father Rafael's murder, his character and the direction of his pastoral work. It seems to me that this is a case of a priest who was misunderstood and whose pastoral work has much transcendence—especially in the Christian base communities.

 **Monday, June 25**

We spent the whole morning from breakfast on at the house of the Passionist Sisters on the road to Planes de Renderos to study the circumstances of Father Palacios' murder, the situation of the Church's internal life and its effects on the world around us. I took with me the professor I mentioned yesterday, who knows about Father Palacios' life in great detail, so that she could tell us about the murder itself and about prior circumstances that could have led to this situation. They were very important revelations, especially with respect to the details that made Father Palacios' life so hard in his relationship to the hierarchy and to other priests.

We continued our reflection. Father Moreno made an extensive analysis of how he sees the intraecclesial situation and also the relationship of the Church with the outside. Valuable opinions clarified the panorama that, at the same time that it worries us, gives us an optimistic view of the life of our Church, which doubtless continues to mature but suffers from grave problems, especially from internal divisions and in its relationships with the government and the people.

In the afternoon, I talked with Father Jesús Delgado and Father Rafael Moreno to sketch the outline of the pastoral letter I plan to release on August 6. We hope to get numerous opinions from priests and from the base communities, since we are taking a survey with respect to the questions this pastoral letter will try to answer in response to the dialogue initiated for opinions on the situation and a possible solution to the situation of our country. Our pastoral letter is intended to be a truly ecclesial, pastoral voice, and to indicate the problems and the possible solutions as we may pastorally express them. This consultation will continue in the next meeting of the clergy, where this rich material will be collected in order to turn it over to the different groups who will prepare the first draft of the pastoral letter.

## Tuesday, June 26

We spent the whole morning meeting with the Committee on Pastoral Work. This meeting, as I see it, is most important, since the diocese exists in order to do pastoral work, and this committee will help to coordinate, motivate and serve the pastoral work of the archdiocese. I have been very pleased that the vicariates, the representatives of the women religious and of the laity of each vicariate are beginning to share the pastoral ideals of the archdiocese.

Today we studied the goals of this Pastoral Commission. I was pleased to find they remember the 1975 pastoral week, which outlined the steps the archdiocese is taking now, requiring the formation of Christian base communities, the formation of leaders or pastoral agents. This was the major part of the reflection. Several other aspects show the vitality of our diocese. We have thanked God and have asked him to continue to bless us.

We had agreed to meet with members of FAPU in the afternoon. There to represent us were Father Moreno, Miss Doris Osegueda, Bachiller Roberto Cuéllar and I. We talked especially about overcoming certain prejudices that FAPU has against the Church. I think the meeting was useful if they truly accepted our explanations.

## Wednesday, June 27

Before I went to the office, I received some interesting visits: from Father Ramiro, a Passionist priest whom we need to continue lending us his services in our archdiocese; from Father Urrutia—Rafael—who has some projects related to the minor seminary and pastoral vocations in the archdiocese; and Carlos Francisco Palacios, brother of Father Rafael Palacios, who expressed to me his concerns as a young man who wants to enter the seminary, but who first wishes to do pastoral work. I indicated to him the post left vacant by his brother Rafael's death in the parish of San Francisco and he was very pleased to be able to work there.

In the seminary there were also other visitors before I could go to the meeting of the Vicariate of Mejicanos. The parish priest of Colonia Atlacatl has a problem with threats made by clandestine organizations against a family. The Church wants to help them and is, thank God, doing so. Also Mrs. Raquel...continues in hiding due to the threats of the White Warrior Union.

The meeting of the Vicariate of Mejicanos also turned out to be interesting, since it was a continuation of the one we had last week that so enthused Father Rafael Palacios. There is no doubt that his spirit is with us, for there was sincerity in the expression of shortcomings, obstacles, difficulties; but they were clarified in discussion so that around noon I was able to present a very optimistic reflection: suggesting that our meeting this morning was similar to those in Acts and that we should try to reach that ideal of a Christian community. The best way to resolve all problems is when we all try truly to be the Church of Jesus Christ.

The Passionist Sisters who work in San José Villanueva came to report how they have also been persecuted there, how someone tried to burn their little church and how they have had to take all the images to the places where they live in order to avoid any major damage.

In the afternoon I met with the workers of the Criterio printing house. The purpose was to celebrate the day of their patron saint, St. John, and to dialogue with them about their working conditions. I was accompanied by the general administrator of the archdiocese, Ingeniero Galván, and by Miss Doris Osegueda, in charge of the communications office; also by María Isabel and Silvia, whom I have asked to work to promote a sense of community among these workers.

We managed to achieve an atmosphere of trust so that they could talk about a series of anomalies in the human relationships at the press. They complain mostly about two of the shop supervisors, who seem to treat them rather badly. Although we made them think about their responsibility to carry out their duties and to try to understand the shop supervisors, I also promised them that I would attend to their requests once I had analyzed them in a frank conversation with the chief of personnel. It was, I think, very useful to be able to tell them that, above all, that we should be linked by one spirit since we are collaborating with the Church in such an important task as editing a newspaper, supporting the press that, thank God, our archdiocese has.

In the evening, Father Rafael Urrutia came to see me along with the seminarian Joaquín, and they gave me their opinion of the minor seminary of Chalatenango. I asked Rafael Urrutia, in conjunction with the person in charge of the minor seminary of San José de la Montaña, to take charge of the parish of the same name, to use it as a base to develop a pastoral vocations project.

 **Thursday, June 28**

I began my work at the office with an interesting meeting with Father Rafael Urrutia and Father Sigfredo, both young men, to whom I communicated my wish to make the parish of San José de la Montaña central to pastoral vocations work. Father Urrutia has accepted the idea very enthusiastically. Father Sigfredo has his doubts because it focuses more attention on the seminary. But I believe that together they can carry out this beautiful work from a parish that was created as a function of the seminary and that has limited itself almost exclusively to celebrating Mass. Father Salvador Colorado, a member of the team of the major seminary who belongs to our archdiocese, also has shown his willingness to cooperate. Because of this, I hope that we will be able to make this idea reality very soon.

There were several visits, among them one from the chargé d'affaires from Venezuela, who very attentively offered his services to our archdiocese—even, if necessary, financial support. I thanked him and we will remember this.

I had lunch with Mrs. Rodríguez, mother of Sister Nelly Rodríguez, with whom I became good friends in San Miguel during my time as a parish priest in that city.

In the afternoon, an interview with an English journalist. Also a meeting with the typesetters at our press, Criterio, at which we discussed some very specific labor problems. I will try to make their difficult situation more human.

Also a visit from Mr. Arturo Meza, who told me about the difficult working conditions in the La Constancia company. I offered to explain to them the Christian principles that govern, according to the ideas expressed in the Gospels, the relationship between owners and workers. God willing, we will talk about this next week.

**Friday, June 29**

I celebrated St. Peter's feast day today in the girls' school, Colegio Santa Inés, in Santa Tecla, where the sisters, the teachers and the students were celebrating the Day of the Pope. I spoke to them of the importance of the two saints honored on this day: St. Peter as head of the Church and St. Paul as a representative of the Gentile world, that is, all of us who form the non-Jewish world, but who together with the Jewish Christians form the one Church of Jesus Christ. After Mass, there was a nice program that showed the role of the pope in the contemporary world. After sharing some moments of joy with these young people, I left to spend the rest of the day at the house of the Oblate Sisters of Divine Love in Planes de Renderos.

 **Saturday, June 30**

The principal event today was the single Mass, agreed upon in a plenary session of the clergy as an expression of the solidarity of the entire archdiocese in the matter of the death of Father Rafael Palacios. The nine days of prayer held in several communities have ended, and today at noon there was a large assembly of communities from the entire archdiocese, priests numbering close to one hundred. It was quite solemn and there was great participation. One could tell the communities had been well developed and, united in one cathedral, they gave a magnificent impression of active participation in the Eucharist.

In my homily I interpreted this single Mass as a gesture of solidarity on the part of the archdiocese for three purposes: first, to reaffirm the infinite and divine value of the Eucharist, which is profaned by excessive individualism and celebrations held for reasons that are not always consistent with the divine will. Second, we were also expressing our appreciation for the priesthood, specifically in memory of a dead priest, vilely assassinated, and showing what the Church is like when it is empty of the Eucharist and of priests, as were all the churches of the diocese on this day of one single Mass. And in the third place, to show the united voice of the people of God, a people who prays, a people who protests the attacks that have been made against it, but does not do this out of hatred or a desire for vengeance, but as a people who calls for sinners to be converted.

This morning at breakfast we had, as is our custom on Saturdays, the review of the week to prepare the news I should focus on in my homily.

And, in the evening, a meeting in Santa Tecla with the Christian base community that had been encouraged by Father Rafael Palacios, to give them pastoral guidance.

# July, 1979

 **Sunday, July 1**

The Mass at the cathedral does not decline in numbers, thank God, and the Gospel and the other readings gave us the opportunity to present Christ as the divine power that gives life in the form of love and justice, which is the key to resolving the social problems of our country.

After the Mass at the cathedral, I went to a Mass in the Tinetti Market, which made those people very happy. I preached to them on the Sacred Heart of Jesus, congratulating them and encouraging them not to let this devotion die, but rather to cultivate it as it merits.

At five o'clock in the afternoon, I preached the Holy Hour in the Divine Providence Hospital with incredible attendance. The second Sunday reading from St. Paul,[182] recommending that a collection be taken up in Corinth for Jerusalem, gave me an opportunity to talk about the spirit of poverty, the true solution to the social injustice in our reality. And I promoted the collection the hospital is making to buy new land on which to continue their charitable work on behalf of their patients and especially with all the orphaned children of the women who die in this hospital.

---

[182] 2 Corinthians 8:7, 9, 13-15.

**Monday, July 2**

Today the vicar general, Monsignor Urioste, returned to the office after a month's vacation in the Holy Land. Father Cristóbal Cortés had replaced him during his absence.

For the last three weeks, very early on Monday mornings, Miss Coralía Godoy has been training the secretaries of the chancery in order to coordinate our archdiocesan files. I attended, too, along with the vicar general and the chancellor, so that we may all use the same norms.

The nuncio has returned from Rome and wanted to talk to me. I went to the nunciature because it is more peaceful there, and he told me that the Holy Father and the Sacred Congregation for Bishops are worried about the division among the Salvadoran bishops and that they expect great cooperation from me in achieving unity. I explained to him what I have expressed many times: that there is a personal factor with some of them and that this makes this task very difficult for me; nevertheless, I will do everything within my power. I especially mentioned my difficulties with the auxiliary bishop, Bishop Revelo, and with Bishop Aparicio, both of whom clearly show personal animosity to me. Nevertheless, I am willing and, with the grace of God, I will do what I can to achieve unity, for I am the first one to realize the bad effects of disunity.

I also explained to the nuncio my concern about Father Rogelio Esquivel. I was not trying to intervene but, as a friend, I had promised to try to help him. I had also promised him, after explaining to him that he is the one who has left, but I also believe that this is a priestly work of charity and I told him that I would do whatever I could because he had come to me, and that I would try to fix things as best I could, always in line with our pastoral work and respecting the opinion of all of the priests.

The nuncio showed a great desire to help me with my difficult pastoral tasks. I could tell that something had been said to him in Rome, for he is extremely friendly to me; on my side, I indicated that I had no dislike for him, but that I had noticed his partiality toward the group of bishops who are not in agreement with me, and that this undoubtedly greatly influenced the division; that if he were more impartial and truly tried to help us to achieve unity, then unity would be achieved.

In the evening, a prayer vigil took place in the cathedral. It was promoted by the confederation of men and women religious, but numerous priests attended and many of the faithful from different communities, among them prayer groups of the charismatic renewal movement. The spirit was very good. I explained to them at the time of the homily that I had great hope for a diocese that puts its trust in prayer.

**Romero offers a blessing on the occasion of his ordination as bishop, June 1970. Accompanying him are Archbishop Luis Chávez y González and Bishop Arturo Rivera Damas (his predecessor and his successor as archbishop of San Salvador). At right is Father Rutilio Grande, S.J., his friend, who was ambushed and shot near Aguilares on March 12, 1977.**

**The San Salvador cathedral and its plaza were the setting for many of the events described in this diary.**

**Archbishop Romero tries to coax a smile from a very young member of his flock. The diary details his many visits to villages where people were living in miserable poverty.**

**Military personnel stand guard at a Salvadoran army post.**

Archbishop Romero lived in this little house constructed for him on the grounds of Divine Providence Hospital.

Archbishop Romero's crosier or shepherd's staff, symbol of his office as bishop, lies on his bed. The picture of the Crucifixion on the shelf was also his.

An assassin's eye view of the chapel at Divine Providence Hospital shows the altar behind which Archbishop Romero was standing just after his homily when a single shot was fired.

Visitors pray at Archbishop Romero's tomb in the San Salvador cathedral. The tomb has since been moved to the crypt.

**Tuesday, July 3**

I celebrated Mass at seven o'clock in the morning in Tinetti Market. Thus the market and the ladies who work there ended their festivities in honor of the Sacred Heart of Jesus, which had lasted throughout June. They are very warm people and I felt good among them.

Afterward I went to the meeting of the clergy, which was interesting. The first principal topic was a study of attitudes toward the death of Father Rafael Palacios. They very frankly pointed out successes and failures. They especially called for greater solidarity and sensitivity on the part of all priests so as to not sabotage the agreements which are reached. A committee was named to be on guard so that these difficult situations do not catch us by surprise; rather, there will always be someone to take the necessary initiatives from the beginning.

The second topic was the consultation for the pastoral letter I am writing. Numerous parishes and communities turned in valuable contributions.

In the afternoon I had a meeting with the major seminarians of the archdiocese. Through these meetings I have seen them mature a great deal, and they talk over their problems very freely with their archbishop. I congratulated them and I told them that the content of the meeting, as much as the way in which they presented it, had pleased me a great deal and that I hope they would be well prepared for the priesthood, as God wants them to be in such a time.

I also received a visit from the Canadian chargé d'affaires, who wants to have contact with the Church in order to learn about the situation of the Church and the country. She feels she does not know much about us because her base for all of Central America is in Costa Rica. I offered her the services of the communications office and I expressed to her the Church's willingness to aid her in this way.

 **Wednesday, July 4**

In the morning, I celebrated a solemn Mass at the María Auxiliadora church. The Mass was sponsored by the Mercedarian Sisters of the Blessed Sacrament on the occasion of the religious profession of two of their sisters.

In the chancery, a meeting of the women religious who do pastoral work in parishes. Also a meeting of the executive committee.

In the evening, a visit from a young student, Armando Castro, who is going to an ecumenical conference of university and high school students in the United States. A good and generous boy, he was very interested in my candidacy for the Nobel Peace Prize. I thanked him and I wished him good luck on his upcoming trip. I said that I had faith in him; he has a great evangelical sense, since he is a member of the Student Ecumenical Movement.

My Wednesday interview program was broadcast.

 **Thursday, July 5**

I held an advisory breakfast to present the contributions that have arrived from different parishes and communities for my next pastoral letter. Present were Father Fabián Amaya, Father Ellacuría, Father Sebastián and Father Moreno. Some other priests and laypeople I had invited were unable to come but are willing to help. I gave them the material and we discussed ways to incorporate all these suggestions. Initially, the plan will be to look at, to present, the reality of the country; to search for and include criteria, especially from the Puebla document, and to suggest pastoral steps that will produce a consistent Church stance and, from there, to give perspectives and direction for the search for solutions to the country's situation.

Afterward, at the chancery, I had an interesting meeting to study filling the post in the parish of San José de la Montaña. My plan to transfer Father Cortés from the basilica to San José de la Montaña was accepted; and to fill the position at the basilica by the transfer of Father Efraín from Chalatenango; along with Father Cortés and, as counselors, Monsignor Urioste and Father Urrutia, who will be in charge of the minor seminary. Sigfredo, who is presently in charge of the minor seminary, will go to Chalatenango to fill the post of Father Urrutia in the minor seminary there with, as counselor, Father Salvador Colorado, archdiocesan member of the team for formation at the major seminary. The purpose of San José de la Montaña is to be not just a parish, but also an archdiocesan center to promote vocations.

Father Efraín was unable to come in the morning, but arrived in the afternoon. He accepted gladly. We will only have to wait for the appropriate conditions to make these transfers.

In the afternoon, an interesting private meeting that could have great transcendence. Directors from the La Constancia factory, who have come to the archdiocese several times in search of guidance from the Church for the owner-worker problem at this big company, came to a meeting I set up in order to present to them in depth the social doctrine of the Church. I was well assisted by Mr. Antonio Orellana, Father Walter Guerra, Bachiller Roberto Cuéllar and a North American sister who is a social worker on one of the great estates of the diocese of Santa Ana.

The valuable contributions of all these individuals profoundly impressed the Mezas, who thanked us profusely and suggested it would be good to have further meetings if it were not a great bother to us. I have the feeling that these capitalists' coming to the Church in search of Christian solutions for the country's social situation will have great transcendence.

I could not attend the Mass at the Liceo Salvadoreño where the Federation of Catholic Schools was offering a Mass for the eternal rest of Brother Blanco, killed in Nicaragua.

 **Friday, July 6**

The archdiocesan Caritas held a meeting today with directors from all over the country.

In the chancery, I met with Father Joaquín Brizuela to talk about the problem of the pastoral work in Ciudad Arce. I have great hopes for him. I think we can change the problematic situation if we keep talking. The seminarians assisting are well disposed to follow the same pastoral line as the rest of the archdiocese. Mother Josefina's leaving will also be beneficial for the unity of the pastoral work of that parish.

At five o'clock in the afternoon, I met with a reporter from *El Mercurio* in Chile.

 **Saturday, July 7**

After breakfast with my advisers to prepare the homily, I went to the Good Shepherd Center, where Sister Luz del Perpetuo Socorro, a very old lady of the Institute of the Cross, a branch of the order of the Good Shepherd, has died. Today we will have the funeral Mass. I felt the great affection this community has for its pastor and the strength of the prayers that rise from there to heaven for the intentions of the bishop and the diocese. I thanked them and tried to give something back to them in my homily, in which I encouraged them to be faithful, like the sister who has left us.

At my residence a suffering mother was waiting for me, along with her son's wife, to tell me that her son, a fifth-year medical student, has disappeared. She shared her story with me and I understood the depth of her pain and promised to do everything I could. More than anything else, I encouraged her not to lose hope and to put great trust in prayer. Tomorrow in the Mass I will mention this new case of injustice.

In the afternoon, I responded to an invitation made me by the Santa Tecla market, along with the priest of the parish of Concepción, Father Alvarenga. We went and received a very cordial and affectionate reception on the part of the men, women and children who work in the market. I spoke to them about the Sacred Heart of Jesus. I told them they should continue in their love for the Church, that all of us are Church and that we have to make the Sacred Heart of Christ present for our holiness, for our justice, for everything that makes our lives nicer and more fraternal. After Mass, a large crowd accompanied me to the convent of Concepción, where I said good-bye with the affection of those people.

 **Sunday, July 8**

The Mass as usual in the cathedral at eight o'clock, very well attended. The Scripture readings gave me the opportunity to talk about the theme of the prophet. The title of the homily was "The Prophet Is the Presence of God in Society." I developed this topic, discussing how the initiative always comes from God, how the prophet is no more than the instrument of God and how society accepts or rejects God in the person of the prophet.

The day passed without any significant events. In the afternoon, I went with the Oblate Sisters of Divine Love on an outing to their farm, where, thank God, I rested.

## Monday, July 9

We began the week with a meeting of the secretaries for instruction by Miss Godoy. This has principally to do with records, but today we have expanded it to include concerns about different aspects of the archdiocesan offices, especially having to do with my secretary.

After attending to other official matters, I went to the town of Paraíso, in Chalatenango, where the Bethlemite Sisters had invited me to have lunch and found they had organized an *atol* festival for me.[183] It was an interesting pastoral experience, very agreeable, since that church and convent, which seemed to be dead before, are today a central meeting place for the faithful, especially the young people, who come there to live the Christian life near the sisters. The atolada took place near the river where the young people had woven tree branches into a shelter, and where the different groups of women, young people and children presented simple speeches and artistic acts that expressed, more than anything, the sincerity and simplicity of these people. We ended with a Mass in the parish, in which I expressed to them my appreciation and encouraged them to continue developing their community, since they already have a substantial base and because it would be a shame to lose everything they have done because of a lack of perseverance.

## Tuesday, July 10

As we usually do on Tuesdays, we had a meeting of the executive council of the chancery. Besides me, it consists of the vicar general, the chancellor, the administrator and Ingeniero Silva, representing *Vivienda Mínima*, who offers us valuable advice.

As in previous weeks, we spent today's meeting studying how the radio is working, but we have now added more general aspects of the chancery: the records and different aspects of the way the archdiocesan government functions. These meetings are very useful and I believe that they will result in greater efficiency and order in our pastoral and administrative work.

There were visits from several priests, but especially from Father Manuel Reyes and an evangelical minister to propose to me a project of

---

[183] *Atol* is a thick drink made from ground corn, traditionally drunk warm from a gourd. A popular festival where *atol* is drunk is an *atolada*.

ecumenical benefit and to ask for aid for the project which is, in part, already begun. I congratulated them and encouraged them to continue because it seems to me a good project that will benefit Father Reyes's parish, the Diez de Septiembre, as well as the evangelical community of the other pastor. I told them that well-studied ecumenism was a true spiritual movement toward conversion to an authentic gospel.

In the afternoon, a meeting with Father Pedraz, the secretary of communications and the vicar general to specify the workings of the radio. We agreed in substance on naming Mr. Napoleón Navarro Oviedo to the position of director-manager.

 **Wednesday, July 11**

I spent the entire morning in Domus Mariae, in Mejicanos, at an interesting meeting of the Vicariate of Mejicanos. The very active executive committee advises the vicar, Father Samuel Orellana. The meeting today was to organize the different functions of the parish, dividing it into three committees: one for social promotion, one for growth in faith and another for the physical church structures—the outline from Medellín, fleshed out by the committees required by the different needs of this parish. After lunch the meeting continued to reflect on the new sense of the Church.

 **Thursday July 12**

Today we met with the shop supervisors of the Criterio Press because there have arisen problems with the workers. It became clear that the workers, many of them apprentices, are partly responsible. They do not produce well in their work and they make demands that the supervisors try to resolve in a just way. We will study, in light of the clarifications made by the shop foremen, the batch of petitions presented by a group of workers. I have urged them to be very careful in this situation in order to avoid any labor scandal and to try to develop a more humane attitude in the relationship with our workers at this Catholic press.

Afterward, the entire morning was full with visitors and interviewers who came to the chancery.

At four o'clock in the afternoon I went to Soyapango to see the Church land where Caritas wants to build its warehouse. The parish priest also went, and the ladies of the archdiocesan Caritas committee and [Father] Luis Alonso Machado, representing the administrative committee of the archdiocese. And we agreed to ask the committee that had recommended selling this land, which is worth a great deal, and buying land elsewhere for a warehouse, to reconsider. But this land seemed more appropriate to the [Caritas] committee, which has promised to build and maintain an educational project and a social project there, which would benefit the parish of Soyapango. I think this request is good and I shall support it, since it provides for a Church presence in an area where it has not existed previously.

Father Nicolás González was also there, and he commented very enthusiastically on the pastoral work of the archdiocese.

After dinner I met with the team from the central major seminary of San José de la Montaña. We discussed different matters having to do with the seminarians of the archdiocese as well as with the life of the seminary and the handling of the seminary property as agreed upon by the archdiocese, which owns it, and the team that administers the seminary.

 **Friday, July 13**

Three pastoral activities stand out today. The first is a meeting at breakfast with those advising me on the fourth pastoral letter. They presented their studies very competently, and we also summarized the survey taken of priests and different communities. In them all is a wealth of material to use to discover the opinion of the Church at this time when a national dialogue has been called for. We can speak as Church, and from the very base of the Church, using the official vehicle of a pastoral letter. I ask God that what comes next—putting these different parts together better and making a final draft—be blessed by the Holy Spirit, who enlightens in this moment the paths of our Christians.

The second meeting was at the house of the Passionist Sisters on the road to Planes de Renderos, a very interesting meeting that tried to bring together the families of the five priests who have been murdered. Except for the family of Father Ernesto Barrera, they were all well represented and spoke, with the familiarity of those who have known them since childhood, about these priests who were called by God to give the greatest testimony, their blood, for Jesus Christ, for justice, for truth. We agreed to record all of these memories as an example for Christians. And we also discussed other options of a legal nature and also of a pastoral nature, so that the example of these martyrs not be lost and also so that the justice of God may be seen in them. It was edifying to see the spirit of forgiveness and the call for conversion that dominated the comments.

Finally, in the afternoon, I went to the beach at Acajutla with the seminarians, who are going to have a get-together there. It will last until tomorrow, but I could only be there this afternoon. I stayed until well after dark and had dinner with them. We had our first discussion, in which they shared the problems they have with the integration of the two archdiocesan seminaries, major and minor. This discussion was the main purpose of this gathering. I noted their frankness, their courage and their sincerity in saying what they do not like, and also their sincere desire to look for answers so that the future priests of the archdiocese be well prepared for their mission with more of a sense of unity and teamwork.

 **Saturday, July 14**

I went to Comasagua, where Father Chalo González had prepared a group for Confirmation. I was very surprised when I arrived at the hour agreed upon, nine o'clock in the morning, and did not see people either in the church or around it. I expressed my surprise to the priest there, perhaps showing a little disgust, and he told me that is how cold these people are. I insisted that perhaps there had been a lack of motivation on the parish priest's part. When the bells began to ring, some people arrived, but we only confirmed one little boy.

In the Confirmation Mass, I tried to express myself well in discussing indifference to God and to ask those present to activate their community through the goodness of the Lord. After Mass, I invited the people to stay and talk to analyze the situation. Besides the parish priest, several other people admitted that, yes, there is coldness, and also there is fear because of the situation of the country. But also some laypeople stated very frankly that the priest also needed to be more active, that with the previous priest there had been many catechists and more life in the countryside and in the town (although less in town). I talked in a fraternal spirit with the priest, encouraging him, since the work he has to do in that town is very hard.

**Sunday, July 15**

This eve of the Feast of Our Lady of Mt. Carmel[184] requires a great deal of work, indicative of the fervor of our people for this devotion to Mary. I dedicated the Mass at the cathedral to the honor of the Virgin under the title of Mt. Carmel and I used her as the model that the Christian should imitate to live the gospel which, in this case, invites us to participate in the prophetic mission of Jesus Christ. And I spoke of the Virgin's faithfulness to the word of the Lord, as a collaborator in spreading the message of God.

After Mass at the cathedral, I went to Colegio Belén, where the Carmelites of St. Joseph were celebrating the profession of seven new sisters. Following the inspiration of the second reading from St. Paul, I spoke of the religious life as testimony to God's eternal love for humankind, to Christ's redemptive act, and of the eschatological transcendence to which the religious life provides witness among humankind. After Mass, I shared some agreeable moments with the community.

In the afternoon, in the parish of Mt. Carmel in Colonia Roma, the Carmelite Fathers had prepared a lovely group for their First Communion, which I had the honor of celebrating.

And in the evening I was visited by the vice president of the Movement of International Reconciliation,[185] which has its headquarters in Vienna. She came to offer us their cooperation to promote in El Salvador an activity related to nonviolence or, more positively, to justice and peace. I liked her idea very much, but I felt I could not accept it on my own and, because of this I asked if we could meet again tomorrow evening, along with some of my advisers.

 **Monday, July 16**

The feast day of Our Lady of Mt. Carmel. I celebrated my first Mass in Merced Church beside the pontifically crowned statue, encouraging the historic brotherhood of Mt. Carmel to preserve this tradition, but to try to bring a new spirit to it, the new spirit of the Church.

At nine o'clock in the morning, the solemn and traditional Mass in El Carmen Church in Santa Tecla. The church was completely filled. The

---

[184] In Spanish, *la Virgen del Carmen.*

[185] Hildegarde Goss-Meyer, of the International Fellowship of Reconciliation (IFOR).

theme of my sermon was to present the Virgin as the model for the Church: the inspiration for the national religious spirit and an example of our union with God and our union with our neighbor. I explained that whatever interferes with our union with God is sin and that every Christian must fight to the death against the kingdom of the devil and against the enslavement that comes from there, and commit to humankind according to the vision of God—including being willing to give up life itself for God and for our neighbor.

In Concepción Church in Santa Tecla, we continued the tradition of holding Confirmations on the feast day of Mt. Carmel. But, in contrast to previous years, we had a very beautiful group of children who were older than eight, already possessing the consciousness to receive, after the appropriate preparation by their parish priest and catechists, the sacred anointing during the Mass.

Afterward, in the evening, in El Carmen in Colonia Roma, another celebration of the Mass and afterward a lovely procession with lamps. It looked like the torch procession at Lourdes, singing the Ave María of Fátima, but for the Virgin of Mt. Carmel. I congratulated the Carmelite Fathers and the faithful of the parish, reminding them that a people devoted to the Virgin will not perish. And we prayed the Salve Regina; I gave them my benediction and we left for our homes very happy.

 **Tuesday, July 17**

The whole day in a meeting of CEDES, the Episcopal Conference of El Salvador. The agenda involved the election of new officers, from president on, and discussion of the seminary. I had written a letter before, referring to our lack of unity and pleading that the elections be postponed and that, instead, we spend the time reflecting on this situation that must be resolved: the lack of unity among the bishops. We spoke frankly about the many deficiencies of our hierarchy. We acknowledged some blame, but I am concerned about how strongly some of my brother bishops feel against the kind of pastoral work I am doing. It is clear that they do not want to see it continue. It pains me that they are not sensitive to the situation of the country and that they feel more comfortable with pastoral work—with preaching—that is not purifying, that does not lead to our people's liberation from this terrible situation. We were unable to arrive at any solution, but we talked about it rather thoroughly and

I think that the ground is fertile to continue when we have our next meeting in August.

In the evening, I met with the major and minor seminarians who just had a meeting on the integration of the seminaries. I was very pleased to hear the conclusions they had reached at the gathering and to feel the spirit of unity that is motivating them to make the seminaries of the Archdiocese, both the major and minor, into one compact unit with the ideal of preparation for the priesthood.

I also had a visit at the little hospital from the interim rector of the National University, with whom I talked at great length about the very difficult problem of our most important center for culture.

 ### Wednesday, July 18

The first visitor today arrived exactly at breakfast time. It was Father Rogelio Esquivel, who told me he wants to work in this archdiocese, since he feels part of it and sees no reason to go anywhere else. I told him very frankly about the direction we follow in our pastoral work and that I did not want to make a hasty decision. I merely told him that I was glad he had returned and that we were willing to continue discussing it.

At eight o'clock we met with the vicars of Mejicanos, Nejapa and Aguilares, who have organized a day of prayer and reflection in the cathedral to mark the thirtieth day since the death of Father Rafael Palacios. I encouraged them to be very careful what they say and suggested it would be best to write it out in advance. We planned the celebration of the Mass that will be concelebrated at twelve o'clock on the twentieth. Throughout the morning of the twentieth until Saturday the twenty-first at noon, there will be different acts and reflections; many of these programs will be broadcast on the radio. Also present were the secretary of communications; Father Pedraz, who is in charge of the radio; the vicar general, Father Cortés; the person in charge of communications as an adviser, Father Rafael Moreno. And we all agreed it should be a dignified celebration that will promote awareness of the mission preached by our Church.

Among the most significant visits this morning was that of Mr. John McAward, of the Peace and Justice Commission[186] in the United States—an interesting conversation about the desire of the members of the United States embassy and the members of the Peace and Justice Commission to serve the cause of human rights in our archdiocese.

Also a visit from Mr. Gabriel Delgado, formerly Brother Julio, who presented his impressions of the divisions among the bishops and the religious ignorance of the people. I asked him for his help, especially with the teachers, to encourage them to promote Christian formation. I agreed to give him a list so that he can get them together and work with them. Along this same line, the Federation of Catholic Schools also gave me the names of their new board today, and we talked, expressing the wish that the Catholic schools be true instruments of the pastoral work of the archdiocese. I shared words of encouragement with Dr. Napoleón González, director of *La Crónica del Pueblo*,[187] which just had a fire last Saturday. I shared words of encouragement with him and promised him I would take up a collection to help his newspaper.

In the afternoon, a meeting at the cathedral with those in charge of liturgy, sound and other aspects of the preparation for the upcoming Feast of the Divine Savior. As always, there is great enthusiasm for this year's celebration of the feast.

Afterward I went to visit the burned building of *La Crónica del Pueblo*, but it was closed.

 **Thursday, July 19**

Today we had the breakfast to discuss the second draft of the pastoral letter. We talked today about how to organize all of the different contributions into one text, using the material from the survey, which is abundant and very good. Father Fabián Amaya has done that work, and we analyzed it carefully and gave our opinion of the whole thing, the way the letter is written now. After we discuss some of the details again, Father Fabián will be in charge of taking all these opinions and doing a second draft that will be more organized and richer, incorporating the suggestions made today.

---

[186] The Unitarian Universalist Service Committee, which funded in El Salvador a publication called *Justicia y Paz.*

[187] A small popular paper.

**Friday, July 20**

In the cathedral, beginning at six o'clock in the morning, several vicariates have organized a long day of prayer—forty hours, which will last until tomorrow noon—in memory of Father Rafael Palacios, who was tragically killed in Santa Tecla thirty days ago today.

At twelve o'clock I was to concelebrate with almost all the priests of the archdiocese. When I arrived at the cathedral to concelebrate, we were surprised to find it surrounded by the police and the National Guard. It seemed that a false alarm had been spread about an occupation of the cathedral or that a political demonstration would arrive to take advantage of this prayer vigil. But, thank God, we were able to concelebrate.

In my homily I alluded to the prayer and reflection taking place, and about taking the message of God's word and taking advantage of the prayer for Father Palacios' soul. I also mentioned his charisms and what his death means, asking how it can be possible that we have come to this crime of murdering priests. And I answered by analyzing the situation of injustice and sin that a priest must denounce. And that means being unappreciated, being a persona non grata, to society, which, like Jerusalem, kills prophets and those who are sent to them. The vigil continued all afternoon and it will last all night with great fervor on the part of the communities that have come from different parts of the archdiocese.

Father Luis has returned to the country. He is a young Belgian who will work in Zacamil with Father Rogelio [Ponseele]. He was very glad to be back for this event at the cathedral. I also greeted Father Juan Macho Merino there; he was pastoral vicar during the time I was in the diocese of Santiago de María. He is a Passionist who is returning from Spain, now assigned to establish a house of formation here for their young men with vocations. I suggested several possibilities to him and told him that I would gladly accept whichever he chooses: the convent of San Francisco in Mejicanos or the St. Theresa House in Apulo or the parish of Guazapa. These three are currently available. There would still be the possibility of a change if none of these proposed houses meets their needs.

## Saturday, July 21

As I had promised, I went today to the town of San Miguel de Mercedes in Chalatenango. I was traveling with Father Fabián and, when we got to Chalatenango, we learned there that there were military checkpoints at the entrances to San Miguel, at each end, to prevent people from arriving in that town at the appointed time. In fact, when we arrived in Mercedes, a group of soldiers made us get out of the car and searched it, perhaps thinking there were weapons in it.

We saw that many people were being detained there, whom we greeted and with whom we tried to begin the journey into the town, which was now nearby, on foot. The leader of the squad, however, told me that they could not go any further, that I should go in the car, that it was an order from above. I commented that it was an irrational order, since these are peaceful people, mostly women, who had come because of a desire of their faith. But reason does no good with these people and I was very sorry to have to leave the people who had been detained. I expressed my solidarity with them and asked them to pray with me—them there and me in the church—and then I went on.

A few steps away a large group of people from the town and those who were able to get into the town were waiting for me in spite of the checkpoints, "*montiando*,"[188] as they say. With them I headed to the church, which was almost filled up. There they told me that there were even more people at the other entrance to town, most of the people from San Antonio los Ranchos, and I sent word to them to go back there and, when I finished my commitments in San Miguel, I would go to San Antonio to thank them for coming and to talk with them. I celebrated Mass. The mayor was present; he does not agree with these interventions that destroy the tranquility of the city, of the people.

In the homily I described the nature and the mission of the Church; the role of the bishop, who should visit the communities; the function of the communities, which are a source of great good for the people. I then deplored that this mission of building a true community is so disturbing as to cause attacks even on faith and the freedom of belief.

After the Mass I met with the pastoral agents: women religious, priests and, especially, many catechists from different villages and from the town of San Miguel, with whom we share the pastoral concern with a generous spirit for continuing the work on their part. I was glad to see how the Sisters of the Assumption, based in Chalatenango, who work in that town along

---

[188] Driving off the road or cutting across the fields.

with Father Fabián Amaya, have really managed to create great enthusiasm among the youth. I stayed to have lunch with them. There was a feeling of joy in the convent and, when I said good-bye to them, I felt the nostalgia that one feels in such a situation in spite of the trial we all had to bear, a trial we overcome with Christian joy.

Then after lunch, I headed to San Antonio los Ranchos and, as I expected, at the Shrine of the Cross were nearly one hundred persons who had not been able to come in because of the checkpoints. So we shared there—prayed, sang, talked. An interesting dialogue with questions and answers, ideas, suggestions—in summary, an atmosphere of family, of joy, faith and hope. I gave them as keepsake pictures of Pope John Paul II, telling them that they were for them, that I had put them aside for them and that I had not given any of them away in San Miguel. I promised to come back again another day especially to go to San Antonio los Ranchos; it will be in August.

When I got back to my residence, I learned about two very sad cases of repression: A mother, father and brothers and sisters had come from La Unión to tell me of their distress because a young man from their family had disappeared. He was taken prisoner near Pasaquina and they have not heard anything about him, even though several days have gone by. The other case is that of a gentleman, the owner of a press in San Salvador; he also was taken prisoner and nothing has been heard of his whereabouts since.

And, finally, the parish priest of El Calvario, Father Federico Sanggiano, notified me that the church has been occupied by FAPU, precisely to protest the disappearance of the latter gentleman.

 ## Sunday, July 22

In the eight o'clock Mass, I began my homily with a greeting to Nicaragua, since this week they achieved the beginning of their liberation by throwing out the regime of General Anastasio Somoza and installing a junta as the new government.[189] We prayed for the country of Nicaragua and we reflected, drawing conclusions from this event.

The theme of the homily came from the Scripture reading:[190] the shepherds Jeremiah uses to refer to government rulers, but that the

---

[189] On July 19, 1979, the Sandinistas took over the government in Nicaragua.
[190] Jeremiah 23:1-6.

Church applies to the bishops as well and to all of those who are pastoral agents or who participate in the government. We reflected on the problem of the peoples who are badly governed, the distinction between good and false shepherds, and how Christ is the true shepherd-king presented in sacred Scripture, in whom we put our hope to resolve the problems of all peoples.

After Mass, an interesting discussion with the young people in the choir from Quetzaltepeque, which participated in today's Mass. There was also a group from Santa Lucía parish in Ilopango, who want to work with the chancery to see how to bring back Father Astor Ruíz, who was expelled from the country when he tried to come in from Colombia and was sent to Guatemala the day before yesterday. I told them that I had already talked with Father Astor and that tomorrow, Monday, we would meet to study this case more carefully. And that this very evening I would go to Santa Lucía myself to celebrate the seven o'clock Mass and to talk with the community, which pleased them a great deal.

There were other interesting visits after Mass. It is a good way to meet with the people, especially those who attend Mass at the cathedral.

In the evening I celebrated Mass at Santa Lucía. After Mass, they showed me what they do and, really, it is a parish in which they are living Christian community in a very vibrant way. A catechist explained their work with the children, a young man, their work with the youth and a lady, their work with adults. And afterward we discussed the matter of Father Astor's situation. They proposed writing an open public letter, but I told them that it would be better to wait for the decisions of the Priests' Senate and that they could send a representative to learn their conclusions there.

 **Monday, July 23**

Today we had a meeting with the vicar general, Father Cortés; with Father Brito, the chancellor; and with Father Villarán, vicar of Ilopango, to which Santa Lucía, Father Astor's parish, belongs. A lay representative of the parish and Father Moreno also attended. Our idea was first to ask for a meeting with the Minister of the Interior and find out the reasons for Father Astor's expulsion, then to visit Father Astor to see how his spirits are. Since it seems he is concerned about other dangers, it is possible that he will not want to come back into the country yet. After that, we will do what is necessary publicly, both in this country and in other countries, since we should say something about these abuses.

I went to have lunch with the seminarians from the minor seminary at Chalatenango and had a very interesting conversation with them. They are young men who are eager to know more and more about their vocation and the problems each man who wants to embrace the priesthood faces. I had a good impression of that young community: recently ordained priests like Rafael Urrutia and Ezequiel Gámez; a deacon about to be ordained, Jaime Paredes; a seminarian already in theology,[191] Joaquín; and some Sisters of the Assumption, also young but with a strong sense of the pastoral work and teamwork. The young men of the seminary are growing in this atmosphere and that seems to me to indicate great promise.

Father Brito informed me when I got back that Father [Christobal] Cortés had talked at length with the Minister of the Interior, who seemed surprised, for the minister did not known anything about what had happened to Father Astor. The minister promised to find out and let him [Father Cortés] know tomorrow. The trip to Guatemala, then, is also postponed.

 **Tuesday, July 24**

The first visitor of the day was Father Walter Guerra, who asked me to mediate in the case of the strike by the workers who assemble brassieres. The workers are holding a group of the directors hostage, but the general manager does not want to go there for fear he will be held hostage, too. But they are willing to grant a great many of the workers' requests.

Father Walter promised me that the owners would come to talk to me and then I could call the leaders of the strike to mediate with them. I said that I would be very happy to do this. But after we had decided on a time and I had agreed to mediate in this case, Father Walter himself called to tell me that it was no longer necessary and that everything was in the process of being resolved—thank God!

I had the Tuesday meeting with the Executive Council of the chancery. We particularly discussed the problem at the press [Criterio], which is also in the process of being resolved. There are many apprentices and a more experienced hand is needed to operate a press that is in the process of modernization; but, at the same time, it is necessary to consider the justice issues involved in removing the apprentices.

---

[191] The final four years of seminary study.

We also talked about station YSAX. The solution will be worked out according to the suggestions of the current director, Father Pedraz. A commission has been named to resolve the problem, composed of the present director, Father Pedraz; Ingeniero Galván, administrator of the chancery; and Father Fabián Amaya.

We also discussed some other aspects of the administration of our archdiocese. Everything appears to be moving toward a coordination that will produce better results. Also, Miss Coralía Godoy is working with the secretaries to better organize the secretarial service, just as the administrator of Holy Family School, Doña Elizabeth Arias, is helping me to arrange some of the material aspects of the chancery. I thank the Lord, then, that all of these things are improving the workings of this office, which is the center for the pastoral work of the diocese.

We talked about pastoral work all morning with the Pastoral Commission, which had scheduled a meeting today. It was clear that the coordination of the pastoral work has been working well, since the office has been in operation, although Father Astor, currently expelled from the country, cannot head it. Father Octavio Cruz, who has talked with him and who has a real pastoral sense, will be in charge of this office along with Piquín, who has also proved to be a good lay administrator of the lay part of the Office for Pastoral Work.

In this meeting, which was rather long, we evaluated the vigil in the cathedral. We very frankly noted the negative points and the prevalence of positive values, in particular the greater consciousness on the part of the communities in defense of their priests, since it was in commemoration of thirty days after Father Palacios' death. I recommended very strongly that they use this situation to explain the thinking of the Church very clearly— the Church that is not to be used by anyone for other ends.

In the afternoon I went to celebrate a Mass for the family in Apopa, where I greeted a beautiful community that was gathered there and had dinner with my family.

**Wednesday, July 25**

The feast day of St. James the apostle. I celebrated the Mass for the patron saint, St. James, in the ancient parish of Aculhuaca. I mentioned the emotion I felt celebrating Mass in a church that links the ancient indigenous civilization with the Christian civilization brought to us by the Spanish missionaries. I spoke of the need for the spirit of St. James in this hour of persecution of the Church.

After Mass I spent some very pleasant moments with the community and especially with the priests of that town: Father Crespín, parish priest of Santiago [St. James] Aculhuaca; Father Nicolás González from Paleca and Father Guty [Gutiérrez], from San Sebastián—all three from Ciudad Delgado.

I was surprised upon my return to discover that the workers of Criterio Press had begun a work stoppage that day, demanding salary increases and other benefits. But, thank God, the administrator of the chancery, along with the vicar general and the communications secretary and Father Pedraz, administrator of the press, have already done some initial mediation; I talked with them before going to the agreed-upon meeting with the strikers. A renovation plan was proposed: Since the majority of the workers are apprentices, a group of qualified operators would be hired and those who are unhappy would receive severance pay and leave their jobs. But when this plan was proposed, the representatives of the group asked for an extension until tomorrow so they could propose the plan to the whole group and bring back reactions. I hope there are no complications.

In the evening, a visit to Dr. Semsch, very encouraging as far as the archbishop's actions and for the archdiocese. I have received a great deal of mail and until very late tonight, I have been resolving different problems.

 **Thursday, July 26**

My principal concern this morning was the strike at Criterio Press. My two correspondence secretaries came at breakfast-time to talk to me about their concern about it, too, because they thought it was being handled as a company would and not in a very Christian way. I made them see that there is a labor, management, factor that must be observed and I also asked them to encourage the Christian spirit in the young men on strike, so that they will also proceed in a Christian way.

I myself spent a while with the three representing the strikers to try to make them see, from my point of view as a pastor, without going into the labor issues—which the administrative side is handling—that they should proceed rationally and, above all, with Christian spirit. I told them they can count on my friendship whatever the solution may be. They thanked me, but it seemed that their principal posture was to stay on legal ground. They threaten to go to the Labor Ministry and take other measures. I told those in charge of the administration about this so that they could keep it in mind, for it seems they will meet again this very evening to resolve this problem.

Among this morning's visits, I had the pleasure of greeting someone from the town where I was born, whom I have known since I was a child: Mrs. Susana Castro, who encouraged me to continue on the course I have begun, in spite of her awareness, through other old friends of mine with whom I have lost touch, of the objections to the evangelical demands of our Church. I thanked her for her words of encouragement and asked for her prayers.

Also the father and sister of Father Trejo, who is in Venezuela right now, came to ask me to give him an extension. I made them see how, since there is a great need for priests, it did not seem very priestly to stay away from the country that needs him so urgently. But I agreed that I would discuss the matter with the presbytery, with the Priests' Senate. I asked that they bring in writing his own request so that it might be adequately studied.

Also, a journalist came, with whom we talked about the situation of the Church and its mission in the present situation of the country.

Members of the community of San Francisco in Mejicanos came to express their pastoral concerns, which seem to me to be in agreement with the initiatives of our archdiocesan pastoral work.

In the evening, a meeting with the archdiocesan Caritas committee in which, primarily, we studied the matter of the construction of the archdiocesan Caritas warehouse; the financial situation and the new programs that are developing; the good impression being created by this new way of running Caritas. I encouraged them not to get discouraged and, in spite of the difficulties, to continue our Caritas's work as a true school of charity.

**Friday, July 27**

For the second time, Father Rogelio Esquivel came to see me. He told me he has an opportunity to go to Guatemala to serve in the parish of Bishop Ham,[192] who is going to the United States for a while. He wants always to be considered a priest of this archdiocese. I discussed with him the problems he has with the clergy. I gave him my approval and encouraged him to use his time in Guatemala to develop friendship with Salvadoran priests because, when his stay there is finished, he could come back to become a fully functioning member of our clergy.

The situation of the strike at the press is the same. It was complicated today by conversations with certain employees at the chancery who seem to support totally the young men on strike at Criterio Press. There were meetings of the administrative council of the chancery with the employees of the archdiocese to explain to them the position of the press, which seems to be very fair; but they think the solution of getting rid of the apprentices at the press is not very Christian. They will continue to discuss these points.

In the evening, a private visit from a major in the army who admitted the degree of corruption that exists among the highest-ranking officers and how there is a group of sane officers who want to preserve the honor of the military. I encouraged him to continue to be honorable within the military instead of retiring as he wants to (it seems to him that he cannot be the man he should be in the kind of situations an army man is faced with these days, amid so much injustice, stealing supported by the same high-ranking officials), so that many of them are working to promote honor within the military, not taking advantage of the situation as others do. I congratulated him and I encouraged him to continue living as the yeast in his own dough.

 **Saturday, July 28**

In our Saturday meeting, we clarified the situation at the Criterio Press so that we could make some determination of how to arrive at a solution to the problem that has arisen there. Bachiller Roberto Cúellar, who has been apprised of the situation, suggested to us some possible ways to resolve it and we authorized him to try them. But unfortunately, although everything appeared to lean toward a solution, the

---

[192] Maryknoll Bishop Richard Ham, then bishop of Huehuetenango.

strikers used delaying tactics and said that it would be better to leave a final decision for Monday.

In the afternoon, in Colegio Don Bosco, I administered Confirmation as part of a very beautiful Communion liturgy to a group of young students of the school. The church was filled by those being confirmed, their parents and their godparents. It turned out to be a true catechesis of this great sacrament that, thank God, is attaining the importance our pastoral program wanted for it.

 ## Sunday, July 29

I mentioned in this morning's homily Father Santiago Garrido's fiftieth anniversary as a priest. In the homily, I presented Christ as the solution to all of our problems, provided that humankind works with him. And I also had the opportunity to denounce the many abuses being committed in the country. German television was present, filming the events taking place in our cathedral. After Mass that same television asked me for an interview and some Italian journalists as well; it took place in the convent of the cathedral and included questions about the situation and the possibilities for the future that the Church sees in this country.

In the afternoon, in Instituto Ricaldone, I went to speak at the final session of a Marriage Encounter. I spoke to them about the three themes they had discussed in their groups: the responsibility of parents, communication with their children and living the Christian experience in their homes.

 ## Monday, July 30

In the morning, a refugee at the archdiocesan offices, who had been in danger of being killed, thanked me. For he was going to leave but, before doing so, he wanted to leave his testimony of the cruel persecution and tortures he had been subjected to during his political struggles. He is part of the extreme left, but what they have done to him is an indication of the incredible lack of respect for people in our country.

There were some other very important visits, including an interview with two journalists from the United States. One journalist is connected with Georgetown University and she brought me greetings from there, since on another occasion they gave me an honorary doctoral degree. The topics discussed were very important, for they are highly intelligent journalists.

In the evening, in El Calvario Church in Santa Tecla, the forty days' Mass after Father Palacios' death; it took the form of a reconsecration after the sacrilegious murder of this priest.

We went over the draft of the pastoral letter with Father Rafael Moreno and Father Fabián Amaya. It is shaping up rather well. I received a letter from Father Astor Ruiz, a very Christian letter, very priestly, in which he expresses his deepest feelings on being unexpectedly expelled from his own country. But I am glad for the greatness of the priestly spirit with which he is offering this trial to God.

 **Tuesday, July 31**

Among this morning's visits, that of Dr. Morales Ehrlich stands out. He had been in exile in Costa Rica and was a candidate for vice-president of the republic in the last election, which ended with the candidates, Colonel Claramount and Dr. Ehrlich, going into exile. They belong to the Christian Democratic Party. He came to say hello to me along with another member of his party, David Trejo, and to offer to work with the Church, which he feels is his Christian duty. I thanked him and told him that the Church many times takes the role of advocate of human rights and of the gospel—many things that are, precisely, things that the political parties should be doing—and that I hope his return to El Salvador meant he would take on this responsibility. He seems to be very optimistic in spite of the enormous political difficulties in this country.

Also, an interview with a radio station in Costa Rica. My message was principally about the example of Nicaragua. I always kept a pastoral and evangelical perspective and avoided any answers of a political nature.

At noon, I went to concelebrate with the Jesuits in honor of Father Santiago Garrido, who completed fifty years in the priesthood this past Sunday.

# August, 1979

 **Wednesday, August 1**

Today I had an interesting meeting with the entire chancery staff to assess what has happened at Criterio Press, since there was a letter signed by the employees of the chancery. I tried to explain to them the process the administrators had followed and asked them also for their hierarchical loyalty to their bishop, necessary in a diocesan chancery, since we form a team which leads the entire archdiocese and should provide a good example of solidarity. There was interesting discussion, very sincere, and I think the balance has been positive toward increasing solidarity and true service to the hierarchical Church.

Father Octavio Cruz was present; he will be in charge of the Office of Pastoral Work. I talked especially with him. He has well-balanced criteria for carrying out the pastoral work I have always dreamed of, following the present course of the Church without any extremism, one that is able to understand the moment through which our country is living. I think that we have heading our Pastoral Commission a priest who will produce much fruit, God willing.

I celebrated the Holy Hour at the Divine Providence Hospital and I used the theme of liberation, from the point of view of liberation from sin and of raising humankind to the level of God. Immediately afterward two journalists, one from Brazil, from *O Globo*, and the other from Venezuela— a very interesting interview because the two journalists are very intelligent, in which we tried to analyze the role of the Church in El Salvador.

**Thursday, August 2**

With the chancellor's help I caught up with a series of letters and commitments. The rector of the cathedral let me know yesterday afternoon that the cathedral is under occupation by the Popular Leagues of February 28.[193] It is a new organization that protests in this way to try to obtain the freedom of some of their members, who have been taken prisoner and have disappeared.

In the afternoon Father Pedraz notified me that a representative of this group wanted to talk to me. I told him that I was at their disposal, for I was interested in negotiating the matter of the cathedral. I did not want to be in this situation on Sunday, August 5, and especially not on Monday, the sixth, as it would keep us from being able to use the place where traditionally we celebrate the patronal feast of the Divine Savior. He agreed to come tomorrow at nine o'clock in the morning.

Another interesting conversation was the one I had with Silvia, my private secretary, who indicated she is suffering because of the way the strike at Criterio Press was resolved. She and her friend María Isabel think that what happened was not just, that money and machinery were considered more important than human beings. I tried to make her see that these things have to be judged more impartially and that it is also necessary to consider the interests of the press, not neglecting human concerns but carrying out one of the most serious duties of the bishop—to protect the goods of the Church—and that I had promised to speak individually with the terminated employees to help them to resolve their problems. But they did not wait for them to be resolved as had been planned, but rather began the strike beforehand, and during it some offensive terms were applied to the hierarchy. She told me that all of the employees of the archdiocese, men and women, shared her and her friend's feelings, which seemed to me to be rather exaggerated. I still say that if anyone is not happy working in the archdiocesan office, the best thing is to leave and look for a job where that person will be more comfortable.

At any rate, this and another private conversation I had with Father Pedraz have made me think that we need to review the personnel we work with and try to inspire in them a spirit in line with the thinking of today's Church, which is my great dream, and in no way betray the principles I preach. (Silvia also insinuated that there is a contradiction between what is preached and what we do.) I have prayed to God for his illumination and also asked him to always keep me faithful in my effort to follow the gospel.

---

[193] A largely student-dominated organization named after the 1977 massacre.

In the evening, a visit from a reporter from the United States who represents three newspapers, accompanied by a translator from the United States embassy. We had an interesting conversation about what the Church thinks about the violence and about the hope it tries to inspire amid the situation of the country.

## Friday, August 3

I have spent today exclusively on the study of the pastoral letter.

## Saturday, August 4

I was also able to spend time studying the pastoral letter, as I did yesterday. Nevertheless, in the evening I had a rather long meeting with Father Moreno and Bachiller Cúellar, who brought the week's news. We commented on the latest happenings in the country. Today in San Esteban Catarina, Father Napoleón Alirio Macías, parish priest of that town, was gunned down. In the afternoon I went there and found out directly about this tragic event, which had been planned far in advance. The priest mentioned *judiciales*,[194] a group of men watching outside the church who took advantage of a moment when the priest was alone to go in and kill him between the door of the sacristy and the main altar.

## Sunday, August 5

I made a special intention for Father Macías at the Mass at the cathedral. The choir organized by the Sisters of Charity in Tepecoyo came to sing, some seventy voices strong—truly a joyous celebration in the cathedral. And at the Offertory, they also offered the

---

[194] Members of death squads.

fruits of the land from that community along with the bread and wine. The people applauded this gesture of sympathy and solidarity.

In the afternoon, the traditional *bajada*[195] was very impressive. A float symbolized the storm at sea, with the inscription "Lord, save us! We are perishing!"[196] I greeted the crowd, since the whole ceremony was broadcast by Radio YSAX and there was ample opportunity to present a message during the two hours that the procession lasted.

## Monday, August 6

The Mass was concelebrated by almost all the priests of the diocese, and the great participation of the communities enlivened the singing and filled the street outside the cathedral and a large part of the park. It was truly a Mass that was patronal and of the people. The presence of the Lord could be felt in our liturgy, and a joy that was based on faith and Christian hope was noticeable. Instead of a homily, I presented the outline of the fourth pastoral letter. It was interrupted repeatedly by applause, through which the people showed their solidarity with the central theme of the letter: the mission of the Church in the country's present crisis. "I hope," I said to them at the end of Mass, "that as you leave here, each of you will be a builder of this new civilization based on the love that our country needs so greatly."

I greeted many people once the Mass was over, people who had come from many corners of the country, in whom I noted a true cordiality toward their pastor.

In the afternoon, another magnificent turnout! Perhaps the greatest that the town of San Estebán Catarina has ever seen, the town whose parish priest, Father Alirio Napoleón Macías, was murdered two days ago. This afternoon at four o'clock he was to be buried in the parish church. Bishop Rivera, Bishop of Santiago de María, presided in his role as parishioner of that parish (he was born in San Estebán) and because the bishop of the diocese, Bishop Aparicio, was not there; he was in Mexico. An immense crowd of priests, and the park and the adjacent streets completely filled with the faithful.

---

[195] A procession through the streets with a statue.
[196] See Matthew 8:23-27.

Bishop Rivera gave an inspired homily, saying that such great pain is necessary for such great redemption, and that the death of so many priests is a sign that the hour of liberation is approaching. The people applauded many of his ideas.

At the end of Mass we processed around the park. The crowd did not move; it was too large. They only opened a path through the street for the priests to pass through. Perhaps some one hundred priests assisted in this funeral and afterward the body was brought into the church where it was buried.

There was a moment of terror during the Mass, for a false alarm spread and a panic began; several people fell on top of each other but, thank God, calm was quickly restored and the rites continued normally. The comments, those about the priest's death, those who killed him and especially those about the positive effects like this demonstration of faith give great hope to the Church.

### Tuesday, August 7

A meeting of the Executive Council of the archdiocese. Also several visits which, although they were important, were not outstanding.

### Wednesday, August 8

I made a trip to the east to give my condolences to some families in San Miguel—the Giralt family and Argüello family. I visited Miss Aurora Asturias, young Miss Angélica de Mena and especially a couple who are very humble, very affectionate: Don Luis Aparicio and Doña Avelina. Very elderly, they have sanctified their pain, their infirmity. She, in a hammock with her legs amputated, offers everything to God; he, also a good Christian, has offered the weakness of his old age to the Church.

At noon, I had lunch in Jucuapa with Dr. Jiménez Barrios, who told me in great detail many events of his interesting life.

In the evening, a meeting with the seminarians to examine certain criteria with respect to Father Macías' death and also about the patronal feast August 6. Their reflections were quite appropriate and gave me the welcome impression of vocations to the priesthood maturing well. I invited them to take these same ideas to the priests' meeting that will discuss the same topic and to the meeting on pastoral work, where they will be able to incorporate many of their ideas for the patronal celebrations.

 **Thursday, August 9**

I spent almost the entire morning with a group of priests from different dioceses who were preparing for a national clergy meeting next Saturday. Very welcome news was that Bishop Barrera of Santa Ana would release a declaration of solidarity, and we in the archdiocese will join in it, and by telephone Bishop Alvarez and Bishop Rivera also added their solidarity. I think that in this way Father Alirio Macías is making the great wish of my prayers a reality: the unity of the bishops and the clergy. We pray to the Lord that this gesture of solidarity resulting from Father Macías' death be the beginning of the unity of all of the bishops and the clergy that would be so useful for the people of God in our country.

 **Friday, August 10**

We had breakfast at Colegio Belén in order to meet there with others interested in the communications media. A new presence was Mr. Munés, a publicity specialist.

During the day there were several visits from priests and some groups and, in the evening, an interview with a journalist.

**Saturday, August 11**

In the Guadalupe room of the San José de la Montaña Seminary, representatives of the clergy from all over the country met. At the same time, the nuncio had invited the bishops to the nunciature. Both meetings were to discuss the death of Father Alirio Macías. While the meeting of the priests was cordial, enthusiastic in defending the clergy and in solidarity with the diocese of San Vicente, unfortunately that of the bishops was a....[197]

The bishops' meeting in the nunciature confirmed the division existing among us. We could agree only on officially denouncing the assassination of Father Macías. The nuncio also offered to support this declaration in his next visit to the president of the republic. But when we tried to look at the causes, the meeting was dominated by the prejudice that there is Marxist infiltration in the Church. It was impossible to overcome that prejudice, in spite of my trying to explain that many priests are persecuted because they want to be faithful to the spirit of Vatican II, translated for Latin America by Medellín and Puebla. This was understood very little. Rather, the blame was laid on the instruments of Marxism which, according to them, the Church is serving. I offered this test of my patience to God, since I was being blamed in great part for the evil occurring in the country and in our Church.

I left before the end of the meeting because I had to go to San Antonio los Ranchos, where I had promised to be. And, although I had postponed the meeting with those good people until the afternoon, the attendance was large. We celebrated Mass and shared a beautiful Christian get-together, which compensated for my disappointment in the morning.

 **Sunday, August 12**

Mass could not be celebrated in the cathedral because it is occupied by workers who are on strike. We had to hold it in El Rosario Church. The homily, which was a commentary on the sixth chapter of John's Gospel, gave me the opportunity to talk about the flesh that Christ offered to sanctify human flesh and what human flesh becomes when it does not feed itself with Christ. At noon, I had lunch with my family, who were kind enough to celebrate my birthday with me in advance.

---

[197] Tape ends here.

**Monday, August 13**

Nothing special, since the many visits at the office were routine in nature.

 **Tuesday, August 14**

In the Carmelite house in Santa Tecla, we had the meeting of the Priests' Senate, in which we principally talked about the problem of the division among the bishops. This group of priests will get representatives of the clergy from the other dioceses to confront this problem directly with the bishops. We also tried to clarify the accusation of Bishop Aparicio that our archdiocese offended his vicar with the funeral Mass for Father Macías. The testimony of all of those who attended was requested, for they can say that this is all false and is nothing more than the product of Monsignor Fredy Delgado's resentment.

The committee set up to coordinate the decisions made in the meeting of clergy and women religious told me that they had postponed the commitment on the part of a group of priests and women religious to fast because they cannot count on the solidarity of all the dioceses and because they think it might be premature. It will be postponed and they will work for greater solidarity on the part of the priests to carry out an action that will achieve the proposed objectives.

Later the employees of the chancery honored me with a birthday celebration. It was very nice, held in the meeting room.

In the evening, more journalists interviewed me in the Divine Providence Hospital.

 **Wednesday, August 15**

The students of the seminary surprised me with a lovely serenade. Then we went to celebrate Mass and to have breakfast, and we visited the patient rooms. They were happy hours, very Christian, filled with great charity; but at nine o'clock I had to go celebrate the patronal Mass at Mejicanos, where Our Lady of the Assumption is the patroness. Father Orellana had prepared a group for Confirmation, which added to the patronal Mass. And I ate lunch with the parish priests of the Vicariate of Mejicanos, with whom we had an interesting conversation about our pastoral work, especially about the Christian base communities.

At seven o'clock in the evening, in the church of San José de la Montaña, the seminarians had prepared a Mass with participation from many different priests, many women religious and the faithful. It was truly a homage that filled my heart to overflowing. Before my homily Father Cortés introduced the homage as the best gift they—the priests and the people of God—could give me on my birthday. After Mass, a young man from the Student Christian Ecumenical Movement read a letter in support of my nomination for the Nobel Peace Prize and asked everyone to sign in support of this petition. With their applause, they showed their willingness to sign—which happened later when the service was over.

After Mass there was also a fellowship time with the seminarians and other communities, which was also joyous and very nice.

 **Thursday, August 16**

At eight o'clock in the morning the Sisters of the Sacred Heart, the professors and the students of Marie Paul School paid me a very affectionate tribute.

At eleven o'clock I celebrated in Chalatenango with the communities of that central point of the vicariate and with the seminarians and all the priests and nuns. But before I got to the Mass, they made me get out of the car at a military checkpoint, treating me as if I were a suspect. It is clear that they like to show their power over the Church. Also, during the Mass the soldiers were watching us—may God forgive them!

At seven o'clock in the evening, the patronal Mass for San Jacinto[198] in the neighborhood of the same name, a Vincentian parish. It was also a very cordial ceremony.

---

[198] St. Hyacinth.

## Friday, August 17

The meeting of the bishops had been scheduled for today. I arrived at the time agreed, but Bishop Aparicio had convinced the other bishops to cancel this meeting out of fear that the priests who were also meeting might try to force a dialogue with the bishops. Although Bishop Rivera and I opposed canceling the meeting and wanted to hold it as usual, the idea to cancel it prevailed—even though the priests had no such intention.

At twelve noon a sister from the United States came to give me a greeting from her congregation. She also brought greetings from some of the bishops, especially from those who work with Latinos, and to express to me the feeling of solidarity of all of those dear churches in the United States.

At six o'clock I had dinner with the third-year students at the seminary. I will try to promote this kind of intimacy more, since they will soon be our priests.

## Saturday, August 18

Today a group of priests, women religious and Christian communities began three days of prayer and fasting in El Rosario Church. They have explained their objectives to me and I respect their project, although I recommended that they use great prudence so as not to compromise the archdiocese in any way. The coordinating and information committee has kept me informed, and I believe that this is a priestly, ecclesial project. The spiritual value of prayer and fasting will dominate, and they assure it will produce a prophetic denunciation in an effort to stop this wave of crimes, of abuses, of which priests have also been victims.

I had to go to Usulután to preside over the graduation of the Technological Institute of Usulután, since the ceremony had been named for me and, out of a feeling of gratitude, I went there to be with them. I presided over the *Te Deum* in the church and the cultural program where the graduation took place, in the Alameda Theater. I expressed my appreciation to them and addressed a few words of guidance and encouragement to the young people, who with their title of *bachiller* represent more hope for our country.

I visited the Franciscan Sisters, who received me very cordially. I brought them to that city and I am glad to see how their school, St. Augustine, has flourished, as well as their other pastoral projects in that city and in nearby towns.

I went to have lunch in Santa Elena. The parish priest, Father Rodas, was a classmate of mine in the seminary. Bishop Rivera was also there, since they were celebrating the feast of the patron of the town. There were several priests at lunch, with whom I shared some cordial moments.

I returned [to San Salvador] to celebrate Mass for the Sisters of the Good Shepherd in the novena for Sister María Mercedes, who died nine days ago.

 **Sunday, August 19**

Since the cathedral continues to be occupied by the workers who are on a hunger strike, I celebrated Mass for the second Sunday in El Rosario Church. The priests who began their three days of prayer and fasting yesterday asked me to let them concelebrate with me and I did so gladly. At the time for the homily, I explained to the people why so many priests were there, and I asked one of the priests to explain the purpose of that prayer and fasting. I clarified, so that the people would not be confused, that this is not an occupation of the church or a hunger strike, but rather an ecclesial action that I see no reason to prohibit. It is an action involving the strengths of Christianity—that is, prayer and fasting—and the purposes seem to me to be healthy as well since they want to obtain greater unity in the Church, especially in the hierarchy and, at the same time, cry out in the name of the people, who are hungry because of the great injustice with which they are being attacked.

Father Moreno explained their objectives after my homily, and I think the idea was very clear. After Mass, many of those attending expressed their solidarity with the group and stayed with them all day long.

After Mass I went to the village of Los Sitios in Dulce Nombre de María, where they were celebrating the Mass for the corn festival. At the entrance to the town, a military checkpoint, the now-familiar search, for they do not respect the figure of the archbishop, who is going to visit a town for reasons of his ministry, and are so suspicious that they look at everything he has in the car. May God forgive them and enlighten them!

The ceremony was very nice even though the sun was hot. We celebrated Mass. I preached to them about the Bread of Life, to whom the bread of the earth should be offered, the tortilla from our corn. And I said that we should thank God and also that we should offer to God these gifts he gives to us. I called for a world based on love. The National Guard, who had arrived during the Mass, was listening to this homily and watching the group, although there was no need for this military presence.

In the evening, I ate dinner with Ingeniero Carlos García Prieto and his wife, Antonieta. Our conversation was interesting, although it seemed to me slanted toward capitalism. There was even criticism of the present course of the Church, but always presented in a very respectful way.

 **Monday, August 20**

I celebrated Mass in the Church of San Antonio Abad, where this Mass culminated the patronal festival of the Assumption of the Virgin, which had been going on through today. In the normal routine of the chancery, several visits.

 **Tuesday, August 21**

Committee for Pastoral Work. An interesting meeting, led by Father Octavio Cruz, the new secretary of this committee. I was only able to be there for the end and I was told it had gone well.

There is a special report [in the files].

This morning I went to celebrate Mass at Colegio de Bethania in Santa Tecla for Sister Rosa, a very old sister, one of the founders, who died yesterday. I preached on religion, the religious life, the testimony of a Baptism carried to its ultimate consequences, imploring that the Baptism our people receive be taken more seriously so that we do not have a people formed of baptized pagans. In this Mass I had the disagreeable experience of encountering a lady who said that I was not the same as before and that I had deceived them. I did not say anything at all. I understand that this calumny is common in those who do not want the Church to touch their petty interests.

In the afternoon a visit from our sister, Paula, a Belgian Christian who helps us with great affection from that country and will help us, I hope, concerning the proposal I made to her to construct an episcopal house.

I also had a visit from Mr. Carlos Borgonovo and the rector of the university to talk to me about the current situation in the country and to search together for solutions we can point out to our beloved country, which is so bloody and suffers so. I told them that the simple fact of being concerned and meeting is already a sign of hope and that we must continue searching; that, for myself, I cannot give any illumination of a technical nature, but that, yes, as a pastor, I can encourage hope and inspire those who do have the knowledge to collaborate with their knowledge and their experience. Possibly there will be some meetings for this kind of consultation at the university.

 ## Wednesday, August 22

A very busy morning with many visits at the chancery. But I mainly had to attend to a meeting I had promised to have with the Administrative Council to evaluate the good work this council has done in advising the archbishop on the administration of our assets. I recognized some deficiencies on my part and promised to correct them. I encouraged them to continue their work since their advice is extremely useful to us in the administration of the chancery.

A visit from some young people from Mexico who were very favorably impressed with the work being carried out in our archdiocese. Also a visit from a representative of the Christian Democratic Party of Latin America, with whom we spoke about the situation of the country. He said that the Church is carrying out a good role.

The Mass to close the days of prayer and fasting was held in El Rosario Church. I asked the advice of the Priests' Senate and they advised me not to go, since it was a controversial action and my participation could divide rather than unite the clergy of the archdiocese.

**Thursday, August 23**

An interesting evaluation with the priests who are attending the dialogue with the Christian Democratic Party and the business sector in San Salvador: Father Estrada, Monsignor Urioste, Father Jesús Delgado and Father Cortés. In summary, the different meetings that have been held have been characterized by progress in mutual understanding. The Church has had the opportunity to clarify several misunderstandings, and they are making positive headway, learning more and widening their horizons, which will favor a solution to the crisis of our country.

I met with the new management of YSAX and of Criterio Press, along with the administrator, the vicar general and other parties interested in the media. It was very interesting to see the affection and enthusiasm with which they are working to spread the ideas of the archdiocese. Different shortcomings were pointed out. Some improvements that will be beneficial for the dissemination of our thought were reported.

In the afternoon, visits from journalists and television in the Divine Providence Hospital. And at seven in the evening, a meeting with the seminarians from the archdiocese, in which we were able to clarify a little the conflict that exists with the seminary team because several students of the major seminary participated in the days of fasting and prayer without having consulted that group. Naturally, I encouraged them to ask for forgiveness and to make peace and to talk about this and, in the future, not to make such decisions on their own.

 **Friday, August 24**

Today I went to celebrate the patronal feast of Arcatao in honor of St. Bartholomew, the Apostle. It was a picturesque journey, but the road was rather bad because of the rain, which was still falling this morning. At the Sumpul River we were stopped at a checkpoint formed by troops from Chalatenango and agents of the National Police. They made us get out; there were priests from Chalatenango, some sisters and I. They kept us there for a long time. We were patient and, after their inspection, were able to go on.

When we got to the town of Arcatao, a strong contingent of the National Guard stopped us again. For the first time, they made me put my hands on top of the car and they searched me. They searched all of us. A North American journalist from Boston was with me; he realized what was happening and was alarmed. Above all, he realized how helpless our people are in the face of the armed forces in our country.

After their inspection and search, witnessed by the sisters from Arcatao, who were very close by, we continued to where the people awaited us. They greeted our arrival with enthusiasm and we went on to the church accompanied by a great number of the faithful. One of the military leaders told me that they had orders to protect me and that I should allow them to do so and that they would be on guard in the church. I told him that it was not necessary, that it would be better for them to guard the town and that, given the situation of the country, the military presence in the church was no honor. But we continued on our way. And it seems that they were in the church at first, but that later one of the sisters convinced them it would be better if they were not there. And they went off to take prisoners elsewhere once they had created a climate of nervousness there.

But the church was completely filled with the faithful. And when I spoke to them about St. Bartholomew, I told them that he had been skinned alive precisely because of his faithfulness to the gospel, and that God sometimes requires sacrifices of us, that we should be calm and courageous and continue to spread the teachings of Jesus Christ. It was a nice gathering. Afterward we went to the convent, where there was a program of songs with beautiful messages and where we conversed informally with some of the people and, at lunchtime, with the catechists from the different towns, who began a very interesting dialogue with their pastor.

We got back rather late and the appointments I had in the evening were kept by Father Moreno and the sisters at the Divine Providence Hospital.

 ### Saturday, August 25

I celebrated Mass at San Juan Opico because a lovely group of young people had been prepared for Confirmation. Many children came, young people from the neighboring parish of Tacachico. It was a lively Mass. The church filled up and we gave the liturgy all its importance in relation to the Confirmations.

After Mass, which several priests from the vicariate attended, I talked with a very significant group of catechists, true supporters of the parish priest. A group that was to be confirmed but was delayed due to problems with transportation was confirmed in the parish hall, which turned out to be another lively ceremony for the catechists.

In the afternoon I celebrated Mass at the Liceo Salvadoreño for a family celebration—a young girl who had her fifteenth birthday and whose family belongs to my former diocese, Santiago de María.[199]

 **Sunday, August 26**

The Sunday Mass was very well attended, as always. I had to celebrate it at El Rosario Church, since the cathedral is occupied by some political groups. There were several journalists and representatives of foreign television stations at Mass.

This afternoon I went to the village of El Salitre in the parish of Tejutla in the department of Chalatenango. There we observed the second anniversary of the death of the catechist Felipe de Jesús Chacón, who was cruelly murdered, the skin removed from his face, two years ago. An admirable man who left a marvelous witness, remembered with great affection, especially by those of the Cursillo de Cristiandad since, after attending a Cursillo, he committed himself to working for the Kingdom of God in a very edifying way.

The Mass was so well attended that we were unable to hold it inside the church and had to take the altar outside. I was not able to share afterward with the different communities that had come because I had another commitment in the community of La Palma, where they were celebrating the second anniversary of the *La Semilla de Dios* Cooperatives.[200] This is an important and unique social project, because it has managed to raise the level of such a poor and helpless region. It is picturesque, on top of a hill. We celebrated Mass outdoors in the fresh air and many people attended. I tried to present the message that work and prayer are the strength of humankind.

[199] The *quinceañera*, the celebration of a girl's fifteenth birthday, marks her passage to womanhood.

[200] The "Seed of God" cooperatives produce crafts which have become identified with El Salvador: small wooden decorative pieces enameled with colorful designs of people and animals.

**Monday, August 27**

The ladies of the archdiocesan committee of Caritas invited me to lunch. I tried to leave there also a message of love, which is what the Church needs so greatly today.

**Tuesday, August 28**

The most important event this morning, which was a very busy one at the chancery, was the visit we had with Mr. Poma and Mr. De Sola, two leaders in private industry who are very worried about the situation of the country. They wanted to share with me their opinions on this matter since, according to them, the Church is the only entity that has the moral force to give leadership for the country. I thanked them for this tribute. I tried to listen to their opinions and to also give mine very frankly. Although we do not agree on everything, I believe that they accept the hard demands of the gospel, that it is only possible to have true peace if there is true justice. And I emphasized strongly the necessity of changing the social, economical and political structures of the country—at the very least, for the people to see a serious beginning of this transformation, for otherwise we will be unable to stop the wave of violence.

In the afternoon we had a very important meeting at the house of the Passionist Sisters at Planes de Renderos to evaluate the results of the conversations that the industry leaders, the Christian Democratic Party and other leading sectors of our society have been holding along with representatives of the Church: the vicar general, Monsignor Urioste; Father Cortés, Father Jesús Delgado and Father Estrada. We evaluated the place of the Church in this atmosphere—and frankly, it was like taking the temperature of our own Church and orienting our pastoral work better. We were unable to finish and agreed to meet tomorrow at noon in the Divine Providence Hospital.

In the evening I had dinner with a Christian base community that Father Rafael Palacios had organized in Santa Tecla. His memory was present in everything, in beautiful testimonies to a man who did so much good almost in secret. For my part, I spoke to them about the relationship between the bishop and a priest and, very concretely, with Father Rafael and how through the priest, the bishop and the community manage to become one spirit, one family. I encouraged them to preserve that in a truly communal and ecclesial way.

**Wednesday, August 29**

I could not go to San Juan Cojutepeque, where they are celebrating their patronal feast today. I attended to visits of different journalists and representatives of foreign television in the chancery.

In the afternoon a Franciscan priest came, one of those who work in Gotera, along with a sister. He is Irish and she is British, and they told me the results of their trip through their countries during their vacations and how they were able to create an atmosphere of great solidarity with our country. On a personal level, they brought me some very meaningful greetings and an invitation to go to Ireland, which I told them would be very difficult for me, given the situation and especially because of the barrier of a language that I cannot speak perfectly.

There was another journalist in the afternoon and one in the evening and, although they try one's patience, I still think it is a marvelous opportunity to spread the words and ideas of the pastor.

 **Thursday, August 30**

An important visit from the Central Peasants' Union,[201] a group of workers from the country who expressed their desire to be in solidarity with the Church and to ask it for some specific help. For my part, I told them that I was willing to do so with great pleasure.

Another nice meeting was with the parish priests of the Vicariate of Mejicanos. In the Belgian sister's house, next to Domus Mariae, we had a very friendly and intimate conversation on their relationship to their bishop. I began by expressing to them my desire to hear very frankly their suggestions—even complaints—in order to improve my relationship with them. And second, their relationship with each other was very frank. They brought out all their defects and encouraged each other to develop their good qualities and their friendship, which is obviously very great. And finally, their relationship to the laity, which is when many psychological and pastoral difficulties came up. But the atmosphere was extremely cordial and encouraging.

---

[201] FECCAS/UTC. FECCAS was the Christian Federation of Salvadoran Peasants; UTC, the Union of Farm Workers.

**Friday, August 31**

Today is the first anniversary of the death of our well-remembered Bishop [Rafael] Valladares.[202] Starting on Sunday, I asked for prayers for him, since I always feel him to be so near.

Several visits at the chancery. The principal one was from a committee from the parish of Colonia Dolores, with Mr. Tomás Sánchez Zelaya, an old friend, who are now ready to build the convent, since they have almost finished the church, and also to continue by building a parochial school. I expressed my enthusiasm to them; they also have the support of their own organization and its generous help.

I had lunch with Don Pepe Simán, who is just about to leave for the United States. The cordiality of his home, where I am given great friendship, also provides an oasis for me in the middle of my work.

I could not have the meeting with the third-year students at the seminary, but we moved it to next Wednesday.

# September 1979

 **Saturday, September 1**

We held the usual Holy Hour at the Divine Providence Hospital and many people came. The Letter of St. James,[203] which is read this Sunday, gave me a wonderful opportunity to talk about the Father who is greater than all the light from the stars and from whom everything good comes, and who invites us to be close to him. There was a Baptism at Mass, which I also used to teach about the baptismal commitment of Christians.

---

[202] Former auxiliary bishop of San Salvador.
[203] James 1:17-18, 21b-22, 27.

**Sunday, September 2**

Some time ago, Father Manuel Loarca and the Daughters of Charity who work in that region [Ateos] had invited me to confirm a group of young people. The crowd was huge; it did not fit in the church and we had to hold the service in the nearby school. They were well prepared and had true youthful enthusiasm, for the majority of the young people were fifteen years old. There was a beautiful offering with baskets of products from that region. A cordial atmosphere and a joyful one that made us think about how beautiful a liturgy can be when it is truly understood as relevant to life. Many communities are constantly being built up by those pastoral agents—parish priests, women religious and many laypeople— who are catechists with a truly serious commitment.

 **Monday, September 3**

The principal event today was my visit to La Chacra, an extremely poor region where the Sisters of the Assumption work. Swiss television wants to take back images of the Church in all our sectors and so, as they were with me in Ateos yesterday along with some other journalists from Mexico, today they were filming different aspects of the miserable but happy and Christian life of the community of La Chacra. I went in houses where the rain that is falling is making the walls and floors damp. Often, the wall is the cliff itself, to which a metal roof has been attached. When they left, the journalists were impressed by this situation of misery and human proliferation—there were children all over the place.

My day ended with a dinner at the Carmelite Institute. Since the postulants[204] leave this week, they had invited me to come and gave me a warm reception. I encouraged them to continue to be faithful to their vocation and, in a joyous and intimate way, we spent a few moments together that were inspiring for our lives.

---

[204] Persons preparing to ask admission to a religious order.

**Tuesday, September 4**

A meeting of the clergy. We spent the whole day on the topic of base communities. There was a very serious discussion of the article published by Father Luis Montesinos, in which he criticizes different aspects of the archdiocese. And I was very pleased to see the solidarity and unity the body of the clergy feels with their archbishop, except for a few. And those not for lack of communion but, rather, because they do not agree with many things, but they also express themselves frankly. At the end of the meeting, I said that, as long as we maintain communion, having tensions is a healthy sign; and that we manage, if nothing else, to make the supreme values of charity and unity prevail.

 **Wednesday, September 5**

I heard a recording made in Arcatao by Swiss television with representatives of ORDEN, who openly call the sisters instigators of subversion in the different villages. I already referred to this in Sunday's homily as a lie and it truly is one, for these people have not understood what almost all of the people have understood: the evangelizing mission of these sisters, who are doing great good in that region.

The Oblate Sisters of the Sacred Heart also came. They will be taking over the parish of Jayaque, since there is no priest there. They are also filled with the spirit of pastoral work.

A group of priests from the different dioceses met in the parish hall of San José de la Montaña to evaluate their program of prayer and fasting held at El Rosario Church.

This whole week Swiss television has been among us with the idea of filming different aspects of the archbishop's life. Because of this, we have seen them in the eight o'clock Sunday Mass, the clergy meeting and in the chancery offices, as well as at the Divine Providence Hospital, filming scenes in the dining room there, in the chapel and with the patients, to show where the archbishop lives. A journalist from Sweden has come, too, one who has visited different sectors of our national life and also wanted to interview the archbishop about the pastoral aspects of the situation.

**Thursday, September 6**

A morning of great activity, including visits and meetings, and ending with the lunch I had been invited to by the priests of Opus Dei. They told me about their work with professionals and university students and also with workers, servants. It is a quiet work, very spiritual. After lunch I was able to see a report from Italian television on the founder of Opus Dei, which emphasizes the value of prayer and of the sanctification of the lay vocation. It seems to me that this is a source of wealth for our Church: the sanctity of the laity in their respective professions.

In the afternoon the nurses who work for Social Security had asked me to celebrate a Mass, which I did with pleasure, in order to thank God that they had been able to resolve the problem of their just demands in a rational, peaceful way. I told them that I wished that all the conflicts in our country could be solved in a similar manner and that one day we could give thanks to God not just for a part of the socioeconomic problem, like the situation at Social Security, but also for the entire country in its diverse, complex problems.

I went to have dinner with the secretary of the Cursillos de Cristiandad. It was a family dinner, and I introduced a topic that was explored in a very Christian and evangelical way: the theme of unity; asking them to suggest to me in a fraternal way what I can do to achieve unity with my dear brother bishops. Because if I am the cause of any obstacle to this unity, then I am willing to fix that. I was very pleased by how frankly they spoke to me, and most of it was positive. They told me that unity must involve the criteria expressed in the Gospels; that unity is one of the fruits of the Holy Spirit and that the people many times interpret this Spirit better than the hierarchy itself does; and that, according to this evangelical criteria and the Holy Spirit, there was no doubt that the course we have adopted in the archdiocese is the work of God. And that if they distance themselves from it, criticize it and work against it, unity will never be achieved outside this Spirit. Rather, we should ask that all of us be converted and I myself should try to be faithful to the Spirit and the gospel, being guided ever more by his inspiration.

**Friday, September 7**

It was a tragic day. We woke up to the news of the assassination of the president's brother,[205] a retired professor who lived in Apopa. The secretary—actually, the subsecretary—of the Ministry of Defense, Colonel Iraheta, came to see me and told me that he had talked at the viewing of the body with the president and the minister of defense and other men in the government about the danger I am in, and that they are offering me whatever protection I want, even a bulletproof car.

I thanked him and sent my regards to the president, my condolences on his brother's death, saying respectfully that I cannot accept this protection since I want to run the same risks as the people do; that it would be an antipastoral witness were I to ride in such safety while my people are so insecure. I took the opportunity to ask him, rather, to protect the people in certain zones where the checkpoints, the military operations, do so much damage—or at least create so much terror. I told him that I myself had been the object of this kind of abuse when, upon entering Arcatao, they had me put my hands up and searched me.

He was surprised; he begged my pardon and said that they would investigate, that many times underlings go beyond the orders given them. I also talked with him a great deal about this situation in which certain crimes seem to be tolerated: I mentioned the murders of our priests, which have not been investigated. Sometimes the suspension of these investigations seems to be intentional. All in all, it seems to have been a useful conversation, since I was able to denounce certain things in a respectful way to someone who can do something about them.

Today is First Friday and many people have received Communion.[206] I went to confession in the Church of Carmen with the Jesuit Fathers, where I saw how the devotion to the Sacred Heart of Jesus is flourishing.

I had promised to go to El Paisnal to celebrate a Mass at Father Grande's tomb, since Swiss television also wanted to film the tomb of Father Grande, who was the first to fall in this series of crimes against our clergy. But I was advised that, given the crime that had occurred in Apopa, there would be many operations around there and that I could be taking a risk; that it was not worth it, since it was not for a pastoral end but rather for the television crew. Because of this, we announced on the radio that we would not have the Mass, and that next Sunday, when I go to celebrate

---

[205] José Javier Romero, murdered by the Popular Liberation Forces (FPL).

[206] Popular devotion to the Sacred Heart includes receiving Communion on consecutive first Fridays for nine months.

another Mass in that same part of Aguilares, we will visit Father Grande's tomb.

In the evening, a meeting with the archdiocesan students at the major seminary. They spoke about the meetings they have had with the rector, Father Goyo, about the days of prayer and fasting in El Rosario Church—five meetings in which they have been able to analyze this and draw very positive conclusions. But, at the same time, they have discovered problematic areas, which we tried to discuss in this meeting.

At the beginning of the meeting, there were two representatives of the ecumenical movement in the United States: The man was a minister of the Methodist Church and the woman, a Brazilian, works in the ecumenical secretariat[207] in the United States. They shared with the seminarians for a while in a very warm manner and then left, very happy about their visit.

With the group of seminarians we went into great depth about the theme of unity, about the topic of mutual respect with the team, so that the seminary might truly be a center of unity for bishops, priests and the seminarians themselves. In summary, I think it was a rich meeting, in which I also began the work so that the committee of priests can take responsibility for working more intensely in the formation of our clergy and in building a good relationship between the archdiocese and the formation team of the seminary.

 **Saturday, September 8**

In the evening I prepared my homily for tomorrow with the information I receive every Saturday to complete the part announcing current news and denouncing abuses in my homily.

The afternoon was also very beautiful in Santa Luisa Chapel where, to commemorate the twenty-fifth anniversary of the Walter Deininger School, we celebrated different sacraments: Baptism, Confirmation and the weddings of several couples. A beautiful way to demonstrate how a school is a center of pastoral work that extends beyond the school when the work is given the evangelistic character it should have in a Catholic school.

---

[207] Rev. Paul McCleary, of Agricultural Missions, and Theresa Drummond, a U.S. nun who had worked in Brazil, both then with the National Council of Churches.

## Sunday, September 9

For the second time, I had to celebrate the Mass at the Sacred Heart Basilica since the cathedral and El Rosario Church continue to be occupied. The congregation appeared larger. Someone pointed out the great number of men who attend this Mass. There was also a Methodist pastor from the United States and a secretary from the Council of Churches in that country. The homily inspired by the miracle of the cure of the deaf-mute[208] gave me the occasion to present Christ as the true Liberator, who does not destroy but rather remakes, and who shows all the dimensions of humankind: the transcendent and the socio-historical.

After Mass, I went to preside over the solemn profession of perpetual vows of a Passionist Sister in Concepción Church—a very beautiful ceremony that allowed me to issue a call to all those who are baptized to take Baptism seriously and reflect it in their lives, since the profession of a religious is not a separate sacrament. Rather, it is the same Baptism carried to consequences that are serious and holy and provide great cooperation for the Church.

After a frugal lunch at the Passionists' house, I went to Aguilares, where we were going to celebrate the ninth day after the murder of Jesús Jiménez, a great catechist whom they called there "the man of the gospel." In spite of being illiterate, he had his biblical notes from which he would select according to the circumstances, and he was very faithful to his responsibility as coordinator of the communities. And he died, murdered mysteriously.

His body had already been taken to the mayor's office, from which the women had to take it to the village where the Mass that I went to celebrate was held, at some distance from the center of the parish. There was a large attendance of communities, which are developed in those areas—a very emotional Mass. The Swiss television people, who wanted to film this Mass, told me their impressions, very pleasant, very original.

After Mass, we went to visit Father Grande's tomb in El Paisnal. The Swiss television also went there to film some scenes of that place, which is venerated in the archdiocese. The fear in the atmosphere was noticeable. The people watched us from a distance, but they did not come near us. An "ear,"[209] as we say, was very close to us, watching what we were doing. And we could see that the National Guard, where they had their headquarters about half a block away, was also rather nervous. In summary, an abnormal

---

[208] Mark 7:31-37.

[209] The word *oreja*, "ear," is commonly used for someone eavesdropping or observing others' conversation, a spy.

situation, a psychosis that has been created in all these places so tormented by the repression.

### Monday, September 10

This morning I assembled the council on the seminary. Father Sigfredo, rector of the minor seminary, is in charge of its affairs, and I have pressured him so that we study, with the commission that was named and that has yet not done any work, the delicate situation of the relationship of the interdiocesan seminary to the archdiocese—a tension that, especially among the bishops, has caused a division. For Bishop Aparicio has removed almost all his students from the seminary to take them to Mexico. The seminary team is also studying a series of problems that it sees in its relationship to our archdiocese. The young men in the major seminary are unhappy and it is urgent that we prevent a greater disaster, the expulsion of several young men who could be very worthy priests. The whole problem was discussed at length and we saw the need for dialogue with the seminary team. But, in order to have that, we need to prepare the material better. We will meet next Friday to continue this dialogue.

I went to have lunch at Colegio Guadalupano, where I saw the provincial [of the Guadalupana Sisters], who is Salvadoran. And I encouraged the sisters who work in Arcatao and who have practically been expelled from there because of the situation of the government. I tried to justify to the provincial this work, which is so misunderstood by many of the people of that region. Meanwhile, the sisters from Arcatao are helping me in the chancery.

In the evening, I went to an ultreya. The Cursillos de Cristiandad greeted me very affectionately. And, after my presentation to the entire group, I invited them to stay to discuss a project for an urban pastoral work. Some very good suggestions were made, but the main one was that Cursillos, which has as one of its charisms infusing the Christian spirit into different situations, is going to study those of the capital and its metropolitan zone as a base for the study of an appropriate pastoral project.

**Tuesday, September 11**

Responding to a wish of the nuncio, I went to see him. He was very cordial and told me that the principal reason for the visit was to tell me about the president's concern for my safety, that he sees great danger and that he is offering me protection. I repeated to the nuncio what I had told Colonel Iraheta, who also came in the president's name to offer me that same protection: that I was prepared to run the same risks as the people, that it would be very difficult for me to accept protection while the people continue to be unprotected. And that we have faith that God will protect us.

The nuncio praised my homily last Sunday and told me that I had spoken well and that he understood that I was caught between two enemies, the right and the left, and that he understood that I was in a very delicate position. I thanked him for his deference. I talked about some other matters, such as the Church tribunal,[210] which urgently needs to be reorganized, and I asked him to intercede with the episcopal conference so that this part of the Church might function in a unified manner on a national level.

There was a meeting of the Committee on Pastoral Work, which was lively. We evaluated the recent meeting of the clergy and planned different aspects of the pastoral work, speaking very sincerely and frankly.

I talked with Father Gámez, who has problems in Chalatenango.

Catholic Relief Services[211] also came to visit me to tell me about the problems that exist with the Carmelite congregation in Santa Tecla: The center that has been operating there had been intended, with help from Catholic Relief Services, for a different purpose. I promised I would intervene so that this would be resolved in a fair way and especially for the good of our pastoral work. This North American agency, CRS, is also willing to help me with the problems the Church has to face because of emergency situations. I told him that we are living in a state of emergency, that there are many families whose members have disappeared, been murdered, taken prisoner, and that something must be done to help them. And he agreed that it would be good to create a fund for this kind of help and he will try to see to that this kind of aid can be better institutionalized.

In the afternoon we had a meeting with the communications office. The secretary, Miss Doris Osegueda, was there; the manager of the radio; Father Moreno, who is in charge of the Communications Committee; the vicar general, Monsignor Urioste; Father Torruella. We discussed different

---

[210] Court for matters under canon law.

[211] The overseas aid and development agency of the United States bishops' conference.

aspects of the radio, the press and related publications. Father Fabián Amaya was also present. He proposed some changes that would, without a doubt, improve the workings of the radio, which would benefit our pastoral work, catechesis, liturgy—the objectives of our Church.

In the evening, a telephone call at the hospital telling the Mother Superior that they were coming to collect the ten thousand colones[212] that I had offered them to kill someone. The Mother Superior was very alarmed and made me go sleep somewhere else, even though I told her, "These anonymous calls are intended to sow fear; don't worry." The alarm spread nevertheless, but nothing happened.

 **Wednesday, September 12**

A morning with many individual visits. Among them, the interview of Radio YSU[213] stands out. It will be transmitted on a Central American network; the principal question was on the situation of the Church in the midst of the conflict of the country.

I had lunch with Fathers Ellacuría and Jon Sobrino, who have just returned from participating in some conferences or meetings of a scholarly nature. Both of them told me that our archdiocese has a good reputation in other areas. In Germany, Father Sobrino saw my homilies translated into German and conversed with some Protestant ministers who are praying intensely for our archdiocesan program; they also promised me the prayers of thousands of their fellow Church members.

Father Ellacuría encouraged me greatly by telling me about his meeting with Father Arrupe in Rome and, at the same time, the meeting of Father Arrupe with the Holy Father. The pope asked Father Arrupe specifically about me, and he [Arrupe] praised my pastoral work to him, also my preaching. It appears this has greatly influenced the Holy Father's judgments. He also noticed that the Holy Father was surprised when Father Arrupe told him six priests have now been assassinated in the country. It makes us think that they do not give the pope objective reports on the situation of the Church in our country. Thank God, everything related to these two Jesuits' trips to Europe has been very positive with respect to our archdiocese.

---

[212] About $4,000.

[213] A major private station.

In the afternoon, another interview with Swiss television, after meeting with the president of the republic, who said that I preach politics, that this is a violation of the constitution and that this shows the freedom there is in the country. I used this opportunity to explain to Swiss television that my preaching is not political but rather evangelical, that it illuminates politics as the Council orders when it reminds us of the Church's right and duty to illuminate with Christian ethics different human activities, which include political activity.

Another interesting interview this afternoon was that with Mother Teresa Margarita, superior general of the Carmelites of St. Joseph, to recommend to her that CESPROR, a promotion house of the Carmelites in Santa Tecla, not be used for a different purpose than the one it was intended. According to Catholic Relief Services, which has helped this project a great deal, it appears that they want to suspend the work on behalf of women that has done so much good and use this house for the purposes of the congregation. The mother superior seemed surprised that I knew about this and told me that it was going to be a temporary suspension, that the work would be continued later, because they did not have the money to continue the work any longer. But I sensed in everything she said that she is afraid of the pastoral direction of the archdiocese, doubtless due to influence from somewhere else—I suspect from the nunciature itself—and that this makes the Mother Superior back away from a work that we all see is obviously of great benefit for our pastoral work. I said that I would talk to Catholic Relief Services which, for its part, promised me that it would continue to provide help so that this project will not have to be suspended.

 **Thursday, September 13**

The morning newspapers, *Diario de Hoy* and *La Prensa*, carried a full-page text of the homily Bishop Aparicio gave in San Vicente last Sunday. It is a strong condemnation of his priests. He says that he cannot defend them and almost accuses them himself, exposing them to possible assassination. He says that the priests who have been killed were purged by the left and that there are priests committed to the left who cannot pull back without the left killing them.

We have met with other priests who are very angry about such dangerous accusations. Radio YSAX harshly criticized the bishop's attitude as not at all pastoral, and the priests have committed themselves to studying how to confront Bishop Aparicio to make him see how serious his accusation is, and, at the same time, to express their solidarity with the priests of that diocese.

We had a meeting with the Executive Committee on Pastoral Work, mainly with Monsignor Urioste, who until now has been vicar of pastoral work, so that he could share his experience with us and help us with the administrative aspect. He was very understanding and said that he would leave everything in the committee's hands. He offered to continue giving his service for the good of the diocese.

I clarified that this reorganization does not take anything away from Monsignor Urioste, since he is vicar general and as such works very closely with the bishop to oversee all the pastoral aspects of the diocese. Besides that, he is the administrative vicar, which involves the other part of the present organization of the pastoral work of the diocese, for the principal committee is the one on pastoral work, to which all the administration is subordinated. As vicar general and administrative vicar, he is the best connection between the pastoral life of the archdiocese and the Committee on Pastoral Work. He understands perfectly and is working closely and cordially with this new effort to infuse life into the Committee for Pastoral Work, which will direct all this work that is central to the work of the archdiocesan Church.

At lunchtime I was pleased that the Guadalupana Sisters, who are taking care of the secretariat for me, are now also taking care of the small kitchen and the personal dining room, where we had lunch with them as a very cordial community and talked about the problems of the diocese. It seems to me, then, that this is a time of consolation for me as a pastor, very useful in my life and for the life of the chancery.

In the afternoon, after I had rested in my own room that I had prepared in the chancery—which I have almost never used—I met with the seminarians who had requested an audience with me. I also saw this as another advantage of staying here for lunch: to be able to spend the early afternoon hours on this useful task of personally guiding the seminarians. The four seminary students who had asked for the audience had some personal problems, and I realized how necessary it is for the pastor to know his seminarians in a more intimate way.

The day ended with dinner at the home of Licenciado Viéytez, where the conversation was very current and rich in experience of the world and of politics.

**Friday, September 14**

Today is the Feast of the Triumph of the Cross, and the Colegio de la Divine Providencia, directed by the Passionist Sisters, is having Mass for the school today. It was held at Concepción Church. I went to preside at it; it was offered for the eternal rest of José Mauricio Flores, an engineering student who was murdered yesterday—the son of a teacher at the school, Don Mauricio Flores. In the homily I said that this young man who was killed and his suffering family symbolize the many people and families who are suffering during this moment in our country's history, and that this should remind us of the meaning of the cross. I encouraged them to be faithful to their duty, to create a country not by killing but rather by giving life, carrying out their duty as they should.

In the chancery the Seminary Committee met to study the qualities we want to see in a seminarian from our archdiocese who is being prepared to take part in our pastoral work. Father Fabián Amaya, Fathers Rafael Urrutia and Sigfredo presented a beautiful study based on Puebla and other documents having to do with seminaries. They were asked to develop some norms that would be our institutional rationale and to propose the dialogue with the seminary formation directors aimed at a mutual understanding of the relation between the archdiocese and the seminary team. This matter is very delicate and it is necessary to face it courageously, for the seminary is the hope of the archdiocese.

I was visited by a journalist from the United States. I also participated in the meeting being held in the Divine Providence Hospital by priests from the diocese of San Vicente. I offered them my help and told them I would do whatever they asked of me, since their own bishop disowned them in his homily last Sunday and almost accused them of following a dangerous ideology that is repressed by the government.

I was unable to go to Cojutepeque for the Confirmation being held this afternoon because there have been many disturbances in the city and there are many military checkpoints on the highway that goes to Cojutepeque. In the city, the BPR, the Popular Revolutionary Bloc, was organizing a demonstration that was broken up by fire from the security forces. There are dead and wounded. Buses were burned and the demonstration was broken up. There are anxieties about tonight and tomorrow, September 15,[214] since we have heard many times that serious things will happen in September. God grant that tempers calm down and that peace begin to reign.

---

[214] Salvadoran Independence Day.

**Saturday, September 15**

Today is a very sad Independence Day. Besides the rainy day, there is an atmosphere of violence, of tragedy. The day began sadly because, due to the disturbances yesterday, the bus service has been shut down and there is an atmosphere of fear. In spite of this, I was able to go to Colonia Dolores to celebrate the patronal feast of the Virgen de Dolores, Our Lady of Sorrows. I asked the people to make it not just the colonia's Mass, but a Mass for the entire country. We should be in solidarity with the great needs and problems of the country and, asking the Virgin to be our intercessor, we should ask the divine Redeemer for the grace of salvation for our beloved people.

There were a good many Confirmations of older girls, some older boys, already eight years old. And I could see the effort Father Mamerto, a Sister of Charity and other catechists had put into preparing them properly to receive this sacrament of the Holy Spirit.

I also met with several members of the committee[215] of that church, encouraging them to continue their work, not only to finish building the church but also to build a convent and a parochial school.

I spent the rest of the day at the hospital, preparing my homily and meditating on the situation of the country.

In the evening, the Guadalupana Sisters from Arcatao notified me that they have been given an appointment with the Director of Immigration in order to clarify their situation. They fear that they will be expelled from the country. Monsignor Urioste will go with them and I tried to give them encouragement and serenity. I told them that I would see them after Mass tomorrow.

With Father Moreno and Beto Cuéllar we prepared the summary of current events during this week, which are very tragic: violence, kidnappings, labor problems. May God always inspire my words so that my assessments are fair.

---

[215] Parish council.

**Sunday, September 16**

The day started out to be a very rainy one. We still cannot have Mass at the cathedral because there are still many things to do there as a result of the occupation by the Popular Revolutionary Bloc, which was a long one. There were, however, still many people at the Sacred Heart Basilica. There were television crews from other countries and a reporter from *Le Monde* in France. I received a very warm reception, especially when I told them in the homily that the Holy Father had asked about me, which was the gist of the news that Father Ellacuría had brought me about a conversation Father Arrupe had with him after having traveled through Central America. And that Father Arrupe had praised the actions of the archdiocese of San Salvador, principally with reference to my teaching in my Sunday homilies. There was other news, especially the request the pope made during an Angelus for prayers for El Salvador.

With this beginning, which the people applauded, I began the homily about Christ, the true Messiah. And I explained the false messiahs since the readings suggested....[216]

In the evening I went to the parish of San Francisco in Mejicanos to turn it over to the new parish priest, Father Juan Macho Merino, a Passionist priest, since their congregation is going to take charge of this sector of the archdiocese and will have a group of theologians and philosophers there preparing to be part of that congregation. At the same time, they will go to the seminary, San José de la Montaña, or to the UCA [Central American University] for their classes. Afterward, there was a joyous, cordial gathering in Domus Mariae, which is near the church.

 **Monday, September 17**

The Priests' Senate met in the tranquil atmosphere of the house of the Carmelite Sisters of St. Joseph in Santa Tecla. The principal topic was to analyze the serious accusations that Bishop Aparicio made in his homily this last Sunday, in which he said that the priests who have been murdered have been killed by leftist groups that will not let them back away. The other topic was an analysis of the occupation of the churches.

---

[216] Tape ends here.

On the first point, it was agreed to go visit Bishop Aparicio on behalf of the archdiocese, which feels itself concerned in this, to make him see how serious his accusations are, the support this gives to those who kill priests; to ask him for proof because we need to see it, if it really does exist; and to ask him to try to be in unity with the bishops' conference to defend the rights of our priests and our people, not attack them. At the same time, we are preparing information that is as objective as possible for Rome.

With regard to the occupation of churches, it was agreed rather to study this more carefully in a special meeting that Father Federico Sanggiano, parish priest of El Calvario Church (which has been one of the churches most affected by occupations) will be in charge of organizing.

Father Quinteros was expected to arrive—he has asked to be reconciled with the Church—but he never came. Father Sanggiano was also authorized to talk to him and suggest to him that he make a spiritual examination and, at the same time, undergo psychiatric treatment.

Father David Rodríquez arrived at the end of our meeting and had lunch with us. He told us that in another homily by Bishop Aparicio this Sunday there had been serious accusations against the archdiocese and that he had prohibited the families in his diocese from reading the newspaper *Orientación*.

After lunch, Monsignor Urioste came to see me to tell me about the meeting with the Director of Immigration, in which they had discussed the situation of the Mexican nuns in Arcatao. The Mexican consul who, in spite of what the Immigration Office had said, did not know anything about it, went with them. The Director of Immigration was very rude to the representative of the chancery, Monsignor Urioste, although later he apologized to him for his direct attack on the program of the archdiocese, asking him to forgive him because that had not been his intention, as it was not that of the president or that of the government (Monsignor Urioste had asked him if the attitude he personally was taking toward him reflected an attitude of the government).

Monsignor Urioste also gave me three messages from progressive military officers, who are planning—secretly, of course—a change of government to a more democratic one. This is very hopeful and I hope that soon El Salvador will breathe better air than the present atmosphere of violence we live in.

While I talked with Monsignor Urioste, I got a telephone call from Argentine television asking me to give a one-minute analysis of the situation of the country. I spoke from my position as archbishop and gave a brief pastoral view of how conflict-filled and explosive our situation is and about the mission of the Church, preaching peace based on justice—the same as always, reduced to one minute.

**Tuesday, September 18**

In the morning we held the general assembly of the society of YSAX, the Panamerican Voice. The new manager, Licenciado Teto Samour, reported on the year's activities, almost all of which had been directed by Father Rogelio Pedraz, who recently had to resign because, as a Jesuit, he had work to do in Guatemala. He has left a very big hole in this task of dissemination. I already have written to him expressing to him my profound gratitude and my desire that, when circumstances permit, he can come back and work with us again.

Also a financial report. We needed to name an auditor and chose my brother Arnoldo. We talked about different aspects of the radio. There was discussion of new equipment and a new antenna, about which I had also written a letter to a friend who has some land near Tonacatepeque. We hope that from there the range of the Panamerican Voice will be greater. There was an optimistic tone, one of understanding of this work that, praise God, is providing so much service to our archdiocese and to the entire Church in El Salvador.

In the afternoon, another very important meeting: this one of the team from the seminary with the seminary committee of the archdiocese. Bishop Rivera was present as the person in charge of the seminary for the bishops' conference. In this role and as bishop of Santiago de María, he made valuable contributions to the discussion between the team and the committee that, at first, seemed tense and prejudiced. But, thank God, the tone softened and it became cordial. This involves a sector that is very important to the work of the Church: the formation of our future priests.

We named as coordinator for the archdiocese Father Sigfredo Salazar, rector of the minor seminary—with whom the formation team also had problems, but which also seemed to smooth out. It seems that God has greatly blessed this meeting. We also agreed to meet more often in the future to talk about so crucial a theme.

In the evening I went to the meeting of the archdiocesan Caritas group, but it was already over and I was only able to express my apology to Miss Elsa Herrera, at whose house it took place.

## Wednesday, September 19

The work in the chancery began today with giving time to two photographers from magazines in the United States who asked me to pose for them. They kept me some fifteen minutes, taking so many photographs that I told them that this was the first time I had been asked to do as many poses as a movie star.

After that came the interviews: the majority of them today with people who are very poor or upset about situations of injustice and mothers of the disappeared, to whom I tried to say a word of encouragement or to give some direction to follow with their problem.

The meetings this morning ended with one on the financial situation of the work on the cathedral. The occupations have brought major disruptions in the celebration of Mass there and in the construction of our cathedral. The Administrative Commission discussed the problem cordially and proposed three solutions to avoid suspending the work because, once suspended, it would be difficult to begin it again and all of the money involved in building the dome structure would be lost. And that, for this reason, it was necessary to put in more money to finish the dome, even if that meant getting it from somewhere else. One idea was to help us get a bank loan in the form of an additional mortgage; or to ask Father Saenz, who has received a loan for the construction he is doing, to pay it back sooner; or, lastly, to ask the priests' cooperative to speed up buying the building it uses—which it has proposed doing. Each of these possibilities was delegated specifically to one of those present—all of whom, I repeat, have the goodwill to make this work. We also talked about the possibility of a trip to Europe to visit different foundations that might aid us in solving this problem of funds, to which we could add the need to build a house for the bishop (since he does not have one) and chancery offices, which are also needed in the archdiocese.

I had lunch with the Claretian seminarians in Santa Tecla. It was a nice group of nine young men and a priest who works with them. We shared a few moments that brought back memories of the spirit of the Claretians who were my teachers in my first seminary, the minor seminary in San Miguel. The conversation at lunch and afterward was interesting and they were, I think, very pleased. They also were encouragement for me.

In the afternoon, my work began with a Mass held for a little boy only a few years old who was a victim of cancer. I spoke in my sermon to his suffering parents and friends of how God, when he takes away these little flowers from the world, is telling us that all is not lost and that, amid so much hate and so much violence, so many bad things, the world can offer to the Lord the best flowers for his throne: our children. And, second, that this suggests to us the necessity of suffering in this world to gain salvation, that the crucified Christ continues to redeem the world through its suffering and its pain.

Afterward I went to the meeting to study the criteria and attitudes we should have in regard to the occupation of our churches. Bishop Rivera advised us on the basis of canon law, and Father Fabián added a very good pastoral reflection. We could see how, in normal times, these occupations are profanations prohibited by law. And that, in reality, their effect is bad, particularly as it de-Christianizes our people. But the situation is not normal and as Christ said, the sabbath was made for man, not man for the sabbath and, as it is permitted in certain abnormal circumstances to eat the bread which is stored [for the offering],[217] in the same way the occupation of churches, when all the channels of expression have been cut off, is a minor evil. And because of this, our reflection should only be to refine our criteria and not appear to reject a need on the part of those who must express the concerns of the people.

We decided, however, to close the cathedral and El Rosario and Calvario Churches specifically, since these are the three most often chosen, without making that decision public; and for them to remain closed while we look for a place besides the church buildings to hold Mass until this situation ends.

Finally, very late in the evening, I received a visit from Sister Judith, who had been expelled. Thank God, she has been brought back from Guatemala and will continue working in El Paraíso in Chalatenango.

Also a family came to see me and, crying, they told me: "We come as children to their father to tell you how we feel because they have burned a bus that was our business, our livelihood, and this has left us in great debt now." I offered them words of encouragement and I told them I was glad that he is in Alcoholics Anonymous. The family itself has progressed in the maturity of their faith and their hope with the charismatic inspiration of the Holy Spirit, and I told them that they had the key to the solution in their great faith but that, at the same time, they should work hard because God will have to bless them as he is testing them.

---

[217] See Mark 2:23-28.

**Thursday, September 20**

The first problem we discussed with the vicars general and the episcopal vicar and the representative of the provincial of the Guadalupanas was the situation of the Guadalupana Sisters who work in Arcatao. The sisters' concern is the lies and persecution they have been subjected to. The mother general recommends that they not return, although others would be sent. An important condition for this is that some priest would oversee their work and go there, even if only every two weeks. This was resolved by Father Fabián Amaya, episcopal vicar, and Father Isidro, Jesuit, agreeing to provide this spiritual support. The other sisters, who cannot return to Arcatao at present, will work in the chancery secretariat and will see in what community or what work near the capital they can do their pastoral work, for they do not want to give it up.

During the morning, there were several different visits from priests, women religious and the faithful. In the afternoon I saw a representative of LP-28, the Popular Leagues of February 28, to arrange another visit for the next day to present to me a common platform that has evolved through discussion among the people, which offers peaceful solutions to the situation of the country.

Afterward, I left for Cojutepeque. In San Juan parish, Father Raymundo Brizuela had prepared a large number of young people and children, all over eight years old, to receive Confirmation—a community that is alive, joyous, which participates a great deal in the service, which also renewed its baptismal and confirmational commitments. Afterward there was friendly sharing with the people coming out of Mass and with the priest in his rectory.

I was unable to go to the seminary meeting tonight as I had promised, but they met with the rector of the minor seminary.

Also I was notified today that two Venezuelan bishops who are my friends, Bishop [Domingo] Roa [Pérez][218] and Bishop Ovidio [Pérez Morales],[219] had arrived from Nicaragua en route to Mexico. I told them that tomorrow we could concelebrate at the little chapel at Divine Providence Hospital and then, after breakfast, go out to see some of the area around our capital.

---

[218] Of Maracaibo.
[219] Of Coro.

## Friday, September 21

A morning full of visitors. One that sticks out in my mind is an interview with Radio Cadena Central,[220] which wanted to contrast my opinion with that of Bishop Aparicio. But I told them I did not want to discuss polemical topics. I had to protest when, several times during the conversation, they tried to push this confrontation. I took the opportunity to reaffirm the archdiocese's position on pastoral work.

Also very important was an interview with a Brazilian journalist who is a reporter for some large newspapers in that country and for the BBC in London. He gave me a list of questions and asked me to think out loud. So it was not really a conversation; rather, he would name a topic and I would then develop it as he had suggested, as if I were thinking out loud. And it turned out to be a reaffirmation of the position the Church has when faced with misunderstandings, and the lack of comprehension and the persecution it is subjected to in this country.

I had lunch with the Guadalupana Sisters who are working in the secretariat for us, since they have already redone the little kitchen in my apartment. I had also invited Father Nicolás González and Sister Rosa María, who is suffering as the result of the very serious lack of understanding of the Carmelite Sisters of St. Joseph, who have dropped her from the congregation and have told her to go home, back to her country in South America. She wants to stay and work with us, which she can do, since she is no longer dependent on a congregation once she has been dropped from it. I encouraged her and then she stayed to talk to the vicar of Chalatenango.[221] He suggested different ways to continue her work with good spirit.

After lunch I spent my time meeting individually with the third-year students at the seminary, who have to decide about their ministries. Some of them want to get them now; others want to wait. I pointed out to them that the priesthood is getting closer and they need good preparation in order to fulfill the hopes of the archdiocese.

And in the evening, in the Divine Providence Hospital, some representatives of political parties and popular political organizations gave me their common platform resulting from dialogue of the people in an attempt to unite the people around a common platform. It seemed very good to me and I think it is one more rational path offered to our people. I congratulated them and promised to lend them all my support on the part of the Church.

---

[220] A commercial radio network.
[221] Father Fabián Amaya.

## Saturday, September 22

Today I went to Guazapa to administer Confirmation to a group of young people fifteen years and older, prepared by the parishes of Guazapa and Aguilares. The people were very aware and participated a great deal in the ceremony. At the end, the young people gave very beautiful testimonies of their commitment to the Church, and they truly felt the presence of the Holy Spirit. After Mass I met with the catechists so I could hear about their work and resolve any doubts they have. I had lunch with the Carmelite Sisters of St. Joseph, who are worried that their order does not seem fully to understand their pastoral work. We decided that tomorrow we would have a private meeting with the other sisters in Apulo, where I will go tomorrow.

In the evening, I received a visit from the ambassador of Germany, accompanied by a member of the West German parliament. The conversation, on topics about the Church and the country, was very interesting. They offered me their total support. The ambassador promised to visit me so he could be informed of whatever we might need in order to help us.

Afterward I met with Father Moreno and Beto Cuéllar to analyze this week, which has been very full, especially of public statements and of violence.

## Sunday, September 23

The Mass was in the basilica, since we have decided to close the cathedral in order to avoid the problem with the occupations. The attendance was large. There was a great deal of applause during the homily. I explained that this does not make me swell up with pride; that, rather, they make me feel myself more of a servant of the people and that I try to interpret this communion of feelings expressed in their applause. I asked them to be very committed to prayer and to following Christ with his cross.

After Mass, I met with Italian television, which was also present at Mass taking detail shots, and with a journalist from London.

After Mass I went to celebrate the patronal feast of the Virgen de Dolores [Our Lady of Sorrows] in the village of the same name, Dolores, in Apulo, near the Lake of Ilopango, in the parish of Ilopango. It was a very picturesque festival since the chapel has a beautiful view of the lake and the people are very affectionate, very attentive to the Church's message.

We celebrated the Mass there with lively participation from the communities, a group that seems to be very aware. During lunch, groups of young people shared some joyful music. I spoke to them about my pastoral letter. The theme of the homily was an exhortation to the devotion to the Virgin, which I plan to put at the end of the letter as one contribution of our Church to possible solutions to the country's crisis.

After Mass, we had lunch with the Carmelite Sisters of St. Joseph, the novices who had come to sing and representatives from the different communities, making it a very happy moment in the dining room at Apulo. After a very private conversation with the four Carmelite Sisters who do pastoral work there and who feel that their pastoral work is not understood by a congregation concerned with form but lacking the ecclesial spirit to understand the pastoral work done by our archdiocese. I told them that as long as there was no substantial change, they should continue to be faithful to their Carmelite vocation, obedient to their superiors, and that I would take it upon myself to talk to the congregation, to try to make it understand this pastoral work that many do not understand, especially when there are so many lies and so many misunderstandings. And that we should pray a great deal to continue asking God what he wants from us in our situation.

When I returned to Apulo, I was faced with the sad spectacle of some young people being chased by people with stones trying to kill them. People next to a van where all the commotion was seemed extremely worried, but I could not do anything, given the level of these peoples' fury. I hope these young people managed to escape in spite of the violence.

In the evening, a visit from an Italian television crew, who had been unable to film several things they wished to because they were short of supplies. But what they needed is coming from Nicaragua and they wanted to get some more information.

**Monday, September 24**

Feast of the Virgen de Mercedes.[222] I celebrated Mass at the women's prison, where the Sisters of the Good Shepherd have prepared a good group of young women and some married women to receive the Sacrament of Confirmation. The theme of the homily was the Holy Spirit given through Confirmation; what the Spirit did in Mary, the perfect woman. And I asked them to have the kind of Christianity inspired by the Holy Spirit during these times. I had lunch with the prisoners as they had invited me to, and in a very nice program, the Lions Club of Mejicanos offered different recreational activities.

I ended the afternoon at the little farm the Sisters of the Holy Family have, having a very nice rest.

In the evening, I went back again to celebrate the patronal Mass for Our Lady of Ransom in the parish of La Merced, under the guidance of Father Torruella. It was well attended and gave me opportunity to speak about devotion to the Virgin as characteristic of Latin America—but a devotion that, as the pope and Puebla advised, must develop according to the needs of the people.

 **Tuesday, September 25**

A morning of intense visits, especially from priests, since I dedicate Tuesdays to seeing priests. Nevertheless, there were also some emergencies among the laypeople. A visit from a military figure to talk to me about the difficulty of the situation and about their secret plans, which we will discuss with some other groups at a meeting he is organizing to be held in the next few days. Also visits from journalists, who are always interested in our situation.

In the afternoon, there was a meeting of the committee on the seminary with the formation team of the interdiocesan seminary. I was unable to attend because they did not let me know in time and I had another commitment with the Union of Salvadoran Peasants.[223] Very interesting— they offered me their complete cooperation and asked the Church to guide them in being able to respond adequately to the moment we are living. I encouraged them to keep their identity as peasants, as an organization, and

---

[222] Our Lady of Ransom.

[223] UTC (*Unión Trabajadores del Campo*, Farm Workers Union).

I thanked them for their expression of concern for the Church which, in spite of all the lies being told, does not bear any ill will but rather has the desire to serve people and to guide them sincerely according to the gospel.

I made the tape for the conversation to be broadcast on the radio tomorrow.

And in the evening, a visit from a business leader who brought me up to date on what young businessmen are doing in order to bring together the diverse groups on the right and the left who are clamoring for social justice. I congratulated him and I promised the Church's help. It cannot, of course, commit itself to any political group, but it does have the duty to guide and support anything positive in this search for solutions for the country's problems.

 ## Wednesday, September 26

This morning's first visit was from a Jesuit missionary from India, who has heard a good deal about our archdiocese and who told me that he had really enjoyed hearing my homily last Sunday. He is taking back as a souvenir of his stay in San Salvador several of my homilies, which have been distributed in printed form, to show to his colleagues in India as an example of a Church that is inspirational for all and which he considers to be almost a miracle. I thanked him for such glowing descriptions and I also offered him our appreciation, shown in our prayers for India, in the same way that we also ask for the solidarity of the prayers of their Churches there.

Another interesting visit today was one from a Venezuelan journalist and political analyst, who recorded impressions of our way of thinking about the situation of the country and of the Church. He showed special interest in the life of our Church and in its coherent defense of human rights.

Also several priests and several laypersons came during this busy morning of work and visits to our archdiocese. The missionary priest took away a very good impression of the attitude of the chancery. I thank God for this witness that our Church is giving and, as I told the missionary father, I will use his comments to encourage our Church to keep itself faithful to its gospel.

At noon I went to have lunch with the priests in the Vicariate of Mejicanos, in the church of Mejicanos, where Father Samuel Orellana took care of us very kindly. They were celebrating Father Nicolás González's degree. He gave me a copy of his thesis, and read me the affectionate dedication he had written for me on its first page. I appreciate this new proof of priestly solidarity. The thesis is on a specific author and on the theme of love as expression of personality. During lunch, he was explaining to us different philosophical aspects of his topic.

Several priests of the San Vincente diocese and Father Clemente Barrera from the Santa Ana diocese came at noon, accompanying Miss Ana Echeverría, daughter of Doña Guadalupe, a noble woman from Mexico, who was very hospitable toward these priests when they were seminarians. She came to visit me, surrounded by all of these priests. And because of that, I praised her spirit of hospitality and the great reward from God awaiting those who care for his priests in this way. She was very moved and I also felt deep gratitude to the Lord because his priests, in spite of being persecuted, always find a Bethany[224] that treats them very affectionately.

 **Thursday, September 27**

Today the Somascan Fathers had invited me to concelebrate the Eucharist with them in the Basilica of Guadalupe in Colonia La Ceiba in honor of their patron, Our Lady Mother of Orphans. I had the pleasant surprise of finding not only the Somascans but also the priests of the Vicariate of La Asunción in Flor Blanca, who are doing the Spiritual Exercises in the novice house of the Somascan priests this week. The women religious, their novices and their students also attended, along with the Somascan seminarians and the students from their school. It was an intimate gathering and, at the same time, a very solemn one.

In my homily, I preached about the deprivations orphans suffer—that is, the deprivation of the fullness of life, deprivation of unity (since the mother is the unifying force of the family and when she is not there, it is as if it falls apart) and deprivation of guidance (when there is no mother there is also a lack of loving guidance for the child). I related these three deprivations to the great needs of our people, for which we have to pray to the Virgin, our Mother. Without her, we are orphans and we—like El Salvador—suffer a lack of life, especially spiritual, a lack of unity and a lack of guidance.

---

[224] A reference to Christ's friendship with the family of Mary, Martha and Lazarus at Bethany.

After Mass we went to have lunch with all the priests at the novice house, a very cordial and familial gathering.

At two o'clock in the afternoon I met with the ambassador of the Canadian embassy, who brought an offer of thirty-two thousand colones[225] for projects to be organized through Caritas. And he promised there will be more next year. I thanked him and I will have to keep him informed so that we can present the proper project for this offer, which we appreciate very much.

I went to celebrate the feast of St. Vincent de Paul in the Santa Luisa chapel, where we also inaugurated the Stations of the Cross. It turned out to be very pious, with the participation of the sisters and students and the Daughters of Mary. We also had a cordial dinner there with the parish priests of El Calvario, who are Somascan Fathers, and with the Sisters of Charity. A familial dinner atmosphere, very cordial.

We heard on the radio the interview with Bishop Aparicio in which, sadly, he continues condemning priests with false accusations and leaving them exposed to great danger.

Tomorrow, God willing, I will go to Ciudad Barrios to spend two days there in response to an invitation from the sisters and, at the same time, out of a great desire to see even briefly my dear town.

 ### Friday, September 28, and Saturday, September 29

I was in Ciudad Barrios Friday, September 28, and Saturday, September 29, visiting my town, encouraging the Maryknoll Fathers, who recently took over that parish, and the congregation of Carmelite Sisters, who have been helping in that pastoral work for some years now. The memory of my infancy, the contact with old friends, renews in my life my enthusiasm to continue the vocation God gave me in the humble town of Ciudad Barrios.

When I got back, I felt a little ill; I think I am getting the flu.

---

[225] About $12,800.

**Sunday, September 30**

I celebrated Mass at the basilica with a rather large attendance. In the afternoon, in spite of not feeling well, I went to celebrate the anniversary of the Legion of Mary in the Divina Providencia parish in Colonia Atlacatl. A very warm reception; a little party. I was only able to be there for the beginning; then I had to go home to try to take care of my health a little better.

# October 1979

**Monday, October 1, to Saturday, October 6**

Beginning Monday, October 1, I had to stay in bed. I had a flu that kept me from carrying out any of my commitments this week.

Thanks to Monsignor Urioste and Father Brito and others who helped, I was able to send representatives to fulfill my commitment to say Mass at the Carmelite Institute. I was able to preach the Holy Hour at the Divine Providence Hospital. I was not able to attend the course on Christology directed by Father Arias, a Jesuit, held at the Externado San José this whole week with some sixty attending, including priests, women religious and laity from the vicariate. I was also unable to go to the meeting in Ayutuxtepeque on matters pertaining to the parish council. Monsignor [Modesto] López Portillo kindly administered Confirmation at the children's home, Hogar del Niño, and at Colegio Santa Inés in Santa Tecla. I also sent representatives to the Mass for St. Francis' feast [October 4] at Concepción Church and in the parish of San Francisco Morazán in Chalatenango. Monsignor Urioste also went to install the Sisters of the Sacred Heart in Jayaque, where I had promised to go this Saturday, October 6.

Thank God, I am feeling better at the end of the week and, with certain limitations, I am going to try to fulfill my duties on Sunday. I was attended by a very dear doctor, Dr. Suárez, a cardiologist, who has assured me that my medical condition is normal now, although I should be careful and be sure to rest.

 **Sunday, October 7**

I was unable to attend the gathering of young people that had been organized by the seminarians at San José de la Montaña or the Confirmation prepared by the sisters in Zaragoza, but Monsignor Modesto did go there, and Monsignor Urioste attended the gathering. I celebrated Mass in the basilica with many people present.

After Mass, an interview with three foreign journalists. And at six in the afternoon, I went to El Rosario Church (today is the Feast of Our Lady of the Rosary) to celebrate the Confirmation of young people who had been prepared by the Dominican Fathers. I preached on Our Lady of the Rosary and thanked the priests for their pastoral work in that parish.

At night, a visit from two military men who talked with me in confidence about their plans to change the government. We will be expecting something during the week; meanwhile, I offered them my prayers and all the moral assistance that the Church can provide in such delicate matters.

 **Tuesday, October 9**

There was a meeting of the Pastoral Commission. I was able to be there only at the end because I received visits from many priests.

At twelve o'clock, as I had promised, I granted an interview to Voice of America, which is broadcast on the radio from Washington, about the Holy Father's visit to the United States and his speeches at the United Nations and the Organization of American States.

In the afternoon there was a meeting at the seminary of the seminary committee and the formation team. I was not able to go to this either, because I did not feel well and stayed at my residence to rest.

**Wednesday, October 10**

In Colegio Belén in Santa Tecla, I met with Monsignor Urioste, Father Jesús Delgado, Father Fabián Amaya, Father Ellacuría, Father Estrada and the laypeople Román Mayorga and Héctor Dada Hirezi[226] to get their advice as to what attitude the Church should take if there is a coup d'etat, as planned. They were very cautious, advising me that above all we should wait, that even in the best of circumstances, we would have to wait and see what form things take and not be precipitate in any gesture of solidarity that could be compromising. They brought up many conditions that have broadened my criteria for such a difficult situation. The principal conditions to ask for would be: first, a purge of the army; a proposal for profound structural changes; and the participation of the people and of all opinions in a true democratic opening. The Church will express the reaction of the people and the hopes they may have in a government that might improve the present situation.

In the afternoon, I celebrated Mass for the soul of Doña Abigail de Giralt, benefactress of the hospital and a good personal friend.

 **Thursday, October 11**

A visit from the ambassador of the United States together with the political officer. On my side, I was advised by Monsignor Urioste and Father Estrada. The meeting had to do with responding to some questions from the State Department as to the Church's assessment of the present situation of the country and what would be the most efficient solution. We said that, in theory, this would be a democratic opening but that, in practice, this route was blocked by the repression and by the limited signs of credibility on the government's part, and that what we could see coming was a violent solution or a coup. We asked the government of the United States to use its influence to accelerate what, in theory, seems to be the most useful method but which, in practice, is being destroyed, since the signs previously mentioned are missing.

I had lunch at the Colegio Guadalupano to greet the mother superior of that congregation, who has arrived from Mexico.

---

[226] Christian Democrat member of the second junta from January 9, 1980, to March 4, 1980; social scientist at the UCA. Mayorga had been a member of the first junta from October 16, 1979, to January 3, 1980.

In the afternoon, I was at the San José de la Montaña Seminary with a group of priests from the Vicariate of Cuscatlán who are doing the Spiritual Exercises. It was a very fraternal and cordial meeting, in which we spoke freely and made proposals to improve our relationship and our efforts for an authentic pastoral work.

In the evening, interviews in the Divine Providence Hospital with Dutch television and with a representative of the Costa Rican press.

### Friday, October 12

A visit from two representatives of the International Red Cross, who had come from Switzerland at the government's request to report on the abuse of human rights. They say that this is not their function, that they are intended to give humanitarian aid and that they cannot give the testimony the president has requested. They asked the Church for its opinion, and we informed them in depth through Father Moreno and Beto Cuéllar, who are in charge of the files in the Legal Aid Office and the accusations that come to the archdiocese.

There was a meeting of the Vicariate of Mejicanos in Domus Mariae, but I could not go.

I had lunch at the home of Don Pepe Simán, who told me about his impressions of his trip to the United States where, in New York, he was able to see the Holy Father go by in person.

In the afternoon, a nice Mass and *Te Deum* in the chapel of the Colegio del Espíritu Santo, where some thirty Franciscan nuns, Mercedarians of the Eucharist, Passionists, Carmelites of St. Joseph and of St. Teresa, Sisters of the Good Shepherd and Josephite Sisters were graduating. I spoke to them about the image the Church must have today in Latin America: as evangelizing the culture of our people.

**Saturday, October 13**

I went to Nejapa, where the Vicariate of Quezaltepeque had prepared a group of young people for Confirmation. It was very impressive to see young people who had been prepared with such care by catechists and parish priests. After being confirmed, they gave testimonies of their desire to work for the Kingdom of God with all their youthful fervor.

In the afternoon there was an ecumenical program at El Rosario Church, but I could not attend because I was expecting Dr. Badía, who was bringing me important information about the confidential news I have referred to previously. It looks like there has been some betrayal of this group of military officers. They are very tense, but still determined to do what they have planned.

 **Sunday, October 14**

The Sunday Mass in the Sacred Heart Basilica with a large attendance in spite of the bad weather. It rained a great deal all through the night and it was still stormy this morning.

At six o'clock in the evening, in María Auxiliadora Church, an impressive Confirmation ceremony with groups from different parishes in this vicariate. Nearly one hundred boys and girls, after having made a spiritual retreat all afternoon with their parish priests, came to receive the gift of the Holy Spirit in all awareness.

 **Monday, October 15**

I celebrated the Mass of St. Teresa of Jesus[227] at the hospital and I asked for special prayers for the situation of the country, since today is a crucial day.

In fact, a little before eight o'clock, Father Jesús Delgado told me that the military group will take all the barracks at eight o'clock in the morning and after that demand that the president step down. I had a commitment in the parish of San Juan Cojutepeque to attend a Bible competition at the

---

[227] St. Teresa of Avila.

parochial school, and I left word that if anything happened to let me know at that parish.

It was an extremely interesting morning. Father Raymundo Brizuela and Professor Don Luis Molina have done wonderful things with the biblical reflection, the Bible study of the children, and it showed today in the contests of oratory and biblical catechism. These children and young people are formed in a very biblical atmosphere, truly steeped in a Christian spirit. I saw great demonstrations of eloquence, of poetry, of memory, of intellectual ability. This was the impression I reflected to them when I congratulated them and thanked them for the rich experience they had given me.

At noon, while we were eating with the teachers, word came that a coup d'etat was rumored, and they warned me that it would be dangerous to return to San Salvador. Nevertheless, I did return, and everything seemed normal. I was tense because I knew what I had heard in the morning and I did not see any results; I thought that they had failed. But rather late, around five o'clock, we began to hear the news on the radio that President Romero had resigned and left for Guatemala. Taking over the barracks had apparently been effective because it left the president with no support. He tried to take refuge in one of the barracks, but all of them had been taken. And the coup was, as they say, "scientifically" prepared and executed in such a way that there was no apparent change in the people: life as usual, not one drop of blood except in San Miguel, where there was some opposition from the commandant and a bodyguard died or was wounded. Everything else appears to be normal.

In the evening, I reflected on this with Monsignor Urioste at his house, since he is ill, and also with other priests and laypeople in order to receive advice as to what the Church's attitude should be. They said that it would be wise to wait and see what direction things take but that, as pastor, I could go ahead and issue a call to the people, exhorting them to be cautious in order to avoid any extremism of either the right or the left and, at the same time, issue a call to the new government in the hope that, if it keeps its promises, this will give it the credibility the government has lost among the people.

Tonight I prepared a message to be broadcast on the radio tomorrow. The atmosphere seems to hold a breath of hope, although at the same time there is fear that, because it is a military coup, there may be a reaction from the forces of the left, who are calling for a popular uprising. There is also fear that the extreme right will feel threatened by the declarations made by the new government, promising many reforms in economic and social matters. We hope to God that their goodwill be understood and that together all of us will find a way out of the crisis of the country.

**Tuesday, October 16**

Also a very important day. Early this morning, I was still preparing the archbishop's message; Father Moreno and Father Gregorio Rosa helped me. At nine o'clock, a visit from representatives of the new presidential junta. They asked me to issue the call for prudence quickly because the reaction from the leftist camp is already beginning. In Mejicanos, in Soyapango, there have been outbreaks of violence, threats, provocation, and they—the new government—did not want to allow themselves to be provoked. I moved up a radio conversation with Father Jesús Delgado, in which I went ahead and talked about what my statement to be issued at noon would say.

### Pastoral Statement in Regard to the New Situation in Our Country

Beginning yesterday, El Salvador has arrived at a new and delicate crossroads in its history. A military uprising deposed the government of General Carlos Humberto Romero. Our Church which, given its identity and the demands of the gospel, has committed itself to be with the people in all of their vicissitudes, has the responsibility to speak its first words about this new situation. This is not a political declaration; rather, it is a reflection in light of our Christian faith. Because of this, before anything else, we look up to God in prayer and from him receive illumination and energy to guide our people and to explain to the new government the Salvadoran people's just desires for liberation.

*Primero Dios,* God willing, whatever God wants: This characteristically Salvadoran expression comes from the deep religious sense that the Church cultivates in the soul of our people. This is its first comment and its initial position. We raise up our prayer to the Lord of history because, "Unless the Lord build the house,/they labor in vain who build it./Unless the Lord guard the city, in vain does the guard keep vigil" (Psalm 127:1).

Our prayer is also the act of giving thanks to God because, according to the information that we have received up to now, the shedding of blood has been avoided during these events. Our prayer, then, offers up to the Lord as well all the suffering and pain of our people, whose blood has watered our soil. Let this price have been high enough for God to give us a future of true justice and peace.

Finally, our plea to the Lord becomes a prayer of reconsecration and a call to conversion, because hate and vengeance can never be the path to true liberation. The road that leads to genuine well-being always goes through justice and love.

To the people: After addressing ourselves to God, our words, which are the words of a pastor, are directed toward the people as a call for caution and as a promise of service. We understand that the patience of our people, who have endured so much, is running out, and we fear that the expectations created by the military uprising could turn into dangerous impatience or degenerate into new violence—even more so, because innumerable martyrs and heroes have come from the people and provide a dramatic testimony of these last nightmarish years. In this crucial moment we are living, however, we want to encourage our people to act wisely, because wise people wait and watch before they judge and act. An impatient and violent attitude would be as guilty and unjust as the oppression and repression that our poor country has been buried in.

Our call is also directed to those who, in order unjustly to defend their interests and their economic, social and political privileges, have been guilty of so much unrest and violence. Allow me to remind them that they should listen to the voice of justice and the voice of the poor as the voice of the Lord himself, who calls them to be converted and who is to be the judge of all humankind.

To those who are active in political parties or popular political organizations: We want to invite them to show true political maturity, flexibility and a capacity for dialogue. Only in this way can the people be sure that they are, in fact, motivated by what is truly good for the country. Fanaticism or idolatry of their own party or organization would be, today more than ever, a grave sin against the common good. The crisis that our country is trying to overcome cannot be resolved by one group alone; it has to be the work of all.

All the people together, then, should build a common framework with justice as a basis for their interaction. Our message is not just a call for prudence; it is also a promise. The Church commits itself once more to continue giving disinterested service on behalf of the people. This new juncture of the country does not alter at all this willingness to serve. It was this sincere desire to serve and defend the people that led the Church to be in conflict with the previous government; because of this, such conflict can only be resolved when we have a government that is also the servant of the people.

To the new government: Our message is finally directed to the new government that has arisen from the military rebellion that overthrew the previous regime. We have studied with care the declarations that express the official positions of the new government. In them we can see goodwill, clarity of ideas and a clear awareness of their responsibility. Nevertheless, we want to make it very clear that this government will deserve the confidence and the cooperation of the people only when it demonstrates that the beautiful promises contained in its proclamation, issued this morning, are not merely hollow words, but a true hope that will begin a new era in our country. On our part, in my role as pastor of the Church, I am ready to talk with the new government and to cooperate with it. We insist on just one condition: that both the government and the Church always be conscious that our reason for being is to be of "mutual service in the measure of the different gifts bestowed on each" (*The Church in the Modern World*, #32).

These are our first words with respect to the difficult task beginning today, which we hope, with God's help, to continue to illuminate through the gospel of Christ. May the divine Savior guide the steps of all people of goodwill who are working to bring justice and peace to our country.

*San Salvador, October 16, 1979*

In the evening, I learned that there have been very positive comments both on my conversation with Father Chus and on my pastoral declaration. The leaders of the movement itself, the two colonels, [Jaime Abdul] Gutiérrez and [Adolpho] Majano, chosen by the armed forces as a whole as the leaders at this moment and representatives of the Military Civic Committee, came at one o'clock in the afternoon to thank me for this support and to put themselves at my orders. I took this opportunity to explain to them the Church's opinion that, above all, they must demonstrate concrete actions. The ones which would most affect the people are a general amnesty and accurate information about the disappeared, allowing the return of those in exile, etc.

They promised me they would do all of these things and said that they appreciated these suggestions. It is clear that they are inexperienced for such an incredibly difficult task as the one they have taken on almost without previous planning. They say, however, that the coup was in planning for over a year, and they believe that the success their efforts have achieved obligates them to be faithful servants—also the confidence the entire army has placed in these two. And also they are all aware that it is imperative to incorporate civilians very soon.

In the afternoon I received reports of outbreaks of violence that have occurred in Mejicanos, in Soyapango, where Father Villarán has disappeared as well, taken away in a group of prisoners. But the governing junta has itself notified me it begs our forgiveness because he was unwittingly taken to the Treasury Police headquarters and that he will be released. I put a group of priests and laity in contact with the government to report on these incidents, which could destroy the hope the people could have in them, and to insist that they demonstrate that they are motivated by goodwill and that they show it through concrete actions.

There have been many calls from journalists, but I have responded with the statement I just read. There is information on different kinds of reactions and we are still waiting. On our part, the position of the Church has been defined: always at the service of the people with the guidance of the Gospels.

 **Wednesday, October 17**

Last night, I was to have had dinner with Ingeniero Román Mayorga, rector of the Central American University, but it was postponed because of what is going on, since Ingeniero Mayorga will form part of the new civilian-military government.[228] This morning I spoke with him on the telephone. I will talk about this at the end of today's entry.

This morning, with Monsignor Urioste, I taped the radio interview to be broadcast at noon, in which I reaffirm the Church's position in this moment of transition in the government. We wanted it to be very clear that the Church is not committed to any concrete political plan and, on the contrary, will always maintain its independence in order to be able both to praise the good things and to criticize the bad.

There have been many visits from priests and laity, which I have used to enrich my thought and to give guidance from the Church to illuminate this historic moment for our country. Several journalists have also come to ask the Church's opinion and we responded in the same way to all inquiries.

In the evening we talked with the third-year seminary students, as we have in previous meetings, about the hope the Church has in these six new members who will become part of the clergy next year. We spoke of their pastoral work with the youth and for vocations in the parish of San José de la Montaña, but with a view to the entire archdiocese. And I am pleased to see how they have united to do this work that will doubtless result in great good for the seminary and for the youth in general. They have already named a committee for the pastoral work with the youth, which also included other young people who met two Sundays ago.

---

[228] The first junta also included Román Mayorga of the UCA, Guillermo Ungo from the Popular Forum and Mario Andino from the Chamber of Commerce and Industry.

They also criticized some of the attitudes they see in this moment of transition in the government, even my statement, especially because it was broadcast on the state channel. They think that the Church is being manipulated to show support for the new government, and that the Church should show more independence. I appreciate this critical sense and I told them that it was good, whenever there are doubts, to bring them up and that they will come out of them with greater solidarity with the Church. And in this specific case, I told them that I am responsible for what I wrote and for what I said and not for how it may be used by one side or another. The fact that it was broadcast on the state channel does not seem to me to compromise the Church, especially since the message given there was precisely my declaration of autonomy, of independence from the new government, of prudent support—naturally, because it is not fair to criticize it and attack it without waiting long enough to be able to judge it by its actions.

They were satisfied. I also told them that this is the risk of any prophetic mission of the Church, to be criticized even by your own people and even to find yourself alone, but able to feel the satisfaction of having tried to be faithful to the gospel.

The telephone conversation with Ingeniero Mayorga was in order to set up a meeting we had, in which he asked my opinion of his becoming part of the civilian-military junta. I told him that he is a person to be trusted, that he would inspire confidence in a large sector of the population and that, given his Christian spirituality and his academic knowledge as rector of the Central American University, he was the appropriate person to provide rational support to a movement that up until now has only been only a military one.

In a gesture of humility, Ingeniero Román Mayorga told me that he believed he heard in my voice the voice of God and that he would agree to do it. I also told him that it was not a commitment made unconditionally, that if things began to go wrong, he would have to resign, and that if I saw this happening, I myself would tell him. He knelt down and asked me for my blessing. And I believe that he is a man we can trust totally, one who sincerely reflects the Church's thinking in the difficult area of politics.

## Thursday, October 18

Among this morning's visits I received one from the ambassador of Sweden, who was interested to know the Church's thought at this time. Also Arquitecto Adalberto Morales, who gave me a very valuable written exposé of the media, which in this transition in the government will have to explain their attitudes, which were servile to and made them accomplices of the previous government in their defamation of the Church and in their attacks on respected people and institutions.

I have also received a similar letter from Napoleón Navarro, who also asks the new governing junta not to spend so much on arms and to return the fifty million dollars that the previous government took away from different ministries to give to the Defense Ministry for arms. Navarro also criticizes the attitude of the government of the United States: When it lifted the sanctions on aid to El Salvador, it immediately offered it military aid. This letter says that it is not military aid we need, that we are tired of bullets and weapons, that what we need is hunger for justice. We need justice and aid that will help our people.

I also received an important visit from Ingeniero Tato Osegueda, who worked for a time in the previous government, but who followed the voice of his conscience and resigned and is today in complete agreement with what the Church has done. He wants to cooperate with us in this. He told me that this hope of redemption given by the coup is, in great part, the fruit of the awareness planted by my preaching. I thanked him for this endorsement and, on my side, I am pleased, naturally—not in a vain way, but rather thanking God that his justice and his Kingdom are gaining ground through his servants in the Church.

Several journalists came today as well. And at seven o'clock in the evening, in St. Ignatius Church, I presided over the graduation exercises of the young ladies of Colegio de la Sagrada Familia. At the end of Mass a bomb exploded very near the school, destroying the power station in that area and a gas station also. The power went out and we finished the ceremony in the dark.

In my homily, as a message to the new graduates, I pointed out the double synthesis that the Church expects of all of those who receive their educations in Catholic schools and institutions: a synthesis of faith and culture and a synthesis between faith and their lives.

**Friday, October 19**

We had made an appointment around ten o'clock with all the journalists who had been asking for a press conference. Dutch television was there, as well as Mexican television, and radio and press from other areas and also from our country. I reaffirmed to them my thoughts about the Church and its relations with the new government.

This afternoon I went to San Rafael Cedros with Father [Leopoldo] Deras, parish priest of that town, who had set up a meeting with his collaborators for me—principally the catechists, with whom we shared the concerns of the Church and the hopes it has for the laity. It was a very interesting dialogue....[229]

Afterward, I went to the opening of the sewing exhibition at the San Rafael dressmaking academy, which was founded and is still directed by Father Leopoldo Deras, parish priest of that town. He greeted me warmly and in an intelligent way. I responded by praising the work of the Church—not just in the area of spiritual evangelization, but also for these social projects. I encouraged the young ladies to continue to make the synthesis between faith and their lives. We ended the afternoon by going to the church to celebrate Mass. It was full and a group of nice young people especially stood out—a group that had been prepared to receive Confirmation. I used the opportunity to try to excite that town about using the charisms and vocations given by the Holy Spirit in the service of the people, above all living our Confirmation.

 **Saturday, October 20**

I went to funeral of Don Marcel Weil, a great friend from way back. Although he was not Christian but Jewish, he was a man who respected each person's faith; and his personal honesty is truly a guarantee that God has received him in heaven. A very close family with whom I am really friends and at whose house I feel at home.

In the afternoon today I also went to the school of Lourdes, directed by the Sisters of the Assumption, to celebrate the First Communion of a group of girls and boys. I praised their work in that poor neighborhood and I called on all those present to work with them.

---

[229] Tape ends here.

When the Mass was over, I got a phone call from the presidential house. They wanted me to come there because they needed to consult with me, but I asked them to come instead to my residence, since my presence at the presidential house could be misinterpreted. They understood my reasons and Colonel Majano, the minister of defense and another officer came to the Divine Providence Hospital with a large retinue of bodyguards and detectives, which was bothersome in the situation of simplicity at this hospital.

Nevertheless, the topic of conversation was very interesting: They came because they were worried about the criticism by our radio station YSAX for the naming of Colonel Rafael Flores Lima as director of the military school. The Catholic station criticized his actions under the previous regime as chief of the Office of Information in the presidential house. He is the one responsible for the distorted news, the campaign of calumnies against the Church, for the falsity and lies which were spread from the presidential house.

They tried to defend him. We maintained our position that, if more drastic changes are not made in the image of the military in the country, this coup d'etat will not work and the people will suffer the consequences of another failure.

We also brought up the question of how the defense minister, who was there, was named, because he was named by the military before the civilians were incorporated into the junta. Colonel [José Guillermo] García, the defense minister, said there in our presence—Father Estrada was with me—that he resigned as defense minister effective immediately until the civilians could ratify his appointment, which had been made by the two colonels.

I also used the opportunity to denounce the abuses the Church is suffering even under the new government, as well as the people's fear of repression from the military operations carried out this week. They tried to explain that they are making purges, changing the mentality with new ideas, but the task is difficult. They asked us for our understanding and patience. They are sure that there is a great deal of corruption and they are even replacing leaders, which creates a new risk because they know that meetings are being held and there could be a countercoup from the right.

In summary, a cordial conversation that ended with a cup of coffee, offered by the sisters, in a cordial atmosphere, even though we had spoken very sincerely, very frankly. We promised to help each other, but always at the service of the people.

Later I continued to meet with Father Estrada and Father Moreno to prepare the data for my homily. Very late in the evening, Father Moreno left—and, unfortunately, he took the papers. But thanks to a helpful friend,

Salvador Barraza, whom I disturbed at midnight and asked to go get these papers for me at the Jesuit residence—I told him he would have to hurry because it was eleven o'clock at night and martial law began at twelve o'clock—thank God, everything turned out all right, and I continued working on my homily until four o'clock in the morning.

 **Sunday, October 21**

Mass was celebrated at the basilica. There was a great deal of anticipation because the people wanted to hear the Church's judgment and its position with respect to the new government. The Voice of America interpreted my statement as conditional support and, in fact, that is what it is. I have called for collaboration with the just proclamations of the new government, to be prudent and not to attack before forming an accurate judgment. But I also accused them of some violent actions, some military attacks that occurred this week, and the slowness we see in carrying out their promises to defend human rights, insisting principally on an accounting of the disappeared and justice for all of the guilty parties.

I have received many congratulations on the fair and impartial position the Church is trying to maintain. At the same time, it supports the hope that this new coup d'etat can bring. If it is done sincerely, it could be the rational solution the pope urged for the problems of Latin America when, at the Organization of American States, he said that there is no need to resort to violence, since all our problems can be resolved through rational means. There was much applause during different parts of the homily, which indicates that I was expressing the people's feelings. And I told the governing junta that this is not a negative judgment, but rather a support and a stimulus to carry out those same ideals before our people become frustrated.

After Mass there was an interesting press conference held there at the basilica. Representatives of television, radio and print media asked very complicated questions, and a great number of people were gathered around listening to this dialogue, among them Father [José] Inocencio Alas, whose presence surprised me. I greeted him warmly, promising to see him later.

In the evening, Father Inocencio Alas talked to me about his current activities in the United States and his current work with companies in Nicaragua. He insisted that I should go to the United States, that there are many Latin communities there who support me, and that I ought to go thank them and, at the same time, encourage them to continue their solidarity efforts. I promised him I would go. We even added the cities of San Francisco and Los Angeles, California.

 **Monday, October 22**

I have received positive comments on yesterday's homily. This opinion is based on my trying to be fair, given the present situation, protesting to the new ruling junta several things that have happened that detract from their proposals and promises, but, at the same time, criticizing the violent, intransigent and impatient attitude of the groups on the extreme left.

This morning there were many visits from priests and the faithful at the chancery. I went to have lunch at Don Pepe Simán's house rather late, since we had to delay it because of these visits and consultations. I felt quite overwhelmed at not finding understanding of the present political moment and of the attitude the Church is taking toward it.

At four o'clock in the afternoon, I had an audience with some members of the Popular Leagues of February 28, who have an intransigent attitude. I offered to arrange for them to talk with the new governmental authorities, but they said that they would have to consult with their leadership and that they did not think that this would be useful, since they totally disagreed with them because this junta is nothing more than an obstacle to the revolutionary process of the people. I tried to make them understand, but they are very stubborn.

At five o'clock in Externado San José, the Legal Aid Office had organized a press conference with foreign and national journalists; families of the disappeared and of political prisoners were also present. The presence of real families who really do cry and suffer because of the disappearance of a family member was very moving. The Legal Aid Office had an opportunity to explain its position, which is in perfect harmony with the archdiocese's program: defending human rights, filing protests and accusations against all of those who abuse these rights, and taking a decisive stand in continuing to demand the freedom of prisoners about whom Legal Aid has definitive documented proof.

**Tuesday, October 23**

We had a meeting of the archdiocesan Executive Council to discuss the difficult situation of the country. Fernando Valero Iglesias was present; he has brought an invitation from Holland for the Archbishop of San Salvador to be the keynote speaker for a program of an ecumenical organization in Holland in December. On previous occasions they have had Archbishop Helder Cámara[230] and Bishop Méndez Arceo,[231] and they want to have Latin American bishops connected with their ecumenical movement, which offers assistance to Latin American projects.

It was also a morning filled with visits, among them those of Fathers Majano, Rivera and Rodas from Santiago de María, who came to invite me to come for the twenty-fifth anniversary of that diocese on December 2. They propose a three-day celebration, with each day dedicated to a bishop of that diocese,[232] and offered to dedicate the second day to me in honor of the most Blessed Virgin and have a program for me after the Mass. I would stay until Sunday for a concelebration they will ask all the bishops to attend. Naturally, I accepted, since it is a diocese I have served in and where Bishop Rivera, who is a true pastoral support for me, now serves with such great affection.

Pepe Simán and Father Goyo Rosa, Father Fabián, Monsignor Urioste and the manager of the radio analyzed the attitude of the radio and the media, which is a delicate topic at such a difficult moment in the history of the country. Also Pepe Simán and Monsignor Urioste arranged and coordinated the trip I will soon make to the United States.

I went to have lunch with a group of priests who were having a spiritual retreat with the Opus Dei Fathers at Clara Luna. The theme we meditated on was the letter sent by Pope John Paul II to the priests during Holy Week of this year.

Father Fernando told me about a letter that has been leaked from the Congregation for the Bishops and seems to have been distributed out of ill will, in an attempt to defame the work of Opus Dei. I told him that I needed to study the matter and would talk about it with him later.

In the afternoon, an interview with Swedish television at the hospital. Also an Italian journalist—as always, with the same idea of getting my thoughts on the position of the Church at this time in the country. The ideas I expressed are the same as those in last Sunday's homily.

---

[230] Archbishop of Olinda and Recife, Brazil.

[231] Bishop of Cuernavaca, Mexico.

[232] Romero was bishop of Santiago de María from 1974 to 1977.

I had to cancel my visit to Dr. Semsch because I had to record my program for tomorrow; I will not have time tomorrow because I have to go to La Libertad. And in the evening I also had a dinner at Dr. Chávez's house along with Monsignor Urioste, Father Estrada, Dr. Morales Ehrlich of the Christian Democratic Party, a new minister—the minister of planning— and two young industrialists. It was a rich conversation because of our different experiences, with criteria that were relatively open. I received the impression that there are also some very trained minds in the business world that are very sensitive to social issues. On my part, I believe I expressed to them the true thought of the Church and called on the powerful classes to facilitate the change our people need.

 **Wednesday, October 24**

Today is the Day of the Hospital. In my radio dialogue I referred, among other things, to this event, reminding people that the patient is the center of the hospital and that we thank and admire the doctors, nurses, etc., around them, who work, I hope, with the spirit of Christ, for everything that is done for a patient is done for Christ himself.

But my pastoral activity today was all in the parish of La Libertad. At nine o'clock in the morning, a lovely group of three hundred to be confirmed, all over twelve years of age, well prepared in their respective communities in the villages in the neighborhood of La Libertad. And afterward, at two o'clock in the afternoon, in the village of Cangrejera, another group to be confirmed, one hundred and fifty young people who were also very well prepared. Thank God, we concelebrated with two priests from the United States and Father Manuel, who works in Ateos, and thus were able, among the four of us, to do the Confirmations and maintain the liturgical enthusiasm of the crowd. I thanked the priests, the women religious, the catechists and all their helpers, and urged the people to take advantage of this infusion of the Holy Spirit to promote our Christianity more as a community and, at this time in the nation's history, to be truly Christian at the level the moment requires.

In the evening, I was visited by Mr. Gerson Meyer, of the World Council of Churches of Switzerland, who came to see me along with Valero Iglesias just to chat as a farewell greeting since he is about to return to Switzerland.

There were calls from the presidential palace that I could not answer because I was away from the chancery, as I have said, in La Libertad.

**Thursday, October 25**

This morning I had an interesting consultation on the political situation of the country. Very educational, since one of the participants is a specialist in this kind of analysis. We decided we need a longer time to reflect. We agreed to spend the entire morning next Monday in Belén and to invite others who play an important role in the governance of the archdiocese.

In the evening, a meeting of the major and minor seminaries with the archdiocesan committee on the seminary. The idea was proposed to merge those two bodies so that the seminarians will perceive only one group of priests representing the entire presbytery, offering them the cooperation of all the priests, so that the seminarians may be introduced to their future ministry, where they will be working along with all the other priests.

At eight o'clock at night I went to the home of Ingeniero Román Mayorga Quirós, member of the junta of the revolutionary government. I could tell he is very tired and very worried about the situation, especially about the rebellion of the extreme left. But I tried to offer him encouragement and to tell him that their responsibility at this time is very great and that God will have to help them. Our meeting was at Mayorga's house and his wife attended us with great courtesy.

 **Friday, October 26**

I celebrated Mass at the Carmelite Institute, where I had promised to celebrate Mass some time ago; today it was held to mark the closing of the school year.

Lunch was at the house of the ambassador of the United States who, along with two assistants, had invited Monsignor Urioste, Father Estrada and me. It was an interesting conversation, especially about the change in government. We tried to suggest what help the United States could offer in this transition to help assure that the change is a peaceful one. They offered to do everything they can.

At four o'clock in the afternoon, I celebrated Mass for one of the young men killed in the repression in San Marcos last week.

I was visited by Colonel Jaime Gutiérrez, one of the main figures of the revolutionary government, who explained the difficulties in responding to our demands, especially those having to do with the disappeared. I could tell there are real internal difficulties in the army. We stated clearly that we will be concerned if this matter, which is such a delicate one, is not resolved to the satisfaction of the people. We also offered him our services, within the limits of the autonomy of the Church, and also were able to emphasize certain things that could offend the Church or retard the process they want to initiate and carry out to achieve the peaceful changes the country needs. It was an interesting conversation. Monsignor Urioste and Father Estrada also participated in it.

I had dinner at the home of Fernando Valero Iglesias, as he has prepared a memorandum for me, helping to plan the trip I will soon make to Holland at the invitation of an ecumenical organization.

In the afternoon, we had a brief meeting with the archdiocesan Caritas committee. The problem today has to do with the manager, Rafael Medrano, who has written a very insolent letter to the director, Father Rutilio Sánchez. It has been necessary to fire a supervisor due to certain abuses committed in the office itself, the result of which is a pregnant secretary. (She will continue to work the time legally allowed.) In spite of all this, we continue to see negative behavior. It is a difficult situation but one, I told the ladies of the archdiocesan committee, that they can mediate and resolve. On my part, I offered to talk to Father Tilo and to the manager to see if I can facilitate a more practical solution—for example, for Medrano to resign, since it seems that he is not happy at this institution.

 **Saturday, October 27**

I went to confirm a large group of young people and children, who had been prepared in Tamanique by the Maryknoll Sisters. I greeted Mother Juanita, who has been away because her mother was ill and later died. Now she is concerned about leaving her father alone, but she is very dedicated to this community. The community of Tamanique seemed to me quite vibrant. The Mass, at least, was very fervent and the celebration of the Confirmation was a true liturgical sacrament, very encouraging.

In the afternoon, I celebrated Mass at the minor seminary as a closing ceremony for their year's work. At the time for the Gospel, all of us together did the reflection, and it was a very beautiful participation as a way to give thanks to the Lord at the end of the school year.

In the chancery there were several visits at this time and a short interview with press and television, since there were journalists from Venezuela and other countries who have to leave very early tomorrow.

We were waiting for a member of the government junta, Ingeniero Mario Andino, but he never came. I had to call the presidential palace about something else and they were in an emergency session.

 **Sunday, October 28**

The Mass at the basilica was very well attended. The homily has received a good deal of praise, although there has been no lack of voices who disagree, voices of those who have a political line they wish we would follow.

In the afternoon, I went to the parish of Colón in the village of Delicias; there was a beautiful ceremony of Confirmations and weddings. Fourteen couples had been instructed by the catechists in that region. After the Mass, which was very solemn, we had a gathering with the pastoral agents who, speaking at the microphone, expressed their enthusiasm for the pastoral work and their solidarity with the pastor. I received an impression that pleased me a great deal: that the work being done there by Father Nicolás Menjívar with the Sisters of the Sacred Heart and the laity truly represents hope.

I forgot to say that after the Mass at the basilica there was a press conference with the press and television, with participation of journalists from Germany, Venezuela, Honduras, Guatemala and I do not remember which other countries. I also gave an interview to Radio YSU, which asked for my opinion on the current political situation. I gave it from my perspective as a pastor, as I always try to make clear.

 **Monday, October 29**

We spent the entire morning at Colegio Belén in Santa Tecla, along with Monsignor Urioste, Father Estrada, Father Ellacuría, Father Fabián Amaya, Father Moreno and an expert in political science from the Central American University, in order to reflect on the present political situation of the country so that we may take appropriate pastoral measures. The political scientist explained to us the revolutions in Peru and Bolivia in order to use them as a point of reference for our situation. And then we got into the analysis of the situation of our country.

I found in the variety of opinions a great wealth of thought because I understood that both the government junta and the popular political organizations, which are in conflict with the government at present, have their positive points and also their negative points. And therefore the position of the Church must be to encourage the good things, to support them, in both the junta and in the popular organizations—and also, from our love for the country and for the cause of justice, to protest those things which impede the revolutionary process that seems to have begun. At any rate, we believe there is something new happening and that we have to watch closely the signs of the times.

There has been a great deal of violence today. When we were en route to Santa Tecla, they were just finishing burning some tires in front of the Basilica of La Ceiba. And around noon there was gunfire downtown, where there were also some deaths. And in the afternoon the minister of defense called me on the telephone to tell me that shots were being fired at the National Palace from the cathedral, but that the security forces were under orders to be patient and not to return the fire unless it was absolutely necessary. He asked me to intercede with those in the cathedral.

I sent Father Sigfredo, who met there with Monsignor Modesto López, rector of the cathedral, and they walked around the cathedral to look but did not see anything out of the ordinary, other than that the church was occupied, closed and from within, yes, the usual slogans of the Popular Revolutionary Bloc were being called out on microphones. There is uncertainty in the atmosphere, but we place our hope in the Lord that everything will turn out all right.

The ministries of labor and the economy, which have already been occupied for several days by the Bloc, have announced that the hostages will be freed today—except for the ministers, who will continue to be held.

Radio YSAX asked me to make a brief commentary on the situation. I condemned the acts of violence and expressed my joy at the freeing of the hostages but, based on the right to freedom, I asked that all of them be freed very soon. Also I was asked about the situation of the cathedral and I told them what I have already said, that we have not seen anything unusual but also that the occupation of churches, ministries and other such activities are not constructive—especially when dialogue has been called for. I suggested more creative political thinking, learning political language instead of using the language of violence, since it is very dangerous to use violence in such an explosive atmosphere. On the contrary, it would be very constructive to express the opinions of different sectors of the country through legitimate pluralism. I argued again for peace and for a more rational path toward justice and peace.

The Catarina Di Maggio School, directed by Sister Socorro, sent a delegation of students to give me a check for five hundred colones,[233] which has been collected through different activities at the school to help our station YSAX. We had a nice conversation, expressing complete solidarity with the position of the Church.

In the evening, Dr. Chávez invited me to have dinner, along with Ingeniero Napoleón Duarte, who has recently returned from exile in Venezuela. He was the [presidential] candidate for the Christian Democratic Party at the same time as Colonel Molina, who became president, rumor says, through a fraudulent election. Therefore, Duarte considered himself president during all the time he was in exile. The new government junta has canceled the decrees of exile and Duarte has returned.

There in Dr. Chávez's house, we watched Duarte's speech on television. He praised me as the one who has kept the hope of the people alive and he offered to collaborate from the political arena in this struggle of the people. It was a very solid and inspirational speech. In our face-to-face conversation with him, we expressed our different points of view about the present situation of the country. Dr. Chávez said that Duarte and I were two people, each one in his own field, whom the Lord had provided to guide the people. On my part, I want to thank him for this assessment that honors me and that is the result of my trying to carry out my evangelical mission. Also, I agree that Ingeniero Duarte has leadership qualities and that, clearly, he is a charismatic person for this moment. He ought to be very careful because he has many enemies who do not want him to be so influential with the people.

 **Tuesday, October 30**

We held a meeting of the Executive Council, principally to discuss the Secretariat of Communications proposed by Fernando Valero Iglesias, who wants to ask for help from Holland to set up a good communications office. We also tried to coordinate the aid for Radio YSAX, since all our advertisers have canceled. It is a good opportunity for us to have a truly independent radio station totally dedicated to culture. The manager, Teto Samour, and Father Gregorio Rosa were authorized to take care of the final details for this campaign for support for the radio.

---

[233] About $200.00.

I went to see the doctor, Dr. Basagoitia, after taking him blood samples for analysis. Thank God, he says my health is good, even better than the last time he examined me. I thank God and I promise to continue using my life to serve his Church.

In the afternoon I celebrated Mass at the Divine Providence Hospital for the eternal rest of the four dead peasants, among them one I knew well: Polín. These four peasants died from gunshot wounds received from the military on the road to Santa Ana.

In the evening, a meeting with the third-year bachillerato students at the minor seminary; there are fourteen young men, all of them willing to continue their studies toward the priesthood—some as diocesan priests and others in the religious orders. We spoke a good deal about their vocation, about the current problems of the country, about the hope they have for the future. The sisters from the hospital served us pupusas and hot chocolate. It was a nice meeting.

In the evening I worked on the speech that, God willing, I will give at the Council of Churches in New York. I still have not been able to finish it.

 **Wednesday, October 31**

Today I got up very early to continue working on the pastoral message that I have been asked to give by members of the National Council of Churches in New York. I have continued working in the moments I can, but it has been a very intense morning, with visits beginning at seven-thirty in the morning, when I went to tape the program for noon on the situation of the country and on other issues the people are asking about.

I also had a meeting with the Vicariate of Aguilares to talk about the matter of Father Joaquín Brizuela and the pastoral work in Ciudad Arce. It appears that Father Brizuela would prefer to go to another vicariate, possibly to the one in Cuscatlán in the parish of San Rafael Cedros, whose priest, Father Leopoldo Deras, suggested to him that they change places and that he would go to Ciudad Arce.

I had interviews with British and Guatemalan television and with other journalists, who are always interested in knowing what the archbishop thinks about the present situation of the country.

In the afternoon, I could not go to the Mass at El Paraíso, where I had promised the children I would consecrate them as Montañeros, but I asked Father Sigfredo to go as my representative. Today I wanted to finish the speech I have mentioned for my trip to the United States.

# November, 1979

### Thursday, November 1

I had lunch with the seminary team to discuss some matters dealing with the relations between the interdiocesan seminary and our archdiocese in San Salvador. They especially concerned the location, San José de la Montaña. Although it is the property of the archdiocese, it seems best to leave it completely for the interdiocesan seminary. For that reason, the team suggests that the archdiocesan offices should be moved to avoid problems that occur because of the conflict with the other bishops. We also talked about the matter of using seminary rooms as offices, which is related to the previous topic.

The most important thing is the report on the seminarians—that this not cause conflicts between the seminary and the archdiocese, as happened last year. I suggested to them that to achieve this it would be good to continue what has already begun, thank God: greater dialogue between the team and the archdiocesan community through the committee of priests from the archdiocese. It is a group of priests of diverse tendencies who can also provide guidelines for the team for a joint report about our seminarians.

This morning there has been a great deal of work in the chancery. Among other visits, that of Don Lencho Llach, who is worried that in the occupied ministries there are also people who work in the coffee industry who were there to arrange some matters of small- and middle-sized coffee growers, and trapped by the occupation.

Also, some representatives of the Popular Revolutionary Bloc came, and I expressed to them my opinions—different, naturally, from theirs— about the current situation. I used this opportunity to ask them for a prompt resolution of the occupations of the ministries. They are very dogmatic in their ways, and it is hard to have a dialogue when someone has fixed ideas. Nevertheless, I tried to be as pleasant as I could in order to keep open the possibility for dialogue with them.

I went to have lunch at the home of Don Pepe Simán, where Bishop Rivera and Monsignor Urioste were also present. We talked about the usefulness of our trip to the United States—although it always depends on circumstances that change so quickly at the present time.

In the afternoon I celebrated the Holy Hour with a large attendance in the hospital chapel, where I spoke with several people who are in the government at the present time or who have very interesting views about this situation.

Today I finished and typed my speech—or rather, the pastoral message—that I will present at the National Council of Churches in the United States on November 8.

When I was finishing this work at almost nine o'clock at night, I received some very alarming telephone calls from the presidential palace. They asked me to go and intercede at El Rosario Church, occupied by the Popular Leagues of February 28, for they have taken a member of the National Guard prisoner. The Guard headquarters is demanding that the governing junta and its commanders let it go in and rescue the Guard member, dead or alive.

I tried to reach Monsignor Urioste and Father Rogelio. We went to El Rosario Church, where the leaders of the Leagues informed us that it was true, that they had taken the soldier prisoner because he secretly entered the church, armed. They thought that his intentions were bad because there were two other armed agents with him, whom they were unable to capture. They had been trying to notify the attorney general so that he might come in an official capacity to get the prisoner, but they had not received any response from the attorney general.

I asked if they could turn him over to me, and they said they would, with a document and witnesses. I informed the presidential office of this. They were very happy that the solution was so easy, but I did not think that it would get so complicated, since later the Leagues insisted on turning him over to the attorney general directly as a better guarantee. Monsignor Urioste communicated with the attorney general and asked him to come because his presence was absolutely necessary at that moment. The delay in the attorney general's arrival complicated the situation. At almost 12:30 we began to see members of the National Guard arriving in the areas around El Rosario Church. I tried to get information from the leader of this operation, who told me that there was very strong pressure in the National Guard headquarters.

Around one in the morning, they all wanted to come; I tried to calm them. The colonel who was in charge of the operation listened to me, but I noticed that the troops were very aggressive. They even said very strong things to me. It was obvious that they would not be patient any longer and were ready to begin at one o'clock in the morning, which was only a few minutes away. I told the Leagues that they needed to speed up the surrender of the soldier. The document had already been written; the attorney general was also in agreement, and so we turned him over.

But, on receiving the soldier, in spite of visible relief in the tension, they began to say that there were also two policemen and that they had come to get them as well. We denied that they were any more prisoners, but they did not believe us and, apparently, they complicated the situation by involving the National Police.

The soldier who had been freed calmed the headquarters of the Guard, where the aggressiveness ended, but the police headquarters was ready to rise up demanding the return of the policemen they said were prisoners. We conferred. The attorney general was very nervous. Also the colonels who had come from the presidential palace and from the police felt that there was something uncontrollable. We proposed a search, that policemen acquainted with those who had—according to the police—disappeared, search the interior of the church. But the Leagues asked that they enter unarmed.

And so it was that I accompanied two policemen dressed in civilian clothes, unarmed, along with Father Alejandro Peinador, pastor of that church, a Dominican and a member of the Human Rights Commission. We accompanied the two policemen, who went along looking one by one at everyone inside of the church and also in the caskets (twenty-one bodies that are going to be buried in a grave that is being dug inside the church because, according to those occupying the church, it would be very dangerous for them to take them to the cemetery to be buried).

Thank God, there was no sign of the policemen. At the same time, we received word that one of them had been located at his home. This also brought relief of the pressure from the National Police and thus the atmosphere calmed. Nevertheless, those occupying the church asked me to stay, just in case, and the Dominican Fathers gave me a room. They did the same for Monsignor Urioste, and other people involved with human rights also stayed to spend the night there.

**Friday, November 2**

All Souls' Day. At six o'clock in the morning, I returned from El Rosario Church. Later, I received telephone calls from the presidential house to thank me for my mediation. I used the opportunity to describe how I see the situation of the security forces: Yes, there are some officers who are better trained and want tranquility, but there are some members who could rebel and who, in a moment of disobedience, could produce fatal consequences. I was glad that I had intervened, and I told him that I am at his service, that the service of the Church was available for these matters.

I have spent the day resting because lack of sleep is very hard on me. Nevertheless, at noon I celebrated the three Masses for the dead.

In the evening I had expected a visit from some young military officers, who had asked for an audience with me through Father Guty [Gutiérrez]. But at the last minute they notified me that they had received an emergency call from the presidential house saying that they were very sorry, so this meeting was postponed until a later date.

 **Saturday, November 3**

I spent the entire morning in the parish of La Palma, Chalatenango, where the Franciscan priest, Father Vitto Guaratto, was holding graduation from the dressmaking school for a new group of young people who have been preparing themselves for two years for this art. We also blessed the house under construction, which Father Guaratto intends to use for spiritual development and to house courses to promote all the different social sectors within that beautiful parish. A fresh atmosphere, very good people. They are developing a good work of promotion, as much by the parish priest as by the Semilla de Dios cooperative, an industry being used to create tourism. All in all, it is a very beautiful combination of work and prayer.

The Carmelites of St. Joseph also have their house there. Their novices were at the Mass and then they took us to visit their beautiful residence.

In the afternoon, rather, in the evening, I saw Colonel Claramount, who has returned from his exile in Costa Rica. We discussed the delicate situation of the country if the military junta does not get guidance from the older military experts, among whom Colonel Claramount would offer disinterested help.

Afterward, we met with two representatives of the Popular Leagues of February 28, with whom I discussed the occupation of El Rosario Church and the burial of twenty-one bodies in that church. I clarified several situations that official sources blame them for and that, according to them, happened differently. I encouraged them to be open to the possibility of dialogue and cooperation, but they really cling to their ideas. It will be difficult to get these people to agree to dialogue about cooperation for the common good of the country; their only desire seems to be the triumph of the ideas of their organization.

Afterward, I was with Father Moreno, Monsignor Urioste and Beto Cuéllar to review the week. We arrived at guidelines that will direct what I do in my homily tomorrow. It involves balancing a very delicate situation: abuses on the part of the security forces, the goodwill of the junta, the rejection by the popular political organizations. But with the help of God, the inspiration of the Holy Spirit and my sincere desire to be just and truly to help the people, I think that I have developed good enough guidelines to be able to encourage them and to denounce abuses in tomorrow's homily, in the light of God's word.

 **Sunday, November 4**

I concelebrated in the basilica with four priests who were celebrating their twenty-fifth anniversary as priests: Father Antonio Vides, Father Andrés Alvarenga, Father Joaquín Brizuela and Father Oscar Martel. There was one from San Vicente, but that couldn't be helped. At the same time, Father Ramiro Jiménez, a Passionist priest, concelebrated with us, since he was named parish priest of the basilica that same morning.

I used the homily to talk about the eternal priesthood of Christ, while the priests who exist in time are replaced. From the Epistle to the Hebrews[234] and from the other readings,[235] the question of what the ministry of the priests is: the defense of monotheism in the face of so much idolatry, also builder of the civilization of love and the ministry of the true

---

[234] Hebrews 7:23-28.
[235] Deuteronomy 6:2-6; Mark 12:28b-34.

worship of the living God. And I denounced the idolatry of our society, as I do in my pastoral letter.

After Mass, we shared with the priests and some of their communities some simple refreshments in the convent of the basilica, where a press conference was also set up with foreign press and television journalists, as well as one local journalist. This kind of interview is becoming a tradition after the Mass, as are other private interviews, which give a pastoral and familial spirit to these moments after Mass.

In Metapán the Franciscan Sisters of the Immaculate Conception were celebrating the centenary of their founding. They had invited me to lunch, but I was only able to mention it in the Mass and begged them to forgive me for not going. I was also unable to go to the fellowship gathering of the catechumens who were celebrating the Rite of Exorcism[236] in a retreat house in Planes de Renderos.

I went to have dinner with the sisters at Colegio de la Sagrada Familia at their little farm in Planes. The atmosphere was restful and cordial.

Again tonight I waited for the young military officers who, according to Father Guty, were going to come, but again they were unable to come.

 **Monday, November 5**

At eight o'clock in the morning I was visited by three journalists, one of them Dutch, another from Ireland and another who is Salvadoran but works in Guatemala. Always the same questions, but this gives me the chance to adapt what I say and to be more precise each time about the situation of the country and the work of the Church as Church.

I received a letter brought by a Salesian nun from the nuncio[237] in Costa Rica, in which he tells me in confidence that the Vatican Secretary of State has asked him to notify me that they have received there, from a reliable source, reports of a threat against my life by the extreme left. This future threat, which could become reality, is intended to create problems for the new governing junta and to increase the confusion among our people. It is not that it does not worry me, given the seriousness of the way it was reported; I have received many of these warnings just as popular rumors. But, even so, I think that I will give it the same importance that I

---

[236] One of the rites connected with the catechumenate process.
[237] Archbishop Lajos Kada.

have always given these things: Take prudent care but without exaggerating.

I consulted with Monsignor Urioste on this, and he agrees with me that these may be the same rumors that are also reaching the high levels of the Vatican.

I also discussed this with two personages of the government who came to visit me. They told me that it was appropriate to denounce it publicly and that, if I wanted, they would give me protection, even an armored car. But I told them that I wanted to continue to run the same risks as my people, that it would not be a good example for me to have this kind of security. I took the occasion to urge them to speed up events that will prove something to the people, who will become disillusioned if they do not see quicker action from the government. They explained to me that in some of the leadership positions of the military forces there are certain people they do not trust, who could be the source of some betrayal, but that they are going to purge those positions. We talked about other aspects of the new government. I thanked them for their confidence and I offered them my services insofar as I am able as a pastor.

I went to visit the nuncio, who had asked me for an audience, in the evening. We discussed the news from the nunciature of Costa Rica. He offered to notify them that the letter had been received, as that nuncio had requested.

We also discussed the situation of the bishops. I asked him to do everything possible to encourage unity among us, but one based on a serious reflection on the situation of the country. He said that I was right and promised to do everything he could. We also talked about the situation of the country. He is concerned that the Vatican still has not given its approval to the new government, which worries him because he does not want to be left behind. He finds it strange that the new government, especially the new Minister of Foreign Relations, still has not made any contact with him. I noted a diplomatic concern in our nuncio.

From three o'clock in the afternoon on, members of the governing junta met in the Nicaraguan embassy with members of the leadership of the Popular Revolutionary Bloc in order to negotiate the release of the hostages in the ministries of Labor and the Economy and, specifically, the numerous demands that the Bloc wants to achieve at any cost. The negotiations lasted until nine o'clock at night and were adjourned to be continued tomorrow at eight o'clock.

With my collaborator in the talks, the seminarian Octavio, I prepared a brief presentation to announce the threat to which I referred before and to give my impressions of serenity and tranquility—to say that it is normal for one who dedicates himself to preaching truth and justice to be at cross-purposes with the world and for his voice, even though it be silenced by death, to continue to be heard in the conscience of those who think as he does. I also referred to the cancellation of my trip to the United States, given the precariousness of the situation of the country. And I thanked the Minister of Foreign Relations of Honduras for his words, in which he mentioned me as a possible contact to work for peace with that country. And other points that I have forgotten for the moment, but which are included in a mini-interview that YSAX wanted to begin to offer, collecting different opinions about the present events and the crossroads at which we stand.

 **Tuesday, November 6**

This morning, since it was the first Tuesday of the month, the clergy meeting took place, attended by many priests of the archdiocese, numerous women religious and members of the laity who participate in the pastoral work of our archdiocese. The topic for study was learning about the popular political organizations. The three principal ones had been invited—that is, FAPU, the Popular Revolutionary Bloc and the Popular Leagues of February 28. Today both the Bloc and the Leagues had other activities and could not come, but we heard a very interesting explanation of the ideology and strategies of FAPU. They are involved in a struggle for a government by the people, for the people, according to the secretary general of the group.

Afterward, we divided into groups by vicariates to ask ourselves two questions: first, what pastoral opportunities are presented in this reality of the popular political organizations and, second, the attitude of the Church. The reflection in groups was very enriching because, when we went back to the plenary, we generated a list of very positive ideas that more closely link our pastoral work of presence in the national reality, connecting it specifically to the identity of the Church.

Therefore, in conclusion, I told them that I had been impressed by the clarity with which the organizations present their ideas, the nature of their organizations and their strategies, and that I hoped that we, as pastoral workers with a complete theology, a whole tradition of the nature, mission and life of the Church, become each day more conscious of this and know how to express it—not only to explain what the Church is, but also to live our true identity as Church without going outside of our ecclesial direction, from which we can affect the political realities positively only insofar as we are authentically the Church of Jesus Christ.

Also I expressed to them how these men from the popular organizations appear to be very dedicated to the work of liberating the people and that we understand this completely. But we are distressed to think that this struggle is only immanent, only against earthly slaveries and realities—political, economic, etc.; that we can understand all of this and be in solidarity with the liberating forces but from our own perspective, which is much more complete because it is founded on liberation from sin and raises humanity to the dignity of children of God, heirs to the eternity of God. Because of this, we are more able to understand liberations on earth and guide them toward the great liberation of Christ.

I also told the pastoral agents that the unity that these forces demonstrate is the secret of their effectiveness and that we also, since we have a theology of communion, should try not to be so divided among ourselves and even less should criticize each other and even less separate ourselves from the ideals and the objectives that the bishop, as the person principally in charge of our pastoral work, indicates for the pastoral work of the archdiocese. When there are differences, we should talk and understand each other and try never to break our communion as Church.

I also announced the invitation from the Diocese of Santiago de María, which is going to celebrate its twenty-fifth anniversary this coming December 2. It was a very cordial meeting, rich in ideas and pastoral initiatives.

In the afternoon one of the Franciscan priests from Gotera, who came with another priest from a diocese in Ireland, taped a television interview with me about the reality of our Church and our country to take back to his country.

This afternoon we were involved with a meeting of the seminary committee with the formation team from the seminary. It was very enriching, for we are establishing a great deal of trust between these two sectors that before seemed to be somewhat antagonistic. We have as the objective of our meeting and our mutual work the good of our future priests, for the more united they see the clergy and the formation team to be, the more they will also be motivated to an authentic priestly formation.

In the evening the new Minister of Health, Doctor Badía, visited the community of the Divine Providence Hospital. I shared with them a pleasant conversation in which there was great optimism and great goodwill to serve the country in such a very necessary area as its health. Dr. Badía, the new minister, is perhaps the doctor who is most knowledgeable of social medicine and knows the health problems of our people well. And he is a man of great goodwill, honest and competent. For this reason, I think that he will do much good. He had already come to offer his services to this hospital. He has gotten some subsidies as well—not official ones, but rather from some charitable institutions. This indicates his desire to be of service in this kind of effort.

 **Wednesday, November 7**

As I had promised Dr. [Jorge] Lara-Braud, I telephoned New York to confirm my decision not to attend the ecumenical meeting of the National Council of Churches that begins tomorrow, Thursday. This afternoon they had planned to hold a Mass in St. Patrick's Cathedral for the Salvadorans and Central Americans of that great city. I expressed by telephone my regret at not being able to go but, at the same time, I explained to him my pastoral commitment to be with my people. He understood perfectly and expressed to me, rather, the admiration of that meeting, and that they will keep the situation of this country in their prayers. I dictated to him by telephone some ideas from the message that I had prepared and that has been sent by mail, as well as a message for the Salvadorans who are to meet this afternoon in the cathedral in New York.

The telephone interview was recorded and was broadcast on the interview program that I have every Wednesday at one o'clock in the afternoon. In the one o'clock interview I also tried to shed light on problems such as that of the recognition of the new government by the Holy See.

At four o'clock in the afternoon, there was an interview on the Catholic radio with FAPU, which complains that there are commentaries that do not clearly explain their work and which confuse it with that of other leftist groups. They clarified many misunderstandings, and we told them that, when there was something they need to clarify, we would gladly give their clarifications as long as they were consistent with the truth and were always positive ways of building the common good of the country. Also, in a meeting at the radio after this interview, we agreed on the naming of the new accountant, the auditor for YSAX.

Afterward, two interviews with German and British television and, finally, a visit from Dr. Lores,[238] who is going to the ecumenical meeting in New York and wanted to give me his greetings. I sent with him my greeting and an embrace for that group. I also gave him copies of my address in Spanish and in English, in case it had not arrived. It was a very nice meeting,

---

[238] Ruben Lores of the National Council of Churches, U.S.A.

and he understood perfectly that I cannot go. We talked a great deal about the situation, and that we will look forward to what Dr. Lara promised me by telephone—that he will come to bring their greetings and solidarity from that meeting.

I also had a private interview with Dr. Saca and Dr. Badía, in which we discussed very confidentially some different aspects of the new government. We promised to help support their goodwill and any good that they do. Also, as for myself, I repeated to him my intention to be faithful above all to my Church, which has to be the conscience of history, and for this reason also has to criticize the obstacles and always support what progress humanity makes toward the Kingdom of God.

 ### Thursday, November 8

I accepted an invitation from the Vicariate of La Resurreción to go to the sea—actually, to Coatepeque Lake—to celebrate Father Vides' twenty-fifth anniversary in the priestly life. We spent a very fraternal day in Hotel El Lago with Father Ramiro, two Augustinians from Colonia Miramonte and a Josephite Father from Colonia Centroamérica.

The conversation always revolved around the present circumstances. Concretely, I asked them—and the dialogue was very interesting—how we can help achieve a true cleansing of the armed forces, especially of the security forces. Father Vides, who was the chaplain of the Guard, has been a witness to many abuses that were committed there and of the sincere desire that has always existed in some officers to rebuild this armed force according to the constitution. For if it is not providing security for the country, it becomes armed terrorism. There is goodwill. I announced to them that this very evening the director of the National Guard is coming to talk with me because he wanted to ask me for guidance and moral support, and that I thought that, in good conscience, the Church has to accept these challenges but also to know how to serve in truth and sincerity. They gave me many practical suggestions. I had also invited Father Fabián Amaya and Father Jesús Delgado to come this evening to advise me.

When I returned from the outing to Coatepeque Lake in the evening, the director of the Guard arrived, Colonel Eugenio Vides Casanova. In a very respectful manner he expressed that he had been listening to my homilies for a long time and that, when he is not here in San Salvador, he has his son tape them so that he can listen to them later. He congratulated me on the ideology, which he has tried to understand and which he thinks is what the country urgently needs. I was glad about this affinity and about this desire in a man who is not only a military officer but also a professional man who has studied abroad, who truly desires that all the obstacles that existed during the previous government be removed and that there be true renewal in the body of the National Guard. He accepts his post only as a sacrifice and a service to the country.

We commented, together with Father Fabián and Father Jesús Delgado, on the different abuses and anomalies that were seen in the Guard throughout the past administration, especially in zones like Chalatenango and other highly repressed zones. We also complained about the lack of understanding of our pastoral work and we offered to do everything that was within our power to cooperate in the noble effort one day to have security forces that are truly respected and not feared.

He expressed to us the fears the new government has because it is faced with the existence of extremists on both the right and the left. But, with God's help, they think this can be overcome and they can begin a renewal that will be continued by a government elected by the people once democratic conditions have been created in the country.

 **Friday, November 9**

Amid the intense activities in the chancery this morning, I received an interviewer from foreign television and another from national television—more specifically, from the university. Also a meeting with the Indigenous Association, which came to explain to me some important points of their indigenous group, which participated in the episcopal meeting at San Cristóbal de Las Casas, where several bishops, with Bishop [Samuel] Ruíz, did a study of this aspect of Latin America. Among us there is a small group of indigenous people in Izalco who want to be able to count on the support of the Church in maintaining their individuality and a true sense of identity and not to be merely an object of exploitation for tourism in El Salvador.

They left me the report that they studied in Mexico and that we are going to publish here so that there can be more knowledge of such an important subject. Also a group from the workers' federation came with sociopolitical concerns to ask for guidance from the Church and to indicate their complete solidarity with the ideas of the Church at such a difficult moment as that in which we are living at present. These consultations and their approaching the Church give me much consolation, since they show

how the Good Shepherd, Jesus Christ, can continue to provide through his Church a word and a voice of hope and guidance for so many different human groups.

I went to have lunch with the priests of the Vicariate of Mejicanos, who are doing the Spiritual Exercises at the house of the Somascan Sisters near the sea in the port of La Libertad.

Another very interesting invitation for the evening: a meeting of ex-priests who have found in this fraternal group a way of sharing their concerns and their situation as priests retired from the ministry. They were very happy that I was with them and they told me of their plan to create a Christian base community. I encouraged them in this objective, since the fact that they have left the ministry does not mean that they have stopped being members of the Church. May the priestly character that they have enable them to do the work of the Church, which a true Christian base community is—one in which they must live the missionary and sanctifying nature of the Church. I see great sincerity, great cordiality and a great sense of loyalty to the hierarchy.

 **Saturday, November 10**

In the morning I talked with Rafael Medrano, manager of Caritas, who is having problems with Father Tilo Sánchez, director of Caritas. Together we agreed that it would be better for both of them to resign and leave the leadership of Caritas to a Christian community or a religious community. I asked for his cooperation in this. We thought specifically of the community of Aguilares, that they might direct Caritas efforts for the entire archdiocese.

Also at breakfast, I talked with Father Jesús Delgado about certain situations in the present governing junta, and especially about the role the Church can play at this time. In the army there is a willingness to receive Christian guidance, but we thought that as long as Bishop Alvarez is the military vicar, this will be very difficult. Father Delgado had already suggested to the new government that they should concern themselves with resolving this matter, for the Minister of Foreign Relations, Mr. Héctor Dada, is a man of the Church and understands this hierarchical problem perfectly. He will be interested in finding a solution—not just to the matter of the military vicar, but also to other matters pertaining to the bishops and their relationship to the government and the Holy See. Specifically, I proposed to Father Delgado that, even if these changes did not take place, it was to our advantage to consider in a pastoral way the Christian orientation of our army, and that he would be a very important part of this since he has many friendships with the army, as does the Jesuit Father Estrada.

Afterward, Dr. Chávez arrived—a good analyst of the current situation from the perspective of the Christian Democratic Party. He explained to me his points of view: a strategy with the objective of connecting with the movement that has begun with the new governing junta, and having the courage and honesty to cooperate with them for the good of the country. I told him that from my pastoral perspective, without leaving aside my identity as Church, I was open to any work for the good of the country. He has proposed that the military officers in the government junta meet with me and with another member of his Christian Democratic Party—just a friendly meeting to appraise the situation. It seems that next Wednesday, God willing, this meeting will take place.

At noon, Father Gregorio Rosa and Miss Doris Osegueda suggested to me a good criterion to use to organize my homily about the week's events. It is a very centered approach and one that, if I consider it along with what Father Rafael and Bachiller Cuéllar usually bring me in the evening, will give me a more just and impartial orientation.

 **Sunday, November 11**

I celebrated Mass in the basilica with a very large number of people in attendance. I tried to be very fair, discussing the situation of the governing junta which offers us true hope—which some do not want to see, but which it is my duty to encourage—and the perspectives of the leftist opposition, which is each day more intransigent and which, in armed groups, resorts to violence that cannot be tolerated.

I spent more than an hour explaining the reading about the widow of Zarephath and the widow of the Gospel,[239] presenting in my homily the three factors that can bring true liberation of the country: a spirit of poverty, a sense of God and our firm hope in the mystery of Christ. Only from this threefold Christian perspective can a Christian view liberation. For that reason, this is not a political perspective but a pastoral one, which permits me to be autonomous and independent in order to support what is good in any sector and also to denounce what is evil in any sector.

---

[239] 1 Kings 17:10-16; Mark 12:38-44.

At noon, I went to celebrate the Mass for the patron, St. Martin, in the city of San Martín, where there was great rejoicing in the popular festival and also great fervor in the church. The communities brought me their greetings and information about their work. We also had a very interesting dialogue during our gathering at lunchtime. They put forth their political views, which concerned me somewhat as it seems that their political criteria prevail over the pastoral orientation offered by their bishop.

I felt this concern again in the evening in Colonia Santa Lucía, where I also went to celebrate Mass. After Mass I offered a time for sharing, especially with the young people, who were also very involved in the politics of the popular organizations, but a good part of them are grounded in the pastoral vision of the Church. These two gatherings have left me very concerned. I have to look, along with those who work directly with me in the diocese, for a way to improve religious instruction, so that the Christian criteria might prevail over the political analysis.

 ### Monday, November 12

Today I went to rest at the house of the Sisters of the Sacred Heart, where I spent the day. But in the evening, a meeting was held with a group of young military officers (some ten of them, including captains and majors), coordinated by Father Gutiérrez, in which I was accompanied by Father Estrada and Father Jesús Delgado. It was a very interesting conversation. I saw the goodwill of these young officers, their sincere wish to offer the country a contribution to true liberation and an effort to learn the thinking of the Church, so that this moment of democratization may be better. We explained the ideas of the Church, and they also spoke with total frankness from their political and military perspectives. We agreed that these meetings should continue and should always be understood from a perspective of mutual autonomy: our perspective, a pastoral one, and theirs, political and military.

## Tuesday, November 13

As usual on Tuesdays, I concentrated my attention on the priests, although there were some visits from members of the laity—for example, Dr. Jiménez Barrios from Jucuapa, who gave me a volume of his poems with the idea that, if we published it, the proceeds would go to the seminary. We talked at length about other things and I thanked him for his generous gesture to the Church, especially when one considers that he is a convert who has found his happiness in his conversion to Christ.

In the afternoon I received Don Pepe Simán, who has been named president of INSAFI.[240] He has decided to accept this position, but he wanted to know my opinion and have my blessing. I told him that the only things that worried me were his salary and the insecurity of the situation he was putting himself in, since this is a transition government and there is a great deal of conflict. He said that he had already thought of these two things and that they did not worry him much. He wants to serve his country and even if, because of this, he gets burned, he considers that it would be an honor for him to have served his country in a disinterested way. I congratulated him, encouraged him. He knelt to ask me for my blessing, which with great pleasure and fervor I gave him for himself, for his family and for his new position.

There was a meeting of the major seminary and some of the priests. I receive great satisfaction from the fact that the clergy and the major seminary—that is, the future clergy—are drawing nearer to each other.

We talked at length about an evaluation of the work of the seminary, in the light of the parable of the talents, and I directed this examination concerning the seminary as a community and concerning each one of them—so many talents—as a group of young men who ought to have their own configuration as the seminary of the archdiocese. Many views were expressed in an effort to define the characteristics of the major seminary of the archdiocese. One of the ones that I liked best said that it was a balanced social sense, under the guidance of the bishop. I told them that I approved of all of this, and that, in particular, they should be characterized by their piety, by their closeness to God, by being men of prayer such as our people will need one day as their priests.

---

[240] *Instituto Salvadoreño de Fomento Industrial*, the Salvadoran industrial development institute.

We also talked about planning an assembly of young people for this coming Christmas, when it has been announced that there will be a visit from the prior of Taizé, with whom I became friends at the Puebla meeting. Since then he has been promising me this visit to our country so that we might celebrate next Christmas together here. There is enthusiasm among the seminarians, who will assemble the young people during their vacation, and I think that it will turn out to be something really fine, due to the charism of the prior of Taizé, who has a very special grace in his dealings with young people. On this occasion, four of the six seminarians in the third year of theology will receive their ministries.[241]

Father Goyo Rosa, with a military officer of the rank of major, paid me a confidential visit in which the officer revealed to me sensational things about the disorder that reigns in the army, of which he has also been a victim, but with the good spirit that youth has to clean up the army of El Salvador. I told him that I especially appreciated his confidences that had to do with the attacks in Soyapango and those on the factories the day after the coup d'etat. All of this was the result of an erroneous interpretation of an order, which left him in such a bad position that he had to move to another barracks. With appropriate reservations, he confided in me, and I thanked him for an enlightenment that will be very useful to me.

 **Wednesday, November 14**

I spent the morning in a meeting of the Administration Committee that was being held especially to discuss the bishop's residence and the archdiocesan offices. The committee's opinion is that there is no need to spend money on this, since its present situation in the seminary is fine, and that it provides a better testimony of poverty and austerity.

I explained to them the reasons we had raised with the seminary team, particularly regarding the tension with the other bishops, why it would be better to build a separate building for the archdiocese, even if it were on the seminary grounds itself; and that, for me, personally, I did not need a residence since, thank God, I share the community of the Carmelite Sisters at the Divine Providence Hospital, but that I did not want my successor to be left without a place to live. Besides, I informed them of the offer of help from European institutions for this project; because of that, it would not

---

[241] The institutional ministries of reader and acolyte.

cost us anything. But if we designed a simple, functional project, everyone agreed that we should consider not only the present, but also the future, since the life of the archdiocese, thanks be to God, is growing noticeably and it will need new offices in order to continue to function. Since the seminary is also growing, it will need its space exclusively for that.

I am very glad about the agreement of opinions, after there had been such divergence of opinion.

In the afternoon, a meeting planned some days ago with Licenciado Jorge Acosta who, along with Licenciado Valero Iglesias, publishes popular editions of the papal documents, as they also did with my pastoral letters. The title of their little booklet is *El Guanaquito*. They explained to me how they manage to approximate the language of the peasants and reach them, even though they may be illiterate, with the ideas of these documents. It is a truly brilliant project and, according to what they told me, it has attracted attention in other countries, who want to imitate this effort of approaching the peasants. I congratulated them, gave them some ideas and said that they should continue with work that is so useful to the Church and especially for the Christian education of our people.

Afterward I went to visit the group of priests who are making their retreat in the seminary. It is for the Vicariate of Quezaltepeque, but there are priests from other vicariates. We talked about the current situation of the country and the role of the Church, the different aspects and opinions that are held by the clergy itself, and by the laity. I insisted to them that our orientation should be totally pastoral, even though it should not ignore the political problems that must be illuminated.

But I liked the second part better, when we talked about the human aspects of our relations with the priests of the archdiocese. There is great goodwill. We told each other of the defects that can impede this communion, which is not just of faith, but also psychological. I thanked them for pointing out my deficiencies, which can interfere with relations I wish were more cordial. There were useful comments for each one of those who participated in this meeting.

The evening, as usual, I spent looking over my correspondence. Thank God, I can count on my good secretary, Sister Nicolasa, a Guadalupe Sister, who gives me a summary of the letters. I make notes of the ideas that must be included in the answer on the letters themselves. A great deal of mail arrives every day and, thank God, I think that we are carrying out true apostolic work through our brief replies and timely messages.

## Thursday, November 15

I forgot to mention that yesterday I received a telephone call from the president's residence. It was Colonel Majano calling just to say hello to me and to express his solidarity, since he had heard about the death threat of which I have been the object, and to tell me that they are very hopeful about the situation of the country and that they think the project they are supporting for some necessary changes and for a government that responds to the people's desire for justice will continue growing stronger. I thanked and encouraged him and I also told him that the Church is always open to the service of the people and that, in this sense, they could always count on the Church, as it would also always keep its freedom to denounce anything which violates the human rights of our people.

Today, Thursday, the fifteenth, I went to Candelaria in Cuscatlán, where Father Salvador Interiano had invited me to preside over the patronal feast of Dulce Nombre de María [the Sweet Name of Mary], which is celebrated there on this date. I spoke to them in the spirit of Puebla of how devotion to the Virgin is a part of our Latin American identity, but it is a devotion which should be up-to-date. As Puebla declared, for both the present and the future it is Mary who is the inspiration for our suffering people—not in a passive way, but rather with the spiritual energy which sees pain in its redemptive sense and supports God's project to transform injustice into an order which is more humane and just.

We talked later with Father Modesto López, rector of the cathedral, who was present there. We had lunch together—a fraternal sense that I wish would increase always among us priests.

When I returned to the hospital, I was told about several telephone calls, to which I tried to respond—especially those from the Minister of Foreign Relations and the ministers of the Baptist Church, who were doubtless very enthusiastic about the coming of Dr. Lara-Braud next Sunday.

I also had a meeting with the psychologist, Dr. Semsch, whom I have not been able to see for days now. Meeting with him helps me to verbalize problems that, with his help, I try to resolve more serenely and surely.

## Friday, November 16

Several groups of people who have been victims of violent actions by groups of the extreme left have come to the chancery. It seems that the left has become more repressive than the repressions that they were denouncing before. We have expressed our solidarity with all of these workers, who have suffered serious consequences in their family and economic situations.

At noon, we had a nice Mass for peace in the Sacred Heart Basilica, organized by the parish council of the basilica. At the time for the homily a lady, young Lydia de Pineda, delivered a very profound, deeply felt speech about peace. I stressed the concept of peace she had spoken of and invited the laity to take the message of Christianity to the world, as she had done. In the same way, I took the opportunity to emphasize devotion to the Virgin of Peace as the mediator of this great gift that our people need.

I had lunch with the Jesuit Fathers. We especially spoke about the topic of the current situation of the country and the role of the Church.

Today the closing ceremony for the major seminary was held. I was unable to attend the Mass as I had been invited to do (Father Cortés represented me) because, at the same time, at six o'clock in the evening, we were going to have a meeting with one of the members of the ruling junta and some others from the Christian Democratic Party in order to analyze and offer help to the new government.

It was a very interesting gathering. Colonel Majano came and, with total frankness, we discussed our points of view for cooperation with the government, which he liked. This meeting will be repeated on an emergency basis in whatever moment they may need advice, and also weekly in order to keep working to identify goals and projects in support for the junta that are urgent in our situation and, more than anything, in order to speed up the structural changes that the country needs.

This afternoon, Dr. Jorge Lara-Braud arrived from New York. He brings a message from the National Council of Churches for our archdiocese, which he will present next Sunday in the Mass at the basilica at eight o'clock in the morning.

**Saturday, November 17**

In the morning I had an interview with a Dutch journalist at the hospital.

Afterward I went to El Calvario parish, in Santa Tecla, where the priests, women religious and laity of the Vicariate of La Libertad were meeting. The principal theme was the explanation of my fourth pastoral letter, which we reflected on in groups. We ended with a plenary session with very practical applications for the pastoral life of that vicariate. The Carmelites came to explain to me certain situations in their congregation, which we discussed with great understanding.

In the afternoon I went to celebrate Mass at the resettlement community in Chalatenango, where close to one thousand families have been resettled after having lost their lands and their houses in the flood of Cerrón Grande. The feast day they are celebrating today is that of St. Teresa, the patron saint of their old village, which is now flooded. Dr. Jorge Lara-Braud, who has come from the United States bringing a message to our archdiocese from the National Council of Churches, participated and he praised the pastoral work of our archdiocese. Dr. Lara also took part in the homily here. After Mass there was a cordial reception and fellowship with those Christians, who gave beautiful testimonies over the microphone.

 **Sunday, November 18**

The Mass was held in the Sacred Heart Basilica. After Mass, an interview with a television reporter—Swiss, I think.

In the afternoon I went to give the blessing to the shrine in the village of El Carmen, in the parish of Santo Tomás. Father Teodoro Alvarenga, the priest who has directed that parish for more than twenty-five years, is very respected and the people are very close to the Church; I received a truly ecclesial welcome. I felt myself a shepherd and felt that the affection of the pastor finds a marvelous echo in these peasants, also in those who arrive from the small villages.

There had been a meeting scheduled for today with the young military officers, but I could not attend it because of my visit to Santo Tomás. I asked Father Estrada to represent me.

## Monday, November 19

This morning and this afternoon also, the episcopal conference of El Salvador met to elect the new officers. At the beginning, the nuncio greeted us and pressed us on unity, since he had not yet been able to achieve greater unity among the bishops throughout his time in the nunciature. He offered to spend his final days—for he thinks that early in the new year he will come to the end of his assignment—doing everything possible for such unity. He recommended for this the naming of two bishops, specifically, Bishop Rivera and Bishop Revelo, who would constitute a committee to work for the unity of the bishops.

But afterward the bishops, principally Aparicio and Alvarez, rejected this proposal of the nuncio that I, for my part, supported. I said that it would be to our advantage to name it and for it to do its work even before we had our elections, for the atmosphere was not propitious, since we were polarized. There was no possibility for the elections to unite us. Rather, they would make the division in our group even greater.

In fact, the elections were held and the process was very biased and arbitrary, so that the majority—Aparicio, Alvarez, Revelo and Barrera—did what they wanted with the voting. The election of the president proceeded canonically and did not produce an absolute majority in the first three votes. In the eighth, Bishop Rivera obtained a slight relative majority, which we, unfortunately, did not realize in time. Only after the ninth vote, the ninth tally, when the canon was read, I realized that in the eighth tally a relative majority had occurred in favor of Bishop Rivera. Nevertheless, as he was not an "acceptable" candidate to the majority, they said that the realization came too late and went on to a tenth round, in which Bishop Alvarez obtained a relative majority and the position of president was given to him.[242]

I myself have written a letter to the nuncio which I have asked him to present to the Congregation for Bishops, calling attention to this anomaly, which removes all credibility from the new president, since he was elected in such an arbitrary way.

The other positions as well, very important committees, were assigned according to the opinion of this majority; the one additional vote[243] that the president has was cast by Bishop Alvarez as new president.

---

[242] According to canon law, a majority is required for election of an episcopal conference president only on the first two ballots. After that, a simple plurality will suffice to elect. This provision had escaped the bishops' notice.

[243] The tie-breaking vote.

In my letter to the nuncio I have asked for this anomaly to be corrected and the presidency given to the one to whom it corresponds canonically, Bishop Rivera. Furthermore, he is the best person, as he is the one who is most conciliatory as far as providing unity, as well as the most prudent and intelligent. He could give a new image to a conference that has been very discredited and will be even more so with a president who is identified by his political and social position with the previous government and whose imprudent criteria and superficiality of judgment do not give a good impression of the Salvadoran bishops. I hope that my letter is heeded but, at any rate, there will be a record of my disagreement with the process used.

 ## Tuesday, November 20

There was a meeting of the archdiocesan Executive Committee especially to discuss the building of archdiocesan offices and of a house for the archbishop. This is planned for the land next to the seminary, on the side facing east. The architects have presented a very functional and practical plan. Based on it, a request will be made for the subsidy that has already been set in motion in institutions in Europe.

Afterward, I went to meet with the Vicariate of Soyapango. Almost all of the priests, the communities of religious, the faithful and the laity who participate in the pastoral work attended. In the dialogue with the bishop the problem of the political and the pastoral came up and I clarified it from my perspective. I am worried about the excessive politicization of some communities and of some pastoral agents.

In the evening, an interview with Father Rafael Moreno, about whom some doubts have arisen in spite of how loyal his service has been. Lately I have been concerned about his being too partial to the popular political organizations.

I went to have dinner with Ingeniero Román Mayorga Quirós, member of the junta of the revolutionary government. In an atmosphere of great trust he told me of the projects and work of the junta and how they have managed to make the junta more compact and arrive at a political consciousness of the structural changes that have to be made. I saw that he is rather optimistic. I also felt that my hope in this change, in spite of the enormous deficiencies of the beginning and of the criticisms of the opposition, is a grounded hope. I ask the Lord that it may be so and, with this principal intention, I will make my pilgrimage to the Virgin of Peace on her day tomorrow, November 21.

**Wednesday, November 21**

The Feast of Our Lady of Peace. I went to participate in the concelebration with my brother bishops in the cathedral of San Miguel. The cathedral was completely full. The service was broadcast on the radio. I felt, frankly, great sorrow that the homily, which could have been a message for this people who are hungry for guidance and for inspiration, was disappointing, largely because the nuncio gave a homily that was very colorless and abstract. I respect his responsibility and his mission, but frankly, the prophetic role of the Church was not carried out here on such a beautiful opportunity as a feast day of the patroness of the country, whose people are in need of a message that is more vibrant, more alive and more profound.

I noted in the bishops the same desire to marginalize me. The people, on the other hand, gave me a warm ovation when I left the church, which I had sensed would happen. Because of that I left last, so as to not offend my brothers, who left more privately, with this kind of popular rivalry. I thank the people. I do not feel any vanity, but rather joy in my harmony with a people who expect from their prophets and pastors an increasingly deep solidarity.

 **Thursday, November 22**

I wrote a letter to Ingeniero Pacheco, whose land borders the land of the Divine Providence Hospital, to support the petition that the sisters of this hospital have been making for a long time: to collaborate to establish the limits of the property of the sisters, since he has encroached on their boundaries for this land. I pointed out to him that he was not being asked for charity but for justice and that, even were it charity, it was worthwhile to help this center of such great sacrifice for the patients at the hospital. Therefore I pleaded with him to help so that this conflict may be resolved soon, implying to him that, on the other side, I would have to denounce publicly his maneuvers, which have already done great harm to the hospital land.

At nine-thirty in the morning, we began the meeting of the Pastoral Committee. It is interesting to hear the report of each one of the vicariates, because it can be seen that there is a great deal of activity in the different sectors of our diocese. There is much creativity; there is a true blessing of the spirit of God among us.

But the principal purpose of our meeting was to study a declaration that has been published by a group of priests, women religious and laity from Christian base communities and parishes from all over the country. It is anonymous; no one has taken responsibility by signing it. In examining the present political moment, they come to conclusions that are at times negative and offensive to our Church. They tried to justify this as an effort to bring light into the midst of confusion.

There were some very strong arguments, like those of Father Fabián, Monsignor Urioste, Father Torruella, some women religious and some others. But there were also those who defended the criteria used in the document. When I spoke, I pointed out to them that it seemed to be more of a political analysis and not a pastoral document. I told them that we must try to build a Church and not do politics and that, in this sense, I was calling for total sincerity with the archbishop and trust in him, especially from those who make up this Pastoral Commission so that, joined together in unity of criteria, we can work together for the building of the Kingdom and from that perspective look at the different realities of the country.

The discussion was very fruitful and although there were some heated moments, trust—in which opinions were expressed sincerely in such a difficult area as this one of faith and politics—prevailed.

In the afternoon I received the visit of a member of the political party MNR[244] and of an old friend, Arturo Gallegos, who extended to me an invitation from the governing junta of Nicaragua. We discussed the reason for this invitation. I explained to them that, as long as we did not have more information about the relationship of that government with the hierarchy of the country, I could not undertake a trip even in response to an invitation, out of respect for and solidarity with my brother bishops—and that, in any case, I would consult them.

Arturo Gallegos expressed to me the concern that the government ought to have an office for advice and technical information in order to create an atmosphere that corresponds to the mystique of the revolution that the officers began after the coup d'etat on October 15. I tried to understand the whole scope of this initiative and I gave him my support, while at the same time expressing the independence the Church maintains, that it cannot identify itself—even in a desire to cooperate—with any concrete political movement. That if the plan was to educate people to create civic consciousness, we have been happily doing that and will

---

[244] *Movimento Nacional Revolucionario*, National Revolutionary Movement, the Social Democratic Party, founded in 1965.

continue to do so. I promised to get him an audience with one of the members of the junta, so that he may talk directly with him.

In the evening Beto Cuéllar of the Legal Aid Office came to inform me with great emotion that they had found near the garrison of the Treasury Police an underground place where numerous prisoners had evidently been tortured; they had left markings on the walls. And that, like this unexpected discovery, there are undoubtedly other secret jails, which existed under the previous government in violation of the constitution. I encouraged Cuéllar to continue his investigation and to keep the investigating committee[245] informed, as a contribution of our Church.

 **Friday, November 23**

In the morning, a meeting of the Priests' Senate. We gave priority to analyzing the actions of the Church at this political juncture in the country. We took into account the declaration of a group of priests that seems to be more a political analysis than a pastoral one. I was very satisfied in feeling the solidarity of the majority of the senators and in discovering, providentially, the priests who agree more with the political line of the popular organizations than with the pastoral direction of our Church.

I expressed my profound sense as their bishop of not being able to count on the sincerity of some of my closest collaborators, and I exhorted them that we build the Kingdom of God among all of us and for the good of the Church. And from this Kingdom of God, which we should feel deeply in faith, we could then better illumine the political realities and what is good for society in our country. We touched on several matters of interest to the clergy; it was a most constructive meeting.

In the afternoon I went to a gathering of catechists of the catechumenate movement in the Rinaldi Institute in Planes de Renderos. I celebrated Mass and expressed to them my joy on seeing this movement flourish. Using the Pope's document on catechesis, I asked them to find a way to connect in their lives the catechumenate with the sacramental life, with the community, with the service of the people of God to our society, and to connect the catechumenate with the *kerygma*[246]—that is, that proclamation, which should have made us find Christ but which did not in

---

[245] The Investigating Committee for Political Assassinations and Disappearances.
[246] The basic proclamation of faith in Jesus Christ, crucified and risen.

our Baptism or in our earlier life, should from now on be a continuing encounter with the Lord, so that *kerygma* and catechesis may achieve their true role in the evangelization of our lives and in those with whom we are to share our lives in a fraternal sense.

When I returned, I found Colonel Abdul Gutiérrez, member of the revolutionary junta, at the hospital, along with Dr. Saca. We discussed cordially some confidential aspects of the government itself. Colonel Gutiérrez even said to me that he was the main agent of the coup d'etat, giving me some very private details of that day, October 15—so much so that it surprised me. I was glad for the trust with which they spoke of this matter.

I also took the opportunity to give my ideas, with the intention of helping them handle this difficult hour for the country with greater sense and balance, for so many dangers could doom to failure this hope for our people's liberation. Colonel Gutiérrez shared these concerns with me but, at the same time, the confidence that God will help it all come out well.

Specifically, we spoke of the division that some of the military officers seem to want to create between the two officers in the junta. He said that it was possible this would happen, but that also they were doing everything that they could to keep anything from dividing them because it could be tragic, as much for the army as for the country, if there were a schism between the two of them. I also expressed to them my concern about the disappeared and I offered the cooperation of the Legal Aid Office, which already exists, and spoke about other matters. I think that it has been a very useful conversation, as well as a very long one.

 ## Saturday, November 24

Today I spent preparing my homily. In the mail was the news that the University of Louvain has decided to award me an honorary doctorate and they will give me this title on February 2, the patronal feast of that university, along with two other people—a man and a woman—chosen for this honor because of their intellectual abilities and their work in the social sphere. They also are asking me to give the speech in that session.

Father Juan Deplanck, who doubtless is the one who has taken an active interest in this happening, writes to me also telling me not to turn it down, to answer immediately, and that he will help me with whatever I need. I have given thanks to God for this new demonstration of divine love and encouragement. Father Rafael Urrutia translated the French for me, and also added a note congratulating me. This has been a great encouragement for me because it is a stimulus for the effort that we are making to have a liberating pastoral. I think that I ought to accept, since it is not merely a personal honor but, rather, encouragement for a cause in which the Church needs a great deal of support.

In the evening we analyzed the events of the week with Father Moreno, Monsignor Urioste and Bachiller Cuéllar. It has been a very full week which I will report on in my homily tomorrow.

 **Sunday, November 25**

I celebrated Mass in the basilica. It is the feast day of Christ the King. We made the consecration to the Sacred Heart of Jesus, as Pope Pius XI had recommended on establishing this feast. At the same time, in the basilica where we have held Mass for several Sundays because of the problem of the occupations of the cathedral, we said these prayers as a kind of leave-taking, for I announced that next Sunday, to begin the liturgical year, we will have Mass in the cathedral again. If there is some new disturbance, we will return to this church or to one that is open.

At eleven o'clock in the morning, Confirmation in the church of Corazón de María—a nice group of young people prepared by the parish priests of this vicariate. It surprised me a great deal that the priests of the church themselves, the Claretians, did not come to the liturgy. I should ask for an explanation of this.

In the afternoon, in the parish of San Francisco Mejicanos, I attended the profession of religious vows of two Passionists, young men who have dedicated their lives to this congregation. The Central American provincial was there and Father Juan Macho, the parish priest, and other Passionists and other women religious, also Passionists. Afterward there was a very nice fellowship in the neighboring Domus Mariae, but I was unable to stay for all of it.

**Monday, November 26**

This morning I went to Chalatenango. In the minor seminary they are conducting an interesting course for those with late vocations to learn about their cultural level and to encourage an adequate formation to prepare them for the priesthood which they still desire. We are not talking about very advanced ages; these are young men who thought that it would no longer be possible for them to enter the priesthood. I received a good impression from this testimony of dedication and from the joy that is visible in them when they see that achieving their ideals is possible.

I visited the community of the Sisters of the Assumption in Chalatenango; I also again visited the Passionists in the parish of San Francisco. I wanted to see the provincial who, unfortunately, was not there. I had a very interesting talk with Father Juan, however.

 **Tuesday, November 27**

I had an interview with the Swedish ambassador, who is interested in the situation of the country and the role of the Church. Another interesting interview with an expert in social communications, an Argentinian who lives in Mexico, and another man from Uruguay, who also has been exiled and now lives in Mexico and is a specialist in creating for the radio; he works with CERPAL.[247] Their interest was to meet me and ask me something about what, they say, surprises them in the Sunday Mass: the communication with the congregation. I told them that one sometimes does not think about the technical aspects that they are familiar with, but knows that the grace of the Holy Spirit guides the Church and makes the word fruitful. I attribute to this all the success that they seem to have seen in my homily, the same as in my pastoral work. I trust in the Holy Spirit and I try to be its instrument, to love my people and serve sincerely, grounded in the gospel. The conversation about other matters relating to the reality of the country was very interesting.

This morning was filled with the meeting of the Pastoral Committee and the Priests' Senate scheduled in order to study, along with other priests, the approach that the Church ought to take in the current political

---

[247] *Centro de Educación Radiofónica para América Latina* (CERPAL), a center for promoting radio schools in Latin America.

circumstances of the country. In the light of these principles, we analyzed the document that a group of priests have published, in which they criticize greatly the attitude of the Church. It shows criteria more political than pastoral. The discussion went very deep. We spoke frankly and we found that many priests and communities are more interested in the political aspects. We tried to orient them more completely toward the pastoral task and to be a sign of unity in the midst of this great variety of parties and political organizations.

In the afternoon I visited a group of women religious in the pastoral work who are presently doing spiritual exercises in Planes de Renderos, under the direction of Father Rafael Moreno. We talked in the afternoon, principally about the difficult aspects of the pastoral work in such a politicized atmosphere. I tried to tell them in all frankness to be valiant in disseminating the message of the gospel and to be truly Church, which neither depends on political developments nor fears change, because it goes on preaching the Kingdom of God and seeks to illuminate the realities of the earth. It was interesting to see how this group of women of different congregations feel themselves so united in the pastoral work. And this was one of the testimonies that pleased me most: They feel that the direction of the archdiocese is so well defined that they feel that each one of them always walks in Christian maturity.

In the evening I went to have dinner at the home of Licenciado Viéytez, where Dr. Chávez, Monsignor Urioste, Father Ellacuría and Father Estrada were also present. We talked about topics related to the present political situation and the role of the Church, principally analyzing the specific situation of the junta and of the government in general.

 **Wednesday, November 28**

In my radio interview today I reminded the listeners that today is the anniversary of the death by assassination of Father Ernesto Barrera and also, nine years ago today, of the first of the murders of a priest that occurred in our archdiocese, Father Nicolás Rodríguez, whose body I, along with other priests, went to get near San Antonio los Ranchos in Chalatenango at the request of Archbishop Chávez.

In memory of these two anniversaries we celebrated a solemn Mass in the afternoon in the parish of San Sebastián in Ciudad Delgado, where Father Neto Barrera was parish priest at the time he was killed. It was a very beautiful Mass, beginning with a very cordial meeting which Father

Gutiérrez organized for me, starting at the entrance to the town of Ciudad Delgado. A joyous and warm reception, and also a very enthusiastic Mass. There were some Confirmations, and I took the opportunity to tell them about the people of God, anointed by the sacraments, among whom their priests distinguish themselves for their service to the people and are obliged to provide a priestly service to the people—that they cannot be confused with other services of a strictly political character and that, for this reason, they have to maintain a difference, a holiness Christ wishes, precisely so that they may be more fruitful in their work for the liberation of the people.

In the morning there were many visits from journalists and other people, priests and seminarians. Rubén Zamora's[248] wife, Doña Ester, offered her services in the secretariat of our archdiocese at no charge. We will use her in the communications office and also as a private secretary to the archbishop. She already began to work this very afternoon.

Today there was also a search of the convent of San Martín. The police had received information that Father Tilo Sánchez had arms and that they were going to be picked up, but they agreed to notify the archbishop, who called Father Tilo to tell him of this accusation. He immediately offered to accompany some official of the police and a witness from the archdiocese to search his convent. This was done, proving the information the police had was false because there were no arms in the convent.

I took the opportunity to thank the police for this procedure, which was wiser than that followed before, and said that in any conflict I hoped that they would have this kind of dialogue beforehand, thus avoiding situations which could be very serious without the participation of the Church. The police also understood that and expressed their thanks. They agreed that we should follow the same process in future situations.

Monsignor Urioste went to the airport to meet Monsignor [Emil] Stehle of Adveniat, but he did not arrive. Perhaps he will come in very late at night. Anyway, we expect him. We are grateful to Adveniat and have new projects for which we would like their help. Monsignor Stehle's visit was announced as one of solidarity with our Church. In the same way he will also go to Nicaragua to offer them the valuable services of Adveniat.

---

[248] UCA professor, member of the Justice and Peace Commission, at that time member of the Christian Democratic Party; later head of the Democratic Convergence Movement and speaker of the national assembly.

**Thursday, November 29**

In the chancery this morning I received the secretary general of the political party UDN.[249] He is a Marxist and had words of praise for the work of the Church. He said that it was very different from other days, when his Marxism called the Church the "opium of the people"—that now, on the contrary, the Church was the best consciousness-raiser and that a great part of what was happening in the country that contributed to the transformation was the work of the Church. He wanted to offer me the opportunity for a dialogue to look for ways to cooperate in a solution to the problems of the country. We agreed to have this dialogue next Monday and identified the people they would invite.

There was an interview with a Colombian journalist who writes for newspapers in the United States.

At lunch in the home of Doña Aída de Muyshondt and with a group of the Ladies of Charity,[250] I celebrated Mass for the eternal rest of several deceased family members of these ladies. And at lunch and in our conversation there were some very constructive ideas about Caritas, whose manager will be a religious sister, as will be those who do the visiting, sisters with this charism for charitable works and promotion among our people.

In the afternoon I went to visit the Eucharistic Sisters[251] who are making the Spiritual Exercises. We shared dinner with thirty sisters and afterward a very interesting fellowship, in which I responded to different concerns they had. I have gotten them to promise a catechesis in the cathedral and to help me to support the liturgy of our Sunday Mass.

I went to see Fernando Valero Iglesias this evening. He is home preparing for surgery, since they have found some rather serious symptoms in his lungs. I tried to raise his spirits and in this way to thank him for his many generous contributions.

---

[249] *Unión Democrática Nacionalista*, National Democratic Union, legal expression of the outlawed Communist party, founded in 1969.

[250] An organization of laywomen who carry out activities to benefit the poor.

[251] The Mercedarian Sisters of the Blessed Sacrament, popularly known as "las religiosas eucarísticas."

**Friday, November 30**

In the morning I had a very important meeting with the editors of the YSAX commentaries. A letter from Monsignor Urioste to Father Ellacuría suggesting they take on the responsibility for these programs has resulted in a letter from the editors in which they explain their support for the archdiocese and that they don't think they should be removed from this work, which is so closely related to to the archdiocese. This was the topic of discussion for the entire meeting, in which some very clear ideas came out, although there was also some resentment. I think that, in general, the meeting was positive, since everyone present—laity and priests—will continue to work and will look for a way to be in harmony with the direction of the archdiocese without seeming to be an official voice of the Church, for that is the heart of the problem.

Also this morning there was a meeting of the seminary committee, in which we analyzed several points related to the reports and the life of the seminarians. But it seems that there is a deeper problem: the ideological problem that is making inroads in some communities where the true sense of Church is being lost. We will try to be very faithful to the theological thought of the Church and use this thought to illuminate the task of the diocese and the seminary.

Monsignor Emilio Stehle from Adveniat arrived. We had lunch with him in the Divine Providence Hospital. We visited the group of women religious who are doing the Spiritual Exercises in Planes de Renderos. He spoke to them and we expressed gratitude to him that, thanks to Adveniat, these women religious can carry out their work. We talked with him about the other programs. More than anything else, he offered greetings of solidarity with our archdiocese. He also visited the Central American University and the cathedral; there are hopes for some help with these efforts.

In the evening Father Estrada had prepared a dinner-interview with a simple and good family, professors at the Central American University. A peasant couple also there were very happy for this opportunity to meet with their pastor. Our sharing was very close: the two couples and the two priests, a frugal dinner and, above all, a very cordial friendship.

# December 1979

 **Saturday, December 1**

I celebrated the Mass for the closing of the course for the Fe y Alegría[252] schools in the chapel of the Externado San José. A large group from five schools for men and women offered there the fruits of their work in the programs this academy offers.

The representative of Misereor[253] also came and I talked to him along with Father Ramón Vega, who is with us now, and Monsignor Urioste, about the many different projects for which Misereor is giving us economic assistance.

This afternoon I went to the diocese of Santiago de María, where yesterday they began celebrating the twenty-fifth anniversary of the creation of that diocese. This day, dedicated to the Virgin and to women, is also dedicated to the second bishop[254] and it is for this reason that I am going to celebrate the Eucharist.

In the evening there was a very nice dramatic program, dramatizing the martyrdom of St. Thomas More, in which some priests and several laypeople participated actively. Father Medrano, Father Rodas, Father Cabrera and other great friends among the clergy there, where I worked for two years, gave me a very affectionate reception, as did Bishop Rivera and many lay members of the community.

---

[252] A widespread program in Latin America, initiated by Jesuits, providing skills training for poor youth.

[253] An agency of the German Catholic Church founded in 1958 to combat hunger and illness in the developing world.

[254] A different bishop was invited each day and the day dedicated to him; Romero was the second bishop of the diocese.

**Sunday, December 2**

After a very cool night in Santiago de María (although its silence was interrupted by the Popular Revolutionary Bloc, which spent the entire night singing and giving speeches in the main park), we awoke to celebrate the twenty-fifth anniversary of this diocese. It was a joyous morning in the city streets.

After sharing the closeness of prayer and breakfast with Bishop Rivera, we went to the cathedral, where we joined with the other bishops and all the clergy of the diocese and numerous pilgrim groups who had come from different parishes for a solemn celebration of Mass. Father Majano gave an appropriate, very eloquent homily, during which he presented the bishops who have had the honor of directing that diocese.

After Mass, medals and certificates were presented by the city government and the diocese to Bishop Machado, who was the bishop of San Miguel when this part of that diocese was separated in order to form the new diocese of Santiago de María. Bishop Machado was brought especially for this from his retirement home in San Juan Nonualco. Archbishop Chávez y González also participated, as he was the archbishop when this division of the diocese took place, and also the rest of the active bishops. A silver tray was given to Bishop Rivera, as the bishop observing this twenty-fifth anniversary of the diocese.

After Mass the president of the bishops' conference, Bishop Alvarez, called an emergency meeting, in which certain doubts about his own election as president and the other positions were clarified. I presented the protest which I had sent to the nuncio, who had called for this meeting through the president of CEDES. Bishop Aparicio also mentioned an irregularity, which was in his favor. My protest was in favor of Bishop Rivera, who had received a relative majority that was not acknowledged; because of this, Bishop Alvarez's presidency is not legal. Nevertheless, I myself proposed that, *pro bono pacis*,[255] we leave things as they are, but with our protest on record.

After a discussion that left me, as always, embittered about my relationship with the bishops' conference, since the personal dislike of me is obvious, nevertheless offering all of this to the Lord, I went to the meeting being held in the Colegio Santa Gema Galgani, where they also gave us a nice lunch.

Upon returning to San Salvador, I found several problems waiting for me. The intervention of the archbishop is requested by the South African embassy in order to help free their ambassador, who was kidnapped and

---

[255] For the sake of peace.

has been a prisoner for several days. They thanked me for my intercession in writing and on the radio on behalf of the ambassador and against all of the violence that is tearing the country apart. In Santiago de María, the nuncio also congratulated me and said that it could not be better.

Also another problem: a meeting with the Jesuit provincial [Father César Jerez] and Father Moreno, specifically to discuss various political views within our Church. They were very understanding and the dialogue was completely open; it was an attempt to identify what true pastoral work is at such a difficult time for the country. Father Moreno, in spite of my many reservations about him, is a man of the Church and is an appropriate adviser for the archdiocese precisely because we need to understand the ideology, the mindset and the strategies of the popular political organizations, which he understands, I think, from a true Church perspective. He will continue, then, to be an adviser but, at the same time, we will complement his judgment with other perspectives in order to form a complete judgment of reality. Along with Father Moreno, I proposed inviting to a meeting about these criteria Monsignor Urioste, Father Fabián, Father Octavio Ortiz or Walter Guerra.

Another problem is the occupation of the factory of the Cotton Cooperative of Zacatecoluca by the popular organizations. The governor called me, asking for the support of the archdiocese in going tomorrow to negotiate with those occupying the factory and in avoiding possible violence. I asked Father Cortés to go, also Beto Cuéllar, representing the Legal Aid Office, and they have gladly agreed to do this.

Finally, at eleven o'clock at night, a priest, the bishop's secretary from Los Teques, Venezuela, where the Salvadoran priest, Father Roberto Trejos, is at the present time, was waiting to see me. The father came to ask me, in the name of the bishop of that diocese, to permit Father Trejos to stay there since he is doing such good pastoral work. I told him that I am in great need of priests and that now that they can come in,[256] a call has gone out to all of them. But I said that I will leave it to Father Trejos and the bishop to decide how important it is to extend his stay for a reasonable period of time, and that I considered an honor the missionary nature of his work or the simple fact of our Church's communion with the diocese of Los Teques. The priest was very pleased and, after discussing some matters of a general nature about bishops and old colleagues in Venezuela, he left. He went with Father Gregorio Rosa, rector of San José de la Montaña Seminary.

---

[256] Under the previous government, several priests had been expelled from El Salvador, others denied entry.

**Monday, December 3**

I invited the Minister of Foreign Relations, our friend Héctor Dada, to breakfast with me; Don Pepe Simán; Father Jerez, the Jesuit provincial; Father Estrada; and Monsignor Urioste, to try to make use of his authority as foreign minister in his relations with the Holy See in order to provide information and, as a Christian, to seek the Holy See's cooperation with the pastoral line of Puebla and Medellín, which the archdiocese tries to follow. And, in this sense, to speak frankly about the actions of the nuncio and of certain bishops, who are very far from this pastoral approach.

This conversation was very interesting since, besides his authority as the Minister of Foreign Relations, Mr. Dada stressed that he will also act as a Christian who deeply shares the concerns of the Church. Possibly he will entrust Don Pepe Simán with a special mission to take information, suggestions and specific requests for our Church. We spoke specifically of the military vicariate, which has not been functioning as it ought in its pastoral role, about certain attitudes concerning the government and the ruling class which some of the other bishops have and, especially, about the lack of unity among the hierarchy.

In the morning the provincial of the Good Shepherd sisters came to see me. She brought the news that the Good Shepherd sisters, who for such a long time have worked in the women's prison, are going to have to leave because of some internal problems in the prisons and with the Ministry of Justice, and also because they lack sufficient personnel to keep up this ministry. I am very sorry that they must leave an area where there is such great need, but she offered their help with the prison ministry—not just in the women's prison, but also in other detention centers in the archdiocese. I emphasized the need for this work and that I would lend every support to whatever collaboration they wish to offer in a sector so needy as that of the prisoners.

Among today's visits, I received one from a Polish writer and journalist, who showed great interest in knowing the Church's view of this situation of violence in the country. He has written several books. More than a journalist, he is a writer who does studies of such situations.

Another very important visit was the one from Dr. [Aristides] Calvani and other Latin American members of the Christian Democratic Movement, who talked with me about the position of the Church and the political actions of their party. It is interesting to know that there is so much human and Christian ability among the laity for the development of our Latin America.

Very interesting also, in the evening, a meeting of different elements of the Popular Forum,[257] who came to the Divine Providence Hospital to talk with me. I had with me as advisers Father Estrada and Father Ellacuría. We touched on some very important points about the government attitudes and about how to promote political, civic consciousness in our people. I offered the use of our communications media, especially the radio and the newspaper, and they expressed their appreciation and said that they would take the opportunity to use them for the education of the people.

Today I prepared the recording for this coming Wednesday, since tomorrow I plan to leave for a short vacation in Guatemala.

 ### Tuesday, December 4

I sent some letters. I attended to different matters, especially to the requests that will be made to Adveniat, Misereor and other European institutions that aid Latin America. Monsignor Urioste will personally present these petitions on his trip with Bishop Rivera to Holland the day after tomorrow. Besides, Monsignor Stehle, the director of Adveniat, and Dr. Córdova, director of Misereor, have come in person. This is assistance that has been requested before and should be renewed, as well as some new projects.

After this very intense morning, I left in the afternoon for Guatemala, where I will spend this week, which will culminate on Saturday with the profession of vows of the Carmelite Sisters in their retreat in Carmel Juyú.

Tonight we arrived in Guatemala and I have felt what good a short vacation can do in the middle of such great activity as there is in our ministry.

---

[257] A broad coalition of moderate progressives from business, labor, academic and Church circles, formed in 1979 to press for reform.

**Wednesday, December 5**

This morning in Guatemala, I visited the Loyola bookstore, where I found several books that will be of great use to me. I also encountered several Guatemalan priests, who showed me their great respect and affection. I have thanked God and them for this demonstration of brotherhood that, thanks be to God, occurs even in countries where one does not expect to be so well known.

We traveled from Guatemala City toward the property of the Carmelite Sisters, which is some three hours away, along a road which is very picturesque—especially near Lake Atitlán, on the banks of which is located the beautiful house that we reached after dark. I celebrated Mass with the Carmelite community, which is very cordial. They gave me a warm welcome; after Mass we had dinner and shared good memories of the life of their congregation and in El Salvador. In a very special way, I feel great gratitude because they have welcomed me into one of their houses, the Divine Providence Hospital, which is practically my only home and family.

 **Thursday, December 6, to Saturday, December 8**

Three days at this summit that the Carmelites call Carmel Juyú because it is located in a village called Juyú, in the territory of Panajachel, near Lake Atitlán in Guatemala. The novices, who are preparing for their profession of vows on the eighth, are the center of affection in this community.

Some of the sisters accompanied me on a visit to the town of Chichicastenango, with its traditions that go all the way back to indigenous paganism existing right within the Christian church itself, where herbal doctors and faith healers, following their own customs, offer incense, send up prayers, use petals of different colors to express their intentions before the patron saint of the village (who is perhaps confused in their minds with their pagan idols). It is a very interesting instance of popular religiosity.

On the eighth, we held the Mass in honor of the Immaculate Conception in which the six new Carmelites took their vows. The superior general of the congregation was there, and a large number of sisters from Mexico and from Central America. I celebrated Mass and spoke in my homily of my admiration for this place and about my episcopal service to the religious life. I concelebrated with the vicar general and a Carmelite priest.

On Saturday afternoon I returned to El Salvador and, after a four-hour trip, I met with Father Moreno; Beto Cuéllar; the vicar general, Father Cortés; and the chancellor, Father Brito, who has already returned from the trip he took because of his health, so that they might inform me and suggest guidelines for my homily about the life of the country during this week that I have been gone.

 ### Sunday, December 9

The Mass was held in the cathedral. When it began, there were not that many people there, but by the end, as usual, the cathedral was completely filled. The second Sunday of Advent gave me my theme: God saves the people through their own history. And God needs the people themselves to save the world: communities that, like John the Baptist, are not identified with any political movement, but which shed light on all of them, as they also do on all the concerns of the people. After Mass, there was a press conference with journalists and television interested in the themes mentioned in the homily and in other aspects of the mission of the Church in El Salvador.

I went at eleven-thirty to share the celebration of the children making their First Communion and their parents, catechists in Divine Providence parish in Colonia Atlacatl—an atmosphere that is truly alive. I congratulated the Redemptorist priests; I expressed my pleasure in this event to the catechists and to all those who collaborate in the work of the parish. And I gave a short message to the many boys and girls making their First Communion. I had lunch with the parents.

At four o'clock in the afternoon I was arriving at the village of El Espino of the parish of San Pedro Perulapán, where Father Solórzano had assembled a large group of people to celebrate the feast of the Immaculate Conception this Sunday. I had the chance to carry out a true catechesis through the Mass and the homily. I was very satisfied; at the end the priest himself and numerous laypeople also expressed their wish to work in evangelizing our people.

In the evening I attended the closing ceremonies of a Cursillo de Cristiandad for women, which was held at Planes de Renderos. There was great faith; this new encounter with Jesus Christ has engendered great enthusiasm. I used my message to tell them that the Cursillo, with its charism of conversion and new encounter with Christ, is only one piece of a larger group of elements involved in evangelization, and that they should try to achieve the other aspects so that their evangelization might be complete. I was referring specifically to catechesis, or to the more systematic study of religion, to the sacraments which are the signs of our belonging to a community—the community which works, not for itself, nor for a small group who have made the Cursillo, but rather for the whole parish, for the whole diocese and apostolate. Everyone who has been evangelized should evangelize the rest. It is a wonderful group of women; they come from the capital, from Jucuapa, from Santiago de María, from Santa Elena and from Jocoro.

 **Monday, December 10**

I went to spend the morning with the Dominican Sisters at the Colegio de Fátima; the superior general is there and the chapter[258] is meeting to elect the new provincial. The same provincial was reelected: Mother Nieves, who has really done a great deal of work. They have great affection for her and treat her with great respect. There are a number of young sisters who are a hope for the future sharing of the life of our people. I congratulated them for the way they carried out the election, their unity, and, at the same time, the humility of the new provincial, who had asked that her selection, which had been made, be postponed because she had something to explain to the superior general, who was with us. After an hour for reflection, the election was ratified and the new provincial expressed her willingness to serve the congregation. Afterward, we sang the *Te Deum* and I expressed my congratulations and my hope that this congregation will continue offering their valuable pastoral service in our archdiocese.

In the afternoon I went to celebrate the twenty-fifth anniversary in the religious life of Sister Nelly Rodríguez and two other Sisters of the Sacred Heart, and the fiftieth anniversary of Miss Mariíta, who is a lay oblate. They had arranged for the families of these sisters to come to the Colegio Sagrado Corazón, and we concelebrated with Father Isidro. I spoke in my homily of the courage required for the religious commitment and how the vows are a sign of how the social situations of our time can be resolved. The disinterestedness of our religious vows truly underscore the irrationality of certain extremisms of our times.

---

[258] A gathering of the members of a religious order.

Before going to the dinner at the home of Sister Nelly's brother, Dr. Abraham Rodríguez, I returned to Divine Providence Hospital, where two of the young military officers needed to talk with me immediately about their concerns over certain attitudes within the military brotherhood itself. They particularly expressed their unhappiness with the Minister of Defense, who is an ally of the past and endangers the spirit of change that the young officers have. I expressed carefully that the Church supports everything that is just and everything that brings renewal and I urged them, as the protagonists of this moment of transition in the government, to act in accordance with their consciences. They promised that other officers would also come to see me—men who, according to what they told me, have great faith in what I say. I will always try to keep the pastoral direction of our archdiocese safe.

There was also a meeting with the community of Zacamil, since they have decided not to distribute the newspaper *Orientación*. They expressed their unhappiness with the present direction of this weekly publication. They feel that they are being referred to when it mentions the division within the Church and groups which are more political than ecclesial. I tried to listen to all of their concerns, their complaints. I told them sincerely what the pastoral direction of our archdiocese is and I invited them to continue this dialogue with those who are in charge of the press and the radio. I think that this dialogue was very positive. They left satisfied that they had been able to have this conversation and were able to explain their ideas but, at the same time, hear other opinions.

 **Tuesday, December 11**

The community of Zacamil, as I had invited them the previous afternoon, came to talk with those who are in charge of the newspaper *Orientación* and of the radio station YSAX. I could not attend myself, so I left it to the Vicar General, Father Cortés, who coordinated the meeting and guided them peacefully to a reflection that kept the dialogue open, so that our communications media may be more responsive to the concerns of our entire Church.

I was unable to attend myself because there was, at the same time, a meeting of the Pastoral Commission that was very lively. A letter that a group of priests had published as a manifesto said that they could not come to this meeting because the atmosphere would not be right for a dialogue, that the Church was again seeing itself as the teacher, that they were unhappy with certain publications, that the previous meeting had turned out very badly, especially because of the incorrect interpretation of the archbishop. For this reason, they suggested other topics for discussion and not the topic which had been announced to continue the previous reflection.

I tried to remain calm and said that the Pastoral Commission was a consultative body for the bishop: that he chose the topics for discussion according to what he wanted to consult them about; seeing that the consultation had already been planned and announced in the agenda, it should take place as it had been planned; and that those who had decided not to come had, in this way, showed how little desire they had for dialogue. I invited them to express calmly, in dialogue with the bishop or through the organizations that the archdiocese has set up for dialogue, their own points of view, and examine them and either change or reconcile different ways of thinking. A dialogue is not for defending positions or for expressing resentment, but rather to search for the truth and share the love and the unity of our Church.

In the afternoon we had a meeting with the personnel of the chancery: the vicar general, Father Cortés; the chancellor, Father Brito; the vice chancellor, Father Rafael Urrutia; the secretary, Sister Nicolasa; and the administrator, Ingeniero Galván. We talked principally about how to improve the diary of the chancery. I am keeping this diary on cassette tapes to be typed up later, but it takes in only the views and activities of the bishop himself and I wanted it to be a diary of the entire chancery team and of the whole life of the archdiocese. This is the history that will be of most interest, especially of such busy days as these in which we live. Father Rafael agreed to gather the work of all the sections of the chancery and, using these personal notes of mine, to write the diary that we want. Later we will decide how to recreate the information on all the time that has passed, the details that we have not been able to record for the diary.

In the evening I went with Father Javier to celebrate Mass in honor of the Virgin of Guadalupe in Colonia Las Delicias in Santa Tecla. Later we went to the home of Miss Carmen Chacón, where we always receive a very cordial welcome.

**Wednesday, December 12**

The Feast of Our Lady of Guadalupe. I went to celebrate Mass in the parish of the Dulce Nombre de María in Chalatenango, which is directed by the Maryknoll Fathers. The theme of the homily was Mary, teacher and model of evangelization: how she was a collaborator in bringing us the great evangelizer, Jesus Christ; how, in the second place, she is the model of the person evangelized; and, in the third place, how the evangelization of a person turns one into an evangelizer, and Mary is the great evangelizer of our Latin America.

There was a meeting planned for tonight with the president of the Supreme Court of Justice and some other lawyers but, at the last minute, they said that they would not be able to come.

I went this evening to celebrate the Mass of Our Lady of Guadalupe in the Colonia de Guadalupe in Soyapango. Father Eliodoro Orellana is the chaplain there and the church was completely filled. There were Confirmations and the message that I gave in my homily was the same as what I gave in Dulce Nombre de María this morning.

Afterward I went to have dinner with Paco Calles, a resident of that parish. There was also with him a group of young people who are part of a community. The parish priest of Soyapango, Father Villarán, and Father Eliodoro, from the chaplaincy I mentioned, were also present.

 **Thursday, December 13**

The Feast of St. Lucy. This patron saint of Suchitoto brings together this very fervent people in the parish church of Santa Lucía, where Father Jorge Benavides, who had invited me to preside over this celebration, is parish priest. I took advantage of this opportunity to direct the rich life in Suchitoto—a people very engaged in politics and in practical affairs—to tell them that the light we ask for from St. Lucy be not only for our material eyes but especially for the eyes of faith. And faith requires of us today to resolve the problems of Latin America and our country—specifically, the three views that the pope cited in Puebla as a theological base for our pastoral reflections; that is, the truth about Christ, the truth about the Church and the truth about humankind, which I tried to apply to the circumstances of our country. After the Mass, we spent time with several priests of that vicariate and had lunch in Father Benavides' convent.

I went with Father [Ernesto] Abrego and we talked about some very interesting things, especially about problems of our priests. I will be sure to be more careful and to pay more attention to this, since they constitute the main part of our pastoral work and there are dangers of misunderstandings and of divisions. I ask the Lord to free us from all of these evils and to give us a clergy united, saintly and efficient for our situation.

In the afternoon I went to the Policlinic to visit two Belgian sisters who work in Quezaltepeque and who, several days ago, were in a traffic accident that has left them in rather serious condition, since they are in casts. I tried to encourage them. They have great spirit and are willing to continue their work in the parish of Quezaltepeque.

In the evening I received a delegation of workers' organizations from Holland, Belgium, the United States and from unions in our own country. It was an interesting meeting, in which they showed their admiration for the role of the Church in the defense of the organization of workers and peasants and of their rights. They offered their solidarity and, at the same time, economic support to the extent they are able in countries which have always helped our Latin American countries. I thanked them and tried to respond as honestly as I could to their questions about the situation of the country and especially about the role of the Church in our country.

 **Friday, December 14**

In the morning, a meeting of the executive committee of YSAX, the Pan American Voice, principally in order to discuss the matter of the auditor and the change of manager, since Héctor Samour has a grant to go to Germany and will leave this coming January. Two candidates were presented. Of the two I prefer Napoleón Navarro because he is better known and we need someone we have confidence in for this post.

Later we went to Domus Mariae to have lunch with the staff from the chancery, from the press and the radio. It is a very large staff, around fifty people, and I felt that it would be necessary to have more of these meetings in order to define our identity within our criteria of service to the Church in such important posts.

I could not go to the meeting of the Ana Guerra de Jesús Center of Promotion. I delegated it to the Dominican priests, who are nearer. It is an educational center for women in the market, where Miss Refugio Alvarez is the principal organizer of a program that is yielding great fruit.

In the evening I went to the Colegio de Fátima to see the superior general of the Dominicans of the Annunciation. They have just had their provincial meeting. They showed me a beautiful movie about the beatification of their founder, Father Coll, a beautiful ceremony in which I participated personally, since these sisters of the Colegio de Fátima paid for my trip.

There was a rumor that the situation was serious in San Salvador and they did not want me to leave Santa Tecla, but I insisted. The rumor was false because, really, the situation is always tense, and there was nothing out of the ordinary.

Also this afternoon we had an important meeting with the seminary committee and some of the members of the Priests' Senate to study the situation of the bishops' conference after the December 5 meeting,[259] in which the officers were changed, with Bishop Aparicio becoming president again. They had named as secretary of the committee on social affairs Father Juan León Montoya, who is not in harmony with the archbishop, and eliminated from the seminary five professors who have the approval of the archdiocese.

We discussed whether it was time to have our own seminary and not to continue to be victims of so many injustices on the part of the bishops' conference. We agreed also to prepare a report for Rome on how the conference in our country does not offer the services for which the episcopal conferences were created, and how there is an attitude which amounts to a personal dislike of the archbishop and the archdiocese. We entrusted to Father Fabián the preparation of this report and also authorized Father Rafael Urrutia to call Bishop Rivera tonight wherever he is, in Holland or Belgium, so that he can take this information to Rome.

 **Saturday, December 15**

There were so many activities in the chancery that I could not spend the time reflecting on my homily. I also went to Apopa with my brother Mamerto for a family commitment, and in the afternoon to Santa Lucía, a parish where they have prepared many children for First Communion and young people for Confirmation. The ceremony was very impressive. There was great participation by the people, and I truly felt that the sacraments are the glue which binds the Christian community

---

[259] The bishops met with the nuncio but without Romero and Rivera.

together. I thanked that community and I urged them to join together and never lose that unity, in spite of all of the temptations that at present polarize our country.

 ### Sunday, December 16

The Mass in the cathedral at eight o'clock gave me the opportunity to focus, from a pastoral perspective, on the most important news of the week, the agrarian reform,[260] which is truly necessary. I have the impression that this commentary has made a good impression in general and that it has better defined....[261]

After the Mass at the cathedral, I went to the Colegio Eucarístico, where the catechists from the Divine Providence Parish in Colonia Atlacatl were having a gathering. There I participated in a panel in which there were some very interesting questions about the pastoral work of our archdiocese. The majority of those who participated were young and gave me the impression of being very mature. I congratulated the parish priest, a Redemptorist Father, and the sisters of the Colegio Eucarístico, who have a positive influence on the pastoral work of catechesis in that parish. I invited them to collaborate on the archdiocesan level with the Pastoral Commission, to focus on this aspect that we are still lacking, the catechetical aspect.

Afterward I went to celebrate a Mass at San José de la Montaña Seminary, where a group of priests who have left their ministries were meeting for spiritual reflection. Several of them were there with their wives, and I had the opportunity to talk with many of the men and women and to celebrate the Eucharist, which was very pleasant. Afterward we had lunch together on the terrace of the seminary, and there were very warm and enthusiastic comments about forming a base community—which, given their theological and pastoral preparation, could be of great service to our archdiocese.

At seven o'clock in the evening, we had a beautiful Confirmation ceremony for some young people in the parish of Monserrat. I greeted this very warm people with great affection. Afterward I shared some time in the

---

[260] The government announced a program of land reforms in mid-December.
[261] Tape ends here.

intimacy of the convent with Father Molina and Father Sanggiano, pastor of El Calvario, and some young people and adults from the parish community of Monserrat.

 **Monday, December 17**

I have spent this morning with the four seminarians who are preparing to receive their ministries this coming Sunday. We analyzed the reports the seminary team made on them, which contain a significant number of negative points. I think that the situation is not that serious—rather, that there is some lack of understanding of the concerns of our archdiocese and of our youth.

I also held a consultation, or dialogue, with some journalists.

I went to visit two doctors about my health, but it is not anything serious. On the contrary, they gave me encouragement since, thank God, I am enjoying very good health these days.

We spent the afternoon taping the program for Wednesday, since tomorrow will be very busy with the priests' meeting and another visit to the village of Ciudad Delgado.

In the evening, in the Casa San Pablo at the Sacred Heart Basilica, they held the Christmas ultreya for the Cursillos de Cristiandad.

 **Tuesday, December 18**

This morning was the monthly meeting of the clergy, which was postponed[262] in order to be closer to Christmas to make this meeting into a fraternal Christmas gathering. Nevertheless, a theme was proposed for study. The meeting took place at San José de la Montaña, and a young priest, Jorge Benavides, spoke about the unity of our clergy. He gave his evaluation and this stimulated a discussion of the many positive things there are in the archdiocese and also pointing out some negative aspects. It was truly an examination of conscience which was later continued in reflection groups according to vicariates that ended with a

---

[262] From the first Tuesday of the month.

plenary session, which contained some very valuable and optimistic contributions.

I concluded this series of reflections, telling them that Christmas gives us the meeting point at which all of us should come together in spite of our personal differences, and that Christ is the great mystery both of transcendence and of immanence. Within these two tendencies we can have our differences, but the balance of Christ gives us the guidance to live as priests, always trying to be Christ's representatives in the world.

Christ is the Word made flesh, the mystery of immanence; God becomes man and takes part in the human realities and illuminates all of them, but is always God. And the priest has to live the identity of his Church, of his mission to illuminate all of the earthly realities—political, social, economic—but without ever losing his own identity. The other tendency is transcendence, for if Christ became man it was to raise everything up to God, and this is our role: to transcend things from within ourselves, not to stay in immanence but rather transcend. As Christ was able to say at the end of his life: "I came from the Father and have come into the world. Now I am leaving the world and going back to the Father" [John 16:28].

Afterward, they served us a lunch, which the priests and the nuns all shared together.

This same afternoon, I went to the village of San Laureano, in the parish of Ciudad Delgado, in order to celebrate the patronal festival of la Virgen de los Remedios. They had prepared weddings and Confirmations for this occasion. A very loving people, with a profound joy that makes one forget all the disagreeable things.

I had dinner with the archbishop of Maracaibo, Venezuela, Archbishop Domingo Roa, an old friend from the Pío Latino, who has come expressly to see me and offer his collaboration and also that of the president of Venezuela, in whatever way they can in the difficult situation of El Salvador. I have decided from the beginning that I would act as a pastor, as I have always tried to do. As to the political aspect, the president of Venezuela has already had opportunities to study in depth the political problem of our country with Ingeniero Duarte, who lived in Venezuela for a long time. But from the pastoral point of view, I would only ask for international influence to soften the extremes of the left and the right and, perhaps, for political aid to the different parties in our country, but this is in the area of politics. My desire as pastor is to look for unity, to defuse so much violence. If they can do something in this sense, it would be, pastorally speaking, a true collaboration with the Church, which we would appreciate very much.

**Wednesday, December 19**

Today the parish of San José Quezaltepeque is celebrating the feast of its patron saint. Invited by Father Roberto and the community, I went to celebrate Mass there, during which there were a good number of young people confirmed and children who made their First Communion. The attendance at the Dominican Sisters' school was very large. (It could not be held in the parish church, which is still occupied by Father Quinteros.)

While we had lunch in the dining room of the Dominican Sisters of Quezaltepeque, I received word by telephone that the archdiocesan offices had just been occupied by the popular political organization, Popular Leagues of February 28. I then communicated with the person responsible for the occupation to ask him what their goals were and to protest this unwarranted occupation of the chancery. He said they wanted to speak with me in person. Nevertheless, I was able to discover their objectives: that we help them to find the bodies of those killed in the evictions that the security forces have just carried out; seek the return of those taken prisoner in these evictions; and, third, denounce the demagogic way in which the junta treats the problems of the people.

In the afternoon a group of priests from the Priests' Senate, invited by the vicar, Father Cortés, to discuss the situation of the occupation. At the same time, Father Rogelio Ponseele, a Belgian who seems to be very involved with this occupation, arrived to tell me that the occupying group requests that I go talk with them. I got a little angry and I told him that he should not represent the interests of an organization so directly, seeing that he is a pastor of all the Christians. There was some argument with him and other priests, but afterward I ended up being reconciled with him and telling him that I had confidence in his priestly and pastoral ability to understand this delicate situation that we are living and not to become biased.

I went with a delegation of priests and with the director of the Legal Aid Office, Bachiller Cuéllar, to talk with those occupying the chancery, who repeated the objectives I have already mentioned. We talked at length about different matters; I even heard them express great lack of confidence in the way that the Church has acted, as if it had turned around one hundred and eighty degrees—their phrase, showing their attitude toward God, as if we had betrayed the interests of the people, which bothers me a good deal given the sincere way that I always try to defend the interests of our people from the perspective of the gospel.

I said that, for today, I was not so interested in this general discussion, but rather that we should return to the concrete situation of the occupation.

We also spoke with the group of hostages—there are fifteen of them, among them four priests, secretaries and other employees, who had been arguing that it was not necessary to pressure the archbishop to issue denunciations or act in favor of justice, since this has always been the role that he has played in the Church. They also feel themselves to be prisoners and, for that reason, this is not a peaceful occupation, even though the occupiers are certainly unarmed. They are violating the liberty of the hostages. And other considerations that seem to me to be valuable and just, among them permission for the women to leave.

I said that I would stay if what they are looking for is security, that the presence of the archbishop would be sufficient and that they should let all the other hostages go. But they—the hostages—said that they understood my generosity, but that they would prefer for me to be on the outside so that I would be able to act more freely in whatever other aspect, and that they would be glad to continue their solidarity with the archbishop from inside. Nevertheless, analyzing things later, I find some small ambiguities in some who seem to be in solidarity with the cause of those occupying the offices.

Later I was in communication by telephone with Colonel Majano of the junta. It was he who called first, but I took the opportunity to ask him for his support in this situation and to say that the Legal Aid Office would go soon to explain the details more explicitly.

Also this evening I had an appointment to talk with Ingeniero Mayorga Quirós, who told me in confidence of his fears about collaborating with a government that still continues to use a great deal of repression. Nevertheless, I encouraged him because, in spite of the repression that can be seen, there is also another, higher level group that is looking for just solutions in more intelligent ways. He is on this level, and it would be a shame to see the civilians involved, in whom we have such faith, abandoning this effort. This does not imply approval of the junta, but rather a hope of being able to find ways that are not violent and bloody.

It was already very late in the evening, almost eleven o'clock, when I headed to the dinner that the Cursillos de Cristiandad were having at the home of Sigfrido Munés, where we talked at length about the situation of the country and the attitude that Christians should have in this moment. I was consoled by the spirit of understanding and dedication of these laypeople.

**Thursday, December 20**

At breakfast I talked with the Minister of Foreign Relations, Héctor Dada, a very fine Christian, with Don Pepe Simán and Father Fabián Amaya. We analyzed the situation, which looks extremely serious. Nevertheless, we have faith in God, and I encouraged the civilians in the government to influence the military corps to join with the efforts for true social justice that motivates the junta. Then we discussed the ecclesial aspect, putting particular emphasis on a visit by a special envoy to the Holy See. In principle, we agreed instead to name as ambassador Don Pepe Simán, who knows well the problems of bishops and priests of our Church. I hope that this mediation will be good for our Church. The minister said that, in the present situation, on the contrary, the nunciature is saying that there is no hope for changes in our Church in this sense.

In the name of the archdiocese and by request of the Popular Leagues of February 28, who are occupying the chancery, Father Cortés and Bachiller Beto Cuéllar went as representatives of the Legal Aid Office to talk with the military officers in the presidential residence. They received the impression that there is goodwill and, this same afternoon, they agreed to resolve the problem as the Leagues request, that is, the situation of those captured or killed during the occupations, who were violently removed by the security forces. From the cathedral, Monsignor López informed us that it has been taken over again by the Popular Revolutionary Bloc and that they are standing watch over the body of someone who died in a confrontation and will be buried from the cathedral.

I talked this afternoon with Don Ernesto Rivas Gallont who, as consul of South Africa, came to clarify something related to the kidnapping of their ambassador, of whom we have had no news.

 **Friday, December 21**

Because the chancery is occupied, we met at the Divine Providence Hospital—Father Fabián Amaya, Father Cortés, Father Brito and Miss Doris Osegueda, secretary of the communications office—in order to study a bulletin that describes the occupation of the chancery. The analysis of the occupation was very interesting. From there, we went on to the ideas of all of these organizations that are a bit fanatic and in which there are Christians and even priests involved. It seems that Father Rogelio, parish priest of Zacamil, has been decisive in this occupation. I do not want to judge with certainty, but I do have suspicions about him as well as of other communities of the same parish.

We agreed also to celebrate the Mass in the basilica, since the cathedral is occupied by the Popular Revolutionary Bloc. They say that the door is open, but that would expose us to the possibility of the Mass being manipulated. It was also decided that we would cancel the meeting of young people that was going to be held on Saturday and Sunday, but we will still have the ordination to the ministries of the four young men in their third year of theology.

Dr. Badía, Minister of Health, was gracious enough to bring personally the data that the Legal Aid Office had asked him for about the wounded who are in the first aid centers and who were wounded when members of the Popular Leagues of February 28 who had taken over land were forcibly removed. The visit from the doctor was a valuable experience, since he is one of the ministers most interested in the changes of the new government. But he also sees realistically the difficulty of moving ahead when there is so much opposition from the two extremes.

Miss María Julia Hernández,[263] who has been in charge of the homilies, of editing them, has brought me three volumes that cover the liturgical year. I have thanked her and congratulated her for this work of publishing my thoughts—something which I think is doing some good. And today, upon seeing the three volumes elegantly bound, I realize the inspiration that the Holy Spirit has given to the word in our archdiocese. Blessed be God! I hope that the Lord may bless this sowing of his word and shed light on the realities that week by week we try to illuminate through his divine word.

Finally, in the evening Monsignor Urioste, who has returned from Holland, arrived with Father Cortés and we talked about the situation of our country, as well as about the events of his interesting trip.

Also rather late at night, Colonel Guerra and another colonel, who was in exile and has returned, came to visit me. They seem to be quite pessimistic about the current situation—a shame, because this depression of spirit could be fatal in men who today need to face the situation with great courage, precisely because it is so difficult.

Monsignor Modesto López, rector of the cathedral, was kind enough to represent me at the feast of the patron, St. Thomas,[264] since I preferred not to go out because of the circumstances. Besides, I think that I have a touch of the flu. Also I asked him if tomorrow, when I am supposed to go to

---

[263] Presently head of Tutela Legal, the archdiocesan human rights office that replaced Socorro Jurídico, Legal Aid.

[264] December 21 was formerly the feast of the Apostle Thomas.

the village of La Esperanza in San Pedro Perulapán, he will represent me, which he will do very willingly.

When I listed the priests with whom I met this morning, I forgot to mention Father Rafael Urrutia, rector of the minor seminary and archdiocesan chancellor, who has acted in a very dignified manner, with courage and with great faithfulness to his bishop—characteristics that also distinguish the other priest, Aníbal Romero, and the two seminarians who have stayed to watch over the property of the archdiocese. I express, then, my appreciation and a very special congratulation for this spirit of priestly fidelity.

 **Saturday, December 22**

Because of the situation of the chancery, taken over by a popular political organization, I did not believe that it was a good idea for me to go in person to carry out my commitment in the village of La Esperanza of San Pedro Perulapán. Monsignor Modesto López kindly went and there, along with the parish priest, Father Solórzano, the vicar Father Montesinos and the priest of Suchitoto, represented the Church well in a village that is terrorized by the violence that, in vengeance, was inflicted there by armed revolutionary elements. It was, then, a great consolation on the part of the Church even though, as they told me, there was great fear and there were not as many people as they would have liked. There had even been an evil rumor that I was going there with the intention of bringing down more violence on that poor village.

Those poor people—they have endured so much suffering, first, from the official side, ORDEN and the National Guard, and today, in revenge, from the groups of the left. May the Lord grant these poor hearts the tranquility they have lost.

The Mass, they say, was celebrated very well, with all the assisting priests participating in the commentary on the Gospel.

I also had to forego attending a Confirmation ceremony in the Lourdes School, but I was represented there by the parish priest of El Calvario, Father Federico Sanggiano. Also, for the same reason, the vigil of young people that was going to be held this afternoon and evening was canceled, since Father Rafael Urrutia, who was the principal organizer, was unable to take care of the last-minute preparations because he is a hostage in the occupied seminary.

Toward noon, the occupation of the archdiocesan offices of San Salvador was ended. We were sorry that so much disturbance in the workings of this office had been caused by the Popular Leagues of February 28 and that some Christian individuals participated actively in this occupation of their own chancery. This is incomprehensible but, in these moments of confusion, we must try to understand.

 **Sunday, December 23**

The Mass was held in the cathedral, in spite of the advice to the contrary (because the cathedral was taken over by the Bloc this last week, and it was thought that there might be some interruption in the ceremony). But it was finally held very successfully in the cathedral. And in this Mass their ministries were conferred on four seminarians in third-year of theology. They are four rays of hope in the near future for the priesthood of El Salvador; possibly next year we will be ordaining these four young men, who now begin their ministries.

After Mass the people greeted them very affectionately at the door of the cathedral. On behalf of the seminary, we had a small celebration for them at the Divine Providence Hospital.

This afternoon, accompanied by Monsignor López, I went to Cojutepeque to bless the new El Calvario Church, which has been paid for by Miss Mercedes Barriere, now deceased. A beautiful church, which will house an ancient and venerable statue of Cojutepeque, the Lord of Mercy (el Señor de las Misericordias). I used the opportunity to preach on the Christian sense of redemption, without which other redemptions on earth do not make any sense. Very warm people, they made me feel the joy of a community that, in their simplicity, truly lives the Christian faith. The parish priest, Father Cayo Ayala, the Belgian sisters who work there, the Franciscan Sisters (who also have a school there) and a large group of the faithful made up the crowd at this beautiful ceremony of the blessing of the new church.

In the evening I was invited to Colonia Atlacatl to a posada,[265] but I felt very tired and asked the parish priest to excuse me.

---

[265] A Christmas custom in which a couple dressed as Mary and Joseph go from house to house for a series of nights looking for lodging and end up on the last night in *la posada*—the inn. Each night they are followed by a crowd with candles, and the evening ends with a celebration.

## Monday, December 24

Christmas Eve. We had breakfast with the vicars general and the two chancellors and Father Amaya to make some assessment of the current problems of the archdiocese—principally the occupation of the chancery, the pastoral attitude of some of the priests, the seminary and other things that were discussed and analyzed well, from a very pastoral and cordial perspective and with the concern of the archbishop. It took the whole morning, and we had barely gotten up from the table when it was already time to go for lunch. But they left to make preparations for Christmas in their various church responsibilities.

In the afternoon, in Colonia Roma, in the church of the Carmelite priests, I presided over a First Communion ceremony—a beautiful group prepared there to celebrate in this way the coming of the Christ Child.

At eight o'clock in the evening, I celebrated the Christmas Mass at the cathedral in spite of the fear and of the advice I received that it would be better for us to close the church. It turned out to be a very beautiful Mass with a great many people. We shared, in this way, the celebration and our Christmas greeting.

The message was based on three phrases from today's Gospel.[266] The first refers to the "Good News": God is the Good News; his presence in the world has brought a seed of renewal to history. There is always hope when there are changes in history, because God is with us. The second quote, the sign that the angels gave to the shepherds ("You will find an infant wrapped in swaddling clothes and lying in a manger"): Christ is God who clothes himself in human misery and takes on all pain and suffering to give it a redemptive value. And third, "Glory to God in the highest," is the goal of all human life, doing everything for the greater glory of God.

At ten o'clock at night, I celebrated Mass at the Divine Providence Hospital. There was great attendance in spite of the fear in the air that this Christmas was going to be a black one, without light or water. Nevertheless, it went off peacefully—thanks be to God!

---

[266] Luke 2:1-14.

## Tuesday, December 25

I went to preside at a First Communion and Confirmation ceremony in the parish of Huizúcar, where Father Benito Tovar and the Passionist Sisters had prepared the children and young people quite well.

In the afternoon I prepared the recording for tomorrow's radio program. Octavio[267] came from Sonsonate, which showed his great willingness to collaborate in this apostolate.

And in the evening I went to have dinner with the family of Miss Angélica de Mena, the Argueta family, where we also shared beautiful memories of San Miguel. It was our Christmas dinner, since we could not have it the day before because of my pastoral duties.

## Wednesday, December 26

In the Divine Providence Hospital I received several important visits, the most important being one from the provincial of the Augustinian Fathers, who has a very good impression of our archdiocese and of the priests' work. He will found a kind of vocational school, where young people who want to follow the way of Augustinian spirituality will gather.

This morning Father Cortés went to Quezaltepeque, where it had been promised that Father Quinteros, who has been an intruder for a long time, would leave the convent and the church today. But the mission failed because a group of about twenty-five persons were supporting the rebel priest with their physical presence in the convent, under the pretext that they were not going to replace a Salvadoran with a foreigner. Father Roberto, who is the rightful parish priest, is Belgian and perhaps this is a problem for a peaceful resolution of this situation. We will see if it is a good idea to change priests, but we will insist that Father Quinteros has to surrender what does not belong to him.

---

[267] A seminarian who helped with the taping.

**Thursday, December 27**

Today the priests' cooperative held its Christmas party in San José de la Montaña Seminary. I could not go because today, the Feast of St. John the Apostle, I was invited to San Juan los Planes, on top of the volcano of San Salvador in the zone of Quezaltepeque, where many Christians, organized into communities by the university students who have been working there for days or years under the direction of Monsignor Urioste, are celebrating their patronal feast. It is an exemplary Christian base community led by some apostolic laymen. There was a beautiful First Communion, a wedding and, most importantly, the Christian base community itself. Father Roberto was there, parish priest of Quezaltepeque, who knows this project very well.

When I returned, I heard on the radio about a crisis in the government. There has been a confrontation between the ministers and the armed forces. It seems they are preparing a statement, which is really a threat to resign, because they think that the army has become rightist and is encouraging the aspirations of the oligarchy. The ministers, who came in inspired by the proclamation of October 15, want the profound structural changes that our people need to take place. We are waiting to see what happens in this crisis that is taking place within the government.

In the evening I had a meeting with the Seminary Committee, in which we studied the attitudes of the episcopal conference and of the seminary team. It is a very concerned group of priests, and I think that this situation will be resolved by having the pastoral formation of our seminarians from the archdiocese more directly under our control although they would go to the interdiocesan seminary for their academic formation, as do the other groups of religious seminarians.

A visit in the evening with a member of the UDN Party was impossible because I was involved in this other meeting. And when I indicated that he could come later in the evening, he responded that he had another commitment at this very difficult time for the political parties.

 **Friday, December 28**

The Feast of the Holy Innocents, which has a special place in the parish of old Cuscatlán. I could not go because there are so many things pending, since many members of the government and the army are coming to consult me. It is an indication of the Church's prestige, and I try to help in all sincerity without abandoning my pastoral role. Because of the political situation of the country, at this time I must be at my post to attend to these consultations. I could not go either to the gathering with the seminarians at San José de la Montaña—the seminarians from the archdiocese (but Monsignor Urioste was with them), or to the meeting at the María Eugenia House in Planes de Renderos to celebrate the catechumens' preparation for the scrutinies.[268] Nor could I go to the meeting of Christian Renewal in the Spirit, which is taking place in the Rinaldi Institute in Planes de Renderos under the leadership of Monsignor [Carlos] Talavera, who has come from Mexico. Nor could I go to a pastoral meeting that we were going to have in the parish of San Sebastián, Ciudad Delgado. But everyone understands that my role now is to be offering services in these problems and that I cannot move from my office.

 **Saturday, December 29**

For the same reasons, I had to cancel my visit to Candelaria, Cuscatlán, where Father Interiano had prepared a large group of young people for Confirmation, but Monsignor Modesto López went to represent me. I was also unable to go to San Antonio los Ranchos, where they were celebrating the traditional festival of the corn. Father Fabián, episcopal vicar of Chalatenango, was there with other priests and brought me the affectionate greetings of that community and a gift—a hat made of corn husks, woven as if it were made of rattan and decorated with corn silk—and a nice letter from Potonico, a true expression of solidarity from those good people.

Over lunch, I asked for the advice of Monsignor Urioste, Father Fabián and Miss Doris Osegueda on the historical focus for tomorrow's homily.

---

[268] Rites connected with the catechumenate process.

**Sunday, December 30**

This has been a Sunday of intense pastoral work. I celebrated Sunday Mass in the cathedral, where some four hundred young people, who had held a vigil in San José de la Montaña Seminary, came as a finale to their night of prayer. One of them gave a beautiful testimony at the end of Mass. The Mass was timely: the Feast of the Holy Family. I put special emphasis on the young Jesus in his family to give a message to these young people, who had made such a wonderful gesture of prayer and reflection. They have come from different communities and show how community life is being renewed in our parishes.

Afterward I went to Tonacatepeque to celebrate a Confirmation and First Communion service. Father Luis Casares was waiting for me on the banks of the Tonacatepeque with the traditional groups—the Daughters of Mary, the Nazarenes,[269] the Altar Society[270]—and a very large group of people. We then headed joyously, with song, applause, confetti, to the church, where we held a beautiful celebration. I again spoke about the Holy Family, but in the sense of the Spirit of God, which is given in Confirmation and which gives a holy meaning to all our Christian families. At the Offertory, the priest had prepared a procession with very generous gifts that really overwhelmed me, crowning the altar with these loving gifts from the people.

We had lunch with the family of the priest and other friends. I have the impression that Tonacatepeque has a very intense parish life.

From there I returned to be in the National Gymnasium at two-thirty in the afternoon. The National Movement for Renewal in the Spirit was having a huge gathering there. I think that some eight thousand Christians from different parishes, with twelve priests presiding over the concelebration, gave a truly rich fervor to this special Mass. At the end Monsignor Talavera invited me for a laying on of hands to reaffirm the commitments of Baptism, Confirmation and the presence of the Spirit in that large crowd. I said that they should go out as the messengers of the Spirit, of peace, of truth, of justice that our country needs so much.

And, finally, in the evening I celebrated in the Church of Carmen the Mass that the Marriage Encounter movement had planned and also a small meeting with the secretariat to assess and plan new pastoral projects having to do with family pastoral work.

---

[269] A confraternity whose main public act was the Good Friday procession.

[270] A women's group that cares for the altar.

**Monday, December 31**

I had breakfast with Dr. Chávez, secretary of the Christian Democratic Party. I did not have very much time to talk with him because some young military officers were waiting outside for me, the officers who make up the Permanent Council of the Armed Forces. We talked for a long time about the situation and their intention to see that their proclamation, which gave rise to the new government, remains in force. In all frankness, I warned them of the risks and of the things I think have to be changed in order to survive this crisis of confrontation with the civilian ministers.

Later, I went to the airport with Monsignor Urioste to meet Cardinal Aloisio Lorscheider, who had notified me of his visit. The nuncio and Bishop Revelo were at the airport. I asked the nuncio if he planned to take him to the nunciature; he told me that he did not know anything about it. I had arranged for the cardinal to stay at Dr. Chávez's house, where they would receive him with pleasure, if he wished. The Cardinal told me that he would prefer to be at the seminary, but when we got to the Divine Providence Hospital I told him that I had a modest residence there that I would be pleased to let him have. He liked this last idea more because, he said, "This way I show that I am with you." This gesture of support for my work on the cardinal's part has encouraged me greatly.

After that, there began this very afternoon a series of visits and interviews so that he may learn about the reality of the country and the situation of our Church. He realized the political intensity of the moment in this conflict among civilians and the military; he gave me considerable guidance, since his experience in Brazil is similar.

I had the opportunity to advise many people today and this evening. The cardinal visited Bishop Revelo this afternoon, the nuncio, and also generously received several laypersons. Ingeniero Román Mayorga, member of the revolutionary junta, had lunch with me. In the evening I celebrated Mass at the cathedral at seven o'clock and in the Divine Providence Hospital at nine o'clock, ending the year with a "family" dinner with the sisters and some friends who had come to the Mass, which was very solemn. At midnight, the end of the old year and the beginning of the new was greeted with many fireworks, which gives the impression of a true liturgy of the time—as Father Segura, may he rest in peace, used to say.

Among the most important visits today was that of Dr. Badía, Minister of Health, who suggested that I bring together the opposing elements of the government to invite them to a dialogue in the presence of the Church. After analyzing it, it seemed to me that I should offer this service. I asked the doctor to invite the civilian part and said that I would invite the military part of the junta, which I did. Colonel Gutiérrez suggested to me that it would be a good idea also to bring the High Command. I told him that, for my part, there was no problem, as long as everyone had a sincere desire to dialogue with the civilians in the government. The meeting was set for this coming January 2.

# January 1980

 **Tuesday, January 1**

New Year's Day. The country awoke today to the tension of all of the internal problems in the government. A crisis among the ministers is becoming more and more defined. It seems that the civilians in the government are convinced that the military government is moving to the right and that they cannot continue in such a situation. I try to understand and guide them and, above all, tell them that they must think of the people, for they must serve them.

As on the first of every month, we celebrated the Holy Hour in the Divine Providence Hospital at five o'clock with an incredibly large attendance. I spoke of the fullness of time of which St. Paul wrote[271] and of how God is carrying out the history of salvation in natural history, how Christ became a part of history and gives a supernatural meaning to time.

 **Wednesday, January 2**

I woke up very concerned, because I have to facilitate this very important meeting today. But I am assured of the prayers of the patients, the sisters and of everyone who realizes what a crucial moment our country is passing through.

---

[271] In Galatians 4:4-7, the second reading of the day.

At the meeting, Monsignor Urioste and Father Estrada served as my advisers. The civilian ministers and the other civilian members of the government arrived promptly at nine-thirty. It appears that the military officers were mistaken about where the meeting was to be held and went to the Hospital; they came, however, even though they were late. They did not want to come in without talking with me first; it seemed they had not understood that they were going to talk with the civilian members and were reluctant to do so.

I told them that dialogue on behalf of the people should take precedence and that it was necessary to talk; that I had told them clearly that it would be a meeting with the civilian ministers. After talking for some time with the officers, Colonel Gutiérrez said that he was open to dialogue and that he would demonstrate it by attending the meeting. I thanked him and I took him to join the civilian members, who were in the top part of the seminary, in the library, where the meeting took place.

I apologized to them for the delay, since it was almost eleven o'clock in the morning. I encouraged them—as a bishop, representing the Church, and as a Salvadoran representing a large sector of the population, I asked them in the name of the Church and of the people to have a frank, sincere dialogue. I told them that they could find a solution that would be good for the country, that they should not give our suffering people a new reason for frustration.

They listened to me with great respect. I thanked them and I encouraged them to begin their dialogue, looking at the roots of the problem, of the conflict, looking later for the many points that the two sectors in conflict have in common and, finally, pointing out the differences between their positions in order to try to overcome them.

Dr. [Rubén] Zamora, Interior Minister, began explaining the root of the problem: the ambiguity of the military, the "move to the right," as they call it, which they do not feel comfortable continuing to work with. Rather than being the accomplices of a military government that continues to favor the right, they would prefer to resign. The dialogue began very frankly between the officers and the civilians, although I had the impression that the civilians were reluctant to believe the promises of the military, or that they did not see them offering their clear support for the declaration which the government had promised to defend.

At the end, I summarized the meeting, saying that I saw an ideal they are trying to promote: that is, the revolutionary process. I also saw difficulties and pointed out what I had heard during their discussion: for example, the ambiguity of the officers and other negative points impeding the progress of our people. And, third, I told them that I had also heard some possible ways of resolving the problem, the most important factors being sincerity, communication and everything that promotes rapprochement. And among the possible ways to look for a solution, I offered the services of the Church, which it is already giving and is willing to continue giving.

It appeared that a cordial atmosphere was achieved; the final good-bye when they left was very different than when they arrived. Unfortunately, while we were leaving, we heard on the radio that the Permanent Council of the Armed Forces had already issued a response in which they affirmed the military position in favor of the declaration, but which rejected several of the ministers' points as unconstitutional.[272] And this was influential because, at three o'clock in the afternoon, when the meeting was to be held to learn the response of the military government, it was already on the radio; they did not even send the response but made them go pick it up. All of these things made the situation worse again and have motivated the resignations of the first of the ministers, which will surely be followed by others.

At noon, I had been invited by the nuncio to a lunch in honor of Cardinal Lorscheider, but since the meeting here went on until almost two o'clock in the afternoon, I asked him to excuse me because of this situation, which he understood completely. The cardinal had already warned me that perhaps I would be unable to go and said that he thought that my meeting with the government was more important and that I should not worry if I could not get there—views that he repeated to me when we saw each other after the meeting and lunch. The cardinal had to leave for the airport and I went with him; we had a very cordial talk.

He is taking away good impressions of my work, based on people he has talked to; he thinks that he will personally suggest to the pope the need for strengthening the episcopate and finding a more radical solution to the situation of our Church. He thinks, after having read my pastoral letters and the homilies and after having conversed with people who are impartial and concerned about the life of the Church, that my efforts represent a work that deserves support, which has again given me confirmation of our pastoral effort.

---

[272] The ministers and other officials had sent an ultimatum to the government about their lack of control over the military and the continued repression.

**Thursday, January 3**

Breakfast with Don Sigfrido Munés and Dr. [Fidel] Chávez [Mena], with whom we talked about the difficulties of the moment. Dr. Chávez, an adviser to the Christian Democrats and the government, told me that for some days they have been negotiating the participation of the Christian Democratic Party and that now, in this crisis of the government, it is going to negotiate its political role [in the government] in an attempt to save the situation. After breakfast, he left for the presidential residence, where they have been meeting all day.

I had visits from some members of the government. I have received great satisfaction from their confidence in the Church and from the good we may be doing by guiding them from a pastoral perspective.

 **Friday, January 4**

I spent this morning in a meeting with five priests from the archdiocese with whom there are some difficulties in our close relations because of the political aspects of their ministry. But in talking in depth and looking sincerely for the solution to these problems and mistrust, I encountered great human, Christian and priestly merit which we will continue to encourage in further meetings. I recall that those who came were Father Rogelio [Ponseele], Father Benito Tovar, Father Trinidad Nieto, Father Rutilio Sánchez, Father Pedro Cortez; also present were Father Juan Macho [Merino] and Father Walter Guerra, who were of great help because of their very well centered and priestly suggestions.

In the afternoon I had a visit from the ecumenical committee of Sweden, who brought me news of a peace prize awarded to our archdiocese by the Christians of the "Free Churches," as they call the Christian communities in Sweden, since the Lutheran Church is the only official one. They said that in May they will announce the prize of which they have brought me news and for which I also thanked them in the name of the archdiocese.

I also was visited by Dr. Guillermo Ungo who, along with some other politicians, has just resigned as a member of the junta of the revolutionary government to analyze the situation and to see how there can still be hope of a way out of such a difficult situation. He spoke by telephone to another member of the junta who has resigned, Ingeniero Román Mayorga. He is going to Mexico to rest.[273]

 **Saturday, January 5**

At noon the two military members of the junta, Colonels Gutiérrez and Majano, came. I met with them accompanied by Monsignor Urioste and we had an honest dialogue about how they see the problems and their hopes for a solution. I took the opportunity to restate my ideas, always in an effort to serve the people, so that they will not have more reasons to be frustrated. They think that the mass resignations have been a good experience—a crisis, but not really a failure. They are optimistic about their negotiations with the Christian Democrats and also with the negotiations that they are going to initiate with the popular organizations in order always to have a government that is of and for the people. They had lunch with the priests who were with me to help reflect on the situation for my homily tomorrow.

In the afternoon, a visit from the rector of the seminary and Father Rafael Urrutia, in charge of the minor seminary and of the Seminary Committee. I asked Father Urrutia to be like a private secretary for me, for us to be closer (since he is a young priest, intelligent and active) and therefore to try at least to telephone and to come from time to time to eat at the hospital. We discussed different matters about the seminary.

While we were talking, Father Jesús Delgado arrived and gave us some marvelous suggestions, including that of creating, already this year, a propaedeutic year,[274] so that those starting their first year of philosophy could begin this way and be introduced to the spirit of the priestly vocation and all that a kind of novitiate would involve. So it is very necessary for us that they know where they have come, those who have come sometimes from schools where they have heard nothing of seminaries or vocations.

We will try to do this at Domus Mariae; we will ask for the collaboration of Father Juan Macho Merino, who has a group of Passionist students there in the neighboring parish of San Francisco de Mejicanos. We also talked

---

[273] Within days, all those who had signed the ultimatum, including government officials and members of the Supreme Court, resigned. The only cabinet minister left was Colonel García, Minister of Defense. The third civilian member of the junta, Mario Andino, also resigned.

[274] A kind of transitional year for seminary candidates who may not have had adequate pre-seminary training.

about giving a diaconate year to those going into fourth year of theology. This will prepare them better for their future priesthood, in greater communion with the people. In sum, several very useful initiatives concerning seminary and a youth apostolate came out of this impromptu meeting.

 ### Sunday, January 6

It has been a Sunday full of work and pastoral satisfaction. I celebrated the Epiphany Mass in the cathedral. In my homily I compared this moment in El Salvador with the turbulence that the Gospel speaks of in Jerusalem, when the three wise men were looking for the King. I said that we are looking with the same spirit for the salvation of our people, which God surely holds, for Epiphany shows us that God came for the salvation of all the peoples. After Mass there was a small press conference, since during the Mass there were a great many representatives of the press, television and radio. We talked at length about the points I had discussed in my homily and other aspects of the present situation of the country. A Swiss journalist also asked me for a more private interview tomorrow at the hospital.

After ward I went to the parish of Aculhuaca, where the catechists had prepared a good group of young people and children for Confirmation. I also used the celebration of Epiphany to talk about this life of God which Christ has brought us and which continues to be given through the sacraments.

After lunch, a meeting with the small pastoral group. I could see that there was a good deal of division and lack of direction and that they blame the parish priest greatly for a lack of attention to the communities. I think that Father Crespín noted all of this in order to provide a practical response to this situation of his parish.

After lunch and a short rest, I went to the community of Rosario de Mora, where the Oblate Sisters of Divine Love work. They have created a community that is full of life. I could see how very close the young people and children are. One sees that they are truly living the pastoral spirit there and that they follow the pastoral direction of our diocese with true solidarity. We held a First Communion; the liturgical preparation had been very well done. Afterward, there was a celebration with the pastoral workers amid the joy of the children breaking their First Communion piñatas—in other words, a family atmosphere, which is what Christ wanted when he founded his Church, the family of God.

In the evening, with Father Moreno, we had a meeting that had been scheduled with a member of the Popular Revolutionary Bloc, who explained to us their present thinking, their analysis of the situation of the country. I saw that there has been a big change in their openness to dialogue with the other organizations, including this invitation to the Church. We want to take advantage of this to inspire the pastoral follow-up we want to make with all those who have joined these popular political organizations, in order to try to save the faith of the people in these militant groups. This dialogue seemed to me to be a very hopeful sign and we agreed to continue talking.

Colonel Guerra was also supposed to come; he is the only military officer who, along with the civilians, signed the document resigning from their ministerial positions. Doubtless because of this, he has been the target of an attempt at revenge: His car was machine-gunned but, miraculously, he was not hurt. It was a shame that it was already rather late and he did not come, although I tried to contact him through Father Chus Delgado. I hope that nothing tragic has happened to this colonel at such a moment.

I also spoke on the telephone with Héctor Dada, who was the Minister of Foreign Relations and who has resigned along with the cabinet, but who, as a member of the Christian Democratic Party, has become part of the revolutionary junta. He had come looking for me in the morning, and I called to greet him. He said that he had only come to say hello to me and to talk with me about a tragedy that has taken place in Chalatenango, where they announced today that some seventy people have died. I told him that I did not know any more than what I had denounced in the Mass, about some four deaths; but that this was very interesting information and that we would find out, and for him to pay particular attention to this kind of situation because it can destroy the goodwill toward the government. I predict that they will be successful and told him that we will pray greatly that the country will find a solution in the choice that has just been made: calling the Christian Democrats to help the government resolve this crisis.

## Monday, January 7

I went briefly to the chancery. I saw a great deal of activity at the different offices. In the Pastoral Committee they are preparing a study of the Christian base communities; in the vicar general's office they are dealing with judicial matters pertaining to the diocese. Different people—priests, nuns and laypersons—came for different reasons to the offices. I talked with Father [Eduardo] Alas, who works in Concepción Quezaltepeque—an exemplary priest, with whom we shared various pastoral ideas that seemed to me to be very centered, very priestly. Thanks be to God, we have priests of great spiritual and priestly depth. I also realized that they were preparing for the meeting of the clergy tomorrow, a spiritual retreat to mark the presentation of the licenses,[275] which will take place in a solemn ceremony.

I spent the rest of the day at the farm of the Oblate Sisters of Divine Love for a short rest. But when I returned in the evening, I had some very important meetings about this moment of crisis in the government and of the country. Many came seeking advice and there were other visits with which, thank God, I dealt with what light the Holy Spirit gives me and for which I give great thanks, asking that the Church always be worthy of being present in the periods of our history.

## Tuesday, January 8

The meeting with the clergy was especially rich in its spirituality and theological reflection about the reality of the Church and, in a special way, about the sense of communion and mission. Thus, the presentation of the ministerial licenses to the priests and the letters that are for the first time given as documents of authorization to the communities of sisters had a profoundly theological meaning. It was my task to set forth the mediation in depth and to propose some points for reflection that later were discussed in a brief plenary session before Mass in the chapel of the seminary, where the solemn concelebration of the Eucharist took place. At the end, as a mission to the entire archdiocese, we presented the documents that authorize the true mission of the priests in the parishes and towns where they will work.

---

[275] The ministerial licenses, authorizing the priests to assume their parish assignments.

In the afternoon I went to Santa Tecla; I visited the Salesian Sisters of Colegio Santa Inés. I wanted to give my condolences to Doña Concepción de Viguer, but I was unable to find her.

There were some telephone calls at the house. I watched Dr. Morales Ehrlich on television present the ideas of the Christian Democratic Party, which has made a commitment (but a conditional one) to help the Armed Forces resolve this crisis in the government. I think that it was a very clear, very solid explanation: a call to the people to join together in a democratic solution, which is the most rational one at this moment. Any other would come from the extreme right, which would bring with it tremendous repression, or from the extreme left, which would mean a revolution that would also cost a great deal of blood.

In the evening I tried to return some other telephone calls that had come in during the day.

 **Wednesday, January 9**

The first meeting today was with a group of Carmelite Sisters of St. Joseph who are going to leave their congregation in order to develop a pastoral experiment. They are going to live in community and with their religious commitment, but without belonging to their congregation any longer; they will be in the parish of Guazapa. I encouraged them to treat this problem very seriously and use this experiment for the good of our diocese. One of these Sundays, I will go there to celebrate Mass and to explain this experiment to that community.

Another very important meeting was one with Bishop Rivera and Father Vega and David,[276] who is in charge of the bishops' Social Secretariat, in order to clarify the situation, since Bishop Aparicio, recently named president of that committee, has named Father Juan León Montoya secretary—a priest who is not in agreement with our pastoral work[277] and who could create many impediments to our work. Because of this, we are trying to return the Social Secretariat to its origins in the archdiocese, distinct from the social action commission of the bishops' conference.

I received a visit from Dr. Chávez, who has spent the night at the presidential residence discussing the agreement between the Christian Democrats and the Armed Forces. He was finally satisfied to have gotten

---

[276] David Alvarado Mixco.
[277] Montoya had written newspaper articles attacking Romero as a Marxist.

the approval and the acceptance of the army on all the points proposed by the Christian Democrats, although he told me there are some minor points which could still involve some risk if they are not carried out soon—for example, the resignation of the Defense Minister,[278] something they made the junta see (even quoting from my last Sunday's homily) would be very important because it would remove a figure of the repression that military control can imply. But Dr. Chávez noted that there must be some secret agreement, since all of them support this minister, whom the people in general reject. In general, however, Dr. Chávez is very optimistic that this reorganization of the junta with members of the Christian Democratic Party and other independent progressive individuals could provide a good solution to the very grave crisis of our country.

Father Mauro Yáñez visited me, an old friend from our studies together in Rome. Although the visit was rather brief, it was warm and we recalled many memories.

I went to the Vicariate of Mejicanos, but the priests had finished their meeting and I was only able to talk with Father Juan Macho, whom they have just elected vicar of that vicariate—a result I am quite satisfied with, since he is a very pastoral and spiritual priest. We talked about different problems of the vicariate. He thinks that by restructuring things to give the work to the vicariate team, all these problems will be resolved, with the help of the Lord. I gave him my picture for his community, another for Domus Mariae and another for the Belgian nun who cares for that house, where they hold pastoral meetings and which will possibly serve as the place for our propaedeutic year for the major seminary.

On the official radio station we heard at noon the complete makeup of the junta, formed by the two military officers, as before, Colonels Majano and Gutiérrez, with three civilians, two of them Christian Democrats—Dr. Morales Ehrlich and Ingeniero Héctor Dada—and a representative of independent progressive interests, a doctor with the last name of Arévalo,[279] I think.

Popular political opinion still has no faith in this solution: the alliance of the Christian Democrats with the army. One hears, rather, the option of popular revolution promoted by the leftist groups. They have received a great deal of publicity, for the ex-Minister of Education, Licenciado [Salvador] Samayoa, has announced publicly that he will go into hiding as part of the Popular Liberation Movement, Farabundo Martí.[280] This news has caused great consternation and has provoked very different reactions.

---

[278] Colonel García.

[279] Dr. José Ramón Avalos.

[280] *Fuerzas Populares de Liberación–Farabundo Martí* (FPL-FM).

In my interview on the radio I said that, first, we have to respect his choice—for he had certainly made it after searching his conscience—and then learn from this choice, which is an indictment of the extreme right, who will not allow for a peaceful solution but only the violent means that some of the leftist groups propose. It also indicts the army, which has gotten used to repressing the will of the people and which thinks that there is no other way for it to defend itself than by using the same weapon: violence!

I hope, I said in my commentary, that the case of Licenciado Samayoa will make us realize that there is very little margin left for rational peaceful solutions, and that we must urge those who are able to do what they can so that a peaceful and rational solution can bring about the changes, there is no need for the bloodbath that we can see coming.

Don Ernesto Rivas Gallont brought me the response of the South African government and the family of former ambassador Dunn,[281] who has been kidnapped. In their answer they ask the kidnappers to take into account the efforts being made and to not ask for things beyond the ability of both South Africa and the Dunn family. I am the mediator; I hope that the clandestine group will come to get this correspondence, to which I will add a letter from me in an attempt to save Mr. Dunn's life.

We talked with Father Moreno and Monsignor Urioste about matters related to the communications office. We were expecting to meet with members of the Popular Revolutionary Bloc, but they did not come.

 **Thursday, January 10**

The superior at the Colegio de la Divina Providencia brought a letter from the Superior General of the Passionists, telling me that they can no longer maintain the community of sisters at San José Villanueva. We talked privately about different things that have brought about this withdrawal. The Mother General has offered to explain it to me in more detail when she comes at the end of the month.

There were three very important meetings in the chancery this morning: one with the vicars and chancellors to discuss matters relating to some of the priests and parish situations; another concerning the seminary, to study the reports on the seminarians; and another on YSAX to study the

---

[281] Romero mistakenly refers to Ambassador Dunn as the "former ambassador" throughout the diary.

legal aspects of the corporation, and the auditor—at present we have none—and, in the matter of disseminating viewpoints, to study the noon-time commentaries on YSAX. The principal conflict with the new manager, Mr. Napoleón Navarro, is that he wants to have more knowledge and even be able to exercise censorship in this area that is so important. It seems to me that this desire is reasonable but, on the other hand, I do not want to lose these valuable commentaries that reach so many listeners on our station.

In the afternoon I was visited by the priest in charge of Central American matters for the Society of Jesus in Rome, a member of the Jesuit curia there. With him were other Jesuits with whom we talked about different aspects of our present situation and the Church. Father Arrupe sent me a special greeting which I returned with fraternal affection, thanking him for his support and solidarity.

The other important visit this afternoon was from the Minister of Defense, Colonel García, along with his subsecretary. They spoke at length about their desires for the transformation of the country and how it was unfair for him to be accused of turning the movement to the right. Concretely, he referred to my denouncing him on Sunday when I called for his resignation. That seemed to me to be the best thing, since all the other ministers have resigned and he continues to be a figure who weakens the credibility of this process of change in the country. It was a long conversation; it lasted for almost two hours.

A visit also from members of the Emmanuel Baptist Church in order to discuss matters related to the upcoming celebration of the ecumenical week.

Finally, Father Gregorio Rosa made some comments to me on the text that I plan to present in Belgium; I need to rewrite some of it.

 **Friday, January 11**

This morning there have been several visits of a private nature, but also some with a more official and transcendent character—for instance, the interview with the manager of YSAX, clarifying the problem of the noon commentaries. The conflict has arisen specifically because of a commentary about the option chosen by Licenciado Salvador Samayoa who, after being Minister of Education, has gone into hiding, with the FMLN. There has been a commentary virtually praising this attitude and encouraging people to follow him, since there seems to be no other option at the moment. This seemed to be an incitement to revolution and, because of this, its presentation on the radio was not permitted, which has caused tension in the group that prepares the commentaries. Father Estrada came and talked with the manager, Navarro, and with Monsignor Urioste; he was persuaded by the reasons they had for suppressing this commentary. For myself, I asked them to continue offering this service in solidarity with the thinking of the Church.

Another important visit was that of Dr. Rubén Zamora of the Christian Democratic Party, who came more in a private capacity looking for a little strengthening, for comfort and guidance, since this is an extremely difficult moment for the party; it has been left to it almost alone to try to save the situation of the country. And, on the other side, the popular organizations are uniting to fight this alliance of the Christian Democratic Party with the army. I tried to tell him how, as a man of faith and of hope, he has to serve the country generously and accept the difficulties and risks with the right intention. I think that he was satisfied with his visit, which was more of a spiritual nature. I think it is important for me to encourage the hope of all who feel concern for the country at such a difficult moment.

Also, the new manager of Caritas, who has great goodwill, to explain to me the disorder he sees in the Caritas office. I told him not to become discouraged and that we had named him precisely to help us have a true Caritas functioning in the archdiocese.

Father Ramón Vega, who is going to be the secretary of the Social Secretariat, will also be in charge of Caritas. I have signed the appointments of the cooperating vicars. I have given the chaplaincy of Asilo Sara to Father Bernardo Amaya. The priests at the Oratorio, who have been dissolved as such[282] and are looking to work in the archdiocese, serving in the parishes of Colonia Luz and the Diez de Septiembre, have organized themselves into a team to administer those two parishes.

Father Brito showed me a very impressive letter from Father Fernando Abad, who is in Colombia, somewhat uncertain about his pastoral and diocesan status. I sent word that he should come back, that there is a great deal of work to do and that we would organize things so that he will not feel the same difficult psychological situation that he is enduring now.

The deacon Pedro García, who has come from La Ceja, Colombia, has left me with a negative impression because he wants to impose his desire to become a priest as soon as possible and does not want to go through the test of the diaconate which, from our experience, we have to have in our diocese. His latest effort has been a letter asking for excardination[283]

---

[282] There were just three members of this religious congregation in the country. When one became a diocesan priest, it was decided to dissolve the group.

[283] Transfer to another diocese, requiring the consent of both bishops.

because he cannot work within the pastoral direction of our archdiocese, saying that he has a bishop willing to receive him. We are going to ask what bishop he is referring to, because I have to give a report on his attitude. Before that, I will speak to him pastorally so that he may reconsider what he is doing.

In the afternoon, a very important visit from a journalist who writes for eighty different media sources. We spent more than an hour in an interview in which, thanks to God, I was able to express the Church's position with the greatest possible care. He told me that in all parts of the country and in the different sectors with which he has talked there is great respect for me and solidarity. I thanked him and said that my position is one of being free to judge the actions of all in the light of the gospel. And doubtless this is the reason the truth will always shine forth.

In the evening a Vincentian Father who is going to be in charge of the group of students came to visit me to work out the last details about his stay in our diocese. It has been decided that they will take over the parish of Lourdes and, because of this, it will be communicated—I have already told Father Cortez that, as vicar general, he should communicate to Father Mateo Quijada that the parish of Lourdes, which until now has been under his authority, will be turned over to this Vincentian community. The Vincentian students, like the Passionists before, will be in charge of the pastoral work in the parish of Lourdes in addition to their study in the seminary.

I was also visited by a Catholic and two Baptists who are organizing the Week of Prayer for Christian Unity. I thanked them for their initiative and have offered them all my help, since ecumenism is one of the ideas that the Council has given impetus to for the modern Church.

I also talked with a young progressive business leader, who feels the tremendous conflict of the moment—faced with an oligarchy of which he is a member, according to his economic status, but from which he is very distant because of his social consciousness. He and others of similar sentiments are trying to cooperate in the transformation of the country. They ask for guidance and support, which I gladly give on my part.

I have made other telephone calls to several persons who wanted to talk to me. We finished our work very late, but with the satisfaction of having done something for the Kingdom of God.

I forgot to say that also Father Chus Delgado and Aníbal Romero have helped me to express my pastoral views better in the speech that, God willing, I will give at the University of Louvain on the occasion of receiving an honorary doctoral degree February 2.

**Saturday, January 12**

Around noon, Colonel Gutiérrez called me from the presidential house to ask if I could be the intermediary in the matter of the occupation of the Panamanian Embassy, where the ambassador of Costa Rica is one of the hostages. A lawyer from the Legal Aid Office went on behalf of the archdiocese to talk with those occupying the embassy, the Popular Leagues . They refused to accept this mediation, for they have already asked the ambassadors of Venezuela and Mexico to do it. I told Colonel Gutiérrez, and he thanked us for our willingness, at least. But the situation in the embassy of Panama continues unchanged.

We learned in the afternoon that the two Guadalupana Sisters in Arcatao had been taken as hostages for a member of the National Guard who was captured by one of the popular organizations. We went to the Minister of Defense, who sent the National Guard to investigate. Thank God, at midnight the sisters returned. They said that it was true that they had been prisoners; they were separated, with the threat that if the soldier who had been captured by the popular organization was not released, they would be killed.

I had lunch with the priests Fabián Amaya, Rafael Urrutia, Monsignor Urioste and with Miss Doris Osegueda to get their advice regarding the events of the week. The perspective of Church which guides this consultation, and which I consider necessary for my homily, is very interesting.

In the afternoon, a visit from a Mexican journalist who writes for some eighty different places. The conversation lasted for more than an hour and it was very interesting. We talked about the situation of the country and of the role the Church is playing in this moment.

 **Sunday, January 13**

As usual, I celebrated the Sunday Mass at the cathedral with a large attendance. The theme was the Baptism of the Lord and our Baptism, which commits us to be better citizens. There was applause, as at other times; there were television people from Guatemala and another country.

After Mass, some workers on strike from factories took over the cathedral. They told me that it was not intended as an offense against the Church, but rather to pressure for talks with the owners, who have refused during this strike that is affecting many workers. They asked me to serve as mediator, to approach the owners and talk to them. I offered them my services, but also I told them that it was not good for them to take over the church because it disturbed our worship. Nevertheless, it has continued to be occupied the whole day.

After Mass I held a press conference, with television also, in which they asked the usual questions about the situation of the country. The journalists are afraid of what might happen, especially if it is of a bloody nature; because of this, they say that they have to stay here in El Salvador. We hope that everyone will act wisely and will negotiate in time. It is a shame that there are so many people embued with this spirit of violence who are almost calling for a popular insurrection.

In the afternoon I went to San Pedro Perulapán, where Father Solórzano was coordinating a meeting of the laity of the entire Department of Cuscatlán. I talked with them, and it is clear that there are very good laypersons who are a hope for our Church. In the Mass Sister Beatriz, one of the two sisters who were taken prisoner in Arcatao, addressed the group and explained the situation in Arcatao, where they had received threats that, if by two o'clock in the afternoon the member of the Guard who was a prisoner had not been freed, they were going to begin a very cruel operation in that region. A call was issued both to those who have the soldier, asking them to free him, and to the National Guard, asking them not to act in a spirit of vengeance.

Also, an ecumenical committee spoke at the time of the homily to invite us to the celebration of the Week of Prayer for Christian Unity which, as usual, will take place from March 18 to 25.

 **Monday, January 14**

This morning we had a meeting of the Priests' Senate; we talked about my upcoming trip to Belgium. They recommended that I go to Rome to deliver objective reports to counteract any bias that might have reached there. We also talked about the changes in the Senate and in the vicariates this coming March.

Then we began to analyze the political situation of the country. I was very pleased to see the maturity of my priests in this realistic reflection in spite of their having different political views. Nevertheless, there is a single pastoral vision and I noted a growth in their sense of being Church. I congratulated them on this and I begged them to continue to advise me so that, in this turbulent sea of politics in the country, our Church may be guided by evangelical and pastoral principles that will enable it to be helpful in the whirlwind that surrounds us.

I was waiting for messages from the FPL with regard to the kidnapping of the South African ambassador, but they did not come. I hope that tomorrow they will come to take back an interesting answer.

In the evening I made an analysis of a psychological nature with Dr. Semsch, who confirms that the position that I am trying to maintain is the correct one, a straight line that honors the preaching, the thinking of the Church. We analyzed some negative points. It was for me a psychologically very enriching reflection.

Today I also went to visit the two Guadalupana Sisters who suffered recently in their community in Arcatao. A member of the National Guard was taken prisoner by a group from the popular organizations and they wanted to hold the sisters as hostages, and also a brother who was working with them there in Arcatao. They took them to a jail and threatened that, if the guardsman did not appear, they would suffer the consequences: They would kill them! We went to the government here and, thanks to this intercession, they went to get them. It seemed that would be very difficult to do, since the director of the National Guard said that when their agents rebel, they do not respond to any authority. But, thanks be to God, the sisters were released. They got back at midnight, actually at almost two o'clock in the morning. After being taken first to the headquarters of the Guard, they were turned over to us in the chancery, where Father Rafael Urrutia and Father Salvador Colorado received them. They were very concerned about the suffering of the people there, since, if the soldier were not freed, there would doubtless be very cruel acts of revenge in the entire sector.

Very late at night, the director of the Colegio Guadalupano called to tell me that the superior general had ordered the two sisters to go to Mexico until any danger they may be in here has passed. I objected, saying that it was not that serious and that they could spend a few days there in the school. Nevertheless, it is an order from the superior. Tomorrow the vicar general, Monsignor Urioste, will go talk with the sisters to tell them what the opinion of the archdiocese is and see if, in this dialogue, the conflicted situation can be smoothed over.

**Tuesday, January 15**

This famous day of the Lord of Esquipulas is celebrated in our archdiocese in San Bartolomé Perulapía, in Colón and in Aguilares, where the Christ is called the Lord of Mercy. I went to this community to celebrate Mass; the Church was filled with people. We went to open the first aid clinic that will be staffed there by a very self-sacrificing doctor, along with Father Octavio Cruz and the Oblate Sisters of the Sacred Heart. There are many catechists and very lively communities, memories of Father Grande and of the Jesuits who worked so intensely in that pastoral effort.

I was very satisfied with the vitality of that liturgy. My message focused on the crucified Christ and the mystery of incarnation, crucifixion and resurrection as the way and goal of human development, as we all must in our evangelization.

In the afternoon the messengers of the FPL came to get the answer from the family of Mr. Dunn, the former ambassador of South Africa, who has been kidnapped. I sent an answer to the FPL through the people in charge of this kind of communication. It contained the response of Mr. Dunn's family and also a letter of mine that appeals to their humanity, urging them to free this poor man, whose wife is seriously ill.

In relation to this same kidnapping, Don Ernesto Rivas Gallont came and, independently of Don Ernesto, another relative who prefers for me to represent the family as the only way to speed up the resolution of this sad situation.

A representative of the Popular Revolutionary Bloc also came to talk with me and, with Father Rafael Moreno, I received him. Their capacity for analysis is remarkable; their political ideas are very clear. For our part, we tried rather to view that which engaged the mission of the Church.

Along with an ecumenical group, I prepared the recording for the program tomorrow. The topic was the very agreeable one of ecumenism, developed in its different aspects in the form of a natural conversation.

Monsignor Urioste informed me about his visit to the Guadalupana Sisters, who have decided to send the two sisters who were persecuted in Arcatao to Mexico. Monsignor also told me about the meeting with those who do the commentaries on YSAX, trying to resolve an impasse that exists with this program. There are still some things to be resolved later.

**Wednesday, January 16**

Last night at about eleven o'clock Father Fermín Sainz told me that the wife of Don Jaime Hill would visit me. He has been kidnapped by the ERP,[284] and they have said that he will be killed today at seven o'clock in the evening if the family has not complied with the conditions that they have imposed. They explained to me, confidentially, that it involves some twenty million colones.[285] They have tried everything possible and have not been able to get that amount because the banks are frozen and because of other laws that make it impossible for them to get such an exorbitant amount, even in the form of a loan.

They came to ask me to intercede, to say a few words on the radio (so that the captors will hear them) about the difficult situation faced by the family and to ask for an extension to this arbitrary deadline and negotiations to discuss these conditions. I recorded a statement to be broadcast on YSAX, an appeal to them. It will also be broadcast on other radio stations.

I left later for San Miguelito in Chalatenango, where there was a celebration of *Corpus*. They greeted my arrival very affectionately— children with pine branches in their hands. A picturesque ascent with a group of students to the summit to the shrine where we had Mass with a large number of people. In the Mass some of the laity spoke, expressing in a very simple but cordial way their solidarity with their pastor.

When I returned in the afternoon, I was concerned about getting some answer to my appeal, but there had been nothing more other than a confirmation of the conditions broadcast on some stations, saying that they would extend the deadline, but only for a short time; that this family could perfectly well use the money that they have outside the country and that they will not accept any other negotiations.

I also received a visit from Father Estrada and Eddie Stein, who are concerned about tomorrow's program at noon, the commentary on YSAX. I understand the advantage of the station having its own voice, but I have asked them to submit things for previous approval to avoid the conflicts that have caused the suspension of this program for several days.

I also talked with Monsignor Rivera by telephone in order to tell him of my surprise about the bishop's conference and my intention to not go to the next meeting.[286]

---

[284] *Ejército Revolcionario del Pueblo*, People's Revolutionary Army, one of the armed groups that would later form the FMLN.

[285] About eight million dollars.

[286] Because of the impending trip to Belgium.

I received a call from Archbishop Marcos McGrath of Panama, who had also been asked to issue an appeal about the kidnapping I have mentioned. He told me that he had done so, thinking that I would not have any problem with his doing so. And he had used the occasion also to issue an appeal for a peaceful solution in El Salvador. I also learned from the Central American Radio Network that the matter had been referred to the archbishop of San José in Costa Rica as well.

I gave an interview to a Brazilian journalist on the situation of the country and the role of the Church.

Today a series of studies on Christian base communities which is going to last three days began in Domus Mariae. Unfortunately, I had gotten confused about the date, and I had committed myself to go to La Palma for the next two days. For that reason, I asked Monsignor Urioste to go and make sure that the meeting keeps its ecclesial nature. According to what he has told me, the first day's work was very positive and he is not worried, since everything seems to be proceeding very well.

Today we finished the speech that I am going to give in Belgium. Tomorrow, God willing, I will send it air mail special delivery. The details of my trip have also been finalized. I will fly Iberia to Madrid and Rome, to handle in Rome some matters with the Congregation for Bishops about the seminary, and to visit Cardinal Pironio and, if possible, also the Secretary of State. And from there to Belgium.

 ## Thursday, January 17

I had breakfast with Bishop Rivera. We discussed the situation of the bishops' conference and our pastoral relationships.

Then I went to La Palma, where Father Vitto Guaratto has prepared a two-day pastoral visit for me. We left La Palma immediately for San Ignacio, a village that is part of this parish, where a small but very affectionate group of Christians welcomed me. We celebrated a lovely ceremony of Confirmation and First Communion in the church. At the end, we talked with the group that works most closely with the priest. They asked me to bring a community of sisters there, and we talked with the priest about the possibility of bringing two or three Franciscan sisters there.

We had lunch in La Palma and we went immediately to the picturesque heights of Las Pilas by a very steep highway. The jeep broke down about halfway, but we were able to use the jeep driven by the sisters who work in Citalá, another village that is part of the parish of La Palma. We went through a place that is called Miramundo. It is the highest point in El Salvador, some 2,200 meters high.[287] From there, we descended a little toward the picturesque valley of Las Pilas, surrounded by pine trees, where other small villages are located on the heights. We celebrated a beautiful Eucharist outside the church because the crowd would not fit inside. A very warm reception. We celebrated several First Communions and many Confirmations, which had been prepared by the catechists of that place.

It was night when we descended after listening to many testimonies from those fervent Catholics. The Holy Spirit is doing marvelous things with this simple people, who are also motivated by the Renewal in the Spirit, which this Franciscan priest encourages with great balance.

After a peaceful night in La Palma, we celebrated Mass there in the morning with a concentration of the faithful who had come from different regions of the parish. The church was full. I heard many confessions; we gave a general absolution with the condition that they make their confessions later. And we celebrated First Communions and many Confirmations, which had been well prepared. In the evening, we had held a meeting with the leaders of the parish who principally work with the priest. I talked with the priest later about the project that they are building: a center that is a true peasant university—a great deal of work, but very well done—where they will give courses, or hold spiritual retreats, etc.

The result of this visit has been very positive. It seems to me that it can be characterized by an awareness of the Holy Spirit through the catechesis for the Confirmations. I received the impression that they are people who are very capable of understanding the revelation of the Holy Spirit Christ brought us, and that they are living it with great intensity, with great piety. I thanked them for the valuable prayer that comes from there. It is like the lung, the breath of the Church. After lunch, crowned by the qualities and affection of this people, I returned to San Salvador, where a very busy afternoon awaited me.

This evening the ecumenical meeting was to begin—eight days of prayers for Christian unity. But I could not go to the opening ceremony because there were some very important visits at the hospital related to the problems that abound these days. We also had a dinner meeting to reflect on the reality of El Salvador, which seemed to me to be very insightful despite the complexity of the situation.

---

[287] More than 7,200 feet.

**Saturday, January 19**

This morning can be characterized by the general meeting of CONFRES, where I discussed the theme of service through the religious life in the present situation of the country. I encouraged them to be identified with the direction of the archdiocese, since one of the signs of religious authenticity is knowing how to adapt to the pastoral work of the local Church where one works.

I received visits from the families of those kidnapped: the Hill family and that of the former ambassador of South Africa. They still have hope; they have great confidence in the Church. They come to it; they appreciate all its intercession. I try especially to give them comfort and great trust in God and to encourage them to accept God's will and to keep high their spirit of prayer and trust.

Father Moreno, Miss Doris and Father Rafael Urrutia met with me to work out the summary of the week that I will use in my homily.

 **Sunday, January 20**

The cathedral is occupied by unions that are demanding that their factories, which they say have been unjustly closed, be reopened—a dispute in which the Church has also acted as an intermediary, trying to get the owners to participate in a dialogue. But we have not achieved this and, for this reason, the cathedral is still occupied. We had to hold the Sunday Mass in the Sacred Heart Basilica with the attendance of those who normally come to the cathedral. The passage from the Gospel on the wedding at Cana[288] gave me the opportunity to give an optimistic and joyous homily, since God wanted to reveal the mystery of Christ and of the redemption through the symbol of a wedding celebration and since, in spite of the difficulties and the problems (like those that Mary discovered at that wedding), we can always trust in the Church because Christ is present in the problems and difficulties.

After Mass I went to San Francisco in Mejicanos, where they were ending a prayer vigil with a profession of faith. It had begun in San Antonio Abad, where Father Octavio Ortiz died a year ago, along with four young

---

[288] John 2:1-12.

men who were making a spiritual retreat. This campaign took place across from the San Francisco church, in the school being built by the Carmelite sisters.

A large crowd attended the Eucharist that we concelebrated with the priests of the Vicariate of Mejicanos and other friends of Father Octavio's. I spoke in the homily of the two levels of our message of Christian liberation: the transcendent one, from which Octavio and the other dead speak to us, which is the goal and the destiny of our kingdom on earth; and the earthly one, the earth where we still have our feet planted, where we are to embody this transcendental message insofar as we work for the liberation of our people, for the Christian redemption of the world. Thus we will also have a place in that heaven that is the transcendental prize of our work on earth. It was difficult for me to leave because there were many people who wanted to greet me.

I went to have lunch with the Oblate Sisters of Divine Love at the Colegio de la Sagrada Familia. I was very sorry not to be able to accept the invitation of the parish priest to join all of the priests who were going to have lunch at Mejicanos, but I had already made a commitment to this religious community and they were waiting to take me there.

In the afternoon, a new meeting with the families of those kidnapped. I also received a message from the captors of the former ambassador of South Africa. We talked about the difficult circumstances that are created by the conditions they impose. For the same reason, the daughter of the ambassador also called me from the United States, very disturbed; I tried to give her courage and suggest to her some things that she might do.

In the evening Dr. Saca paid me a visit to say good-bye because he is going to the United States with his family, to settle them there and then come back. He told me that Colonel Gutiérrez, one of the members of the revolutionary junta, is ill and at his clinic, and I asked him to take me to see him. We talked; I tried to cheer him up and to give him the comfort that the Church usually provides. He seemed to me very calm, although I know that the problems in the government are very difficult.

**Monday, January 21**

This morning I had a meeting with the Priests' Senate to continue and bring up to date our analysis of the situation of the country: specifically, to decide on the attitude that, as Church, we ought to take in the archdiocese. We said that there is a psychosis in the atmosphere, as if everyone were expecting a civil war very soon. The demonstration that has been announced for tomorrow by the popular political organizations has created a strong impression, an expectancy almost equal to waiting for a civil war. We have analyzed the situation and it is certainly serious. But our duty as Church is to keep hope alive, to stay above all the false rumors and to try to live in reality and, especially, in our intimate consciences, with God. To instill this in our communities is our primary responsibility at this time.

With respect to my trip to Belgium, we agreed that we will meet again within two days, after the demonstration, to see how things are and to see what we should do. We also canceled the pastoral meeting that had been scheduled for tomorrow because of all the nervousness.

Among the visitors who came was Deacon Pedro García, who has caused me great disappointment. After his formation in La Ceja in Colombia, he has insisted on leaving the archdiocese because he believes that he cannot in good conscience follow the pastoral direction of our archdiocese. I tried to convince him of his error and also to make him aware that in our diocese there is a healthy pluralism in which any tendency can find a place as long as it is legitimate in a pastoral sense. Nevertheless, he is determined to go. I have given him two conditions: first, that he tell me what diocese he is planning to go to so that I can, in good conscience, make a report on him and thus fulfill my responsibility; and, second, that the archdiocese recover the money that it has spent on him.[289]

There was also some contact with the kidnappers of the ex-ambassador of South Africa, who want information on the doctor they have said can go see him. I took the opportunity to send them some other information that they should know, always with the intention of obtaining the release of this poor hostage.

At the radio, in relation to the commentaries, I have tried to put on some pressure so that we do not let ourselves be controlled by cowardice. Real prudence, yes; censorship, also, if it is rational; but we should not

---

[289] Education and travel expenses.

abandon the program of commentaries, since they are of great usefulness to orient our listeners in such a confusing time.

The most comforting event today was the celebration that we had at noon in Apulo in the Santa Teresita Home, where the seminary for late vocations has been opened. A group of young men who had thought that it would be impossible for them to study in the seminary have found with Father Fabián, episcopal vicar of Chalatenango, an opportunity to bring their studies up to date and to continue their ecclesiastical studies. It was beautiful to hear them, their joy in their reborn hope.

Along with this experience, we were surprised by the promise of three young women, who for months have been thinking of becoming a community, taking religious vows for a year and living as part of the community of Ilopango. Another experience we had is that of five Carmelite sisters who have left the congregation but who will stay together without abandoning their religious spirit and their service to the communities of the archdiocese. They will live in Guazapa and, on my return from Belgium, we will go celebrate the ceremony of their incorporation into that community.

Also on this occasion when the Holy Spirit showed us so many gifts, I confirmed a Jesuit novice who has to go to Panama to finish his preparation and who received in the midst of that very charismatic atmosphere this precious gift of the Holy Spirit.

 **Tuesday, January 22**

Today was marked by tragedy. On this day in 1932 was begun the great massacre by General Martínez against a so-called communist revolution in the western part of the country.[290] To commemorate this anniversary, the popular political organizations and other leftist organizations organized a joint demonstration in San Salvador— the largest, they say, in the entire history of our nation. And truly, it started at the statue of the Divine Savior and went on for blocks and blocks toward the center of the city. But when it reached the National Palace, machine-gun fire broke up this beautiful demonstration, which was really a popular fiesta. They dispersed in all directions, taking cover in the cathedral, in El Rosario Church, in the stores and all the places nearby where they could

---

[290] *La Matanza*, "the slaughter," was the government's response to the revolution led by Farabundo Martí (from whom the FMLN takes its name). Thousands of peasants were massacred by the army.

hide. Several dead bodies were left in the streets; also many wounded, who were taken to the first aid centers. The dead bodies were taken away after having been seen by the judges. In the cathedral alone there were eleven bodies by the evening.

It is mysterious. They called me immediately from the presidential palace, alarmed by what had happened. I received word from Ingeniero Héctor Dada, member of the revolutionary junta, who informed me that the gunfire did not come from the security forces because they were all in their barracks; that they had seen some people disguised as members of the military participating in the demonstration; and that the complaint that was made from El Rosario Church by Marianela García, member of the Human Rights Commission of El Salvador, who had said that there were police agents around the church and asked that they be pulled back, was false—because, according to the government, there were no such police; the bullets that have been found did not come from the security forces, etc.

On the other side, reporters who were present at the events and the testimony of many witnesses indicate that soldiers on the balcony of the National Palace had fired on the crowd. Some are sure that there was some provocation before this action on the part of the soldiers. The truth is very confused. As for the Church, we have calmly begun an investigation in order to make an informed judgment.

We have tried to cooperate in this tragedy, helping to evacuate the people who were in the cathedral—some three hundred refugees—who were taken to the chancery, where they were provided with food and a place to sleep. The sisters and other Catholic institutions have been very generous in collaborating in this aid given by the Church.

A large part of the crowd took refuge in the university, where they estimate that there are some forty thousand people. The night has been a tragic one. There have been bombs in different parts of the city. One of them was placed, doubtless by those of the extreme right, in the antenna of our Catholic radio station, YSAX, which has suffered some damage, although it is not serious. Domus Mariae, where the antenna is located, also has suffered some damage to its structure.

In another intercession at the presidential residence, I asked Sigfrido Munés, who is in charge of the Information Office, not to link all of the private stations to Radio Nacional because that would take away the spontaneity and the pluralism of information. But Mr. Munés told me that it was a way to prevent the news being twisted around and that all of the services will be joined through the national radio network. I insisted that this not be done permanently. Nevertheless, this national network has continued, removing in this way all initiative and all participation of the different stations that have been providing such good social and informational services.

There has been further contact with the government and with different sectors of the people in the intercession that the Church has offered voluntarily. As far as the work of the chancery, almost everyone has been infected by the psychosis of the country. There has been no lack of visits to the archdiocesan offices, with the same nervousness caused by this violent situation.

 **Wednesday, January 23**

Beginning in the early hours, we were asked to intercede so that they will withdraw the military forces who have the National University surrounded. More than forty thousand persons feel trapped there and want the military to withdraw so that they can leave and return to their homes. In the presidential residence, where we went with this request, they told us that the intention of these forces is not to imprison those who are in the university but rather to defend them from any attack from the right, who caused the tragedy beginning yesterday and who could continue their attacks on the crowd when they leave the university. Because of this, they set up these checkpoints to keep them from causing problems for the people.

We have insisted that the people would have a hard time understanding this interpretation. We were asked to send a committee from the archdiocese along with the Red Cross and the Human Rights Commission to intercede at the university, where this crowd is already rebelling against the National Guard, so that we can try to convince them that these forces will be withdrawn and to be prudent and calm when they leave and not to misinterpret the presence of the military forces. Those who went were Father Cortés, vicar general; Father Jesús Delgado; Father Rafael Moreno and Licenciado Roberto Cuéllar. They carried out their role as negotiators in the National University. They managed to get the military forces withdrawn and the people were able to leave peaceably.

In the afternoon there was a mass of people in the park next to the cathedral and in the cathedral, where along with several other priests I celebrated Mass for those who had died. I directed my message to the crowd who surrounded the coffins containing the dead. The burial was not held this afternoon, but rather will be tomorrow morning—which rather surprised me, seeing that they had asked me to celebrate Mass for the purpose of the burial—but that is the way that these organizations are. They twist or misdirect things to serve their own purposes. At any rate, the cathedral is offering its services to the poor.

This morning I had two important meetings: one with the Priests' Senate to analyze what happened during the demonstration yesterday and, more than anything, to decide what action to take at this time. One of the decisions we came to was to send the committee to intercede at the university. We decided that we would continue our analysis tomorrow, particularly in order to determine what the role of the Church should be at this moment.

The other meeting took place in the convent of the parish of La Asunción, Flor Blanca, with the committee that administers the property of the archdiocese. We analyzed the work that this committee is doing with such great sacrifice and such goodwill and, at the same time, pointed out the deficiencies in its work as well as those of certain people in the work of the chancery. I have tried to give more authority to this committee and to reorganize the way the financial aspects of the chancery function. The administration of its property will be completely controlled by this committee.

In the afternoon I received three important visits with the assistance of Monsignor Urioste and Father Estrada. The first was from the ambassador of the United States along with an undersecretary[291] of the United States State Department who is a specialist in the affairs of Central America and the Caribbean. The visit lasted an hour, during which we carefully analyzed the situation. The United States seems to support the government. They told us in confidence something about their projects and of their goodwill toward El Salvador. On our side, we very frankly set forth our ideas.

The second visit was from members of the Supreme Court of Justice which, concerned about yesterday's events, is trying to conduct an investigation. Because of this, they came to visit the Church, which they praised for its work in providing information, and for the carefulness of its denunciations, and for what it does for those who have suffered abuses in our country. We talked for a long time, and we realized the desire these lawyers have to make the Supreme Court have the excellence a judicial system should have in a democratic system. According to what they told us, there are existing organisms which, according to the traditions of our country, are completely inoperative, but which should be revived in order to defend the rights of the people. It was a very cordial conversation and the ideals were especially patriotic.

---

[291] James Cheek, then deputy assistant secretary for Inter-American Affairs.

The third visit was from the Spanish Ambassador, along with the state secretary for Latin America. We talked at length about matters of Spain and of Latin America. We also analyzed the situation of El Salvador a little, which was what most interested this representative of the Spanish government. He told me that my name is well known in Spain and brought me congratulations and greetings for the pastoral work we are doing here.

Even later in the evening, Ingeniero Rosa, Father Gregorio Rosa's brother, came to talk to me about his experiences and his testimony of yesterday's events. He was on the balcony of the cathedral and could see what happened at the National Palace clearly, especially the group of National Guardsmen who, according to what he said, did in fact fire on the crowd.

Today also we decided in the council of the Priests' Senate that this was not an opportune moment for my trip since the people are suffering. Nevertheless, we will decide during the days that are left. At any rate, I authorized Father Gregorio Rosa to organize a trip for me that would take the least time possible and to see if it would be possible to send someone to represent me. Father Goyo talked to Father Juan Deplanck in Belgium, who told him it would be better to cut down the events planned for ten days in Belgium, but that I should still go, even if only to receive the honorary doctorate I have been offered by the University of Louvain. At any rate, they have organized a very short trip for me. I will decide in the next few days whether I will go or not.

 **Thursday, January 24**

A telephone call from Father Juan Deplanck in Belgium has made me decide to travel to that country, since he explained to me that they have made some preparations. Although they can reduce the program a great deal, he still thinks that it is essential that I go to the ceremony to receive the honorary doctorate in Louvain. He also agrees that the situation in our country is very serious; because of this, he will do everything possible to shorten the trip even further. According to him (and I agree), it would be a service to the diocese. Because of the support that it means for our pastoral work, I think that I should make the sacrifice and go. I will arrange it, then, so that I can leave Monday of next week, to be there on Saturday, after being in Rome, where I have some things to take care of. I could begin the return trip the following Monday, or Tuesday as Father Juan is still asking.

We had a meeting of the Priests' Senate, which has been meeting more frequently in order to analyze the very difficult situation of the country and how to carry out the mission of the Church in the best way possible—a very frank analysis. We put together the elements to write an information bulletin, using the criteria of the Church, about the disturbances that ended the demonstration two days ago.

In the seminary there are many refugees from villages where they are persecuted, but they are leaving now. The Senate was informed about the actions that the representatives of the Church have been carrying out in getting the refugees out of the university after the military were withdrawn. It is difficult to understand the true motive of these military activities since, according to the civilians in the junta, it is to protect the refugees themselves; while the organizations and the people in general suspect that it is to suppress demonstrations by the popular organizations.

I talked at length with my brother about the organization of the financial administration and of the combined administration of the property of the archdiocese. With goodwill, he and the priests on the committee are prepared to offer me good advice.

The superior general of the Passionist Sisters, who are in charge of the village of San José Villanueva, also came to the chancery. In order to renew their vows they will have to leave this mission. We have insisted it is important that they not abandon this area and that they continue to attend to it, even if it is from the Colegio de la Divina Providencia. The mother superior promised to study the case and to make a decision before leaving for Mexico.

In the evening I received a visit in the hospital from the manager of Caritas to inform me about what is being done with the refugees. It could be misinterpreted, since there is prejudice against the popular organizations. I told him that in such cases what must prevail is human need and Christian charity.

Also, in the evening a delegation from FAPU came. I was accompanied during the visit by Father Rafael Moreno. We talked for about two hours about FAPU's analysis of the situation and the peaceful solution that they offer: a perspective of unity, an alliance among the popular organizations, the young military officers and the sensible part of the government, all in behalf of the people. Father Moreno pointed out that this proposal largely coincides with what I said this last Sunday in my homily. I offered the full collaboration of the Church to unite forces in order to save the country.

**Friday, January 25**

This morning, the provincial of the Spanish Missionary Carmelites, a congregation that has taken charge of caring for the Salvadoran Policlinic and two base communities in the archdiocese, Plan del Pino and La Laguna in Chalatenango. We talked in detail about the work that they do and about the situation of the country. She showed her satisfaction in working with this Church, for which I thanked her.

Also, in the morning a committee came from PUCA, the Central American Union Party, to ask me to use the weight of the Church on behalf of the unity of Central America, which they think would be the best solution for the crisis in each country in Central America. They ask concretely that I help them to get the "juridical personality"[292] and to get the offices and functions of ODECA assigned to this party, which can better involve itself in the Central American matters.

At noon, Bishop [Luís] Bambarén came. He is the bishop of a diocese [Chimbote] in Peru and president of the Commission for Social Affairs of CELAM. He said that he had come expressly to visit me and also to invite a representative to the next meeting of this commission of CELAM, which will take place in Panama. When I told him that the president of that commission in the episcopal conference of El Salvador was Bishop Aparicio, he told me that he would not like for him to come because of the experiences they had in Puebla, when the bishop caused great discomfort. He said that it would be better to invite someone else to come even as only a guest. We did this, talking by telephone with Bishop Rivera, who accepted the invitation with pleasure.

We talked a good deal with Bishop Bambarén about our situation. I felt that he was very understanding. He agrees with the pastoral direction of our archdiocese, since he follows a similar line in Peru and has also been the object of misunderstandings, as we are here.

He stayed in my room here and shared the life of this community. While he went out, I had a meeting with the vicars general and the chancellors to talk about my absence during my trip to Belgium. Monsignor Urioste thinks that I should not go, given the gravity of the circumstances of the moment. But, on thinking it over, I think it will, as Father Juan Deplanck from Belgium said, be good for the Church and will strengthen our pastoral direction with the honor that the University of Louvain has prepared for me. For that reason, I think that I should go and

---

[292] A kind of legal recognition that enables qualifying organizations to function.

be absent from here for the shortest time possible, a period of some five to seven days, giving sufficient authority to those who will be in charge of the chancery.

 ## Saturday, January 26

This morning I went to the airport to take Bishop Bambarén, who was very cordial and happy. He asked me to give him a collection of my homilies. I promised to send them to him, because I did not have them there. He says that he read the one from last Sunday in *Orientación* and he thought that it was very good. He would like to have more of them, other homilies. I will be glad to send them to him. It was very encouraging for me.

I had a meeting to prepare the homily; coincidentally, Father Ellacuría and Father Estrada arrived beforehand. We talked about the perception of El Salvador in the United States, from which Father Ellacuría has just come. It seems that they were alarmed by my last homily, in which I talked about a popular project and did not support the Christian Democrats as much. Because for the United States, the Christian Democrats are the solution; they have promised to help them. We said that we do not have to please the United States or anyone else, but rather to look for the solution that is best for our country. And the advisers who were with me agreed with what I had said in my homily.

We continued talking about a statement which, after hearing the views of the Senate, Father Moreno had written about the demonstration that was broken up by gunfire. It seemed fine to me, but was also improved by the opinions of the others. It will denounce the many bloody incidents that have occurred this week, always emphasizing the Church's pastoral and evangelical aspect.

In the evening, in accordance with what Father Moreno had told me, he came with a young man from one of the clandestine groups to talk about their political projects. I had the opportunity to tell him what the Church thinks about solutions that involve violence, which is what these organizations advocate and which has caused so many problems in recent times. They have their ideology and their way of thinking; it would be difficult to get them to change. I think that praying for all these people is the best way to help them and to give the country a solution that is not based on blood, hate or violence.

**Sunday, January 27**

Again the Mass had to be held at the Sacred Heart Basilica because the cathedral continues to be occupied. The attendance was very large. The theme was Christ, prophet; the prologue to and beginning of the ministry from the Gospel of St. Luke[293] gave me the opportunity to explain the meaning of the homily. When Christ says, "Today this scripture passage is fulfilled in your hearing" [Luke 4:21b], he gives a true homily, a living actualization of the word of God.

I referred also to the major event of the week, the demonstration that ended in tragedy and, after my consultations with several priests, I analyzed the responsibilities of a moment in which everyone must give up their polarized attitudes and dedicate themselves to harmonizing different ways of thinking for the common good of the country.

After Mass I held a press conference. There were people from British television, journalists from Switzerland, the United States and Mexico. We always talk about the situation of the country and the role of the Church.

At noon Colonel Majano of the revolutionary junta came, as he had said he would. He is very simple in his ways when in private, and we spoke in great detail about the situation and about his projects. They are very concerned about the present moment, but are confident that they will be able to earn the goodwill of a people they are trying to serve.

I offered him my observations, as I had in my homily, that what is necessary is sincerely to associate oneself with the people, to take their organizations into account, and to stop the repression of these organizations, since that gives the impression that they are not in control of the National Guard or of the other security forces. And with the vengeful and violent attitudes of these security forces, the government loses the prestige and credibility necessary to inspire goodwill.

We had lunch with the sisters from the hospital. Colonel Majano was very cordial and even offered different services to the sisters of the hospital.

I spent the afternoon packing my suitcase for my trip tomorrow to Europe. Nevertheless, I had several things to do at my desk and had to attend to some visitors, such as Father Alliet, who brought me the addresses of Belgian priests and nuns who work among us and whom I hope to be able to visit there.

Also, a meeting that we were going to have with the national coordinators of the popular organizations had to be canceled because only those from the Popular Leagues came. The others gave the excuse of

---

[293] Luke 1:1-4; 4:14-21.

other activities, among them the burial of some of the members of the UDN who had been killed.

And I went to see the nuncio, who wanted to give me something. It turned out to be a letter in which they observe that I have given my support to an ecumenical meeting in Brazil and that has a theme which they see as criticizing Puebla and the division among the bishops—and that they recommend that I take personal responsibility if I go to this meeting. I explained to the nuncio that this surprised me, because I had not expressed such support, and that I did indeed thank them for the invitation but made my excuses, since I could not go so soon after having returned from Europe. The nuncio said that he would report this. I think that he was satisfied.

When I returned, I talked by telephone with the son of Mr. Dunn, who is held captive. I tried to give him some hope, that we should have confidence in God.

 **Monday, January 28**

Today I began my trip to Belgium to receive the honorary doctoral degree from the University of Louvain. The route they planned for me was to fly Pan American to Guatemala, Miami, Madrid, Rome—where I will spend two days working—and then to Louvain, Belgium. The plane left at eight o'clock in the morning, after I had said good-bye to my sister, other relatives, some nuns and priests.

The scenery has been very picturesque and I have felt a great peace, even though I am worried about what could happen in my country. But when I was leaving, Mother Luz, superior of the Divine Providence Hospital, reminded me of the Psalm we prayed this morning: "The Lord shepherds his people."[294] She said I should be calm, that everyone would pray that the Lord would pasture this flock that I am leaving, even though I do not want to. I am going to carry out another responsibility that is also in service to the Church, because I believe that this honor I am receiving is not merely a tribute to me, but also provides support for the pastoral work of our archdiocese. It is also general support for everyone whose pastoral work follows the direction indicated for the Church by the Second Vatican Council.

---

[294] See Psalm 95:7.

Around noon we got to Miami, where we had to wait for several hours, since the flight for Madrid was not leaving until five o'clock in the afternoon. After a very short night, we arrived at Madrid at dawn, although our watches said eleven o'clock at night. The winter makes the morning very dark; it seemed to be night, not seven o'clock in the morning, when people were beginning to go to work.

Around nine o'clock in the morning, after a wait in the Madrid airport, we took the flight to Rome. I had the same emotion that I always do: Rome for me means a return to the cradle, going home, returning to the source, to the heart, the brain of our Church. I have asked the Lord to preserve my faith and my loyalty to Rome, which Christ chose to be the seat of the universal pastor, the pope.

Father Juan Bosco drove us to the Pensionato Romano; he had been so kind as to come to the airport to pick us up. Our first visit after lunch was to St. Peter's Basilica. The expedition that I have always liked to make: the visit to the Blessed Sacrament, the visit to the tomb of the apostle St. Peter, the visit to the tomb of St. Pius X and the visit to the tombs of the popes, where I felt a special emotion on praying at the tomb of Paul VI. I remembered so many things from his conversations with me, in the visits in which I had the honor and the blessing to be admitted to a private audience.

Afterward we went to look for Cardinal Pironio, but he was very busy with the Dutch Bishops' Synod. He will let me know when he is able to receive me.

We walked around the streets adjacent to St. Peter's Square. All of this makes me remember my seminary years in the Pío Latino and renews my faith and priestly enthusiasm. The Dominican Sisters invited us to dinner. They had come to meet us, but we had not made a definite arrangement and so we arrived before they did and they did not find us. They had also prepared a room for us in their house at Monte Mario. To try to repay this generosity a little, I was pleased to go to dinner with them and talk to them about what is happening in our country.

**Wednesday, January 30**

Today has been very full of God's grace and of great personal satisfaction. It started with a telephone call at seven o'clock in the morning which, given the time difference, I think was very early in the morning. It was Father Juan Deplanck, calling from Belgium to welcome me, to ask me to extend my stay in Belgium until the following Monday in order to be able to go to France, and to tell me that the people are looking forward to my arrival and to my talking with them. I told him that I would be glad to do it, that I only ask that they make the arrangements for me to travel on Tuesday, that is, the following day.

Afterward, en route to my appointment with Cardinal Pironio, I went first to the Secretariat of State to arrange for us to go to the public audience of the Holy Father. I also visited Monsignor [Leonardo] Erriquenz, who is in charge of Central American matters at the Secretariat of State, to tell him that I wanted to talk to him. But he told me that it would be better for me to talk with the Secretary of State himself, Cardinal Casaroli, and that he would arrange the audience for me.

Then I talked to Cardinal Pironio—a brief but very encouraging conversation. He told me that he also wanted to see me to tell me that he was very happy that Cardinal Lorscheider's visit had been so positive, and that the pope himself had received a very good report about me. Cardinal Lorscheider had told Cardinal Pironio that I was right, that in El Salvador things are very difficult and that I am the one who sees the situation and the role of the Church clearly and that they must help me. This seems to be the gist of what Cardinal Lorscheider told him about his trip to El Salvador.

I thanked Cardinal Pironio very much and I also encouraged him, because he told me that he also suffers a great deal precisely because of his efforts on behalf of the peoples of Latin America, and that he understands me completely. He recalled to me a verse in the Gospel which has special meaning for him: "Do not be afraid of those who kill the body, but after that can do no more" [Luke 12:4b]. His interpretation is that while those who kill the body are terrible, those who wound the spirit and destroy a person with lies and defamation are even worse. And he thinks that this is exactly the martyrdom I face even within the Church itself and that I must be strong. On the whole, it was a very powerful encouragement and left me in better spirits to talk with the Holy Father at the public audience.

At ten o'clock in the morning, we entered the public audience along with an enormous crowd of people who went into the Paul VI Room. It is an immense hall, but it was filled with the faithful who sang, applauded, prayed. The Holy Father came in at eleven o'clock. It was a long time from the time he came in until he reached the platform where his throne is, since he was greeting people here and there as he walked by. That took him almost an hour.

The address that His Holiness gave at the general audience on this Wednesday, January 30, was a continuation of the meditations on Genesis that he has been presenting in the general audiences. He spoke about the dignity of humankind, given the two human aspects of the body, masculinity and femininity; how happiness is found in innocence and that the shame related to the human body is a sign of original sin—a reflection that I thought was very beautiful, but which was also very deep. I think that many people had difficulty understanding it. Someone told me that the people are fascinated by the pope's entrance and when he greets people personally, but that during his talk there seems to be more distance, a lack of understanding. It is really a shame, because it is a moment at which the people are very attentive; any idea that is understandable, however simple it might be, could have a good effect on the listeners.

When the audience ended, he called for the bishops present to come join him in blessing the people. I had the pleasure of being immediately on his right. Afterward, when we—the bishops—greeted the pope, he told me that after the audience he especially wanted to talk with me. But I had to wait a good while because, after he greeted the bishops, a circus that had come to honor the Holy Father and to ask for his blessing began its performance. They performed artistic and comic numbers—they were very funny—that filled the entire public and, of course, the Holy Father with joy. He also spoke at length with a chorus that had come from Poland, his country. He had a cordial conversation with them, also with the sick people and everyone who had a privileged position among the crowd.

When he finished this long good-bye, he received me in a room where he holds special audiences. He received me very warmly and told me that he understood perfectly how difficult the political situation of my country is; that he was concerned about the role of the Church; that we should be concerned not only with defending social justice and love of the poor, but also with what could result from a score-settling effort on the part of the popular left, which could also be bad for the Church.

I told him, "Holy Father, this is precisely the balance that I try to keep, because, on the one hand, I defend social justice, human rights, love of the poor. On the other, I am always greatly concerned for the role of the Church, and that by defending these human rights, we not become victims of ideologies that destroy feelings and human values." I said that I very much agreed with his discourses and they gave me great strength and material for my actions and my preaching. I mentioned his speeches in Mexico, specifically the one in Oaxaca, and told him that my teaching—

what I preach and what I try to do—can be found in those speeches. The pope said that he agreed with everything that I was saying and, at the end, he gave me a very fraternal embrace and told me that he prayed every day for El Salvador.

In this conversation I have felt the confirmation and the strength of God for my poor ministry. It was almost three o'clock in the afternoon, and I went to the Jesuit curia where unfortunately, because I got there so late, I was unable to have lunch with Father Arrupe as I had been invited. Nevertheless, I had an extremely interesting conversation with him. He was very glad when I told him about my conversations with Cardinal Pironio and the Holy Father, and he reaffirmed his solidarity with me and the support that the Jesuits give me.

Very frankly, he told me also of the fears there can be in the Society of Jesus, but also how much good there is; and that the speech that the pope made to the Jesuits that was commented on as a condemnation was really totally different, for the pope has great affection for the Jesuits and wants to prevent any possible errors on their part. He does not deny that, as human beings, they have their defects and make mistakes; but he says that, in general, there is a strong spirit of service to the Church.

From the Jesuit curia, I did an interview by telephone with Radio YSAX in El Salvador. I was able to do the Wednesday interview on the telephone with Monsignor Urioste, who told me the news of the country—which was sad, because he told me of killings and crimes but, at the same time, about the work of the Church. For my part, I told him about my trip and what I have already mentioned about the audiences that I had this morning and how I would soon have the other meetings that pertained to the archdiocese.

In the evening the Passionist Sisters who live in San Giovanni e Paolo Square came to visit me. They invited us to dinner; we went there with Father Jesús Delgado and with the other two Jesuit priests who kindly accompanied us here in Rome. It was a very cordial dinner, very warm; it was also, for me, a refreshing sign of the kinship of the Church. These sisters assured me that they are continually praying for me and that they are totally in agreement with the pastoral direction of the archdiocese.

Upon my return to the Pensionato Romano, they had details for me on tomorrow's interviews with the Secretary of State, Cardinal Casaroli, and with the Cardinal Prefect of the Congregation for Bishops, Cardinal Baggio. We will also try to get an interview with the Congregation for Catholic Education to talk about matters related to the seminary.

It is already evening, but I am very satisfied with this day, which has been filled with blessings for the archdiocese and for its pastor.

**Thursday, January 31**

It was another day filled with great satisfaction and many pastoral achievements. The first visit today was that of the South African ambassador to the Holy See, who came to thank me for my concern about the kidnapping of Mr. Dunn, former South African ambassador in El Salvador, who has been kidnapped and for whom I have been interceding. He wanted to have more information, which I was able to give him. He was pleased because, he says, he is a great friend of Mr. Dunn, the ambassador.

Two Sisters of Bethany also came to see me—Salvadorans who work here. I greeted them, asking them if I could do anything for them. Because of this, I have a letter to their superior general, who lives in Santa Tecla.

Later I went to the Secretariat of State, where I had an appointment with Cardinal Casaroli. He received me very cordially and asked me about the situation of the country and the functioning of the Church. He told me that the ambassador from the United States had come to see him to express some concern about my being part of a popular revolutionary line, while the United States is supporting the government of the Christian Democrats. I made it clear to the cardinal that it is not a matter of political choice, but simply of searching for justice in the solution of our people's problems. He told me that he was not insisting on that, as the visit from the ambassador was not of an official character and that, anyway, the Church does not act in order to please earthly powers but rather in accordance with its faith and in awareness of the gospel.

The cardinal was also concerned lest the defense of human rights and the people's desire for justice result in the Church being beholden, or in Christian ideas being subjugated, to ideologies. I told him, as I told the Holy Father yesterday, that it is also my concern to preach social justice and defense of human rights, but at the same time, to warn the popular forces seeking justice about the danger of falling prey to foreign ideologies. I also explained to him that we could not talk about anticommunism without the danger of being identified with the injustices perpetrated by the rich, who talk of anticommunism not in order to defend Christian principles, but rather to defend their materialistic interests. I could tell that the cardinal was satisfied with our conversation. He assured me that he prays a great deal for El Salvador.

Another thing that I must explain is that the cardinal saw that my perspective was just, that we must manage to preserve what good there is in the present government and join to it and support the good that exists in the popular efforts. He told me that he thinks that this is the true way out of our crisis. All of this confirmed in me my desire to continue defending the rational part of the government and to press it to dialogue with the popular forces, who also must be warned of the danger of losing Christian ideals in achieving a temporal liberation.

Afterward I went to the Congregation for Bishops, but Cardinal Baggio was not there because the pope had invited him to the Mass for the closing of the Dutch Synod; neither was the undersecretary, Archbishop Moreira, a Brazilian whom I met when I was leaving and who had told me he would return shortly.

This gave me the opportunity to go talk with the Congregation for Catholic Education to talk about the matter of the seminary. I found the undersecretary there, which was very fortunate because his mind is open to the progress that many times scandalizes the more traditional part of the Church. He told me, very confidentially, that he is afraid of this lack of openness in the Church. He is glad to find similar criteria in me.

We spoke at length about the situation of the seminary and he promised to do whatever was within his power to help and that he would let me know. He urged me to be of good spirit and to keep in mind that whoever follows this progressive direction of a Church that is truly faithful to the principles of Vatican II will suffer much and be held in suspicion, but the consciousness and the satisfaction of serving God and the Church is greater than any persecution.

I went later to the Congregation for Bishops. Cardinal Baggio was not there, but Archbishop [Lucas] Moreira [Neves] received me with great understanding, and I was able to leave the letter I had written to Cardinal Lorscheider with him. It was a summary of our conversations in San Salvador; I especially urged him to resolve the situation with the auxiliary bishop and to take seriously the suggestion to revitalize the bishops' conference with new members, open to the new ideas of the Church. He listened very attentively to all the problems I could explain to him. I also left him some documents from the episcopal conference. He promised to study them and talk with Cardinal Baggio and, on his own part, to do everything that is in his power.

When I was finished there, I went to the Pensionato Romano to pack my suitcase and have lunch. Then the Dominican Sisters came to take us to the airport, where we headed to Belgium on Alitalia.

It was four o'clock in the afternoon and our trip was a happy one. We arrived in Brussels, where Father Juan Deplanck and other Salvadoran and Belgian friends were waiting for us. Their welcome was very warm. Father Juan said that there were plans for the evening, a meeting in Brugge. We headed there without stopping to have dinner except for a small sandwich on the way.

After about an hour or a little longer on the road, we arrived in this picturesque city that I saw only at night. A great number of the faithful were gathered in the parish hall: members of Christian base communities begun there by Father Pedro at the express wish of the bishop, Bishop [Emiel-Jozef] DeSmedt, who was also at the meeting. Father Rogelio [Ponseele], who is on vacation, was in charge of the meeting. He introduced me and I was received with warm, seemingly endless applause. I greeted the crowd with a feeling of communion. I was happy to feel at home, to greet Bishop DeSmedt—to thank him for all of his cooperation with our Church—and all the Belgians, who have given us such valuable aid in the form of people, economic assistance and all kinds of help for our pastoral work.

Afterward were some other greetings—expressions of solidarity. I was invited to say a few words, and I chose as my theme the topic of my speech for the ceremony awarding the honorary doctorate: faith and politics. I talked about what faith has to offer to the political realities, using my pastoral letter: the services the Church gives in this time of crisis, starting above all from its identity as Church. And second, what faith receives in exchange for its service to the world: maturing of its belief in God, a deeper sense of sin and a deeper knowledge of Jesus Christ, his incarnation and redemption. There is a reciprocity between the Church—the good it does when it illuminates politics—and politics, when it deepens the faith of Christians in their own reality.

After receiving several greetings and some gifts from the families of the priests, especially Father Pedro's mother, I went to the bishop's residence at the invitation of Bishop DeSmedt, where we talked for a long time about the situation of the Belgian priests in El Salvador, concentrating most on the situation with Rogelio, which the bishop understands. He has the same reservations that I do, so we were able to share our worries. We propose not to make a victim out of him but rather, to be of fraternal help through dialogue so that he may be a good instrument of the pastoral work of our diocese. In the same way we spoke about the problem of Father Esteban Alliet.

I was very glad to be able to give him good news about the other priests and sisters from his diocese. Bishop DeSmedt asked me what else he could do. He said he had no hesitation in helping us, that divine providence would help him. Even when priests want to go there, he will be happy to give them permission. I was amazed by such a generous spirit in a bishop who truly loves the universal Church and does not see only the needs of his own diocese.

It was already midnight. It was strange to leave Brugge in the middle of the night. We returned to Louvain, where we were able to get a little sleep in the House of Formation for Latin America that the Belgian priests direct in order to prepare pastoral agents from Europe, principally Belgium, for the Latin American dioceses.

A beautiful room was waiting for me. Thus the long day that I have tried to describe in this diary ended as the new day was beginning.

# February 1980

 **Friday, February 1**

Scarcely four and a half hours of sleep and Father Juan Deplanck was already calling me to go celebrate Mass, to have breakfast and then to the different commitments on his program.

The first was at the House of Parliament in Brussels, where the prime minister received us. He is in practice the supreme authority of the country and was very cordial and attentive. He asked us about the situation of our country and the role of the Christian Democrats, since he belongs to that party. I talked to him very frankly about the realities of the political and ecclesiastical situation of our dear country.

Later we went to the press conference that had been organized at the University of Louvain. There were twenty-five or more journalists, representatives of the press, television and radio, with whom we talked for more than two hours—an interesting, intelligent conversation. They also asked about the situation of the country, the situation of the Church in Latin America, the problems that they see within the Church and within the political situation. I tried to stay within my pastoral role but answered all of them. Father Jesús Delgado helped me a good deal, making valuable contributions to this dialogue, as did Father Juan Deplanck, especially in his translations into Flemish and French.

After the meeting we went to have lunch at a nice restaurant in Louvain. This gave us a short rest. Then in the afternoon we went to Brussels again to visit the headquarters of the Christian Democratic Party, whose president received us very attentively and expressed great concern for our situation and about what help they could provide from Belgium for the political situation of our country.

The second visit was to the headquarters of the World Labor Federation,[295] an international confederation of unions, where we experienced fully the human warmth of a gathering concerned about the situation of our workers and concerned about what could be done, given the terrible crisis for the workers, peasants and the poor of our country. It was a very positive, very Christian conversation. In the ideas expressed we found great harmony between much of the ideology of that organization and the gospel of our Lord Jesus Christ.

Finally, we went to the Ministry of Foreign Relations to visit the Ministry of Development, where they provide aid for countries of the Third World. The undersecretary received us and explained to us very broadly that they could provide a great deal of aid to our programs, as long as we presented them through organizations with legal status, and that they would approve anything that would contribute to our development. The undersecretary, who seems to be from a Latin American country, told us that he knows Father Ramón Vega. Because of this, I told him that we would take advantage of the help they are offering (since Father Vega has a great deal of experience in these matters and is a friend of his) and present aid programs directed at the needs of our country.

It was eight o'clock at night when we returned to the seminary, where the rector was waiting for us. He was so kind as to have dinner with us and then invited us to his room for a drink and some crackers. We talked at great length as brother priests about some problems related to the Belgian priests in El Salvador. He promised us his help in a friendly and priestly way. How much can be accomplished when we talk in a fraternal way! And so ended another providential day of our trip to Europe.

 **Saturday, February 2**

It was the Feast of the Virgen de Candelaria, a day of great emotion and a great deal of communication and useful contacts. I celebrated Mass in the chapel of the Colegio Latinoamericano with Father Juan Deplanck.

---

[295] WCL, originally founded in 1920 as the International Federation of Christian trade unions.

After breakfast I dressed in my bishop's cassock to go to the University of Louvain to the ceremony awarding the honorary doctoral degree. A procession with all the professors in their robes moved toward the church at the university, where they sang a Gregorian Mass. The Mass was celebrated very solemnly, with a homily that expressed the importance of the life of our Church in the archdiocese. It was in Flemish, so I did not understand, but I heard very dear names from Aguilares: Jesús Jiménez, Father Rutilio Grande. I realized (and afterward they told me) that it greatly praised the pastoral work of our diocese. Four honorary doctorates were awarded, but the address was directed particularly to me.

When we returned to the university, we got ready to enter the great hall, full of dignitaries. The prime minister was there; the bishop of Brussels, Bishop DeSmedt; all the professors; the four candidates for the doctorate; a very select audience; and seated above, a very select group of students.

The rector gave the opening remarks and then introduced me, since I was to give the main address about the political dimension of faith. When I took my place on the platform, the crowd greeted me with warm, seemingly endless applause, which naturally I appreciated very much. I said a few words that had been translated into Flemish for me, to tell them how sorry I was that I could not speak their language, but that I would speak the language of the poor of my country, whom I was there to represent. This effort to speak their language was received with more warm applause.

And so I began my speech in Spanish about the political dimension of faith, beginning with the poor. In summary I talked about what faith can do in the area of politics, the task of our archdiocese in its commitment to the country and, in the second part, how our faith becomes enormous, the mysteries become deeper through these same political realities when we are conscious of the preferential option for the poor. I talked for forty minutes and I could see that they were paying incredibly close attention. Even though I was speaking in Spanish, Father Juan had prepared a Flemish translation they were all following.

When I finished, the applause was extraordinary. I felt truly overwhelmed by their enthusiasm and the reception—especially by the youth of the University of Louvain, who encouraged the entire audience to keep applauding.

Then they continued the ceremony, awarding the doctoral cowls, reading to each one the citation praising them: a woman from South Africa, a literary figure; a medical doctor; an engineer; and me. I was also recognized in a special way by the public when the person presenting me—a monsignor whose name I cannot remember but who was very pleasant—spoke about me, about my life. They translated it into Spanish for me at another time, and it was very complimentary. When this presentation ended, as he had done with the others, the rector put the sign of the doctorate on me, the cowl, which was also applauded.

Finally the doctor, speaking on behalf of the four of us, expressed our gratitude. And then there was a cordial, lively reception for all of those attending, where I was able to greet many of the relatives of the priests and nuns who work in our diocese and many acquaintances from Latin America— a true celebration of the Spirit and of culture. Afterward we went to a typical room in the university, where they served a lunch to all those who were part of the university and their guests.

The greetings of all of these people especially were very encouraging. All of them told me that it had been a very timely message and that it had made many people think about the situation of our country and about the Christian and theological perspectives of our pastoral work. A theologian who had some reservations about liberation theology told me that he had understood many points he had not previously understood, and that he thought that Latin America truly has its own theology without its ceasing to be the theology of the Church. Many testimonies, especially from young people who feel the desire for a faith that is more committed to the realities of the country, etc. Thank God and the Virgin for this desire and the moral support that I have felt in these events.

It was already five o'clock in the afternoon, and some Salvadorans were waiting for me in Father Juan's room to share their concerns about our country. Afterward we went to Brussels for a meeting that had been organized with Latin Americans. There are about five thousand of them in Belgium, many in exile, others who are students. There was a very cordial atmosphere of questions and answers about the problems of Latin America, about the Church and especially about El Salvador. All of us were quite satisfied with such a cordial dialogue.

Finally, we went to have dinner at the home of an Uruguayan, a good friend of Father Juan, who lives with his wife and his family in one of the university residences. We were joined by another couple and another friend with whom we shared an interesting dialogue. And thus this very intense day finally ended around midnight. It is almost Sunday, February 3.

### Sunday, February 3

After Mass, celebrated with Father Juan and Father Chus in the chapel of the Latin American College and after seeing some visitors—a woman from Germany who has come especially to talk to me about the areas in which a German group in solidarity with El Salvador can help us, and a very old couple, a priest and an old woman who asked me to take a donation to Father Rosa and the others who studied in Belgium to help with whatever they wish—we left with Father Juan and Father Chus to go to the home of Father Juan Deplanck's family. I do not remember the name of the town where they live, but we had lunch there and greeted his family, which is very close, very numerous.

Afterward, we went to the motherhouse of the Sisters of St. Nicholas in another town in the very southern part of Belgium, where were gathered all the families of the priests and nuns who work in our archdiocese. The warm reception they gave me was very moving. So was the fellowship we shared first in the chapel, where we read a text from the Gospel about the mission of those sent by God to preach the gospel and a homily in which I tried to comment on the feelings that joined us there and our memory of far-away loved ones, the product of these families which are so close, so warm, so Christian. Later we shared a delicious snack during which we had another opportunity to greet one another and to have pictures taken in family groups. All in all, it was an unforgettable afternoon. It was heartening and of great Christian sense. I will take the memories of this afternoon back to our dear Belgian collaborators in the archdiocese.

It was already night when we started for Paris, where we have an intense schedule tomorrow. The route was very picturesque, in spite of the fact that it was raining. Everything was new for me—also our arrival in Paris. It is the first time that I have seen this beautiful city. Even though briefly, I have had the satisfaction of seeing it with my own eyes.

### Monday, February 4

We stayed in Paris, in the house of a community of Dominican priests whose superior organized the full day we will spend in Paris tomorrow. We celebrated Mass with the community, had breakfast and then began our work.

First we went to see the offices of INODEP,[296] an information and solidarity organization for the Latin American countries. We had a brief meeting there, in which we informed them about the situation in El Salvador and the relationship of the Church to this situation. I thanked them for what I know about this organization's efforts on behalf of the Salvadoran people.

Later, accompanied by Father Jardines, a pleasant young priest who speaks French and Spanish very well, we went to visit the secretary-general of the French bishops' conference. The secretary received me very graciously, and I was able to talk with him at length, to inform him about the situation of the country, about the situation of our Church. With fraternal frankness, I talked to him about the division that exists among our bishops. I asked the French conference to do something in a fraternal way to help with our problems among the bishops in El Salvador. He wrote down some information and will present it to the president, Cardinal Etchegaray of Marseilles. He placed a call to the cardinal, and I had the happy honor of talking with the cardinal, who speaks Spanish and who very cordially regretted not being able to see me in person. But he offered me all his help and said that he was truly very glad for my presence there in the office of the French bishops' conference.

Afterward we went to a meeting with Cardinal Marty,[297] who was extremely nice and a very interesting and effective man. He won my confidence by his very fraternal reception. I talked with him in depth about the problems with the bishops, about the nunciature, about my relationship with the Holy See. He promised to help me with everything, since he is good friends with Cardinal Lorscheider and Cardinal Pironio, whom I told him he could consult to get a more impartial view of what I was telling him. He indicated that he agrees with the progressive ideas of our archdiocese and he agrees with me on the matter of those who do not want to progress in the direction indicated by the Council. He told me that it was a problem for the entire Church, since all of us are concerned that the advances begun by the Second Vatican Council not be blocked, that there are many traditionalist groups in the Church who try to use the actions of the pope to justify a step backward—which is false, since the pope has always had a very great love for the Council and its advances. I felt great harmony with the cardinal's ideas and great hope in his promises to do something for our Salvadoran Church in his dealings with the Holy See.

---

[296] Ecumenical Institute for the Development of Peoples.
[297] François Marty, archbishop of Paris.

Later we went to have lunch with a group from Justice and Peace and other organizations in solidarity with our country. It was a lunch of some fifteen people, who were very interested in asking questions about our Salvadoran situation and about what they can do to show solidarity with us. I felt that this meeting was very useful because it offers much hope for our people.

We went afterward to a meeting of Amnesty International, a small office from which they do all their work of cooperation, solidarity, with other countries. We discussed the situation of the disappeared and what they can do to keep bringing up such a delicate subject and about other forms of repression against our people.

Then we went to an address that was a Catholic house, where we had a very interesting meeting with the press. There were some forty journalists from the most important newspapers in the country. I greeted them and gave them an outline of the current situation of the country and the role that the Church is playing. This began an interesting dialogue in which they asked about matters related to the country and the Church, in which I had the chance to clarify my ideas and thank them that they, with their marvelous news media, will get this information to the whole world. Father Jesús Delgado helped me a good deal, translating and adding several ideas.

After this meeting we went to the Church of St. Mierlie, where we held an ecumenical service with a Protestant minister who had come especially from Marseilles, where they had also wanted me to come had I had time. He very generously came and participated with me in this ecumenical celebration dedicated especially to the pastor and the archdiocese of San Salvador. There were songs, an appropriate reading from the Gospels, a commentary first by the minister, in which he praised the archbishop of San Salvador; then I gave a message in Spanish that a young woman translated as I spoke. The translation was very bad, and I felt that much of what I wanted to say was lost.

It was a summarized version of my speech at the University of Louvain—about what Christian faith can do in the service of the world and how the Christian faith is enriched as it receives from the world the reflection of what it cultivates in the world. Those who understood Spanish— almost everybody there—thanked me at the end for my message, which they seem to have appreciated. They mentioned the names of Aguilares, El Paisnal and all the names of these people and places of our archdiocese that have written pages of love for our Church.

After the ecumenical service I had the pleasure of greeting there several exiles from Latin America and many friends from El Salvador, with whom we had dinner at the community of the Dominican priests. It was already rather late when we started back to Louvain, and we arrived there at two o'clock in the morning.

 **Tuesday, February 5**

I have spent today almost entirely attending to different letters, messages and other documents which, because of the activity of the previous days, were all disorganized. In particular, with Father Jesús Delgado we organized the different economic contributions that have been given to us here for the needs of our Church. I also wrote letters of thanks and of excuse to all those groups who had organized a meeting for me which, for lack of time, I could not attend, since I had to shorten my trip and could not carry out the entire program Father Juan had originally planned.

Around three o'clock in the afternoon, along with Father Jesús and Father Juan, we communicated by telephone with the radio, where Monsignor Urioste in El Salvador interviewed us. We told him what had happened, my last moments in Rome, the doctorate at the University of Louvain and the different meetings with groups in Belgium and in France. When I spoke, I particularly emphasized the meetings with cardinals, bishops and other people who represent so much hope for our archdiocese.

There were also some visits or telephone calls that required more time. Around six in the evening we were in the Brussels airport to begin the return trip. Father Rogelio was there with his family and Jaime Meléndez, who works as a diplomat in this country, a Salvadoran who is greatly esteemed by many families. I left Father Jesús Delgado and Father Juan and, along with Father Rogelio, we went on the flight to Madrid.

At nine o'clock at night in Madrid, we arranged our continuing flight with Iberia, which leaves at one o'clock in the morning.

**Wednesday, February 6**

Today began very early, boarding at one o'clock in the morning the Iberia flight that was to take us during a very long night (since we are flying toward the west) to our America. The airplane trip in this seemingly endless night was pleasant—comfortable seats, a movie and also classical music through the headphones, reading or sleeping. And thus we arrived when it was still very early in Santo Domingo, where we had a short layover, and then we left for Panama, where we arrived at seven o'clock in the morning in America, seven hours later than the time in Europe.

In Panama I was able to speak on the telephone with Archbishop McGrath, who invited me to come greet the other bishops who were at a meeting of the social action section of CELAM. It was a meeting of several bishops from Central America, Mexico and the Caribbean. There I had the opportunity to greet (besides Archbishop McGrath) Bishop Rivera, Bishop Flores, another Guatemalan bishop, another Mexican bishop, Bishop Vega from Nicaragua and several other bishops who are involved in social action work in different countries. The president of this CELAM commission is Bishop Bambarén. I was unable to talk to him because he was not there, but I would have greeted him with great pleasure, since he came personally to El Salvador to invite Bishop Rivera to this meeting. I also learned about Father Pedro L'Eclair's pastoral work in Panama and that he will be coming to El Salvador soon.

From Panama, after a short wait, we flew to Costa Rica, then to Managua, where Fathers Plácido, Piquín and Paco boarded the plane. There was a problem that forced us to wait longer than scheduled. We were two hours late; we arrived in El Salvador at four o'clock in the morning instead of two o'clock as scheduled. I was sorry for the people who were waiting for us and who received us so warmly.

It makes a strong impression on me to return to the country after a period in which, given the intensity of our history, there are many events and changes—about which Father Urrutia, who had come to meet me with other friends, began to tell me on the forty-five minute drive back from the new airport to the Divine Providence Hospital.

Here I found a huge quantity of mail. The joy of the sisters who met me, the first little comments—how pleasant it is to return home after being gone for a period of days! Nevertheless, the worries have begun. Already some letters have to do with the kidnapping of Mr. Dunn. I also received telephone calls from the Spanish Embassy, which is occupied by the

Popular Leagues of February 28, and other calls that show me the necessity of my staying here in my post unless there is a compelling reason to leave.

 **Thursday, February 7**

I have spent almost all morning meeting with the vicars general and the chancellors in order to find out about the activities of the chancery. At the same time, this has permitted us to analyze the political atmosphere found in our Church. I am satisfied with the loyalty and the industry with which my closest collaborators have been exercising the authority of the diocese during my absence.

I received a call from the ambassador of Spain, who is a hostage in his own embassy, which is occupied by the Popular Leagues of February 28. I tried to give him courage and I promised to go visit him. At the same time the person in charge of the occupation, Mr. Argueta, talked to me. He said that he also wanted to talk to me in person to clarify certain things and thought that the call from the ambassador might have confused me about the internal situation in that embassy. I promised I would go visit him.

I also communicated with the presidential palace to greet Colonel Majano, who expressed his cordial congratulations for the honor of the doctorate that I had received in Louvain, and who also commented on the way that the media has twisted this news and my interviews on the radio as well. He told me that he had realized during the time he has been in the government the ways in which our media misuse the news, slanting it in favor of the oligarchy that controls that media. He told me that he would come to see me very soon. I told him that he already knew the time we preferred, which was to have lunch together.

Twice today the ambassador of Italy and the special ambassador from Spain came to talk about the occupation of the Spanish embassy. They told me about their efforts to negotiate with the Popular Leagues and with the government. The situation is even more difficult since there is little information about what the National Guard is doing in its military operations or why the Ministry of Defense will not clarify this. I expressed to them my willingness to intercede, always in the character of my position, in whatever way I can in the embassy as well as with the popular organizations, although not everything is within my power. Nevertheless, I have sensed a respect that could cause them to listen to me and which I could use to alleviate the conditions that the hostages are suffering in the Spanish embassy.

There were requests for newspaper interviews from foreign journalists who are in the country—some from Argentina by telephone and from Spain, also by telephone. But, since I am not well informed about what has happened during the days I was gone, I thought that it was wiser not to do them and to postpone them all until after Mass this next Sunday, when we will have a press conference as usual.

 **Friday, February 8**

At breakfast I met with the Jesuit provincial, Father Jerez; the two Jesuits, Ellacuría and Estrada; Father Fabián Amaya; Father Cristóbal Cortés; Father Rafael Urrutia; and Licenciado Roberto Cuéllar, who is in charge of the Legal Aid Office, in order to analyze the political reality of the country and talk about what is the best approach for the Church to take. It was a frank meeting, very enriching, in which we analyzed the role played at this moment by the government, the Christian Democrats, the popular political organizations and especially the very closed reaction of the extreme right and of its armed groups that are doing many bad things, causing such violence.

I took notes so that in this way I can explain in the next homily the situation of our Church, which always has to be that of announcing the Kingdom of God; of supporting all that is positive in the myriad political and military attitudes; also of denouncing the abuse of human rights and of looking for ways out other than by violence, while denouncing the different kinds of violence and evaluating them fairly and judging them from the perspective of the Kingdom of God—which is not of a political character and does not support any particular political project, but is rather the illumination of faith for justice based on our faith and our Christian sentiments.

Again I received a visit from the ambassadors of Spain and Italy, who are somewhat depressed because their meetings with the highest levels of government have been effectively blocked by the lack of information from the security forces. And they think that the demands of the Popular Leagues of February 28 with respect to the captures and disappearances will not be resolved; this will mean that this siege at the embassy will continue until they get better information. They asked me to try to influence the Leagues so that they will leave the embassy. They also promise to continue working. They realize the need for extraordinary means in a situation in which so little importance is given to the human rights that are justly demanded by these organizations, but there are eight lives in the embassy—not that they are in danger of violence, but, yes, through their discomfort and being deprived of their freedom.

I have spent the afternoon organizing a great deal of correspondence that arrived during my absence. I am going to begin to assemble the notes I will use for my next homily.

### Saturday, February 9

The special activity today was the dinner meeting to get information for my homily. Father Fabián gave me a good summary of the outlines of the three political projects that are proposed in El Salvador: the government plan, that of the popular political organizations and that of the right. We have grouped the different acts of violence—there have been many this week—around these three groups, and the possibilities for a solution without the necessity of resorting to violent armed rebellion, which would be terrible if it should break out in El Salvador. I worked until late in the evening, organizing my notes. And I got up very early to find the best way to explain the situation of the country and the role of the Church, inspired by the readings for this Sunday that speak to us precisely of the God of history who calls for human beings to collaborate with God in building the history of each people.

### Sunday, February 10

During the Mass, which was held at the basilica because the cathedral continues to be occupied, I received a warm reception after my trip. I felt a special affection in that church, which was very full; the crowd continued to swell as the Mass progressed. The homily went on for almost two hours. I think I may be going on too long, but I feel, even so, the need to guide these people, who are listening to me avidly. I talk for so long precisely because I do not see my audience tiring; they seem always attentive. I hear that they also follow the radio broadcast with the same attention.

After Mass I had a press conference, principally with foreign journalists from Latin America and Europe. There was not much for them to ask since, as they themselves said, everything had already been said in the homily. Nevertheless, it was a very cordial moment in which I felt myself a friend of the journalists. There was also a large crowd standing around this meeting, enjoying the dialogue to which they, the common people, also contributed some interesting comments. The homily was broadcast at a later hour because the recording was made and then taken to the radio station, since it is more difficult to broadcast directly from the basilica.

I went to have lunch and spend the afternoon with the sisters from the hospital, who came to the house of the Oblate Sisters of Divine Love, and with the sisters from the Colegio de la Sagrada Familia, who also came. We enjoyed a very nice familial atmosphere, which strengthens our efforts for a Church that, in its difficult struggles, must also feel the tenderness of the love God has always given us in order to strengthen our work for the Kingdom.

 **Monday, February 11**

I went to celebrate the patronal feast of the village of Lourdes in the parish of Colón. The church was filled to overflowing, and there was a warm reception for their pastor. I preached about Our Lady of Lourdes, presenting her as a symbol for the Church, and how what had happened in Lourdes between the Virgin and Bernadette showed the exact role that the Church should have with human beings: to bring humankind closer to God to pray, to make them see their mission—to make the commitment God shows to each human being and to live it. The Virgin tells Bernadette what her mission is and to carry out the work of the Church in conjunction with its pastors. The Virgin tells Bernadette to tell the priests that she wants a church built on that spot.

Using these three ideas, I exhorted the congregation to be obedient to the Church and to build, together with their pastors, the Church our diocese wants to have so that it may be the true Church of Jesus Christ. Father Nicolás Menjivar, the parish priest, opportunely and generously read to the people the reasons for my being awarded an honorary doctoral degree at Louvain and asked them to show their solidarity with the bishop, which they expressed through very warm applause. The same thing happened at the end of Mass, when I asked the people for testimonies of their sense of being Church. I could feel a great spirit in the expressions of solidarity and communion which these Catholics live.

In the afternoon I received a visit from the ambassador of Nicaragua who, besides coming to greet me, invited me to go to his country to learn at first hand of the interesting experiment taking place there.[298] I expressed my wish to go there to see Archbishop [Miguel] Obando [Bravo] and also to take advantage of the opportunity to know what he was offering me.

Dr. Jiménez also came, a former Venezuelan politician who had been at the Sunday Mass and who expressed his appreciation for my ministry, which, without losing its spiritual nature, is also trying to orient the politics of the country so that it may develop according to God's plan. He was very frank and mentioned to me some points in which he wished that the Church would give more support to the Christian Democrats in their efforts to save the country. I told him that I agreed, but that, above all, I want to be true to my people and demand of a democracy what the people demand of it—the kind of democracy which is possible today—especially by making the army end its repression, which is so violent against our poor people.

There was also an engineer who came to tell me that his office had been occupied by the Popular Leagues; he asked me to intervene. I did this through the Legal Aid Office. Licenciado Cuéllar will go there to mediate and to offer the archdiocese for this negotiation.

The seminarian Miguel Rodríguez also came. His family has been a victim of this repression in the Department of La Unión, where they live. His mother has been an example of Christian strength, but the suffering of his family is very great. I have offered him all the help of the Legal Aid Office and have asked him to give me the details of this attack so that I can denounce it, as is my duty.

In the evening I went to visit the Chacón family and share with them these human feelings of being family, feelings so necessary in these times of great tension.

 **Tuesday, February 12**

The morning began with a visit at the hospital from Ingeniero Villacorta, the undersecretary of agriculture, who very graciously gave me a copy of the agrarian reform plan he has developed along with his assistants at the ministry. He explained to me some of the more difficult points. He brought this document to me because he wants to

---

[298] The Sandinista revolution.

know the Church's reaction to it, especially in relation to Christian social doctrine. I told him that I would study it with my advisers. We discussed at length how difficult such a step is, but how crucial it is for the Christian Democrats to determine whether or not the armed forces are in favor of the transformation of the country that would be required.

Afterward, Don Ernesto Rivas Gallont was waiting for me in the archdiocesan offices, along with the son of the former ambassador from South Africa, Mr. Dunn, to talk about the proposal to be presented to the FPL in the matter of the kidnapping of Mr. Dunn, which is being negotiated.

Mr. Rivas Gallont and Mr. Dunn's son authorized me to tell Mr. Dunn's kidnappers that they are making an intense appeal in South Africa to collect funds so that they can ransom Mr. Dunn, but that they cannot give them any more than they can collect, since the family personally is poor and they do not have the support of the government in this. Mr. Dunn's kidnappers will come to see me this week in my role as mediator in this painful matter of the kidnapping.

There were a great number of visits from priests and laity at the chancery, while in the meeting room there was a dialogue taking place between the owners and workers of one of the factories that is having conflicts and strikes. The archdiocesan offices are being used for many negotiations, which shows the reputation that it has for impartiality and justice.

The most important meeting today was the one that we had with Father Octavio Cruz in his role as head of the Pastoral Commission. I was quite satisfied with the information he has given me about the intense work he is doing to promote the pastoral work.

The principal event was the course held by the Christian base communities in Domus Mariae and preparation to participate in another meeting of these communities in Brazil. There was also activity related to the different groups in the seminary and other aspects of our pastoral work. I was interested in what Father Octavio told me about the spiritual and cultural formation of the priests, who perhaps feel they are very poor, humanly speaking, for having neglected their efforts at aggiornamento.[299]

Also interesting was the meeting with Dr. Mario Levy, who commented on different aspects of the pastoral direction of my pastoral letter and certain inconsistencies he finds when it deals with the political groups of the left. His letter is very interesting, and I began to comment on it in the radio program we taped this afternoon for tomorrow's program. We talked specifically about how the people must be organized—not

---

[299] Bringing up to date; a term associated with Vatican II.

necessarily belonging to one organization or another, especially if it is not good for the people, but, yes, to awaken the critical faculties of the people, so that they will cease being merely part of the mass and can be a people organized for the common good.

I also received an emergency visit from Rubén Zamora and another member of the Christian Democratic Party to tell me about the most serious event today. A group of students celebrating the victory won in the Ministry of Education was holding a demonstration, which was broken up violently by certain elements of the right along with the army, which followed the disbanded crowd until it entered the Christian Democrats' building, which is occupied by the Popular Leagues of February 28. There gunfire left several dead and many wounded.

The committee of Christian Democrats came to ask me to give asylum in the seminary to two women, members of the Leagues who were occupying the Christian Democrats' headquarters, who came out in the guise of liberated hostages. One of these women saw her own husband fall dead during the gunfire and is extremely nervous. We managed to arrange for them to go to the Colegio de la Sagrada Familia. Because they are women, it would be difficult to give them lodging in the seminary, which is in session.

In the evening I received a visit from a journalist who wanted an interview for a magazine in Argentina. We talked at length about the situation of the country, the role of the Church and some personal information about me.

 **Wednesday, February 13**

I talked during breakfast with Father Ramón Vega, whom I had invited so that we might talk about matters concerning the social secretariat. He explained a series of problems to me and I see that it is progressing in a direction that is good for our diocese. He is managing to get intellectuals who belonged to the association of university students, many of whom are professionals today; we hope that they will collaborate with a Christian consciousness. I told him that sometime I would come to those meetings and that I always count on the advice, which is so necessary for me, so that I can respond as Church in such significant moments in our history.

Immediately afterward, Dr. Rubén Zamora arrived to tell me about the bloody events of yesterday—how they had dislodged the members of the

Popular Leagues who were holding several people hostage in the headquarters of the Christian Democratic Party, and how this military operation, which left so many victims, took place against the wishes of the government, who had expressly ordered the Minister of Defense not to proceed militarily to dislodge them. He told me horrible things that the security forces had done, and how since last night they have been analyzing within their party what they should do: of course, to ask for the firing of the present defense minister and, as a party, to bring more pressure on the army. And some are even talking about pulling out of the government. The matter is very delicate, but it is time to take measures that truly show they want an end to the cruel repression in the country.

I had agreed to grant several audiences in the chancery but, in addition to the ones scheduled, there were several unexpected visits that I attended to as well as I could. The vicars, the chancellors helped a great deal in seeing many of the people who come in such critical circumstances in the politics of the country.

After lunch I spent the afternoon studying. In the evening there was an interesting meeting of the major seminary, in which they expressed to me their doubts, their concerns in a frank dialogue. I think that I tried to resolve them and that they were satisfied and will continue to work for the formation of the kind of priests that the Church needs at this time. It was satisfying to find myself surrounded by these twenty-one young theologians and philosophers who truly represent the hope of the Church.

 **Thursday, February 14**

A brief interview after breakfast with the vicars general, Monsignor Urioste, who has returned from a brief vacation, and Father Cortés, who informed me of some of the activity in the chancery in my absence. We tried to evaluate our work and we found a lack of communication; because of this, some decisions are made more than once or contradicted. Monsignor Urioste told me with fraternal candor that many times my attitude seems to countermand something that the vicars general have decided and that this interferes with the functioning of their authority. I recognize this, but I stressed that we need better communication. Therefore we have decided that every day at eight o'clock we will meet to see together what must be done in the diocese. This brief and unexpected meeting seems to me to have been very useful.

I went immediately afterward to Domus Mariae and in Sister María's house, as I had promised before my trip, I met with those priests who have been identified as being most linked with the left. I had a very fruitful conversation with them. This meeting today has also brought us closer together, for many times it seems that we are separated and that there is more danger, when really they are making sincere pastoral and priestly efforts.

At the same time, I used the opportunity to express my fears and to insist that, amid the fluctuations of politics and of our affinity for the popular political organizations, we truly be signs of the Kingdom of God, because this is why we are in the Church: to give witness of a transcendent presence amid our work on earth. They offered their comments, according to the gospel, on this thinking. I will continue to ask God for them to be, as the bishop of Brugge said to me in Belgium, not enemies or victims, but true collaborators.

In the afternoon, an interesting meeting with representatives of the popular organizations. There was one representative of the UDN political party and another from the Popular Leagues of February 28. The other two, FAPU and the Popular Revolutionary Bloc, could not come, because they were delayed at the last minute—possibly because the funerals of the victims of yesterday's repression were at the same time.

But this conversation with the two representatives of the political groups, which I took part in for the Church along with Father Moreno and Monsignor Urioste, was fruitful. I had the chance to express my concerns and to point out the areas of competence of the Church, to defend the Christian sentiments of the people, and to search, all of us, as true Salvadorans, for the most peaceful and honorable solution to this crisis in our country.

We agreed to continue these meetings and that the Church would offer its services without ever losing its identity as Church. We ask especially that they hurry efforts to have a plan of government that comes from the people and that is presented to the people to solidify the people in these organizations. In such a project the Church can offer a double service—to illuminate with the gospel the technical areas that are not its areas of expertise and to judge the humanistic aspects according to evangelical principles. On another level, to the religious and human aspects (for example, how religion is looked at), to the element of justice in this new project, the Church could bring all the richness of its teaching. At the same time, I said that it must be clear that we would not take part as a political force, but rather as Church, with the light of the gospel. It seems that this clarification was beneficial and that there is a new aspect to our relationship with these organizations.

In the evening, a brief interview which had been announced with a representative of one of the underground organizations, with whom I am negotiating the release of a hostage and, at the same time, trying to shine the light of the gospel on activities that many times are not in harmony with Christian thinking. I felt that my message was received and that, because of this representative, my message will also reach the whole organization through its leaders.

 **Friday, February 15**

As I had promised, at eight o'clock in the morning I was at the meeting with those who are responsible for the chancery so that we may have better communication and a more communitarian governance. That was the topic for today's meeting: to see what weaknesses we are suffering from and what we can do to correct them. Several concrete topics surfaced which, if we look at them as a group, we can resolve much more intelligently and permanently. Afterward an intense number of visits, some scheduled and others impromptu.

A group of young people came from Sonsonate[300] to ask me to bless a clinic there and celebrate Mass. I thanked them for their kindness and promised to visit them privately on another occasion. They insisted that I come to the inauguration of the clinic. I told them that for that they must ask permission from their diocese; they agreed to let me know. This points up the wisdom of the Church in dividing its territory and also the esteem of the people, which I cannot reject but should guide.

In the afternoon there were several visits in spite of none being scheduled. Given the immense number of problems, occupations, hostages and similar cases, they must be attended to without delay.

---

[300] In the Diocese of Santa Ana.

## Saturday, February 16

Today, although I wanted to spend the whole day on the preparation of my sermon for Sunday, I had to go to the cathedral in the morning to carry out a commitment to bless the image of San Rafael that will be taken to the village of the same name in Candelaria Parish in Cuscatlán. It will be received there by Father Interiano. I did not want to deny this petition from the humble peasants, since in them I always feel the presence and the call of God.

This gave me the opportunity to talk with those who are in charge of the occupation of the cathedral, two young people who belong to a sector of the Popular Revolutionary Bloc. They are Christians, but feel obliged to carry out these actions because they do not see any safety outside the church. It involves housing there a number of peasants, many of them women and children, who have fled from small villages in the territory of Las Vueltas in Chalatenango, where the National Guard and ORDEN persecute them cruelly. Others have had to flee to the hills and these have taken refuge in the cathedral.

I told them that I understood all of that, that the Church always offers this kind of hospitality and that it was not necessary to occupy it as they were doing. And I asked them to put me in touch with the leaders of the Bloc so I could talk to them about the occupation of churches, since Lent will be starting soon and the people have a right to their places of prayer. By talking with the Church, they can find other ways of achieving the ends for which they are occupying the churches.

In the evening I got still another visit about a labor situation in which there has been conflict. Specifically, two organizations, the Popular Revolutionary Bloc and FAPU, are working against each other instead of trying to work together to help in the case of a factory that is closed but is in the process of reopening. An occupation by the other organization has blocked this process. I will denounce this and call for order tomorrow in my homily, God willing.

In the afternoon I went to Guazapa for a most unusual service celebrated in the parish convent itself, where the Carmelite Sisters live. Today they have changed their position but with their same religious goals, for they have separated from their order, the Carmelites of St. Joseph, and have begun—five of them—a house in which they will serve the people in a pastoral way and still carry out their religious commitments but without ties to their former order.

All of this has been done in an orderly way and, although the order perhaps does not completely understand this step, I sense that the people have understood it very well, and that if they are truly faithful to their present goals, they can do great good even as regards the religious life itself, bringing it closer to the people and making it more appealing in their midst. In fact, they told me that several young women want to join their group, but that they want to proceed prudently, insisting on all the things that the gospel requires for a religious life. We held, then, a very intimate Mass with the relatives of these new sisters, along with the community that cooperates in the pastoral work. It was a very understanding atmosphere of much prayer, much reflection. For me it also provided enrichment through the Spirit of the Lord.

I went back to prepare my homily, listening to the counsel of those who met with me today: Father Moreno, Miss Doris Osegueda, Licenciado Cuéllar, Father Cortés and Father Urrutia. They give me very valuable help to learn more about the events of the week and how to illuminate them evangelically through my Sunday homily. I have worked until the early hours of the morning, and it is already Sunday, February 17.

 ## Sunday, February 17

The homily lasted for an hour and forty-five minutes. I talked about poverty, using the guidelines of the Medellín document, presenting it as a denunciation of the injustice of the world; as a spirit that is lived, relying on God; and as a commitment, that of Jesus Christ, who committed himself to the poor. And from this, the Church also carries out the mission of Christ to call all people to salvation. And with the light of the Beatitudes, which were read today in the Gospel,[301] I illuminated the reality of the country to condemn the selfishness of the rich who insist on maintaining their privilege and also to give direction, beginning from the needs of the poor, to the politics of the country. It has been greatly discussed, because in the evening I was with the Jesuits at the Central American University, to take them some mail, and I found a very warm reception there—along with some other laypersons who had also heard it.

In the afternoon—rather, at seven o'clock in the evening—I went to Santa Lucía, a parish in the territory of Ilopango, where the new parish priest, Father Luis Recinos, was being installed. He has come from Nicaragua to continue his studies here, and he will provide us with this pastoral service, attending to the parish of Santa Lucía, since the former

---

[301] Luke 6:17, 20-26.

pastor, Father Astor Ruíz, was unable to get back into the country and has been working precisely in Nicaragua. So there was an exchange of priests, someone who left Santa Lucía for Nicaragua and someone coming from there to Santa Lucía. It was also a very pastoral moment, talking with the different committees, encouraging them to continue, congratulating them because in the year they have been without a priest they have shown themselves to be a truly Christian community.

After I returned from this Mass, I delivered the secret letter that the family of the kidnapped Mr. Dunn sends to his kidnappers through this secret connection.

 **Monday, February 18**

In the meeting that we are now used to having during the first hour of work, we analyzed some points about the priests and their assignments in the parishes. We concluded that it must be studied at a deeper level, together with the Priests' Senate and the Pastoral Commission. But, since it deals with a rather confidential matter, we will choose one or two people from each of these groups to study in a conscientious way the situation of our clergy with the goal of locating each of them in the most appropriate place, given their qualities.

Afterward we had a meeting of the Priests' Senate, which was very interesting in that it dealt with current events, such as the occupations of churches and the problem of violence in the country.

In regard to the occupation of churches, there was a great deal of discussion about the expediency of writing a document about what the Church thinks so that all of us might see this from the same perspective. But they thought that it would be more timely to take direct action with those who cause the occupations. Those priests who have most contact with the organizations were asked to get the leaders of these groups to engage in dialogue with me to talk about how to keep these occupations from occurring—or so that, in a case of urgent necessity, they may happen after previous agreement with the person responsible for the church.

In the afternoon, another very important meeting in the Catholic University center with the administrative board, the vicars general, the administrator of the chancery, Ingeniero Galván, and the person in charge of the center, Father Ramón Vega. In that very place where Archbishop Chávez planned to build the archdiocesan office and the archbishop's residence, we studied whether this work should be continued or if it would be preferable, as we have thought recently, to build it next to San José de la Montaña Seminary. This latter opinion prevailed after lengthy discussion.

As for the place that had previously been designated for that, it was agreed to build the warehouse for Cáritas there and also the church that is a condition for that donation. Father Ramón Vega was in charge of asking for a subsidy from the appropriate organization to help us with both construction projects. As for the construction of the archdiocesan offices on the seminary land, it was reduced a great deal to a simpler structure. There is hope of receiving subsidies from some foreign institutions, added to the money that we already have from the sale of some of the seminary land during Archbishop Chávez's time, which was earmarked for this project: the residence of the archbishop and the archdiocesan offices.

In the evening Father Estrada and Father Ellacuría came to find me to tell me that last Sunday's homily has caused a furor in Rome and that the Father General of the Jesuits communicated to them—that is, to the Central American provincial—the comments that are being made in the Secretariat of State itself. Tonight they will talk with Father Jerez, who is in Panama, so that if it is necessary he will go to Rome to explain the situation and show how the words of the homily are appropriate to the difficult situation of El Salvador.

Specifically, the letter to be sent to the president of the United States, which was read during the homily and which seems to be the principal motive for these comments, is inspired by the increasing danger that is represented by the military aid to El Salvador, especially, the new concept of special warfare, which consists in eliminating in a murderous way all the efforts of the popular organizations, using the pretext of communism or terrorism. This kind of war purports to do away not only with the people directly responsible but also with their families who, according to this theory, are totally poisoned by these terrorist concepts and must be eliminated. The danger, then, is great, and the letter is to ask the president of the United States *not* to send military aid that would mean great injury to our people because it would mean the destruction of many lives.

## Tuesday, February 19

They awakened me with an urgent telephone call from Sister Maria from Domus Mariae to tell me that a bomb had gone off in the base of the YSAX transmitter and that it has been completely destroyed. I asked if there were any injuries; I am glad that the damages were only of a material nature that can be repaired.

Tonight at the same hour, around eleven o'clock, another bomb exploded in the library of the UCA. Obviously, these are plots of the extreme right against the voice of the Church and against the calls for social justice.

In the chancery many priests and laity came to express their solidarity after the attack on our radio station and to offer now, from the beginning, their help to get it back in operation soon. Bishop Rivera also expressed his solidarity when, at eleven-thirty, we had a meeting of the bishops at the nunciature. None of my other brother bishops mentioned this matter of the radio station, nor did any of them mention my honorary doctoral degree or any other aspect of our archdiocese except to criticize it, always implying that the pastoral direction is in error.

The meeting was called by the nuncio on behalf of the Sacred Congregation for Bishops which, in the name of His Holiness, has declared the election of the president of the bishops' conference invalid and tells us to hold a new election, but after having reflected and prayed. The nuncio commented on some other things and got us to agree to meet next Tuesday for a spiritual retreat in the morning and to hold the elections in the afternoon. The atmosphere of these meetings always seems to me very cold and very strange. I chose not to say anything, since everything that I say is misinterpreted because of the ill will that, without a doubt, exists on the part of some of my brother bishops. We had lunch at the nunciature.

In the afternoon I expected the seminarians, since I have offered to spend my Tuesdays continuing this interesting dialogue with the future priests. And I ended the work day at the home of the Godoy sisters, where they gave me dinner with all the affection this family can offer.

I also had a visit from the ambassador of Spain, who has been freed and is no longer a hostage in the embassy, along with the state secretary for Latin America, who had come from Spain because of this problem, and the Italian ambassador. We talked very amiably with all three of them, and with a great sense of solidarity for our diocese and gratitude for our collaboration in the problem of the occupation of the embassy.

**Wednesday, February 20**

Today has been an extremely full day. The archdiocesan offices are increasingly crowded with the people who come to visit, who want advice, who come for meetings. The vitality is noticeable, and I thank God for it. We had our meeting at the chancery with the vicars general and the chancellors to examine some areas with great frankness. I think that every day this meeting is more useful, although I said that we should be more punctual and efficient. I put Father Rafael in charge of setting the agenda and of being sure that the meeting is always held, even though someone may be absent.

Among the visits I had a meeting with the press at about eleven-thirty, in which there were journalists from the United States, Switzerland, Germany, France. It was an impromptu thing but rich in questions and in orientation from the archdiocese.

Also Miss Marta Benavides, a member of an ecumenical group who is very active, came to offer all her help. I asked her to help us in the area of social communication. She accepted this idea gladly and has begun to do so with great interest.

In the afternoon I went to meet with the seminarians of Santa Tecla, who are doing their propaedeutic year. After explaining to them the purpose of this year and the hope that we have in them, we carried on a lengthy dialogue. With great frankness, I asked them to consider me more of a friend than an authority figure. There was a very cordial atmosphere, trust that enabled them to express their dreams, the joy of finding themselves in this new experience in the seminary, as well as their fears for the future. I have promised them that what has begun openly cannot become closed; rather, taking into account the suggestions, the constructive criticism, we will continue improving with them the formation of the future priest.

After having dinner with them, I went to the Sacred Heart Basilica where, in a very solemn service with a large crowd, I celebrated the beginning of Lent and distributed the ashes after inviting the people, as the representatives of the entire archdiocese, to walk with their pastor in this pilgrimage of sanctification, of austerity, that leads us to Easter, so that we can offer the country a renewed Church in Lent, with new men and women who can be the true, authentic liberators of the people. After Mass, there were journalists who were still interested in talking; it was also interesting.

It was nine o'clock at night and, when I got to the hospital, I had two important commitments: one with Father Estrada, Father Ellacuría and a banking expert who wanted to explain to me a project related to the agrarian reform and the problem of the banks.[302] I listened to him attentively, but I told him that it involved technical matters and that I could only ask him to continue developing his ideas so that later we can compare them with other projects, principally those proposed by the people. What is needed today are concrete projects; because of this, I offered him my congratulations and my hope that he will always work with such enthusiasm in this kind of collaboration with our people.

The other meeting was an impromptu one with the National Coordinating Commission of the Popular Organizations,[303] which was to meet today with some of the young military officers, but they were unable to come. Nevertheless, this contact with the leaders of the organizations was fruitful, although we did not talk about anything in depth. We agreed to meet tomorrow with different sectors of the Church to talk about some aspects of the relationship between the Church and the popular political organizations.

 **Thursday, February 21**

After Mass the day began with breakfast with Father Ramón Vega to talk about matters related to the Social Action Office and problems having to do with Caritas.

After that, a meeting of the Pastoral Commission in the chancery. In my opinion, it is the most important committee in the diocese, since it helps me to coordinate the different activities of the vicariates of the archdiocese and to guide our pastoral work based on its suggestions. Father Octavio Cruz, as secretary-general, is giving great impetus to this office, as is the layman, Francisco Cuéllar.

I could not stay for the whole meeting because at ten-thirty in the morning I had a meeting with a representative of the United States government, who is representing U.S. interests in El Salvador until the new ambassador[304] arrives. The principal topic of the meeting was to talk about my letter, sent this last Sunday to President Carter, president of the United

---

[302] A program of land reform and nationalization of the banks to be announced on March 1.

[303] The CRM, *Coordinadora Revolucionaria de Masas*, an executive committee of the popular organizations formed in January 1980.

[304] Robert E. White.

States. The representative told me that, in the first place, the president had not received the letter, which has been widely distributed worldwide. He wanted to talk to me about the principal purpose of the letter, which had to do with military aid to El Salvador—explaining to me that it was not to put weapons in the hands of the security forces but rather to improve some aspects in which the army is still deficient, and other explanations of this kind.

I then tried to answer this, telling him that my letter was based on information that I had received and that I had made my comments with respect to this information. And that I was still afraid that military aid, even of the kind that he explained to me, would cause greater repression of the people, since it is the Minister of Defense himself who directs both sectors of the military institution and that, no matter how much I was told that it was not for the armed forces, this aid (in the amount of five million U.S. dollars, no less) could end up there, in more arms and greater repression of the people.

And with respect to the influence of the United States in this country's politics, I told him that aid to the government, which does not enjoy popular support, would be interpreted by the people as an imposition; and that what we would most appreciate would be for them to push for the process in which the people have already made a great deal of progress and not to impede it by imposing another way that is not what the people are building as creators of their own destiny.

There were other topics as well. The most important idea was that the ambassador should suggest that this military aid be conditioned on beginning to carry out the reforms that have been announced so many times and the elimination of the repressive tendencies that obviously prevail in the present government.

Another visit of great importance was that from Catholic Relief Services to offer me help with the emergency needs that could arise in El Salvador and to talk with me about other aspects of the cooperation between that institution from the United States and our archdiocesan Caritas.

In the afternoon I went with Father Alliet to visit the sisters in Quezaltepeque and Father Roberto, all of them Belgian, to convey to them greetings from my recent trip to Belgium. I am very pleased that these priests and nuns are doing such good for a people in such great need. Unfortunately, that is where there is the controversy with Father Quinteros, who lives in an outrageous way and continues usurping the convent and the church. But Father Roberto has managed to make the chapel of the school run by the Dominican Sisters the center of the parish life.

On the way back, we also visited Sister María, who is in charge of Domus Mariae, where I was able to see in person the tremendous damage done by the bomb that destroyed the transmitter base of our radio station YSAX, the Pan American Voice.

Returning from this trip around four-thirty, there was a meeting scheduled at the seminary with the National Coordinating Committee of the popular political organizations. Among the agenda items, we decided to begin the discussion with the occupation of the churches. First, the organizations explained the reasons why they occupy churches; immediately afterward, the priests, mainly those from El Rosario Church and the one from El Calvario Church, explained the disturbance those occupations cause in the life of the parish. And then we discussed whether we could reach some kind of agreement so that these occupations will not cause the problems they do and still have the same effect the organizations say this tactic has—that is, for pressure, for self-defense and for denouncing injustice.

Another meeting late in the evening with a member of the FPL, the Popular Liberation Forces, a secret organization which we fear greatly (they have carried out several kidnappings). But we have been able to enter into dialogue with them for the purpose of expressing the views and the thinking of the Church and to make them understand that the respect for these Christian sentiments of the majority of the people would be a necessary condition for them to have the popularity they lack now, when they are attacking these feelings.

 **Friday, February 22**

On this Feast of the Chair of St. Peter we celebrate the third anniversary of my taking over as archbishop. The priests remembered the date and told me that they wanted to celebrate it. I told them that I was willing to do so eucharistically, celebrating Mass with them at noon. And so this commemoration was organized—an anniversary that calls up, above all, a great sense of responsibility and a great sense of prayer.

Before Mass, we spent the morning in reflection with a team analyzing the political situation of the country. There was a professor from the Central American University along with the rector of the same university; Father Estrada also; the priests Urioste, Fabián Amaya, Cortés, Urrutia; Father

Moreno and Bachiller Cuéllar. We ate breakfast together discussing the topic.

The meeting was held in the dining room of the Divine Providence Hospital, in spite of having been planned for the Santa Eugenia House in Planes de Renderos. The change was at the request of Mr. Héctor Dada, member of the governing junta, who wanted to be able to meet with us because he had a message for us from the junta itself.

The topic was presented by the expert and commented on by all of us. A pre-revolutionary situation exists in El Salvador, but it is progressing rapidly toward a revolutionary phase. The message brought by Mr. Héctor Dada, representing the government junta, was to ask the Church to use the power of its words to ask the left for a truce—a truce to give the government time to carry out its projects for transformation.

We analyzed this request from the government and said that it was not the Church but rather the people who should negotiate this truce with the government; and that the government ought to try to get popular support and not impose reforms, especially if the people have realized that it is with the support of a foreign power, such as the United States. As for us, we want nothing more than to cooperate with transformations that will benefit the poor, but we cannot ignore the fact that the people and the popular leftist organizations cannot cooperate with a project in which there is, at the same time, the reality of repression. And we asked that the saner part of the government—for instance, the goodwill of the Christian Democrats, represented by Mr. Dada and Dr. Morales Ehrlich—help to create this credibility for the government by removing all of its repressive aspects.

On the other hand, we said that it is not only the left that should be asked for a truce, for it is the right that is the principal source of violence at this time, and it can be controlled by the government and thus kept from provoking violence from the left. In other words, we discussed a very important topic with total frankness, and it took the whole morning for all to have a chance to express themselves freely.

At noon we went to the basilica for the concelebration of the third anniversary of my becoming archbishop. The ceremony was very fervent, intimate. There were not many people, but there were representatives from the different communities in the archdiocese—a good number of priests and nuns, who celebrated with true fervor and affection.

The homily was given by Father Cristóbal Cortés, who was very generous in his praise—above all in talking about the teaching of the pastoral letters, which he analyzed as the expression of the archbishop's ideas and of the pastoral direction of the archdiocese. Afterward, very affectionate greetings upon leaving the church. The seminarians in the different preparatory classes for priests gave a note of joy and hope to the celebration.

In the afternoon I went to visit the Belgian congregations of Cojutepeque and Santa Cruz Michapa. In the evening I had a visit from the secretary-general of an organization against torture, which has its headquarters in Milan, Italy. He brought their greetings and the news that this year the organization will concentrate its activities on El Salvador.

I was also visited by the Passionist provincial, along with Father Juan Macho, with whom we shared ideas on the pastoral life of our archdiocese which, without a doubt, are very flattering. In a special way we spoke of the seminarians and of vocations, since they have a group of Passionist students with us and want the best for them because they are the hope of the order. To this end, we discussed whether the preparation in philosophy and theology their students are receiving in the Central American University is sufficient. I explained clearly my thoughts, saying that we should leave it to the judgment of Father Juan to fill in what deficiencies may exist, which seems to me to be the safest course. Nevertheless, this gave me an idea of how our own seminarians could also get a more autonomous preparation, more in line with our archdiocese, since there are many complaints from them and from the priests about the preparation currently being given in the interdiocesan seminary. We do not want to lose this interdiocesan connection, but we also want people who can form part of the pastoral work of our archdiocese.

 **Saturday, February 23**

This morning I went to the village of Botonsillal in the parish of Colón, where we were going to celebrate some wedding ceremonies prepared by the catechists in that place. I was accompanied by a team from British television, which wants to have information on our pastoral life in the rural areas. They were very impressed and took a great many photographs for their report. The event was very cordial, and, at the end of Mass, several of the young people and other people from the area expressed their feelings of solidarity with the archdiocese.

In the afternoon I went, at the invitation of the young people there, to Sonzacate, a town near Sonsonate, even though it is not in my diocese but is in Santa Ana. They had gotten the permission of their bishop, which I confirmed when I saw Bishop Barrera in the nunciature; he told me that it was no problem. There were doubts about whether I should go in order to avoid a conflict [with Bishop Barrera], and also because I have received death threats. The nuncio in Costa Rica has advised me of the danger of threats against me again, and he has told me that I should be careful. Nevertheless, I felt a special obligation to these young people and so I went. And, frankly, their reception was very warm; my absence would have caused great disappointment. I tried to fulfill their expectations, later blessing a first aid clinic that they have built on their own initiative. I believe that, even though it is outside my jurisdiction, it is still Church and provides encouragement for the efforts of all humankind.

When I got back, we held the advisers' meeting that the Office of Social Communication and Father Moreno and Bachiller Cuéllar usually have for me. This has also been a very conflictive week, with much violence. There are many things to denounce, as there are also many things to encourage our people, who suffer so.

 **Sunday, February 24**

We still held the Mass at the basilica. Even though the cathedral is no longer occupied, it is still very dirty and smells bad. It will take some time yet to get it ready to be used for Mass after having been occupied for a month. The inconvenience caused by the occupations is great, but we understand that our people need to be able to find refuge in the church, given such a horrible situation of oppression as the one that we are living.

The attendance at Mass was extraordinary, largely due to the fact that the radio station has not been on the air since Monday, when a bomb blew up there. When I referred to this event at the beginning of my homily and commented on the many expressions of solidarity and sympathy and aid that are coming in, the people applauded enthusiastically. All of this represents a hope that we can rebuild the station rapidly.

A representative from the Radio News of the Continent, of Costa Rica, offered us the services of their station on shortwave, thirty-one meters, in order to transmit my entire homily. He will send the tape today and he offered, if necessary, to do it directly next Sunday, using a telephone. This gesture was also much applauded.

I also announced, to the great joy of the people, that the technicians from the Central American University and other people who are experts in this field have offered their help to build a tower that is stronger than the one just blown up. The people's rejection of this action is evident and their support for our station has also become more evident.

After Mass there was a press conference. It was very eloquent, for the journalists were from different parts of the world and they showed great interest in learning about the opinion of the Church with regard to the present situation of the country and also great interest in the threat against my person that I denounced in the Mass. Several of the people who were gathered around this press conference also spoke, asking the journalists for their support for our diocese, for our radio station, for their archbishop.

At noon I went to close the gathering of the major seminarians, which has been taking place with the seminarians of our archdiocese at San José de la Montaña since last Friday. Before Mass we talked very openly. The youthful restlessness of these future priests is admirable. We do not want to mute their enthusiasm at all but rather to direct it toward a pastoral work that is in accord with the concerns of this archdiocese, which also feels itself young and enthusiastic.

In the afternoon I had to decide whether I was going to Guatemala or whether I was going to cancel the trip. The priests at the chancery held a private meeting in which they discussed the danger of my going to Guatemala for my Spiritual Exercises. There is more danger there than in our own country; also, my presence here could be more beneficial in these hours of conflict. Finally I decided not to go. I will be able to do my retreat at the Passionist Sisters' house in Planes de Renderos.

 **Monday, February 25**

At breakfast time the priests from Chalatenango who were going to go with me to Guatemala to do our Exercises at the Carmelite house, Carmel Juyú, arrived. We all had great expectations for this fellowship in such a picturesque place, but the reasons presented by the group from the chancery, who also talked to them at that time by telephone, had convinced the group to cancel the trip and to do the Exercises here along with me at the house belonging to the Passionist Sisters, who have very generously accepted the idea in spite of its impromptu nature.

Around nine o'clock in the morning, we were already in the Finca Lourdes House on the road to Planes de Renderos, a picturesque place, beginning our Exercises, which Father Fabián will coordinate. All of us joined in a discussion that was very cordial and profound. Today has been a rich time for reflection, since we have planned to have only one guidance session in the morning and another in the afternoon and have left as much time as possible for personal reflection, which we will discuss later, at noon and at the end of the afternoon.

In the evening we had another rich dialogue of a very pastoral nature, which was directed tonight to the pastoral visit proposed by the Vicariate of Chalatenango: to three zones in which there will be an acting vicar to help the episcopal vicar. In each zone we will spend two days working with the pastoral agents; afterward we will design parochial programs, which I will go visit in the next trimester. In this way we can have a pastoral visit for evaluation, for planning and a more technical one for a joint pastoral effort. The Pastoral Commission will be asked to finish this project so that it can be begun during the week of next Pentecost.

 ## Tuesday, February 26, to Friday, February 29

Beginning today and through Friday, February 29, at noon, I have been doing my Spiritual Exercises at the Lourdes farm belonging to the Passionist Sisters, on the road to Planes de Renderos. These have been days of deep reflection and of very fraternal and intimate fellowship with the diocesan priests who work in the vicariate of Chalatenango. Father Fabián Amaya, episcopal vicar of this vicariate, led us in two daily meditations, which we reflected on in individual prayer afterward and then discussed in fraternal dialogues at the end of the morning and the end of the afternoon, during the Eucharist; and in the evening we had a dialogue of a pastoral nature, in which many initiatives that would benefit that vicariate and the diocese in general came up.

During these same days there was also a private meeting in the chancery of the popular political organizations with other political groups in order to analyze the platform that the organizations are proposing for a democratic revolutionary government. The Church has offered its services within its areas of human and Christian expertise.

Also during these days they have begun the work on the antenna at YSAX, the radio transmitter that was almost totally destroyed by the bomb that has left us without a Catholic radio station. Father [Philip] Pick, a Jesuit from the United States who is working with radio stations in Honduras and Panama, has been brought here; he is directing these efforts along with Father Pedraz. The technicians of the Catholic university and the technicians of ANTEL have also offered their help. With so much help and such great popular support, we hope that our station will be back on the air again very soon.

Friday afternoon, after I finished the Exercises, I visited the work on the transmitter at YSAX. I found Father Pick working along with everyone else in clearing up the ruins of the bomb, along with other construction workers who were trying, under the direction of the engineers from the Central American University, to rebuild the little house where the new transmitter is to be installed. This is provisional, for the final location will be outside the city; we already have a piece of land for it.

# March 1980

 **Saturday, March 1**

The most memorable event today was the ordination as a priest of Jaime Paredes, a young deacon who is a descendant of a distinguished Salvadoran family. He studied in Mexico and returned to spend most of his diaconate in El Salvador. He is a priest of great promise. Currently, he is directing a group of seminarians who are doing their introductory or propaedeutic year and will also work in other pastoral areas. The ceremony was very impressive in its simplicity, especially the moment of the laying on of hands, since there were many priests participating in this consecration. His parents and friends who were present watched and then greeted him with great affection. The presence of the seminarians was very moving—our five seminarians came and it seemed to be a celebration of vocations among the young people, which, I am sure, was greatly stimulated by Jaime's ordination. After Mass, there was a simple but very cordial reception in which everyone took part—not only the distinguished guests, but also all the peasants who had come from the communities of Chalatenango.

Also after the ceremony, I gave an interview to a journalist from the United States. They are always interested in learning about the crisis of our country and the role of the Church in it.

In the afternoon I celebrated the traditional Holy Hour of the first day of the month in the Divine Providence Hospital with a large attendance. I talked about the Gospel for this coming Sunday,[305] which speaks of the transfiguration of the Lord, calling us to participate in the life of Christ and of the Church at a time when Christians have an important mission to undertake in our country.

Also today I had a meeting with some specialists on agrarian reform whom the United States has here in El Salvador, but who are promoting the government plan, which is not very popular. It does have the support of the United States but, in a situation like this, one has to be skeptical about aid that would restrict the authentic desires of the people to a plan that is imposed. I thanked them. I was interested in hearing the details, which are really very technical, but I intimated my concern that the project, with all its economic aid, should always take into account the views and wishes of the people and not merely support a government that, because of its repressive aspect, loses more popular support each day.

In the evening we had the meeting with my advisers to prepare the homily for the next day.

 **Sunday, March 2**

The second Sunday of Lent. Because the radio is not in operation, many people came in person to the basilica and it was more crowded than usual. The services of the Radio News of the Continent from Costa Rica carried the sound of the Mass on shortwave, especially the homily. Afterward, I heard comments that it was heard—and rather clearly—not just in this country, but also, since it was on shortwave from Central America, in the entire isthmus and also on the continent.[306] I also learned that radios in Venezuela and Colombia had collaborated in this effort. It really impressed me to think that, for the first time, the voice of a homily given by the archbishop of San Salvador reached beyond its borders and was heard in all the continent. In such a situation, I was conscious of the fact that the listeners were not just of my diocese but from all over Latin America, to which this Church directs its efforts in accordance with the very clear norms given at Medellín and Puebla.

---

[305] Luke 9:28b-36.
[306] South America.

After Mass there was an international press conference in which some ten journalists participated; also many of the people from the Mass, who are making it a habit to also participate in this dialogue, which many times provides clarification in reference to points in the homily or other matters of interest to the newspapers that visit us. All of them were foreign journalists.

In the evening I went to the parish in the neighborhood of Lourdes, where Father Mateo Quijada had prepared a group for Confirmation. The church was filled to overflowing with the faithful. Their reception was very affectionate. I had to tell them that there would be a change in this parish and that, in spite of the fact that they are very fond of him, their parish priest will have to go to another parish. Next Sunday we will turn over the parish here to a group of Vincentian Fathers, who will help us work in this poor section of our diocese. At the same time the present parish priest, Father Mateo, will go to the village of El Carmen in the parish of Christ the Redeemer, where he will be listed as assistant vicar.

## Monday, March 3

After a week's absence, I returned today to the chancery, where I began my work with our usual meeting with the vicars and chancellors. Monsignor Urioste could not come because he is somewhat ill with the problem that causes him to suffer so—problems with his circulation and with the veins in his feet.

We discussed that, because of certain defects in my character, I can provoke different kinds of resentment or divisions, but that I should not have any doubts about the loyalty of these collaborators. I told them that they were right, and I told them that this had been one of the points of my examination in the Spiritual Exercises last week. I had returned with the idea that, with their help, we would try to be more united in our work, to communicate better, and that we would correct each other in those things which could weaken our work in community, which is so interesting. And that, as I proposed during the retreat, we are going to have this meeting at the beginning of each day in our chapel, so that it may also be a moment of prayer and evangelical guidance for the work of directing this archdiocese.

Immediately afterward we went to the meeting of the Senate that had been set for this morning. Some had forgotten it; therefore not many people were there. Nevertheless, we discussed some very important points, such as planning tomorrow's meeting of the clergy, in which the new Priests' Senate will be elected.

We also touched on other points related to the mission of the Church in such a politicized atmosphere, in which the Christian base communities run the risk of losing their identity and becoming more political than evangelical. I tried to clarify, as well as I could, the transcendent problem that the Church at this time cannot ignore—such a great political problem, what is happening with our people—because we cannot take the risk of staying on the sidelines at such a historic time. But we must be sure that our presence has a true ecclesial identity. We also discussed other points in a familial and trusting atmosphere.

I went to have lunch with the Belgian priests, since Father Pedro Le Clerq has arrived from Panama. And with this I finished this first day at work with one of my most important principles, that of sharing my life more, even in private terms, with the dear priests of the diocese. We had a very fraternal conversation in which I was able also to express my fears about the criticism that exists about the Belgians' work. When I am with them, I see that it is a very Christian work, but one which requires great care on the part of the pastor of the diocese. Also they told me that there have been telephone threats and that they prefer not to sleep in their residence. I was able to arrange, with some reservations, for them to spend as many nights as they wish at a school.

In the afternoon, along with Father Moreno, I studied a document that we have decided to present in the name of the Church and the two universities abut the situation of the country. It will also serve as a call to the people to take part in deciding their own destiny and not to expect the political groups to do everything; rather to take advantage of the efforts to achieve unity and openness in the popular organizations so that the people may also give their opinion of the present situation and try to search for the ways that are best. In this way, it will be the people themselves who are working to shape their own destiny. I have some reservations about the document and asked for more time so I can study it with a group of priests at the clergy meeting to be held tomorrow.

During the night, we heard explosions for almost an hour—an assault of the People's Revolutionary Army on the barracks of the National Guard....[307]

---

[307] Tape ends here.

## Tuesday, March 4

As usual on the first Tuesday of the month, we held the meeting of the clergy today. The women religious did not come because this meeting was mainly to elect a new Priests' Senate to serve for the next two years. First, there was a meditation on Lent presented by Father Juan Macho Merino, and afterward, the election of representatives of the different sectors of the clergy to the Priests' Senate. By the end, we had selected a group that is representative of the different sectors of the clergy: a young man, four priests working in a rural area, two diocesan priests from urban areas and two religious. The election was well managed. I will name another five and thus complete the Senate, which will come together soon for its first session.

I also realized that the work is progressing in Domus Mariae, both the work on the little building where the new transmitter of YSAX will be installed and the technical work on the transmission, which is being directed by Father Pick with the help of technicians from ANTEL and the Central American University.

In the afternoon, an interview with the North Americans who are advisers to the agrarian reform project. I was accompanied by Father Juan Ramón Vega, and we discussed the project. They have decided to support it totally, and we hear that tomorrow this law will be issued by the governing junta. Our principal concern is whether the governing junta will have authority with the two extremes of the right and of the left, which are fighting it so much. Nevertheless, for myself, I support everything just in this reform. I promised the moral support of my prayers and expressed my wish that it be carried out for the benefit of our people.

I could not go as invited to the parish of San Antonio in Colonia América where, in the Chapel of the Andes, they gave out Bibles today to the followers of the catechumenate movement, which is doing a lot of good among us.

I also emphasized to the priests that I intend to dialogue not only with the priests in the consulting body—that is, the Priests' Senate—but also to talk individually with the priests. I asked them to pardon me for not being able to go, told them that they always have my goodwill and asked them for their help in opening channels for these personal conversations.

**Wednesday, March 5**

After breakfast I was surprised by the ecumenical committee on humanitarian aid. They had been told that they were to have a meeting with me at eight o'clock, but I did not know anything about it. I expressed to them briefly my concern that there is such dissipation of energy with different committees of a charitable nature and invited them to come at four o'clock in the afternoon, when I would call a meeting of the other sectors, Caritas and the archdiocesan emergency committee, in order to unite our efforts. I later consulted about this in the meeting with the chancery officials, who share my concern. But we cannot have the meeting this afternoon because several people cannot come. We will leave it for another time. It seems that there are divisive forces or people who want to take advantage of this activity to use the archdiocese for political ends. I will be very alert, and we will try to be sure that it is a true charity, as befits the Church.

The meeting with the vicars and chancellors is always very useful. We look at many aspects of the life of the chancery and of the diocese. I think that it is absolutely necessary to have this meeting every day.

During the morning, many individual audiences which had been scheduled and, toward noon, an interview with journalists from the United States and from Europe. Miss Marta Benavides translated. She is working in the chancery offices—ecumenically, since she is a Protestant—and is providing a good service to the archdiocese.

It was already rather late when the government press secretary, Don Sigfrido Munés, came to visit me at the Divine Providence Hospital to invite me to the presidential palace tomorrow at eleven o'clock. But he could not tell me why, which I told him was rather absurd; that I could not go if I did not know why I was going. From his conversation, I deduced that it had to do with the dissemination of the law of agrarian reform and that the other bishops had also been invited, along with the entire cabinet and the government and other people who could be interested in supporting the government in this effort to change the agrarian system.

I expressed my ambivalence, of course, at being invited without being informed of the purpose. I also expressed my reservations about these social, economic and political reforms when, at the same time, the people are being massacred. Even though I know that there is great goodwill in one sector of the government, what prevails and offends the people so much is the repressive nature which, as long as it exists, means that the Church cannot feel full confidence in the government. I told him that I appreciated the invitation anyway; that I want to maintain my personal friendship with him and with other members of the government, but only on a personal level; that he should understand my reservations as the pastor of the Church and the responsibility my presence implies.

I promised him, however, that I would think about it and reflect on it and that I would decide according to my conscience. He agreed to that and said that, whether I did or did not go, he would not be concerned and would not feel that his friendship with me had suffered in any way.

In the evening I went to a meeting of the movement of Catholic intellectuals that Father Ramón Vega is trying to reactivate. There were professionals, some twelve of them. We discussed the subject of the need for professionals to enter fully with all their abilities into the process of the people and for them to make their Christian conscience a part of the life of the nation. There were doubts whether this organization should be continued or whether it is not worth the trouble, but I encouraged them. I told them that this work of the Church among the professionals is essential and that for the pastors themselves and especially for the archbishop, being able to rely on this group of intellectuals to discuss things in case of doubt is a great help.

Finally, I went to the Jesuit residence, at the UCA, to consult them about whether or not to go to the gathering at the presidential palace. The criteria that I had expressed prevailed, and we decided that it would be better for me to send a representative, but not to go myself, and that I should express my approval and support for what is good in it in my homily next Sunday, and also express my reservations, always in support of the people.

### Thursday, March 6

At breakfast I consulted Monsignor Urioste about the wisdom of accepting the invitation to the presidential house today at eleven o'clock for the proclamation of the agrarian reform law. He saw very clearly the positive aspect, which would be to support a cause which will be of benefit to the people, but he also saw the negative side of a government that is characterized by a very repressive policy. And we decided, as we had last night, that I would not go in person, but that I would instead send Father Cortés as my representative.

At eleven-thirty on a radio-television network the law of agrarian reform was solemnly proclaimed by Colonel Majano from the presidential house. Immediately, a state of emergency[308] was declared in an attempt to avoid the uproar this decree could create.

In the afternoon I talked with members of the Popular Leagues of February 28 and also with a member of the FPL. Both of them discount the government measure as a reform that does not make changes at a deep enough level to meet the needs of the country but is instead another way of putting a patch on an unjust situation, looking good in international circles and allowing the intervention of the United States. There are many points in these fairly profound analyses that Monsignor Urioste and I questioned— he was present at the first meeting—and these worker and peasant politicians answered the questions with great conviction. There is no doubt that they are analyzing the real situation of the country in great depth. We ask God that the violence that we see coming will not accelerate, since the left and the popular political groups do not see any other way to achieve a real transformation of the country so that the....[309]

 **Friday, March 7**

I spent the morning in the Aldeíta, Father Gabriel Rodríguez's house, where we have the four seminarians who are in the fourth year of theology doing their year of diaconate. We had a very interesting meeting in which they presented to me their project for spiritual, pastoral and academic experiences. It would be a year in which these young people would interrupt their regular studies and enrich themselves with a great experience but would not get out of the habit of study or neglect their spiritual formation. I saw that they were very happy and that Father Gabriel was also very optimistic.

After this meeting, we went to celebrate the Eucharist in the church of Aldeíta with a community that filled the small church with great affection, with a faith I could see was quite vital. We know that Father Gabriel, and now the four seminarians, work intensely with this community of faith.

When I returned, I had a meeting with the ecumenical committee on humanitarian aid to clarify its relationship with Caritas and with the

---

[308] A curfew and the suspension of many civil rights; martial law.
[309] Tape ends here.

emergency committee of the archdiocese. We do not want to multiply or complicate the charitable work but rather to coordinate all the efforts, the initiatives for the service of our neighbor. I believe that all of this activity will then show a true example of love to this community of the archdiocese. We will try to build a warehouse for Caritas, along with an office, on the land where the university center is located. We will also try to get the archdiocesan Caritas board to become a full participant in this coordinated effort for charity and beneficence.

In the evening the reverend bishop[310] from Sweden came. He is bringing me the 1980 Peace Prize[311] that was awarded to me and will be given to me next Sunday. We had a long conversation in which he explained to me what the religious life is like in his country. The Lutheran Church is the official Church of the country, while all the others, including the Catholic Church, are called "free Churches." They have organized an ecumenical office, and it is they who have chosen me along with the Church of the archdiocese to be honored with the 1980 Peace Prize.

He told me that when he asked the consent of the ministry for religious affairs, they were very pleased and said that "for Archbishop Romero and for the diocese of San Salvador, anything they want from Sweden." He told me that the ambassador of his country in El Salvador and Guatemala would be present at this tribute. He also told me that the Catholic Church, which is a very small minority in Sweden, with a German bishop and many Latin American immigrants, felt very pleased by this choice and took up a collection to help the needy in our diocese. He has brought this contribution, which represents much sacrifice and great affection on the part of the Catholics of his country. Next Sunday we will have a ceremony during the Mass. They will award this prize, which is also a stimulus for the entire community.

I also had a conversation with an English journalist. We talked about the situation of the country and the mission of the Church in such a difficult moment, in which the social and economic reforms seem to mean great good for the people, but nevertheless can be a screen to hide the true repressive intention that continues to be very cruel toward our people. I think that this is a very difficult moment for discernment for the Church, but I rely on the light of the Holy Spirit who, I hope, will not fail me in guiding my ecclesial community.

Also, the translator for the minister from Sweden wanted to have a meeting with me. He is Lutheran; he works in the Swedish embassy in Guatemala and will take part in the ceremony next Sunday.

---

[310] Rev. Per Arne Aglert, general secretary of Swedish Ecumenical Action.

[311] A kind of alternative Nobel Peace Prize, given by this Swedish group.

Finally, a brief interview with Mr. Ernesto Rivas Gallont about the kidnapping of Mr. Dunn, which seems to have gotten more complicated. It is clear that the collecting of funds in South Africa is a failure, and they cannot offer a large sum for the freedom of Mr. Dunn. Mr. Gallont has been called to Washington to talk there with the South African ambassador and see if they can find a new way to deal with this serious problem. I promised, as mediator, to do what I can, but I see it is a very grave situation. May the Lord help us to save this life and help the Church to make its service useful in the name of Jesus Christ in order to obtain the liberty of Mr. Dunn.

 **Saturday, March 8**

At ten-thirty I went to bless the church of the village of El Salitre in the parish of Tejutla. A little more than an hour on the road and the people were waiting at the detour to accompany me, in spite of the dust, on foot to the shrine, where Father Valerio and Father Gabriel Rodríguez, along with some seminarians, were presiding over a good-sized group of people who were also waiting. I preached on what a church means: a center of unity for the Christian family, an encounter with the Lord and a sense of the transcendence of life.

After Mass there began a dialogue with great confidence. The parishioners asked several questions of a religious and practical nature and also made some suggestions. They applauded greatly when I told them that our transmitter would possibly be broadcasting tomorrow. If not, it is because there are very serious problems that we are trying to overcome, that we were not sure that they would be resolved that same day, but that if they wanted to listen, possibly the station from Costa Rica, Radio News of the Continent, would also broadcast it on shortwave.

I went to visit the elderly father of Felipe de Jesús Chacón, who had died violently, killed[312]—a catechist who is considered a martyr for our faith. These people are also very warm. They receive one with great affection and go out of their way to share the little that they have.

In the evening, with Father Ellacuría and Father Estrada, Monsignor Urioste, Miss Doris Osegueda, Bachiller Cuéllar and Father Rafael Urrutia, I received advice for the informational part of tomorrow's homily.

---

[312] In August 1977.

The family of the young Castellanos couple, who were killed yesterday after being kidnapped eight days earlier, came to ask me to have their bodies at the eight o'clock Mass at the basilica because they especially wanted me to celebrate the Mass for their eternal rest. From this gracious gesture, I decided I should grant their petition. I warned them, however, of the festive atmosphere that exists in our Masses—but looked at with a spirit of hope and prayer, this atmosphere will not clash with the sadness in that home.

It was very late when they told me that they had not been able to get the new transmitter base of YSAX to work. Because of that, they will be unable to broadcast tomorrow's Mass. I insisted that they contact Radio News of the Continent in Costa Rica, which had offered to provide this service as long as YSAX is not in operation.

Today the cathedral was taken over again by FENASTRAS to stand watch over nine bodies, victims of this repressive wave in which we are living. There are other dead whose funerals will be held elsewhere. They asked me if I could celebrate the official Mass in the cathedral. I told them no because I had already arranged to have the Sunday Mass at the basilica because of the uncertainty of the occupations. And I begged the leaders to think about, evaluate these occupations, taking into account the difficulties that we had discussed in a previous dialogue. They said that they had not given previous notice of the occupation because it had to be a rapid action, since the Popular Revolutionary Bloc had been going to take it over to use it as a protest, and that they had a urgent need to take it in order to have the bodies there for the viewing this evening.

 **Sunday, March 9**

I consider this a very special Sunday, and I thank God for the immense satisfactions that I have received today. The Sunday Mass was exceptional in the sense that there were two events that do not happen every Sunday.

First, because of the announcement of the 1980 Peace Prize awarded to me by Ecumenical Action of Sweden. Since I was unable to go there, they very graciously sent the secretary-general along with another member of the Lutheran Church to make the solemn presentation to me in the cathedral. The ambassador from Sweden[313] was also present. The minister who gave me the prize—a testimonial and a check for ten thousand dollars, plus another check for twenty-five hundred dollars from a collection among Catholics in Sweden—spoke before the presentation, expressing the feelings of those Christian Churches with words of high praise. The ambassador himself presented me with the prize, linking his country officially in solidarity with this ecumenical gesture coming from his country.

The other event was the presence of the bodies of two people who were murdered in these last few days after being kidnapped. They were found dead, and they had been horribly tortured. They are the couple Roberto Castellanos and his wife, a young Danish woman, whose mother was unable to come. Roberto's mother had specifically asked for them to be here at this Mass, in spite of my warning her that it could perhaps offend her sense of sorrow. She told me that her son had worked hard to improve the situation of the country and greatly admired the stance of our Church. Also, she felt drawn to this Mass and begged that the final prayers for them before they are taken to the cemetery be said here.

For these two reasons, the crowd at the basilica was very large. The immense basilica was not large enough to contain the people, a great many of whom had to stay outside.

My homily was inspired by these two events as I linked them to God's message about personal conversion as an essential condition for salvation.[314] I also referred, as application, to the two attitudes that have been most obvious this week: the growing repression of the government against the people, especially against the popular organizations and, on the other hand, the two laws of agrarian reform and the nationalization of the banks.

My view was that these were good laws, but that they ran the risk of being unenforceable as long as the repression is not stopped and there is no attempt to dialogue about the projects the people propose, and that seeking to defend the government projects with an intransigence that regards the right and the left as equally enemies is unjust. It is true that the right is affected by these changes, but its attacks that try to destroy the organizations of the people are not repressed. I said that the left does not oppose projects that are good for the people. The left, defined as the

---

[313] Henrik Ramel.
[314] The Gospel was Luke 13:1-9.

popular organizations, does not present projects that contradict this; rather they could coincide for the benefit of the people. The government must listen more to these voices of the people if it wants to find support and efficacy in its projects.

The exit from the Mass was very moving. We put the two coffins at the head of the procession, with the sorrowing family, the priests representing the Central American University who concelebrated with me (the wife was a student there), the representatives of Sweden and then all the people in general—who, on leaving, expressed their condolences to the family and their congratulations to me.

Afterward we went to the convent of the basilica, where the Swedish mission had prepared a general reception with soft drinks and cookies for the people. At the same time, there was a very interesting press conference, since there had been many journalists from television, radio and the press from other countries at the Mass. Father Ellacuría, rector of the Central American University, participated; his answers were very intelligent. We asked them to take back to their countries a true image of a situation that is very difficult to understand; for at the same time that reforms that will benefit the people are being put forth, there is also a repression that terribly offends the dignity of our people.

At noon I went to the closing ceremony of a gathering of young people in the San José de la Montaña Seminary—some forty young people aided by the seminary committee for pastoral work with young people. The Mass was very youthful, indicative of much promise for our Church. I was very pleased at Communion time, when almost all of these young people were able to take the Eucharist. I told them that a life in grace, always open to Communion, was a guarantee of God's blessings and of a successful pastoral work. And I invited them to work with the young people of the entire diocese.

At five o'clock in the afternoon I went to the basilica again to preside over the funeral Mass for the soul of Dr. Mario Zamora,[315] who was also assassinated last week. I expressed my condolences to the family, to his father, his wife and the rest of his family and relatives. Taking as my theme the first reading,[316] in which God tells Moses of his will to liberate his people and to offer them "a land flowing with milk and honey" [Exodus 3:8b], I told them that the merits of those who work in politics and for the liberation of the people are immortal when they have worked with Christian

---

[315] Recently named Procurator General for the Poor; brother of Rubén Zamora.
[316] Exodus 3:1-8a, 13-15.

hope in their hearts. This land of milk and honey is not to be found in this world but is a utopia that continues to build the paths beyond history. This was the measure of Mario Zamora who, as a Christian, had worked for a more just and humane world in El Salvador.

Finally, at seven o'clock in the evening I went to give possession of the parish of the sector of Lourdes to Father Juan Martínez, a Vincentian priest. Their provincial, Father Chacón, Father Juan and I presided at the Eucharist. Father Juan will come there with a group of Vincentian theology students, who are studying at the seminary and who are going to share the pastoral experiences of that poor neighborhood. The people were very warm, especially the Sisters of the Assumption, who already work there and seem to be very eager to cooperate with the new parish priest. So do the Sisters of Charity,[317] who are there because the parish priest is a Vincentian; they also offer their collaboration.

There is hope of improving the pastoral effort, which Father Mateo Quijada, the parish priest who is moving to a different location in Colonia Escalón in the village of Carmen, was unable to develop truly in the direction followed by the archdiocese because he had some prejudices against the liberation of our people. He always tried to protect certain privileges which make it impossible to live the logical radicalness which the gospel demands at this time. Father Mateo did not attend the ceremony, but last Sunday, as I have already said, he was present at the Confirmation ceremony that he had prepared as his farewell to the parish.

There were some rocks thrown at the church during the ceremony, doubtless by people who are not happy with a pastoral direction that tries to be very true to the demands of the gospel.

 **Monday, March 10**

I began my day's labor with an interview with a journalist from Chile, who had come especially on behalf of the Vicariate of Solidarity[318] and who was interested in meeting me and in asking some questions about my views on the Church and this moment in the history of the country. Another interview—this one with French television, which

---

[317] Also founded by St. Vincent de Paul.

[318] An organization of the Archdiocese of Santiago created during the Pinochet dictatorship, which provided different kinds of aid—legal, medical, etc.—to the victims of repression and their families.

was also filming yesterday during the Mass in the basilica; also, a brief series of questions about the current situation of the country.

Afterward I went to celebrate Mass in the presence of the bodies of nine people killed by the military repression, which have been in the cathedral since yesterday. Other priests came as well, and we concelebrated this Eucharist. I used the message of the homily to say that those bodies are a lesson about the elevated destiny that human beings have—eternity. They are an indictment of the sin that rules on earth to such an extent that it can kill in this way. And I offered a word of encouragement for all of those who continue to struggle for the liberation of their people.

Afterward I went to take part in a meeting of a group of priests who meet in Domus Mariae every month. They are the priests who could be called "progressive." It is very interesting to have these conversations in which we learn more about each other.

In the afternoon Father Ramiro came to tell me that a very powerful bomb had been found in the basilica and that it could have gone off yesterday, possibly while we were celebrating the Mass at five o'clock for the eternal rest of Dr. Mario Zamora, at which there were many people. The bomb, which had been placed near the altar of St. Martha, was disarmed by police experts, who said it was strong enough to have destroyed the entire basilica and everyone who was there at the time. I thanked God, who has freed us from this new danger and has also saved this old church, of which the people of the capital are so fond.

I also went with Father Ramiro to El Rosario Church to see the Dominican priests and to learn in more detail about the gunfire directed against it the night before. According to these priests, the group that had taken refuge in the church was attacked by two rounds of machine-gun fire. The first one possibly came from the neighboring buildings; it could have been rightist groups. The second one was when the police appeared, and the shots directed at the church came from the Monumento de la Libertad.[319] I realized how awful these bullets are—they can pass through iron, destroy outside and inside walls. Thanks be to God, no one was injured, but there was great damage to the church. The priests said that perhaps some one hundred bullets had broken stained-glass windows, metal arches, walls and other parts of the church.

In the evening, a visit from Licenciado [Alberto] Arene to talk to me in some depth about the crisis within the Christian Democratic Party and about his resignation, along with other long-standing Democrats, all intelligent individuals. In analyzing the situation they think that the

---

[319] A monument to liberty, commemorating Salvadoran independence from Spain.

Christian Democrats should not continue in power because they are serving as a cover for the terrible repression that the government is carrying out against our people. Licenciado Arene has received death threats and is leaving for the United States—not only in order to avoid danger but especially because, he says, an international effort is urgently needed to provide objective information about this situation, in which the presence of the Christian Democrats contributes to a situation that is truly repressive against the people.

Finally, at the invitation of Monsignor Urioste, I went to have dinner with Dr. Delgado, Monsignor Urioste's cousin, and with Dr. Granillo, president of the Supreme Court of Justice. The conversation dealt with my homilies. They criticized me for not having supported the agrarian reform project and the nationalization of the banks in a more decisive way. I told them that I had approved of the good aspects but that, at the same time, I pointed out the great risks that could make these laws ineffective. For as long as the terrible repression against the people is not stopped, the people cannot believe in or cooperate with a government that is offering reforms but at the same time gives them repression. The discussion of other aspects, mostly having to do with my homilies, lasted the whole evening, until we had finished dinner. But we ended by saying that the frankness that had reigned in this atmosphere made us realize the need for greater communication in order to get information from other sectors with which we do not normally have contact.

Back in my room at eleven o'clock at night, I received a call from a radio station in Nicaragua about doing an interview about the present situation of the country and other aspects that also concern Nicaragua. I especially defended the Christian sentiments involved in all revolutionary movements so that they may truly be beneficial for the people, who are deeply religious.

 **Tuesday, March 11**

The first news of this morning is the bomb that was placed at the priests' cooperative. I went to see it at noon and, thank God, it had only ruined the door and the merchandise that was near the door. In spite of the cooperative having been wide open from one o'clock in the morning until five o'clock due to the bomb, when those in charge arrived, nothing else was lost. Indeed, it was an attack for which we have no explanation, but there are some political implications since it coincides with the naming of Ingeniero Duarte as a member of the governing junta.[320]  His brother is the former priest Alejandro Duarte, who is considered to be the same as the political figure. There could have been other causes. Some say that it is because it has to do with priests, but the first explanation is more likely.

After several months, we again held a meeting of the Executive Council of the archdiocese. Monsignor Urioste was there, Father Cortés, Father Brito, Ingeniero Galván, Licenciado Mauricio Silva and myself. This is a meeting that we want to have every Tuesday from eight to nine to evaluate the functioning of our chancery. We studied several matters, as can be seen in the minutes that are prepared each time. I was very pleased with the concern for achieving better communication among the different coworkers at the chancery and greater attention and order in the reception area.

In the afternoon I went to an audience with the nuncio of Costa Rica, who has come on behalf of the Holy Father to work for unity among the bishops in El Salvador. He gave me a letter from the Cardinal Secretary of State,[321] in which he asks my help in better achieving this end.

We discussed different aspects of this lack of unity. I explained my position in the Church. He made several comments and I tried to persuade him of my convictions, which I hold in all good conscience. But I noticed in him a certain resistance to my way of doing things. In spite of my explaining to him what a difficult atmosphere we are living in and how well the people accept this direction, he has certain fears that the popular organizations may be communist. This factor, the fear of communism, affects some of his judgments.

I told him that I was very careful to avoid this infiltration, that it was one of my concerns and that he should not worry that my support for the popular organizations might mean a sympathy for the left—even less, ignorance of the danger of infiltration, of which I am very much aware. But I also see that among us anticommunism is many times the weapon that the economic and political powers use for their social and political injustices. I think that I made my position clear. I accept, of course, that in any accidentals in which I can yield, I am willing to do so on behalf of achieving peace, but never in my convictions about faithfulness to the gospel, the new directions of the Church and my dear people.

Late at night I received a telephone call from a newspaper in Mexico to interview me about the situation of the country and the opinion of the Church.

---

[320] Duarte replaced Héctor Dada, who resigned on March 10.
[321] Cardinal Agostino Casaroli.

**Wednesday, March 12**

Today is the anniversary of the death of Father Grande.

We are going to have a meeting of bishops in Ayagualo, called by the Holy Father himself—his suggestion that we pray and try to achieve unity. This coincided with the arrival of the nuncio from Costa Rica, who has come precisely on this mission. The meeting took place in Ayagualo in the Salesian retreat house. It began with the celebration of Mass by the nuncio and all the bishops. During the homily the nuncio made a plea that he wanted to implement after Mass in asking for a dialogue in which we would talk about the two different sides of the episcopal conference.

On my side, I expressed that it was my desire for faithfulness to the gospel and the doctrine of the Church that always becomes conflictive when it is not just approved in theory, but when we also try to live it. I pointed out that these divisions already existed in the time of Archbishop Chávez and that they always took the form of criticism against the archdiocese, which is trying to be faithful to the orientation of the postconciliar Church. I also said that there was a great deal of criticism of the archdiocese and that the other dioceses do not offer living examples to imitate. What I asked was some respect for the archdiocese and that each one of us respect his own jurisdiction. Bishop Rivera also explained the situation very intelligently, since he can refer to the functioning of our archdiocese starting after the Second Vatican Council, making reference to exact historical and doctrinal information.[322]

The statements made by the other bishops, of course, were against the direction of the archdiocese. They presented many superficial arguments, although I acknowledge those things in which there could be some error on my part and I am willing to correct them.

After lunch we continued this interesting meeting until four o'clock in the afternoon. We had the voting to elect the new president and vice-president. They heeded my call to unite to elect Bishop Alvarez and thus ratify our earlier election, but I was surprised that they did not do the same thing with the vice-president. Rather, they took the position away from Bishop Rivera and put in Bishop Aparicio as vice-president. This has left me with great uneasiness about the incoherence in our attempts to achieve unity.

Among other things, it was agreed that we will issue a joint statement about the situation of the country, which will principally be a Lenten appeal,

---

[322] Rivera had been auxiliary bishop of San Salvador during the Council (1962-1965).

as a sign of our unity in the teaching and the discipline of the Church. We also agreed that, when we make declarations that affect the entire episcopate, we should take this into account and consult with the other bishops. I understood that this referred to me personally, but I said that I would accept these conditions also, as long as they would also consider that many times they make declarations in the other dioceses that are very unwise and that also compromise the Church.

All in all, it was very fruitful, although I fear, given the aggressiveness with which Bishop Aparicio and Bishop Alvarez attacked me, that we have not achieved much with respect to deep feelings of unity. The Lord will judge. On my part, I want to offer up all these sacrifices and all this unpleasantness so that the gospel may triumph and that we may all be converted to the truth and to the service of God and our people.

I was visited by Doña Gloria, the wife of Ingeniero [Héctor] Dada Hirezi, who came to seek comfort and to thank me for the moral support I gave him after his resignation as a member of the council of government. She clarified several things for me about the accusations of disloyalty that have been made against her and her husband by the Christian Democratic Party and the governing junta. I told her that he can be at peace, since he had followed his conscience and had given testimony of faithfulness to his conscience.

 ## Thursday, March 13

In the chancery meeting we listed the members of the Senate and the vicars. We agreed to write a commentary, create a document, in which we would again express our hope for renewal that would occur in the same way as these changes in personnel have.

This morning there were a number of visits, but the principal one was that from the Movement of Independent Professionals, an organization that already has some one hundred fifty members. It includes professionals and technicians who believe they have found their place within the people's process. Without choosing a single political option, they want to be a nucleus for the enlightened promotion of all the political life of the country. We talked a great deal and I saw that the ideas of the Church and their way of thinking have much in common. Based on that, we concluded with the offer of mutual service: that of the Church in a pastoral area and theirs in professional and technical aspects.

At noon the nuncio from Costa Rica came to see the situation of the archdiocesan offices and the San José de la Montaña Seminary, which share the same building. We tried to show him that the interference of which the other bishops accuse us does not exist. But the nuncio seems to have a predisposition that doubtless reflects the mission he was given, therefore his insistence that we should build other offices for the archdiocese as soon as possible and leave the whole building for the seminary. This is what I have wanted to do for a long time, except that, in an economic sense, we do not have the means, but, with the help of God.... And I told the nuncio that. At precisely that moment, Ingeniero Galván, who is a witness to our efforts in this area, arrived.

The nuncio went with me to have lunch at the hospital where, after lunch with the sisters, we discussed his latest recommendations in a more intimate atmosphere—always from the perspective that I am greatly to blame for the lack of unity among the bishops, in spite of my attempts to remind him of yesterday's meeting and the fact that he has to recognize that there was a great deal of passion involved, especially on the part of Bishop Alvarez and Bishop Aparicio. Nevertheless, even recognizing this passion and that it is personally directed against me, he insists that I should give in as much as possible, which is also what I think—but not in substance, not when it has to do with being true to the gospel, to the teaching of the Church and especially to this suffering people, who would find it hard to understand this.

After a nap, I went with Father Alliet to visit the community of Belgian nuns who are in Santiago Texacuangos. We spent a very cordial and happy time with that community, which is working intensely, especially in the area of health. They are experts in nursing and have almost a hospital—I should say, a very efficient first aid station in what was the convent and is today, we could say, a very well-stocked first aid center.

Upon returning, we talked with journalists from Italy, Venezuela and the United States. It was a rather in-depth interview about the ideas of the Church, especially with regard to the violence and in the context of the reforms in the country.

Doña Inga de Gavidia also came on behalf of Caritas. We had dinner together to talk about this problem, which interests me a great deal since it has to do with organizing the charitable works of the archdiocese.

At seven-thirty in the evening, we had the meeting with the minor seminary, which was very pleasant after I told them that our relationship as bishop and seminarians must be based on faith and on a very supernatural sense of obedience and understanding. Many questions came up—an interesting dialogue about vocations, in which we ended up telling each other how our vocations came about. I began by telling them my story and they also felt they could talk freely about how the Lord had called them. I asked them to relate their personal stories, since no two vocations are alike and this would serve for our mutual edification.

Around nine-thirty in the evening I went to visit the Jesuits: Father Ellacuría; Father Jerez, who has recently returned from Rome; and Father Jon Sobrino, who has just returned from a conference of Third-World theologians in Brazil. All of them told me about very positive aspects of the relationships on their trips, about how there is certainly support for my pastoral work. It is admirable how this work which means such great sacrifice is understood and regarded with affection in other countries, while in our own country, my brother bishops show such a lack of understanding of this work that seeks, very sincerely, to be of service to God and to the gospel. I ask the Holy Spirit to make me walk the paths of truth and never let me be guided by flattery or by fear of offending anyone other than our Lord!

## Friday, March 14

I began the day with a working breakfast with the priests from the chancery. We finished looking at the appointments of vicars, since next Monday there will be a meeting of the Pastoral Commission and the new vicars and pro-vicars will need to attend. We are preparing a statement expressing the hope that this change of personnel will also mean a renewal of spirit and a desire to work toward the goal of building up our archdiocese well.

We also studied a document that they want the archdiocese to sign, along with the universities and other institutions that are independent of politics, for the purpose of condemning the tremendous repression and expressing an opinion in favor of the poor about the agrarian reform that is being carried out and about the other reforms.

Father Cortés, Father Fabián and the others who were at the meeting were left with the task of finishing it, since Monsignor Urioste and I went at nine o'clock in the morning to meet with the recently named ambassador from the United States, who had requested an audience. Father Estrada was there also. We had a very interesting conversation. He seems to be a man who is more than a diplomat, a man who has great respect for human rights, who has also been under fire in politics. He wants to be a true collaborator in the process of our people. He recognizes the errors that have been committed by his country in our Latin American countries and is willing to work to create another image of the United States. We felt sufficient trust to point out our fears, the errors that we see and especially our desire to defend the poor people from so much oppression and from so much injustice.

He also gave me the answer to the letter that I had sent to the president of the United States, asking him not to send military aid as long as this aid would cause more repression of our people and saying that he should be very careful about intervening politically—although we certainly do need the help of that country as one more developed than we are. The letter is written by the secretary of state[323] of the United States. They also provided a translation into Spanish, which we studied.

After this meeting, I went to see the property at the University Center, where Bishop Chávez had planned to build the archdiocesan offices and the bishop's residence. Given the needs at the time, it was impossible to do so.

With Arquitecto Morales, Arquitecto Jovel and Father Vega, we considered the possibility of building there instead a house of development for the clergy. That is, a residence for priests where they can also hold courses of renewal for our priests and where there would also be some rooms for priests and bishops who pass through San Salvador and sometimes do not have a church place to stay. But, more than anything else, a place for programs for priestly renewal with a chapel (which is a condition for the donation of the land) that can be used for the university pastoral work, the intended use of the house that already exists, the University Catholic Center. I have given thanks to the Lord for this project, which has been accepted with great enthusiasm by those who have shared in these deliberations. We will have the plans for this project drawn up so that we can also ask for aid from other countries.

At four o'clock in the afternoon, an important meeting of the Confederation of Catholic Schools at the Liceo Salvadoreño. It concerned involving the schools in pastoral work. I congratulated them on this effort to give a pastoral aspect to the schools. In coordination with the bishop and the pastoral plan of the diocese, the schools may become true centers for the formation of pastoral workers, of Christians who live in solidarity with their Church and who are formed to *be* Church at the service of the transformation of our people. Therefore, it is necessary to leave behind all this activity on the fringes of pastoral work and to become fully a Church effort for the pastoral and evangelization work of the archdiocese.

There was a very interesting dialogue, and it was agreed to incorporate the Confederation, through a representative, into the archdiocesan

---

[323] Cyrus Vance.

Pastoral Commission, and that each Catholic center would try to form a true community for Catholic education—a community that would truly be Church, open to the archdiocese and to the universal Church—with the students, the teachers, the parents, others who work in administration, former students, etc.—which would mean, around each school, a great human and ecclesial community.

In the evening, a meeting with the ambassador of Italy, who was rather critical of the situation of the Christian Democrats and who promised to promote a meeting with leading members of the party so that, as pastor, I could tell them the thinking of the Church and its responsibility in the area of politics.

After all that, I had dinner with Colonel Majano and Dr. Morales Ehrlich, members of the government council, rather, of the revolutionary junta of the government; also Monsignor Urioste, Father Estrada. We principally discussed the process of the agrarian reform in the different sectors of the country.

They have great hope. They feel real happiness at having taken such a daring step, for which I also congratulated them. But I also pointed out the risks and dangers and doubts that motivate my criticism, which was discussed in a very cordial way by all those at the dinner. It was cordial and, I think, constructive for the good of the country.

Principally, I identified as deficiencies and dangers the agricultural reform being linked with the visible wave of violent repression by the security forces, which takes a great deal of the credibility away from the agrarian reform; it lacks the support of the people. Secondly, they have not assured more popular support by trying to dialogue with the popular forces—they should not consider all of them leftists or communists—with the desire to discover there what are the true interests of the people and their claims for justice. The extreme right is not the same thing because it is not working for justice, but rather to maintain its privileges. The third aspect that I criticized was their seeming to be so subservient to the will of the United States—that they could receive aid, but that they should be sure to preserve the autonomy of our country.

They accepted all of these points of view and indicated that they form part of what they are concerned about and that they wanted to ask my help in achieving this dialogue with the people. I also spoke to them, in this sense, about the collaboration of the movement of professionals and technicians that has just formed, which they did not know about and that they thought represented great hope. I thank the Lord for a day that has been so intense in terms of relationships that can benefit our Church and our people.

**Saturday, March 15**

I had breakfast with Father Jesús Delgado, who usually comes on Saturdays. I used this opportunity to talk with him about the projected center for priestly renewal, suggesting that he talk with Father Vega and that together they prepare plans for this to be built on the land where the archdiocesan offices were to be built. That cannot happen because of a lack of funds, which the archdiocese cannot provide, given its economic situation. But a house of study and a residence for priests would be a very good objective. Father Jesús Delgado also suggested adding a small hospital for priests who are ill, since it is right in the hospital zone. It seems that the hand of God is pointing out this path, which is something that I have wanted for a long time: a house where we can better tend to our dear priests, bringing them up to date, taking care of their health, their rest, their friendship.

With Father Jesús, we also went to Domus Mariae to see the work on the radio station. There we met Father Pick and the engineer who, along with the father, is doing this work. They told me that it was ready to go on the air, but that it would be good to strengthen part of the building so that this transmitter, which cost so much, will be better protected. Nevertheless, they will see if it can be working in time for tomorrow's homily. I am not in a hurry; rather, I allow God to show us his signs. Certainly, it would be a very good service, since they say that the new transmitter is more powerful and the radio will be heard better—even in this provisional form, since a new tower and antenna will be built on different land, which is now being prepared.

In the evening Father Astor Ruíz came to visit me. He is currently working in Nicaragua and is trying to clarify whether it would be better for him to come back now or to stay there until the storm passes, preparing himself to be able to give better service. I did not have time to discuss this in depth. I told him that it would be better for us to talk in the next few days, since during dinner I was busy with Father Ellacuría, Father Estrada, Father Rafael, Miss Doris Osegueda and Bachiller Cuéllar, preparing the information for my homily.

**Sunday, March 16**

This has been a day of great pastoral work and great satisfaction. The Mass at the basilica went on until ten-fifteen. I realize that I overdid the preaching, but the themes—the focus on a reality that is so dense—and the attention of the people encourage me not to neglect this opportunity to continue developing the Lenten catechesis, our thinking about the mystery of Christ that we are preparing for Holy Week, and also to give Christian guidelines for interpreting the very complex realities of our country.

Today I highlighted the repression, which has not ended but, instead, is getting worse. It is causing great pain and the Church must denounce it. I also referred to the process of agrarian reform which is being developed and of which the Church approves, but which I wish did not have this repressive side that makes it lose credibility with a people that feels itself to be the victim of the government itself. I also referred to the state of emergency and to the strike that is being organized for tomorrow, a general work stoppage which, I said, has as its objective to focus attention on the repression. It is a legitimate cause, but they should be very careful that it does not degenerate into a new tragedy of the same repression they are trying to denounce. And other aspects of the Church and also the civil life—a very intense life this week.

Later we went to Aguilares where, at eleven-thirty, we celebrated Mass for the soul of Father Grande on the third anniversary of his death. The Jesuit provincial was there and a great many Jesuits, maybe nearly all of them, as well as priests from other congregations and other diocesan clergy. We made an impressive group for the concelebration.

On the other hand, I noticed the absence of many of the people of Aguilares, for the church was only half-filled and I could tell that the majority of them were communities that had come from elsewhere. This shows that the military repression in a zone that has suffered so much is having the desired effect of terrorizing the people and of distancing them from those who can help them in their awareness and in organization.

I used the opportunity to preach about this very thing, using the Scripture reading[324] that speaks to us about Christ reconciling the world through his death and his blood, of how the mystery of our Church asks us to sacrifice in the way that Father Grande was asked, and for us to make an effort for the integral liberation of our people without being afraid of anything happening.

---

[324] 2 Corinthians 5:17-21.

It is hard to live in this region. The priest and the sisters told me that many people have left the towns and the villages.

We went later to Tejutla to the village Los Martínez, where they were celebrating the feast of the patron saint, San Salvador de Horta. He was a Franciscan, and the parish is under the care of the Franciscan Fathers. I took the opportunity to preach to them how the saint must be the human being of the day and that our imitation of him should not be literal but rather in the spirit, in order to be people of our times, in these difficult commitments that we are living.

After Mass I gave time for dialogue. I noticed that there are complaints about Father Valerio among the people. A Franciscan, he is very zealous, a very hard worker, but he wants to impose a direction that the people do not accept completely. They want the direction of the archdiocese, which speaks of Christian base communities. Father Valerio says that he fears these communities. I tried to open him to a confidence and understanding of the people's complaints, but always in linking them to the hierarchical sense of the Church.

Fortunately, two of the seminarians who are doing their year as deacons in that region and who seemed to me to be very mature in their knowledge of this matter helped me to understand the situation. I charged them to keep working according to the guidelines of the archdiocese, which wants to have these communities in all the parishes. I understand that Father Valerio, being a foreigner and not understanding our situation and our pastoral approach, may have these reservations. We must understand that, but we also have to push him so that he does not extinguish the very vigorous spirit that is felt among the people.

In the evening the Dominican priests were waiting for me in the hospital, one of them the vicar of a section of Madrid. He is very interested in knowing the orientation of our pastoral work and in helping us spread our thought, as it already receives broad acceptance in this area of Spain. He would like to send out information through the countries of Europe, Latin America and Africa. This is, then, a good informational service, which we will offer every help. Father Luis Bourguet, who is also a Dominican and was also present, will be in charge of putting the Spanish initiative into practice.

## Monday, March 17

They told me that there was a great deal of gunfire coming from the direction of the National University last night. I slept very soundly and did not hear anything. Nevertheless, at daylight we received word that there are security forces surrounding the university and that there is an exchange of gunfire. Naturally, there is more from the security forces. The requests to intervene begin to arrive, both from within the university and from the civilians who live in the area. Even the rector and others from the university came to the archdiocesan offices to ask for our intercession. Father Cortés received them and then went to the presidential palace to talk to Colonel Majano and to ask him to halt this repression, which is causing great terror in that sector. The colonel, once the situation had been explained to him, promised to order the withdrawal of the troops.

According to what we learned later, not even the junta itself was able to control them. At any rate, the situation still continued in the afternoon. Around four o'clock I talked with Colonel Majano myself. He promised me again that he would order the troops to withdraw. A few minutes later another member of the junta, Dr. Morales Ehrlich, spoke with me and told me that they were going to withdraw from this military operation.

I spent the entire day in meetings with the Pastoral Commission in the María Eugenia House in Planes de Renderos, which belongs to the Sisters of the Assumption, with the new vicars, not all of whom were able to get there because of the situation of violence that is in effect today. The Mass Movements Revolutionary Coordinating Commission ordered a work stoppage for today, and this has caused disturbances in different parts of the country. There has been news from Colonia Santa Lucía, from the neighborhood of San Jacinto and from other areas of the capital.

We were able to hold our program peacefully. I was able to tell them what I expect from the Pastoral Commission—that is, a coordination that will bring harmony between the two sectors into which our pastoral agents tend to be divided. Some of them do not want to commit themselves to the pastoral program of the archdiocese; others perhaps go to the other extreme, thus causing the others to mistrust them. There was serious discussion of these facts. Father Octavio Cruz, who was coordinating the meeting, gave us a very good analysis of what the pastoral project of the archdiocese consists of, taking his information from the documents that have inspired this project: for example, the pastoral week, the pastoral letters and the Puebla document. It is a very specific, well-defined direction and is clearly supported by the Church itself, which finds the excuses of those who do not want to adapt to these ideas unacceptable. And it will be the work of the Pastoral Commission to give this specific form in our archdiocese.

The meeting ended at six o'clock in the evening with a Eucharist that was very intimate and in which there was great participation.

Meanwhile, there is news of violence, such as that at the Hacienda Colima, where there is word of twenty-three dead, and other places where violence has also taken place.

This day ended with a visit from the Minister of Agriculture, the Minister of Planning and two other men from the government to talk to me about how the process of agrarian reform is going, their desire for this to resolve the problems of the country and how sorry they are that this has become a point of contention on the right, which does not want these changes, as well as on the part of the left, which is putting on pressure and creating tension. And how—and this is the most important part—in sectors of the government itself and among those who should be collaborating in the changes, there are apparently ambitions, personal interests, which are destroying the hope for reform. They ask me, in my role as pastor, to denounce this corruption, this egotism, and also ask, inasmuch as is possible, for a truce so they can carry out in peace these reforms that will benefit the people. We discussed the situation for a long time. There was, I saw, great frankness and a desire to make the program work—not in order to achieve personal glory, rather for the good of the people.

After this visit, Father Astor Ruíz was waiting for me. He has been working in Nicaragua and has come to see if he can come back to El Salvador again. He has concluded that it is not wise to stay, since there is an atmosphere of such repression and mutual mistrust. The fact that he would be coming from Nicaragua could cause him problems. At the same time, he wants to continue his pastoral work, which is principally with workers in the Diocese of Estelí in Nicaragua. I was very edified by his way of seeking advice and by the humility with which he knelt down at the end to ask for my benediction. May God bless him, and may we always have this sense of our priesthood which identifies us with the virtues of Jesus Christ.

 **Tuesday, March 18**

For the first time, the Franciscan priest of the parish of La Reina has invited me to visit his parish—specifically the neighboring town of Agua Caliente—where he has prepared a large group of young people and children to receive the Sacrament of Confirmation. It is a rather remote place in the department of Chalatenango, but there is a new wide highway that is making access easier.

The reception was very warm, the people very fervent. But they seem to have a charismatic spiritual formation; they live in intense piety but with no apparent commitment to the present moment. Nevertheless, I have hope that the new Pastoral Commission of the archdiocese will take the pastoral project of the archdiocese to all the parishes. I repeat, however, it was a morning that was very intensely lived as a community of faith and prayer.

In the evening I had a brief private interview with a representative of the group that is holding Mr. Dunn captive. I insisted that everything be done to free him as soon as possible. The representative promised to do what I had suggested, but it depends on the high command of this group. I ask God to return Mr. Dunn to his home soon, since he has been a captive for several months now. Mr. Jaime Hill, who had also been captive for several months, has been freed within the last few days.

In the Divine Providence Hospital they held a raffle to raise money for their work. It always brings economic support for this work—truly a sign of God's providence.

In the morning we had the meeting of the Executive Council in the chancery to talk specifically about the radio and the Office of Social Communications. There was also a note from the presidential palace, relaying a complaint by the commandant of Cojutepeque against Father Ricardo Ayala, whom he accuses of indoctrinating a group of peasants with Marxism and of telling them that he will soon travel to Nicaragua and Cuba to bring back arms for revolution. This is blatantly ridiculous, since Father Ayala is a very balanced man. This accusation actually made him laugh, as it did our vicar general, who met with him. We will respond, then, that these accusations are ridiculous and that a just government does not give credence to this kind of information.

In the María Eugenia house in Planes de Renderos, today was the end of the meeting of the Pastoral Commission with the new vicars and with new projects for the year's work. I could not go today because I had gone to the town I mentioned before.

In general, there is an atmosphere of tension and violence. There are military all around the presidential palace. This creates a very bad impression and could provoke more violence from the left. As long as the repressive spirit of the armed forces does not change, it will continue to cause great harm. On the other hand, the agrarian and banking reforms are progressing, but the people cannot accept them as long as this horrifying repression is felt in all sectors. In the little town I went to and also in the place I went on Sunday, there are many complaints but, since there is also great terror, they cannot talk freely about what is happening.

In the evening I also received word that an ecumenical commission will come from the United States: Bishop Arzube,[325] along with a minister from the National Council of Churches and another representative of human rights and amnesty, to learn in person about what is happening in our country. I told them I would receive them with pleasure, and I hoped that the bishop who is coming will participate in the concelebration this coming Sunday.

 **Wednesday, March 19**

Today, St. Joseph's feast, I celebrated the first Mass at the Colegio Cristóbal Colón, run by the Josephite priests. I told them that St. Joseph is the model for the man that our country needs today: with a commitment to a sense of justice, with a sense of collaboration and with a sense of faith.

Professor Moreno said a few words of praise for the bishop on behalf of the entire school. The professors also presented me with a donation for YSAX. The collection taken up in that large gathering also went to our radio station, a gesture for which I thanked them cordially.

I visited the repair work at YSAX in Domus Mariae. I found Father Pick there. He was on his way to the health center because he feels somewhat ill. The silent labor of these Jesuits, who are helping to repair our radio YSAX in a very professional way, is admirable.

I went to the chancery for a while. There were a large number of visits, the most significant one from Fathers Torruella and Mejía, who came to share with me some ideas from a group of priests who are concerned about the politicization of some of the priests. They invited me to a reflection so that we may have a dialogue among the different sectors of the clergy and, if possible, an inquiry in order to neutralize anything which might divide us as priests. I thanked them for such a valuable suggestion, and I asked them for their cooperation.

With my brother Arnoldo, who helps me organize the financial and other aspects of the administration of the chancery, we talked about the deficiencies that we see at present—principally on the part of the

---

[325] Juan Arzube, auxiliary bishop of Los Angeles, then chairman of the U.S. bishops' Committee for the Church in Latin America.

administrator and in the Office of Social Communication, especially in the press and in the office itself. I asked him to help me to resolve these serious problems. Tomorrow we will have a meeting toward that objective.

At four o'clock in the afternoon we had a meeting with the council or committee for humanitarian aid, an ecumenical committee of which Caritas is part. It was to discuss a problem that has arisen in the refugee centers. What is happening is that the agents of the popular political organizations are using these people for their political activities. We have tried to make it clear that a refugee center should not be a headquarters for their operations. There was a great deal of discussion. I always have the impression of extreme politicization in the declarations made by Father Rogelio and Father Tilo Sánchez, as well as by others who participated in the meeting. But I was also very glad to see the very balanced position of some of the priests and some of the members of the Protestant Churches who collaborate with us in this ecumenical work. The manager of Caritas, Miss Carmen, was also very prudent in her orientation.

I went afterward to celebrate my second Mass for St. Joseph's feast at the Somascan seminary, where there was also a group of refugees from Cojutepeque and from Chalatenango. The homily was along the same lines as the one at Cristóbal Colón School. After Mass we had dinner with the seminarians and the priests and had a very interesting conversation about problems of the situation of El Salvador, the role of the Church and some information that the seminarians tried in a very intelligent way to get.

Finally, tonight the president of Cor Unum came, the pontifical office that coordinates the different organizations of promotion, charity and social action. I told him frankly about the lack of efficiency of our national Caritas and our desire to make the diocesan Caritas more active in the formation of Christian love. He promised that he would help with the programs of the archdiocese, but that we should present these programs to him, which we will do tomorrow with Caritas and the ecumenical commission on humanitarian aid.

 **Thursday, March 20**

At eight o'clock in the morning, I had a brief meeting with the Administrative Commission, which my brother Arnoldo also attended to give a report on the accounts and the financial situation of the chancery. The situation is rather worrisome, since we have been spending only money from subsidies and we do not see a way to finance our expenses ourselves. I said that I was willing to accept any suggestions that they had, especially relating to changes in personnel, the elimination of some positions.

I left them studying this, since I had to go to the Senate meeting in Planes de Renderos, in the María Eugenia house, which belongs to the Sisters of the Assumption. This was the first meeting of the new Senate. I urged them above all to work for the unity of the clergy, since all the different currents and ways of thinking among the clergy are represented in the Senate. I also told them that we had to base our meetings on a human sense of trust, friendship, sincerity; that the sense of faith and of the supernatural with which we think about ourselves in the context of our priestly vocation is not enough. Rather, this human base of friendship is what will give a pleasant, practical and efficient sense to our work as a team, in working principally for all of our priests, whom we represent.

After recalling the statutes and the duties of the Senate, they went on to hold elections. They elected as president Father Cristóbal Cortés and, as vice-president, Father José Luis Bourguet. The atmosphere was very warm, and in this atmosphere we discussed the first points, especially how to make the service of the Senate more efficient. It was decided to designate the leadership as a permanent council who will stay abreast of any situations of the diocese and the bishops and will inform the body of the Senate rapidly, in order that it may serve the bishop's need for consultation according to the circumstances, however unexpected they might be.

Later, in an attempt to serve the clergy better and with a view to our realities, three committees were organized: one which will be intended principally to cultivate the unity of the clergy; another to orient the relations between the clergy and society, all the sociopolitical aspects that many times divide us or prevent us from working together as a group; and a third committee, which we called the Infrastructure Committee, in charge of the different practical aspects of the clergy—for example, culture, spirituality, health, social benefits and subsistence, etc.

After that, we talked at length about the practical problem of the differing political senses that divide us, since we live in a situation in which the country is so politicized, so polarized. At one o'clock, we ended the meeting with lunch in an atmosphere that was always friendly and greatly optimistic.

In the afternoon, a conversation with representatives of the Popular Leagues of February 28, with whom, since I could not do so myself, Father Rafael Urrutia and Licenciado Roberto Cuéllar met on my behalf.

At the same time, I was meeting with Father Pedraz, a Jesuit who has great administrative ability, to ask him, according to the meeting of the Administrative Committee, to help us reorganize our archdiocesan administration. I gave him the authority to review the different aspects that we had discussed in the meeting with the administration and said that the Administrative Committee would act in accordance with what he said. He told me that he is always very willing to serve and that he asked only that I give him a few days to decide, possibly until Sunday or Monday. I hope that his answer will be affirmative, so that soon we can resolve this situation that has me worried with regard to the financial situation and administration of our archdiocese.

I also had a meeting with the manager of Caritas and a representative of the ecumenical council on humanitarian aid to look at their projects and work on behalf of people in need so that we can present them to the representative of Cor Unum, from Rome, who is here with us. And we went to visit him at the nunciature. He has shown himself to be receptive, understanding of the difficulties and projects of the work of the archdiocesan Caritas and of the present emergencies.

# Afterword

Archbishop Romero taped no diary entries after March 20, 1980.

YSAX was back on the air on Sunday, March 23, broadcasting the eight o'clock Mass in the Basilica of the Sacred Heart. In his homily Romero addressed the soldiers of the security forces, entreating them to follow a higher law and refuse to turn their guns on their fellow citizens of El Salvador.

On Monday, March 24, 1980, the archbishop went to the Divine Providence Hospital to celebrate a memorial Mass at six p.m. in the chapel there. As he finished his homily and extended the invitation to prayer, a single shot rang out from the chapel doorway, and Romero slumped to the floor with a bullet in his chest. He died soon after in a hospital emergency room.

His funeral Mass the following Sunday was also interrupted and never finished when a bomb exploded in the crowded plaza outside the cathedral. Shooting followed and forty people died, most of them trampled in the ensuing panic.

In the next decade the United States increased the flow of military aid. The violence escalated into a civil war which claimed the lives of an estimated seventy-five thousand people. Among them were Ambassador Dunn, four women from the United States—three nuns and a layworker—raped and murdered in December 1980 and six Jesuits, machine-gunned to death with their cook and her daughter in November 1989.

On February 1, 1992, under the terms of a peace accord negotiated by a United Nations commission, the FMLN began demobilization and the government started to reduce the strength of the security forces.

Carol Luebering
Editor
St. Anthony Messenger Press

# Glossary

**Adveniat:** An international organization formed by the German bishops, concerned with solidarity with Third World countries.

**AGEUS (*Asociación General de Estudiantes Universitarios Salvadoreños*):** General Association of Salvadoran University Students.

**ANDES (*Asociación Nacional de Educadores Salvadoreños*):** National Association of Salvadoran Teachers.

**ANEP (*Asociación Nacional de la Empresa Privada*):** National Association of Private Enterprise.

**ANTEL (*Asociación Nacional de Telecomunicaciones*):** The state-owned telecommunications company.

**BPR (*Bloque Popular Revolucionario*):** Popular Revolutionary Bloc, a coalition of popular organizations.

**Caritas:** The main social assistance group in most Latin American countries.

**CEDES (*Conferencia Episcopal de El Salvador*):** The Salvadoran bishops' conference.

**CELAM:** The administrative body of the Latin American Bishops' Council.

**CLAR:** Latin American Confederation of Religious.

**CONFRES (*Confederación de los Religiosos de El Salvador*):** The organization of men and women religious.

**CRS:** Catholic Relief Services, the overseas aid and development agency of the United States bishops' conference.

**CUTS (*Central Unitaria de Trabajadores Salvadoreños*):** United Confederation of Salvadoran Workers.

**ERP (*Ejército Revolucionario del Pueblo*):** The People's Revolutionary Army.

**FAPU (*Frente de Acción Popular Unificado*):** United Popular Action Front, a coalition of popular organizations.

**FARN (*Fuerzas Armadas de Resistencia Nacional*):** Armed Forces of National Resistance, an armed resistance organization.

**FECCAS (*Federación Cristiana de Campesinos Salvadoreños*):** Christian Federation of Salvadoran Peasants.

**FENASTRAS (*Federación Nacional Sindical de Trabajadores Salvadoreños*):** National Trade Union Federation of Salvadoran Workers.

**FMLN (*Frente Farabundo Martí para la Liberación Nacional*):** Farabundo Martí National Libertion Front, a coalition of five militant popular organizations.

**FPL (*Fuerzas Populares de Liberación*):** Popular Liberation Forces, an armed resistance organization.

**Mass Movements Coordinating Committee:** A coalition directing popular organizations.

**MNR (*Movimiento Nacional Revolucionario*):** National Revolutionary Movement, the Social Democratic Party, founded in 1965.

**National Guard:** A largely volunteer force used for internal security.

**National Police:** The ordinary police force.

**ORDEN (*Organización Democrática Nacionalista*):** Democratic Nationalist Organization, the government's antisubversive paramilitary organization, composed of peasants.

**Priests' Senate:** An advisory body composed of representative clergy.

**Security forces:** A blanket term which includes the army, the National Guard, the Treasury Police and the National Police.

**SEDAC:** Episcopal Secretariat of Central America and Panama.

***La Semilla de Dios:*** God's Seed, a cooperative encouraging local handicrafts.

**Treasury Police:** A small professional force used to maintain internal security.

**UDN (*Unión Democrática Nacionalista*):** Democratic Nationalist Union, the legal representation of the Salvadoran communist party.

**UGB (*Unión Guerrera Blanca*):** White Warrior Union.

**UNO (*Unión Nacional Opositora*):** National Opposition Union, the opposition coalition in the 1977 election.

**UTC (*Unión de Trabajadores del Campo*):** Union of Rural Workers.

***Vivienda Mínima:*** A group working for decent housing.

# Index